THE
BOOM

ENERGY HISTORIES, CULTURES, AND POLITICS

SERIES EDITOR:
Petra Dolata, Associate Professor, Department of History, University of Calgary

ISSN 2562-3486 (Print)   ISSN 2562-3494 (Online)

This series features original research at the intersection of energy and society. It welcomes works that contribute to international discussions on the history, culture, and politics of energy and speaks to the energy humanities and energy social sciences. The series has a strong interest in, but is not limited to, North American issues.

No. 1   *Imperial Standard: Imperial Oil, Exxon, and the Canadian Oil Industry from 1880*
Graham D. Taylor

No. 2   *Energy in the Americas: Critical Reflections on Energy and History*
Edited by Amelia M. Kiddle

No. 3   *The Boom: Oil, Popular Culture, and Politics in Alberta, 1912–1924*
Paul Chastko

 UNIVERSITY OF CALGARY
Press

PAUL CHASTKO

OIL, POPULAR CULTURE, AND POLITICS
IN ALBERTA, 1912–1924

Energy Histories, Cultures, and Politics Series
ISSN 2562-3486 (Print) ISSN 2562-3494 (Online)

© 2025 Paul Chastko

University of Calgary Press
2500 University Drive NW
Calgary, Alberta
Canada T2N 1N4
press.ucalgary.ca

All rights reserved.

This book is available in an Open Access digital format published under a CC-BY-NCND 4.0 Creative Commons license. The publisher should be contacted for any commercial use which falls outside the terms of that license.

Library and Archives Canada Cataloguing in Publication

Title: The boom : oil, popular culture, and politics in Alberta, 1912-1924 / Paul Chastko.
Names: Chastko, Paul A. (Paul Anthony), author
Description: Series statement: Energy histories, cultures, and politics, 2562-3486 ; no. 3 | Includes bibliographical references and index.
Identifiers: Canadiana (print) 20250237822 | Canadiana (ebook) 20250237873 | ISBN 9781773856667 (hardcover) | ISBN 9781773856674 (softcover) | ISBN 9781773856704 (EPUB) | ISBN 9781773856698 (PDF) | ISBN 9781773856681 (Open access PDF)
Subjects: LCSH: Petroleum industry and trade—Political aspects—Alberta—Turner Valley—History—20th century. | LCSH: Petroleum industry and trade—Corrupt practices—Alberta—Turner Valley—History—20th century. | LCSH: Petroleum industry and trade—Social aspects—Alberta—Turner Valley—History—20th century. | LCSH: Oil fields—Alberta—Turner Valley—History—20th century. | LCSH: Petroleum—Prospecting—Alberta—Turner Valley—History—20th century. | LCSH: Swindlers and swindling—Alberta—Turner Valley—History—20th century. | LCSH: Turner Valley (Alta.)—History—20th century. | LCSH: Alberta—Politics and government—20th century. | CSH: Alberta—Politics and government—1905-1921.
Classification: LCC HD9574.C23 A54 2025 | DDC 338.2/72820971234—dc23

The University of Calgary Press acknowledges the support of the Government of Alberta through the Alberta Media Fund for our publications. We acknowledge the financial support of the Government of Canada. We acknowledge the financial support of the Canada Council for the Arts for our publishing program.

This book has been published with the help of a grant from the Federation for the Humanities and Social Sciences, through the Awards to Scholarly Publications Program, using funds provided by the Social Sciences and Humanities Research Council of Canada.

  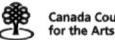 

The manufacturer's authorized representative in the EU for product safety is Mare Nostrum Group B.V., Mauritskade 21D, 1091 GC Amsterdam, The Netherlands. Email: gpsr@mare-nostrum.co.uk

Copyediting by Peter Enman
Cover image credit: Edited photograph of George Edward Buck by Sarah Deschamps. Original photograph Provincial Archives of Alberta, GR1972.0026 Box 1 File 1C. Courtesy of the Provincial Archives of Alberta. "View of Dingman #1 and Dingman #2, Turner Valley, Alberta." Summer 1914, (CU1558287) by Unknown. Glenbow Library and Archives Collection. Libraries and Cultural Resources Digital Collection, University of Calgary. Colourbox 20750164.
Cover design, page design, and typesetting by Melina Cusano

Contents

List of Figures and Tables		vii
Introduction: "The Wildest Boom That Ever Hit the West"		1
1	"Scientific Oil Finding:" Turner Valley's Anticline	17
2	"The Formation of These Companies . . . Should be Stopped:" Speculation and the Newspaper Feud	53
3	"The Difference Between Poverty and Riches is Action!" Dreams and Reality of an Independent Oil Boom	93
4	"I'm Going to Go Through With It Even if it Leads to Jail:" George E. Buck of Black Diamond Oil Fields	123
5	"A City So Blessed Cannot be Checked:" Oil! . . . Sort of	145
6	Reign of the Charlatans	189
7	Boycotts, Consumer Protection, and Private Detectives: Responses to the Boom from Voluntary Associations to the Pinkertons	215
8	Reforming Self-Regulation: Taming the Brokers and the Calgary Stock Exchange	249
9	Public Interest Versus Private Rights: Judge Alexander A. Carpenter's Commission and the Big Boom's Big Hangover	269
10	"I am Not Going Back to Canada:" The Law Comes for Buck	295
11	"A Matter of Public Concern:" The Lees Commission and Monarch Oil	339
12	"The Most Important that has Ever Been Tried in the Province:" The Trial of George Buck	373
13	"It is to be Regretted that Such a Scoundrel Should Escape Punishment:" Buck's Appeals	397
14	Conclusion: Buck and the Boom	419
Acknowledgements		427
Bibliography		431
Notes		445
Index		487

List of Figures and Tables

Figure 0-1	"A Square Deal in Oil," *Calgary Morning Albertan*, February 2, 1914, 11, CU1709303. Early Alberta Newspapers Collection, Libraries and Cultural Resources Digital Collections, University of Calgary.	3
Figure 0-2	"Prosperity and Oil." *Natural Gas and Oil Record*, June 13, 1914, 1.	8
Figure 0-3	"Today's the Day." *Edmonton Journal*, May 25, 1914, 1.	10
Figure 1-1	"William Stewart Herron, petroleum pioneer in Turner Valley, Alberta," Hess, c. 1930, CU1125948. Glenbow Library and Archives Collection, Libraries and Cultural Resources Digital Collections, University of Calgary.	24
Figure 1-2	"Gas and petroleum claim being staked by the City of Calgary," June 12, 1911, CU189401. Glenbow Library and Archives Collection, Libraries and Cultural Resources Digital Collections, University of Calgary.	27
Figure 1-3	"Archibald Wayne Dingman," E.B. Curlette, c. 1930–1933, CU181710. Glenbow Library and Archives Collection, Libraries and Cultural Resources Digital Collections, University of Calgary.	31
Figure 1-4	Canadian Western Natural Gas Company ad. *Calgary Herald*, June 14, 1956, 38.	33
Figure 1-5	"Calgary Petroleum Products #1 well [Dingman #1], Turner Valley, Alberta," I.H. Sinclair, c. 1914, CU1217652. Glenbow Library and Archives Collection, Libraries and Cultural Resources Digital Collections, University of Calgary.	37
Figure 1-6	"Drillers at Dingman #1 well (Calgary Petroleum Products #1), Turner Valley, Alberta," c. 1914–1917 CU1134522, Glenbow Library and Archives Collection, Libraries and Cultural Resources Digital Collections, University of Calgary.	38
Figure 1-7	"Group of men standing at well-head of Dingman #1 (Calgary Petroleum Products #1), Turner Valley, Alberta," c. 1914–1917, CU1134205. Glenbow Library and Archives Collection, Libraries and Cultural Resources Digital Collections, University of Calgary.	42
Figure 2-1	"New 'Arms' of Alberta," *Calgary Morning Albertan*, December 11, 1913, 1, CU1701012. Early Alberta Newspapers Collection, Libraries and Cultural Resources Digital Collections, University of Calgary.	91

Figure 3-1	"Which is it to be?" R.C. Edwards, *Calgary Eye Opener*, July 3, 1915, 1. Early Alberta Newspapers Collection, Libraries and Cultural Resources Digital Collections, University of Calgary.	94
Figure 3-2	"The Greatest Gift," *Natural Gas and Oil Record*, November 8, 1913, 1.	95
Figure 3-3	"The Men Behind the Gun," *Natural Gas and Oil Record*, May 23, 1914, 13.	101
Figure 3-4	"Pessimists and Otherwise," *Calgary Morning Albertan*, October 23, 1913, 8, CU1699923. Early Alberta Newspapers Collection, Libraries and Cultural Resources Digital Collections, University of Calgary.	103
Figure 3-5	Excerpt from "A Great Future," *Natural Gas and Oil Record*, December 12, 1913, 6.	105
Figure 3-6	Piedmont Petroleum Products Company ad. *Calgary Morning Albertan*, May 12, 1914, 7, CU1300898. Early Alberta Newspapers Collection, Libraries and Cultural Resources Digital Collections, University of Calgary.	118
Figure 3-7	"The Difference Between Poverty and Riches is Action!" *Calgary Morning Albertan*, May 16, 1914, 9, CU1301220. Early Alberta Newspapers Collection, Libraries and Cultural Resources Digital Collections, University of Calgary.	121
Figure 4-1	"9th Avenue SW, Calgary, Alberta. Palliser Hotel and Canadian Pacific Railway Station are visible on left side," c. 1920, Calgary Photo Supply Co. PC005483. Peel's Prairie Provinces—Prairie Postcard Collection. Available at https://library.ualberta.ca/peel.	126
Figure 4-2	"Important Announcement," *Calgary Morning Albertan*, February 3, 1914, 9CU1701489. Early Alberta Newspapers Collection, Libraries and Cultural Resources Digital Collections, University of Calgary.	134
Figure 4-3	"Heart-to-Heart," *Calgary Morning Albertan*, March 23, 1914, 7, CU1701176. Early Alberta Newspapers Collection, Libraries and Cultural Resources Digital Collections, University of Calgary.	136
Figure 4-4	"Giant Gusher," *Calgary Eye Opener*, May 23, 1914, 3, CU11428707. Early Alberta Newspapers Collection, Libraries and Cultural Resources Digital Collections, University of Calgary.	143

Figure 5-1	"Dingman #1 blowing in, Turner Valley, Alberta," May 14, 1914, CU1554074. Glenbow Library and Archives Collection, Libraries and Cultural Resources Digital Collections, University of Calgary.	148
Figure 5-2	"The Scarecrow," *Natural Gas and Oil Record*, May 18, 1914, 1.	152
Figure 5-3	"The Greatest Magnet in the World—Oil!" *Natural Gas and Oil Record*, May 30, 1914, 1.	153
Figure 5-4	"Investors waiting to buy oil stocks in Calgary, Alberta," Progress Photo Company, May 15, 1914, CU1149999. Glenbow Library and Archives Collection, Libraries and Cultural Resources Digital Collections, University of Calgary.	156
Figure 5-5	"Investors waiting to buy oil stocks, Calgary, Alberta," c. 1914, CU1554077. Glenbow Library and Archives Collection, Libraries and Cultural Resources Digital Collections, University of Calgary.	157
Figure 5-6	"Investors waiting to buy oil and gas stocks outside Huron and Bruce Oil and Gas Company, Calgary, Alberta," c. 1914, CU1145708. Glenbow Library and Archives Collection, Libraries and Cultural Resources Digital Collections, University of Calgary.	160
Figure 5-7	"Calgary Restaurant," *Calgary Morning Albertan*, June 1, 1914, 1, CU1302322. Early Alberta Newspapers Collection, Libraries and Cultural Resources Digital Collections, University of Calgary.	163
Figure 5-8	"The Small Investor gets best chance," *Natural Gas and Oil Record*, July 11, 1914, 18.	164
Figure 5-9	"The Flame and the Moth," *The Toronto Daily Star*, May 30, 1914, 30.	170
Figure 5-10	"Men in cars and on sidewalk waiting to invest in oil stocks, Calgary, Alberta," Harry Pollard, c. June 1914, CU1137947. Glenbow Library and Archives Collection, Libraries and Cultural Resources Digital Collections, University of Calgary.	179
Figure 6-1	"Birds of Prey," *The Toronto Daily Star*, June 15, 1914, 14.	201
Figure 6-2	"Picnic group at site of Dingman #1 well (Calgary Petroleum Products #1), Turner Valley, Alberta," c. 1914, CU1136172. Glenbow Library and Archives Collection, Libraries and Cultural Resources Digital Collections, University of Calgary.	205
Figure 7-1	"J'Ever See Such Luck?" *Calgary Morning Albertan*, May 23, 1914, 1, CU1301447. Early Alberta Newspapers Collection, Libraries and Cultural Resources Digital Collections, University of Calgary	224

Figure 7-2	"Caravan of automobiles en route to Turner Valley, Alberta," c. 1914, CU192892. Glenbow Library and Archives Collection, Libraries and Cultural Resources Digital Collections, University of Calgary.	243
Figure 7-3	"Duke and Duchess of Connaught at Dingman number 1 well (Calgary Petroleum Products #1), Turner Valley, Alberta," Progress Photo Company, July 28, 1914, CU192442. Courtesy of Glenbow Library and Archives Collection, Libraries and Cultural Resources Digital Collections, University of Calgary.	244
Figure 8-1	"Calgary Oil Proclamation," *Calgary Morning Albertan*, October 14, 1914, 9. CU1702268. Early Alberta Newspapers Collection, Libraries and Cultural Resources Digital Collections, University of Calgary.	250
Figure 10-1	"George E. Buck Wanted Circular," c. 1916, GR1972.0026, box 1, file 1C. Provincial Archives of Alberta.	307
Figure 11-1	"Charles Stalnaker pouring nitroglycerine down torpedo tube inside oil rig, possibly Montana, United States," c. 1935, CU1217942. Glenbow Library and Archives Collection, Libraries and Cultural Resources Digital Collections, University of Calgary.	347
Figure 14-1	"Flare at Turner Valley oil field, Alberta," Lane's Studio, c. 1930s, CU1153082. Glenbow Library and Archives Collection, Libraries and Cultural Resources Digital Collections, University of Calgary.	425

Table 1-1	Geologic Time, Turner Valley.	18
Table 2-1	Value of Building Permits in Calgary, 1910–1915.	64
Table 5-1	Calgary Bank Clearings, Selected Months and Weeks, 1913 & 1914.	162
Table 5-2	Calgary Stock Exchange and Calgary Oil and Stock Exchange Values Compared, June 8, 1914.	176
Table 5-3	Average Professional & Tradeswomen's Salaries in Calgary, 1913.	181
Table 6-1	Selected Alberta Stock Prices, May 15–June 6, 1914, Published by the *Natural Gas and Oil Record*.	202
Table 7-1	Distribution of Corporate Headquarters of 1914 Turner Valley Companies by Province.	233

Introduction: "The Wildest Boom That Ever Hit the West"

HE WHO DOES NOT PULL FOR OIL IS A TRAITOR, and should be shot. He who thinks Western Canada is going to the dogs is a fool and should be sent to Ponoka.

—J.L. Tucker, Editor
The Natural Gas and Oil Record
August 9, 1914

George Edward Buck is proof that every good story starts with a bad decision. Born March 20, 1867, in Esquesing Township (now Oakville), Ontario, George Buck was part of a large family of nine children. His formal education consisted of what he picked up at a one-room rural school where the Bible served as the chief reading material. Historian John Schmidt writes that, as a young man, Buck was devoutly religious and hard-working, if only because there was little else to do given his conservative upbringing, limited education, and opportunities in the rural Ontario of his childhood. In his early twenties, Buck moved to Toronto and found new prospects in the commercial world as an insurance salesman. He married Elizabeth Ada Beaty in 1894 and started a family. At age forty in 1908, Buck suddenly uprooted his wife and five children from Ontario and moved to Alberta, where he believed more opportunities existed for someone with his ambitions. In addition to his job as an insurance salesman, Buck was an itinerant evangelical preacher and missionary, and quickly became a leading figure within the Christian Church (Disciples of Christ) Calgary congregation. Fiercely independent, highly decentralized, and unrelentingly evangelical, the church espoused a theology that demanded adherents seek a personal relationship with their creator.[1]

After stints as a real estate promoter and coal mine operator, Buck read *Oil Finding,* a book on petroleum geology published in 1912 by the eminent British geologist Edward Hubert Cunningham Craig. At a time when divining rods and doodlebugs (a pseudo-geophysical device allegedly capable of finding oil) stood as good a chance as anything else at predicting where drillers would find oil, Craig's book sat at the cutting edge of the search for oil's gradual transition from art to science. Free from technical jargon and easily accessible, Craig's text demonstrated how to methodically, and rationally, identify potential oil fields.

The book was a revelation for Buck, particularly because two oil companies—Archibald W. Dingman's Calgary Petroleum Products and McDougall-Segur Exploration Company (named after partners David McDougall and Ira Segur)—had begun drilling for oil in Turner Valley. All at once, Buck saw his present and future as an oil promoter laid out before him with one outsized aim: to realize Jesus Christ's prayer that "all His followers be one" and unite all Christians to accept "the word of God as their only rule of faith and practise."[2] In a future fuelled and funded by oil, Buck dreamed of establishing the Kingdom of Heaven along the foothills of the Rocky Mountains. Sustained by his faith and secure in his conviction that he was engaged in God's work, Buck began his project with the purchase of mineral rights from the Dominion government on a parcel of land along Sheep Creek in Turner Valley near Black Diamond. Buck convinced his wife, Ada, his mother-in-law, and a few other family members to form the Coalinga Syndicate, which Buck then made himself president of with control over all financial decisions. The syndicate's board of directors consisted entirely of family members, including his wife and his cousin, Jennie L. Earl.[3] On paper, it all looked and sounded official enough, but in practice the directors never formally met or kept any records. "I know nothing about the business end of it at all," confessed his long-suffering wife, Ada, when questioned about company affairs. "I leave everything to Mr. Buck to look after."[4]

The Coalinga Syndicate operated as a holding company, managing the assets of the partners and providing them with a layer of separation in case anything went sideways. Buck then chartered a new oil company, Black Diamond Oil Fields, to carry out exploration. Legally, the company was its own entity separate from the syndicate, but in practical terms the two were one and the same. With a few minor changes, the company shared the same board of directors and president as the Coalinga Syndicate. Then Buck, as president of the Coalinga Syndicate, sold Buck, acting as president of Black Diamond Oil Fields, the mineral lease purchased from the Dominion government at an obscene 158,990 percent increase over the original purchase price for cash and shares. The terms of the sale were such that Black Diamond Oil Fields sold stock to investors and used the revenue they generated to repay

> ## ---a square deal in oil, for you
>
> This is addressed to intelligent people who do their own thinking and who know what's what. After much public and private criticism of oil development methods, some fair and well informed and some most unfair and downright ignorant of everything pertaining to petroleum and its finding, the people of Calgary have at last a square-deal oil proposition that is such as to meet at all points the absolute approval of every intelligent and fair-minded person in this city and elsewhere.
>
> Mr. E. H. CRANDELL, alderman and capitalist of Calgary, a man of eminent business ability and integrity, has accepted the voting trusteeship of a majority of all shares issued of The Black Diamond Oil Fields, Limited (which shares belong to the former leaseholders and are placed in trust) to insure the fair and square administration of the Company's affairs in the interest of oil finding and of all the shareholders alike. Mr. Crandell is not interested in oil or oil lands, nor in this Company or in any other Company, but has consented to act in this semi-public capacity and lend his talents for business to the most efficient and business-like testing of the Black Diamond Oil Fields.
>
> THE TRUSTS & GUARANTEE COMPANY, LIMITED, assets over $11,000,000.00, has been appointed the Registrar and Transfer Agent of all the Capital Stock of The Black Diamond Oil Fields, Limited, which will insure a proper, accurate and business-like handling of all the stock of the Company.
>
> J. H. SINCLAIR, M.S., has been retained as geologist and petroleum engineer for the Company. Mr. Sinclair's first-hand and extensive knowledge of the fields, his previous experience in the U.S. geological survey in the California oil fields, and his acquaintance and association with such men as Cunningham Craig, Dowling and other eminent geologists in their work in these fields, is an assurance of first-class service along petroleum engineering and geological lines. Mr. Sinclair unhesitatingly pronounces 34-19-3-W5, the property of The Black Diamond Oil Fields Limited, the most favorably situated oil leasehold, without exception, for testing the petroleum possibilities of the whole field southwest of Calgary. He fully expects this Company to reach the Dakota sands, the acknowledged reservoir of petroleum in these fields, at a depth of only 400 feet from the surface of our holdings, where the drill is now working day and night.
>
> The drilling actually commenced Thursday, January 29, and now proceeding rapidly, is in the hands of The International Supply Company, Limited (Martin & Phillips) the acknowledged best drilling firm in all Western Canada. At Medicine Hat they drill 1,000 feet in depth easily in 30 days and have drilled 1,000 feet in 12½ days. The contract given the Black Diamond Company is at a most reasonable price on account of the many advantages 34-19-3-W of 5 possesses from the point of view of rapid and easy drilling and petroleum finding.
>
> The property of the Company, 640 acres of the very best oil land in the whole district, is regarded as large enough for TEN oil companies in a proved and producing region, and should be easily worth $3,200,000.00 upon the striking of oil in large commercial quantities, which we expect to do in at most from 30 to 45 days from this date. This should make each $1 share worth over $10.00 per share.
>
> Only 50,000 shares of the treasury stock of The Black Diamond Oil Fields is now offered for sale at $1 per share. 87½ per cent. of this is to be expended on actual drilling of perfect wells.
>
> Every intelligent person wishing to participate in the prodigious profits in petroleum and under the most favorable circumstances in the whole field and who wishes ACTION in development and security for the fair business administration of his oil investments should place his funds with this Company and without delay. Any information at the Company's office.
>
> Shares may advance NOW any day and WILL advance as drilling progresses, and without notice.
>
> Address all communications, or better, call personally for the purchase of shares or for information upon the
>
> ### SELLING AGENTS of the BLACK DIAMOND
> OIL FIELDS, LIMITED

Figure 0-1 "A Square Deal in Oil"
Ads for Black Diamond Oil Fields were among the most colourful that appeared in the winter of 1913/14, with Buck trying several tactics to separate investors from their money. (University of Calgary Libraries and Cultural Resources CU1709303)

the partners in the Coalinga Syndicate for the mineral rights, enabling the partners to recoup their initial investment first whether the well had oil or not. Using the oratorical skills that made him such a charismatic preacher, Buck convinced family, friends, and members of his congregation to invest everything in his new oil company for a chance to strike it rich. But when sales faltered and failed to raise enough cash to carry on development, Buck's faith in the unproven field proved so strong that he liquidated other assets and even signed over the title to his family's house to creditors as collateral for a loan to pay for rental of the derrick and drill crew.

As a promoter selling stock to the public, Buck hustled with the best of them, keeping his name in the press and on people's lips. He readily embraced a role that required him to be carnival barker, ringmaster, and circus sideshow all rolled into one, with just the occasional whiff of the unpredictable to spice things up. Once, Buck ordered an armed sentry to fire a few live rounds from his rifle over the heads of potential investors on a pre-arranged visit to the well. He didn't mean any harm but said he wanted to build a sense of mystery and danger around the well. On another occasion he took out a full-page newspaper ad labelling his rivals "fake" oil companies and claiming that the oil underneath his "scientifically selected" location lay 1,000 feet closer to the surface than in other parts of the formation. Even if it were true—and it was not—Buck had no way of proving it. In fact, it was a lot of fun being George Buck. He loved driving fast cars on Calgary's narrow streets in the company of "high priced women," and playing practical jokes on the guys in the office.[5] There was only one problem: as an oil man and promoter, George Buck never drilled a successful well in his life. In itself, this was an uncomfortable truth but was not necessarily fatal to his business pursuits. After all, Thomas Edison found thousands of different ways not to make a light bulb before he discovered one that worked.

Through the cold, grey winter of 1913/14, brassy newspaper ads trumpeted that his company engaged in "scientific oil finding," as practised by the eminent British geologist Edward Hubert Cunningham Craig. Yet, for six months after "spudding in" (the start of drilling) the well, instead of the instant success he had dreamed of, Buck pursued a hand-to-mouth existence of selling just enough stock to fund exploration. Even this meagre existence foundered in the middle of a worsening depression in western Canada. His congregation soon tapped out and a deal to sell a large block of shares worth $10,000 to a private investor in Saskatoon fell through. Financial salvation remained frustratingly out of reach. By the spring of 1914, he could no longer beg, borrow, or steal any more cash to keep the company afloat. Buck stared into the abyss of bankruptcy, not to mention personal ruin. A line of creditors, including the drilling company he hired, International Supply run by "Tiny" Phillips and "Frosty" Martin, were at the end of their tether. Their original contract stipulated the company would drill a hole 1,500 feet deep for $10,000 with payments for every 200 feet drilled. Buck and Black Diamond also agreed to supply fuel for the driller's boiler. However, run on a shoestring budget, Black Diamond and Buck quickly fell into arrears on their payments and never bothered picking up the tab for the boiler's fuel. Growing weary of Buck's non-existent payments but endless excuses, by the early spring of

1914 Tiny Phillips told driller James Hayes to complete the hole to the contracted depth of 1,500 feet as quickly as possible and then pack up the rig and move on. Hayes later testified that, due to Buck's inability to make payments, International Supply would not stick around one minute longer than necessary.[6] More importantly to Buck, however, if the drill bit reached 1,500 feet and Buck's balance owing remained outstanding, International Supply Company's lawyers would be able to seize all the assets of Black Diamond Oil Fields. Buck, who had used all his property, including his coal mine and family home, as collateral to finance operations, would lose everything.

Like a desperate gambler on a losing streak, Buck did his best to delay International Supply's inevitable departure, but time, luck, and circumstance began conspiring against him. Black Diamond #1 now approached the 1,500-foot depth where, in October 1913, Archibald Dingman's Calgary Petroleum Products #1 had produced a show of naphtha that excited investors and captured the public's imagination about southern Alberta's oil potential. Given the proximity of the two wells, and Buck's continuous stream of self-promotion, both investors and interested observers expected Black Diamond #1 would produce a similar show.[7] So far, however, Black Diamond #1 had reported signs of natural gas but no seepages or traces of crude oil. Buck clearly believed these hurt sales of Black Diamond stock and hindered his ability to generate enough revenue to keep paying the drillers.

Multiple legal imbroglios added to his considerable burdens. On April 25, 1914, the man Buck originally asked to head his oil company, Grant S. Wolverton, sued Buck for $1,500 in damages and filed for an injunction against the sale of some Black Diamond stock. The clash with Wolverton originated months earlier when Buck included 10,000 Black Diamond shares as part of an incentive package to woo Wolverton from his present employer, Oscar Devenish, to take over as president of Black Diamond. But Wolverton got cold feet and stayed with Devenish. That left the disposition of the shares used to try and entice Wolverton as the issue between the two parties. Wolverton claimed he tried to return all the certificates when he refused the post but said Buck allowed him to keep 2,000 shares for his troubles. There matters rested until March 1914, when Black Diamond experienced its credit crunch and needed to make a payment to International Supply. On March 25, 1914, Buck and the board of directors of Black Diamond demanded the return of the remaining stock certificates, claiming Wolverton had not provided the services he promised in exchange for the shares. Five days later, company secretary and treasurer Jennie Earl wrote Wolverton insisting on immediate payment of $2,000.[8] Wolverton sent the letter to his attorneys and decided to sell a block of 1,000 at two dollars per share, less a fifty-cent commission per share for the broker. Only after the deal closed and Wolverton tried to transfer ownership did he learn that Buck had cancelled the certificates and claimed that he was the rightful owner. Wolverton sought a court order to compel the company to register transfers and asked for damages totalling $1,500 to recover his costs from the scuttled sale. Making matters worse, Wolverton intended to go to trial.[9]

As Buck battled Wolverton in the courts and less than promising reports accumulated from the oil well, the unmistakable pall of failure began shrouding Buck and his company. One of Black Diamond's directors, Dr. H.E. Hall, tried cashing out before the collapse, placing a large block of stock on the market at a low price, drawing the ire of Buck, who immediately fired off a letter to shareholders lashing out at "unfriendly interests" that included two of the three daily papers, *The Calgary Morning Albertan, The Calgary Daily Herald,* and an industry broadsheet, *The Natural Gas and Oil Record.* Due to an earlier dispute with the owner/editor of the *Record,* Buck characterized the latter as little more than a "weekly yellow sheet devoted to knocking genuine oil developments." Buck claimed all three editors envied his success, and questioned their objectivity; all three, he complained, held substantial investments in other companies. As for Dr. Hall, Buck resorted to name calling, denigrated him as being "last of his class" at medical school and a selfish "loser" who should tender his resignation as a director. The letter closed with the cryptic comment that this might be the last letter "until we make our full announcement of our very successful developments"—a bold statement considering how close Buck was to financial ruin.[10] Buck's real problem was that he had invested his own money in the well, staking his personal future on the success or failure of the business.

Two weeks later, Buck told Black Diamond's employees the company was on the verge of bankruptcy and that he, personally, would lose everything if it went under. Increasingly desperate, Buck openly talked around the office, and especially on trips out to the well to driller James Hayes, about finding a way to artificially stimulate the price of Black Diamond so he could pay his bills and get more time. It is not clear how or when Buck began thinking of salting his well—pouring oil down the well and bringing it back up, thus creating the appearance of an oil strike—but the conspiracy came together remarkably quickly. In a matter of days, Buck created a self-made combination of crude oil and gasoline to salt the well with and came up with a boiler room scheme to sell as much stock as he could. "If you go along," Buck told his co-conspirators, "you'll be looked after."[11]

Hayes later remembered that Buck raised the issue with him three or four times in April 1914. "He didn't ask me to put it in," Hayes later told investigators. "He talked about putting it in himself." However, since nothing could happen at the well without Hayes knowing, Buck wanted Hayes's consent before going ahead with the scheme. So it should hardly come as a surprise that after midnight on a moon-filled night in May 1914 Buck sat on the corner of a bed pleading with the driller to just let him salt the damned well. Otherwise, he, his family, and friends would lose everything. The driller initially refused, holding firm against outright deception of shareholders, but Hayes's resolve began to waiver as Buck continued to talk. "Finally," testified Hayes, "he hung so much—he said he would lose all of his property, and his home was mortgaged and he would have no place for his family, and so I told him that the boys could put it in in the morning."[12]

The next day, Buck delivered the news that the Black Diamond well had produced a show of crude oil, ostensibly demonstrating the same promise as the Dingman well. But word of Black Diamond's strike barely caused a ripple, despite stories in all three major Calgary dailies, including one on the front page of *The Calgary Morning Albertan* on May 8, 1914. Frustrated and desperate, Buck followed up with the *Albertan* and arranged for a feature story the following day, but the public reaction remained underwhelming. Fortunately for Buck, less than a week later, Archibald Dingman's Calgary Petroleum Products #1 produced a modest show of crude mixed in with a much more voluminous show of natural gas, proving definitively that crude oil existed beneath Alberta. It also unleashed eleven weeks of unbridled excesses and debauchery that saw a stock market frenzy capable of lifting all boats, including that of George Buck, who found a temporary salvation from personal financial disaster but now longed to use this new opportunity to secure his future.

In many ways, this is the "origin story" of Alberta's oil culture that takes place a generation or two before the 1947 Leduc discovery during the Turner Valley boom of 1913–14. Oil culture can be defined as the attitudes, assumptions, values, beliefs, and actions associated with, and arising from, petroleum development that reflect, and direct, the socio-economic, political, and cultural dynamics in a jurisdiction, in this case the province of Alberta. Exploring the province's first boom helps identify and define the origins and persistence of several aspects of Alberta's petroleum culture, including an abiding faith in entrepreneurialism, unvarnished capitalism, individual initiative, the wisdom of the free hand of the market, and the importance of progress, reason,

Figure 0-2 "Prosperity and Oil"
Several ads in the winter of 1913/14 emphasized that petroleum would bring a better future for Calgary and Alberta.

and technology. Born in increasingly dire economic circumstances as both the province and the global economy adjusted to the waning of the prolonged economic boom (1898–1912), finding oil in Alberta encouraged the belief that the new industry would insulate the province from the pain of an impending economic downturn. At bottom, most decided the oil industry provided a better life than the one they currently possessed. Given the onset of economic tough times that descended on the province, and much of western Canada, following the collapse of the wheat economy in 1912–13, the prospect of finding oil in Alberta took on added urgency and promised to transform the city, province, region, and possibly the nation. Oil culture gave the city—and the province at large—its swagger. As one Vancouver paper noted at the height of the boom, "Nobody appeared to have the slightest doubt that within a short time he or she (for the women were as heavy buyers and sellers as the men) would be taking his or her ease in a Pullman bound for a holiday in some southern clime.... Everybody seemed to be making money; had made it, or was about to make it, and was confident that he or she would make it."[13]

After commercial quantities were discovered by Edwin L. Drake in Pennsylvania in 1859, petroleum's energy density, utility, versatility, abundance, and relatively low price compared to other fuel sources marked it as a crucial strategic and economic commodity as it gradually evolved from its primary utility as a source of illumination in the nineteenth century. As commercial uses for petroleum and refined products expanded dramatically, the search for additional supplies grew increasingly urgent. In the 1860s, only three countries produced commercial quantities of oil—Canada, Russia, and the United States. By 1914, substantial discoveries added Romania, Indonesia, Burma, Mexico, Iran, and Venezuela to the list of producers. But the size, scope, and scale of the US industry dwarfed all competitors as discoveries in California, Kansas, Oklahoma, and Texas enabled petroleum's rise as the premier fuel source for the burgeoning transportation revolution at sea and on land.[14]

By the early twentieth century, oil also acquired a significant strategic dimension in part because of its importance as an industrial fuel. In 1890, historian and former president of the US Naval Academy at Annapolis, Captain Alfred Thayer Mahan, published *The Influence of Sea Power on History*. In this widely read book—it went through fifteen printings in ten years—that could be briefly summarized as an exploration of how the rise of the Royal Navy led to Great Britain's rise as the pre-eminent economic and political power in Europe, Mahan argued that there is an intimate relationship between economics and the effective use of naval power that any state could achieve. Maritime trade was an important way for states to generate and maintain wealth in peacetime. In the event of war, the state that controlled the sinews of world trade—while disrupting those of its opponent, could dramatically shift the balance of resources in its favour.[15]

But the advantage technology offered with one hand, geography and fate took with the other. While Great Britain had abundant supplies of coal, it did not have domestic supplies of crude. Indeed, as late as 1913, the British empire accounted for less than 2 percent of global oil production, ensuring Britain remained dependent on international suppliers to provide fuel for the Royal Navy. As historian Brian Black observed, by the early twentieth century petroleum emerged as a strategic commodity capable of establishing a state as a global power, transforming international oil exploration into a veritable arms race between countries.[16] The United States, with whom the British empire competed for influence and trade in South America, exported almost 80 percent of Britain's fuel requirement with Standard Oil's UK affiliate, Anglo-American, alone accounting for between 60 and 75 percent of the United Kingdom's fuel and refined products.[17] Anglo-Persian Oil (now British Petroleum) had a large concession in Iran (then still called Persia), ensuring that most of the British government's attention in the 1910s focused on the petroleum potential of the Persian Gulf, but finding energy sources inside the empire became increasingly important. By 1913, the Tulsa, Oklahoma–based *Oil and Gas Journal* noted substantial exploration efforts underway in New

Figure 0-3 "Today's the Day"
The *Edmonton Journal* contemplates the possibility of the Royal Navy running exclusively on Alberta oil. Despite not having a source of petroleum within the Empire, the Royal Navy converted its ships from coal to oil in 1913 and commenced a global search for petroleum. Many believed that the discovery at Turner Valley would secure Alberta's—and Canada's—economic and strategic future.

Brunswick, Ontario, Manitoba, Saskatchewan, and Alberta.[18] Developments in Alberta, especially the oil sands deposits in the north, received particular attention from the Admiralty, and Alberta's staunch anglophile population dreamed of making an important contribution to British power.[19]

After months of drilling by three different oil companies—Calgary Petroleum Products, McDougall-Segur, and Black Diamond Oil Fields—just south of the city, in May 1914 Archibald W. Dingman's Calgary Petroleum Products produced commercial volumes of gasoline. Technically, it produced a wet gas condensate known as naphtha so pure that, even unrefined, it served as fuel in the engines of motor cars. The discovery unleashed months of pent-up anticipation and excitement in a sudden flurry of celebration mixed with avarice. Historian Earle Gray wrote that "within a few months Calgarians woke up from that monumental speculative spree with such a hangover that more than half a century later the city still remembers the event as the wildest boom that ever hit the west." Despite the frenzy of speculation, and the estimated $4 million invested (equivalent to $108 million today, adjusted for inflation), returns were paltry. Over 500 oil companies formed; fewer than fifty drilled for oil and, by 1919, six produced wet gas laced with petroleum condensates. As Gray observed, between 1914 and 1924, Turner Valley "produced only 65,945 barrels of oil, an average rate of less than twenty barrels a day. Seldom had there been so much excitement generated over such little oil."[20]

Despite the failure to strike crude oil in commercial quantities, the boom nonetheless witnessed the beginnings of Alberta's petroleum culture that still influence the perceptions and politics of the province, particularly the veneration of the market and oil's transformative abilities. Both during the boom and in its aftermath, a series of institutions and practices, both formal and informal, emerged with the goal of taming reckless speculation and providing structure and predictability to an otherwise chaotic industry. Not surprisingly, the negotiation of Alberta's oil culture relied to a large degree on pre-existing values and beliefs about the role of the state in the economy, based on the two conservative bedrocks of southern Alberta's political economy—ranching and the railroads. This, in turn, necessarily touched on the complex interplay of such forces as morality, politics, market forces, and debates in the public square about the competing meanings of freedom, liberty, and entrepreneurialism. As historian of the early oil patch John Schmidt noted, "[it] being a new product, the average man didn't know much about [oil's] nature except that it would make people rich."[21]

Oil's boosters emphasized petroleum's transformative qualities as the path to a better future of wealth and prosperity and sharply limited the role of citizens and governments to serving as handmaidens to development. Editorials and advertisements reflected traditional attitudes toward business and commerce while directing emerging beliefs about the new industry. Discussions covered a wide variety of topics, such as the proper role of the state in economic development, trade-offs between democracy and capitalism, and the tension between individual rights and collective responsibility, along with more mundane matters, such as the difference between speculation and investment. These debates shaped perceptions about the decidedly masculine characteristics of the prototypical Alberta "oil man"—usually middle aged, male, staunchly conservative, steadfast in his support for unvarnished or bootstrap capitalism, and possessing an unswerving belief in the importance of progress and industrialization. The state should play a minimal role, just strong enough for the protection of property rights but weak enough to not intervene in the economy except to encourage resource development. Despite the vicious boom and bust cycle of the oil patch, already well established by 1914, in most cases oil's "boosters" believed the transition to an oil-based economy and society would ensure prosperity, both individual and for the province—perhaps even all western Canada. Eventually, and at its most ambitious decades later, some believed Alberta's petroleum wealth would ultimately enable the province to remake Canada in its own entrepreneurial free-market image.

A variety of sources, including archival records, local, regional, national, and international newspapers, oil company advertisements and prospectuses, and corporate and private records, as well as the transcripts and evidence collected during various investigations and trials, can be called on to illustrate some of the assumptions inherent in Alberta's early oil culture, particularly the petroleum industry's growing association with progress, prosperity, modernity, and industrialization. Newspaper articles, cartoons, and advertisements produced in the cold and dreary winter of 1913/14 emphasized oil's growing importance to a modern industrial economy. For a considerable number of boosters, those voices urging caution, or expressing hesitation about oil's future, the so-called "knockers," were not just mistaken in their views, but wicked, or worse. Who else, besides drunks, fools, or the malevolent, would oppose progress?

But as *The Boom* reveals, contemporary debates regarding Alberta's emerging oil culture were far more contested, more diverse, involved far more people—both inside and outside the province—and were less one-sided than one might assume. While Alberta's contemporary political climate is typically described as staunchly conservative, in the context of the boom, the presence and influence of different strands of populism and progressivism meant that, at critical junctures, important voices wondered whether government has a responsibility to protect "the people" from "the interests."

Alberta's two main political parties in the first decades of the twentieth century embraced progressive reforms. As historian Howard Palmer pointed out, very few real ideological differences existed between the Liberals and Conservatives. Both were dependent on the support of British Canadians, advocates of laissez-faire policies for economic development, and shared a belief in the inevitability of growth of the province of Alberta. Both also believed the province's economic future depended on the deployment of modern science and technology. Nevertheless, the deciding factor for voters at the turn of the century might have been that provincial Liberals were more responsive than the Conservatives to implementing a liberal reform agenda, including suffrage, prohibition, and direct democracy (initiative, the referendum, and recall). The Liberals dominated provincial politics between 1905 and 1921, winning four successive provincial elections. Thus, as the province experienced the shock of a dramatic transition from rapid economic growth to depression and frenzied speculation in 1913–14, individuals, organizations, and groups emerged or formed to protect "the people" from "the interests," seeking to tame the excesses of an unfettered market. Indeed, the problems and perils of unvarnished capitalism became readily apparent and structural issues, such as conflicting lines of jurisdiction, made self-regulation of "wildcat" speculation largely ineffective and inflicted irreparable damage on the province's reputation as a good place to do business. Repeatedly, bitter experience revealed the inadequacies of this system, inviting different impulses to "do something" that resulted in more populist responses.

Prairie populism, like its variants elsewhere, exists more as a framework for discussing political and social questions as a contest between "the people" and a set of "elites" or interests who exert outsized or undue influence over the masses than as a fully developed political party, movement, or ideology.[22] In the context of the boom, populism can be used to explain a group of civic leaders, promoters, and investors joining to create the Calgary Stock Exchange to try and tame rampant speculation by so-called "curb brokers" in order to preserve investment capital for companies. A more libertarian strand of populism could explain why at least ten other independent stock exchanges operated during the boom. Populism also informed responses to the boom from outside Calgary, when civic leaders both in Canada and the United States resorted to self-help measures that included informal, but nonetheless effective, campaigns against Calgary oil to protect consumers. Journalist and historian James Gray wrote that after the boom, burned by promoters promising big returns but delivering little more than unpaid bills and broken dreams, "everyone not totally stupid came to regard shares in oil companies as something akin to shares in mining companies, the Brooklyn Bridge, and gold bricks—as downright swindles."[23]

In his magisterial volume about the Alberta Energy Board, University of British Columbia historian David Breen concluded that the stain left by May–July 1914 saddled Calgary oil companies with a poor reputation requiring a generation for Albertans to erase. "For the next decade legitimate local petroleum companies starved for capital were able to proceed only intermittently."[24] For this reason alone, George Edward Buck is arguably the most notorious, and influential, oil promoter of the first Turner Valley era (1912–1924), even though he never produced a barrel of oil. Indeed, the shadow cast by Buck over the Alberta industry is greater than that of all but a few of Alberta's oil pioneers. Convinced of the righteousness of his cause and secure in his belief that he was doing God's work, Buck approached business with a winner-takes-all mentality. He also promised investors "action," and always delivered. Sometimes, action meant a picnic at the Black Diamond well site. On other occasions, it meant creating a spectacle by insulting the press as hypocritical or branding another oil company "fake." Buck always made himself and his company the centre of attention and used a combination of wit, brazenness, and guile that, for a period of eighteen months, made him the most infamous oil promoter in all of Canada and parts of the United States. In the process, he revealed and exploited the fundamental weaknesses of the self-regulating institutions and difficult-to-enforce criminal statutes imperfectly serving as the province's oversight system for petroleum development in the early twentieth century. His egregious conduct and outrageous behaviour included the company-wide conspiracy the Alberta attorney general's office alleged defrauded investors of half a million dollars (approximately $14.4 million, adjusted for inflation), and singlehandedly compelled the government of Arthur Sifton to abandon its hands-off approach to regulation.[25]

The Boom, therefore, is a different account of the first Turner Valley era precisely because it rescues the failures, miscreants, and charlatans from obscurity and returns them to the story. Dismissing their misdeeds as unfortunate, and mostly harmless, aberrations minimizes the outsized influence these wildcatters exercised over perceptions of the values and beliefs of Albertans held by many outsiders. To many non-Albertans it appeared that con men and schemers far outnumbered honest operators by a sizable margin. Worse was the growing belief outside Alberta that the provincial government was both unable and unwilling to do anything to restrain their bad behaviour, prompting those jurisdictions to respond using their own self-help measures, such as boycotts and information campaigns. For careful observers of contemporary Canadian energy issues, these provide striking and obvious parallels with current debates over environmental protection, pipelines, and access to tidewater. In 1914, no less than today, perceptions matter. The privileging of individual rights and the desire to pursue economic profit regardless of the social and political costs overrode what observers believed was the province's obligation to protect "the people" from "the interests," and produced an object lesson in collective responsibility for development. The result was irreparable damage to both Alberta's reputation and its nascent industry as investment capital dried up before the outbreak of the Great War. By mid-June 1914, despite the importance of securing additional sources of crude to ensure energy security, investors outside the province steadfastly refused to invest in "Calgary oil" because of the perceived moral failures of Alberta's political and economic elite at curbing the bad behaviour of the rogues and charlatans among them.

The marginalization of people like George Buck owes itself to the fact that, as James Gray points out, the first generation of editors and publishers telling the story of Alberta's early oil industry celebrated the triumphs but tended to overlook its shortcomings. "They were people of faith in the present and future of the oil industry," wrote Gray. "So deep was that faith that it prevented them from reporting the failures with the same care with which they reported the successes."[26] Thus, while Dingman, Herron, and Calgary Petroleum Products remain part of the story, in this book the focus expands to account for the regional, national, and international dimensions of the Turner Valley discovery.

And, like every good story before it, it starts with a bad decision.

1

"Scientific Oil Finding:" Turner Valley's Anticline

> *Turner Valley is structurally probably the most complicated oil field in North America.*
>
> —Theodore A. Link
> *Association of American Petroleum Geologists Bulletin*
> November 1934[1]

Turner Valley, just outside of Calgary in the foothills of the Rocky Mountains, sits atop a massive oil deposit estimated to contain approximately a billion barrels of oil. Knowing a little bit of the basic geology of the Turner Valley field and the capabilities of the best available drilling technology of the time spoils some of the suspense of the first Turner Valley boom. The combination of the subsurface geology of Turner Valley and the limitations of cable rig technology made tapping into the main oil and gas reservoir in 1914 virtually impossible. Informed geological opinion generally held that if Alberta possessed petroleum reserves, they would reside in Cretaceous era rock, the Dakota sandstone, less than 2,000 feet from the surface (see Table 1-1). In Turner Valley, however, commercial quantities of oil and gas lay much deeper (6,820 feet) below in the Mississippian, making commercial development of oil virtually impossible given the limits of drilling technology and the incomplete knowledge about the subsurface features of the Valley. Only in the 1920s did it become clear that Turner Valley's Dakota formation did not contain a true Dakota conglomerate, making it unlike any other western Dakota oilfields. Furthermore, the faults in the valley were far more complex than preliminary surveys by the Geological Survey of Canada revealed. But the entrepreneurs, promoters, and investors of the boom, to borrow a phrase, did not know what they did not know about the Turner Valley anticline and

17

Table 1-1 Geologic Time, Turner Valley

ERA	PERIOD	FORMATION	DESCRIPTION
Mesozoic	Cretaceous	Edmonton Series	Thick littoral, estuarine, and freshwaters series with occasional coal seams
		Bearspaw Shales	Impervious marine and estuarine shales
		Belly River Group	Thick sandstone formation with some coal seams
		Claggett Shales	Marine-estuarian shales
		Cardomin Sandstone	A few thin beds with subsidiary conglomerates
		Dakota Group	
		Kootenay Group	An arenaceous group with many coal seams. Much thicker near the Rocky Mountains
	Jurassic	Fernie	Shales
Paleozoic	Mississippian	Rundle Group	Competent, massive limestones and dolostones
		Banff	Shaley mudstones grading upward to massive limestone
		Exshaw	Black, platy fissile shale
	Devonian		Interbedded clastics (chunks and smaller grains of broken off sedimentary rock), carbonates and evapoprites (layered crystalline sedimentary rocks) grading upward into interbedded limestones, dolostones and shales
	Cambrian		Mature tergenous clastics interbedded with dolostones and limestones

invested their time, attention, and money in drilling for oil, basing their projects on the best possible information available at the time.

Set in the foothills of the Rocky Mountains, Turner Valley, southwest of Calgary, consists of a series of rolling, grass-covered ridges and wide-open valleys. Two rivers, the Sheep and the Highwood, cross through the valley before joining eight kilometers east of Okotoks. The Turner Valley field runs in a narrow belt from north to south, parallel to the Rockies approximately forty-eight kilometres (twenty-two miles) long and 5.5 kilometers (2.5 miles) wide. Surface seepages along Sheep Creek ensured that Indigenous Peoples used the petroleum as medicine long before settlers arrived.[2]

Geophysicist Paul MacKay observed that the study of the structural geology of Turner Valley—that is, of the arrangement of the folds, faults, joints, and fractures of the field—is one of the most dynamic in western Canada. It is important to remember that MacKay's conclusions about the Turner Valley formation represent the culmination of several decades' worth of research, writing, and theorization about the creation of the formation—not all of which was available to drillers and promoters in 1914. "The Turner Valley structure is fascinating," wrote MacKay in 1991, "in that it is consistently represented as a classic example of the latest geologic theory."[3] Little wonder, because the process that formed Turner Valley took place over billions of years. Over time, the rocks, sand, sediments, and shales accumulated as Alberta cycled between periods of land and sea. Life evolved from microscopic single-celled organisms and algae to vertebrates and more complex vegetation. As plants and animals died, they mixed with sand and water, forming layers of sediment subjected to intense heat and pressure. The Devonian period (419 to 359 million years ago) saw a large network of tropical reefs, rich in marine life and lush vegetation covering Alberta. Eventually, these Devonian reefs produced most of the oil and natural gas deposits in the province. During the Cretaceous period (140 to 65 million years ago), a large inland sea covered much of North America.

Plate tectonics also played a significant role, particularly the interaction of the faster Pacific plate (moving northwest at seven to eleven centimetres—three to four inches—per year) with the slower North American plate (moving west-southwest at 2.3 centimetres—one inch—per year) where the two meet as if on a conveyor belt. Normally, the edge of the heavier and denser Pacific plate sublimates (moves beneath) the lighter and more buoyant North American plate. But around 65–35 million years ago, landforms from the Pacific plate too big to pass under the North American plate crashed into the edge of the North American plate, causing the compression of the continent.

The *Imperial Oil Review* likened the results of this collision to dropping a pebble in a pool of still water. "It caused geological ripples which were intense near the point of origin and moderated as they spread outward."[4] Known as the Laramide Orogeny the slow-motion collision, over thirty million years, produced breaks in the earth's crust known as thrust faults. The faults pushed thick sheets of older Paleozoic limestones eastward over younger Mesozoic rocks, producing at least two notable consequences for the Turner Valley field. First, it created the Rocky Mountains, which extend nearly 7,000 kilometres from Alaska to New Mexico. Second, it produced the Western Canada Sedimentary Basin (WCSB), when a wedge of mid-Proterozoic to Cenozoic strata covering 1.4 million square kilometres (640,000 square miles) from the Northwest Territories to the United States "detached from its basement, displaced northeastward, compressed and thickened."[5] Six kilometres thick at its western end in the Cordillera in the foothills of the Rocky Mountains, the strata of WCSB gradually thins to nothing along the edge of the Canadian Shield in the east. The folding and thrusting of the Laramide Orogeny placed thick layers of rock over layers of organic matter contained in lower strata. The combination of the increased pressure and time resulted in one of the largest oil and gas fields in the world, most of which lay underneath the surface of Alberta.[6] Estimates are that the WCSB contained 1.71 billion barrels of oil and 632 trillion cubic feet of gas.

Over tens of millions of years, water and wind steadily eroded the Rocky Mountains. Composed of sandstone, the glaciers of the Pleistocene (Ice Age—2.5 million years ago) carved valleys and troughs through the soft rock. Some glaciers believed to be nearly four kilometres thick eroded rock and minerals from the mountains and deposited sandstone, siltstone, and shales in the valleys and foothills of the mountains, covering the area with a glacial till that hid the subsurface features. Making matters more challenging, oil and gas is not normally found in the strata where it is formed; rather it is typically found after it has migrated through pervious beds and becomes trapped in an impenetrable rock barrier, where it will accumulate in a reservoir that can be flat, folded (anticline or syncline), or faulted strata. While some oil and gas will escape through faults (breaks) between the rocks to the earth's surface, most will remain in the trap. Most oil and gas reservoirs are composed of sedimentary rock (sandstones, grits, conglomerates, dolostones, and limestones), and in the Turner Valley field, dolostones and limestones are the most important.

The Turner Valley reservoir is not a pool of oil as much as it is a narrow ribbon of gas, oil, and water extending from the northeast flank of the formation down to the southwest. Oil historian Earle Gray suggested visualizing the arrangement of gas, oil, and water in the reservoir as sealing a jar half-filled with equal parts oil and water, tilted on a forty-five-degree angle. The trapped air at the top is the gas cap. The gas cap of the ribbon starts in the northeast corner of the formation, underneath about a mile (5,280 feet) of rock. Sandwiched between the gas cap and the water table is the main body of oil, which starts approximately 6,000 feet underground. In April 1957, G.S. Hume of the Geological Survey of Canada noted that the difference in elevation between the highest and lowest well drilled was approximately 5,000 feet. Nevertheless, the producing oil and gas beds occur at a minimum depth of 3,450 feet and extend down to 9,000 feet.[7]

The Geological Survey of Canada (GSC) played a crucial, and sometimes overlooked, role in bringing about the exploitation of Alberta's petroleum industry. Founded in 1842 as a modest, publicly funded but independently directed scientific survey, the GSC thrived and expanded in fulfilling its ambitious official mandate of carrying out "a Geological Survey of the Province of Canada." The task of mapping Canada's geology was a daunting one, but the Survey benefited greatly from partnerships with Indigenous Peoples, who offered critical support by teaching survival skills and serving multiple roles as "guides, hunters, warriors, and as co-leaders."[8] The combination of Indigenous ways of knowing about the land and its resources and the technology of the settlers spurred Canada's economic and industrial development. Through its widespread publication of maps and reports, the GSC drew attention to the area's natural resources and opportunities. After 1871, the survey played a crucial role in transforming the Canadian West by reconnoitring navigation and communication routes and gathering, cataloguing, and disseminating information about the climate, soil, vegetation, wildlife, natural resources, and Indigenous populations of the territories of Rupert's Land transferred to Canada.[9] As Alberta oil patch historian Aubrey Kerr reminds, "These were *public servants*, officers of the geological survey of Canada, not entrepreneurs" who identified, catalogued, and carried out much of the important early work that resulted in Canada's natural resources industries.[10]

Despite a promising beginning—Ontario claimed the first commercial oil well in North America—to a certain extent federal regulations stunted the growth of the Canadian industry, but so too did the relatively poor quality and high sulphur content of Ontario crude, which inhibited the growth of export markets compared to "sweeter" (meaning less sulphur content) Pennsylvania crude in the 1870s and 1880s.[11] Furthermore, Canada's recent colonial past left behind an economy geared toward the export of raw materials and natural resources and a small manufacturing sector. Developing the economy behind the high tariff barriers of the National Policy after 1867 resulted in higher-cost and more inefficient production methods, especially when compared to the US industry. As production declined in Ontario's older fields, Canadian imports of US crude expanded to meet growing demand. The proximity of abundant energy sources in the eastern United States, particularly the prolific oil fields of Pennsylvania and Ohio, combined with a greater density of railroad tracks and cross-border ties between Canada and the US sources, offered a cheap alternative, especially as additions to US proven reserves lowered the price of American crude. Until 1925, western Ontario provided the bulk of Canadian oil production, though it remained limited to the small fields around Bothwell, Oil Springs, and Petrolia.[12]

But there were promising signs in the West. Both the GSC and the Canadian Pacific Railway noted geological features in western Canada where natural gas proved abundant, as the railroad knew all too well. In 1882, as the CPR built the Prairie Route, the GSC looked for coal and water deposits along the route. As construction neared Langevin Station (now known as Alderson) outside of Medicine Hat, instead of water drillers struck natural gas that quickly ignited and burned down the derrick. With proven reserves in the area, the town of Medicine Hat drilled for natural gas, finding it in sufficient quantities to establish its own consumer gas industry after 1899.[13]

George W. Dawson carried out the GSC's mission in southern Alberta in 1881. Dawson also wrote the first mention of a reverse dip along the banks of Sheep Creek in a report published in 1883.[14] For practical geologists, however, the significance of the Turner Valley anticline was that it heaved the Cretaceous-period Dakota formation closer to the surface, giving prospectors the opportunity to drill into these rocks at shallower depths. By the early twentieth century, contemporary wisdom held that the Dakota sands held all of Alberta's petroleum deposits. As a 1913 GSC report on the oil and gas prospects of Alberta concluded on the eve of the boom, the three most promising areas were the Athabasca River district in northern Alberta, around Medicine Hat in central Alberta, and around Bow Island in southeastern Alberta. Of the three, it was only Bow Island, where Eugene Coste's Canadian Western Natural Gas drilled eight wells nearby producing seventy-six million cubic feet of natural gas every twenty-four hours, that enjoyed a degree of commercial success. More importantly, Bow Island established the Dakota sandstones as the key to Alberta's petroleum future. "The wells have a depth of 1,890 to 1,930 feet," summarized the report. "This is believed to be the Dakota sandstone."[15]

The GSC saw its role as being a catalyst to the private sector development of Canada's natural resources, and their reports succeeded in inspiring an amateur geologist by the name of William Stewart Herron. Born in Gelert, Ontario, on February 10, 1870, Herron was the second child in a family of thirteen (nine boys and four girls). Herron left home at age fourteen, to work as a cook's helper in a logging camp in the wilderness of northern Ontario, where he met Ella McKinnon, who came to work in the same camp as Stewart. The two fell in love and were married the following spring. In the meantime, Stewart advanced to be bull cook—the boss of the cookery—and learned the ropes of the logging industry. Between that and his ability to handle horses, he launched the first of a series of business endeavours using horses and sleighs as a contract log hauler. To supplement his income from log hauling, Herron also built ice roads in the winter by levelling the snow and flooding the trails; in the summer he cleared trees and cleared bush from a surveyor's line. In 1896 Herron became a pioneer settler of Cobalt in northern Ontario, where he cleared timber and built roads for the Temiskaming and Northern Ontario Railway and became a member of the town council. It was also during this period at Cobalt that Herron became interested in mining, claiming that he had discovered some mineral deposits near Cobalt but unscrupulous partners cheated him out of his share. "The story," observed journalist and Herron family biographer Frank Dabbs, "became part of his repertoire after he had succeeded in the oil exploration business. When he told it, it was tinged with his bitterness towards men who had tried to deal him out of that opportunity, too." A more accurate story, noted Dabbs, was that he sold his mineral proprieties before development to finance the family's move out west.[16]

Time and circumstances dictated the move to Alberta. Frail in her youth, Herron's first wife Ella grew weaker as she aged. By the time their third child, Archie, was born after daughters Irene and Laura, Ella was practically incapacitated. Then, when Archie died at a year and a half, Ella's physical decline accelerated. As Stewart spent a great deal of time away from home working, he arranged for a nanny to care for the children. Meanwhile, construction on the Temiskaming line ended shortly after the turn of the century, and as mining in Cobalt waned, Herron moved the family first to Haileybury, where he built a new home before returning Ella for treatment to Toronto, where she died shortly after doctors declared her incurable. Suddenly, Herron became a single parent with two young daughters. Given that he spent a good amount of time away from home, and that remarrying quickly was customary practice on the frontier, it is not surprising that Herron would look for a new wife and mother for his children. In short order, he met and married Edith

Figure 1-1 "William Stewart Herron, petroleum pioneer in Turner Valley, Alberta"
William S. Herron has long been considered the "father" of Alberta's petroleum industry. His persistence helped prove the existence of oil in Alberta. (Glenbow Archive CU1125948)

Isabelle Johnston, a widow three years younger than himself who had lost her husband in a logging accident. Edith had a daughter, Mabel, the same age as Laura. But, before marrying Edith in 1904, Herron found himself in the unusual position of having free time on his hands. After placing his children in the care of his own family, in 1903 he set out in search of a fresh start. He travelled through southern Ontario, where he visited the natural gas fields north of Lake Erie before crossing the border to visit the Pennsylvania oil fields. According to Breen, his experience in the Cobalt mine awakened an interest in petroleum geology. In an interview decades later, his son, Bill Stewart, recalled his father was "a fabulous reader" who became a self-taught geologist.[17]

Herron made his way west to Okotoks just south of Calgary, where he bought a 960-acre section of land from the Canadian Pacific Railway for three dollars an acre. In the late summer of 1904, Herron returned to Ontario, where he and Edith married on November 28, 1904. Shortly thereafter, he sold his house, road construction and cartage equipment, and horses in anticipation of moving out west. The family boarded a train in December 1904 to make the 3,000-kilometre journey to Alberta, where he intended to raise workhorses on his ranch. It was a shrewd plan. As Dabbs observed, every aspect of economic life in southern Alberta at the turn of the century depended on cartage. Freight wagons using up to twenty-four horses hauled everything—grain, feed, seed, timber, stone, brick, cement, and coal—and Herron intended to use his ranch to raise animals for the transportation business. But his skill set, like his knowledge of forestry and road building, would prove as useful as his reputation as a hard worker.

The cartage business would take some time for Herron to develop as he built his stock of horses. In the meantime, he worked for William Livingstone and Joe Pugh at their lumber mill in the Crowsnest Pass, where Herron took a money-losing operation and made it a stunning success. Within two years, Pugh and Livingston learned enough from Herron that they no longer needed his services, but they presented him with another proposition. The stock of workhorses in the region continued to decline, prices for the animals continued to rise. Livingston and Pugh proposed that Herron break wild workhorses in the foothills to supply their business with adequate horses. Herron countered with his own proposal. He would help them reorganize and expand production in exchange for 25 percent of the increased output. In practical terms this meant that for every three horses he broke for Pugh and Livingstone, Herron would receive one horse to add to his stock. The task of breaking wild broncos proved easy for Herron, as he hitched them to a heavy coal wagon between a quiet team pulling a shipment of coal to Okotoks. Soon enough, Herron broke enough horses to set up Herron Cartage, and by 1909 the business achieved sufficient scale to contract to supply and haul coal from the mine in Black Diamond to the electric plant in Okotoks. In less than five years, Herron established for himself the reputation as an enterprising businessperson unafraid of demanding work. But his prodigious work ethic, frequent absences, and lack of social standing made him an outcast among southern Alberta elites. Dabbs suggests that this lack of acceptance bothered Herron, driving him to make enough money to force his entry into the right social circles.

One day in the spring of 1911, while waiting for a load of coal, he went to investigate a nearby gas seepage. Well known for the smell of rotten eggs, the seepage along Sheep Creek was surprisingly well investigated. As Calgary Petroleum Product drillers began their work in late 1913, "old-timers" shared stories about the seeps. The Turner family had homesteaded the valley in 1886 and used it to raise purebred horses. The brothers noticed their horses refused to drink from the water near the seepages but dismissed them as swamp gas. But cattle ranchers living on the banks of Sheep Creek dug a hole in the ground with spade and pick through which enormous quantities of gas escaped. Through some undescribed method, they managed to store the escaping gas in barrels so they could burn it for light. John Ware, the famous Black rancher from Texas who now called Alberta home, took some samples in 1888 and sent them to a doctor in Calgary for analysis. The doctor, who pioneered the use of X-rays, proved ill-suited to analyze the sample, saying it was coal gas. The August 3, 1904, edition of *The Calgary Daily Herald* announced on the front page that prospectors searching for coal deposits on Sheep Creek had inadvertently discovered natural gas "in considerable quantities." One of the prospectors stopped to light his pipe but barely struck his match when he found himself thrown through the air and landed on the ground a few feet away hatless and with his clothes on fire. The newspaper noted that if the gas on Sheep Creek could be piped to Calgary, it might become a commercial proposition. Finally, in 1911, rancher Andy Anderson led Calgary Alderman John G. Watson to the seepage, where Watson became convinced that it produced natural gas. Hoping to attract the Canadian Pacific Railway to build their workshops in Calgary instead of Medicine Hat, on June 1, 1911, a delegation from the Calgary city council that included Mayor J.W. Mitchell and Fire Chief James Smart, staked a claim on the property for the City of Calgary. Unfortunately for the city, Mitchell and Smart never filed the paperwork, leaving the opportunity for homesteader Michael Stoos and Herron to do so a few months later in September.[18]

Herron wanted to investigate the seepages for himself. Once there, he spotted an anticline on a rock outcropping and instantly believed that petroleum produced the seepages. More than instinct prompted Herron's belief that oil existed below. His years of reading about petroleum geology had transformed Herron into a confident, self-taught amateur expert on the subject to the point where he could easily, and vividly, describe the subterranean formations of Turner Valley while explaining why it should have petroleum, as he did in an interview with the *Herald* on October 25, 1913. Herron explained that the Discovery well sat on top of an anticline that he described as a "fold in the rock, caused ages ago by pressure or contraction" that formed a natural oil reservoir closer to the surface than it would have if it were located on the largely undisturbed prairie. Describing the different layers of the earth's formation as stratas, Herron delivered a thumbnail sketch of the Turner Valley structure. "The oldest strata studied is the 'Aegean' formation, which contains no animal or vegetable fossils." Subsequent layers from the Jurassic period held the remnants of animal life in the form of lizards and reptiles, followed by the Carboniferous strata containing "a higher order of animal

Figure 1-2 "Gas and petroleum claim being staked by the City of Calgary"
L-R: Mayor John W. Mitchell; "Cappy" Smart; Alderman John "Gravity" Watson; and Frank Harris place a sign on the site of what would become Calgary Petroleum Products #1. City officials forgot to fill the necessary paperwork, enabling W.S. Herron to claim the lease instead. (Glenbow Archive CU189401)

life and luxuriant vegetation" trapped in lower shale formations. Following the coal shale and sand of the Cretaceous, were the vaunted Dakota sands. This formation, asserted Herron, "is considered to be the greatest oil-bearing formation of this district." The tremendous upheavals that produced the Rocky Mountains "have tiptilted these stratas so that now in the mountains we find the earliest stratas cropping out on the surface of the slopes." Herron explained that the ideal conditions found in the Black Diamond district existed because of the series of anticlines running parallel to the mountains. Lest anyone believe that Herron was talking out of his hat, for good measure, Herron provided the source—DeLorme D. Cairnes's report on the Moose Mountain district in "Bulletin number 968, issued by the Department of the Interior, Ottawa."[19] Stewart Herron's trip to Pennsylvania, said his son Bill decades later, "may have had a great deal to do with his recognizing the gas seepages in Turner Valley." So, too, did his dogged determination to read and absorb the materials produced by the Geological Survey of Canada.[20]

Using a metal tub and some jars, Herron collected and sent samples of the gas to universities in Pennsylvania and California, both of which confirmed that the gas sample contained a petroleum derivative. The news spurred Herron into action. Already working eighteen-hour days, for the rest of 1911, he liquidated most of his assets, selling his farm in Okotoks and speculating in Calgary's booming real estate market. The moves provided the necessary capital, at least $40,000 ($1.1 million today, adjusted for inflation), to quietly assemble both the land and mineral rights to more than 7,000 acres of land that included the land both astride and adjacent to the gas seepages on Sheep Creek. Herron paid the Dominion land agent a five-dollar filing fee for a twenty-one-year mineral rights lease plus a first-year rental fee of twenty-five cents per acre. Thus, $165 bought a one-subsection (640 acres) lease while a quarter-section (160 acres) lease cost $45. Two of Herron's purchases along Sheep Creek, including the vital one on Michael Stoos's homestead ($18,000), and another where developers William McLeod and William Livingston ($15,000) already held the mineral rights, cost more. The purchases left Herron in possession of more than thirteen kilometres of land along the Turner Valley anticline but with no capital left for development. As historian David Breen noted, Herron's exertions left him land rich but cash poor. Breen might have added "vulnerable," because the Dominion Land Office required leaseholders to make "improvements" on the land within the first year to retain the lease. Furthermore, at twenty-five cents an acre, subsequent annual lease payments totalled $1,750, nearly double the average annual earnings of $850.92 for male workers in Calgary in 1911. While leaseholders could apply for extensions on rental fees, it was not a viable long-term strategy, particularly given Herron's extensive holdings. Herron needed to become a promoter to secure outside capital, and an experienced driller, just as other investors noticed his activities along Sheep Creek and began their own investigations.[21]

However, Herron proved ill suited to the role of oil promoter. While he was intelligent, ambitious, and optimistic about the future, promotion brought out his worst qualities—impatience, arrogance, and suspicion of others. Believing that developing the petroleum and natural gas of Turner Valley would be his ticket to becoming part of Calgary's financial and entrepreneurial elite where he would gain access to the wealth and respect he craved, he resented needing other people's money to do so. Herron, tactfully concluded oil historian Earle Gray, "was not particularly endowed with social graces." He refused to bite his tongue when the financiers overrode his understanding of geology or drilling, demonstrating little of the confidence, grace, or tact that came effortlessly to others. Most problematic of all, and as his business records reflect, Herron proved to be litigious and held long grudges.[22]

One of Herron's first attempts to secure an outside source of funding involved approaching California oil executive Ira E. Segur. Attracted by the prospects in Turner Valley, Segur made his way to Alberta in 1911 when Herron offered him a partnership. But Segur declined the offer from Herron, partly because he believed finding oil in Turner Valley would be a massive undertaking and believed only those who could afford to lose large sums of money should invest.[23] Segur joined with E.P. Howard and promptly struck a deal with local rancher and businessperson David McDougall to form the McDougall-Segur Exploration Company in 1912.

Born in Owen Sound, Ontario, in 1845, David was the second son of Methodist missionaries George and Elizabeth McDougall, who had moved out west along the Red River cart route. The McDougall family's missionary activities cemented their prominent status. David's father, George, and brother John would eventually build Edmonton's Methodist church—the oldest surviving building in Edmonton—and worked tirelessly toward establishing schools.[24] Unlike his father and older brother, however, David had different interests that led him to receive his education at mission schools (Victoria College, Cobourg, and Rockwood Academy near Guelph) and spend a year in the United States before rejoining his family in 1865 in what was then the North-West Territories. Five years before, the family had moved to Norway House on the north end of Lake Winnipeg. Within a few years the family moved farther west to Fort Edmonton, where Reverend George established a mission. In 1867, David became a trader and a trapper with Indigenous Peoples for a 200-mile radius around Victoria (now Smoky Lake, 60 miles east of Edmonton) on the North Saskatchewan River, freighting his goods on Red River carts each spring to Hudson's Bay Company's headquarters at Fort Garry, near modern-day Winnipeg. He married Annie McKenzie in 1871, and they settled near Morley, where the couple started their family and David established himself as a missionary, merchant, and fur trader. By the turn of the century, he branched out into ranching and real estate in Edmonton and Calgary, becoming one of Calgary's leading citizens in the process. David's granddaughter Eleanor Luxton writes that David's world consisted of local leaders James Lougheed, R.B. Bennett, and Patrick Burns, among others, "who were on councils or boards, and had foresight enough to realize that Calgary had passed the 'cow town' stage . . . . When he moved to Calgary, David naturally took his place." Indeed, the sandstone McDougall School, also known as the provincial government's southern offices on 412 7th Street SW, was named after John, George, and David McDougall.[25]

Capitalized at a meagre $100,000 divided into 100 shares, McDougall-Segur consciously appealed to well-heeled investors largely because the partners believed it made little sense for a company "to get the savings of the poor man to engage in the hazardous enterprise of drilling for oil in an absolutely new field." In short order, the company's directors sold an additional 150 shares to investors in Montreal, Toronto, Halifax, Quebec, Ottawa, Winnipeg, Edmonton, Kamloops, and Vancouver to increase the company's capitalization to $250,000. McDougall-Segur #1 started drilling on a site picked by British geologist Edward Hubert Cunningham Craig, whom they hired as a consultant, about eighteen kilometres northwest of Herron's prime location in late 1912.[26]

In the meantime, by June 1912, Herron's search for a business partner prompted him to approach the City of Calgary to provide "whatever they saw fit" to help develop the field and provide cheaper gas to displace coal for Calgary consumers. Unbeknownst to Herron, a year earlier, on June 1, 1911, Calgary mayor J.W. Mitchell and a delegation of officials staked a gas and petroleum lease on the very same parcel of land where Dingman #1 sat. City officials, however, forgot to file the paperwork in time to prevent the lease from reverting to the Crown, thus enabling Herron to acquire it that September. Frank Dabbs believes that the city's fathers, still smarting from losing the lease on Stoos's property, strung Herron along with no intention of signing a deal. Negotiations with the city continued off and on for at least four months before Herron concluded the city was not serious. Changing tack, Herron approached the Calgary Natural Gas Company's Archibald W. Dingman.

Born at Greenbush, Ontario, in March 1850, Dingman was one of nine children of United Empire Loyalist parents. As a young man, he spent some time working in the Pennsylvania oil fields from 1879 to 1883 before marrying Ida Lane in 1882. After leaving the oil fields, Dingman taught school and dabbled in several other ventures, including bicycle repair and manufacturing Comfort Soap for Pugsley, Dingman and Company. The latter venture nearly made millions for Dingman, but the entrepreneur lost everything when the factory burned to the ground. After the fire, Dingman cursed his bad luck and left for Alberta in 1902, bringing his own equipment to settle back into the petroleum industry. Like Herron, Dingman was a voracious reader of petroleum geology. But Dingman's organizational abilities and managerial acumen truly set him apart. He began his drilling career in Alberta searching for natural gas on the flats of the Saskatchewan River within the city limits of

Figure 1-3 "Archibald Wayne Dingman"
A shrewd businessman and skilled promoter, Archibald Dingman proved a steadying influence against unrealistic expectations both during and after the boom. (Glenbow Archive CU181710)

Edmonton. By 1905, Dingman moved south and launched a new joint stock venture, the Calgary Natural Gas Company, selling most of the original issue of capital stock (5,000 shares at ten dollars per share) to Calgary's elite, some of whom he would turn to again years later when launching Calgary Petroleum Products Company. Dingman found or identified several promising structures in the foothills around Calgary. With development capital in place, Dingman acted as the Calgary Natural Gas Company's general manager to secure the title of exclusive supplier of natural gas to Calgary city council. At the time, Calgary processed coal into oil to provide heat, power, and light. But burning manufactured coal gas proved inefficient and expensive for consumers, and city council looked to lower costs by switching to natural gas.[27]

At first, Dingman tried to secure his own supplies of natural gas by drilling for it in the city. In 1906, Calgary Natural Gas Company #1 spudded in at a drill site found by the Geological Survey of Canada on the Tsuut'ina First Nation. The well produced small amounts of gas but not enough to justify further development, so the company abandoned the well in 1908. Despite finding insufficient quantities of gas, Dingman still regarded it as a positive experience; the well reached a depth of 3,400 feet, a remarkable accomplishment given the rig's limitations, and provided valuable data and experience. Dingman's next well, Calgary Natural Gas Company #2, spudded in August 1908 on the estate of Colonel James Walker in what is now the Inglewood Bird Sanctuary. Completed by May 1909, the well struck gas at 2,900 feet with a modest daily flow of roughly 900,000 cubic feet. A small pipeline linked the well to A.E. Cross's Calgary Brewing Company before additional infrastructure enabled the gas to supply a small part of the city's energy needs.[28]

Dingman needed more production, hence Herron's decision to approach Dingman about Turner Valley. But Herron simply could not match another suitor with deep pockets, Eugene Marius Coste. Born in Marseilles in 1859 to a prominent family and educated as an engineer, Eugene Coste succeeded in finding plenty of natural gas for the CPR on its western Canadian lands. From 1906 to 1909, Coste brought in gas wells all over southern Alberta before setting his sights on securing the lucrative Calgary market, especially after a prolific natural gas well blew in at Bow Island in 1911. To bring the gas to Calgary, Coste proposed building a 383-kilometre pipeline. Herron believed it would be much cheaper and efficient to develop Turner Valley because of its proximity to the city. Coste, however, denigrated the prospects in Turner Valley, claiming that the broken formation there made drilling for oil or gas pointless. The charge owed more to Coste's stake in the Bow Island pipeline project. Dingman hoped he would also receive a lucrative position in the new company, but Coste had other plans, so Dingman began quietly winding down his involvement with Calgary Natural Gas.[29] By the time Herron approached him to organize a new oil company, few others in the province could match Dingman's experience and background knowledge of all aspects of the industry.[30]

Oil patch legend claims Herron convinced Archibald Dingman and R.B. Bennett to invest their money and expertise while on a fishing trip to Sheep Creek. When the party stopped for lunch, so the story goes, Herron pulled out a pan, lit the gas seep and began cooking a lunch of eggs and bacon over the open flame. While colourful and brassy, like several stories of the early oil industry, it is a complete fabrication. Herron himself denied that the cooking demonstration happened; the Herron family maintained a reporter made it up to sell newspapers. But through sheer repetition, it became accepted truth, ensconcing itself in Alberta oil patch lore and the cultural landscape so deeply that the Canadian Western Natural Gas Company featured it in advertisements in the mid-1950s and reporters repeated it as fact into the 1980s. It endured because, as historian Brian Black observed, "the industry's success

Figure 1-4 Canadian Western Natural Gas Company Ad
The enduring myth of the alleged cooking demonstration performed by William S. Herron to attract investors to Turner Valley is highlighted by this Canadian Western Natural Gas ad from 1956. Although the Herron family long claimed that the story was invented by a bored newspaper writer, some authors continued to print the story as fact well into the 1980s.

The Boom that Began with a Cooking Demonstration

In 1911 pioneer rancher Bill Herron lit a gas leak seeping from the rocky floor of Turner Valley. Then he calmly began frying eggs: a convincing demonstration of Turner Valley's rich natural gas potential. In 1914 the Dingman well blew-in with a flow of gas and oil. Meanwhile, other men of vision were piping gas to Calgary from the Bow Island field . . . the beginning of Canadian Western Natural Gas Company Ltd. Since 1922 Turner Valley has been an important supply source for the company's system. Your gas company is proud that its history is closely allied with the "Turner Valley Story" . . . a story that began with a cooking demonstration.

depended on myth." Particularly myths that explain "facts about the region combined with hopes of individual wealth and the potential for petroleum to dramatically improve . . . society."[31] The story succeeds because it is unpretentious—a stunt worthy of Phineas T. Barnum that explained the presence of petroleum in Turner Valley more relatably and easily understood than reports on anticlines and geological theories. Its longevity and persistence suggest Albertans want the story to be true because of what it says about them and Alberta's oil. From this perspective, the story taps into several strands of Alberta's oil culture, including the ethos of rugged individualism, self-sufficiency, entrepreneurial initiative, faith in the power of nature to transform lives, and the romance of the "last best West" where anything was possible. Where else but Alberta could a cooking demonstration conjure a multibillion-dollar industry?[32]

Even though Coste's pipeline project provided adequate volumes of natural gas from Bow Island to the city, securing additional natural gas supplies remained a top priority for the growing city. After all due consideration, Dingman pronounced himself satisfied with Turner Valley's encouraging indications. On July 1, 1912, Herron offered Dingman an option to purchase a 55 percent stake in 3,940 acres of land in exchange for $22,000 in cash and a commitment to spend at least $50,000 drilling a well. With an opportunity to develop a supply of gas closer to Calgary to rival Coste's Canadian Western Natural Gas, Dingman put together a nine-person consortium to create Calgary Petroleum Products Company, Limited (CPP) on July 26, 1912. Capitalized at $150,000, the company included some of Calgary's most prominent citizens: Senator James A. Lougheed, future Prime Minister Richard B. Bennett, lawyer William Henry McLaws, rancher and brewer Alfred E. Cross, and real estate promoters T.J.S. Skinner and A.J. Sayre. The large personalities in the group occasionally produced friction, but no competition would be more compelling than that between Herron and Dingman. Although Herron deserved much of the credit for envisioning Alberta's petroleum future and assembling the mineral leases, Dingman relegated Herron to the fringes of the company and became the public face of the enterprise, creating some hard feelings between the two that only intensified later. Furthermore, Dingman claimed the title of managing director despite investing no capital of his own. After establishing the CPP, Herron signed a second deal with Dingman that saw Herron buy into the company by selling four-ninths of his remaining 45 percent stake in the leases to Dingman as a "service fee" for assembling the consortium. This second agreement provided Dingman a 20 percent stake in the company and reduced Herron's share to 25 percent. Despite holding fully one-quarter of the shares in the company, Herron did not sit on the board of directors. Herron, who was sometimes difficult to work with at the best of times, later claimed Dingman neglected to notify him about the meeting formally electing the board.[33]

Notwithstanding Dingman's sharp elbows, he proved to be an inspired choice to lead the Calgary Petroleum Products Company. The *Herald* called him "the grand old man of Alberta," and Dingman's combination of business sense, experience, and temperament brought a steady hand to a pioneering venture. At the time, Dingman was among the most experienced drillers in western Canada; none of the CPP's other partners had any experience finding, processing, or transporting oil.

However valuable Dingman's practical business experience proved to be, his intangible qualities—his self-confidence, vision, faith, and level-headedness—enabled him to withstand the vicissitudes of a career in the boom and bust of the oil patch and served him well as the public face of Calgary

Petroleum Products Company. "Carry on," he would say. "We want and need more crude oil." It fell to Dingman to give updates and interviews to the press, serving as spokesperson for the syndicate, and to periodically advise various levels of government about pending oil and gas–related legislation. Mostly praised, he sometimes drew criticism from boosters for his caution and secrecy; nonetheless, Dingman remained unflappable and clear eyed, particularly at crucial junctures. Dingman thought strategically about where the company, and the Alberta oil patch, were and where they needed to go. Like a skilled chess player who sees the whole board and plots several moves ahead of their opponent, Dingman calculated the current situation and future needs before acting. The habit served him well and persisted for the rest of his life. After he died, his son, Claude, claimed his father had mapped out a twenty-year plan for the development of Alberta's petroleum industry. Dingman served as more of a steward of Alberta's natural resource wealth, in the best possible sense of the word, than a typical businessperson. Dingman's two children, Claude and daughter Corinne, vividly recalled the poem that served as their father's personal philosophy: "It's all in the State of Mind." Both seemed unaware that their father had adapted the poem from Walter D. Wintle's famous late nineteenth-century poem "Thinking," which begins "If you think you are beaten, you are" and emphasized the importance of perseverance and faith in Dingman's dogged pursuit of petroleum in the province.[34]

By November 1912, Calgary Petroleum Products Company ramped up its drilling preparations. Herron hauled the timbers and began assembling the derrick at the well site, while Dingman travelled to Pittsburgh to buy a standard cable tool rig, equipment, and a drill crew. To be sure, qualified drilling companies already existed in Alberta, including International Supply Company run by US expatriates Albert Parker ("Tiny") Phillips and Walter Randall ("Frosty") Martin. Born January 13, 1873, in Oil City, Pennsylvania, Phillips was the son of driller Samuel Anthony Phillips, who apprenticed as a blacksmith and moved into the oil industry forging tools because it offered better pay. "I was brought up around an oil rig," wrote the younger Phillips in his blue scribbler. "An oil rig was my playground."[35]

But personal rivalries and long-standing grudges also informed decisions. Martin and Phillips drilled wells for Coste and the CPR, and Dingman regarded them as bitter rivals. Instead, Dingman hired two successive drillers from Pennsylvania, William Elder and then Martin Hovis, along with an American crew, to drill Calgary Petroleum Products' first well. Personal history also took a hand. William Elder had served as driller on Dingman's earlier wells for the Calgary Natural Gas Company. Dingman's new company spudded in Dingman #1 along the banks of Sheep Creek in January 1913, a few weeks after the spudding in of McDougal-Segur.

The site itself seemed easily accessible to major transportation links. Its location in Turner Valley meant the nearby railhead at Okotoks rested approximately sixteen miles from the well site. Flat terrain made it look easy to bring in workers and equipment. But Claude Dingman recalled that the dirt roads were either a sea of mud and water or almost impassable with drifts of snow. Torchy Anderson, later the editor of a Vancouver newspaper but in 1914 a reporter with the *Herald,* readily agreed with Dingman, vividly describing Turner Valley roads as "a doubtful adventure of mud, rocks and washouts." Fifty years later, he pointedly remarked that even on a normal day the roads were "bad beyond the imagination of today's motorists." Another reporter, Chester Bloom, added that the two chief enemies to travellers in and out of the oil field were mud and mosquitos. "Wise travellers," said Bloom, "never went anywhere in those wilds without sharp axes" to cut down trees when necessary to build "corduroy" sections of roadway across water and mudholes. Even then, teams of horses proved more practical than automobiles to haul supplies and equipment to the well site.[36]

Once drilling started, the combination of a particularly harsh winter, the depth of the well, the limitations of cable tool rig drilling technology, and scant knowledge of the difficult geology of the Turner Valley formation proved frustrating for even the most experienced American roughnecks. William Elder, and later Marty Hovis, quickly learned that the field was unlike any other they had drilled before. Known in driller's parlance as "crooked hole country," the soft rock, folds, and twists in the formations below dictated caution; otherwise, drill tools would bend, get stuck, require repair or, if lost down the hole, could compel the abandonment of the well altogether. Decades later, Dingman's nephew Charles, who served as the province's chief geologist, realized most wells in Turner Valley were crooked; after a few hundred feet of drilling, the hole would slant off in another direction. Holes purportedly 5,000 feet deep were far shallower than drillers realized because the drill bit began travelling parallel to its intended target as it skidded across the top of the limestone formation. Only in the 1930s would equipment capable of measuring a well's deviation arrive in the province, and in one case horrified drillers learned their wells deviated as much as thirty degrees from perpendicular. *The Western Oil Examiner* later powerfully described the effect as producing holes "that went down like corkscrews and meandered all over the sub-surface of the Valley." As a result, wells in Turner Valley, already

Figure 1-5 "Calgary Petroleum Products #1 well [Dingman #1], Turner Valley, Alberta"
Drilling on the Dingman well started in July 1912 and a few problems and challenges made it deeper and more expensive for the Pennsylvania crew to drill. Turner Valley was "crooked hole country" and it took more than 650 days and more than $60,000 ($1.8 million today) to drill 780 metres (2,718 feet.) (Glenbow Archive CU1217652)

deeper and more expensive to drill than those at other locations and requiring a well depth of over 3,000 feet, could play cruel tricks. The average drilling cost of $12.50–$13.00 per foot did not include the $27,000 worth of machinery bought by Calgary Petroleum Products Company, straining both the budget and the limits of cable rig technology. As Carl Nickle observed, in 1914 drilling beyond 3,000 feet with cable tool technology went beyond reason because of costs but also because of Turner Valley's unpredictable geology.[37]

In the early twentieth century, whether crews were drilling for oil in Texas or Turner Valley, the process was slow, monotonous, and dangerous. Cable tool rig technology used a wooden derrick, usually constructed on-site from hand-cut planks of Douglas fir, and a steam engine to operate like a primitive jackhammer. Working in four- or five-man crews, skilled rig builders normally took six days to complete construction of a cable tool rig, along with the bull wheel, derrick, and machinery housing.[38] Made of tempered steel, the sharp and heavy drill bit, sometimes starting out at twenty-four inches in

Figure 1-6 "Drillers at Dingman #1 well (Calgary Petroleum Products #1), Turner Valley, Alberta"
Apart from overalls, leather boots, and gloves, drillers in the early twentieth century lacked any personal protective equipment. Note the soft hats. Calgary Petroleum Products' drillers Joseph Brown (right) and Martin Hovis (third from right). (Glenbow Archive CU1134522)

diameter and weighing as much as a ton, grew progressively smaller in size and weight as wells went deeper. Suspended from a Manila cable and attached to the end of a steam-powered "walking beam" that rocked like a teeter-totter, the heavy drill bit rose to the top of the 84-foot-high derrick before crashing into the rock below. Periodically, the driller removed the bit to clean the hole of rock chips. When the bit dulled, the tool dresser heated and reshaped the point with a ten-pound sledgehammer. While rotary rig technology existed, it was faster, bigger, more expensive, and required more skilled workers to run. More importantly, early drillers deemed rotary rig technology unsuited to the unpredictable subsurface features of Turner Valley.

Most camps usually had a car available for "the convenience of the camp," to get to the nearest post office or telephone, but when wintry weather arrived, the car was useless. Water had to be drained from the radiator in the fall to prevent it from cracking in freezing temperatures. Health and safety regulations were decades away and few rules governed oil exploration in the early days—only the regulations governing the use of steam engines applied because of the rig's use of a boiler to power the rig. As historian David Breen noted, basic guidelines governed the extraction of minerals. "The essential requirement was that one had to obtain the consent of the mineral rights holder, then one might dig, burrow, blast and drill at will."[39] By 1910, federal regulations dictated that the Canadian Navy (then known as the Naval Service of Canada) could make first claim on oil production from Crown lands, pre-emptively establishing a quasi-form of nationalization that superseded the law of capture, which held that oil production belonged to those who brought it to the surface.[40]

Although the petroleum industry in North America had fifty years of experience by the 1910s, oilfield technology remained in its infancy and regulation and health and safety measures were spartan. After discovery, provisions to protect the environment and guard against waste were very basic. Few early drillers bothered using casing pipe, so if drilling went through a shallow aquifer a well could spoil the groundwater. Furthermore, drillers had little to no control over gas; if the bit struck a pocket of high-pressure gas, it could easily cause a blowout. Indeed, one early well drilled at Pelican Rapids along the Athabasca River in 1897 hit a flow of natural gas estimated at 8.5 million cubic feet per day. As the drillers lacked the capacity to adequately deal with the blowout, the well continued to spew natural gas for the next twenty-one years before it could be shut in.[41] If a well struck oil, metal or wooden tanks stored production; if production exceeded storage capacity, drillers relied on shallow pits to store the excess. Earthen trenches were far from ideal; crude could leak out of them, and since they were usually uncovered, the lighter (and more valuable) fractions, like kerosene, tended to evaporate. Nevertheless, a combination of economics, the primitive state of petroleum engineering, and self-interest meant the well would produce flat out regardless of the consequences. No incentive existed to steward resource development; in fact, several factors argued against showing any sign of restraint. Investment capital and profits could only be realized by selling production. In fact, companies that shut in (left oil in the ground after drilling) production for any length of time were uncertain the well would resume production at its former level. The lack of trained petroleum engineers meant producers risked having the well collapse on itself or become clogged with paraffin.[42]

Beyond well site considerations, no equipment existed, for example, to protect the rig or crew if the drill hit a pocket of high-pressure gas and caused a blowout. Even basic personal protection equipment for rig hands, like steel-toed boots and hard hats, did not exist. Unless down for repairs, rigs operated twenty-four hours a day, seven days a week with two crews, each working a twelve-hour shift and sleeping and drinking in makeshift shacks while off duty because there was nowhere else to go. The shortage of skilled or experienced roughnecks and rig hands meant high wages for those who were around. With an average hourly wage of thirty-five cents an hour in Alberta, drillers earned more in one month (approximately $880) than farmhands or apprentices earned in a year—prompting some to inflate their credentials. "The Americans were expert liars about their qualifications when they showed up in Canada," noted the wife of driller Garrett W. Green, who in 1914 was employed by International Supply Company to drill a well near Viking, Alberta. "Findlay (Ohio) roustabouts [workers who completed whatever heavy work was required] suddenly became firemen; firemen back there could get jobs as tool dressers and tool dressers could easily pass for drillers here."[43] Rig hands earned between twenty-five and fifty-eight cents per hour ($3 to $7 per day), depending on their position and experience, but for most of the single men, the bulk of their pay went to alcohol. "Few outsiders could understand the psychology of oilfield crews and their capacity for whisky," wrote oil patch historian John Schmidt. "They could always depend on working hard the next tour to sweat it out of them."[44]

Spouses, partners, and children of rig workers endured the same dreary and solitary conditions at the drill camps. Living quarters consisted of tarpaper shacks or tents. Given the relative isolation of drill sites, uncertain roads, and lack of transportation, women stayed close to the camp. Livery stable hands from the nearest town usually delivered groceries once a week. When the monthly pay envelope arrived, the women in camp would try to get to Edmonton or Calgary for some shopping, visits with friends, and catching up on the latest news and gossip. "We had variety in this kind of life," recalled Mrs. Green. "From rattlesnakes in the Bow Island country, to the beautifully wooded foothill country; and we loved it all. Early Alberta was a wonderful place for children. There was so much for them to do outdoors." While the snakes often scared the children, the most prevalent pests were mosquitos. "They came out of every pothole," recalled Mrs. Green, "and the only known repellent we knew then was oil of citronella. It was bought by the gallon for the camp." At the Dingman well, from time to time, members of the Stoney Nakoda Nation would pass through, taking parts of the animals that the settlers did not use and trading food for rose petals and wolf willow beads.[45]

Unintentionally, the early Alberta oil patch imposed a spartan hand-to-mouth existence on investors and drill crews. Equipment and replacement parts took days to arrive by train from Pennsylvania and were subject to a 37 percent import duty, straining budgets and patience even further. Companies and drillers became accustomed to scrounging and borrowing material help from anyone who could provide it. Compared to a well in Pennsylvania, where production costs were between $2,000 and $3,000 a well, wells in Turner Valley field were nearly ten times as expensive to drill, costing $30,000 to $35,000 (all figures in 1914 dollars). According to Dingman, the added expenses all had to do with the Turner Valley formation, which required more casing per well and the use of casing deeper down the hole to prevent cave-ins, which slowed drilling and increased costs.[46] At most, the crew could only drill a few feet per day. All too frequently, the rig sat idle as the crew waited for casing, pipe, tools, or parts to arrive by rail. At other times, drilling stopped because the company lacked sufficient funds to pay for supplies, equipment, or wages. Unsurprisingly, given this experience, fifteen years later Herron reminded a separate set of partners grumbling about slow progress and rising costs that they all knew some wells in Turner Valley that took between one and seven years to drill approximately 3,500 feet underground.[47]

From early on, Dingman #1 gave promising signs of being a natural gas producer. At 180 feet, it produced enough gas to replace coal as the energy source for the well's boiler. Other pockets of gas appeared at several horizons (467, 877, 1,205, 1,235, and 1,260 feet). The promising developments prompted visits to Alberta by Standard Oil representatives in March 1913. By August 1913, with the well producing two million cubic feet of gas at a depth of 1,563 feet, Dingman began selling gas to communities around Calgary via a hastily constructed pipeline. In addition, Dingman and the CPP collected and hauled some of the naphtha in tank wagons and drums for sale in Calgary. But Dingman wanted oil, so the search continued. Knowing that people and the press scrutinized every word, Dingman remained cautious in public statements. A public letter published both in the *Morning Albertan* and the *Herald* in May tried to scuttle early rumours of an oil discovery. "The facts are," wrote Dingman, "that the district is not yet a determined oil field and is not yet even a gas field of determined commercial value." Another press conference in early August 1913 illustrates Dingman's deft ability to manage expectations while sustaining optimism. As he did before, Dingman corrected reporters suggesting CPP had developed an oil field, preferring to use the less prosaic term "prospect" instead. Until a field produced oil, he repeated, it was just a field. The presence of so much high-quality naphtha suspended in the gas reminded Dingman of the oil produced in Pennsylvania, and Dingman hoped that its source was oil-based. But, referring to the amount of casing required, Dingman allowed that, compared to Pennsylvania, the Turner Valley field certainly "did not stand up well" to drilling. Still, Dingman confided to reporters, finding the source intrigued him, as did the lingering question whether it existed in commercial quantities. Dingman allowed that pungent

Figure 1-7 "Group of men standing at wellhead of Dingman #1 (Calgary Petroleum Products #1), Turner Valley, Alberta" Interior of the Dingman well drill shack showing the crew watching the well venting, most likely petroleum condensate. Mostly transparent and nearly odourless, condensate is more flammable and explosive than crude oil. Usually composed of propane, butane, or hexane, the rest of the sentence should read condensate can also contain carbon dioxide, hydrogen sulphide, aromatics, and naphthenes. (Glenbow Archive CU1134205)

question to linger in the air for a moment. Just as easily, Dingman dismissed ever-present rumours that Standard Oil would take over the field. "Standard Oil have the money to buy the oil if they want it," Dingman said matter-of-factly, "but the idea that they are following prospectors and promoters around is ridiculous."[48]

The other major company drilling in Turner Valley, McDougall-Segur Exploration, spudded in their first well before Calgary Petroleum Products Company. Their experience revealed several early growing pains with the Alberta oil patch as the new industry took shape. Some problems in the oil business are universal and happen regardless of where operations take place—like a lost tool in the well that delays drilling or delinquent shareholders not responding quickly enough to a cash call. Other problems are the product of an incomplete regulatory environment in a new industry, as when

McDougall-Segur discovered in October 1913 that the owner of the surface rights, Francis Wright, could assert the right to bar them from accessing their first well site. Despite McDougall-Segur possessing the mineral rights, and the fact that drilling had begun ten months earlier, the Dominion's existing Petroleum and Natural Gas Regulations did not entitle the company to enter upon leased lands without the permission of the surface rights holder. Belatedly, the board of directors mobilized to lobby government to pass amended legislation and engaged in protracted negotiations with Wright to ensure the company could access the well site. Thankfully, for the company's sake, at no time did Wright block their access and the two sides reached an agreement in May 1914 granting them access in exchange for $500 and two shares of McDougall-Segur stock. Negotiation and, in time, new legislation resolved these and other similar issues.[49]

As the depth of the Dingman well rose and the volumes of gas continued to increase, the higher costs and longer time required to drill Turner Valley brought structural and institutional changes to address the needs of oil companies and Albertans alike. Both Calgary Petroleum Products and McDougall-Segur began drilling as privately owned enterprises with comparatively modest expectations about operational costs, although both would ultimately become joint-stock companies. CPP committed to spend $50,000 drilling Dingman #1—$1.5 million today, adjusted for inflation—while McDougall-Segur increased their initial budget of $100,000 to $250,000 (approximately $6.6 million, adjusted for inflation.)[50]

Questions about the best way to mitigate risk while still financing exploration loomed over the emerging industry, especially as companies contemplated raising investment capital. Unfortunately, many Canadians doggedly clung to the belief that British investors remained eager to invest in Canadian resource schemes regardless of their size and scale. As London merchant banker Arthur Grenfell wrote to his father-in-law, Earl Grey, the Governor General of Canada, in 1907, "There is no doubt that most Canadians think that they have only to arrive in London with ideas and everyone is prepared to fill their pockets with sovereigns." As the country was only a marginal petroleum producer, Canadian oil companies operating domestically received scant attention from British investors. From 1890 to 1914, British direct investment in Canadian oil never exceeded $5 million, with most of that investment capital funnelled toward Ontario-based exploration companies. The problem for Canadian natural resource projects was that they competed against other opportunities for long-term British investors who enjoyed global investment opportunities. Only the largest, and few proven, producers tended to secure

British capital. However, the size and scale of operations in Turner Valley might warrant the creation of a local exchange prevalent in periodic mining booms—coal in Nova Scotia, nickel and iron ore around Lake Superior, various gold and silver discoveries in Ontario, British Columbia, and the Northwest. According to historian Ranald Michie, all adhered to a rough pattern where the initial rush of discovery witnessed the proliferation of numerous joint-stock companies that justified the creation of a local exchange.[51]

In early August 1913, 200 men gathered outside the Dominion Land Office to try and file on several oil leases. The crowd grew impatient and soon a fight broke out that quickly escalated, requiring the police reserves to restore order. In an increasingly tense atmosphere, three members of the Calgary Petroleum Products board—Sayre, Dingman, and Lowry—recommended to the Calgary Board of Trade (the precursor to the Calgary Chamber of Commerce) that it help form a local stock exchange. Their reasoning was sound. At that time, no organized capital market for resource development existed in western Canada. Railroads spent their own money developing coal mines to fuel their trains. Forestry and other mining projects could count on attracting investors using private capital to finance their endeavours. Borrowing from the banks remained limited. Apart from granting mortgages to farmers, banks in western Canada were ill suited to finance development projects with long investment horizons. In any case, only a handful of banks operated nationwide and small private banks proliferated across western Canada.

Much like those in the United States or the United Kingdom. Alberta's progressives tended to buttress Adam Smith's conception of the market's self-regulating invisible hand with the belief that a freely chosen act was, by definition, a "natural" and moral one as well. Historian Daniel Rodgers notes that the notion of a freely chosen act and this potent combination "stacked that burden massively against state economic action." Instead, members of the emerging professional and middle classes created voluntary associations that not only rationalized their professions but enabled them to exercise political and economic power in the process.[52]

Given the tight margins and highly speculative nature of petroleum development, creating an exchange to raise long-term risk capital seemed prudent. Augmenting their numbers by including other prominent Calgary businesspeople, an eight-person consortium petitioned the provincial government to incorporate the Calgary Stock Exchange as part of an attempt to put into place ideas of self-regulation and governance that travelled hand in glove with idealized notions of laissez-faire capitalism. In the case of the

Calgary Stock Exchange, "the need was felt," reflected R.F. Scrimgeour, the CSE's secretary-treasurer in the 1940s, "for a trading centre where members of a well-regulated and strictly disciplined organization might gather for the purpose of not only of trading in securities in a free and open market but of promoting the best interests of an infant industry." Lacking either the financial resources or the ideological inclination to assume responsibility for regulating the industry, the provincial government found it "expedient to grant their prayer," and issued the CSE a provisional charter on October 25, 1913. The Act incorporating the CSE required it to "compile records and publish statistics, to acquire and distribute information respecting stock, shares, bonds, and debentures . . . to promote the observance of such regulations and requirements as may be by by-law established." Like several stock exchanges that emerged in the western United States and Canada before it, the Calgary Stock Exchange played a key role in securing investment capital for the oil and gas companies operating in the local economy—just not yet. The CSE did not begin operations for the next seven months mostly because, while a dozen or so companies formed and began selling stock, the volume of those trades did not yet justify opening the exchange.[53]

Advocates for the CSE were right to be cautious. The chances of success were minimal; approximately 10 percent of the companies created in the initial rush produced any mined product, be it ore, gold, silver, or oil. Even fewer companies, around 4 percent, turned a profit and paid dividends. Companies typically sought well-heeled British or American investors, but most of the start-up capital for mining ventures was usually both local in origin and highly speculative, meaning that it tended to withdraw as quickly as it appeared, making the firm's long-term prospects extremely tenuous.[54]

Meanwhile, section 40 of the January 18, 1914, federal regulations governing resource extraction addressed concerns about the growing presence of US capital in the Canadian industry. The Dominion government stipulated that companies operating on Crown leases "shall at all times be and remain a British company, registered in Great Britain or Canada and having its principal place of business within His Majesty's Dominions and the chairman and majority of the board shall at all times be British subjects and the company shall not at any time be or become directly or indirectly controlled by foreigners or by a foreign corporation."[55]

Nonetheless, the more fluid and open borders of the early twentieth century meant American prospectors, promoters, and investors regularly operated in Canada and eagerly joined the rush after putting a few locals on their board of directors to follow the letter of the law. This certainly was the case in Turner Valley. As historian Ranald Michie points out, "American prospectors, promoters, and investors regarded Canada as an extension of their own hinterland."[56] Americans found several ways around the legislation, particularly as federal laws did not prohibit US citizens from holding mineral leases on Crown lands, and US entrepreneurs already living in Canada used a combination of their own capital and locally raised funds to gain entry. Appointing local agents, lawyers, and managers to a company's board of directors also addressed stipulations that British subjects comprise a majority of directors for any company operating on Crown lands.[57]

Alberta-chartered companies also actively encouraged the participation of US investors if for no other reason than their omnipresence in the West generally, and in Calgary in particular. The 1911 census revealed that Americans made up approximately 10 percent of Calgary's population of 44,000. However, as historian James Gray argued, the census likely undercounted the number of Americans in Calgary and Alberta, categorizing people according to racial background. Since many Americans were of British ancestry, census takers included them among Calgary's 29,000 British citizens rather than the 4,000 Americans. Plenty of signs pointed to the ubiquitous presence of Americans in Calgary beyond the ambiguous results of the census. The most exclusive residential area in Calgary, Mount Royal, became known as "American Hill." Twenty-four American fraternal societies operated in Calgary by 1908; twenty-five labour union locals affiliated with the American Federation of Labor. Thirty Protestant churches tended to the spiritual uplift of the city, mostly Baptists and Methodists that supported the Temperance and Moral Reform League.[58]

On October 6, 1913, William Elder returned to Calgary from Turner Valley to tell Dingman that, at 1,562 feet, the well produced a few gallons of straw-coloured liquid popularly known as "white oil." Technically, however, the liquid was naphtha, a petroleum condensate usually found in conjunction with crude oil. Although the directors of Calgary Petroleum Products hoped to keep the discovery secret, word already had begun to spread. Calgary Petroleum Products issued a cover story that Elder arrived in the city to secure a spare piece of equipment to repair a break in the machinery. Rumours of an oil strike grew in frequency and intensity, prompting the *Herald* to note on October 9 that "it's very difficult to get at facts in the oil business, and this paper therefore takes no responsibility for the truth or untruth of the report." Indeed, as the *Albertan* observed, rumours of oil strikes floated from Turner Valley every two or three weeks for the previous six months had kept Calgarians in a high state of alert. The *Edmonton Journal* speculated that Calgary Petroleum Products were reluctant to confirm the find until they secured more acreage. Finally, on October 10, 1913, Dingman issued a very carefully worded statement to the press to temper expectations and provide perspective. He acknowledged that Dingman #1 had struck "oil of a very high specific gravity . . . and the quality is equal, if it does not exceed, the finest grades of oil found in any oil territory." However, Dingman warned that the discovery "does not prove or determine that commercial values maintain." More work, money, and time were necessary to prove whether the well would produce enough to sustain industrial development of any scale. "Until this is determined," Dingman stated flatly, "the physical conditions are such that all exploitations must be purely speculative." Dingman reminded reporters that, so far, Dingman #1 had produced mostly gas with traces of oil. Until proven otherwise, it would be safer to assume that the oil was an anomaly, although Dingman maintained it was an encouraging one. Dingman wanted reporters to keep this information in perspective and treated with a healthy dose of caution. In the meantime, Calgary Petroleum Products would continue to drill, "encouraged to hope that it will be able to secure results which will bring about an evolution in our industrial welfare."[59]

Despite Dingman's qualifications and circumspection, many heard only what they wanted, and enthusiasm continued to build. Press coverage of the discovery further complicated matters by using the terms "natural gas," "gasoline," and "oil" interchangeably. Like pilgrims travelling to a shrine, a procession of Calgarians travelled by automobile to Okotoks to see the "Discovery Well" for themselves. Included in the caravan were two of Calgary Petroleum Product's directors, A.J. Sayre and Oscar G. Devenish. Once at the site, they emptied their tanks and drove back to Calgary using the naphtha from the well to demonstrate the quality of the unrefined product. The *Herald* reported that the men were amazed to discover that "the power generated was at least 25 percent greater than that obtained from the gasoline on sale in the city." Observers also noted the heavy sulphur content of the naphtha as the fuel burned. Although it may have been a corny—and foul-smelling—stunt, it proved effective with many who saw it, and Calgary Petroleum Products soon equipped a car with a sign telling people it was powered by gasoline provided directly from the Dingman well. Even though reports indicated a small flow of naphtha and not crude oil in commercial quantities, boosters, promoters, and reporters soon posited that the field contained an oilfield "second to none on the American continent." A stream of reports claimed that the oil was the highest grade ever recorded—pure gasoline without refining. Gallons of oil were handed out in small bottles and the *Herald* reported that more than twenty different companies formed to sell stock based on their leaseholds in the region.⁶⁰

From his room in the Empress Hotel, on Sunday, October 12, 1913, Archibald Dingman set aside some of his earlier reserve and qualifications in announcing that the company had found oil "in commercial quantities," but pointedly refused to provide details as to how much or how little, in gallons or barrels, Dingman #1 had produced. "I have never seen, nor have I ever heard of oil of a similar grade or quality, so far as excellency is concerned, except in what is known as the Cherry Run district of the Pennsylvania Oil Fields." Following his formal statement, Dingman entertained reporters' questions, and revealed some ambivalence regarding developments over the previous forty-eight hours. The director of Calgary Petroleum Products recognized he was in a tight spot. If he emphasized the speculative nature of developments and the risk CPP's investors had taken, he might discourage others from drilling in the field. But If he abandoned his restrain and celebrated the discovery too much, "I might reap, ultimately, recrimination," said Dingman, if other companies drilled without the same success. As he did so frequently, Dingman kept a level head and urged people to temper their enthusiasm. It was impossible to tell how thick or thin any oil-bearing strata were, and he provided an example of a well at Pincher Creek that had demonstrated all kinds of promise but was ultimately a dry well because the broken formation below allowed the oil to seep away. Notwithstanding Dingman's careful qualifications, the October 13 edition of the *Albertan* carried a banner headline: "Oil is found in commercial quantities" even though the evidence did not yet support this conclusion.⁶¹

By October 16, retailers in Calgary bought a barrel for $9.30 ($246.68, adjusted for inflation) and sold gasoline from the Dingman well for thirty cents a gallon. The *Albertan* stated that Calgary had captured the attention of "the big oil world" and reported on the growing outside interest. "California, and Oklahoma and Texas and Pennsylvania have accepted the new field as worthy of consideration and from many of the oil centres of the United States and Mexico are coming experts and operators." The activity coincided with another visit to Alberta by British geologist Edward Hubert Cunningham Craig, this time serving as a consultant for a syndicate of London capitalists put together by Winnipeg financier Mowbray S. Berkeley.⁶² Craig marvelled that "to the best of my knowledge oil, similar to that coming from the Dingman, in its crude form has never before been discovered. It is unique, and if I told experts in the old country that automobiles could be run on crude oil from a well in southern Alberta, I am sure that they would not believe me." The oil produced at the Dingman well was too high in quality to fuel the Royal Navy, declared Craig. But as the well bored deeper to find the source of crude, Craig was certain it would be of a lower calibre more appropriate for naval use. Even though Craig was not involved with Calgary Petroleum Products, he believed that the Dingman discovery "is entirely in accordance with the theory formed and published in my book on the subject of oil-finding."[63]

The Dingman discovery touched off a scramble among promoters to secure mineral rights, and since the Crown held most of the mineral rights within the province (some estimates place the number at 95 percent), this produced a rush to the Dominion Land Office to file petroleum leases. In one day, speculators filed 118 separate applications covering 100,000 acres within a fifty-mile radius of the Dingman well. Several leases changed hands, with one allegedly fetching $33,000. However, those holding the mineral rights on property near Dingman and the McDougall-Segur wells refused to sell for the time being and reportedly were monitoring developments. Speculators filed on so much land that in short order, the only available promising parcels would be leases returned to the market after their leaseholders fell behind on their payments. The competition was so intense for these properties that one local company stationed four men at the land office twenty-four hours a day. "They are filing as far away as Lethbridge," noted one land office official. "If this keeps up, claims will soon be taken down near Coutts and right down south as far as the international border." By the end of the year, the Calgary land office collected $85,000 from leaseholders and the Dominion government received $1.445 million in lease payments for 1913–14. Early in the new year, when expiring mineral leases taken out twelve months earlier returned to circulation because the owners had failed to develop the lease, ugly scenes ensued at the land office, forcing Calgary police to station officers and institute a lottery to draw for places in line to avoid "disgraceful riots." Over two days in October 1913, police oversaw the distribution of 750 lottery tickets for a place in line. On the following Saturday morning, the number of lottery tickets doubled to 1,500 just for the opportunity to bid on land between fifty and sixty miles away from the Dingman strike.[64]

The boom drew new people, workers, investors, and fortune hunters to the city. As early as June 1913, prospectors and oil workers arrived from the major producing regions and finance centres of the United States seeking new opportunities. By sheer serendipity, the Dingman discovery coincided with one of the periodic declines in drilling activity in the United States. Between 1910 and 1913, US petroleum industry drilling increased to 23,094 wells, a 66 percent increase. Drilling activity declined sharply thereafter, dropping to

12,142 wells by 1915. Most of the decline took place in the aging and maturing fields from Lima, Ohio, to Appalachia, prompting an exodus of oil workers from Ohio, Pennsylvania, West Virginia, and Illinois westward in search of new opportunities as the US industry's centre of gravity moved south and west. While Oklahoma, Texas, and Louisiana were frequent destinations for itinerant oil field workers, some made their way to Alberta. In June 1913, *The Oil and Gas Journal* reported that "'Billy' Davidson, an old-time temper-screw artist [driller], left Tulsa this week for Calgary, one of the booming cities of the Canadian Northwest" after hearing reports about the discovery. Upon arrival in Alberta, Davidson conducted his own investigation and was now determined to lease or buy land in the province. If the land refused to produce oil, Davidson figured he would rent it to an ambitious farmer to raise wheat.[65] Other US expatriates, like International Supply Company's Frosty Martin and Tiny Phillips, did not think of coming to western Canada until they were hired by geologist Eugene Coste to drill for oil and gas on the prairies. Head drillers of the Dingman well, Martin L. Hovis and Joe Brown, arrived from Pennsylvania.[66]

Others left the city to drum up investment capital, like local entrepreneur and real estate promoter Clarence A. Owens. Weeks before, Owens had authored a series in *The Morning Albertan* informing Calgarians about the tricks of the trade for real estate "wildcatting" he learned and profited from during the recent housing boom in Calgary. In the petroleum industry, "wildcatting" means drilling for oil in territory not known to be an oilfield. But, in Calgary's real estate market during the boom years before 1913, "wildcatting" referred to misrepresenting the true value of property in anticipation of selling that asset to another investor for a larger profit. Seeing a new opportunity, Owens quickly left for New York, allegedly with samples from the Dingman well, to secure funding for a new petroleum venture. A few weeks later, Owens returned triumphantly, proclaiming the trip a remarkable success because he had found wealthy American investors to launch a new company, Canadian Standard Oil. *The Morning Albertan* reported the company had $5 million worth of operating capital provided by unidentified but "well known oil men of New York" with pre-existing operations in Oklahoma and California. Owens and his new-found partners pledged to buy land, develop, and operate in Calgary.[67]

The assumptions made by Albertans about the boom are quite striking. Many, if not most, were certain that a very large oilfield waiting to be exploited lay just outside of Calgary; some even predicted that it extended as far north as Fort McMurray and as far south as the international boundary. They were equally sure that oil would be easily found in commercial quantities and that they sat on the cusp of the economic opportunity of a lifetime—one that could secure their financial future. Beyond these oft-expressed beliefs, other assumptions reveal few thought carefully, if at all, about the logistics or infrastructure necessary to exploit an oil boom. While exploration companies formed to start drilling for oil and investors dreamed of geysers of oil gushing from the ground, few asked, "What next?" or "What else do we need?"

Calgary and Alberta were not adequately prepared for the appearance of a major oil field. The city lacked storage facilities, transportation, and refining capacity, meaning these capital-intensive facilities would have to be built. Further downstream, more questions remained. What market would Alberta oil service? Perhaps more importantly, would Alberta oil be competitive on international markets? There were already reasons to suspect it might not be, as wells in Alberta and Turner Valley were already among the deepest drilled using cable tool technology, raising questions about the effect this would have on production costs even before transportation costs to markets were included. The sheer distance of the oil field to major urban markets or tidewater either in Canada or the United States raised questions about Alberta oil's ability to displace other crudes from the market, especially given the high sulphur content of petroleum produced in the valley. Nevertheless, many took it on faith that, if oil were found, the city and the province would embark on a new development trajectory and potential bottlenecks would wash away. Boosters claimed railroads would expand their transportation infrastructure to service the oil fields. Additional capital projects would produce investments in extraction plants and refineries, producing new jobs and industries on the prairies. This is what happened in Texas in January 1901 when Spindletop came in with production of 75,000 barrels per day. But Texas oil fields were so prolific that they broke John D. Rockefeller's monopoly over the US oil industry and temporarily drove crude prices to three cents a barrel.[68]

Surely, boosters believed, Calgary was destined to become the next great North American petroleum centre. And heaven help the person who questioned it.

2

"The Formation of These Companies . . . Should be Stopped:" Speculation and the Newspaper Feud

> *It appears to the writer that the conditions demand that those in whose hands the destinies of Calgary are now placed—I refer to the city council and the board of trade—should issue a warning of the most serious character to the investing public of the world, to stand back and not to permit themselves to be carried away with dreams of ready-made fortunes until the actual truth and facts be demonstrated. . . . The gravity of the situation cannot be over-estimated and it behooves conservative business people to apply the breaks [sic] of reason and sound common sense to a situation that is big, and concerns everybody interested in the financial and industrial future of western Canada.*
>
> —"An old oil prospector,"
> Letter to the Editor
> *Calgary Herald*, October 15, 1913

After God had finished making the rattlesnake, the toad, and the vampire, he had some awful substance left with which he made a knocker. A knocker is a two-legged animal with a corkscrew soul, a water-sogged brain and a combination backbone made of jelly and glue. Where other men have their hearts, he carries a tumor or decayed principals. When the knocker comes down the street, honest men turn their backs, the angels weep tears in Heaven and the devil shuts the gates of Hell to keep him out.

—"The Creation of the 'Knocker' Explained"
The Bellevue [Alberta] Times
June 19, 1914

Before the proliferation of radios and well before the introduction of television, newspapers served as the defining medium of the age. Three major daily newspapers, a broadsheet dedicated to oil and gas news, various magazines, and a weekly, epoch-defining paper published "semi-regularly" with international reach vied for readers' attention in Calgary. Each, in its own way, contributed to public debates regarding the development of Alberta's emerging petroleum industry. Newspapers carried wide-ranging discussions about the balance between the public and private sectors in resource development and the allocation of benefits between different groups, as well as offering differing interpretations of what constituted the public good, fairness, and equity.

In the late fall and early winter of 1913, a sharp divide emerged between William M. Davidson of *The Morning Albertan* and the afternoon dailies of George Marshall Thompson (*The Calgary News Telegram*) on the one hand and James Hossack Woods (*The Calgary Daily Herald*) on the other. At its core lay differing views of development, the role of the state in the economy, the operations and efficiency of markets, trade-offs between the public good versus individual interests, and differences of opinion about the role and desirability of speculation in the oil boom.[1] The differing world views of the editors reflected their different priorities and experiences, shaped the way their respective papers covered the emerging oil boom, and illustrated the growing importance of the monopolist/populist debate within Alberta's oil culture.

At one end of the spectrum sat Woods and the *Herald*, who craved the control and certainty of an oil patch dominated by the majors—the integrated corporate giants born in the last quarter of the nineteenth century and best exemplified by John D. Rockefeller's Standard Oil.[2] Calgarians should preserve their savings and refrain from investing in any oil company operating in the province until the field struck oil. Woods reasoned that, with access to larger sources of capital, skill, technology, and industry knowledge, the majors possessed all the necessary means to develop Alberta's oil fields and ensure its rational integration into petroleum's pre-existing, and increasingly global, transportation, refining, and marketing networks. In his writings Woods and the *Herald* clearly conveyed their disdain for speculation, regarding it, as R.H. Mottram did, as the mark of a true gambler who takes risks "for risk's sake, for the pleasure of the thrill and the vanity of success."[3] Woods's world view reflected the social liberalism of British thinkers like Thomas H. Green who saw freedom as being much more than the absence of coercion. Rather, people would reach their full potential within the boundaries of a healthy and vibrant community. Thus, unlike classical liberal thinkers who argued markets are efficient and envisioned a minimal role for the state, social liberals like Woods believed people and markets were neither always rational nor efficient and necessarily believed in a more active role for government that included responsibilities for regulating business and exercising oversight to ensure order and predictability over a chaotic industry.

Davidson and the *Albertan*, on the other hand, expressed more classical liberal beliefs about the infallibility of markets and rational behaviour of investors. Davidson did not trust government regulation and believed individuals made the best possible choices for themselves within the confines of a robust, competitive market. He embraced the populist rallying cry of freedom and opportunity and denigrated the supposed order and rationality of big business as a fool's errand wherein only the rich grew richer. Only through development by many independent entrepreneurs embracing the chaos and cutthroat competition of laissez-faire capitalism would the province and its citizens prosper. Davidson and his contemporary George Thompson at the *News Telegram* argued for development by the independents and financed through speculation, which Davidson saw as inextricably linked to entrepreneurialism and the prototypical independent "oil man." Where Woods saw danger and believed the interests of consumers needed to be protected from the vicissitudes of the market, Davidson countered that petroleum represented freedom and opportunity. Thus, the pages of the *Albertan* argued that the future depended on small investors getting into the industry as soon as possible to realize the greatest profits. The respective views of Woods and Davidson reflected diverging interpretations about the meaning of freedom and democracy, morality, regulation, and the role of the state versus the market.[4]

As their editorials grew increasingly heated, the feud between the editors about the meaning of freedom and democracy involved members of Alberta's new petroleum fraternity, who largely agreed with Davidson's classical liberal argument and took his side, in part because it coincided with early twentieth-century beliefs about local boosterism The feud produced one lawsuit alleging the publication of slanderous remarks and led to the creation of an industry association, the Alberta Oil Development Association (AODA). In turn, the AODA claimed responsibility for countering anything its members deemed "misinformation" about Alberta's nascent new industry. In an increasingly tense and supercharged atmosphere, some anonymous oil industry boosters, likely from the AODA, threatened both the *Herald's* publisher and editor, illustrating the faith oil's boosters had in the industry, their intolerance of criticism, and their single-minded pursuit of economic growth.

James Hossack Woods, the editor of the small "c" conservative *Herald*, came from a prominent Quebec family. Born in Quebec City in 1867, he was the son of Alexander Woods, who served as chair of the finance committee of Quebec, and later as Canada's first consular official in Australia. James Woods began his journalism career as a reporter with *The Toronto Mail and Empire* in 1893, where he later became the city editor and parliamentary correspondent covering the press gallery in Ottawa. Woods also served as the news editor of *The Montreal Herald* and the business manager of *The Toronto News* and founded the Woods-Norris Advertising Agency before arriving in Calgary in April 1907 to take over as managing director and editor of *The Calgary Daily Herald* until 1935, when he retired and became president, a position he held until his death in 1941. The oldest of Calgary's three major dailies, the *Herald* began publishing in 1883 as the voice for the policies of the ranchers, the railroads, and the federal Conservative Party. Canadian popular historian Pierre Berton once described the paper as being "as raw as the frontier," noting that *The Calgary Daily Herald* once assigned a photographer to follow the premier of British Columbia, the Honourable John "Honest John" Oliver "in hopes of catching him drunk enough to run a damaging photo on page one." Although Berton claimed John Oliver as the target, it seems far more likely that the *Herald's* Tory-blue editor would have targeted the former editor of the Liberal-backed *Edmonton Bulletin,* Frank Oliver, who also served as an MP and a minister in Wilfrid Laurier's Cabinet.[5]

Having been at the helm for less than a year, Woods succeeded in attracting friendly outside capital from William Southam of Hamilton to help grow *The Calgary Daily Herald*. With the company reorganized as the Calgary Herald Publishing Company, the *Daily Herald* became the third paper in Southam's growing coalition of newspapers that included *The Hamilton Spectator* and *The Ottawa Citizen* and would soon add the *Edmonton Journal*. Unlike the Hearst chain in the United States, each Southam paper retained mutual stylistic and editorial independence and only followed one central directive from Southam—to have the largest circulation in its market, a process Woods facilitated by helping found a regionally based news association, the Western Associated Press, in 1907, which challenged the unreliable news distribution services offered by the two telegraph companies, Canadian Pacific Telegraphs and the Great North Western Telegraph Company. In August 1907, Canadian Pacific Telegraphs abruptly announced a unilateral rate increase to four times the current rate at the same time they planned to cut services. Canadian papers banded together to create a news service that met their need for increased overseas and international news and that augmented their Canadian news coverage by using their correspondents in other parts of Canada to gather Canadian news. By 1917, this became known as the Canadian Press.[6]

The *Albertan*'s editor William M. Davidson followed a path similar to that of Woods into the Calgary newspaper business. Born in 1867 at Wellington, Ontario, and educated at Toronto University, Davidson began his journalistic career as a staff reporter on *The Toronto World* before moving on to the *Toronto Star*, where he joined the press gallery for the Ontario legislature, demonstrating a subtle and nuanced grasp of public issues over the next seven years before becoming editor of the *London News*. In 1902, Davidson moved to Calgary and bought *The Morning Albertan*, becoming the editor-in-chief as well as proprietor. On Davidson's watch, Calgarians perceived *The Morning Albertan* as the Liberal Party's mouthpiece, and he ran the paper until selling it in 1926. Active in the Alberta Liberal Party and a shameless civic booster, in 1905 Davidson travelled to Ottawa as part of a municipal delegation lobbying Wilfrid Laurier's government to make Calgary the provincial capital of the new province. But Calgary elected a Conservative representative while Edmonton elected Liberal Frank Oliver, settling the matter for the Laurier government. What stung Davidson more, however, was Premier Alexander Rutherford placing the provincial university in his home riding of Strathcona in Edmonton instead of Calgary. An embittered Davidson excoriated the leader of his party, calling the decision "the despotic act of a small dictator."

He also held elected office—once as a school board trustee and twice as a Member of the Legislative Assembly (MLA). Davidson ran the *Albertan* on a shoestring budget. Decades later, one former reporter remembered that, when he was hired, he was told his salary would be fourteen dollars a week—if it was paid at all. The frugal existence of the *Albertan*, complete with outdated equipment, insufficient staff, and not nearly enough cash, became evident when an April 1913 fire caused $50,000 worth of damage to the *Albertan's* building and plant while the paper carried only $25,000 worth of insurance. "It had nothing but nerve," recalled Davidson, "which was not backed by experience or very much real wisdom." [7]

The youngest of the three papers, *The Calgary News Telegram*, also had the youngest of the three editors. The son of a Canadian customs official in Port Hope, Ontario, and a printer by trade, the red-headed George Marshall Thompson was thirty-one when he travelled to Saskatoon in 1906 with his business partner, Charles Elmer Tryon, to launch the *Saskatoon Capital*. The two men ran the *Capital* on a shoestring budget as the paper struggled to survive. One reporter recalled that the two men frequently fought over the use of the one light that served both the business and editorial offices. The arguments occasionally grew heated, prompting several threats to dissolve the partnership. The two struggled to keep the paper afloat or make payroll and often collected advertising money on the weekends to make ends meet.[8] They sold the *Capital* in 1912 and the paper eventually became *The Saskatoon Daily Star*; Thompson and Tryon relocated to Calgary to take over the management of the two-year-old *News Telegram*. As editor, Thompson endeavoured to ensure his paper dealt with issues rather than personalities, but his departure from Saskatoon elicited something stronger than a sigh of relief from rival paper *The Saskatoon Phoenix*, whose editorial page all but frog-marched him out to the city limits. The *Phoenix* accused Thompson of possessing a raging ego and claimed that, under Thompson's influence, the *Capital* represented the worst of "low-type journalism" in the city and succeeded in infuriating Conservatives and Liberals alike. Few would lament his departure for Calgary, as the rival paper also alleged the *Capital's* new owners had changed the paper's name to *The Saskatoon Daily Star* "to get away from the past and the record of the *Capital*." The *Phoenix* concluded its scathing epitaph of Thompson's time in the province with a dismissive wave of the hand: "His end had come, people were not interested in him, nor are they now. There is no reason why he should be further inflicted on this community."[9]

Reporter Fred Kennedy recalled Thompson wore "peg-top pants with a suit coat that reached almost to his knees. He also wore 'American-type' boots with exaggerated toe swell and smoked ill-smelling cigars. He had a large and pretentious private office complete with fireplace. But his pride and joy was a huge brass cuspidor that he could hit dead centre with unerring accuracy."[10] Like Davidson, Thompson was actively involved in the Liberal Party. Often described as a partisan firebrand, Thompson could, indeed, be staunchly partisan but also displayed signs of nuance. He stood apart from his party when it came to the question of natural resources ownership. In 1905, Liberal prime minister Wilfrid Laurier ensured that control of the natural resources of Alberta and Saskatchewan remained in the hands of the Dominion government in exchange for a federal grant of $375,000 annually to offset lost revenues. Indeed, Thompson believed so fiercely that the two western provinces deserved control over their own natural resources that he briefly considered running as a Conservative in the provincial election of 1913. In 1920, Thompson and his wife left the newspaper business altogether, moving to Toronto to become the manager of the Strout Farm Agency of New York until he retired in 1932.[11]

One other major presence existed in the Calgary newspaper market: Robert Chambers "Bob" Edwards and the *Calgary Eye Opener*. As the *Eye Opener*'s sole editor and reporter, Bob Edwards earned the reputation as the prototypical Calgarian and the social conscience of the city.[12] Edwards founded the paper in High River in 1902 before settling in Calgary in 1904, and by the time of his death in November 1922 he had published as many as 500 issues. According to historian Hugh Dempsey, the *Eye Opener* was more "Bob Edwards's personal platform for social content and humour" than a traditional newspaper.[13] To be sure, Edwards did cover news stories, but he had more in common with literary social satirists and progressives like Mark Twain and H.L. Mencken in launching attacks against political corruption and pursuing reform with equal zeal. Although billed as a weekly, the *Eye Opener* possessed neither printing facilities nor a regular staff. A binge drinker and alcoholic who openly discussed his struggles with sobriety in his paper, Edwards published the *Eye Opener* according to his own schedule—"semi-occasionally." If a few weeks passed between editions, Calgarians suspected Edwards was either drying out in a hospital or simply did not have much to say. "I haven't bothered publishing a paper since the December [1914] municipal elections," Edwards wrote to nurse Jessie McCauley Ross in February 1915. "Though I intend coming out on the twentieth of this month just to show the maddened populace that I haven't been killed in the trenches."[14]

Like the muckrakers, Edwards loved nothing more than skewering the powerful while comforting the meek. Edwards tended to mistrust large combinations, like the Canadian Pacific Railway, and reflexively backed the underdog. A staunch advocate for women's rights, he also argued that health care was a basic human right. But it was his literary style, irreverence, humour, and willingness to tilt at windmills that drove the *Eye Opener's* circulation to over 18,500 in 1908 when Calgary's population was 10,000 people, making it the largest circulation between Vancouver and Toronto. His keen eye and biting wit gave Edwards international reach; the *Eye Opener's* subscription list extended across much of Canada, the United States, and Great Britain, and reprints of Edwards's articles appeared in newspapers across North America. "Calgary," allegedly said one prominent New York politician in the early 1900s, "is, I believe, a place in Canada where the *Eye Opener* comes from." The paper and its editor possessed substantial cachet and were more than willing to wield it. Indeed, despite his well-known struggles with alcohol, Edwards's support for Alberta's prohibition movement in 1915 may have proved decisive as Albertans adopted prohibition in 1916. Edwards, wrote Grant MacEwan, "exerted a public influence which probably surpassed that of any western editorial or political figure of his time."[15]

Of the three daily editors, Woods preached a more cautious and pragmatic approach to the possibility of finding oil to the south of Calgary, perhaps because of his previous experience with petroleum investments. Woods owned leaseholds in southern Alberta and joined with partners Fred Lowes and Jim Cornwall to form one of the first syndicates to explore the mineral wealth of Norman Wells in the Northwest Territories. While the wet gas and condensates present in the Dingman well usually indicated the presence of crude oil, the reality is that the main crude structure still eluded Dingman #1. In much the same way that Dingman maintained that an oilfield existed only after it produced oil, Woods remained sceptical of overheated rumours and reports trumpeting oil in commercial quantities. Supposing for the moment that oil existed beneath Turner Valley, Woods knew than no company could absolutely guarantee their drill would find it without suffering from some calamity, like a cave-in, a bent pipe, or running out of cash, and he believed he had a responsibility to educate investors about the risks of investing in an unproven industry.

Conditions were ripe for abuse and the emergence of a bull market reminiscent of recent mining booms in British Columbia and Ontario. During those events, newspapers and magazines such as the Toronto-based *Financial Post* and *Saturday Night* played a crucial role in exposing the unseemly side of stock market promotions.[16] Starting on October 24, 1913, *The Calgary Daily Herald* expressed concern about the sudden appearance of a dozen "bucket shop" brokers (unlicensed share dealers) buying and selling oil stocks on the streets of Calgary, many for recently formed oil companies trying to capitalize on the excitement created by the Dingman discovery. But two additional concerns lurked behind the *Herald's* actions—the fear that unscrupulous promoters were preying on the desperation of the growing number of unemployed congregating in the city in the autumn and winter of 1913–14 and a belief that desperate Calgarians hoped they could resell oil stocks quickly at a higher price.[17]

The prolonged period of economic growth in the Canadian and Albertan economies ended in 1912–13 as several factors converged to bring about the onset of economic hard times. World historians classify the fifty years before the Great War as the first "Golden Era" of globalization, featuring the free flow of capital and labour across national borders with few impediments or restrictions. Indeed, prior to the Great War, Canadian and US currencies were interchangeable at par, cementing the ties between the two national economies.[18] Technological transfer accompanied the movement of people and goods. Since 1897, massive investments to extend communication and transportation networks had underwritten the dramatic expansion of prairie wheat exports and brought international capital and immigrants to both the Canadian and Albertan economies. In a country flush with money and new residents, a construction boom, financed by British capital, produced railways, farms, and homes, and grew the cities. Historians John Feldberg and Warren Elofson estimate that total British investment in Canada from 1900 to 1913 in securities, insurance, and other forms amounted to $1.75 trillion.[19] In turn, the construction boom fuelled the consumer goods sector of central Canada and iron and steel manufacturing in Nova Scotia. But then the economy entered a recession after completion of the two transcontinental railway projects threw thousands of labourers out of work and the two largest sources of Canadian investment capital suddenly dried up. In Great Britain, disruptions caused by the Balkan Wars (1912–13) sharply constricted British investments in Canada and dealt a heavy blow to Calgary investors in construction and real estate speculation. So too did the onset of the recession of 1913–14 in the United States.[20]

Despite several promising signs and record profits in some sectors, most notably in manufacturing and construction, the province's economic growth in the last quarter of the nineteenth century and first decade of the twentieth century was far from even.[21] Not everyone prospered during the long boom of 1896–1912. Despite a tenfold increase in production to three million tonnes between 1897 and 1910, the province's coal mining sector struggled to serve more than a regional market due to high transportation costs and tariff walls that precluded it from more lucrative eastern Canadian and US markets. In agriculture, small-scale, labour-intensive farming dominated through the early 1900s where the combination of arid land, a short growing season, labour shortages, and a lack of specialized equipment limited crop yields and precluded large-scale operations. Alberta's agricultural output increased dramatically between 1900 and 1910 due to a combination of railroad development, increased immigration, the proliferation of dry-farming techniques, crop rotation, better irrigation, and the availability of Marquis wheat seeds (with a shorter growing period and higher yield). But Alberta's production of wheat still lagged behind that of Saskatchewan and Manitoba; the province's farmers produced more lower-priced oats, barley, and rye.[22]

Changes in ranching were perhaps the most dramatic. In less than forty years large-scale commercial "open range" operations rose and fell. As ranching historian Warren Elofson notes, the large corporate combinations initially spread to the northwestern plains as an outgrowth of developments in the United States and attempts by the Dominion government to capitalize on the "beef bonanza" taking place. However, the corporate ranches struggled mightily to overcome the challenges of conducting their business in new territories that were only aggravated by steadily declining cattle prices after 1882. No fences meant no protection against predators—whether wolves or cattle rustlers—or myriad other problems, like disease, poor breeding practices, or the effects of Alberta's harsh and unforgiving climate, all of which raised costs and ate away at profits. Alberta's corporate cattle ranches could neither maintain profitability nor attract enough capital from national or international investors to sustain operations, forcing them to take on debt to survive. The brutal winter of 1906/7 hit large corporate ranches particularly hard. The loss rate, largely due to mass starvation of herds, reached as high as 50 percent, spelling the end for many of Alberta's large-scale ranches. In its place were much smaller operations—perhaps around 100 head of cattle—"family"-run ranch/farms that eventually solved many of these challenges by adopting new methods and techniques.[23]

The general prosperity masked other problems. The first tangible signs of economic distress hit Calgary's construction sector as building permits fell from a record high of $20.4 million in 1912 to $8.6 million in 1913 and continued to slide. By 1915, the value of building permits fell to just $150,500 (see Table 2-1).[24] Construction was not the only sector affected. The recently completed CPR shops at Ogden, designed to employ more than 2,000 mechanics, laid off hundreds of workers and by the summer of 1913 placed the rest on reduced schedules.[25] Wheat prices dropped in 1912 and did not recover until 1915. Also, by 1912, the western land boom ended, and investors began selling urban landholdings. Unmistakable signs of a slowing economy in western Canada intensified after the autumn harvest ended, when an additional 40,000 seasonal workers across the west were unemployed. All 400 real estate concerns in downtown Calgary sat closed and shuttered; by December 1913, Calgary's unemployed reached 10 percent of the population, with 2,000 tradesmen and 3,000 unskilled labourers out of work. In Edmonton, at least 4,000 of the city's 72,000 residents were unemployed, numbers so large that they soon organized themselves into the "League of the Unemployed." On December 31, 1913, an "ill-clad army" of about 1,000 unemployed marched on Calgary's city hall demanding that the city provide work to everyone "regardless whether they are married or single and regardless of color, race and nationality" with a minimum wage of thirty cents per hour and not less than nine dollars per week. If the city could not provide employment, protestors demanded three meal tickets a day, each good for a twenty-five-cent meal at a local restaurant, as well as a clean place to sleep. City hall representatives responded that the city could not do anything more than it was doing. All public works projects continued, and the city provided employment to men on alternate weeks to try and provide the greatest amount of relief to the largest number of people. But city officials confessed that, even if they could begin all the public works projects they could (winter's frost prevented digging ditches and trenches), the city's limited resources could only provide relief for about 500 of the assembled workers.[26]

Yet the slowing economy did not deter the influx of immigrants to the West, particularly large numbers from the United States and Britain in search of better opportunities, exacerbating the economic tough times on the prairies. Private charities throughout the province strained to provide relief. The public debt of the province grew from $1.2 million in 1908 to $56.2 million in 1913, while national revenues dropped from $168.7 million in 1912 to $133 million in 1914.[27] Historian David Bright writes that, even before the onset of the depression, many Calgarians struggled to make ends meet. While wages increased in Calgary between 1903 and 1912, inflation likely outstripped nominal gains as retail prices grew 40 percent over the same period. Thus, even before the onset of the economic depression in 1913, a single wage earner could not support a working-class family. Wage earners turned

Table 2-1 Value of Building Permits in Calgary, 1910–1915

	1910	1911	1912	1913	1914	1915
Building permits	$5,589,594	$12,907,638	$20,394,220	$3,619,563	$3,435,350	$150,500

Data adapted from "Calgary's population," *Calgary Herald*, October 20, 1916, 6.

to a variety of measures—from penny capitalism to prostitution—to supplement incomes.

Given the increasingly dire circumstances, various civic leaders expressed concern that curb brokers and bucket shops would capitalize on the dreams of gullible investors of easy riches won via the stock market. Visiting the city in October 1913, Vice-President George Bury of the Canadian Pacific Railway noted the "great efforts" made by curb brokers to sell oil stock to all passersby. "It is to be hoped that those concerned in the permanent prosperity of the city and province will not allow the wage-earner and the small investor to be victimized," warned Bury.[28] But oil provided a ray of hope in an otherwise cold and grey winter, particularly as new oil companies formed and sought to raise investment capital through the sale of shares to the public, offering them the dream of future riches and financial security. The *Herald* regarded the possibility of Calgarians speculating in oil stocks as the economy slowed with scarcely concealed horror. Even cursory inspection revealed that many companies selling shares lacked both the capital and the inclination to develop an oil and gas field. Some companies did not specialize in the production of oil and gas, argued the *Herald,* as much as they did in separating investors from their hard-earned cash.[29]

To make its point, and to increase public literacy about the difference between real estate investments and stock speculation, *The Calgary Daily Herald* ran a series of front page articles between October 24 and October 31, under the generic headline "the floatation of oil companies." Billing the series as a public warning, the paper went to great lengths to assert its faith in the "character and permanency of the oil field" but nonetheless challenged the fundamental premises of Alberta's emerging oil culture—namely its belief that individualism, competition, and unfettered capitalism would produce the greatest returns for the largest number of people. More significantly, however, the series also dared question the greatest intangible asset necessary for the oil industry—faith in those things unseen. Woods and his paper rationally, dispassionately, and stubbornly insisted on proof. Proof that an oil field existed, not just surface seepages of oil and wet gas. Proof that the company investors placed their money in would drill for oil, not simply sell dreams. For *The Morning Albertan* and other industry supporters, the *Herald's* insistence on proof represented nothing short of apostasy and a breach of the public trust.

Thus, while the parameters of the public debate between the papers and the industry conform to other progressive era clashes between the interests of businesspeople and the professional classes, additional layers of local boosterism and optimism about the West influenced Davidson's writings and complicated his criticism of Woods's approach with the *Herald*. The *Herald* advocated pursuing the development of the oil fields with information and expertise mobilized in service of the broader community. What concerned the *Herald* were "the unwarranted promotions that are being based on present knowledge and reasonable expectations." In its estimation, less than one in ten emerging companies was a fair investment. Less than one in a hundred would provide investors with a reasonable return. Less than one in a thousand would return proportionate interest to investors. This, concluded the editorial, justified drastic measures: "The *Herald* believes that the formation of these companies, or at least the selling of their stock to the public, should be stopped." The campaign enlisted the support and backing of the city's elite, as represented by the mayor, Herbert A. Sinnott, J.W. Campbell of the Board of Trade, and Oscar G. Devenish of the Industrial Bureau. The three men issued a joint statement that emphasized the uncertainty and speculative nature of oil exploration, cautioning that "it is impossible to state whether the oil found merely came from a seepage, or indicates the existence of a large deposit at a greater or lesser distance or depth." As drilling continued, the letter warned the public "against placing too great confidence in circulated reports and particularly urged to exercise care in investments in oil leases, or in the stocks of companies or syndicates which have been or may be formed for oil exploitation." The article on October 25 raised several concerns, including the possible damage to the city's reputation if it produced an oil boom where "hundreds of companies are formed that never make a dollar for their shareholders." Even if the oil field proved productive, the damage done by illegitimate operators and speculators to the city's reputation could be incalculable. In the absence of government action, information and education campaigns were the best way to protect unwary investors and the city.[30]

The articles tried to build financial literacy in its readers by breaking down the process, from the acquisition of oil and gas leases to the drilling of a well. In the absence of "blue sky" laws requiring transparency in company prospectuses, the series taught readers how to read a prospectus critically by explaining the difference between capital stock and promotion stock, the necessity of acquiring access rights from surface rights holders, the potential for litigation, and how to determine if the company was a good investment by assessing its assets and liabilities. To illustrate its points, the articles used case studies provided by start-up companies, like the Paraffin Oil Company and Rocky Mountain Oil Fields, for readers to consider. The two companies were among the earliest start-ups offering shares to investors but had yet to acquire drilling rigs or spud a well. The prospectus of the Paraffin Oil Company provided the substance for the October 25 article while the Rocky Mountain Oil Fields prospectus received coverage on October 27, 1913. The paper studied one last company, Black Diamond Oil Fields, on October 28 before turning to a general discussion of the oil patch. Cumulatively, the articles provided a background primer on stocks, investing, and the emerging oil boom.

In all three cases assessed by the *Herald*, the companies did not hold tangible assets—either existing oil production to sell, or capital plants, like a derrick—to prove to investors their intent to drill. In fact, the *Herald's* articles pointed out that the only asset most of these new companies used to set the value of their shares were oil and gas leases. In themselves, the leases did not hold any actual value, nor did they guarantee an oil find—they were more like gambling or lottery tickets. Individuals or companies could purchase mineral rights from the Dominion Land Office for "about $150.00 a section" (actually $165 per section) or more if bought from a previous leaseholder. The company then converted the value of the lease into cash, stock, or both, at an exceedingly high price relative to its actual cost from the Dominion Land Office. Since securing mineral rights from the province cost twenty-five cents per acre, this meant that some companies now "paid" themselves between ten and twenty-five dollars an acre to acquire those oil leases, an increase of between 3,900 and 9,900 percent over what they paid for them from the Dominion Land Office. This alone, argued *The Herald*, was reason for small investors to be sceptical. But possessing the mineral rights to a parcel of land did not guarantee the oil company the right to access the land if another individual held the surface rights. Unless the company obtained the written consent of the landowner, a company could not prospect, drill, or otherwise do anything to prove up the mineral rights contained in the lease. Furthermore, the land office did not recognize the transfer or subdivision of leases attempted by some companies and only permitted the drilling of a single well for every 640 acres of leasehold. Small investors therefore needed to be alert to the potential for litigation to precede or follow any attempt at development.

The Paraffin Oil Company provided an interesting case study because the company, capitalized at $500,000, paid two men, both of whom were directors, $399,990 worth of shares for oil leases to 1,120 acres of land. In turn, the sellers agreed to drill a well to a depth of 1,500 feet within a year. When drillers completed the well, the sellers would then receive an additional $100,000 of treasury stock. Paraffin Oil would then sell 199,995 shares of promotion stock at fifty cents a share to raise an additional $100,000; of that sum, the company promised to set aside $10,000 to drill a well. Thus, when the public, not the company or its directors, provided the capital to drill, the directors would make a $90,000 profit on 1,120 acres of unproven oil rights plus earning for the directors *another* $100,000 worth of treasury stock. Given such conditions, the *Herald* concluded it impossible to see how any investor could realize a profit.[31]

On Monday, October 27, the paper turned its attention to the prospectus of Rocky Mountain Oil Fields Limited, which had different particulars. Rocky Mountain publicly offered shares to provide $50,000 of the company's authorized capital of $100,000. The prospectus also revealed how the company bought 1,920 acres of oil leases from gentlemen now serving on the company's board of directors. Initially, the company paid these men $50,000 for the 1,920 acres of oil leases, divided unequally between shares and cash—$30,000 worth of shares and $20,000 in cash. But when the Dingman well proved oil existed in the field, the vendors exercised an option in their contract to take their entire payment in stock, meaning the vendors now owned half the total stock in the company in exchange for the leases. This meant the remaining half of the company's stock would necessarily provide the entire working capital for development. The prospectus further claimed that the company would offer no promotion stock and that there would be no promotion expenses. Every cent acquired from the sale of stock would be used in development. The *Herald* then posed three important questions: Is the company paying the promoters too much for the oil leases? Will the sale of the remaining shares provide enough capital to develop the company's leases? Finally, is an investment in Rocky Mountain Oil Fields a good one for investors?

The article allowed that the answer to these questions depended on the individual, but offered a few observations. The first was that the company effectively paid $50,000 for 1,920 acres of unproven oil leases—roughly twenty-six dollars per acre for land that lay between three and eight miles away from the Dingman well. It would be difficult for promoters to claim that these sections of land were any more or less likely to be valuable than any of the other leases that surrounded them. Furthermore, speculators could buy nearby leases for much less than the twenty-six dollars per acre paid by the company. Remembering that half of the company's capital stock paid for the leases, $50,000 hardly seemed sufficient capital to develop the remaining two leases. In its concluding remarks, the *Herald* pointed out that this was not an investment but was, rather, rank speculation. "This company, like all other companies being formed, bases its chief claim to value on the fact that oil has been discovered in the Dingman well," summarized the paper. If the company and its operators had such faith in their property, let them put prove it first by putting machinery on the ground and spudding in a well without asking investors to bear the entire risk.[32]

After assessing the prospectus of Black Diamond Oil Fields on October 28, the *Herald* turned its attention to the attitude of civic leaders, like council member Thomas Alfred Presswood ("Tappy") Frost. Born in Norfolk, England, in 1865, Frost came to Canada in 1887 and decided to study for the ministry at Woodstock Baptist College in Ontario. Ordained as a minister in 1889, Frost arrived in Calgary as pastor of the First Baptist Church in 1896 after serving at five Ontario churches. In 1904, Frost resigned from the ministry and found a second career as a psychiatrist with Alberta's Department of Health. As the first registered cardholder at the Calgary Public Library, Frost had roots in the community that were deep and wide. Described as a Liberal in politics and a Baptist in religion, Frost carved out a reputation of being colourful, honest, progressive, and well-intentioned, ready and willing to deliver a speech at the drop of a hat. Indeed, perhaps the most dangerous spot in Calgary was the space between Frost and a reporter's notebook. He earned the nickname "Tappy" because of the initials of his given names spelled "TAP," as well as for his habit of inspecting the quality of the cement used in sidewalks by "tapping" them with a hammer he carried. During the Great War, Frost served overseas with the 89th Battalion as a quartermaster sergeant and worked for the Department of Soldiers' Civil Re-establishment at war's end. In 1922, he accepted an appointment as psychiatrist at the Ponoka Institution, where he worked until he passed away in 1927. Considering his record of service to the community, in 1915 the *Herald* wrote that the great progressive Republican president of the United States, Theodore Roosevelt, was little more than a "'glorified Tappy' Frost," cheekily adding that "somewhere here there is a large-sized compliment concealed, but who for?"[33]

In 1913, however, the *Herald's* Flotations campaign plainly irritated Frost, as did its general coverage of oil and gas issues. However, his status as a director for Rocky Mountain Oil Fields likely influenced his views. Indeed, the day after the *Herald* published its assessment of Rocky Mountain Oil Fields, Frost responded with a letter of his own to the rival *Albertan*. The council member claimed he wanted to "criticize the Critic," providing investors with all sides of the story. Frost stated he would not directly engage with the *Herald's* criticism of Rocky Mountain Oil Fields and would confine his remarks to the paper's general understanding of the issues related to oil and gas development as it related to two issues in particular: the entry rights of mineral leaseholders to the property and, more generally, the element of risk in oil field development.

Threading the needle carefully, Frost said he did not object to the paper highlighting individual cases "wherever justified" but suggested the *Herald* hire a writer "who has been in the country long enough to know the simple conditions upon which any purchaser of land obtains it from the Crown." The *Herald* found ambiguity around access rights for a property when a different party held the surface rights. Frost claimed the Crown retained mining and mineral rights as well as the right to entry. If the landowner refused entry, wrote Frost, "the crown will enforce entry on application of the lease holder." But the reality was that in the winter of 1913/14, several oil companies encountered stiff opposition from landowners and farmers, some of whom had just learned for the first time that they did not hold the subsurface mineral rights to their property when oil companies appeared on their property. The unwillingness of the provincial government to clarify matters beforehand also caused confusion and uncertainty, delaying the start of more than one drilling operation.

The question of risk, however, proved to be a difference in world view. As Frost saw the issue, the *Herald's* attempt to shield investors from unnecessary risk missed the mark because without risk "no poor man living would have hope of ever changing his position in life." To those seeking his advice about investing in Rocky Mountain Oil Fields, the council member claimed he always replied with a question: How much could the person afford to lose? "Kiss it goodbye with a hope to meet again," he stated. "Because the *Herald* does not know that any company has ordered machinery or done anything that has cost any money is not sufficient justification to use such ignorance in the connection in which it does." Frost then derided the *Herald's* statement that the directorate of Rocky Mountain Oil Fields should personally invest in putting the machinery on the ground without asking private investors for the cash as patently absurd. Frost concluded his letter with the statement "without faith work is dead." The *Herald* replied to Frost's letter that afternoon, and chastised the alderman's statements, saying that Frost's advice "might come well from a bounce-steerer or a race-track tout or an illegitimate stock promoter. It comes poorly from a man who is an alderman of Calgary, and who is supposed, whether truly or not, to represent business sentiment." In any case, the *Herald* pointed to expert geologists like Dowling and Cunningham Craig who questioned the wisdom of the land rush. Dowling criticized the "haphazard mode of taking up leases" and predicted "a great number of these will no doubt be altogether useless." Meanwhile, when asked about the prospects for oil, Cunningham Craig demurred and said he "is not fully satisfied regarding the oil field to the southwest of Calgary."[34]

Taken together, the *Herald's* articles provided a valuable public service. The breakdown and analysis of the three oil company prospectuses alone served as a wonderful primer for beginning investors, alerting them to potential risks, pitfalls, and unanswered questions relating to an oil flotation. The series also illustrated the extent to which the average Calgarian and Albertan remained ill prepared and unknowledgeable about financial matters and investments despite dramatic increases in the number of Canadians invested in the markets.[35] Now was not the time to speculate in risky ventures. "For months back the people of this city and country have been hard up," wrote the *Herald* on October 28, 1913, arguing that people were just paying off debts and only now beginning to save some real money. "Nothing could be worse for them, nothing worse for Calgary, than a boom in oil stocks such as seems to be starting here today." Coming on the heels of the real estate bubble in which so many Calgarians participated, it also illustrated the extent to which speculation in oil and gas stocks represented a different gamble altogether. Real estate retained its reputation as a "safe" investment because investors always obtained something tangible and stood the greatest chance for turning a modest profit. Investing in oil, however, was decidedly different. The risks associated with oil speculation were high risk, high reward. While investors could reap fabulous rewards, the risk came with a greater possibility of losing everything, especially in an unproven oil field like Turner Valley. As one letter to the editor published in the *Herald* on October 30, 1913, argued, "There isn't one of the concerns who are selling oil stocks who would be willing to guarantee that their property contains oil or your money refunded."[36]

Even in these early days, the *Herald* reported that the oil boom attracted some outsiders looking to turn a quick profit. "As one oil man from Kansas frankly put it," informed the *Herald* on October 30, "there are 'easy pickings' to be made." The paper then warned that, unlike the real estate boom, which had kept money in the city, money invested in oil stocks would leave Calgary forever. For Woods and the *Herald*, this fundamental difference underpinned their reticence regarding investing in oil stocks until discoveries proved the field. Archibald Dingman inserted his thoughts in the debate, writing a letter to the editor published in the *Herald* on November 1, denouncing attempts by stock promoters to cash in on the success of the Dingman well. "Up to the present," wrote Dingman, "there is not warrant for anyone to pay over one dollar to any company or proposed company, believing it to be anything more than an ordinary speculative gamble." In the strongest possible terms, Dingman urged potential investors to complete their due diligence before investing and that failure to do so "is not using the ordinary caution exercised in acquiring the money in the first place." Dingman explicitly stated the Turner Valley field was both abnormal and expensive to drill in, requiring liberal doses of time, money, caution, and patience. Calgary Petroleum Products "cannot be held responsible for, nor have we the wish of time, to try and account for the thousand and one lurid reports emanating, most probably, from those who are looking for easy prey." The *Herald* concluded its series much more pithily on November 1: "Save your money, pay your bills, attend to your own business and wait until the Dingman well is finally and fully proved before you even consider putting your cash into these oil stock flotations."[37]

The *Herald's* series attracted international attention, generating plaudits from *The London Globe* and *The Pall Mall Gazette* that, in turn, advised British investors to be cautious until the field could be adequately proven. The series and its conclusions, however, did not sit well with either Davidson, the editor of *The Morning Albertan*, or Thompson of the *News Telegram*, both of whom suspected Woods would actively discourage the "little people" from investing as part of a broader plot to save the oil field for a large major. "The cry of wildcatting," said J. Wadsworth Travers to the *News Telegram*, "which has been so smoothly put forth is having the effect which its promoters thought it would have to some degree at last. The sale of leases has dropped off considerably of late and the small speculator, whose only chance of making any money at all out of the oil strike is to get right in on the ground floor, is beginning to be attacked with cold feet." Given rumours that Woods had recently sold two half sections of oil rights for $5,000, Davidson believed Woods a rank hypocrite. Bob Edwards, editor of the *Eye Opener* and good friend of Davidson, put it most succinctly by asking, "What do you think of a man who will sell a piece of property, then, with his big stick, proceed to make it worthless?"[38]

Starting on October 29, *The Morning Albertan* began its own analysis of the oil companies operating in southern Alberta, starting with Calgary

Petroleum Products. Cumulatively, the articles emphasized the entrepreneurial character of the companies' directors and underscored their standing in the community. The accompanying editorial left little doubt where Davidson stood. To Davidson, the *Herald's* articles smacked of paternalism, betraying Woods's lack of faith in the operation of a free market and underscoring his belief that small investors were like infants in need of protection. Investors, whether large or small, argued Davidson, could decide for themselves whether to assume the risk of investing in the market. "The men who are buying stock in companies at the present time are not the maimed, the halt and the blind," wrote Davidson, alluding to Luke 14:21, "but shrewd business men, many of whom understand that they have better protection in a stock company than in any syndicate that would be formed." A few days later, the temperature in the feud raised a few more degrees. The *Albertan* referred in passing to the region's growing economic crisis and claimed the *Herald* "has declared war upon these companies, and is doing its utmost to destroy the only place where ordinary people, inside or outside of Calgary, desirous of taking a chance, can place their money." Over the course of its response to the *Herald's* series, the *Albertan* opined that oil companies usually failed for one of three reasons: the company drilled for oil or gas in an unsuitable location; mistakes by an incompetent driller—like dropping a tool down the hole and spending all of the money trying to retrieve a failure rather than making a clean start; or profligate spending on office expenses or other "profitless expenses." Thus, according to the *Albertan*, companies with experienced, and proven, business leadership enjoyed a tremendous advantage over those companies that did not.[39]

On November 5, 1913, after charting a "middle-of-the road" course between the *Herald* and the *Albertan* for weeks regarding the issue of speculation, George Thompson published a remarkable editorial arguing that Albertans possessed special characteristics, embedded in the institutions and culture of western Canada, that obligated them to fulfill a quasi-religious "mission" to develop the oil and natural gas resources of the province. Entitled "The Question of 'Oil,'" the piece likened Alberta's first generation of oil and gas entrepreneurs to Christopher Columbus as the "discoverers" of a new world, thus generating an oft-used metaphor during the boom that many still considered flattering. From Thompson's perspective, the global economy and everyday life were already rapidly changing due to the second industrial revolution. The transformations wrought by electricity, chemicals, and petroleum fundamentally altered the economy and society, rewarding some with new opportunities while leaving others behind. The changes were both exhilarating and frightening. Scarcely sixty years before, there was no oil production in the United States, and it was now a multi-million-dollar industry. As the automobile transformed transportation, Calgary would prosper now that the "era of the motor car, and the consumption of crude oil as the motive power par excellence of the age, have just commenced." With rapid urbanization, the proliferation of transportation networks, the employment of "vast armies of workmen," and the creation of hundreds, if not thousands, of private fortunes because of petroleum, the *News Telegram* argued that the pessimists urging caution about developing an oil industry in Alberta "are to be doubted." Referring elliptically but unmistakeably to the *Herald*, the *News Telegram* accused Woods of "usurping the position of local censor and warning the public with the empty and owl-like gravity of the mountebank not to spend one dollar in prospecting for Petroleum by the only method of finding the precious and magic fluid—namely by drilling."[40]

Thompson speculated that in addition to innumerable personal fortunes, petroleum development would increase Calgary's population, wealth, and commerce in the next few years and would infinitely improve the standard of living in the province, region, and country. Beyond this, a whiff of Social Darwinism's emphasis on the survival of the fittest filled Thompson's emphatic message, "WE MUST BE PREPARED TO PAY THE PRICE OF PROSPECTING." Beyond personal fortunes, economic necessity and international competition also argued in favour of development. The sheer size of the Dominion meant that Canada rivalled the United States and Russia, but those two countries produced substantially more oil—approximately 1 million barrels a year each. Failure to develop its natural resources was incongruent both with Alberta's values—here Thompson referred specifically to its "spirit of enterprise"—and the legacy of the region's pioneers, some of whom risked life and limb exploring and developing the resources of the country. Espousing a unique mission for Alberta to develop the province's oil and gas reserves and underwritten by a brand of western Canadian exceptionalism that distinguished the region and its people, the editorial proclaimed that "the excellence of our occidental civilization, the abundance of our wealth, the opulence of most of those whom we call our 'old timers,' ARE THE SELF-EVIDENT REWARDS FOR THE ENTERPRISE AND INDOMITABLE COURAGE THAT WON'T WAIT." In building the province, western Canadians had accomplished in less than ten years what it took a century for "slow-going" eastern Canadians to acquire.

The real question before Albertans was whether they would continue to develop industries, take risks, and grow, or simply quit. Thompson allowed that the decision was both highly individual and collective. While there were "sufficient pessimists elsewhere" in his estimation, there was no reason for pessimism anywhere in Canada due to the endowments of nature and the indomitable spirit of its people. "If we in whose hands its destiny has been entrusted will but do our part faithfully and well, with the great common weal our uppermost consideration," success was all but assured. Alberta's mission provided a powerful incentive to the entrepreneurs of the province to drill for oil, not because it was easy but because it was both hard and expensive. Anticipating critics who suggested that only large multinational corporations and conglomerates had the investment capital to undertake the mission, Thompson swatted their arguments aside. Most of the thirty-four successor and subsidiary companies of Standard Oil concentrated their operations in the downstream sector—refining and marketing. "Only three," wrote Thompson, "are producing companies." Thompson then likened drilling for oil to the insurance business, where strength in numbers mitigated risk. "All that is required for success is ample capital and integrity and skill in the management." Drilling for oil, reasoned Thompson, was exactly like selling insurance. While the death of a single policyholder was a tragedy for his widow and orphans, the insurance company paying out the benefit regarded it as "a matter of little importance" because the company had thousands of policyholders and shareholders to defer the risks. "The same applies to oil prospecting companies," wrote Thompson, because these businesses were "engaged merely in prospecting for oil."[41]

Thompson's strained analogy held that, in certain areas, oil deposits extended under large continuous areas known as fields. In other regions, distinct and separated areas of smaller pools existed. To be sure, even around the "fields" and "pools" companies still drilled dry holes. But oil companies with large holdings either in large areas of a promising location or more numerous holdings scattered across promising stretches were bound to find oil "if provided with sufficient working capital to test their various properties for Petroleum by actually [sic] drilling of wells, *are most scientifically designed to 'strike oil* [emphasis added]."' Oil companies, if "honestly and capably organized, on business lines, and [if] their undertaking of prospecting for oil is carried on with integrity, economy and skill—each company is entitled to as great respect and encouragement from the press as are banks or insurance companies, or any other business organization." Thompson then directly challenged Woods's argument that investors should wait until after an oil discovery before investing, calling it a fallacy like "waiting until a city is fully grown before purchasing a town lot." Early investors received the greatest returns and the largest profits. In this current venture, success depended on the accuracy of the investor's judgment regarding the resources of the region, the "energy and enterprise of his neighbors," as well as his own initiative. In Thompson's consideration of the history of prospecting for oil, "one is forced to the conclusion that the general public are never played properly for 'suckers' until the area is proved to be productive." Once the wealth is proved, investors become overconfident and singularly focused on realizing a profit at any price, becoming easy marks for crooked dealings, by the likes of Daniel Drew, Jay Gould, Jim Fisk, and Tom Lawson, "the hyenas of commerce and industry who have always controlled certain newspapers and news sources for the undoing of the people to serve their own ghoulish greed." The point was that *"the little fellow has a chance to win during the course of development* [emphasis in original].". Thompson closed with the warning to "keep your eye on the people who have been so generous with advice, and you will probably understand the motive in proffering that advice."[42]

For would-be promoters, Thompson's editorial salved their bruised egos following the *Herald's* pointed comments. The very next day, Rocky Mountain Oil Fields hailed the piece "absolutely true, complete, and sane," using excerpts from the editorial in its ads, and printed a couple of thousand copies of the piece to mail to anyone interested. But the broader oil industry and interested observers outside Alberta also began to weigh in and found things to be concerned about. *The Financial Post* stated that it did not want to discourage investigations of the petroleum wealth of Alberta but believed that "prospecting has not gone far enough to warrant the general application being made to the public for capital." *The Petroleum Gazette,* a trade journal published out of Titusville, Pennsylvania, took notice of the burgeoning dispute between the industry and the *Herald* and offered its own sobering take for investors and promoters about the Dingman strike: there was much to be worried about. Citing oil producers working in Petrolia, Ontario, the *Gazette* claimed most wells drilled in the foothills of the Rocky Mountains would produce oil seepages of high-grade petroleum because they underwent a process of filtration. But nothing those drillers saw to date led them to believe Turner Valley distinguished itself from earlier finds at Pincher Creek or Flathead Valley. In those two cases, the fields also presented promising surface seepages but produced no commercial quantities of oil. Predicting that the Dingman well would "cause the expenditure of large sums of money," the *Gazette* nonetheless doubted anyone would earn a dividend from the production of oil. The boom would quickly turn to bust, but only after unscrupulous promoters "get their fill of dollars from the innocent." Their experience told them that the small gas supply and limited quantities of petroleum produced to date did not inspire confidence. Neither did its presence in a broken formation with loose rock and gravel and no cover to trap a large deposit of oil. But the big "tell" for the *Gazette* was that "the Calgary [Dingman] well is guarded and outsiders are not allowed to take a 'peep.'" "Good wells," the *Gazette* noted, "create booms and do not need talk; but poor ones are always shrouded in mystery while a boom is being worked up." The article concluded with a devastating statement: "It is to be hoped that the Canadian press will assist in killing this unwarranted oil boom of the west, and thereby save injury to our country at a very important and critical time."[43]

Unfortunately, the reality remained that every company featured by the *Herald* in its Flotations series presented serious problems that posed undue risks for investors hoping to achieve a reasonable return on their investment. Facing tough questions, and unaccustomed to press criticism, some, like Stephen E. Beveridge and Don M. LeBourdais of Rocky Mountain Oil Fields, lashed out at the *Herald*, arguing that petroleum speculation was no different than any other business. The spat grew into an increasingly bitter back-and-forth campaign on the editorial pages after the *Herald* announced that it would not accept any advertising dollars from oil companies it considered to be engaged in rank speculation. Over Beveridge's signature, LeBourdais penned a letter to the *Herald* on November 3 mocking the *Herald's* announcement that he later claimed went unpublished by the *Herald* and subsequently became part of a Rocky Mountain Oil Fields ad published in the *Record*. "How often, Mr. Editor, have you seen signs ornamenting the whole front of store windows, reading something like this: 'Going out of Business! Forced to raise $50,000 in Ten Days!' 'Everything is Absolutely Half-Price!' Yet you know all along that the advertiser has no intention of going out of business, but was just using a rather flamboyant method of attracting the public," argued LeBourdais. Turning attention to the storefronts of some of the *Herald's* "star" advertisers, LeBourdais declared that they used window displays and decorated storefronts to bring in business. "We venture to say that the sketches used by some of the offices selling oil stock, which you ridicule and condemn today, are mild in comparison." Beveridge and LeBourdais argued that entrepreneurs floating oil companies could use the same methods. The *Herald*'s riposte to this letter, published on November 4, replied that the Rocky Mountain Oil Fields prospectus, filed with the provincial government, remained free from extravagant claims. But Rocky Mountain Oil Fields ads made dubious statements guaranteeing that the company would strike oil. That statement, argued the *Herald*, was obviously untrue. "It was made in order to sell the stock of the company, and the person that wrote it must have known that it would tend to mislead the reader."[44]

Believing his character impugned, Beveridge began plotting his revenge through *The Natural Gas and Oil Record*, a new weekly trade paper about the petroleum industry that emerged as a direct result of the *Herald's* Flotations series. Winnipegger J.L. Tucker revealed that he had no preconceived notions about Alberta oil and absolutely had no intention of starting an oil sheet. But his business took him to several of the leading figures in Calgary oil—Oscar Devenish, Archibald Dingman, Ira Segur, and William S. Herron, among others—who convinced him that oil existed in commercial quantities. Tucker also related that before staring the *Record*, he spoke with Woods to ask him directly if he believed in the oil fields around Calgary. "Mr. Woods answered that he did, and offered to make a wager that there would be an oil refinery started here within a year."[45]

Convinced that the field was legitimate, Tucker moved into the newly opened Grunwald Hotel and operated the *Record* out of the *News Telegram* building. *The Natural Gas and Oil Record* started out as a weekly, publishing its first issue on November 1, 1913. An unabashed booster of Calgary oil, Tucker clearly objected mightily to both the *Herald's* and Dingman's warnings about "wildcatting." "If Mr. Woods had confined himself to the killing off of illegitimate companies he would have been upheld on every side," wrote Tucker, "but he goes so far as to say that no oil stocks are good." Calling their stances hypocritical and pledging his paper "ready to help kill any crooked flotations of oil stocks," echoing earlier comments in the *News Telegram,* Tucker likened "wildcatting" to the Spanish monarchy's decision to finance Christopher Columbus's voyage or the building of the Canadian Pacific Railway. Without wildcatting, he claimed, there would be no Calgary or CPR.[46]

Word quickly spread that Tucker intended to publish an exposé of both the *Herald* and its editor J.H. Woods. The *Herald* heard about the impending article, and warned Charles Pohl, the manager of the Deutsche-Canadier Publishing Company printing the *Record*, that the contents of the article were libellous. If the article appeared in print, the *Herald's* editor and publisher, J.H. Woods, could take legal action and would likely win. After meeting with his lawyer, Pohl, who had previous experience with libel lawsuits, concluded discretion was the better part of valour and informed Tucker that he would not publish the article.[47] Stephen E. Beveridge pleaded with Pohl to print the article regardless of the consequences and promised to assume responsibility for the publication and "would pay any loss it incurred." Beveridge then put his promise in writing and, at a subsequent meeting with Pohl, even offered to buy the printing press to ensure the article appeared. In the meantime, Woods contacted the printer directly, warning Pohl again of the certainty of a libel suit if he published the piece. With the stakes clearly defined, everyone waited to learn what the publisher would do with the fateful November 7, 1913, edition of *The Natural Gas and Oil Record*.

Pohl evidently decided the threat of Woods's lawsuit was too great. However, since some copies of the issue containing the open letter from Beveridge to Woods were already printed, Pohl decided to run them through the presses another time to cover the offending article with a black box. Pohl eventually destroyed those copies when he realized the text bled through. The publisher omitted the story altogether for the reprint. The hastily redesigned front page contained a black box of text that appeared under the headline, "So people may know." Tucker inserted a note in the left-hand margin promising an explanation in the next edition. The November 14 edition of the *Record* admitted that it took issue with the *Herald's* claim of thirty years of public service and decided to document "a number of incidents" of one year with James Woods as editor. While the *Record* maintained that all the stories scheduled to go to print were true, at the request of the *Herald* they had pulled the story because it was not in the public interest to print them.[48] For the time being, the feud settled in Woods's favour.

The key role of small investors even attracted comments from sources outside the city and province, including H.F. Miller, the business manager of the Chicago Association of Commerce, who addressed the Industrial Bureau of Calgary on November 6. Miller concluded that every sign pointed to the development of a large oil field in western Canada and expressed the hope that "some plan will be devised to prevent the buying up of large tracts of property by speculators or by a few corporations, and that your local people will benefit by the development when it comes."[49] On November 15, an op-ed appeared in the *News Telegram*. Published under the name "Petroleus," the piece further attacked what it called the *Herald's* campaign of "abuse and knocking." But what is more interesting about the Petroleus essay is what it reveals regarding popular perceptions about the global petroleum industry. Like other authors, Petroleus began from the premise that Alberta generally and Calgary in particular were renowned for their progressive values, foresight, and push. Petroleus claimed that the people of Calgary responded quickly to opportunities, both as individuals and organizations, producing "better business blocks, more progressive and up-to-date stores, more wealth per capita, than any other city in Canada." The city achieved these feats by "never waiting for opportunity to knock" but rather by displaying individual initiative and entrepreneurship. But Petroleus detected a change when "the biggest opportunity that has ever come to any district is knocking today at our door." What changed? Perhaps Calgarians had lost their confidence because of a generational shift from the pioneers who settled the province to their offspring. The younger generation "have lost their grip, their faith and their belief in our country." Alarmingly for Petroleus, this suggested this generation of Albertans lacked "the stamina, the mind and the endurance to sit in and play a big man's game." During the first few days following the Dingman announcement in October, Calgarians displayed their usual characteristics: "faith and belief and their accustomed push" to take advantage of the bounty that nature provided. They began spending money, taking risks, and displaying faith as part of a frantic push to spur development. This all but disappeared when "news got out to the big money centres of the world, when the big men found out what was in the wind."[50]

For Petroleus, the "big men" were the leaders of the global petroleum industry, whom he depicted as nameless and faceless power brokers who operated in the shadows. After the "big men" learned of shows of petroleum at Dingman #1, they mobilized their minions, and one newspaper editor, to ensure that Alberta's petroleum wealth remained in the hands of the few. "Money talked," explained Petroleus, and doubts multiplied about the existence of oil south of Calgary. Simultaneously, however, "prosperous looking gentlemen" arrived in town, speaking sweetly to buy up acreage and develop the region even as Albertans began to get cold feet. "If we are not ready to fall into their arms then [they] produce the big knotty club" to bring about compliance. Albertans, warned Petroleus, must brace themselves and "take a hand in the big man's game." But "they"—presumably referring to representatives from Standard Oil—were already in Calgary presenting an even greater challenge to Albertans. Theirs was a global organization "so far-reaching that it is even an impossibility for us to get reports on the oil business from the different governments of the world." Like a black hole capable of bending light and ensuring that matter could not escape its gravitational pull, the organization Petroleus described was so perfectly opaque and secretive about its operations that "even in the great oil state of Pennsylvania it is impossible to get a report on the oil business after 1892;" that Ohio could only issue a ten-page pamphlet of statistics; and that California was impotent to make any report on its operations whatsoever. This, declared Petroleus, is the organization Albertans must fight "if we wish to see the Alberta oil fields take their rightful place in the markets of the world . . . [and] see the city of Calgary . . . increasing its population, increasing its buildings, increasing its wealth. This is the organization which we have to fight and down if we desire to retain our just heritage and do as we have always done before—hold our own in the big man's game."[51]

Subsequent editorials in the *News Telegram* revealed just how far Thompson began to move from the view of using scientifically backed development. On November 24, Thompson argued that "the average young man with common, ordinary intelligence, and his wisdom teeth cut right through, does not need any particular guide to tell him just what he should do in the matter of an investment in oil . . . he knows, perhaps, just as much about the chances of striking oil in commercial quantities in this district as any of those supposed experts." As this was a new industry in western Canada, few were qualified to offer advice regarding oil investment, let alone the editor of the *News Telegram*. Promoters and investors needed oil in commercial quantities to make money. "Will it be discovered?" That, reasoned Thompson, "is the question upon which the entire fabric of this whole business rests . . . . After that, it rests entirely upon the honesty and integrity of the men promoting the different companies and upon their business methods, whether or not the investor makes money or whether he loses, just as it ends in every other business."

But this was not necessarily the case. Promoters could be honest, display integrity, and have the most up-to-date business practices and still neither discover oil nor guarantee that their operations would be profitable. The combination of the limits of drilling technology and the complicated nature of the Turner Valley formation caused the greatest problems encountered by McDougall-Segur. Drilling in Turner Valley required deep holes that pushed cable tool rigs to the limit of what they could realistically achieve. Even then, drilling proved slow, expensive, and unprofitable because no one could reach the oil-bearing formations. When McDougall-Segur Exploration began operations in 1912, the company's capitalization was $100,000; by early October 1913, its capitalization reached $500,000. Further contrary to Thompson's confident, yet astoundingly naïve assertion, the oil industry, even at the turn of the century, was not just "like every other business." Rather, it already displayed the sophisticated integration of global supplies, markets, and transportation networks and the use of economies of scale. Simply finding crude reserves was only part of the problem. After all, in 1909, William D'Arcy of Anglo-Persian Oil discovered a prolific oil field but then realized that Anglo-Persian faced several problems in the downstream sector that included refining, transportation, and marketing. There were occasional glimpses indicating that Albertans realized oil was a *global* industry, but the discussions in

1913–14 took place in a vacuum and were therefore more aspirational than reasoned and rational. Repeatedly, press and investor reports assumed the successful development of any oil deposit, regardless of the costs of production, distance from population centres, the capacity of markets, or lack of transportation and refining infrastructure nearby. Indeed, Thompson believed "the whole future of this city and district depends to no small extent upon whether or not oil is discovered in commercial quantities."[52]

Thompson reached the logical conclusion of his argument on November 28, writing that the Dominion government must serve as "lender of last resort" and provide Alberta's nascent oil industry with the necessary capital to establish its proven reserves. The *Herald's* Flotations campaign deterred many Albertans from investing, and Thompson expressed some sympathy for potential investors now hesitating to risk their money. Unable to state with absolute certainty that commercial quantities of oil existed in Turner Valley, governments should now invest public money to develop the field because the "'wise guys in the oil game are not giving away their trump cards." Nonetheless, despite their reticence and caution, deep down, Albertans remained convinced "that there is oil—and plenty of it—beneath the surface of the earth." The industry needed investment capital to prove it existed. If the private sector could not—or would not—invest, Thompson argued that the federal government should do so because oil would be a *national* asset. By serving as a catalyst and investing a million taxpayer dollars, "the price would be cheap at ten times that amount if it were for a surety discovered." Hundreds of thousands of dollars from southern Alberta flowed into federal coffers as people purchased oil leases, demonstrating the faith of Albertans in this endeavour. Federal money "would be the most effective means of putting a stop to the 'knocking' . . . a campaign which has not only turned hundreds of thousands of dollars away." If the "knockers" remained unchecked they might kill a commercial enterprise that, while risky, still possessed substantial "remunerative attractions."[53]

As the attacks on the *Herald* unfolded, the Geological Survey of Canada released a report that said the naphtha found in Dingman well rarely existed in great volume and appeared as the result of filtration through clay strata. Since the total volume of oil in the field remained an open question, the GSC concluded that "the commercial value of the strike is still unproved." The so-called "white oil," noted the GSC, was of exceptionally high quality but usually never occurred naturally in any great quantity. With a wary eye on the economy, the *Herald* argued that 1913–14 was no year for gambling on an unproven oil field because Calgarians "will need their money for their ordinary domestic purposes." Advertisements suggesting those less well off could invest only a few dollars yet still make a fortune were nothing less than dishonest. From the west coast, *The Victoria Daily Times* chimed in and suggested that oil companies were as optimistic in the future of Alberta as an oil producer "but with less reason than real estate men have been in future values of city and suburban lots in western cities."[54]

With newspapers across the country siding with the *Herald*,[55] the feud reached a fevered pitch on November 19, 1913, when *The Morning Albertan* published an ad accusing *The Calgary Daily Herald* of accepting money from Standard Oil to publish critical articles about the oil companies operating in Calgary. Only after the ad appeared did the *Albertan* fully consider the implications of its actions. On November 20, the editorial page of *The Morning Albertan* stated that the paper regretted "the appearance of such an advertisement. Though it has little sympathy with the policy of its contemporary, it has not questioned the sincerity of its motives."[56]

In the meantime, individuals from Alberta's emerging industry began negotiating a set of shared values, interests, and beliefs about Alberta oil that transcended notions of laissez-faire capitalism by adopting the politically defensive strategy of forming a trade association. Citing the need to secure the "protection of their mutual interests," namely the earliest possible development of Alberta's oil and gas resources, on November 24, 1913, a hundred or so promoters, shareholders, brokers, leaseholders, civic officials, and others formed the Alberta Oil Development Association (AODA).[57] With the press excluded from the gathering, the founding members ostentatiously met over luncheon at a Calgary restaurant to launch the organization and proclaim the birth of a new industry capable of transforming the regional economy. Either by accident or design, the luncheon received ample coverage and the new organization did everything in its power to ensure that the press received plenty of quotable material as well as copies of the 429-word resolution the group passed explaining its core values and mission.

The AODA's founding resolution claimed as "established fact" by geologists that the subsurface formations south of Calgary contained a vast oil field "worthy of development and exploitation in a thorough and extensive manner." The second clause identified Calgary as "the metropolis of this district," and declared the unwavering belief that successful development of the oil field would produce benefits and prosperity for the city. The document then acknowledged the need to secure adequate capital from "the money centres of the world to successfully undertake such development and obtain this great storehouse of wealth." Significantly, in this section, the AODA's members shied away from laissez-faire principles to advocate the establishment of a "co-operative organization of the oil interests affected," and the organization pledged to launch a "vigorous publicity campaign" both to inform prospective investors and attract capital. The AODA also awarded itself the responsibility to "correct, suppress or counteract in every legitimate and effective manner the dissemination of any misrepresentative, erroneous, hurtful, or exaggerated statement, opinion or falsehood that may have secured publicity or that is about to secure publication or dissemination locally or elsewhere." What, precisely, did that mean? More to the point, who would determine what was "misrepresentative, hurtful, or false"? Considering the heated reaction elicited by *The Calgary Daily Herald's* information and education campaign, some believed the AODA should serve as a sort of information ministry or "war room" to immediately counter claims they did not like.[58]

For some, like city alderman and municipal booster "Tappy" Frost, economics were a motivating factor. For Frost, oil would prove Calgary's salvation from the recent recession and collapse of real estate prices. "If we can just fasten the word 'oil' to Calgary," said Frost at the organizational meeting, "then the money will be coming in." Frost certainly believed in the potential of an oil discovery around Calgary, serving as president or director for at least seven different oil companies. Another speaker, W.D. Outman, vice president of Herron-Elder Oil Company and newly elected chair of the organization's publicity committee, alluded to the economic downturn, comparing Calgary to Spokane, Washington, the railroad and commercial centre of the "Inland Empire" of Washington, Oregon, Idaho, and Montana that served as the corporate headquarters for several mining companies. Outman said that Calgary's fortunes had taken a nose dive with the recent downturn. "Unless something is done Calgary will go through the same period of hard times that Spokane has. I believe that something has happened to stop it, and that something is oil. Oil is the savior of the situation and I believe that Calgary has a great future based upon oil."

Notable by their absence at the organization of the AODA were the two leading figures of Turner Valley's early development, Archibald Dingman and Ira Segur. Members of the AODA made both men honorary vice presidents of the organization. When questioned whether they would accept the invitation, a clearly surprised Dingman responded that he had not heard of an offer from the organization yet and added, "I don't want to appear discourteous." Ira Segur proved less circumspect in his comments. "Me at that meeting? I should hope not. Don't use my name in connection with it," reported the *Herald*.[59]

One day after the formal announcement of the AODA, the *Herald* questioned, "Will sane men control?" the newly created organization. The pointed question highlighted the tension between two factions the paper believed would decisively influence the direction of the AODA—wildcatters or genuine developers. The *Herald* noted with relief that moderate elements concerned with the overall health of the industry temporarily prevailed, holding prominent positions on the organization's board of directors. A great deal would depend on how the organization interpreted its self-appointed mandate "to correct, suppress or counteract . . . the dissemination of any misrepresentative, erroneous, hurtful or exaggerated statement." The mandate served either as a sword to attack critics or as a shield to protect consumers from exuberant statements about Alberta's potential reserves or the promises of fabulous wealth contained in advertisements. For the *Herald*, however, the most significant issue requiring immediate attention was the standardization of stock values. Different agents sold the same stock at different prices. Indeed, the *Herald* pointed out that some of the most prominent members of the AODA sold stock to "insiders" at one-third the price and wondered what the organization would do about that. The AODA "should see that the public is protected by the absolute pooling of every share of stock of this character that is left in the hands of those to whom the public is trusting its money." The *Petroleum Gazette* sided with the *Herald*, noting that the AODA would be wise to work with critics rather than against them to address any issues that arose. The *Gazette* argued that the extravagant claims of confidence men "and associated swindlers" hurt development more than they helped.[60]

It is ironic, considering the emerging symbiotic relationship between the AODA and the *Albertan*, that the chain of events that led to the demise of the AODA began the next morning. *The Morning Albertan's* front-page editorial launched a blistering attack on Woods and the *Herald*, claiming Woods intended "to destroy confidence in the oil field and to make its development impossible." The fight got personal and dirty quickly when the *Albertan* speculated that the real cause of the problem lay with the *Herald's* "alien ownership," hinting that owner William Southam was really pulling the strings; real Calgarians would know better than to kill the golden goose. Whipping itself into a lather, the editorial declared it remained "the privilege and duty of citizens who can afford to risk and lose some money to help on with the development and exploitation of the oil fields."[61] The attack continued when the *Albertan* printed another blistering, and borderline unhinged, front page editorial that claimed, among other things, that public pressure compelled the *Herald* to hastily "kill" its campaign against oil development. One portion that originally appeared entirely in bold font, capital letters, is worth quoting at length considering subsequent events, and illustrates the increasingly strident tone:

> IF THE DEVELOPMENT OF THE OIL AREAS IS NOT PROCEEDING AS RAPIDLY AS WE HAD EXPECTED, THE CALGARY HERALD IS TO BLAME. IF COMPANIES WILL BE UNABLE TO DEVELOP THESE AREAS, IT WILL BE BECAUSE THIS UNPATRIOTIC NEWSPAPER WAFTED THE DAMP BREATH THROUGHOUT THE COUNTRY IN ITS ATTEMPT TO KILL THIS PROMISING UNDERTAKING. IF THE HERALD TAKES ANY GLORY IN NIPPING IN THE BUD ONE OF THE MOST PROMISING ENTERPRISES, OF PREVENTING THE EXPLOITING OF RICH OIL AREAS, OF RETARDING DEVELOPMENT, IT CAN HAVE THE GLORY. IT HAS DONE IT ALL, SINGLE HANDED AND ALONE. IT WAS NOT A DIFFICULT ACCOMPLISHMENT.[62]

Another subsequent editorial from the *Albertan* on the 28th claimed the *Herald's* "vicious work" had succeeded in keeping not just British capital, but "outside capital from all parts of the world" from the nascent oil patch. Following this editorial, the *Albertan* went silent regarding the *Herald's* campaign.[63]

The *Albertan's* counter-campaign against the *Herald* dangerously stoked and intensified feelings of frustration and anger among promoters, drillers, and investors, both harnessing and channelling those feelings in unpredictable ways. Editorials blamed the *Herald* and its "alien owner," William Southam, for the uncertainty in the oil patch. As economic conditions worsened in late 1913, regardless of whether it accurately represented Southam's beliefs, or simply as a stunt to sell more newspapers, the *Albertan's* counter-campaign tapped into and exploited the fears and frustration of some within the AODA. Like modern-day Cassandras given the gift of prophecy but fated not to be believed, some of the oil men of the AODA saw themselves as part of the vanguard of a new industry capable of delivering economic salvation and prosperity but dismissed by critics and naysayers in whom they saw willful ignorance and malevolent intent. In the AODA, they found a community of like-minded people facing similar problems and challenges. Indeed, speakers at the AODA meeting on November 26 exhorted members to share data and information about the drilling in Alberta, including what kind of drilling tools and machinery worked best to benefit the common good. But it is equally clear that the community also emboldened some of the more passionate boosters, who emerged with a powerful sense of identity—that their status within the oil industry distinguished them from others who lacked such status. At the conclusion of the November 26 meeting, W.D. Outman delivered a passionate speech wherein he pledged himself to do more, both as an individual and as chair of the AODA's publicity committee. The organization needed to advertise "as much as our finances will permit," even if it meant subsisting on coffee and donuts alone. He regretted that so much secretiveness "by some who should have known better" kept the members of the AODA apart when they should be working together. He deplored the tendency of "some sections" of the press to neglect the opportunity presented. The existence of a nearby oil field meant "Calgary has no reason to feel the pinch of hard times. It is Calgary's duty to rise up and stamp out any methods calculated to hurt her in the estimation of the outside world."[64]

The next day, November 27, Stephen E. Beveridge filed a criminal complaint for libel against *The Calgary Daily Herald* and its editor James Woods for the article that appeared in the *Herald* on November 4 discussing the *Natural Gas and Oil Record* incident. Beveridge's evidence remained shockingly thin. The criminal complaint did not specify any part of the *Herald's* article but claimed the entire piece would expose Beveridge to "hatred, contempt or ridicule."[65] When asked to explain his reasons for the libel suit against Woods, Beveridge replied, "He accuses me of inciting a man to commit an offence, and that accusation I consider libelous." Beveridge added that he might initiate civil proceedings if he was unable to get satisfaction in criminal proceedings. Journalist and oil industry historian John Schmidt observed that in a few cases "outright crooks sought to lessen the heat on their activities by resorting to the old trick of bringing slander or libel suits against their honest detractors."[66]

On December 3, 1913, Beveridge's complaint went before Judge Colonel Gilbert Sanders in the city's Magistrate's Court for a hearing. Sanders was a former member of the North West Mounted Police and a veteran of the Boer War, so his twenty-year service as Calgary's police magistrate was a second career for him. Despite having no formal legal training apart from twenty-three years as a Mountie where he held ex officio status as a justice of the peace, Sanders quickly established a reputation as a "common sense" judge. Known as much for the perpetual scowl and monocle he wore as for his deeply conservative values and stern judicial decisions, he displayed a penchant for corporal punishment that bordered on bloodlust. The Harold Boardman case in March 1914 serves to illustrate Sanders's particular brand of justice. Arrested for assaulting and robbing Mary Jeffry, a seventeen-year-old domestic, Harold Boardman pleaded guilty in his appearance before Justice Sanders. Nevertheless, a string of witnesses testified to Boardman's honest and sincere character as a regular church attendee and musician in the church orchestra. Sanders announced that Boardman's offence "is a very serious one, and one which renders you liable to life imprisonment." Before imposing his sentence, Sanders admitted he took Boardman's previously spotless record into account in order that he could impose the most lenient sentence upon him. "I am going to sentence you not only to teach you a lesson but in order that others may be deterred from committing the same crime that you have committed," said Sanders. "I sentence you to six months at Lethbridge with hard labor, with 20 lashes, ten being administered six weeks after the term has commenced and ten six weeks before its close." The stiff sentence for a first offence shocked the city, generated a flurry of letters to the editor, both in favour and against, and prompted the *Herald's* editorial page to question whether the lash, which remained in use in western Canada until 1960, was necessary. Left unanswered was the question of what, in Sanders's estimation, would constitute a harsh sentence. Perhaps that was Sanders's intent.

Notwithstanding the well-earned reputation for an austere brand of justice, Sanders proved a marked improvement over many of the purely political appointees preceding him on the bench. Prior to Sanders's appointment, many judges were derided by critics as "third class men" lacking the requisite morals, character, and abilities to perform their duties. Back in the 1890s, Judge Thomas Ede frequently heard cases and passed sentence while inebriated, and, as was often the case when justices depended upon emoluments to make ends meet, profited from his office by charging fees for holding hearings and witnessing documents, and pocketing fines he imposed. More recently, Sanders's immediate predecessor, Crispin Smith, who also favoured the lash and frequently rolled up his sleeves to serve as executioner for such sentences, had resigned under a cloud of controversy. But significant questions remain about the impartiality of justice practised in the early twentieth century. The justices of the peace and magistrates in the system remained unremunerated by the province except for what court costs they could recover from those they convicted. As historian James Gray succinctly observed, justices may have arrived in court with a built-in predilection to convict because "it cost them money to acquit."[67]

In Sanders's court, however, Beveridge appeared petty, vindictive, thin-skinned, and ill-prepared. Believing that his claims were self-evident,

Beveridge merely presented the *Herald's* article and expected vindication. Unconvinced, Judge Sanders warned Beveridge's lawyer that he had not proved his case.[68] Under cross-examination by A.E. Clarke, who guided Beveridge line by line through the article, Beveridge admitted the substance of the *Herald's* article was true: he had encouraged the editor of *The Natural Gas and Oil Record* to publish a libellous article about the *Herald*. Beveridge also admitted that the substance of the *Herald's* Flotation article about Rocky Mountain Oil was true—particularly damaging admissions included that the company's prospectus listed property it did not own, and that Beveridge personally received $10,000 worth of stock in exchange for mineral leases he paid $160 to obtain. Sanders duly forwarded the complaint to higher court to decide the following week, on December 5, but the complaint quietly disappeared. Over the weekend an anonymous telegram signed "Alberta Oil Men" arrived at William Southam's home in Hamilton and threatened Southam unless the *Herald* stopped its criticism. Southam promptly sent a telegram back to the *Herald*, and emphatically endorsed continuing the *Herald's* campaign. The *Herald* broke the news of the threatening telegram on December 10.[69]

After the editorial on November 28, the *Albertan* went silent about the *Herald's* campaign, possibly because Davidson wanted to cover different subjects, like the intervening municipal election. But it is also possible that the *Albertan's* tacit support of the AODA, as well as its likely rooting interest in Beveridge's libel suit against Woods, induced a temporary ceasefire. On the morning of December 10, the *Albertan's* editorial page attacked in a different direction, criticizing Archibald Dingman's silence about progress of the well. Dingman, wrote the *Albertan*, "seems to wish to discredit any optimistic statement about the well, and gives no information." Calgary Petroleum Products, argued the editorial, was drilling on public land leased from the people, and the success of the well meant a great deal to the citizens of Calgary. "Every day Calgarians have to meet the insulting charges of putting on a fake boom," complained the editorial. "The proof disproving this unfair and dishonest accusation is right on the grounds, but a mystery company will not permit it to be used." Dingman's reticence to provide information, concluded the editorial, justified an investigation by city council. "If the company should refuse such an investigation we must try and get at it in some other way."[70]

Suffice it to say there was plenty to discuss at a previously scheduled meeting of the AODA on the night of December 10. The assembled members had a lengthy discussion of the telegram before deciding not to take any action. AODA secretary C.A. Owens prepared a statement disavowing any knowledge or connection to the telegram by the organization. But clear divisions emerged and polarized the group. Several members, including AODA president J.R. Sutherland and Vice Presidents Beveridge and Herron, pointedly denied that they either knew or participated in the plot whatsoever. Just as vehement were those who believed the *Herald* had reaped what it sowed, perhaps none more than Tappy Frost. The alderman sarcastically concluded that the telegram probably originated from a disgruntled member of *The Calgary Daily Herald* who wanted Woods fired because they could not sell their oil leases. According to the *Albertan*, Frost sang the praises of the province of Alberta, celebrating the pioneering spirit of ranchers and farmers who came before, and mocked the futile attempts "of certain individuals to 'knock' and retard the development and exploitation of the vast subterranean wealth and resources of the Calgary district." The speech, reported the *Albertan*, was well received.[71]

However, the telegram ripped open a chasm between moderates and hardliners in the organization. Just before the motion to adjourn, one AODA member, C. Kipling, held up a copy of the *Herald* and announced that "we should assure this paper that we had nothing to do with the matter in question." The statement, said the *News Telegram*, "brought forth a howl of protest from the assembled oil men. "I make a motion," said Mr. Beattie, the advertising manager for Black Diamond Oil Fields, "that this association do not undertake to remove the dense ignorance of the writer of this article and furthermore I do not think that we should honor the publication by giving any attention at all." With the meeting adjourned, Stephen Beveridge, presumably the person whose honour the telegram sought to defend, unequivocally denounced it in public. With his lawsuit pending against Woods, perhaps he felt there was no other alternative. The next day, *The Natural Gas and Oil Record* assured readers that the *Herald* knew who sent the telegram but claimed Woods would not disclose that information simply "to get a rise out of some of the members and start something. No one here need have any fear that the owners of the *Herald* don't know what's going on through regular channels." Meanwhile, the front page of *The Morning Albertan* published a cartoon for "Oilberta's" new coat of arms featuring the addition of two oil cans flanking an oil well at the head of a story predicting a minimum of twenty wells in the Calgary-Turner Valley district. Lest anyone overlook the point, the paper also proposed a new motto: *Oleum nostrum or nobis hodie*, which translates to "Our oil is for us today."[72]

On the morning following the contentious meeting, association secretary C.A. Owens resigned, publicly blaming a busy schedule that prevented devoting too much time to the organization. But the timing suggested the dispute over the incendiary telegram played a larger part than Owens cared to admit. Rumours swirled that as many as six other directors planned to step down as well over the incident. *The Morning Albertan* downplayed news of a rift and accused the "disloyal and selfish . . . alien newspaper" of stirring up trouble among the oil men and predicted the troublemaker "will get his when all things are made right." The *Albertan's* editorial page stated that all loyal Calgarians should do what they could to help develop the oil fields and suggested no Calgarian "should send a letter abroad without referring to the prospects of rich oil fields in Calgary [and] also saying the oil has been discovered and in paying quantities." At a heated general meeting on December 16, Owens plus six members of the executive committee, including the president, vice president, treasurer, and several other officers, formally resigned. The membership, however, refused to accept the resignations without explanations. Addressing the membership, the resigning directors blamed their decision on the division between two factions. The resigning directors self-identified with the moderate faction and felt they no longer had the trust of most of the organization. After a lengthy discussion, most of the board of directors, except for Owens, agreed to stay on. Owens did, however, pledge to remain at his post for a month until the organization found a replacement. Members then raised $2,000 to help publicize Alberta oil and talked about incorporation as a means of raising even more. When the executive committee met the following day, they adopted a far-reaching plan to advertise "in all the leading papers throughout the world," and confidently predicted that the move would bring a flood of inquiries. The executive committee also announced that it had hired Frank F. Lischke from Portland, Oregon, as publicity secretary. The self-inflicted wounds, however, were too great and the AODA limped into the New Year before suspending operations entirely. The *Albertan's* final mention of the association optimistically said it would meet soon and the executive felt momentum toward development would stimulate interest in the association.[73]

The tragedy of the rapid rise and fall AODA is that, while the organization saw itself as one designed to protect and advance the interests of the industry, it interpreted its mandate very narrowly—to counter every real or perceived slight of the industry—and did not take account of the broader picture. The only evidence of its campaign to promote Alberta's oil development were some non-specific want ads that appeared in newspapers across Canada and the United States.[74] By early January, other issues came into focus that would substantially affect development for which an industry organization could readily have represented private sector interests. Leaseholders who purchased natural gas and petroleum rights in the aftermath of the Dingman discovery

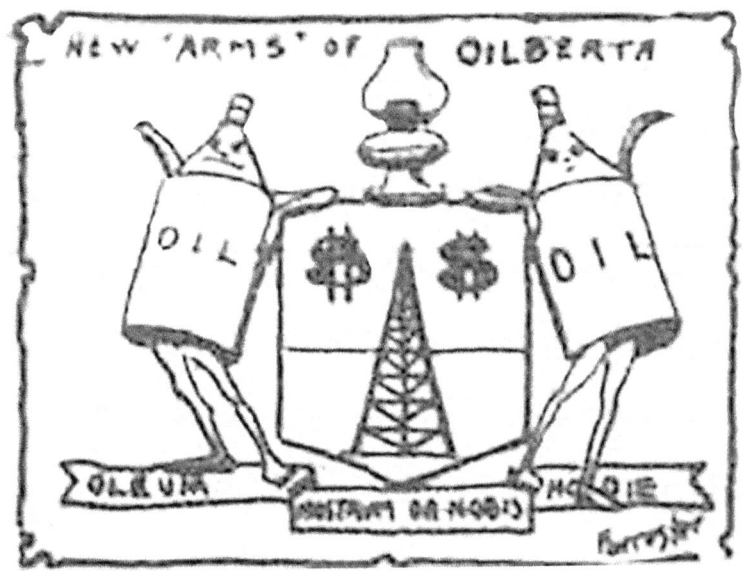

Figure 2-1 "New 'Arms' of Alberta"
In the increasingly desperate winter of 1913/14, the prospect of better times, underwritten by petroleum development, provided hope to many Albertans who believed fervently that oil would transform the province economically and shape its future. (University of Calgary Libraries and Cultural Resources CU1701012)

in October and November were still waiting for the Department of Mines to issue their leases. While the local Mines offices accepted the yearly rental fee before forwarding the paperwork to Ottawa for processing, since August 1913 the Department of Mines had issued no new lease certificates because the department began redrafting regulations. Little understood or appreciated at the time was that, according to the terms of the Alberta Companies' Act, businesses could not sell shares until they were in possession of a physical copy of their lease from the Dominion government. The delay affected approximately 600 leases, meaning that, technically speaking, few companies could raise development capital legally through public share offerings. Perhaps the only redeeming feature was that, until the lease arrived, companies did not owe any rent on their property.

More urgent, however, were questions about the legality of the Dominion government's reservation clause separating subsurface mineral rights from surface rights holders. The Dominion Lands Act (1883), renewed in 1886 and

1906, stated that Dominion lands sales were possible in certain named instances—school lands, or with lands owned by the Hudson's Bay Company. In 1889, an order-in-council passed reserving subsurface mineral rights for the government on all homestead lands. Revisions in 1908 further tightened the Dominion government's authority. Greater clarity, however, highlighted the weakness of the earlier reservation carved out by the order-in-council, and a court challenge in Ontario now questioned the legality of the entire system. *The Natural Gas and Oil Record* warned that the situation remained untenable and could lead to mass litigation and speculated that, perhaps, the reason the Dominion government seemed reluctant to issue mineral leases was that officials were waiting for a ruling before committing to oil leases. Nevertheless, in mid-January the Department of Mines finally issued a brief letter explaining the delay behind the delivery of leases. Given the highly charged atmosphere and growing suspicion in Alberta, some assumed nefarious motives behind the delay, and great relief accompanied the delivery of the first batch of the delayed 100 leases to the land office on March 7, 1914.

The threatening telegram to Woods and Southam broke the fever of the first boom and reined in the more heated commentary from Davidson about Woods and the *Herald*. While Davidson, and Thompson to a certain extent, occasionally directed a pointed barb in the *Herald's* direction, nothing came close to the brand of personal attacks that emerged in October and November 1913. Moreover, the AODA never recovered from the whiff of violence expressed by certain segments of its membership. Although the newspaper feud clearly, and starkly, illustrated the extent to which oil's supporters believed in the future of the industry, it also revealed an extreme aversion to criticism, bordering on intolerance, that was to impart an enduring legacy to Alberta's oil culture.

3

"The Difference Between Poverty and Riches is Action!" Dreams and Reality of an Independent Oil Boom

> Between the two extremes represented by the geologist and the practical driller there is a happy medium. The geologist can indicate the best spots in a given area to drill for oil, but hardly in any case can he prophesy absolutely a profitable production, although he can sometimes be almost certain. On the other hand, we have the very large and efficient body of what one may call practical men, who have been in the oil prospecting and oil producing business for many years, and who declare that nothing but the drill can prove a given territory. It is a combination of these two branches of knowledge that should be aimed at by anyone entering upon work in a new field. Were the two points of view correlated and made use of, much money would be saved and the whole oil industry would be looked upon by investors with greater confidence.
>
> —*The Financial Post*
> February 7, 1914

It is one of the most emotive images of the first Turner Valley boom. Bob Edwards presented the discovery of petroleum as a stark choice between two competing visions of the provincial economy, environment, and society. In a pencil drawing of a farmer leaning up against a barbed-wire fence, two alternative futures are on display. On the farmer's right is a depiction of the province as it currently existed—bucolic countryside and an agrarian economy dominated by wheat as far as the eye can see, where the only

Figure 3-1 "Which Is It To Be?"
Bob Edwards's cartoon presents the province's choice between agriculture and petroleum as a binary option. (University of Calgary Libraries and Cultural Resources CU11540676)

buildings are rustic farmhouses and other outbuildings. On the left is a vision of a future dominated by the oil industry, where dozens of oil derricks, several of which are presumably gushing oil, dot the landscape. Significantly, the illustration hints at the repercussions and trade-offs for the economy, the environment, and society. Reflecting the economic transition taking place in Pennsylvania's oil region following the discovery of petroleum in 1858, once productive fields now lie fallow. Off in the distance, the sun is either rising or setting—it is difficult to tell—on the scene, but perhaps significant is that the sun can be seen in the clear skies over the farm, while its rays cannot penetrate discharge—whether oil or smoke—launched into the sky by multiple derricks. The picture's caption, "Which is it to be?" makes it clear that Edwards believed Albertans, like the farmer in the foreground, were on the cusp of a life-altering choice.

Another image, used regularly in the pages of *The Natural Gas and Oil Record* after its first appearance in the November 8, 1913, edition, suggests that a series of incremental decisions had already made the choice between agrarian and industrial economies alluded to by Edwards. Oil is presented as a part of a balanced regional economy but having global implications. The

Figure 3-2 "The Greatest Gift" Transplanted Winnipegger J.L. Tucker, editor of *The Natural Gas and Oil Record*, consistently presented petroleum development as one part of a dynamic, robust prairie economy where oil and gas coexisted easily alongside agriculture.

capitalist looking at a world map contemplates Alberta's oil as one part of a diversified economy that includes oil and wheat in addition to cattle ranching, coal, and manufacturing. Critically, the image also depicts the transformation wrought by the transportation revolution of the late nineteenth century—railroads and steamships powered by liquid fuels—and the significance of the Panama Canal (then nearing completion and opening in August 1914) providing Alberta products with outlets to global markets.

Calgarians, and Albertans generally, responded in a variety of ways to the prospect of fundamental change to political, economic, and social structures but also to the landscape contemplated by oil development. Some scholars have suggested that the petroleum industry constituted a radical departure from traditional Canadian patterns of metropolis-hinterland economic development described by historians Harold Innis, Donald Creighton, and J.M.S. Careless.[1] Advertisements for stock offerings, company prospectuses, editorials, and letters in local newspapers offer a window into the hopes, fears, and assumptions of various stakeholders regarding the first Turner Valley era. Such documents also helped establish the parameters of Alberta's emerging oil culture in ways that built on or expanded earlier mythologies of "the West's" transformative qualities. Indeed, many of the hundreds of thousands of immigrants from Europe, Ontario, and the United States coming to western Canada since the 1880s believed they could become self-reliant, independent, and perhaps wealthy as small-scale ranchers or farmers. By the winter of 1913/14, oil had briefly replaced ranching and farming as a possible avenue of wealth.

The spectacular growth of the petroleum industry during the first two decades of the twentieth century defies easy comparison. Growing demand for crude and refined products—US energy consumption increased 250 percent between 1900 and 1920—sustained high prices and encouraged greater exploration and development.[2] The possibility of an oil strike produced a populist response from Albertans that manifested a deeply ingrained mistrust of concentrated wealth and prioritized the success of the common man. In this, Alberta's pursuit of an independent oil industry bore more than a passing resemblance to similar responses in Texas in the aftermath of the Spindletop discovery in 1901.[3] Ties between Calgary's urban business leaders and the landowning/ranching elites in its environs reinforced the prevailing view that small business owners were best positioned to serve the public interest. Unlike in Texas, however, where independent oil men relied on state and federal antitrust legislation to keep out large combinations like Standard Oil, Albertans relied on informal measures to sustain the independent character of the boom at this stage.[4]

As discussions between the members of the Alberta Oil Development Association revealed, Calgary's would-be oil barons dreamed of fame and fortune but remained acutely aware of their limited human and capital resources and were far from monolithic in their views. Some feared the large combinations, like Standard Oil, would shut them out of the field if given the opportunity. But other entrepreneurs, like Ira Segur, were prepared either to partner with or sell to Standard Oil from a very early date. Alberta's independents did not speak with a single voice. Crucially, their lack of cohesion and investment capital meant they could not translate their numbers into political power to bar the majors as they had done in Texas, precisely because they needed other people's money to fund exploration and development, or, as R.B. Bennett made plain in 1919, selling to Standard Oil was the only way they could salvage what remained of their investment.[5] Some promoters assumed they did not need special sources of expertise to make a fortune in oil; others readily embraced technical experts such as geologist Edward Hubert Cunningham Craig.

Although typically overlooked in earlier histories of the boom, Cunningham Craig played a pivotal role in publicizing the oil prospects of southern Alberta.[6] Between 1912 and 1914, Cunningham Craig served as a consultant, independent expert, and trusted commentator on oil developments in

Alberta because of his experience with major international oil companies. His specialized knowledge and expertise nurtured and sustained hopes about oil in Turner Valley. Newspapers and promoters as well as the British Admiralty and international investors sought his professional opinion and quoted him liberally, especially during the critical winter of 1913/14. Even sceptics about Alberta oil respected Cunningham Craig's contributions because his long experience compelled him to urge investors to behave cautiously and speak out against what he perceived as irrational speculation.

Significantly, newspaper editorials and advertisements both reflected and directed the community's emerging identity as a new group of socio-economic elites. At their core, the advertisements tell stories, sometimes idealized, about the company, the province, nature, and consumers, as well as about the past, present, and future. As ads for oil companies multiplied after October 1913, they influenced discussion in the public square. Some focused abstractly on oil's ability to provide personal freedom and security, while others dwelt on developing the requisite virtues of bootstrap individualism. Underlying all trends, however, lay the assumption of a vast and limitless oil field beneath Alberta stretching from Athabasca in the north to the international boundary with the United States. This was not merely a case that Alberta's soil held adequate supplies of oil and gas; local boosters brashly asserted supplies were so plentiful that, as historian George Colpitts observed in his environmental history of western Canada, natural resource wealth alone could sustain successive generations of Albertans and Canadians. "No theme," writes Colpitts, "became as integral to western promotion as natural abundance."[7] The celebration of dreaming big dreams provided by capitalism free from the shackles of monopolistic enterprises, and faith in both nature and natural resources as providers, were all common themes. As historian Brian Black has observed, in the late nineteenth and early twentieth centuries few stories were more popular than those of great wealth realized by natural resources. "The idea of the valueless become valuable filled every day with the possibility of locating one's fortune right beneath one's nose." Produced locally rather than by larger national agencies, the ads also reflect the emerging battle over resource development and how the debate evolved as companies responded to various events, such as the *Herald's* information campaign.[8]

In the winter of 1913/14, the unwelcome spectre of John D. Rockefeller's Standard Oil loomed uncomfortably over discussions. A few years earlier, Alberta newspapers followed with more than a passing interest the US justice department's anti-trust case against the company and largely agreed with the conclusion that the company's operations harmed consumers more than they helped. Reprints of *The New York Herald's* exposés of Standard Oil's operations reminded Albertans of their experiences and complaints about the Canadian Pacific Railway. What resonated with Albertans was the way Standard dominated the industry with its ability to manipulate freight rates and monopolize refining. "The Standard Oil Company stands ready to buy every drop of oil produced at the wells for cash," noted one article. "It has built up its businesses to the point of practical monopoly and has paid thirty percent and more dividends on its stock for years." Observing that Standard did not care whether a flowing well was "a thousand barrel 'gusher' or a ten barrel 'pumper,'" the article asserted that the company remained ready to run a pipeline to the field even though "it may be many months, even a year or more, before that particular run of oil is sent through" for refining. The scope and scale of Standard's operations staggered the imagination. "Millions and tens of millions of dollars are thus tied up, invested in crude oil for future use—but the seller gets cash." Major trunklines constructed by the company were "as direct as if laid out with a ruler" and took no account of "rivers, hills, or even mountain ranges, they travel by the most direct routes to their destinations."[9]

As happened in many places influenced by the reach of Standard Oil, the US Supreme Court's ruling in May 1911 dissolving the trust received front page coverage in Alberta and across Canada.[10] When reporters followed up with enquiries about what the ruling might mean for Standard's operations in Canada, it prompted pessimistic conclusions from lawmakers that the judgment would not affect Standard Oil's operations "one iota," perhaps because the assumption was that oil corrupted politics. Standard Oil, said one prominent MP from Nova Scotia, already owned "everything in this country worth owning" related to oil, and the member seemed genuinely surprised to note that Imperial Oil was "one of the subsidiary companies" owned by Standard. Meanwhile, the Department of Labour, which served as the legal arm of the Dominion government responsible for reining in combines and trusts north of the border, claimed it had no official knowledge of Standard Oil's Canadian operations beyond what the newspapers reported. Some weeks later, one letter to the editor of *The Calgary Daily Herald* lamented that the US government had enabled "an octopus like the Standard Oil trust" to throw its tentacles "over the length and breadth of the land" to stifle all business and crush its opposition for as long as it did.[11] The looming issue was whether the development of Alberta's oil would be done by the independent companies rather than a large combination.

Early in the twentieth century, a rudimentary definition emerged in the north American oil industry describing an independent as any oil company unaffiliated with Standard Oil; gradually it evolved by the 1930s to a more sophisticated one that distinguished between the scope and scale of operations of two types of companies—majors and independents. A major is a vertically integrated company capable of carrying out the four basic functions—production, transportation, refining, and marketing—of the petroleum industry. Independents, on the other hand, perform as few as one and as many as three of those functions. Differences in size, scale, and scope of operations reflect the number of companies that fulfill the criteria in each category. There are only a handful of majors compared to hundreds of independents. The sheer size of the majors also enables them to conduct business in multiple pools over one or more countries compared to the smaller independents, which tend to specialize in a single area. Another significant difference is that majors tend to be able to generate investment capital from their existing operations while independents raise capital through investors.[12]

For Albertans in the 1910s, "independent" primarily meant the company did not have any ties to Standard Oil. Furthermore, "independent" meant a company concentrated on exploration and production (with the possibility of moving into downstream operations later). More than anything else, "independent" implied a local company—with investment capital raised from outside the petroleum industry, ideally from private investors in the community so that southern Albertans would benefit the most from development. At the Alberta Oil Development Association meeting on November 27, 1913, W.D. Outman argued that the development of the oil fields of Calgary "will never become great as a transfer station for the Standard Oil. It is the success of the small man that will make the city." Outman then concluded that "any man who prevents the small man from getting into the game is hurting Calgary."[13]

Calgary newspapers reported every whisper about Standard Oil's agents inspecting the fields. Given William Davidson's more populist leanings, *The Morning Albertan*'s editorial pages brooded on the rumour that the oil industry's largest integrated major would soon commence operations in Alberta; *The Calgary News Telegram* countered that Standard Oil would wait until small producers proved the field before assuming control. *The Morning Albertan* struck a defiant, but unmistakably pessimistic, tone based on the experiences of other small producers in the United States. If oil existed in southern Alberta a monopolistic combination would enter the field and strangle the competition in the crib, harming the interests of the people. A couple of legitimate operators would become millionaires and a handful of "lucky" speculators would become wealthy. Davidson expected that a smelly refinery to marginally advance the city's "commercial interests" would be the city's enduring reward. All too soon, Rockefeller's Standard Oil, or some other large monopoly, would take over the field.

Just as Ida Tarbell had described in her exposés of Standard Oil for *McClure's Magazine* a decade earlier, *The Morning Albertan* suggested Standard Oil would crush independent operators. An Alberta industry dominated by Standard would impart no benefits. Oil prices would remain unchanged and real wealth would accumulate in the hands of as few as "less than one hundredth of one percent" of Canadians. Most galling, Standard Oil would benefit from the courage, sweat, and toil of other "legitimate" operators who risked everything to prove the field while Standard sat idly by. The editorial sighed that the entire system was flawed and blurted out that "the resources of the country should not be held up as prizes to the bold and lucky speculator, and to the rich monopolies of the earth. The people should have the wealth." In the face of inevitable monopolistic domination, the government should take possession of the oil fields on behalf of the people. "The wealth belongs to every person. To permit it to be handed over to some monopoly, great or small, which will hold up the price to some fabulous amount, is ridiculous."[14]

The Calgary News Telegram went a step further, arguing explicitly for the exclusion of Standard Oil and its interests from the field, and equated investment by Canadians in the emerging oil industry as an acid test of loyalty and patriotism. Coverage in the *News Telegram* emphasized that the Dingman discovery was the "result of scientific exploration" acquired since the beginning of the modern petroleum industry in Pennsylvania, which had "robbed" the field of "speculative hazard by men who know." An editorial on October 25 argued this was hardly a case of nationalism for nationalism's sake, but it certainly sounded like it. "Compel the Standard Oil combine to keep to the country of its origin and exploit its own industries and resources," stated one editorial. "Canada has no room for alien trusts and octopuses of this caliber." The resource bounty of Canada "must be explored and enjoyed by our own citizens and not exploited by aliens." For the *News Telegram,* the only impediment to autarky was Canada's lack of investment capital, and Canadian millionaires now had a moral obligation to invest in Alberta.[15] At the heart of this debate swirled the question of who would develop Alberta's oil field: large,

Figure 3-3 "The Men Behind the Gun" Stokes-Stephens ad highlights the masculine qualities associated with the prototypical "oil man" of the oil boom.

integrated companies, like Standard Oil or its Canadian affiliate, Imperial Oil, or small investors? The much-contested answer proved to be the first big clash of ideas in the public square regarding the boom.

The downside of relying on independent companies to develop the Alberta oil fields slowly emerged. Local entrepreneurs did not necessarily possess the requisite specialized knowledge, or experience of oil exploration and production, but nonetheless played up the importance of their stature to attract investors. Hoteliers William J. Stokes and Hough L. Stephens operated far out of their field of expertise but marketed shares in the Stokes-Stephens Oil Company based on the quality of their character, previous successes, and the proximity of their leases to those of other known companies. Within weeks, though, the two men hired California oil man Ira Segur to carry out day-to-day operations. Nevertheless, in a somewhat strange ad for the Stokes-Stephens Oil Company published in May 1914, illustrators prominently featured pencilled portraits of the two men "behind the gun" at the company. Setting aside for a moment that companies drill for oil rather than coordinate an artillery barrage, the ad nonetheless clearly reveals much about the aggressive, and masculine, characteristics associated with Alberta's emerging oil culture. Both men were depicted straddling artillery pieces and firing their weapons—both spouting oil—at each other before it puddled on the floor.

Brothers Stephen and Francis Beveridge, who made their fortune in Calgary real estate, emphasized their business sense and deep roots in the community, convincing investors to assume both would translate into oil discoveries and ensure success. Their oil company, Rocky Mountain Oil Fields, organized in October 1913, seemed to run more like a real estate firm than an oil company. Rocky Mountain Oil Fields' prospectus revealed little understanding of the oil industry and reflected the bias of location from real estate. Part of Rocky Mountain's pitch argued that its 2,000 acres of leases surrounding the Dingman well alone were reason to invest. "These buildings [sic] are practically surrounded by companies now drilling for oil and they are geographically located so that, in the event of oil being struck in any one company, Rocky Mountain Oil Field[s] Limited will have lands in the immediate vicinity." With directors that included local luminaries like City Councillor Tappy Frost, rancher A.F. Landles, engineer J.C. Milligan, and tycoon George T.C. Robinson, the prospectus crowed that "the financial solidarity of the concern may be ascertained." While that may have been true, the prospectus failed to specify what kind of practical oil-finding experience Rocky Mountain Oil Fields could draw from.[16]

In the absence of specialized industry knowledge to convince investors of the soundness of their company, Rocky Mountain instead sold dreams. An ad campaign that ran between October 22 and November 10, 1913, highlighted the transition from one generation to the next implicit in discussions about the transformative nature of the West and differences between "old" and "new." The "old" economy of Alberta defined by ranching and farming and subject to periodic booms and busts of commodity prices was compared to the ability of a "new" industry, oil, to transcend economic hard times to fundamentally remake existing relationships between the metropole and hinterland. One ad from October 23, 1913, titled "Pessimists and Otherwise," emphasized the community's feeling of optimism and faith in oil compared to the tired pessimism of the old economic order, a feeling that in many ways illustrated the ability of oil to transform—if not completely overturn—existing economic relationships. In several respects, it was the natural progression of local boosterism practised throughout western Canada in the early twentieth century and deemed essential to ensure regional economic progress and prosperity. Border illustrations framing the ad drove home the point of generational change and renewal by depicting "OIL" as a young, clever man

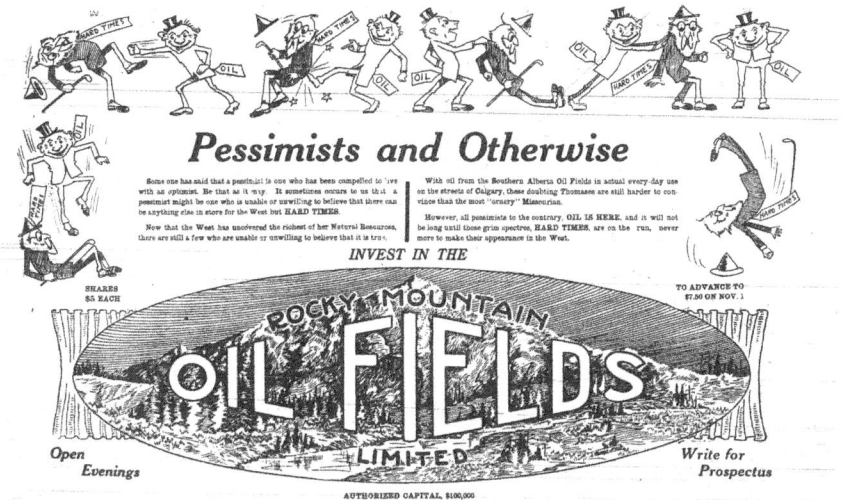

Figure 3-4 "Pessimists and Otherwise"
As tensions between the editor of the *Calgary Herald's* editor, James H. Woods, and the Beveridge and LeBourdais of Rocky Mountain Oil Fields escalated, this advertisement appeared, classifying those opposed to development as out-of-touch pessimists. In what might have been a coincidence, the caricature of "Hard Times" slightly resembles Woods. (University of Calgary Libraries and Cultural Resources CU1699923)

inflicting all kinds of mischievous violence on an older gentleman labelled "HARD TIMES." "Some one has said that a pessimist is one who has been compelled to live with an optimist," began the Ad. "It sometimes occurs to us that a pessimist might be one who is unable or unwilling to believe that there can be anything else in store for the west but HARD TIMES." But now that nature had revealed the full richness of Alberta's natural resources, pessimists "are unable or unwilling to believe that it is true." Even though retailers sold oil from the fields of southern Alberta, pessimists, the ad argued, denied reality, and refused to acknowledge forces, resources, and technologies bringing about the economic transformation of the region. But the ad declared, "OIL IS HERE, and it will not be long until those grim spectres, HARD TIMES, are on the run, never more to make their appearance in the West." A variation on the Pessimists theme infused the "Are You Playing a Longshot?" ad, which used *The Calgary Daily Herald* as a foil by listing the factors in favour of investing against the advice of the *Herald*, which it described as "lone and lonesome" in its opposition to investing.[17]

While Rocky Mountain Oil Fields' ad campaign played on a few other themes over the autumn and early winter of 1913, they constantly returned to the theme that oil development assured a prosperous future. Early in the campaign, the "Okotoks Oil Field" ad claimed the discovery had already produced tangible benefits for the citizens of southern Alberta by loosening credit and shrinking the cost of living. According to the ad, the Dingman strike cut the price of gasoline from forty cents per gallon to thirty cents despite its limited quantities. With future development, the savings to consumers were bound to be larger and gasoline at thirty cents per gallon would be a distant memory as the prices for refined gasoline would assuredly drop. "[T]he time is near when THAT price will be cut in two as a result of striking oil in the Southern Alberta Oil Fields. Can't YOU see it coming?" Near the end of the campaign, partly as a response to the intensification of the debate around the flotation of oil companies, the focus shifted to the struggle of the independents over the majors. While Calgarians could content themselves in the ensuing general prosperity that petroleum wealth would bring, how much more satisfying—and rich—could they be if they supported the independents? Buying stock in an independent oil company and providing the necessary capital to prove the oil field was tantamount to civic duty. Oil would bring about a dramatic economic and social transformation from a sparsely populated hinterland to a modern industrial core. Without specifying how capital or expertise would transfer to the prairie province, the ad predicted there would be "huge refineries, large chemical works, steel plants" and every kind of large manufacturing plant coming to Alberta "because the various products of petroleum lead to the establishment of a great number of industries, and the development of the fields will call for many others." Oil meant well-paying jobs for thousands of men and women "who will come from the ends of the earth to make Calgary their home." It would mean many more profitable railroads to enhance Alberta's ties to the outside world. But most of all, oil would transform Calgary into a world-class city and Alberta into a populous province, brimming with a happy, and wealthy, people. The question that now remained was whether the reader would share in this future. Left unstated, at least in this ad, but present in others for Rocky Mountain Oil Fields, was the assumption that if left to the majors, development would not take place. "By drilling, and drilling only, will the extent and value of the Alberta Oil Fields be determined." Those investors who committed their cash were the steadfast pioneers of a new industry. "When oil is struck in large quantities the pioneers will reap their harvests. Stock in one of the present-day companies will be worth at least ten times its par value then." Future investment opportunities

Figure 3-5 Excerpt from "A Great Future"
Other ads, like this one from Rocky Mountain Oil Fields, emphasized the potential for oil to alter the regional and national economy. Note that Lady Liberty's torch is illuminated by oil

might come along but the late investor would have little opportunity to profit. The ad also reflected how the *Herald's* campaign required Rocky Mountain to switch tacks by adopting the slogan "Investigate and You Will Invest." Ads with a different theme appeared in trade journal *The Natural Gas and Oil Record* on November 21, 1913. "A Great Future's" imagery is striking. Lady Liberty's lamp in the top left corner lit by oil. Merchant ships plying their trade on the world's oceans belch smoke from their stacks fuelled by Alberta oil; motorcyclists and automobile drivers indulge in recreational motorsports secure in the knowledge that lower fuel prices prevail. The ad urges readers to think of the industries that would develop in Alberta "through the agency of Natural Gas and other by-products of the oil industry." Unlike other "sickly" sectors of the Canadian economy requiring artificial protection provided by tariffs, the oil industry is a "strong, healthy" industry "indigenous to the soil" and "natural."[18]

The reality, however, was that the majors enjoyed the *gravitas* that came with access to greater resources—human, material, technological, and financial—than most independent companies busily organizing in Alberta. Combining the practical experience and specialized knowledge of drilling hundreds of wells in many locations, the majors likely could do things that the independents could only dream of. The love/hate relationship with "big oil" came to a head in the autumn 1912 when eminent British geologist Edward Hubert Cunningham Craig arrived to assess Alberta's petroleum prospects and became, in the estimation of D. Austin Lane, secretary of the Oil and Gas Association of Alberta in the 1950s, a St. John the Baptist–like figure—"a voice crying in the wilderness"—regarding the province's petroleum prospects.[19] If Albertans wanted to exclude "big oil" from developing the field, they nevertheless sought the larger industry's stamp of approval to convince investors that oil existed in commercial quantities.

Cunningham Craig represented the emergence of the modern, technically sophisticated, specialized oil industry dominated by integrated oil companies—like Burmah Oil and Anglo-Persian Oil, both of which employed him at some point—with global operations. Born in Edinburgh, Scotland, in 1874 and educated at Cambridge, Cunningham Craig began his professional life as a cartographer for His Majesty's Geological Survey in 1896 before promotion to head geologist five years later. Cunningham Craig left the Geological Survey for the private sector in 1907 but still served as an adviser to both the Royal Navy and the British government. In the estimation of historian Thomas Corely, "he possessed a richly-deserved reputation for being conceited, over-confident and disdainful of other people's opinions."[20] Geologist Arthur Beeby-Thompson, who worked with Cunningham Craig in Trinidad, described him as "a robust, healthy individual of Scottish descent," predisposed to boast about his prodigious physical endurance. No one who worked with him ever doubted his abilities or intelligence, but it is unlikely he was a pleasure to work with. "Never have I met a scientist with greater conceit, self-confidence, and reluctance to listen to the views of others," writes Beeby-Thompson. "Indeed, he never resented a charge of conceit. Craig never hesitated to dogmatise on any subject, and on principle he would find cause to disagree with any observation, even of quotations from his own reports."[21] Granting an interview to the *Herald*, Cunningham Craig boasted that his opinion was so valuable that, while working in Persia as a consultant, a rival company hired assassins to kill him in order to gain a competitive advantage. "The competition among the oil development companies is there very keen," he noted, "and all means, fair or foul, are used in the rivalry of trade."[22]

In part because of his desire to bridge the divide between theoretical and field-based geology, in 1912 Craig published *Oil Finding: An Introduction to the Geological Study of Petroleum*. Billed as a common-sense, non-technical guide, the slim volume (190 pages of text, excluding index) blended the theoretical concerns of "scientists" and the practical observations of geologists in the field to produce a new synthesis about petroleum geology. "So much nonsense has been written and published about oil," claimed the book's introduction, "that many vague but essentially erroneous ideas are current, if not actually accepted." Cunningham Craig lamented that, in practical oil-finding efforts, geology found itself playing a secondary role to engineering. Even in leading textbooks on the subject, geology found itself dismissed, in Cunningham Craig's words, "in a few carefully guarded and colorless paragraphs."[23] Drawing liberally from his own experiences in the field, he hoped to move geology from the fringes to the centre of petroleum exploration. *Oil Finding* covered everything from the organic and inorganic theories about the origins of petroleum and its formation to discussions of rock formations and stratigraphy (the study of the origin, composition, arrangement, and distribution of successive layers of rock). The preface to the 1912 volume, written by Sir Thomas Boverton Redwood, an advisor on petroleum to the British government, suggested that the combination of common sense and technical know-how imparted by Cunningham Craig would enable individual geologists and laypeople "to form an independent opinion as to whether the technical data given in a prospectus are adequate" and allow shareholders in exploratory projects "to interpret reports of progress which at present they find intelligible."[24]

Oil Finding covered its subject comprehensively, starting with one of the most vexing questions geologists had confronted for the previous fifty years—the origin of petroleum. By the early 1910s, geologists and chemists had advanced several different theories to answer that riddle, but none enjoyed widespread acceptance. Three main lines of argument dominated discussion of oil's origins: organic, inorganic, and a combination of the two. Of the three, organic theories that argued petroleum resulted from the decay of plant or animal life were, by far, the oldest and most widely accepted explanation. Inorganic theories of petroleum's origins traced back to Pierre Eugène Marcelin Berthelot, who created organic compounds by chemical manipulation. In 1866, Berthelot suggested that water containing carbonic acid, or an earthy carbonate, could produce oil and/or natural gas if it met metallic sodium or potassium at high temperature. In 1877, Russian chemist Dmitri Ivanovich Mendeleev published his theory that water, percolating down through fissures in the earth's crust, encounters metallic carbides. Under extremely high pressure and heat, a chemical reaction takes place that produces metallic oxides and saturated hydrocarbons. The hydrocarbons ascend into the sedimentary rocks where they are found.[25]

Citing chemical, geological, and experimental evidence, the first chapter of *Oil Finding* argued that petroleum originated as organic matter—either animal or plant—and generated the most commentary from contemporary critics. The question of petroleum's origins had clear implications for the search for new oil fields. If geologists did not know, or could not prove, "from what material and under what conditions petroleum is formed" how could they tell where to find it? "The geologist must consider why there should, or should not, be oil" in a particular formation.[26] Subsequent chapters on the process of petroleum formation and migration discussed how the combination of organic matter in the presence of water with the precise combination of pressure and temperature could explain the differences in grade and class of petroleum, thereby rounding out the theoretical discussion of the volume. The remaining five chapters turned to a more practical incorporation of field observations to finding oil fields. With examples from the oil fields of Trinidad, Baku, Venezuela, Mexico, Burma, Persia, Ohio, Pennsylvania, California, and others, Cunningham Craig distinguished between surface and structural indications of petroleum and discussed stratigraphy and where to locate wells, as well as including two guided lessons (for beginners) in Field Work and Indoor Work. These last two chapters expressed the hope that "here and there among them the beginner may find something that will help him in his practical work."[27]

"It used to be one of the distinguishing points between the amateur and the professional geologist that the former was frequently content with the drawing of a horizontal section, while the latter always pinned his faith to a map, but nowadays the amateur is learning that in any case the map must be made before the section, and that nothing but a map will suffice."[28] Cunningham Craig offered opinions about selecting the proper scale—"the smallest scale that is at the same time sufficiently large to admit of mapping in detail will be naturally selected . . . six inches to the mile"—equipment, and suggestions for mapping in rugged terrain. As for indoor work, the book suggested that two months in the field would require three weeks of indoor work to properly complete maps made from field notes. In his closing remarks, Cunningham Craig made the case that no other branch in geology offered a more promising future than the search for petroleum. "The life of the oil-finder, with its travel in many lands, its contact with many races, and its frequent change of scene, is, taking the rough with the smooth, a thoroughly enjoyable one."[29]

Fast on the heels of *Oil Finding*'s publication, in 1912, Cunningham Craig arrived in Alberta at the behest of the McDougall-Segur company as well as for Mowbray S. Berkeley and John W. Lea's British Alberta Oil Company; both sought his informed opinion on Alberta's oil prospects before committing to substantial investments. Of particular interest was Cunningham Craig's observation that many of the world's largest oil fields flanked and ran parallel to mountain chains, especially when they bordered great plains. Soon, he speculated that the eastern foothills of the Rocky Mountains contained oil deposits. The trip enabled him to complete field work, consult with the Geological Survey of Canada, and keep an eye on developments for the British Admiralty. Cunningham Craig's international reputation meant his appearance conferred immediate credibility to the field. On December 16, 1912, *The Calgary Daily Herald,* citing "one of the greatest experts in the world in oil prospecting—Cunningham Craig" wrote that indications of a rich oil field, "possibly the richest on the American continent, excelling even those of western Pennsylvania," lay just thirty miles south of Calgary.[30]

The rampant land speculation and stock sales that started in October 1913 following the Dingman strike seemed unnecessarily reckless to Cunningham Craig. Unfortunately for him, however, his well-publicized trips to Alberta and statements to the press seemed to encourage speculators despite warnings that discovering oil was far from guaranteed.[31] Furthermore, the carefully qualified statements issued by Cunningham Craig provided fodder for boosters and critics alike to suggest the internationally known geologist backed their position. Indeed, supporters pointed to his enthusiastic declarations that oil existed in Alberta to suggest that the province contained one of the world's largest oil fields. But they were frustrated when Cunningham Craig suggested he might forego issuing a comprehensive statement on the Alberta oil fields before returning to England in early November. "I have not finished my investigations yet, nor am I fully satisfied regarding the oil field in the southwest of Calgary," said Cunningham Craig on October 28, 1913. Citing the need for more time and information to fully form his thoughts, he suggested his statement would likely "take the form of an article in one of the magazines devoted to petroleum matters" to receive the widest possible audience.[32]

Cunningham Craig did relent before his departure on November 4, 1913, and issued a broad endorsement of the oil prospects in Alberta, suggesting that a substantial deposit lay underground in Alberta and that, in his opinion, it would likely justify a "big campaign of development." Cunningham Craig's statement elicited a giddy reaction from *The Morning Albertan,* then embroiled in the increasingly bitter feud with the *Herald* over its Flotations campaign, that his words "will warm the cockles of the hearts of many who have holdings in the new district." *The Victoria Daily Times* concurred, saying that Cunningham Craig returned to the Old Country "with a report which may give rise to one of the most phenomenal developments in southern Alberta ever seen in any portion of the world." Citing a third party, the paper predicted Cunningham Craig would report "there is plenty of oil in Alberta" and that Alberta "is one of the most wonderful oil fields in the world." However, the paper also reported that Cunningham Craig considered the depth of the oil pools the most challenging problem ahead. Believing that the oil sat roughly 2,500 feet underground, the paper pointed to a potential inconsistency; Alberta's altitude of approximately 2,700 feet above sea level might influence the depth of wells before drillers encountered the pay zone. The Victoria paper wondered, "Is it necessary to get below sea level to find any big supply of oil?" Given that reports suggested the Dingman well encountered oil at approximately 1,500 feet, they estimated the drill bit needed to go down at least 3,000 feet.[33]

Meanwhile, critics like *The Montreal Gazette* pointed to Cunningham Craig's more cautious conclusions that "only a small percentage of the leases now filed upon will be of any commercial value." Perhaps more sobering for the *Gazette* was his evaluation of Alberta's anticlines as "small, narrow ones." Based on his conclusions in *Oil Finding* that wells drilling outside the anticlines likely had no oil under them at all, the *Gazette* wondered, "Is this a fair basis on which to ask people of moderate means to put money into heavily capitalized companies?"[34] Although he did not intend it, summaries of Cunningham Craig's positive public statements began appearing in a number of ads, circulars, and letters for newly formed oil companies, including Rocky Mountain Oil Fields, Standard Oil Fields, and Black Diamond Oil Fields. Stockbroker Julian Langner invoked Cunningham Craig's authority in attempts to sell stock in the Peerless Oil Works by claiming that lands acquired by the company "have been FAVORABLY REPORTED UPON BY MR. E.H. CUNNINGHAM CRAIG."[35] The ubiquitous use of Cunningham Craig's comments by other oil companies eventually compelled Mowbray Berkeley to threaten legal action against companies citing Cunningham Craig.[36]

Back in London, Cunningham Craig released a letter in *The Oil News* (London) that highlighted development at the Dingman well over the past year. Noting that many "have heard a good deal about it," Cunningham Craig referenced the wild rumours that meant people were inclined to disbelieve everything they heard. But he wanted to assure readers that he had visited the well site "before any plant was on the ground" and visited again after the strike in October. While Cunningham Craig believed Calgary Petroleum

Products could find the heavier oil, he warned that "they may have to go some distance." His professional assessment of the field would have to wait another occasion, as he was still going over the data. Nevertheless, there was great excitement in Calgary. The letter closed by referencing the explosion in land sales and creation of companies. "You might warn speculators who have filed on ground all over the place that very few have any chance of finding their leases productive." Referring to Cunningham Craig's international reputation, the editor of *The Oil News* assured readers that they could read the assessment "with confidence," but also drew "special attention to the warning he gives against rash speculation."[37]

Guarding against "rash speculation" proved easier said than done, especially during the gloomy winter of 1913/14. The prospect of an oil discovery provided a much-needed reprieve from reality and offered people the chance to dream of future prosperity. As if Calgarians needed more reminders that petroleum was an international business with local implications, some companies used this to their advantage to encourage more investors to buy stock. A full-page ad taken out in the *Herald* by Herron-Elder on December 4, 1913, emphasized the increasingly complex connections in communications, transportation, and business the city had with other parts of the world and the evolution of the global economy. With oil being an international business with multiple competitors clamouring for a share of the market, the ad drove home an inescapable reality—competition between companies carried international implications:

> When that magic message flashes to the uttermost ends of the earth from CALGARY in the next few weeks—perhaps in a few days—even **hours**—then will the great rush be on in dead earnest.
>
> Multitudes will flock to Calgary then.
>
> The wires are all laid.
>
> The scene is well set.
>
> Watchdogs are all on duty—**here and now.**
>
> The drills are busy day and night.
>
> Other drillers, too, who **mean business**, are on the way.
>
> **The big oil treasure will be struck—and soon.**

And everyone with an ounce of information or intelligence, of knowledge or skill, believes it will be **BIG**.

Telegraphs span all the continents, and touch every centre in the whole civilized world.

Cables are laid under all the seven seas of this rapidly evolving globe.

Microorganisms vibrate through all the oceans of air around this earthly planet.

Everybody, **everywhere**, is in touch with **Calgary**.

All eyes are upon **us**.

Everyone is waiting for a trusted whisper from **here**.

Those five words, "**strike** of oil, **big flow**," **with a** Calgary dateline, will set the whole human race agog.

The world and his wife will grab the grips and flock here from afar.

The big CPR hotel here will be filled to overflowing as by magic.

Strangers from far and near will fill all the vacant rooms in town.

Empty office space will have to house the homeless.

Good oil stocks will shoot upward.

Sky high they will **soar.**

"Curb" markets will be held—and crowds of eager buyers will attend.

But the "buying orders" from London, New York, Berlin, Paris, by **night** wires "**day rate, rush,**" **will** be ahead of **you.**

Europe is awake while Calgary sleeps.

Even the "Orient" will have bought while Calgary slumbers.

You will be "out" then if you are not "in" now.[38]

Calgarians eagerly awaited Cunningham Craig's formal assessment of oil prospects in Alberta. Finally, early in the New Year, the *Herald* announced that he would deliver an address to the Royal Colonial Institute in London on January 21, 1914.[39] Attended by a number of oil experts and government officials, the forum allowed Cunningham Craig to advance his argument that oil originated from terrestrial vegetation and place "the incontrovertible geological facts" before his audience that Cretaceous formations (the Dakota and Kootenay), not Devonian limestone, were the primary oil-bearing formations in western Canada. His address began by referencing a similar speech he had given seven years earlier on the development of Trinidad's oil fields. Although Trinidad's prospects were much maligned at the time of his speech, Cunningham Craig reminded the audience its wells now produced flowing oil at 20,000–40,000 barrels per day. Now the only lament expressed in Britain regarding Trinidad was that the best successes belonged to a US-based company. "No patriotic Briton or Canadian can regard with indifference the possibility of the history of new oil fields in Canada taking a similar course."[40]

A brief sketch of the Ontario industry quickly seguéd to "a new field that I wish to call to your attention this afternoon, newer geologically, and so new practically that it has yet to be proved." Cunningham Craig acknowledged that the Royal Navy was "at least partially" committed to the use of fuel oil but faced stiff global competition for supplies. More worrying was the fact that global consumption of oil, and its price, continued to rise. In Canada, declining production in older eastern Canada made developments in Alberta critical. Years before, Cunningham Craig became convinced "on purely theoretical grounds" that the eastern foothills of the Rocky Mountains "probably" contained oil fields. Visiting Canada in 1912 and working with the Geological Survey of Canada and "practical oil men," like Ira Segur and William Herron enabled him to buttress academic conjecture with practical field work. He then guided the audience through a summary of the three geological conditions required to produce an oil deposit with commercial quantities contained in *Oil Finding*. First, a formation with "a sufficient quantity of organic matter from which oil can be formed." Second, strata that "contain porous rocks capable of acting as reservoirs for liquid hydrocarbons," such as sandstone, overlain by impervious rocks, like shale or clay, in sufficient depth to seal the oil reservoirs and prevent the loss of gas pressure. Third, that the strata should be in large enough size to concentrate liquid hydrocarbons into definite locations beneath the surface. For this, a dome, or anticlinal structures, "are almost essential."[41]

In western Alberta, Cunningham Craig credited the GSC with identifying a promising formation 3,800 feet thick showing evidence of "having been deposited in a comparatively shallow sea." Composed of seven strata of rock of varying thickness, the deepest parts of this formation—the Dakota and Kootenay—lay exposed on the western belt of the foothills, but later groups covered them to the east and "do not crop out again except over a large area on the Athabasca and Peace Rivers." A broad and gentle syncline 140 miles across extended to the east of the foothills and an equally broad and gentle anticline followed. Cunningham Craig observed that the formation was so subtle that only "dealing with very large areas of land" made it clear.[42] Noting the GSC's 1913 report surmising that western Canadian petroleum originated in the Devonian limestone, Craig emphatically stated that "all traces of petroleum in this province of Alberta are indigenous to the Cretaceous formation, and had the origin of oil from terrestrial vegetation been more widely known, there could never have been any doubt upon the matter." Specifically, Craig believed the oil had formed in the carbonaceous beds of the Kootenay group where coal beds existed. "The same material under the requisite conditions of sealing and pressure may be converted into oil."[43]

The challenge for petroleum hunters in Turner Valley, according to Cunningham Craig, lay in finding locations where the Dakota and Kootenay groups are not too far down but are far enough away from their outcrops where geological structures capable of concentrating petroleum existed. Ideally, the optimal location would also have all the necessary human and material resources to facilitate development—a good water supply, a population centre, and transportation infrastructure—nearby. Then, with an understated confidence, he delivered the punchline—"All these conditions we find in the foothills west and southwest of Calgary." Cunningham Craig anticipated that the broken nature of the formation presented some challenges. The anticlines were more symmetrical to the east, but exposed shales often sharply folded parallel to the main axis and even contorted, "making the structure appear very complicated." Nevertheless, he had every confidence that the complication was "more apparent than real; these are to be regarded as minor puckerings on broadly anticlinal areas." Drillers need not worry about the broken formation, for Cunningham Craig believed that much sharper, and deeper, subsidiary folds existed in Persia and posed few problems to drillers. While not every part of the field contained favourable structures—toward the south "the favorable structure dies out"—mapping "proves that in several localities excellent anticlinal structures do occur."[44]

Summarizing recent developments of the drilling program of Calgary Petroleum Products and McDougall-Segur, Cunningham Craig noted that both companies were located to give the best results without deep drilling. Both firms struck gas at shallow depths, and Calgary Petroleum Products encountered strong gas at several horizons until, at 1,562 feet, the well made "a very remarkable show of oil, accompanied by very strong 'wet' gas." Admittedly, the show of oil was minor—"at best, only a few barrels per day"—but Cunningham Craig remained doubtful that either well reached the Dakota group, where he believed they would strike the main reservoir. "Alberta," he noted, "is a country of great distances, and it may take many years before complete geographical data are to hand." Nevertheless, Alberta enjoyed all the essential conditions required for a large oil field. Indeed, he speculated that petroleum deposits covered practically the entire province, from the Athabasca River to the south of Calgary. Further to the east, the anticlines were gentler, and Cunningham Craig necessarily believed they required deeper drilling. The real promising formations lay to the north. "The weathered outcrops of the Dakota group on the Athabasca River contain heavy asphaltic oils, [and] the evidence from the Dingman well suggest that any oil struck in the foothills in rocks of the same horizon will be a paraffin base and [of] much greater value." The difference between the oil sands in northern Alberta and the naphtha produced by the Dingman well owed to "the different conditions of temperature and pressure in which the petroleum in each case has been formed."[45]

Building toward his conclusion, Cunningham Craig tackled the question of the Calgary boom directly, observing with slight exaggeration that nearly everyone in the city filed for mineral rights for thousands of land sections. Dominion regulations made it easy to apply for oil leases, but keeping them was a different matter entirely. "Trafficking of licenses and leases is rife among speculators who are not able to defray the heavy expenditure necessary [for] development work." However, the Dominion government would revise the regulations to address the problem. But these changes could not erase the damage done. "Oil leases are on sale in shops and offices throughout the city, and are practically being hawked about the streets. And it is no exaggeration to say that probably not ten percent of those who hold prospecting licenses have any sound reasons for determining whether they are of value or worthless." When he left Calgary in November, Cunningham Craig noted that sixteen companies had formed to develop the oil fields. Undoubtedly, more had emerged in the interim. Some immediately sold stock before making any test to determine if the land they held was worthwhile. "There will be admitted on all hands that such procedure is greatly to be regretted, as the legitimate and carefully organized enterprise is discredited when a host of speculators are in the field doing their best to unload their holdings and the responsibilities upon the public." Most of those companies would fail, predicted Cunningham Craig, because they rushed headlong into development and did not carefully select their sites. Because of this collective failure, he warned that losers would outnumber winners by a wide margin and their failure would harm the handful of companies that went about the work more methodically. Despite this reality, he looked to the long term: "If as much as one percent of the land taken up on prospecting licenses proves to be profitable and productive, Canada would own one of the world's greatest oilfields, an asset to the Dominion and to the Empire of enormous value." A few months of drilling in 1914 "should be sufficient to settle once and for all whether the present excitement has been justified or not, and whether the Empire is to be the richer by a great and growing industry in the development of an oilfield that may eventually rival that of California."[46] Given that annual production from California wells reached nearly 100 million barrels, Cunningham Craig's assessment would cause a stir.

Coverage of the speech evolved as more complete copies of the text arrived over the next two weeks. A preliminary cable provided papers with a synopsis of the address on January 22, 1914. Partial, and then full, texts arrived on February 4 and February 7, 1914, respectively. Among papers more critical of the emerging boom, coverage remained relatively consistent. The *Herald* praised the address as a calm and realistic appraisal of the oil situation in Alberta by "the leading authority in the world on the subject." The paper further pronounced that "three conclusions are irresistible" in the aftermath of Cunningham Craig's statement. First, that oil existed in Alberta "in commercial quantities." Second, that much of the exploratory work done to date "has been futile," and that much of the exploratory work underway "will be unprofitable." Finally, that the *Herald's* campaign against the flotation of oil companies was "more than justified by investigations and development." Developing an oil field "is not child's play and the chances against individual success are very heavy."[47] The *Vancouver Daily World* reported that Craig, whom it believed "largely responsible for the Calgary oil boom," maintained that he confirmed an abundance of evidence indicating oil existed in the foothills of the Rockies but it "could not yet be regarded as a certainty." Of greater concern is the "mischief" done by speculators, the majority of whom would prove failures.[48] The *Edmonton Journal* noted that he "criticized very strongly" the prospecting taking place but "was more than hopeful as to what could be accomplished by proper methods." London papers now carried stories about credulous investors in England buying plenty of Alberta oil stock when a cablegram alleging that "oil has been struck at Calgary in commercial quantities" circulated. The *Journal* lamented that the *Herald's* flotations articles tamed the wildcatters in Calgary but could not do the same in England.[49]

Relentless optimism characterized the *Albertan's* initial coverage, as that paper seized on Craig's statement that if 1 percent of leases produce oil "this will be the greatest oil field in the world, which is not so bad. Of course, if we get oil on 75 percent of the claims upon which we have filed, Alberta will have an oil area seventy-five times as big as any other country in the world."[50] But as the full text became available, the *Albertan* moderated its enthusiasm, especially considering Cunningham Craig's sobering warnings about rampant speculation and the failure of previous exploration efforts. On February 7, the *Albertan* walked back some of its earlier enthusiasm, claiming that the cable extracts sent on January 22 "did not do justice to the full report." Nevertheless, the *Albertan* characterized the report as optimistic, mostly because of what it did not say. "He is not sure that there is oil in the district in paying quantities. There is nothing in the formation to lead him to believe that it is impossible that southern Alberta will not be a second California. He does not say that Alberta oil fields will be a phenomenal success." Overall, the *Albertan* claimed the report was useful.[51]

By March 1914, seven companies—McDougall-Segur, Calgary Petroleum Products, Black Diamond, Southern Alberta, Federal, Western Pacific, and United Oils—drilled for oil in the "Calgary District." The sheer number of companies prompted the *Albertan* to optimistically predict that as many as twenty companies would be drilling within the next three months. The expansion of independent drilling, and the arrival of spring, brought changes to the tone and tenor of some companies' advertisements, many of which tapped into previous schemes to sell mining stock to the public. "The trick," writes historian Michael Bliss, "was to issue huge numbers of shares in very low denominations—a dollar a share or even penny mining stock—and then promote the speculation as virtually riskless." The problem, as Bliss concludes, is that "the line between selling and swindling was almost non-existent."[52]

Piedmont Petroleum Products, for example, billed themselves in their ads as the oil stock "for the man with little money" and likened stock speculation to a lottery where everyone who invested wins. "Buy oil shares at 10 cents," implored Piedmont, pitching their sale to lower income investors with a limited issue of bargain shares that promised big returns and almost no risk. "When oil is struck it will go to at least par, and many times more." The

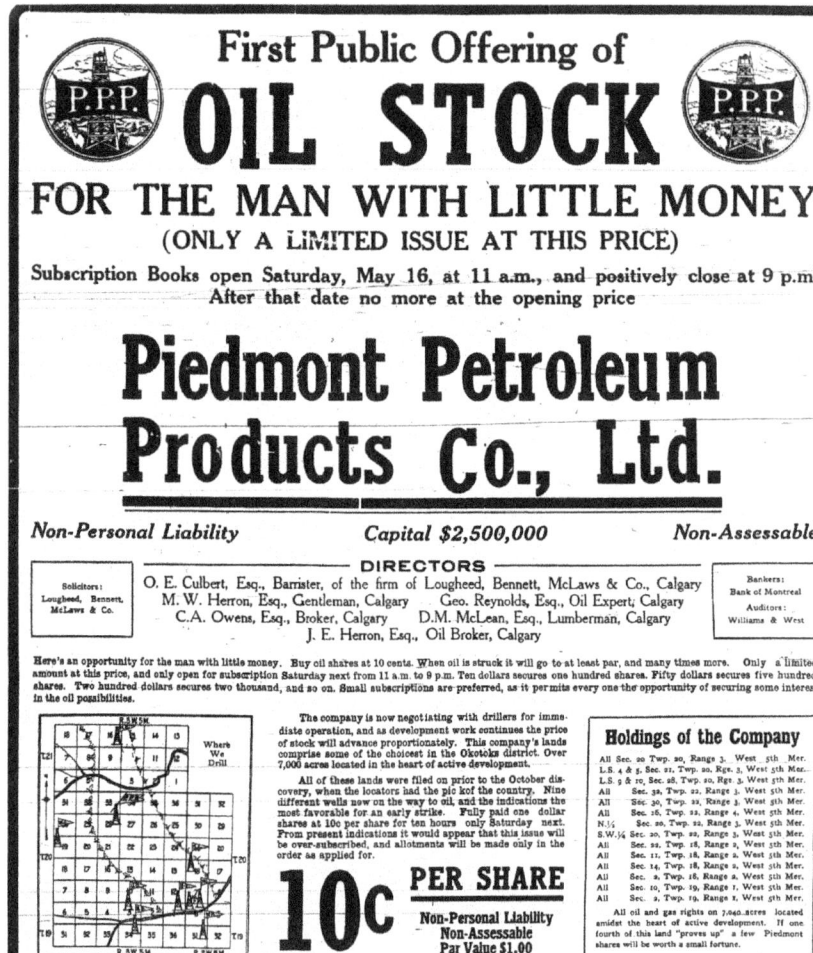

Figure 3-6 Piedmont Petroleum Products Company Ad

Piedmont Petroleum Products targeted small investors with a limited time offer of shares at ten cents and virtually guaranteed a tenfold return on investment "when oil is struck [shares] will go to at least par [$1.00], and many times more." The company held mineral rights for 7,040 acres and projected that if a quarter of the leaseholds contained oil, "a few Piedmont shares will be worth a fortune." (University of Calgary Libraries and Cultural Resources CU1300898) ad assured potential investors that "small subscriptions are preferred, as it permits every one the opportunity of securing some interest in the oil possibilities." A second, more insistent, ad by Piedmont ran the next day, this time urging potential investors to dream big and believe in oil and the market delivering a future of wealth and prosperity without any risk. "Oil shares purchased at ten cents each have been known to 'go' as high as $1,800.00 each," cooed the advertisement, subtly implying that even a minimal investment could produce staggering returns. Even if the Piedmont well was a small producer, the ad reassured potential investors that "the stock will pay mammoth dividends on par value. That means an increase of ten times the opening price."[53]

Scholar Frederick Buell describes the emergence of a "culture of extraction" associated with petroleum development that distinguished it from other extractive industries. Unlike the capital-intensive nature of coal mining, which required a large labour force working underground, oil offered "immense reward for little investment and less hard labor." Once tapped, oil rose under pressure to the earth's surface, eliminating the need for miners to go underground. What could be easier? Furthermore, Buell points to Ida Tarbell's notion that oil extraction signalled a return "of the old epic-heroic ideology of democratic, self-reliant, community- and nation-building individualism." In 1938, Tarbell observed that many involved in oil extraction saw themselves as "men of imagination who dared to risk all they had on the adventure of seeking oil."[54]

One of the most evocative ads that embodies many of these themes was one for Herron-Elder published on May 16, 1914, emphasizing oil's recent history of creating instant millionaires in California, Texas, Oklahoma, and Russia. But it also emphasized the importance of personal choice and individual courage; everyone had the opportunity to act but only a select few would. For readers of *The Morning Albertan*, the Herron-Elder ad proclaimed, "This time opportunity pauses at YOUR door. Will you sleep on or will you act NOW?" In a sidebar to the ad, the company offered a "near parable" about two fictional people, Jones and Smith, each of whom had a dollar. "Jones" saved his money by putting it in his sock and "passed under the judgement of the non-producer." "Smith" sought to invest his dollar and believed that "Nature is the only real producer" and that "Natural Products have been and always will be the greatest boon to mankind." Though he lacked any specialized skills or training, Smith possessed faith in the combination of nature and the free market and "invested his dollar in Nature's gift—Oil." The short parable then delivers its punchline with a wallop. Jones's example of thrift and savings represents no virtue worth celebrating; only wasted opportunity and regret. No traces of the man with the dollar in his sock remain. Jones is, at best, forgotten, at worst a "bad example," someone who lacked vision, faith, or courage. Smith's entrepreneurial spirit and belief in oil's transformative powers, on the other hand, merited celebration. Smith "is hailed as one of the nation's great. He lives on the fat of the land and is honored because he had faith in Nature." Lest anyone doubt the high stakes presented by this choice between faith and maintaining the status quo, the ad said bluntly to "ask Rockefeller," then one of the world's wealthiest men and often invoked in the oil advertisements of the time. The moral of the parable and its celebration of rugged individualism, personal responsibility, and the miracle of oil is as clear as its title: "The Difference Between Poverty and Riches is Action!"[55]

For close readers with even a passing awareness of Herron's background and the events since the founding of Calgary Petroleum Products, it was obvious that the person of "Smith" was how Herron saw himself: as a visionary entrepreneur unafraid of demanding work, and humbled and in awe of nature. Perhaps the ad also betrays the lingering whiffs of resentment about his exclusion from Calgary's elite, and Dingman's power play at the shareholder's meeting that left Herron off the board of directors despite his 25 percent stake in the company until February 3, 1914, when Sir James Lougheed and others forced a motion through giving Herron a seat.[56] Friction then spilled into the courts in the following days as Dingman sued Herron and his daughter for $750,000 ($20.1 million today, adjusted for inflation) over contested leaseholds. As this came fast on the heels of a separate bruising battle over the location of a second well (won by Dingman by steamrolling his partners), it appeared Calgary Petroleum Products would tear itself to pieces.[57] Considering that recent history, the advertisement is thinly veiled wish fulfillment projected on the citizens of Calgary wherein Herron—and investors with the courage to join him—attains the independence, prestige, and financial security provided by oil. It proved to be an incredibly effective campaign. When Herron-Elder closed its subscription at nine p.m. on May 20, 1914, the company's shares were oversubscribed, ensuring that Herron-Elder could finance a well, making it one of the few Calgary-based companies to drill a well during the Turner Valley boom.[58]

Decades after the boom, Calgarians repeated the (supposedly) true story of a man who suffered a nervous breakdown and was sent to the provincial sanatorium at Ponoka. Discharged on the eve of the boom, he sold a section of his land for ten dollars an acre—$1,600 in total (approximately $43,000 adjusted for inflation). When his lawyer asked him what he was going to do with his financial windfall, the man replied that he would invest the lot in

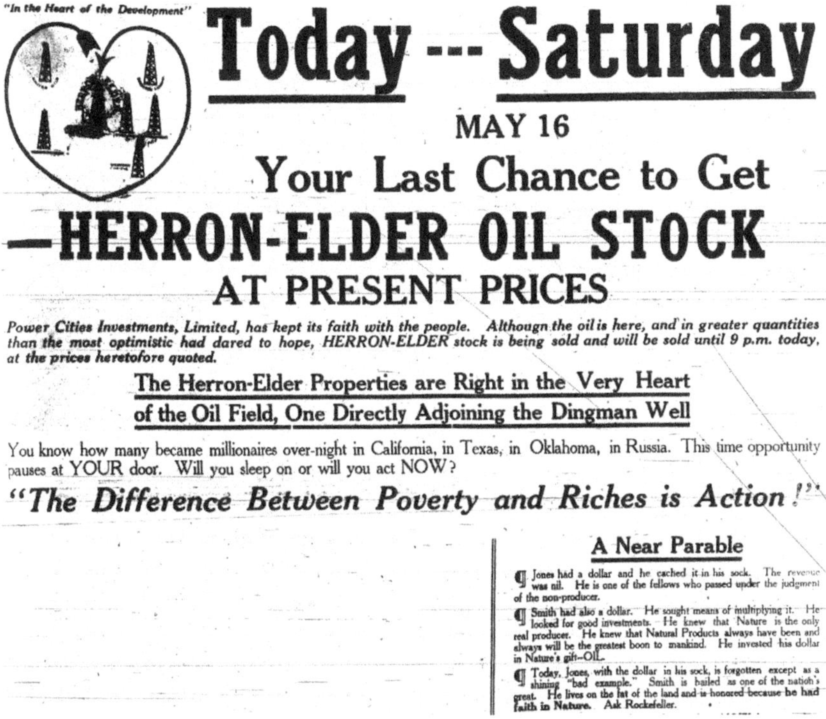

Figure 3-7 "The Difference Between Poverty and Riches is Action!"
The "near parable" in this Herron-Elder ad highlights many of the qualities and characteristics associated with Alberta's budding petroleum industry. (University of Calgary Libraries and Cultural Resources CU1301220)

Monarch Oil shares at a dollar a share. The lawyer looked at him and said he was crazy. "No, I am not," he replied as he pulled out his discharge papers. "I have a certificate to prove it." Of course, when Monarch stock hit forty dollars a share in June 1914, he cashed out and retired to the Okanagan.[59] Compared to the difficulty of growing good crops in the hard prairie soil, some boosters suggested oil would be relatively easy to produce. Unfortunately, bitter experience taught a number of these investors that, while oil was tempting to get into, it was harder to achieve success unless you were lucky, a little bit crazy, or both.[60]

4

"I'm Going to Go Through With It Even if it Leads to Jail:" George E. Buck of Black Diamond Oil Fields

> *Look, Alex, to rephrase Gertrude Stein, a promoter is a promoter is a promoter. If you don't have a heart full of larceny, you'll never make a promoter. The essence of being a promoter is to have your cake and eat it too. You do a deal that enables you to get a promotion going and the objective of all promoters is to wind up owning the deal, or most of it, without risking their own money.*
>
> —James Gray to Alex Freeman
> Winnipeg, Manitoba
> 1937[1]

Approximately one week before Calgary Petroleum Products Company struck oil, on May 8, 1914, Charles Tryon of *The Calgary News Telegram* broke the news that George E. Buck's Black Diamond Oil produced a show of oil at approximately the same depth CPP had the preceding October. For Buck, the discovery did not come a moment too soon. Broke, with his house heavily mortgaged and payments in arrears to International Supply Company drilling the well, Buck was perilously close to losing everything. But rather than a fortuitous turn of luck, Buck's salvation owed itself to a company-wide conspiracy to "salt" the well by pouring oil down the hole and claiming to strike oil. In the excitement that followed, Buck sold enough stock to keep his fledgling company afloat, saving himself and his family from financial ruin.

What enabled Buck to think he could get away with such a scheme? Part of the answer assuredly lies in the context of the boom of 1913–14, wherein what few rules there were seemed easy to break and largely free of consequences.

123

Certainly, the pro-business and small-government ethos that resulted in a lax regulatory environment made it easy for an individual like Buck to flourish. But Buck's evangelical Christian faith also imbued him with the conviction that he was both different from and superior to others. His search for crude oil embodied the spirit of "wildcat Christianity" defined by historian Darren Dochuk. At its core, wildcat Christianity describes the overlapping relationships Dochuk found among many independent oilmen between their faith, labour, business interests, and the church that do not distinguish between these different aspects of life. Buck's evangelism drew him away from the collective efforts at social reform of liberal Protestantism and pushed him toward a more personal goal of earning salvation through struggle and saving souls, one at a time, to earn spiritual rewards in the hereafter. Within his church, the lack of formal structures and hierarchy facilitated the elevation of charismatic speakers like Buck to positions of prominence. Unfortunately, it also allowed him to easily exploit his position of authority to further his own ends. Thus, when combined with evangelism's belief in an active God, and the inevitable return of Jesus Christ, it meant no time could be wasted. To search for oil, which necessarily meant studying the land, was to decipher God's work on earth. Thus, all work, whether drilling for oil, salting a well to raise additional funds, or preaching the gospel, was God's work.[2]

Between 1905 and 1915, the population of Calgary swelled from around 14,203 people to 58,000 as the result of federal immigration policies designed to attract settlers from the United States and Europe. While large numbers of farmers and ranchers still moved to the West, middle-class professionals, like grocer William Georgeson, insurance salesman George Buck, and reporter William Cheely, leavened their numbers. Calgary's growing population stimulated the growth of construction, processing, manufacturing, and service sectors as the local economy transformed the city from "Cow-town to Hub of Industry" by 1913.[3]

As historian Will Ferguson observed, Alberta "was very much a self-selecting venue. The West attracted misfits and outcasts, dreamers, schemers, eccentrics and oddballs, mountebanks, and moneymen. The restless. The lonely. The thirsty. Thirsty for something more, something better. Thirsty for life."[4] Historian Gerald Friesen agreed, calling the prairie west "a land of new beginnings" whose people believed they had a mission to complete.[5] The 1911 Dominion census reveals that the average Albertan tended to be a white male between the ages of twenty-five and twenty-nine. Compared to the national average, Albertans tended to be slightly younger and more likely to be male. In the province, males outnumbered females 59 percent to 41 percent compared to the national average of 53 percent male to 47 percent female. Meanwhile, roughly 66 percent of Alberta's population was twenty-nine years old or younger with an average age of 26.2 years. With fully one-third of the population between the ages of twenty and thirty-four, the prolonged economic boom dominated their formative years. The preponderantly young, male population of the city ensured that by 1912, in the words of historian James Gray, "Calgary was in the process of becoming the booze, brothel, and gambling capital of the far western plains."[6]

At the age of forty, Buck transferred to Calgary as the superintendent of the Manufacturers Life Insurance Company. Due to the western land boom and the arrival of so many immigrants, Calgary was already a boom town when Buck arrived. The first thing to greet Buck in Calgary was likely the smell. Years later, newcomers recalled an unrelenting assault mounted on their noses because across the tracks from the Canadian Pacific Railway on 11th Avenue was the biggest horse barn in western Canada, housing sixty teams of draft horses. Reportedly, stable hands shovelled the manure into a pile on one side until it formed a small mountain before hauling it away. After it rained, the wind could catch the odour and spread it for blocks. Stockpiles of coal in the railyard shed soot and smells with every gust of wind that also stirred up the dust from unpaved streets. Once one was clear of the train station, the smell hardly improved. There were also fifteen livery stables, one for every other block, as well as twelve blacksmiths and the alleys behind the liveries piled high with manure. The narrow streets of downtown Calgary tended to trap the miasma of people and beasts. Directly opposite the train station sat the five city blocks of 9th Avenue, known officially as "Atlantic Avenue" and unofficially as "Whisky Row." Consisting of ten hotels—including the Alberta Hotel's reputed longest bar between Winnipeg and Vancouver (125 feet)—locals claimed all Atlantic Avenue needed to make it perfect was a long brass rail and spittoons at each end. Beyond Whisky Row and the businesses and shops of downtown Calgary sat no fewer than three known areas of prostitution where "saloons and houses of ill repute were cousins, with madams providing illicit whiskey to whet or quench the appetite."[7]

The only way such morally questionable behaviour could openly flourish was with the connivance of the local police, and for much of the province's first decade, both Calgary and Edmonton established reputations as "open cities"—that is, open to vices like liquor, gambling, and prostitution—despite the strenuous efforts of temperance and moral reform societies, making

Figure 4-1 "9th Avenue SW, Calgary, Alberta. Palliser Hotel and Canadian Pacific Railway Station are visible on left side"
The string of ten hotels along 9th Avenue, starting with the Palliser Hotel (top left) and across from the CPR train station (foreground, bottom left), known as "Atlantic Avenue" but more informally as "Whisky Row" due to the concentration of bars. (University of Alberta Library PC005483)

life on the prairies in the early twentieth century decidedly different from Buck's strict upbringing in Ontario. Indeed, scandal rocked the Edmonton police force in late 1913 when Mayor-Elect William J. McNamara, a brash real estate promoter, dismissed the reform-minded chief of police, Silas H. Carpenter. Chief Carpenter, a former Montreal police officer with piercing dark eyes, bushy eyebrows, and an exquisite handlebar moustache, had arrived the year before and immediately launched a campaign to clean up the streets and tackle corruption in the police department. Within the first year, 2,500 drunks were arrested along with the keepers of four dozen brothels, their clientele, and dozens of opium users and vagrants. Carpenter's exertions proved too effective for interests backing McNamara, led by Alderman Joseph Andrew ("Fighting Joe") Clarke, whose patrons wanted a wide-open town—so long as it avoided the worst excesses. How could this be accomplished? Carpenter's predecessor, and subsequent replacement, A.C. Lancey, later testified at a specially convened inquiry into Edmonton Police that he was instructed by members of city council to arrest prostitutes on the street but to leave the estimated 300–400 brothels alone. McNamara furiously denied the claim.[8]

Carpenter's dismissal ignited a fierce public backlash, and by June 1914 McNamara abruptly changed tack and claimed he had fired Carpenter for being too lax. McNamara accused the former police chief of not only tolerating social vices (prostitution, drinking, and gambling) but turning a blind eye to the corruption of the Edmonton police force. Called by McNamara to testify before a public inquiry, Carpenter turned the tables and alleged the chair of Edmonton City Council's safety and health committee of coming to his office and saying, "You come from the east, and you must remember that conditions are different in western cities from what they are in the east. In western cities the people want houses of prostitution, and they want gambling houses."[9]

If Carpenter's accusation were true, it undoubtedly meant that Buck would be busy, because in addition to his job as an insurance salesman, he also happened to be a gifted and charismatic preacher for the Disciples of Christ and began proselytizing at the corner of 12th Avenue and 1st Street. At first, Calgarians did not know what to make of the group, misidentifying them as Mormons and then branding them a "fake" church, prompting a letter to the editor of *The Calgary Daily Herald* introducing the church and its beliefs to the city. "We include in our membership thousands of the best business and most talented professional men of every calling," and, the letter continued, the church included the late President James A. Garfield among its congregants.[10] The sect sought to reconcile and unify the various strains of the Protestant Church based on the teachings of Christ from the New Testament. Described as possessing a "traditionally conservative evangelical outlook," the Disciples of Christ typically embraced the values of small-scale laissez-faire capitalism, individual responsibility, honesty, and frugality while eschewing traditional Christianity and its proclivity to elevate the clergy. Instead, the Disciples of Christ emphasized the individual's relationship with God and embraced the introduction of the social gospel, especially the notion of the scientific method and an emphasis on natural laws. Buck regularly preached in the Disciples of Christ's tent with subjects like "Winning Souls," "Almost Persuaded," and "Seek the Old Paths and Walk Therein," or led Bible studies.[11]

In addition to his abilities to preach, Buck proved a larger-than-life man about town. According to historian John Schmidt, Buck was "an impressive talker who exuded confidence all over the place." Ambitious, enterprising, and extroverted, Buck modestly dressed in a black broadcloth coat and soft dark hat but usually worked a cigar, pipe, or chewing gum underneath his thin waxed mustache. As an active member of the city's automotive club, he loved cars, particularly his red Dodge, and later an eighty-horsepower red McFarlan Six.[12] Although the insurance industry brought him to Calgary, by 1910 Buck branched out into real estate, founding B & R Realty Company with partner and fellow Disciples of Christ member Harry W. Ritchie. The partnership lasted a year before Ritchie resigned and left for Edmonton. Success in real estate led Buck to invest in coal mining when rumours spread that the CPR intended to construct a line from Montana to Calgary and then on to Peace River. In August 1912, Buck bought an interest in a coal mining property on Wolf Creek, but development only showed a coal pocket rather than a seam. By 1913, B & R Realty dealt in farmlands, coal lands, mining properties, and petroleum leases and moved out of the McDougall Block and set up offices in the Patrick Burns building, kitty-corner from City Hall, smack dab in the middle of the city. Buck's (modest) philanthropy—publicly donating one acre of land for the founding of a university in Calgary, and other charitable donations—placed him on the periphery of Calgary's first families. So, too, did his home in Lower Mount Royal—a scant three blocks away from that of Senator James Lougheed.[13]

It was also in 1912 that Cunningham Craig published the first edition of his influential book *Oil Finding*. Buck later claimed that this "standard work" convinced him of the value of "scientific geology" in the pursuit of petroleum.[14] Despite boasting to one reporter that he identified potential drilling locations in 1912, it took Buck until June 24, 1913, to organize and register the Coalinga Oil Syndicate. A partnership consisting of Buck, his wife Ada, brother-in-law John A. Campbell, and cousin Jennie L. Earl, the Syndicate collected all the oil leases held by the four in exchange for a 25 percent stake in the partnership. An ad found in *The Natural Gas and Oil Record* reveals that Buck briefly attempted to sell 5,000 shares in the syndicate, but the company remained strictly a family affair. Coalinga called no formal meetings, kept no records of its decisions, nor, apart from appointing Buck director, did it have a formal executive council. Buck then organized Black Diamond Oil Fields on August 13, 1913, with all the members of Coalinga Syndicate listed as directors in the oil company. Initially capitalized at $750,000, Black Diamond acquired one of Coalinga's leases for $262,500. On paper, the deal saw Black Diamond pay Coalinga $250,000 in shares (par value $1) and $12,500 in cash.[15]

The heavy debt burden from the purchase of leases caught the attention of the *Herald*'s "floatation of oil companies" series, earning the company the dubious distinction of being the final company profiled on October 28, 1913. The *Albertan*, which usually reflexively countered the *Herald*'s criticisms, largely agreed with its rival on this occasion, concluding "the offer is not at all attractive.... Mr. Buck of the Diamond Oil Fields is paying Mr. Buck of the Colinga [sic] Oil Syndicate many times too much for the oil rights. In the second place the company does not have sufficient land. Altogether it is not a good proposition." The critical articles slowed the number of investors willing to place their money in Black Diamond Oil Fields—the company sold roughly 5,000 of the 75,000 shares for a dollar each—so Buck began borrowing from friends and family to finance drilling on the lease. By November 29, 1913, he finally scraped enough together to convince Tiny Phillips and W.R. "Frosty" Martin of International Supply Company to begin drilling the first of three wells on the lease before Christmas 1913.[16] Under the terms of the contract, International Supply Company agreed to drill the well to 1,500 feet at ten dollars per foot in return for $13,000 payable in three installments—an $8,000 payment to start work with another $3,000 due when the well reached 500 feet and $2,000 due at 1,000 feet. Buck's company also agreed to supply all the necessary coal and water to fuel the boiler.[17]

Unusual developments and strange happenings dogged Black Diamond from the start, and George Buck proved particularly adept at drawing attention to himself and his company, although not always for the right reasons. Buck's juvenile sense of humour and penchant for practical jokes suggest he was not entirely a stable business partner. When the cartage team delivered the construction materials for the derrick to the well site in December 1913, they encountered a woman armed with a gun who told them that she owned the mineral rights to the land and threatened to blast the men to kingdom come unless they got off the property immediately. When they stood their ground, the armed lady lowered the weapon and claimed Buck hired her to put on the performance.[18] On another occasion, when the company desperately needed cash from stock sales to continue operations and discussions between Buck and a selling agent reached a critical phase, Buck reported that the conversation ended abruptly because his pipe exploded; someone loaded it up as a joke.[19] Events like these fuelled rumours that Black Diamond and George Buck were not really interested in drilling for oil. Nevertheless, Black Diamond #1 spudded in on December 1913, meeting Buck's deadline, but real drilling started on January 29, 1914. Shortly thereafter the company began an aggressive push for attention, promising to drill day and night (as did most other drilling outfits). What is striking in retrospect is how quickly Buck pivoted from charming, confident, circumspect businessman to outrageous promoter.

The charm offensive began in late January 1914. At a meeting of Black Diamond's directors on January 30, Buck's friend, Edward Henry Crandell, became a voting trustee of the company and proxy shareholder. If the goal was to project stability and competence, Buck clearly chose well. A well-connected, wealthy developer and "captain of finance," Crandell was born in 1858 in Fort Perry, Ontario, to parents of United Empire Loyalist stock. He built his reputation first as the owner and proprietor of a general store in Brampton for twenty years and serving as a city councillor, auditor, and two-term mayor of Brampton (1897, 1898) before joining the Mutual Life Assurance Company of Canada and moving to Calgary as general western agent. In short order, Crandell became one of the most successful insurance and real estate businessmen in the city. As his wealth and stature increased, so did his business interests, adding the Alberta Sewage Pipe Company, the Jackson Wood and Fuel Company, and the Calgary Tent and Mattress Company. Crandell also dabbled in the early exploration for oil in Waterton, as part backer and president of the original Discovery Oil Company that in 1905 held leases near Waterton Lakes. Within a decade, the lake and 7,812-foot mountain near the well site were named after him. Despite an expanding business empire, Crandell also retained his interest in politics, serving as a local school board trustee and one term as city councillor (1914–1916).

Crandell's most enduring legacy emerged from the 1905 purchase of Calgary Pressed Brick and Sandstone Company in the town of Brickburn, then five miles west of the city of Calgary, now the community of Edworthy Park. By the turn of the twentieth century, brick served as the primary building material for the many cities and towns across the prairies, and Crandell produced the material for many of the city's iconic buildings, including the Lancaster Building, the Capitol Theatre, and the Mewata Armoury. Crandell expanded operations to a fifteen-kiln plant producing 45,000 bricks per day—well below its daily capacity of 1.5 million. But Calgarians—and many others around the world—are more familiar with another feature of the 400-acre site. Just off the Old Banff Coach Road and overlooking the Bow River, Crandell built a three-storey, twenty-two-room red brick mansion that initially served as the family's summer cottage and then permanent residence. The family called it "Varsity Heights" until 1920, when the Crandells leased the house and thirty-two acres to the Red Cross for $2,700 per year to serve as the Soldiers' Children's Home for sixty orphaned and convalescing children. The mansion reverted to a private residence when, in 1951, wrestling promoter Stu Hart bought the house and raised his family there.[20]

As for Crandell, his active involvement with the United Church, the YMCA and YWCA, and the Conservative Party, among other charitable endeavours and organizations, projected calm and predictability absent from

Black Diamond's other directors. Two days later, on February 1, the charm offensive continued as Buck invited a few guests, including W.S. Herron and William Elder, to the derrick by car for dinner and a demonstration, generating a small mention in the *Albertan* to go along with a full-page ad addressing itself "to intelligent people who do their own thinking and who know what's what." Somewhat disarmingly, it acknowledged public and private criticism of the company's methods, "some [of it] fair and some most unfair and downright ignorant of everything pertaining to petroleum and its finding." Promising a "square deal in oil," Buck emphasized the company's honesty and integrity, pointing to the appointment of Crandell as trustee and the retention of geologist J.H. Sinclair of California as evidence of the company's goodwill and seriousness.[21]

The following day, Buck took out two ads in the *Albertan*. The first one on page seven proclaimed "everybody enthusiastic about Black Diamond," striking an optimistic, if slightly braggadocious tone that, among other things, claimed the Dakota sands, "the acknowledged reservoir of petroleum in these fields," sat only 400 feet from the surface and that the 640 acres owned by the company will "be easily worth $3.2 million" when they struck oil in "30 to 45 days from this date."[22] The second ad, on page nine, started innocuously enough with Buck claiming he was so pleased with Black Diamond's progress and was so confident of "striking oil in large commercial quantities" that "I do not want to sell one more share of Black Diamond stock at present prices than is absolutely necessary to carry on Black Diamond drilling." To raise capital, Buck, who was not involved with Devenish's much larger United Oils company, apart from owning 1,000 shares in it, offered to sell those shares in United for half the par value of ten dollars. To further turn the screw on his competition, over the next ten days Buck took out successive ads claiming that no one had bought his United shares and began dropping the price in increments until his erstwhile partners, Harry and Ida Fenner, who between them claimed one-third ownership interest in the shares, filed an injunction to prevent him from selling any more.[23]

Buck understood viscerally that the cutthroat competition between companies tapped into deeply rooted social and cultural forms that have, as historian Brian Black has pointed out, shaped the industry since the nineteenth century.[24] In 1914, no level of government established production limits on the amount of oil any single company, promoter, or wildcatter could produce. Buck understood that the industry rewarded and celebrated the ruthlessly independent, rational, free enterprisers among them. Furthermore, in the absence of any other restraint imposed by government, theoretically only three things limited how much oil a promoter or wildcatter could produce: the rule of capture, oil's existence as a liquid under pressure, and petroleum's fugacious qualities. The rule of capture governing North American petroleum development held that whoever brought oil or natural gas to the surface first, owned it. Given that petroleum deposits often extended over a larger area, several leaseholders likely tapped into the same pool, providing an immediate incentive to drill aggressively with as many wells as possible to produce the reserves first. In the Black Diamond field, Dingman #1's well (Section 6, Township 20, Range 2 West of 5th) lay three miles east of both United Oil's well (Section 3, Township 20, Range 3 West of 5th) and Black Diamond #1 (Section 34, Township 19, Range 3 West of 5th); less than a mile separated United's well from Black Diamond #1. As the *Herald* observed in the late spring, "It is thus apparent to the layman that the wells are all in the same general zone."[25] The full implications of the rule of capture become plain upon consideration of oil's existence as a liquid under pressure and its ability to migrate from one area of a deposit to another.

But competition between promoters and would-be oil barons had to be carefully managed. Southern Alberta's oil and gas community (excluding brokers) remained comparatively small—maybe a couple of hundred people in total, from drillers to promoters and financiers. Everyone knew each other. They lived in the same neighbourhoods, sent their kids to the same schools, shared office space in the same set of buildings, and served on one another's board of directors. These circumstances produced a largely insular and self-referential oil patch wherein today's business rival could easily be tomorrow's partner. O.S. Chapin illustrates the point. As one of the original backers of Calgary Petroleum Products, Chapin became a member of the board of directors. But he also invested in William A. Georgeson's Monarch Oil, and Oscar Devenish's United Oils, serving as a director of these two companies as well, even though they were competitors with Calgary Petroleum Products. As the feud between Herron and Dingman revealed, infighting between erstwhile business partners could, and did, take place and participants sometimes turned to the courts for relief. For the most part, however, disputes generally observed a sense of proportion. Dingman, for example, always ensured Herron received proper acknowledgement for his pioneering work on the Turner Valley oil field, despite their personal difficulties.

If the rough-around-the-edges Buck knew these unwritten rules existed, he did his best to ignore them. In Buck's case, his evangelism enabled him to conceive of business generally, and the oil boom specifically, as a zero-sum game where the ends justified the means and winning necessarily meant someone else lost. A no-holds-barred brawler who enjoyed a good fight, Buck did whatever it took to win. In early 1914, after filing the paperwork to incorporate Black Diamond Oil, Buck refused to pay the law firm used to prepare the papers and was promptly sued by the lawyer for non-payment. Naturally, Buck retained arguably Calgary's most famous law firm, Lougheed, Bennett, McLaws, to represent his interests during his very litigious spring and summer of 1914. Buck rewarded their exertions on his behalf by suing them at the end of July for charging too much.[26]

The feud with United Oil and Oscar Devenish, however, proved particularly nasty, prompting local newspapers to refer to it as "the oil wars." What prompted Buck's feud with United Oils? Part of the answer lies in the fact that the two companies were uncomfortably close to one another. Not only did they occupy office space in the Burns Building, but their respective wells were also adjacent to one another, less than one mile apart. In August 1913, Buck initially asked Grant S. Wolverton, then in the employ of Devenish and a director in Devenish's real estate business, to serve as president of Black Diamond Oil Fields. Failing that, Buck asked Wolverton to serve on the board of directors. To help convince Wolverton, Buck and the Coalinga Syndicate transferred 10,000 of Coalinga's 250,000 shares in Black Diamond to Wolverton, unevenly divided between two certificates—one for 8,000 shares, the other for 2,000. Given that Wolverton had worked with Buck on getting Black Diamond up and running, Buck believed the deal was all but done, and even filed a prospectus listing Wolverton as president with the provincial registrar on August 14, 1913.[27] But Wolverton, a vice president in Devenish and Company, wanted additional changes incorporated into the prospectus, as well as having it vetted by a lawyer. After carefully considering the offer, and talking matters over with Devenish, Wolverton refused both positions at the behest of Devenish. Ultimately, the decision likely came down to choosing between doing business with Devenish or George Buck. As a divorcee with a son in college in the United States, Wolverton opted against making a big change. Days later, at the launch of United Oil, Wolverton became one of its directors.[28]

Wolverton knew the 10,000 shares were part an incentive package for assuming an executive position with Black Diamond, so he returned them to Buck at a meeting in early November 1913. Subsequent accounts of the meeting sharply diverge in tone and substance. Wolverton claimed Buck was both gracious and appreciative of the work Wolverton did for Black Diamond, especially on the prospectus. According to Wolverton, Buck accepted the return of the certificate for 8,000 shares but not the one for 2,000, saying

Figure 4-2
"Important Announcement"
The ad that started the Black Diamond/United Oil Feud.
(University of Calgary Libraries and Cultural Resources CU1701489)

IMPORTANT ANNOUNCEMENT ON OIL

Personally, since my visit to 34-19-3 W. 5, Sunday, I am so absolutely confident of the early striking of oil in large commercial quantities on the property of the Black Diamond Oil Fields, Limited, where drilling is now in active progress, fully 30 to 45 days ahead of all others—Dingman and Segur not excepted—that I do not want to sell one more share of Black Diamond stock at present prices than is absolutely necessary to carry on the Black Diamond drilling. Therefore

I hereby offer for immediate sale at only ONE HALF the par and selling prices ($10 per share).

1,000 Shares UNITED OILS At only $5 Per Share

In any quantity desired, delivery of stock subject to escrow, the proceeds from which will be immediately put into the drilling of the well now rapidly sinking on the property of The Black Diamond Oil Fields, Limited.

(Signed) **GEO. E. BUCK,**
114 P. Burns Bldg., Calgary.

that if Wolverton could not be a director he would like to keep Wolverton as a shareholder, and refused to accept its return.[29] Buck, however, remembered the meeting quite differently, claiming that Wolverton told him Oscar Devenish did not want him serving on Black Diamond's board of directors and Wolverton had caved in to the demand. Buck also claimed Wolverton wanted to return the 10,000 in shares, saying "he had not done anything to earn it" and only returned the certificate for 8,000; according to Buck, Wolverton claimed he could not find the certificate for 2,000 shares and promised to return it once found.[30]

The Natural Gas and Oil Record revealed another motive for the burgeoning feud. The surface rights holder of Section 34, the location of Black Diamond #1, claimed Buck did not have his permission to enter the property and that United Oils held the rights, assertions Buck vigorously denied in a three-quarter-page ad in the *Albertan*. In retaliation, Buck announced that he had acquired the surface rights to 1 percent of all United Oil leaseholds. Inevitably, the matter found its way into the courts, where Buck had a caveat issued on the contested Black Diamond leaseholds after he produced an agreement signed by Harry Denning granting the right to purchase the surface rights. United Oils produced its own agreement claiming ownership, and when questioned by *the Albertan*, Buck dismissed United's claims out of hand. "If they have bought anything of this kind, they have bought something from someone that cannot deliver. I have the papers. I let the other fellow do the worrying about such things. I am content to do the drilling." But in the interim, Buck's former lawyer, William Morris, sued Buck for false pretenses when the cheque he sent as payment bounced because of insufficient funds, and had Buck arrested and hauled before a judge. Buck's friends immediately leapt to his defence, claiming persecution. "Mr. Buck has had the nerve and courage to attempt to develop the local oil resources and we are of the opinion that there is an element of persecution in this action," claimed one before adding, "One hundred Bucks with 100 drills dropping might help make of the Okotoks oil fields a second California." Once before Judge Colonel Sanders in police court, the charges were dismissed after Buck managed to convince the court he had made a mistake about the amount of funds in the account.[31]

Buck's defence, and Black Diamond's advertising campaign, elicited pointed remarks from *The Natural Gas and Oil Record*'s gossipy "Sprays from the Derrick" column. "With a crazy man mixed up with all this wet gas and making us dizzy with the prodigious profits to follow, is it any wonder that we cannot keep track of our bank accounts?"[32] The remark may have soured relations between the paper and the company because after March 7, 1914, Black Diamond Oil Fields no longer appeared in the *Record*'s directory of oil companies. Shortly thereafter, the injunction against Buck's sale of United Oil shares lifted and Buck promptly began selling them for one dollar per share. In the meantime, the lawsuit between United Oils and Black Diamond over the surface and mineral rights to Section 34 seemingly resolved itself in the middle of March when Oscar Devenish and United Oils withdrew their complaint against Black Diamond. Less than a week later, however, Devenish sought a new caveat on Black Diamond's lease, enabling Buck to continue running attack ads trumpeting Black Diamond's success.[33]

Typical ads for Black Diamond used what is known in advertising circles as the Barnum style advertisement. Named after Phineas T. Barnum, the Barnum style attempted to entertain, amuse, and divert its audience and saw advertising as a catalyst designed to gain rapid and widespread publicity.

Figure 4-3 "Heart-to-Heart" George Buck used advertisements like this to sell stock and keep Black Diamond in the public eye in the winter of 1913/14. (University of Calgary Libraries and Cultural Resources CU1701176)

a heart-to-heart talk on OIL (read EVERY word of THIS)

---the real PIONEER OIL development company in all Southern Alberta---or ALL Alberta---as everybody NOW knows, is THE ONE that started REAL OIL-FINDING FIRST.

---the FIRST company to start on a real scientific ANTICLINAL location, with AT LEAST ONE THOUSAND FEET LESS to go to the REAL OIL-BEARING STRATA, was BLACK DIAMOND

----the FIRST company to let an oil-drilling contract BY THE FOOT---not by the YEAR---to a FIRM OF COMPETENT, EX-PERIENCED, SKILLED DRILLERS (MARTIN & PHILLIPS) was BLACK DIAMOND.
----the FIRST people in ALL Alberta to get up and FOLLOW the advice and information of CUNNINGHAM CRAIG, B.A., F.G.S., the greatest oil-finding authority and expert of the British Empire, on the whole world, were those of BLACK DIAMOND.
----the FIRST people in ALL Alberta to get busy and select the ABSOLUTELY BEST anticlinal OIL LAND when practically EVERYTHING in ALL Alberta was WIDE OPEN for filing, were those of BLACK DIAMOND.
No wonder, THEN, after a year or more by OTHERS, of guessing and trying, experimenting and discovering (?), BLACK DIAMOND, which starting ACTUAL DRILLING less than TWO MONTHS ago, is ALREADY fully 90 days AHEAD OF ALL OTHERS in the golden quest for OIL---the BIG FLOW that makes MILLIONAIRES over night.
----no wonder, NOW, that BLACK DIAMOND, with all its rapid progress and favorable developments, is its FIRST WELL, is NOW being grabbed at and greedily coveted by grasping persons. We believe O. H. Devenish and his associates have ABSOLUTELY no more just claim to BLACK DIAMOND'S property than YOU, the reader of THIS announcement, have to the Dominion Government post-office site in Calgary, to the Provincial Government's Land Titles Office, or to the ROAD ALLOWANCES of Alberta---and not HALF as much. Devenish, therefore, has NO RIGHT what-ever, to file ANY caveat or claim on BLACK DIAMOND. Yet O. C. Devenish, NOW realising the GREAT VALUE of 50-19-9-W.5 at the ABSO-LUTELY BEST OIL LAND on the whole region, and greedily coveting the development work ALREADY DONE, and further realising from our progress reports of well number one, up to March 10th, that BLACK DIAMOND was on the eve of announcing a great OIL STRIKE, filed a caveat on Black Diamond's property. The Minister of the Interior and the Minister of Justice of Canada, and all the best legal opinion of Calgary, are ALL fully agreed that O. C. DEVENISH NEVER HAD any more claim to BLACK DIAMOND'S property than a JACK RABBIT.
----nearly EVERY valuable PIONEER mineral location, in the EARLY history of practically EVERY mining camp of GENUINE MERIT has similar-ly been attacked by greedy and unscrupulous "CLAIMANTS". BLACK DIAMOND, no exception. The company of Calgary, is no exception. The CROWN and COURTS of CANADA and ALBERTA, however, will quickly clear the air and put the claimants where they properly belong.
----where the title to BLACK DIAMOND is cleared and ABSOLUTELY CLEARED as it will be in the course of a few days, thanks to our excellent solicitors, Messrs. Lougheed, Bennett, McLaws & Co., and the justice of our CROWN and COURTS---we will be able to announce for the benefit of our shareholders the very favorable developments in

BLACK◆DIAMOND

Well Number One since March 10th, when the depth attained was 831 feet, and the drilling was in a hard cap rock.
----should we make our announcement earlier, while the CAVEAT CLOUD hangs over BLACK DIAMOND, our shareholders would be at a great dis-advantage in dealing in at a proper profit at their enterprise and initiative in getting into the PIONEER OIL company and driving the drill downward day and night with their hard-earned dollars on the ABSOLUTELY BEST OIL LOCATION in ALL ALBERTA to PROVE BLACK DIAMOND. Such an announcement NOW would give us no just advantage by our no-strings-lease to Black Diamond (17) company having NO INSECURITIES, and thereby defeating the purpose of drilling, or flooding the market with their own one-sixteenth-no-strings-attached stocks and thereby defeating the purpose of drilling, or flooding the market with their one-sixteenth-no-strings-attached stocks and thereby defeating the holding BLACK DIAMOND stock WORTH perhaps $500 an APIECE, but unsaleable for possibly ten dollars per share. BLACK DIAMOND is determined to protect the interest of EVERY shareholder to the utmost possible way. BLACK DIAMOND'S SQUARE DEAL agreement issued to Z, and is SO FAR AHEAD of the usual DEVELOPMENT AGREEMENT, and also more straightforward and prepared to war TWO WEEKS, or a little more if necessary, to THIS announcement.
----it will also be to our shareholders, when, even up to practically EVERY new coming hold of REAL MERIT, and which is the CANADIAN COURTS are quickly and easily cleared, we feel that BLACK DIAMOND can much better afford to take the present capital for drilling and being ALREADY DONE by offering shares at only $2 per share than most of our shareholders could afford to part with their shares or even a small part of them, at even many times that price per share.

On the printed page, the Barnum style would "manifest an expansive use of space, brash layouts, a liberal use of ornamentations and cuts, and a disorienting variety of typefaces."³⁴

With Buck's legal troubles abating for the time being—they never fully went away—he could now focus his attention on raising capital to fund the company's development program. Buck ran an extensive and aggressive ad campaign in local papers to generate interest through most of February and into March 1914. But sales of Black Diamond stock remained sluggish. In early March, Buck brought in Norman Fletcher, an accountant from Medicine Hat, to audit the books. Fletcher quickly discovered that Buck and his company were on the brink of bankruptcy. Buck and Black Diamond did not have the cash on hand to make the balloon payment owed to the drilling company, International Supply, once they completed the well to the contracted depth of

1,500 feet. Stated simply, Buck needed drilling to slow down to give him more time to raise the money he owed. Operating at arm's length, Buck ordered Fletcher to ask driller Hayes to only drill a few feet per day. Hayes initially refused, arguing there had already been too many delays and he doubted he would be able to keep his job if he failed to make further progress. But Hayes soon knuckled under and slowed the drilling. After making excellent progress, the well agonizingly lingered above the 1,500-foot threshold for weeks, drawing the notice of *The Natural Gas and Oil Record* on April 25, which wrote, "Geologists and others are up in the air about conditions at this well," as reports still had Black Diamond in sandstone.[35]

The bigger problem affecting Black Diamond was that the company was chronically underfunded. The company's prospectus revealed that directors authorized 75,000 shares of capital stock for sale to the public, but the board of directors later reduced this to 50,000 on January 30, 1914. By early May, the balance sheet revealed only 17,715 shares sold, 12,000 of which were to four salespeople—Norman Fletcher, Major Gillespie, E.H. Crandell, and C.L. Whyte—reselling shares for Black Diamond. With a par value of one dollar per share, this left the company with little wiggle room to cover the contracted payment of $13,000 to International Supply and operational expenses. In desperation, Buck pulled Black Diamond stock off the market, perhaps to stimulate stock prices by creating an artificial shortage. But share prices did not budge.[36]

Buck's monetary crisis prompted him to think creatively and led to a multi-pronged conspiracy to inflate stock prices that featured salting the well to simulate an oil strike. Preparations to salt the well began at least a week before a scheduled official measurement of the well's progress by Black Diamond's more sober and trustworthy face, company director E.H. Crandell. But Buck could not proceed until International Supply Company's driller, J.H. Hayes, signed off. At first, Hayes remained steadfast in his objections. But after Buck raised the issue "three or four times," Hayes finally relented. A relieved Buck told Hayes that he would salt the well on May 7.[37]

In the meantime, accountant Norman Fletcher became suspicious when two or three one-gallon cans of crude oil and gasoline arrived at the office. "We did not have any cattle or sheep to dip," reasoned Fletcher, referring to the concoction used by shepherds and ranchers to protect livestock from infestations, "and that is what it is used for." Instead, Fletcher later testified that Buck seemed to be experimenting with the oil and gasoline, blending the two together until "it resembled something that came out of the southern Alberta field." It was messy work, and Buck left traces of his various concoctions all over his desk in his private office. After some experimentation, Buck proclaimed he had found a good mixture and began showing it off to the people in the office. On May 6, the day before salting the well, a visibly agitated Buck gathered everyone together for a meeting. The company teetered on the verge of bankruptcy but Buck nonetheless believed there was enough money in Calgary to salvage Black Diamond Oil Fields. All they needed to liberate that investment capital was an oil strike—or have people believe they struck oil—within the next week. But how could Buck guarantee an oil strike within the necessary time frame? With that, Buck laid out his plan to "salt" the Black Diamond well to sell more stock and keep the drilling rig operational.

Stunned, Fletcher and advertising manager Harry C. Beattie protested the proposal as fundamentally dishonest, but they were in the minority; the rest of the gathered employees readily agreed to the plan, including Buck's mother-in-law, Elizabeth Beaty. Beaty, like her daughter and son-in-law, had invested heavily in Black Diamond Oils. If the company failed, she would lose everything. Buck then asked Norman Fletcher to help deliver cans of oil to the well. Fletcher refused and told Buck he was on the verge of committing a very serious offence. If Buck went ahead with the scheme, warned Fletcher, he was prepared to quit. Harry Beattie also urged Buck to reconsider. "Leave everything to me," Buck now told his fellow conspirators. "I'm going to go through with it even if it leads me to jail."[38]

After the meeting broke up, Fletcher and Beattie left the office to discuss the morning's events. Over lunch, Fletcher adamantly said he would not take part in the plot, but Beattie began to waver because he had sold considerable volumes of stock to his friends and family. What would they do if the company failed? If it meant saving the company, Beattie now said he would help Buck "dope the well." That afternoon, more preparations took place, with Buck securing somewhere between ten to twenty gallons of distillate from Ray Lee, the owner of Diamond Motor Company. At five o'clock, Buck announced that he was going to the well and again asked Fletcher to accompany him. "I took sick right after dinner," said Fletcher, so Buck got Major Gillespie, a salesman with Black Diamond, to go with him. Gillespie brought Buck's car around. In the back of the vehicle, Fletcher saw motor rugs covering something up. After Buck and Gillespie left, Fletcher collected himself and left for Medicine Hat.[39]

That night, Buck and Major Gillespie arrived at the well site only to discover that driller Hayes now had cold feet. At the last minute, Hayes left a written note in the derrick forbidding Buck from salting the well and claimed his conscience compelled him to try one last time to stop Buck. The driller later said, "I made up my mind I didn't want nothing to do with the deal."

Hayes testified that Buck came to his tent after finding the note around midnight and sat down on the corner of the driller's bed to talk for the better part of an hour. A despondent Buck tried again to convince Hayes that salting the well was the only option. "He said he would lose all of his property, and his home was mortgaged and he would have no place for his family, and so I told him that the boys [the tool dresser and the fireman] could put it in in the morning." Buck then told Hayes that he had the oil with him in tins and would leave them out. The next morning, sometime between five and six o'clock, Hayes ordered Roy Minue and Lafe L. Tyrrell to pour several gallons of the oil and gasoline mixture provided by Buck into the bailer, claiming that orders to do so came directly from Buck. Minue and Tyrrell lowered the bailer to the bottom of the well and mixed the concoction with a hand pump. After removing the bailer, they then ran the tools down the well and "discovered" oil and poured it into a barrel. A couple of days earlier, Buck had asked Fletcher if Billy Budge, another watchman, could ride on horseback to the Black Diamond post office to phone Buck and deliver a coded message—"Paul"—to signal "oil is found." Fletcher responded that Budge would follow instructions.[40] After it was done, Hayes later testified that Buck gave some stock to "all the boys" for salting the well, including 500 shares for Hayes himself.[41]

Later that morning, Buck invited Charles Tryon, the managing editor and reporter for *The Calgary News Telegram*, out to the well along with city council member Freeze to witness E.H. Crandell's measurement of the well's depth. Tryon originally knew Buck as a client with an advertising account at the *News Telegram*, but the two began having more conversations about the oil business as time went on. Over five months, Buck cultivated a friendship with Tryon, supposedly taking the newspaper man into his confidence and telling him "secrets" from the business. Buck showed Tryon soil samples from the hole and attempted to teach the reporter about the geology of the field. Tryon, however, could never quite fully grasp what Buck said except for the promoter's belief that the company would strike oil. When Buck asked if he would like to visit the well personally "when the time came," Tryon eagerly accepted the offer. Thus, at around ten a.m. on May 7, Tryon joined the party heading out to the well by automobile. Upon arrival, the group headed straight for the derrick, where Buck introduced the crew before showing the group a barrel of oil supposedly taken out of the well the night before. Buck also ignited gas from the well before removing some oil from a barrel, throwing it on the grass and setting it on fire. With the demonstration complete, Buck then took Freeze out to inspect the sluice running into the creek, leaving Tryon alone with the head driller, J.W. Hayes. Tryon asked Hayes a few questions but found the driller tight-lipped; Hayes later admitted, "I didn't have much to say about it. I was drilling then and working." Tryon also remembered walking down to the stream and seeing indications of oil along the banks.

Shortly thereafter the visitors got back into the car for the trip back to Calgary. Sitting next to Buck in the front seat, Buck asked Tryon for his assessment and the reporter responded that it looked like Black Diamond Oil Fields #1 had found oil. Buck then urged Tryon to phone his editor, Charles Hayden, to arrange a special edition of the *News Telegram* announcing the find. The reporter declined, responding that he would prefer to report it personally. Nonplussed, Buck pressed him to phone the report in from Black Diamond or Okotoks. Once again, the reporter demurred, this time telling Buck they had missed the deadline for the regular edition, only to have Buck press Tryon to call for an "Extra" edition. Told it would cost too much—between $50 and $500 to print—Buck said he would cover the costs and even offered the reporter a couple of hundred shares of Black Diamond for his trouble. Perhaps Buck tried too hard, or maybe the blatant bribe attempt raised Tryon's hackles, but something the reporter heard or saw did not add up, and Tryon refused, opting instead to return to the city. Tryon recalled that the rest of the trip home took place in silence. Back at the *News Telegram* office, Tryon asked for one of the sealed oil samples from the well, but Buck refused with no explanation. Tryon filed what Buck termed a "brief and unsatisfactory account" buried deep in the paper the next day on May 8. An obviously irate Buck called Tryon personally to complain. The *News Telegram* "didn't give him the write-up that was expected," testified Tryon, adding that Buck said, "They could get it from the *Albertan*." In the meantime, Crandell gave an upbeat assessment to the *Herald* for its May 8 edition, describing his visit to the well. "I firmly believe that the drillers have struck a small flow of crude oil," Crandell told the *Herald*.[42]

None of this satisfied Buck. Determined to secure more favourable publicity to drive up stock prices, Buck contacted William Davidson of the *Albertan*. Unlike the *News Telegram*, the *Albertan* carried a front page story about Black Diamond's "find" in its May 8 edition even though its reporter did not visit the well with the rest of the party on May 7. To the *Albertan's* reporter, either in person or on the phone, Buck claimed the well had struck a strong seepage three weeks earlier and when the crew raised the bailer that morning the showings of oil were so prominent that they sent the private code to bring Buck out to Black Diamond #1 for an inspection. "We're happy enough tonight," said Buck. "Ours is the first well to reach the Dakota sand

and the first to strike oil in the crude in Southern Alberta. We claim Black Diamond well No. 1 to be the real discovery well."[43] After a quick conversation, Davidson told reporter and managing editor William ("Bill") W. Cheely that Buck would take him out to the well site. Cheely later recalled that within fifteen minutes the managing director of Black Diamond Oils arrived at the *Albertan's* offices to pick him up.

The son of a merchant, William Winbourne Cheely was born in Denver, Colorado, on February 29, 1868, and grew up amid a changing west marked by periodic mining booms, so-called "Indian campaigns," and cattle trails headed north from Texas. Although he was born in Denver, Cheely's formative years largely took place in rough-and-tumble mining camps. Widely beloved by his colleagues as a true character and storyteller, Cheely claimed as one of his earliest memories seeing an entire mining camp escort a man accused of some kind of infraction. When they reached the outskirts of the camp, someone told the condemned man to run. When he did, a hundred guns opened fire, practically tearing the victim to pieces.[44] "He was something of a wit and a raconteur, having an inexhaustible fund of droll stories with which he regaled his friends and cronies," wrote the editorial page of *The Montana Standard* upon his death in 1939.[45] Wherever Cheely worked, he became a staunch "booster" of the community and its business interests. With his keen sense of humour and ability to craft a grand narrative story, Cheely rarely seemed to meet a person he could not get along with. In 1936, the *Great Falls Tribune* reported that Cheely celebrated his sixteenth birthday with fifty friends. He claimed the younger age because his birth in a leap year provided him a birthday once every four years.[46]

In 1911, Cheely joined the staff of *The Calgary News Telegram*, establishing himself as an excellent reporter with a fine sense of humour. The *Albertan's* Davidson remembered noticing Cheely's writing when the reporter published a report of a speech made at the Women's Canadian Club. "These were the early days of women's organizations in Calgary," recalled Davidson. "For some reason the officials of the club were very shy of the press and placed a ban on reporters." Cheely hid in the pantry to listen to the speech, and his subsequent report "gave a very interesting running story of the happenings, together with some details of his stay in the pantry." The following year, in 1912, William Davidson brought Cheely on board as the managing editor and a reporter for *The Morning Albertan* to boost circulation.[47]

Cheely had spent the first twenty-two years of his career in the newspaper business bouncing around the United States as manager and editor of different newspapers between Butte, Montana, and Minneapolis, Minnesota.[48] To *The*

Morning Albertan, Cheely brought a distinctive, tabloid/sensationalist style resembling the evolution of journalistic style brought to urban daily newspapers in the United States by James Gordon Bennett and Joseph Pulitzer, emphasizing stories and personalities over information. The *Albertan* embraced big headlines and concentrated on delivering one or two big front page stories a day, and Cheely usually wrote the big story. Described as "the Apostle of Goodwill; the Dispenser of Sunshine" and a "highly capable, alert, and pungent writer," Cheely's brief three and a half years in Calgary were eventful personally as well. He married his wife, Nell, and, partially due to his investments in oil leases and oil companies, reportedly became a millionaire because of the boom. "Bill Cheely is the happiest man you ever saw. He owned a whole section of land and several thousand shares of stock in different oil companies," noted one of his friends, Duncan McGregor from Butte. "When the strike was made, he became a millionaire in a day."[49]

Perhaps because of his gregarious nature and outgoing personality, Cheely tended to blur the lines between his responsibilities as a reporter and the stories he covered—sometimes to the point where he became part of the story. Perhaps Cheely sensed that Black Diamond was about to provide a big story. Accompanied by Major Gillespie, Buck drove the reporter out to the well. Cheely added some rhetorical flourishes to his column, writing that the well now resembled an "old baronial castle," protected by armed men, surrounded by a moat, and accessible only by drawbridge lowered after the visitor provided the correct password, which Cheely surmised as a series of hand signals between Buck and the guard. Closer to the well, Buck brought Cheely to the derrick house, where the reporter noted the heavy smell of crude oil before Buck instructed the driller to raise the bailer and dump the contents into the sluice box where it ran off into Sheep Creek. Cheely saw the traces of oil on the surface and smelled the odour of coal oil. Buck then dropped a match or a lit piece of paper or waste into the well, causing an explosion of flame about ten feet high. Pleased with the demonstration, Buck prefaced his remarks with the statement "The oil we have found is just a seepage," and then spoke to Cheely for an hour or two about conditions at the well. While Buck expressed some vindication of his faith in the existence of an oil field, he admitted to investing all his savings in the company and confessed that the discovery released some of the pressure bearing down on him. The main body of oil probably lay further down, but he remained certain they were near it. During the conversation, Buck produced a geologist's report and letter from Kelso Laboratories that wound up in Cheely's possession later in the day and provided quotes for his story. Cheely's report on his visit, complete with

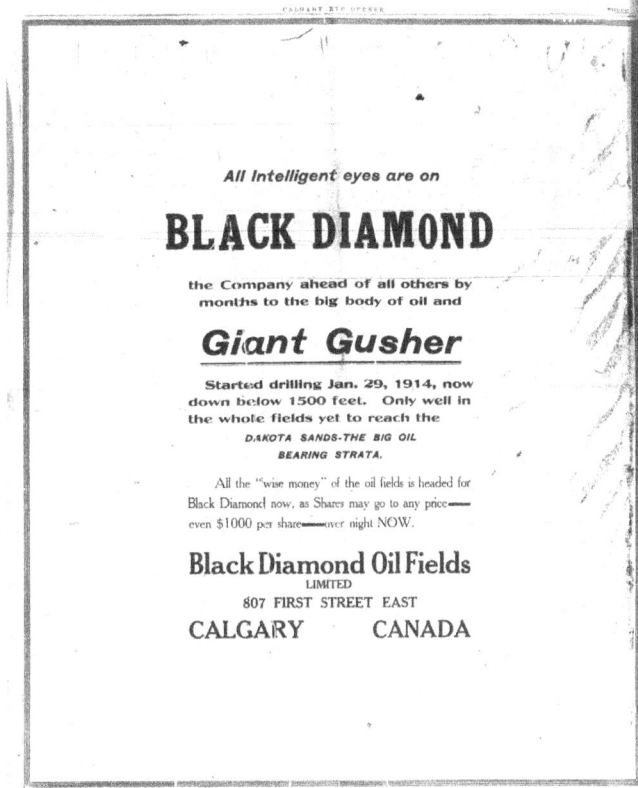

Figure 4-4 "Giant Gusher"
Despite his well-known reluctance to include advertising in the *Eye Opener*, Bob Edwards ran this ad for Buck's company in the spring of 1914. (University of Calgary Libraries and Cultural Resources CU11428707)

direct quotes from the geologist's report, appeared on the front page of the May 9, 1914, edition of *The Morning Albertan*. Cheely's article quoted Buck as saying, "I feel just like Christopher Columbus when he discovered America. I would like to stretch my hand across the centuries and shake hands with his venerable bones."[50]

Salting the well was the first step in a grand plan designed to stimulate interest in Black Diamond Oil Fields, increase stock sales, and generate enough revenue to continue drilling operations. With the first part complete, Buck turned his attention to the next steps. But Buck was a schemer and a promoter, not an oil man, and he faced one very real problem—his well did not produce any oil. At most, he had bought himself some time, depending on how the next part of his plan unfolded. Fortunately for Buck, less than a week later, the Dingman well came in and the rising tide lifted all boats—at least for the time being.

5

"A City So Blessed Cannot be Checked:" Oil! . . . Sort of

I want to say that never, in all the years that I have lived in Calgary, and always meeting with reasonable success, have I felt so great a sense of gratitude as I do over the discovery of this great natural resource. It gives us confidence in ourselves, in our city, and in our province at a time when we need it most sorely. You won't know Calgary in two weeks. It will be the livest place in Canada. People will flock into this city from all parts of the continent. Anyone who has not been in an oil boom cannot imagine what wide interest a real strike of oil creates. It brings thousands of people and millions of dollars to the town or city that is fortunate enough to be the centre of activity.

—Oscar G. Devenish
Calgary Morning Albertan
May 16, 1914

The sights up there are simply wonderful and like old days in the western boom camps.... They have turned hair dressing establishments, barber shops, cigar stores and everything else into shops selling oil stock. They have no exchange up there and they use any old place for their dealings. I saw one place where they were selling the stock so fast that they just threw the money and checks into a big basket and when it was full lugged it off to the bank and filled another one.... Those people up there didn't know what they had. They haven't all waked up to it yet. But it is certainly a big thing and beats any excitement we have seen for a long time.

—Duncan D. McGregor
The Montana Record-Herald
June 2, 1914

George Buck and Black Diamond Oil Fields would have been a simple failed venture if not for two things: the prevailing belief among investors that oil and natural gas existed in commercial quantities in Alberta; and the tendency for a rising tide to lift all boats. Initial public reaction to the "discovery" at Black Diamond remained muted, partially because Black Diamond stock remained off the market at Buck's behest. But Buck's instinctive belief that any discovery would stimulate public enthusiasm proved correct. Black Diamond's salvation owed itself to the success of others, namely Archibald Dingman and the Calgary Petroleum Products Company.

The winter of 1913/14 had witnessed significant changes to Calgary Petroleum Products. As early as December 1912, a controversy over the leaseholds Herron sold to the company erupted when Dingman alleged that Herron did not transfer mineral rights to another section of land held by the Canadian Pacific Railway as stipulated in the original deal creating the partnership. Herron claimed that since he never held those rights, they were not his to sell. But in the interest of holding the consortium together, Herron transferred the mineral rights to another section free of charge. Despite attempts to keep the peace, Herron's hard feelings over relegation to the margins of the company by Dingman became mutual when Herron poached William Elder in November 1913 so the two could form their own company, Herron-Elder. Elder's decision to leave CPP temporarily stopped work on Dingman #1 until Dingman brought in Martin Hovis, another driller from Pennsylvania, to replace Elder. While both sides remained relatively tight-lipped regarding the developments, by the spring of 1914 Dingman and the directors sued Herron and his daughter to recover the property or payment of $750,000. Fortunately, the two sides reached a settlement by early April, temporarily putting the matter to rest. When asked about the dispute, Herron referred *The Natural Gas and Oil Record* to Luke 6:2–30 to "find why certain things have come to pass."[1]

Despite the tensions that existed between Herron, Dingman, and the rest of the consortium members, drilling at Calgary Petroleum Products #1 made steady progress under Hovis's watchful eye. By early April, persistent reports of oil showings on drill bits, well cuttings, tools, and equipment appeared in local papers. Ever cautious, Dingman largely confined his remarks to the other directors and steadfastly refused to comment in the press, prompting the *Albertan* to resort to interpreting his body language or seeking comments from those with whom he spoke. Daily updates increased the tension and built public expectations of an imminent discovery. For months, Ira Segur, the managing director of the McDougall-Segur Exploration Company, drew on his considerable experience to remind reporters and investors alike that "the development of an oil field is not accomplished in a moment. It is really a matter of years." With public expectations growing with each passing day, Segur advised, "Possess your soul in patience. An oil well is not made in a day or in a year for that matter. It might be necessary to drill a number of wells before the oil-bearing sands are tapped."[2]

The California oil man knew what he was talking about. Finding oil in the complex formations beneath Turner Valley increasingly loomed as a more expensive proposition than many had first assumed. By March 1914, the *Herald* reported that during a planned trip east to Ontario and Quebec, Ira Segur and E.P. Howard, the company's fiscal agent, planned to negotiate with Standard Oil to sell all or part of its interests in Turner Valley. "Don't be surprised," said the *Herald's* source, "if Standard Oil appears as a competitor of the Canadian Western Natural Gas, Light, Heat & Power company in the Calgary market. Who else could supply the cheapest gas?" Segur remained tight-lipped about the meeting upon his return a few weeks later, but no deal emerged. Jersey Standard sent a representative to gather a sample of the oil for analysis at the company's Buffalo refinery as well as dispatching two geologists to Turner Valley to survey the field. Their reports were mostly negative, and Imperial Oil largely left Turner Valley alone for the next few years. In the meantime, on May 15, the directors struck a committee to "negotiate with any Company which wishes to secure drilling rights to any portion of the property" owned by McDougall-Segur Exploration. This was part of a

Figure 5-1 "Dingman #1 blowing in, Turner Valley, Alberta"
Technically, Dingman #1 produced a wet natural gas that contained naphtha, a kind of unrefined fuel so pure that it could run automobiles of the time unrefined. Dingman #1 continued producing wet gas until 1939 until it was abandoned. (Glenbow Archives CU1554074)

transition of McDougall-Segur Exploration into a holding company that created development subsidiaries when cash permitted. Directors easily raised $1 million from existing shareholders to fund a subsidiary, Segur Oils, to which it transferred the mineral rights of McDougall-Segur #1. Rumours of a buy-out or merger with a larger company with deeper pockets, like Standard Oil, the Canadian Pacific Railway, or the Hudson's Bay Company, increasingly made sense given the depth of wells emerging in Turner Valley. The latter two were both large landholders in western Canada and retained the mineral rights on lands they sold to settlers. P.I. Naismith, the manager of the Resources Department for the Canadian Pacific Railway, explained that Calgary Petroleum Products "are drilling in the heart of a district which is very largely owned by the CPR and who would be materially benefited by any discovery in that field."[3]

Finally, on May 14, 1914, at a depth of 2,718 feet, Dingman #1 struck a strong natural gas pocket flowing at a rate of a million cubic feet per day. A straw-coloured light oil accompanied the gas. Because of the extremely high gas pressure of the field, the well produced a "gusher," sending oil soaring fifteen to twenty feet into the air, making the strike seem much larger than it was. As Archibald Dingman's nephew, Charles, later recounted, the heavy gas pressure coming from the well made it difficult to calculate how much oil the well produced, so the public concocted their own exaggerated figures well above the actual total of ten barrels per day.[4] News of the strike at the Dingman well reached Calgary late Thursday evening and promptly stopped everything as a raucous celebration began. Friday morning, the front page of the *Albertan* bellowed that 1,000 feet of oil lay in the Dingman well by seven p.m. the night before. Bill Cheely's front page story declared the rate of production at 200 barrels per day but claimed the oil's high quality made it equal to a 3,000-barrel well in California.[5]

An emotional William Herron offered his thoughts to the *Herald*:

> I am not a sanctimonious man. I have been anything else but such. But this great strike has caused me to think more seriously than I have ever done before. The Lord has willed it to be so. He could have willed it to be a dry well or a duster. Coming at this critical time in the history of this great western country, I feel that it is given to us for the benefit of His people and the development of the west. I am happy to think that I am the one that was chosen to lead the people in this undertaking. If wealth should come to me out of it, I shall endeavor to deserve it, as I realize that it could be taken away from us just as easily. Think of the condition of Mexico today with her great oil reserves. We have all got something to be thankful for.[6]

In an interview with the *Vancouver Daily World,* Herron went further in his analysis of the significance of the strike, suggesting that his single greatest contribution lay in assisting the development of the province and the Dominion. Indeed, Herron expressed his greatest regret that "so many millions of pounds sterling" from Canada financed development projects in foreign lands when domestic projects in western Canada languished. Despite Alberta's tremendous agricultural possibilities, he predicted that oil would eventually assume pride of place in the province's revenue-producing industries, in part because British investment dollars would freely and unreservedly flow into Alberta. As an ardent imperialist, he hoped the discovery of oil would not only benefit the Dominion of Canada but the whole Empire.[7]

Herron was far from the only one thinking what the strike would mean for Calgary and its future. Oscar Devenish could barely conceal his excitement, declaring, "This looks to me like one of the biggest things in North America. Imagine an oil gusher of pure gasoline, shooting its precious shower up 60 feet into the air. Practically pure gasoline!" Devenish then juxtaposed the Dingman well with the copper deposits in Butte, Montana. To Devenish's mind, there was no comparison. Profits from the hourly output of the Dingman well greatly exceeded the expensive upfront costs and long investment horizons of copper mining. "Calgary has become the center of interest of an excited world," he told *The Calgary News Telegram*. "Be glad you're here." Then, in his capacity as president of the Calgary Industrial Board, Devenish issued a signed statement crediting the well with producing 150–200 barrels per day, generating $20,000 worth of oil per day—roughly equivalent to $600,000 today, adjusted for inflation. The *Herald's* headline writer enthusiastically declared the "oil discovery will mean that problem of unemployment is solved" over a story about poor relief in the city. A banker at the head of a delegation of Canadian and American financiers predicted the end of budget austerity in the province, while an investor from Wisconsin simply "marvelled at the seeming implausibility of it all."[8]

Meanwhile, the *Albertan* cast aside all pretenses of objectivity and launched itself squarely into the role of civic booster for the next few weeks. On May 16, the paper's banner headline declared, "AND THE BEST IS YET TO COME," a quotation culled from a quick statement to the *Albertan* by geologist Cunningham Craig. The paper gave far less prominence to the qualifications Cunningham Craig issued during his statement. While he believed that this proved "beyond a doubt" that there was an oilfield in Alberta, it did not "explain away all our difficulties yet, and this will not happen until a heavier oil has been struck." Observing that the Dingman well produced petroleum condensates, Cunningham Craig noted that it "is a very valuable oil, but it only shows that there is a great body of heavier oil somewhere near." That heavier oil is what he continued to search for, explaining that "a heavier oil refines into more products and has a much wider market." Underneath the statement sat a picture of John D. Rockefeller, Jr., driving horses. "Please note," read the caption, "that it is quite in fashion to drive horses oneself even although one may own a few oil wells and be the proud president of some distinguished branch of the 'I Should Worry association.'"[9] A few days later, the paper predicted that by the end of June "a forest of derricks" would surround the city. "There will be no excuse for any able-bodied man being unemployed, and the money will all flow into Calgary to be put into circulation in this city.

It seems almost too good to be true, but these are cold, hard facts which can be ascertained at the local telegraph offices."[10]

Images and popular depictions of the power of oil to transform the city, province, and region intensified after the Dingman discovery, and Superintendent Ken McNicholl of the Associated Charities likened the discovery to a deliverance. "If the oil strike proves to be what it appears, it will mean a big era of prosperity for Calgary. And we certainly need it." McNicholl revealed that the number of applications for assistance strained the resources of the association because donations to the charity could not keep pace with rising demand from the unemployed. A permanent oil find would bring with it "a general rise in prosperity and I hope a corresponding increase in the donations for the work of the charities." Meanwhile, *The Morning Albertan* asserted that Calgary loomed as one of the wealthiest cities in North America. "It is situated in the centre of a great agricultural and coal country. It is in the midst of the richest petroleum area. It has cheap power and fairly cheap natural gas. It has the best water and the best climate in the world. A city so blessed cannot be checked." *The Calgary News Telegram* celebrated the find as more profitable and permanent than the recent real estate boom. "A gold field at our doors could scarcely be more valuable than an oil field," wrote editor George Thompson. "It may be accepted that the value of oil will increase rather than decrease and that, therefore, if the Alberta field proves as rich as has been predicted, a flow of money will be directed to Calgary that will effectively banish hard times." *The Natural Gas and Oil Record*, on the other hand, noted that the beginning of the boom meant people were not afraid to meet their banker, butcher, or grocer in the street. Last week, they "wouldn't trust you for air" but now eagerly solicited business. The city was now infinitely more confident. "Where there was doubt, there is belief and that is what makes and accomplishes great things."[11]

Themes of returning prosperity and a new dawn brought by the discovery of oil and gas are reflected in the cartoon "The Scarecrow," printed by *The Natural Gas and Oil Record* on May 18, 1914. As the sun rises in a field dotted with oil derricks behind a scarecrow labelled "Calamity Howler," hundreds of birds named "Oil" and "Gas" arrive to feast and pick apart the straw stuffing of the scarecrow.

The Western Standard proved far more pragmatic in its analysis, emphasizing the commercial benefits of increased capital into the city. People could expect rapid growth in the area around the wells. Railroads to and from the oil region would expand to support drilling operations and the transportation of product by building branch lines. A townsite would be constructed in the oil

Figure 5-2 "The Scarecrow"

The arrival of oil and gas in Alberta makes short work of the "Calamity Howler." *The Natural Gas and Oil Record* played a pivotal role in shaping perceptions about what the petroleum industry meant for Alberta's economic future.

district to provide housing for workers and services for the community. "The production of oil must now be regarded as a local industry, as far as Calgary is concerned," declared the *Standard,* destined "to take its place among the ordinary commercial enterprises of this part of the Dominion." Building refineries and training oil workers would virtually banish unemployment in the process. In the meantime, entrepreneurs should rest assured that they enjoyed several layers of protection. *The Western Standard* noted approvingly that the Dominion's Oil and Gas Regulations stipulated that "machinery must be on the ground and drilling started within a year, or the oil lease will be cancelled," and suggested this meant small leaseholders did not need to protect their holdings with a rifle. Institutions and organizations associated with the province, the city police, and "the best business men, who by organizing exchanges which admit the listing of no stock except producing concerns and companies in a bona-fide state of development," protected the interests of the people. Within the next two or three months, the *Standard* predicted that one hundred wells would be working full time. "While there has not yet been such a rush as there was to Bakersfield, in California, where men and women fought their way through the streets, nevertheless the citizens of

Figure 5-3 "The Greatest Magnet in the World—Oil!"
Much as predicted in the above cartoon, the discovery at Turner Valley brought thousands to Calgary hoping to strike it rich.

Calgary have had a wonderful opportunity to study human nature during the excitement."[12]

In an echo of future concerns about the province's petroleum wealth altering the national economy, the financial editor of *The Toronto Daily Star* predicted a transfer of people from Toronto to Calgary. "Unless something breaks pretty soon there'll be an exodus from this town of a lot of people who like to be at the red-hot centre of gamble, no matter what it is." Meanwhile, *The Ottawa Citizen* reported that two former Ottawa residents, George and William Mackie, had struck it rich in Calgary, each earning $1,000. With combined holdings in oil leases valued at $200,000, both men fully expected to earn a million dollars each. *The Natural Gas and Oil Record* reported that so many people were visiting Calgary in the preliminary stages of the boom that all hotels were at capacity. It was difficult to argue with illustrations of "the New Calgary" with vast amounts of money blown in from Turner Valley fields, or depictions of oil as a huge magnet drawing people and investment capital into Calgary.[13]

The Dingman strike unleashed a second, and much larger, wave of investment and speculation. Suddenly, on the morning of May 15, Albertans everywhere were on the move. In Calgary, seemingly every available automobile drove to Turner Valley filled with people determined to see the well for themselves. In Edmonton, over one hundred people bought tickets for the eight a.m. CPR train to Calgary so they could buy oil stock, including

Edmonton's mayor, William McNamara. Nothing trumped the importance of getting in on the boom and buying oil stock. As an intemperate feud escalated between several members of Edmonton's city council and the mayor, McNamara skipped out of the previously scheduled city council meeting to travel to Calgary with his brother to buy oil stocks. The *Edmonton Journal* attributed McNamara's absence to a case of "Oilitiritis," a fever characterized "as a rush of oil to the brain, resulting in an intense disregard for one's regular business, total absent mindedness for the immediate needs of citizens, and a sudden desire to look after one's self." Several outraged city councillors backed a motion to adjourn the meeting until the mayor returned.[14]

Banks estimated that Calgarians and Edmontonians withdrew approximately $2 million (roughly $1 million in each city—$62.6 million combined, adjusted for inflation) from savings accounts in a little over three months to invest in oil stocks. Since Calgary's population totalled about 55,000 in 1914, that meant every man, woman, and child invested an average of $18.20 ($570, adjusted for inflation) in the Turner Valley boom—just less than half the $40.26 average monthly salary of a male Alberta farm labourer and 77 percent of a female farm labourer's average monthly salary of $23.63. Edmonton's population—72,516 in 1914—invested an average of $13.79 per person. Little wonder *Herald* reporter Torchy Anderson concluded that "Calgary took to oil like a wino to the bottle."[15]

Chance played a part in the frenzy. The Dingman well came in on May 14—exactly one day before the 5,800 or so Alberta-based employees of the Canadian Pacific Railway received their monthly paycheques on May 15, injecting approximately $290,700 into the local economy at exactly the moment for speculators to pounce.[16] It is not difficult to imagine a railway worker or two, feeling flush with cash just after payday, being tempted by the promises of easy money and fortune presented by investing in oil. Calgary Petroleum Products stock on the curb went from $12.50 to $200 a share, causing *The Victoria Daily Times* to note that no one was willing to part with CPP stock. "Everybody wants to buy, and the newer companies are the only people who are willing to sell."[17] New companies immediately formed to take advantage as a previously skeptical public lost all inhibitions. Savings accounts emptied as money flooded the city and province from all over Canada and the United States. At the Bank of Montreal on the corner of 8th Avenue and 1st Street SW, a line of people nearly a block long formed waiting to close out their savings accounts. "The teller," recalled Torchy Anderson, "had a waist-high pile of torn up bank-books." In the offices of oil companies, money arrived so fast they had no time to sort it. At least one business crammed bills into wastebaskets and issued grocery-store receipts. Scenes from the frenzy shocked a visitor from Vancouver. "People are literally standing in the streets and throwing their money into the brokers' offices for oil shares. They cannot get them rapidly enough." Stock vendors sold shares on the street stands while other brokers, overwhelmed by orders, locked the doors to their offices. "Determined investors," recounted an unofficial history of the Calgary Stock Exchange, "shouted instructions through keyholes and threw cash over the door transoms."[18]

Claude Dingman recounted the scene years later:

> Daily the city soon filled with an excited throng, some having legitimate intentions, others ready to "fly-by-night." Printers came in for a rush of business, with an hourly demand for prospectuses, detailing beautiful pictures of "Black Gold" for the asking. Thousands of stock certificates were madly written out, even into the far hours of the night. The land office almost became the scene of a "stampede." Outside and inside excited ones jostled for first position in the line up of buyers of prospective oil lands. But in the main offices of the new oil companies the action was at once wonderful and absurd. The buyers of stock, almost frantic, threw their money over the counter, into any handy box or desk, and even the sight of large bills overflowing into the waste-baskets did not halt the scramble. Some frenzied ones hadn't time to wait on receipts, but ran off rejoicing, and into the melee next door for another chance at wealth. In the blocks with one, two and three stories, elevators were scorned as too slow. Stairways became a seething mass of rushing humanity, with the best speed artists the first served.[19]

In short order, outside capital made its presence felt. Communication and transportation technology—railroads, telegraph, wireless, and telephone—spread the word of the strike and rapidly extended the pool of investors to the rest of Canada and the United States. *The Globe* in Toronto ran a front-page story on May 16 about the Discovery Well (the renamed Dingman #1) and noted the crush of investors seeking oil company stock. The Boston-based *Christian Science Monitor* ran its first story on Dingman's well on May 18 and two days later *The Manchester Guardian* followed suit. Within a week, the *Herald* remarked that every train arriving in the city brought "crowds of people" eager to invest before noting that "money is pouring in from all parts of Canada, the United States and Great Britain like water." Less than a

Figure 5-4 "Investors waiting to buy oil stocks in Calgary, Alberta"
May 15, 1914, one day after Calgary Petroleum Products came in, was the payday for Canadian Pacific Railway's employees and injected approximately $290,700 into the local economy. In less than a two-minute walk from the train station crowds gather outside 801 1st Street SW to buy oil stock while a lone police constable stands in the doorway to control the crowd. (Glenbow Archive CU1149999)

week later, *The Morning Albertan* reported that moneyed elites from Spokane, Washington, made the trip north and claimed "at least fifty men of wealth have floated into the city for the purpose of getting in on the oil game when the getting is good and easy."[20] One man from Tacoma, A.J. La Mar, glumly told the *Tacoma News-Tribune* that Americans were already too late to capitalize on the boom. "When I left Calgary oil claims were taken for 100 miles in all directions. Filing began a year ago," said La Mar a few days after the Dingman strike. "Those who expect to make money in the Calgary oil fields will have to take plenty of it with them."[21]

As the first week of the boom ended, arguably the most influential Calgarian had yet to weigh in on the Dingman strike. Thus, it was no trivial matter that Bob Edwards set aside his caustic humour to deliver an unequivocal statement on May 23 proclaiming the discovery of "the greatest oil field in the world." Edwards raved that the well produced nearly pure gasoline and 2 million cubic feet per day of natural gas. Only two other wells in existence, wrote Edwards, could boast such production. "One is a restricted district in

Figure 5-5 "Investors waiting to buy oil stocks, Calgary, Alberta"
Investors gather outside Acme Oil's head office—216 8th Avenue SW – less than a three-minute walk from the CPR station on 9th Avenue SW. (Glenbow Archive CU1554077)

West Virginia. The other is on the steppes of Russia." Edwards also provided his personal assurance that

> there is nothing fakey, bogus or speculative about this sensational oil discovery. Thousands of visitors have been out to the Dingman to see for themselves. Last Sunday they were treated to the sight of two gushers which each gushed in a most obliging manner for a few minutes for the benefit of the onlookers, one of our genial alderman being drenched with the stuff because he failed to get out of range in time.... This oil search which has been so earnestly pursued for the past five years on the advice of world-renowned experts like Cunningham Craig, has passed the speculative stage and is now right here gushing up out of the ground.[22]

New oil companies, brokerage firms, and stock exchanges sprouted like mushrooms as investors scrambled to make their fortune. Depending on the criteria used, an estimated 500 oil companies formed, thirteen stock exchanges were chartered, and easily over 1,000 brokers appeared to buy and sell oil and gas stocks. Most of the brokers were former real estate agents who fell on hard times when the Calgary housing boom collapsed in 1913. Other companies and agents branched into oil after providing other services, financial or otherwise, to customers. Future *Albertan* reporter Fred Kennedy, a teenager whose family arrived in Calgary two years earlier, sold stocks out of his newspaper bag in the lobby of the Palliser hotel.[23]

The boom quickly transformed the city's skyline. As the *Vancouver Daily World* noted, "the buildings were not higher, but brilliantly colored signs of all sizes, shapes and cuts appeared on the tops of the stores and hotels announcing to the passing public below the quantities and the merits of respective oil concerns and companies who had their offices on the streets beneath," causing people to mill about "like cattle in a roundup." A reporter from Spokane wrote that downtown Calgary "is literally covered with 'Oil Stock for Sale' signs as far out as I have been able to walk, every hole in the wall being occupied by a broker or a promoter." Even the smallest location came at exorbitant cost. "Brokers are asked $200 per month for offices about 10x12 feet, and I understand they are paying $20 to $40 per day for little stands in some hotel lobbies." Meanwhile, *The Toronto Daily Star* reported the Redcliff brokers jumped at the opportunity to secure a small brick-and-tile office not yet constructed out of the back of the Alberta Hotel and began working out of the space for rent at $40 a day.[24]

The Morning Albertan predicted that by August, Turner Valley would have one hundred drilling plants operating in the Calgary district. "One hundred rigs means more than 100 wells," gushed the paper. "It means several hundred and several hundred wells in this particular district may astound the world and make of Calgary the great oil metropolis of the British nation."[25] Meanwhile, *The Financial Post* quoted at length a private letter to the president of the Imperial Bank in Toronto dated May 20, 1914, noting that "small depositors of every kind are drawing their money out of the savings bank and buying scrip. I am informed that yesterday there were 350 such withdrawals from one leading bank alone. There is also a lot of money coming in by telegraph, etc., for investment in the oil stock." The paper advised "investors to keep their money in their pockets. As yet the whole thing is a gamble and there is as great a probability of as much money being spent in searching for oil as will be obtained from the sale of oil discovered."[26]

Orders for stock certificates flooded every printing establishment in the city, resulting in a shortage of printer's stock. *The Western Oil Examiner* concluded decades later that no one really understood what they were doing; they simply joined in the excitement. "Few of the hundreds of promotions that followed the Dingman well had a dog's chance of success. Fewer promotions would have passed an examination of even the village half-wits." Investors simply believed "somehow things would work out and everybody would wind up rich." Behind the psychology of the boom lay a belief that Alberta now possessed global significance. On May 23, the banner headline in the *Vancouver Daily World* declared Turner Valley the "largest oil area in the world" and presented the statements of Malcolm E. Davis of the Alliance Investment Company at face value when he proclaimed, "There is not the slightest doubt that we have tapped one of the largest areas of oil yet discovered." Davis's enthusiasm minimized the risks of investment, practically guaranteeing that everyone who invested would profit. While Davis conceded some wells would be better situated, he crowed, "Every well driven will be a revenue producer and a dividend payer if handled properly by promoters."[27]

Interviews like the one given by Davis exerted tremendous influence on potential investors in Calgary and beyond, as one Chicago newspaper reported that twenty-one Calgarians became millionaires in less than twenty-one days.[28] Few escaped the omnipresent boom. Out-of-town visitors saw men on the sidewalks adorned with signs and advertisements selling shares in oil companies while autos, drays, wagons, taxicabs, and bicycles streaming with banners, placards, and advertisements clogged the roads.[29] The front page of *the Albertan* told the story of a seven-year-old boy who, having sold a copy of the newspaper, went to invest the nickel he earned in oil stocks only to be told that shares only sold in blocks of one hundred. "Tears and sobs rent the small frame as [the nickel] was disconsolately withdrawn." But the boy's tears caught the attention of an older man, Member of the Legislative Assembly R.E. Campbell, who asked the lad what was wrong. "A little sympathy soon drew the cause of woe from the quivering lips of the youthful investor, a brive [sic] five-dollar bill from Mr. Campbell's pocket restored hope, sparkles, and beaming joy." The punchline came with a wallop—"before night those shares had doubled and the youth was wealthy."[30]

Everywhere, people dreamed of striking it rich. "Men went here and men went there," noted one reporter. "Buying, selling, millionaires, masons, street sweepers and society women mingled in one vast throne, buying oil, selling oil, rebuying and reselling their shares."[31] Every train that arrived brought new investors and the city positively hummed. "Business went on with never a stop," concluded one reporter. "Everybody was making fortunes or had made them or was about to make them."[32] A story circulated that one woman

Figure 5-6 "Investors waiting to buy oil and gas stocks outside Huron and Bruce Oil and Gas Company, Calgary, Alberta"

Huron and Bruce was one of many companies formed in late 1913 that waited until May 1914 to begin operations. At the corner of 7th Avenue and Centre Street, investors and a dog wait for their opportunity to buy stock at $10 a share. (Glenbow Archive CU1145708)

arrived in Calgary by train and entered the station where some were selling stocks. She pressed money into the hands of a man she presumably thought was a broker and said she wanted to buy oil stock. When the "broker," who was a visiting railroad inspector from Winnipeg, asked which one, the lady replied that she did not care, she just wanted to buy some stock. Less than a week after the Dingman strike, British-Canadian Oils hired twenty staff members to take money and issue receipts for its initial offering of stock at five cents per share. The company collected three baskets of bank notes and checks based solely on possessing mineral rights around the anticline. One brokerage firm operating out of the lobby of a Calgary hotel averaged sales of $3,000–5,000 per day ($90,550–$130,000, adjusted for inflation).[33] *The Vancouver Sun* reported that Calgary streetcar employees "assigned their salaries for July, August, and September to enable them to purchase more stock."[34]

Calgary bank clearings offer one way of measuring the impact of the boom on the local economy. They provide a snapshot of economic activity, including the volume and frequency of transactions; they suggest how well banks and businesses manage their cash flow; and they provide an indication of overall business confidence. In the first four months of 1914, Calgary's monthly bank clearings reflected the grim reality of the ongoing depression, sitting at an average 23 percent per month lower than over the same period in 1913. Modest improvement took place in the first two weeks of May before the Dingman strike on May 14, but bank clearings were down approximately 14.9 percent over the year before. After the Dingman strike, the sudden crush of investments abruptly reversed the downward trend as clearings matched and soon exceeded reported clearings, pulling even with 1913 totals and, in certain instances, surpassing them. The difference between Calgary and other western cities was so striking it prompted *The National Post* to remark on July 4 when clearings increased by nearly 38 percent that, to a certain extent, "the experience of Calgary has saved the West during the last week of the half year from a somewhat phenomenal contraction in the returns of clearing houses."[35]

Newfound prosperity looked different for different sectors. Newspapers did brisk business, generating advertising revenue and selling papers swollen by advertisements. One issue of the *Herald* held 170 columns of oil ads, prompting *The Toronto Daily Star's* declaration that "the boom is making the newspaper proprietors rich, anyway."[36] The *Albertan* grew from an average of twelve pages to a peak of twenty-six. The *News Telegram* ballooned from an average twenty pages to forty-two. On May 23, *The Morning Albertan* announced a steep rate increase to one dollar per inch of space to advertisers without a contract. "That is a considerable increase over present rates," conceded the paper, "but the unprecedented demand and additional expenses makes it necessary." All of it traced back to the demand created by the oil boom. Oil companies insisted on taking exceptionally large space to make announcements, placing inflationary pressure on newsprint and ink. Meanwhile, the number of printers in the city remained limited, and many of those were now busy printing ornate stock certificates as well, forcing many to work overtime. As the crush of people arriving in the city increased, the city's hospitality sector began to boom as well. "Eating houses are crossing off the reduced prices on the menu cards—signs of the hard times that were, till very recently—and are not only boosting their wares to the original prices of a year or so ago, but in many instances are adding just a little bit more." Many were devoting all their time to oil and stopped going home for lunch or dinner, increasing foot traffic at local eateries. Hotels and rooming houses filled, and several had to turn guests away. Calgary's new Palliser Hotel opened earlier than expected to capitalize on the crush of business. Shops

Table 5-1 Calgary Bank Clearings, Selected Months and Weeks, 1913 & 1914

	1914	1913	% CHANGE OVER PREVIOUS YEAR
January	$16,293,215	$21,680,990	-24.9
February	$12,930,884	$18,680,004	-30.8
March	$14,431,284	$18,072,245	-20.1
April	$16,767,487	$20,116,753	-16.6
Week Ending			
May 8	$3,887,253	$4,566,868	-14.9
May 15	$3,481,008	$4,088,261	-14.9
May 22	$4,809,655	$4,837,229	-0.6
May 30	$4,768,434	$4,837,229	-1.4
June 5	$4,487,120	$4,500,326	-0.3
June 11	$5,648,026	$4,927,770	14.6
June 18	$4,572,030	$4,894,413	-6.6
June 26	$4,424,650	$5,755,055	-23.1
July 3	$5,441,428	$3,944,808	37.9
July 10	$5,711,343	$4,887,946	16.9
July 17	$4,872,429	$4,185,694	16.4
July 24	$4,758,625	$4,363,386	9.1
July 31	$3,783,325	$4,075,447	-7.4
August 7	$4,392,042	$5,063,137	-13.3
August 14	$4,214,989	$3,978,022	6.0
August 21	$3,363,926	$4,361,581	-22.9

Data adapted from *The Calgary Herald* and *The National Post*. Various dates.

reported increased demand for office furniture, and retailers were especially eager to serve budding entrepreneurs. An advertisement for the Calgary Furniture Shop on May 16 announced the store had received a shipment of "office equipment for oil barons and others," consisting of a variety of finished mahogany rolltop desks, arm and side chairs, and typewriter stands. "They have real money, these oil promoters," noted one salesman.[37]

Not surprisingly, themes of rugged individualism and the triumph of the "common people" over "the big interests" became common in the spring and

Figure 5-7 "Calgary Restaurant"

The sudden crush of investors and speculators generated local benefits but also created a bifurcated economy. The restaurant and hospitality sectors, for example, saw the opportunity to return prices to pre-1913 levels. However, the entertainment sector found itself resorting to gimmicks, like offering shares in oil companies with the purchase of a ticket to attract customers. (University of Calgary Libraries and Cultural Resources CU1302322)

early summer of 1914. Acme Oil billed itself as a small, plucky company with big ambitions that gave opportunity to small investors to enjoy life instead of toiling for someone else. The clear message is that investing in Calgary's oil boom was much more egalitarian in scope. The theme was repeated in the cartoon "The Small Investor Gets the Best Chance," published by *The Natural Gas and Oil Record* in May 1914. The cartoon's striking optimism projects the belief that Turner Valley was not quite an investment as much as it was a treasure hunt for untold riches.[38]

The discovery at Turner Valley was more than a local event. It quickly ignited a regional discussion about the potential for oil to transform the economy of western Canada and raised the question of whether Alberta oil should serve national or regional markets. This would prove a crucial debate given the future of the Canadian petroleum industry. *The Natural Gas and Oil Record* called for the construction of pipelines to the Pacific Ocean and the

Figure 5-8 "The Small Investor gets Best Chance"
As many hoped in the winter of 1913/14, local and small investors provided the bulk of investment capital for the 1914 boom. Of the estimated $4 million invested in the Alberta oil fields in 1914, Calgarians and Edmontonians provided roughly half of the capital.

Great Lakes. The frenzied search for oil leases expanded well beyond Turner Valley to cover the entire province. A syndicate, rumoured to consist of capital from Winnipeg and New York, acquired oil leases on two whole townships southeast of Lethbridge and eighteen to thirty miles east of Coutts on the international boundary along the Grand Trunk Pacific Railway. The town council of Macleod considered spending $30,000 to drill for oil before deciding to hold a public hearing on the issue. Meanwhile, in Red Deer in central Alberta, speculators acquired $35,000 worth of oil leases in a single week and incorporated the Red Deer Oil and Gas Company. In Edmonton, an ad for Nakamun Asphalt and Oil Company in the *Edmonton Journal* invoked the expertise of Cunningham Craig and promised readers its holdings contained similar prospects to those at the Dingman well, urging Edmontonians to invest in prospects around central Alberta. Speculators and prominent business leaders filed petroleum rights on 200,000 acres of land around Edmonton and dozens of new oil companies formed in under three days. Other companies, like the Athabasca Petroleum Company, emphasized their holdings in the Athabasca region and its immense oil sands deposits in northern Alberta and predicted that "unlimited capital will now flood Western Canada for oil development."[39]

While "oil fever" in the wake of Dingman extended north to Red Deer and the Olds region, where Monarch Oils drilled, the *Red Deer Advocate* sounded much more cautious regarding oil prospects than even the *Herald* dared. One participant, whom the paper labelled "an interested party," observed that "it costs about $40,000.00 to drill 3,000 feet and you have to get your drillers from the Pittsburgh region as the Western Ontario men have no equipment to go as deep as they would likely have to go here." Potential investors needed to exercise great patience to ensure investments remained in the province and did not go elsewhere. Another interviewee, described as "a citizen of wide travel and extensive experience," lamented the number of "fools" who "launch out their hard-earned savings to line the pockets of these easy money sharks." Observing that Canada's former Governor General, Earl Grey, had recently bought one of the largest companies in California for British investors, the *Advocate* compared the two investments and found Canadian prospects much bleaker. Investing in Dingman for $200 a share yielded a well producing wet gas and condensates. On the other hand, Grey bought so much more in California because included in the sale was all its "wells, equipment, and connections—a tried, going concern which has paid dividends for years." The point was that the nascent Alberta oil patch faced a long, daunting road ahead that the *Advocate* systematically began to detail.

> Where on earth is the market for these scores of wells projected? California oil will meet it at Vancouver from its pipelines to tidewater and the Standard Oil Company product will meet it at Winnipeg. Who owns the storage tanks, the oil cars, the whole transhipment equipment of oil and gasoline through the country? Not the railways, but the Standard Oil Company and its branches. These people who talk of big money in oil stocks either buy to unload on poor dupes or else they are absolutely ignorant of commercial conditions in oil. We have oil in Alberta, it is a good commercial proposition for a limited

amount of capital and a limited number of people increasing as population grows, beyond that there is nothing to it.[40]

Elsewhere on the prairies, the oil boom in Alberta drew attention to the scarcity of oil supplies and the importance of diversifying energy sources. One independent oil company in Saskatoon, the Hartford Oil Corporation, urged investors to think of a future without oil to recognize the significance of developments in Alberta. The company took out a full-page ad focused on the sustainability of future oil supplies, anticipating future conversations about "peak oil," and the ability of Standard Oil to continue to supply refined crude products to consumers. In a cry that resonates to the start of the twenty-first century, the corporation bluntly stated that recent developments proved "It's A Case of Alberta to the Rescue."[41]

By July 1914, *The Vancouver Sun* estimated the aggregate capital of the independent oil companies operating in Alberta at half a billion dollars. Considering the sums of money involved, the west coast newspaper offered the most thorough analysis of how oil could transform the economy of western Canada and make Calgary the core of a hinterland region that extended to the west coast. In an extended essay the *Sun* compared the economic potential of Turner Valley to the California gold rush of 1849. That gold rush proved vital to launching the regional economy with spin-off industries in timber and agriculture. What made oil different from gold, argued the paper, was that it is not just a mineral but an energy source capable of producing immense wealth. With a wellhead price of seventy cents per barrel, the value of California crude produced over the past thirty years, argued the *Sun*, is worth more than the combined output of gold, silver, lead, copper, and citrus crops of the state over the same period. Readers could only dream about the possibilities created by Alberta oil worth several dollars per barrel, and there were plenty of customers waiting by. More than 5,000 factories operated in southern California alone, and while the area around San Francisco had fewer, they were not insignificant. Oil powered all these factories operating along the west coast, as well as fuelling the trains and merchant ships transporting passengers, raw materials, and finished products from San Diego to Vancouver Island. The fact that petroleum consumption vastly exceeded production in recent decades made the Turner Valley discovery even more significant, argued the *Sun*. So too did oil's strategic dimension as the fuel of choice for the ships of the Royal Navy. Britain's coal deposits had enabled the Royal Navy to control maritime trade routes and maintain its empire in the nineteenth century, and perhaps Canadian oil would do the same in the twentieth. Even if peace prevailed, modern petroleum refineries produced thousands of petroleum-based products, from dyes, soap, and candles to chewing gum, cough syrups, and cosmetics. High-grade oil, like the naphtha produced by the Dingman well, could fuel the booming automobile industry. California's oil fields had been flowing for thirty years; although it remained early days—the Dingman well had only begun producing five days earlier—how much oil was there and how long would it last? Based only on known seepages and surface showings, the best geological minds speculated that the Alberta oil fields extended along both sides of the Rockies into British Columbia. Perhaps western Canadian oilfields extended from Peace River in the north to Wyoming and Colorado in the south. Setting that matter aside for the moment, if British Columbia and Alberta developed an oil field a quarter the size of that in California, the article speculated the oil industry would mean more to Canada than it did to California. Thousands of well-paying jobs in related sectors, like transportation and refining, as well as jobs in spin-off industries and support industries—coal, steel, and manufacturing—would relocate to western Canada to support the petroleum industry. The vision of the future was transformative and breathtaking. "If Alberta and British Columbia can produce even a considerable portion of what many of the best mining engineers expect, there will be built up a business that will dwarf the lumber business and will nearly rival the production of wheat in the provinces further east. It will open up industry after industry that will call for the investment of capital from all over the world."[42]

Outside investors from Britain and portions of the United States, however, proved more cautious and skeptical than Calgarians about the implications of Dingman's find and the permanency of the boom. A story filed by the Canadian Associated Press on May 22 noted that London investors and financial advisers were "not yet aroused" by the Turner Valley strike. British investors were prepared to wait for further discoveries before committing their investment capital. More discouragingly for Alberta promoters, the only brokerage firm selling shares in Alberta oil found its offering "roundly condemned by every authority who thought it worth while to refer to it at all." Meanwhile, after describing the broad contours of the Calgary "boom," including a description of Calgary Petroleum Products stock reaching $200 per share, the Edinburgh *Scotsman* dumped a bucket of cold water on expectations with the blunt conclusion that "it is doubtful whether the discoveries justify the excitement, and it is probable that something like normal conditions will soon be restored." The London-based *Financial Times* delivered the cruellest cut of all on May 27 when it declared Throgmorton Street—home to the London Stock Exchange and the Bank of England—had already made up its mind to discourage attempts by Calgary-based oil companies to raise capital in Britain until its value could be "more convincingly established." The *Financial Times* strongly urged potential investors "to analyze with exceptional care any prospectus which may come into their hands hereafter in connection with the mineral deposits of Calgary."[43]

Eastern Canadian newspapers were no less sceptical. By far, *The Toronto Daily Star* proved the newspaper most critical of the boom, fearing rampant speculation would undermine the industry. On May 30, the *Star* published a haunting cartoon entitled "The Flame and the Moth" depicting a smouldering candle labelled "Calgary Oil" surrounded by hundreds of scorched moths. The accompanying caption read "An Old Story About to be Retold."[44] A few weeks later, on June 16, the *Star* ran a very critical piece about the Calgary boom based on the observations of Toronto-based stockbroker R.T. Kemerer. Kemerer visited Calgary immediately following the Dingman discovery with hopes of finding a good investment for his firm. Unlike most critics who still expressed caution because the field remained unproven, Kemerer called Turner Valley a "good oil field." Rather, Kemerer identified structural shortcomings in Alberta's regulatory framework and oversight that he believed precluded investors from realizing any return on their investment. According to Kemerer, problems began with the size of leases that enabled promoters to tie up large swaths of land at cheap prices. Furthermore, even if he found a good prospect to file a claim on, Kemerer noted that the long line-ups of promoters and speculators outside the Dominion Land Office created opportunities for budding entrepreneurs—especially those who joined the queue with the intention of selling their place once it became clear that the Dominion Land Office typically served ten people per day. "Had I had anything to file and been content to await my turn," said Kemerer, "I would have had to wait months." People sold their spots in line for up to $1,000 in late May, but prices fell to $300 just before Kemerer left in early June. Other issues abounded. Despite the opening of the Calgary Stock Exchange, the bulk of the trading in oil shares took place outside the exchanges, either on the curb or in the numerous brokerage offices or uncharted exchanges. While the CSE projected the image of stability and propriety, the reality remained that it handled barely a fraction of the transactions; multiple exchanges operated in the city, but curb brokers and bucket shops handled most trades. Beyond that, the formation of hundreds of companies presented the image of a robust, competitive market that would quickly prove the field, but Kemerer believed scant few were worthwhile investments. The bulk of companies were ones "in which the shareholder has absolutely no chance at all" due to a lack of capital, experience, or will. Perhaps more explicitly than any analyst since the *Herald's* Flotations series, Kemerer demolished the belief that an independent oil boom carried out by small, independent oil companies would strike oil let alone generate a profit for investors. Some prospectuses revealed companies reserving as little as 10 percent of their capital for treasury while promoters received 90 percent up front. According to Kemerer's calculations, companies with less than $35,000 in their treasuries were doomed to failure. "Such amounts of money are useless," argued Kemerer, "as it costs at least $35,000 to put a well down to where the oil is supposed to be." Every indication suggested that the oil in Turner Valley lay below 2,000 feet, and with drilling companies charging an average price of fifteen dollars per foot, companies with less than $35,000 in the treasury ran extraordinary risks. Pointing squarely at the Dingman, where Calgary Petroleum Products had spent approximately $60,000 to date, and McDougall-Segur had spent $70,000 drilling the deepest hole in the field, Kemerer concluded western wildcatters held every advantage over eastern investors.[45]

The *Star* was only one eastern publication casting doubt on the Alberta boom. *The Financial Post* cautioned investors about the "insane orgy" taking place in Alberta. "The regrettable part of the oil boom is that the losers will be recruited very largely from the ranks of those who can least afford to lose their scant savings." *The Canadian Mining Journal,* also based out of Toronto, added its voice to the growing criticism by pointing to the paucity of information about the oil field and the foolishness of investors throwing away their money by falling for cheap sales tricks used in real estate. "The very uncertainty is the salesman's most valuable asset," said the *Journal.* "And if one feature stands out more vividly than any other it is the Western salesman's imagination concerning future possibilities."[46] *The Montreal Gazette* cautioned readers to be skeptical of production reports coming from the province. While noting that some companies anticipated development of "pumping" wells, none were yet on stream. Investors had to remember that pumper wells "can produce much, but it comes slowly and gives a moderate profit. Those who will soon be asked to buy stocks issued on a gusher basis will do well to know the information now given."[47]

Like many others in the oil patch, a well-known driller from Midway, California, H.H. Henshaw, made his way to Calgary in June 1914 and reached mixed conclusions. In a letter written to the *Coalinga Oil Record* on dated June 17, 1914, and published in full by *The Natural Gas and Oil Record* a month later, Henshaw offers a slightly different perspective on the Turner

Figure 5-9
"The Flame and the Moth"

Contrary to the optimism in Calgary, the *Toronto Star*, took a decidedly more pessimistic view of Calgary's oil boom. The caption accompanying this cartoon read, "An old story about to be retold." The original cartoon was published upside down in the paper making it harder to determine what was being pictured.

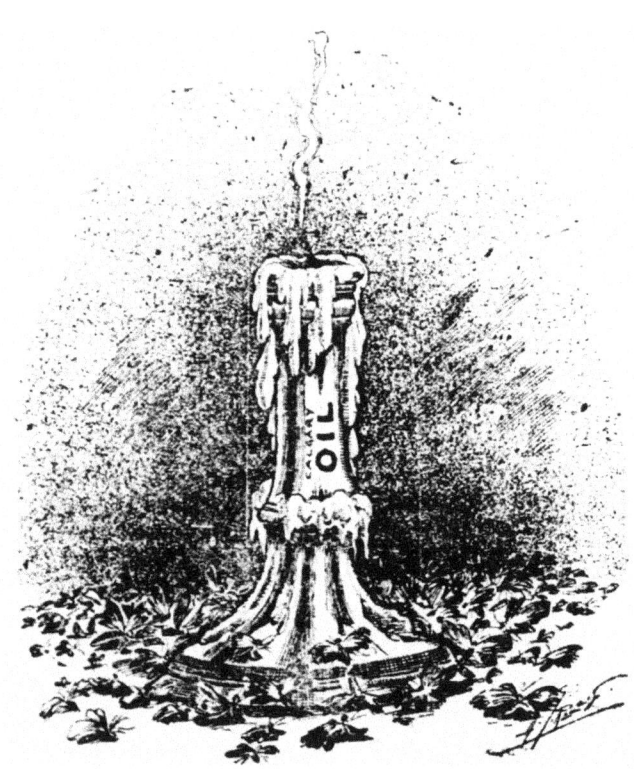

Valley boom. While he "found a very pretty city with lots of activity and prices for all commodities very high," he noted that the oil boom "is practically all over." Virtually all the development was going on with local money and "the Dingman well that caused all the excitement is not on the pump yet, so it is impossible to state what it will make." In stark contrast to local boosters who touted the Dingman as producing a high grade of crude, Henshaw dismissed it as "a poor grade of coal oil." Henshaw also noted that American oil field workers might encounter difficulties crossing the border to find work in Canada. "The American is handicapped about 50 percent here as the Canadian is afraid of him, and it seems as though they are going to force all operators to use their union men so the chances are not going to be so bright for the boys coming here from the states," noting that he saw "several fellows turned back" because customs officers "were cautious about having the country overrun with common laborers. Several of the boys here told us that they had some little trouble getting through, but we experienced none whatever; the inspectors probably took us for capitalists." Regardless,

Henshaw marvelled at the conditions, declaring "this is a fine place for the working man indeed; it is daylight at 3 am and don't get dark until 10:30 p.m. so he has a good chance to get in a full day." In closing his letter, Henshaw advised "the boys" to make sure "they have something in sight before they come, as the best they will get on the ground is second consideration from the Canadians."[48]

Despite Henshaw's pessimism about prospects for American roughnecks in the boom, William Cheely concluded almost the exact opposite in a piece published in the *Spokane Spokesman-Review* on May 31, 1914. After describing the investments made by Albertans, Cheely singled out the prominent role played by US capital investment from California and Washington, such that "one might well come to the conclusion that [Calgary] was a Pacific coast town in the states." Financiers from Spokane negotiated the merger of several companies that would control half a million acres of land. Drilling manufacturers from the both the eastern and western United States busily filled a flood of orders for oil well drilling equipment and machinery.[49] Washington-based Flathead Petroleum Company sold stock to Spokane investors after acquiring an interest in 10,580 acres of leases in the Sweetgrass district near the international boundary. After returning from a week-long inspection of the Alberta fields and securing mineral rights on 2,000 acres, A.G. Hanauer of the Hanauer-Graves Investment company declared to the *Spokesman-Review*, "I regard this as the opportunity of a lifetime for investors. There is an element of risk, of course, but the extent of the district, as outlined by a number of competent experts, materially reduces the chances of loss, so far as investing in legitimate companies is concerned."[50]

Indeed, Spokane newspapers reported on a constant stream of financiers and investors travelling to Calgary and reporting favourable conditions and investment opportunities. As it was the largest and closest US city to Calgary and counted an estimated twenty-six millionaires among its population of 105,000 citizens, mostly from mining investments in silver, lead, and zinc, attracting investment capital from Spokane was critical to the success of the oil boom. US investment capital only became more significant when the outbreak of the Great War in August 1914 removed European capital from world markets. An ad published in the Waterloo (Iowa) *Courier and Reporter* depicted Canada as a welcoming woman to American businesses and reminded readers that "Canada has always 'made good' with the US investor" and would do so again with Calgary oil. Referencing common values and institutions between the two countries, it suggested Calgary oil was a safe investment. The "rigorous" laws of Canada, and the Canadian government, ensure "that every man gets a square deal . . . investments are made by rich or poor with a double sense of security in the development of such legitimate enterprises as this great oil district."[51]

Perhaps because of frustration at the reluctance of British capital to commit, comments like those of the *Toronto Star* and the *Canadian Mining Journal,* and lingering resentment that the province's natural resources remained under federal control, an undercurrent of resentment, leavened by hubris, occasionally erupted in the West. While the Dingman discovery gave hope to those who believed in Alberta's natural resources, it also provided the occasion to revisit past slights, settle old scores, and advance the narrative of bootstrap individualism and entrepreneurialism that made Alberta, and the West, unique. A fair reading of the *Star's* coverage of the boom shows that the paper took its lead from Cunningham Craig—cautious optimism about the prospects but awaiting further proof before fully endorsing Turner Valley's oil-producing status, and concerned that rampant speculation would do more harm than good. This, however, opened the Toronto daily to criticism from *The Calgary News Telegram* for its lack of enthusiasm. In the *Star's* reaction to the Dingman discovery, said the *News Telegram,* "the most auspicious announcement that has ever come out of Western Canada is passed over as if it were but an everyday occurrence." The *Star's* editorial page categorically rejected the characterization, replying that both the press and people of Ontario were hopefully expectant. "It is hoped that there will be plenty of oil," responded the *Star,* "because there is little doubt that there will be plenty of boom." On the contrary, argued the *Star,* the *News Telegram* mistook criticism for jealousy. Ontarians were not upset that Calgary might become an oil producer but did object mightily to the swindlers who were deceiving investors. "In matters of that kind people like to do a little careful discriminating."[52]

Newspapers were far from the only institutions taking note of eastern Canada's reaction. The Athabasca Petroleum Company used space in one of its ads to chastise the "detractors and doubters of Canada's potential oil wealth." It also claimed armchair critics and sceptics alike now sat silenced and discredited by developers with the "courage, enterprise and foresight to carry on their operations in the face of active antagonism." Prior to *The Regina Leader's* decision on June 1, 1914, to ban all advertisements for Calgary oil, Frank L. Runions, a broker in Regina selling stock in Alberta oils, took out a three-quarter-page ad in the paper boldly declaring, "We told you so!" in two-inch-tall letters and surrounded by excerpts from telegrams describing the Dingman discovery in vivid detail.[53]

It is fair to wonder why Albertans generally, and Calgarians in particular, seemed so thin-skinned on this issue. Pride—in the community, city, province, and industry—played a large part in the visceral reaction to outside critics. Equally important, however, was that for all the talk about creating a self-sustaining and independent oil boom, within a week of its beginning, local capital was already committed and Calgarians were already largely tapped out. On May 20, just shy of a week after the Dingman strike, the *Herald* reported that bankers in the city believed their clients' cash would soon run out if it had not already done so. The clear implication was that the boom could only be sustained by attracting outside capital. Attention therefore fixed on investors outside the province—from Toronto and Montreal—as well as from California and the Pacific northwest.[54]

In the meantime, the frenzy of investment convinced even the *Albertan* of the need to impose some kind of order on stock sales, including the need to establish transparency in prices. The *Albertan* noted that prices charged by brokers for the same stock could vary by as much as 30 percent between brokers operating within a block of one another. The paper was much relieved when the Calgary Stock Exchange held its first organizational meeting on May 25. Chartered the previous October, the CSE appointed lawyer Edmond Taylor as the chairman of the board of directors, with Oscar G. Devenish and A.P. Strong as vice chairs. The meeting also approved the CSE's bylaws and formalized the amalgamation of the CSE and the Calgary Oil Exchange, the largest of the independent exchanges in the city. It quickly became clear that Calgary's elites intended the CSE to rein in some of the worst excesses of the industry, especially attempts at price manipulation and wildcatting. They hoped the CSE would push brokers off the streets into the curated confines of the stock exchange, where rules and regulations guided the conduct of both companies and brokers. Perhaps not so coincidentally, enacting these rudimentary practices might also forestall government intervention to protect consumers. "This step," noted the *Albertan* approvingly, "is one of the utmost importance to all concerned in the oil business." Initially, the CSE fixed the number of seats at forty and charged a $500 fee for each, but demand required them to increase it to 100 seats by June 19. To keep the floor from being too chaotic, and to keep a close eye on the brokers, the board granted one seat to every firm or individual broker on the exchange. The CSE required brokers to post a $5,000 guaranteed bond in addition to a $200 annual fee and forbade brokers belonging to the CSE from trading on any other exchange. The exchange reserved the right to approve companies and required a $500 listing fee before listing a new company on the exchange. To eliminate outright flotations, and partially to offer some protection to consumers, the CSE forbade the listing of companies still organizing. Bylaws established a twenty-four-hour window to settle all local transactions, seven days outside the city, and London delivery was offered for sales in England. A schedule of fees adopted wholesale from the Vancouver Stock Exchange established a minimum commission of one dollar but also approved a variable commission schedule based on the sale price of the share. For example, stocks sold for up to five cents per share netted a commission of 1/8 of a cent per share while charging a 1 percent commission for shares over one hundred dollars.[55]

While the CSE trumpeted its provincial charter as evidence of the fundamental soundness of its venture, the lack of a provincial charter did not inhibit others from forming their own stock exchanges, reflecting the overall weakness of the regulatory structure and the province's infatuation with entrepreneurialism and self-regulation. From the province's point of view, the benefit of self-regulation was that it did not require any government expenditure or oversight. The exchange would regulate itself. While this sounded good in theory, as historian Chris Armstrong points out, in practice it presented several limitations. As a voluntary organization with a diverse membership, the CSE remained only as strong as its weakest link. In practical terms, oversight of member companies remained limited in reach and scope. The existence of outside competitors, not to mention the omnipresence of unregulated "curb" brokers, ensured that enforcement would never be too robust. The first local competitor to the CSE, the Calgary Oil and Stock Exchange, emerged shortly after the CSE began trading. Founded by local entrepreneur Marenus Janse, who also served as the president of Bonnie Brae Coal Company and the Janse Drilling Company, the Calgary Oil and Stock Exchange began operations in early June, launching with seventy members. By some counts, as many as thirteen stock exchanges of varying sophistication formed within the city at the height of the boom, including the People's Exchange, the Universal Exchange, the Consolidated Oil Exchange, the Investor's Oil Exchange, the Majestic Exchange (operated out of a converted movie theatre), and the Standard Oil Stock Exchange. Furthermore, several "open call" exchanges ran on Calgary streetcorners. Outside Calgary, the Vancouver Stock exchange attempted to capitalize on the boom. By May 19, *The Vancouver Daily Province* showed the VSE trading twenty-five "Calgary Oil Stocks" on its unlisted section shortly after the Dingman strike. By July, well-known Vancouver broker Harry Bettz opened the Calgary Oil Exchange at 39 Hastings Street East. Chartered by the province of British Columbia and linked to Calgary by telephone and private wire, the exchange limited its membership to fifty and offered amenities like a cigar and bootblack stand.[56] As historian Chris Armstrong notes, "Never in Canada would there be such fierce competition amongst exchanges as during the Calgary oil boom." Indeed, when W.J. Quinlan of the Grand Trunk Pacific Railway arrived in Calgary and claimed it took twenty minutes before anyone tried to sell him stock, *The Natural Gas and Oil Record* published the story under the headline "Brokers asleep."[57]

Some observers hoped competing exchanges would lower transaction costs and broker's fees, and help spread the word of Alberta's emerging petroleum industry. However, what they did not anticipate, and perhaps should have, was that the operation of several exchanges provided conditions tailor-made for stock price manipulation. Prices were completely fictitious as few were based on possession of physical reserves or production; almost all depended on supply and demand to establish their prices. If a block of vendor's stock from a reputable company with good prospects and a drilling rig entered the market, the price would immediately drop and brokers battled either to force prices down or to drive them back up, making good commissions in the process. Furthermore, the value of stock varied between the exchanges, creating many opportunities for profit through arbitrage—the practice of purchasing stock at a lower price on one exchange and selling it at a higher price on another. In the less-regulated financial markets of boomtown Calgary, it was sometimes difficult to distinguish between those employing legitimate trading strategies and others attempting to manipulate the market. Broker R.C. Carlile reflected on this ambiguity decades later. "My partner was Jimmy Robertson," recalled Carlile. "We had Constable on one exchange and somebody else on the other. These two used to do quite a big business buying on one and selling on the other."[58] One striking example of price discrepancy took place on June 8, 1914, one week after the opening of the Calgary Oil and Stock Exchange. Price comparison reveals the potential for profit—as well as manipulation. Not surprisingly, the most glaring difference involved Black Diamond Oil Fields, whose shares traded at $3.25 on the COSE and $5.25 on the CSE, a spread of two dollars. Hypothetically, a broker buying shares at $3.25 on the COSE and selling 30 of them at $5.25 on the CSE would net a profit of $60—approximately $1,560 today—plus commissions, simply by exploiting the price gap between exchanges. Even smaller spreads could yield profit. For example, Western Pacific's bid of $2.10 on the CSE compared to a price of $2.15 on the COSE would result in a five-cent-per-share gain—roughly 2.4 percent—would be above the average 1 to 2 percent daily profit for a typical day trader today.[59]

Table 5-2 Calgary Stock Exchange and Calgary Oil and Stock Exchange Values Compared, June 8, 1914

Company	Calgary Stock Exchange			Calgary Oil and Stock Exchange		
	Bid	Ask	Volume	Bid	Ask	Volume
Alberta Petroleum	$0.13	0.15	1232	$0.13	0.14	944
Black Diamond #1		5.25	30	3.15	3.25	585
Calgary Petroleum Products	82.5	85	5	—	87.50	
Dome	—	0.62		—	0.6	
Federal	—	0.6		0.5	0.55	300
Fidelity	0.2	0.25	217	—	0.18	
Herron-Elder	—	0.8		—	0.7	
Monarch	19.00	20.00	15	—	18.00	
Okotoks	0.11	0.14	800	0.13	0.14	200
Piedmont Petroleum Products	0.27	0.3		0.25	0.27	775
Stokes-Stephens	0.35	0.38		0.37	0.39	550
Trenton	—	0.18		0.13	—	2500
United Oils	18.00	19.00	24	—	18.50	
Western Canada	4.75	5.00	105	5.10		90
Western Pacific	—	2.10	150	2.10	2.15	1822

Data adapted from *The Natural Gas and Oil Record* and *The Calgary Daily Herald*.

One immigrant writer, Basil Clarke, described how he rapidly climbed the ladder to become a curb broker in Calgary in May 1914, providing a striking example of the city's—and the province's—reputation as a land of opportunity with the discovery of oil. Clarke, a reporter for the London-based *Daily Mail*, filed stories about his travels through Canada as a "fortune-hunting" immigrant, and vividly recalled witnessing scenes of wild celebrations in the street as people hugged, danced, and sang about the discovery. Immediately, Clarke wondered how he might be able to turn all the "turmoil and oil interest" to his advantage, as a newly arrived immigrant "with no more than his muscles and his wits to help him, though an immigrant willing (as immigrants here must be) to do anything from pick-and-shovel upwards."[60]

Clarke spent the night wandering around Calgary streets wrestling with the problem, but no solution presented itself until the next day. "Oil share dealing seemed the one business of the City. Every broker's office, every land office, every commission agency and almost every other shop became an oil share exchange. Chemists, clothiers, confectioners, hotels and the rest ran their oil share department and competed with the brokers and real estate men. And there was work for all and more. Queues waited at doors in many cases." After changing into a white shirt and collar bought from the Hudson's Bay Company, Clarke found a real estate office promoting an oil company. "The work of the place was held up through sheer inability of the clerical staff to book orders fast enough." After identifying the person in charge, Clarke asked if he could use another clerk. The man replied affirmatively and waved him over without so much as even looking up at Clarke. "'There's a pen and things. Sit at the table and make out receipts.'"[61]

For the next nine hours, Clarke made out receipts, eating sandwiches from a paper bag at mealtime brought by another clerk. At the end of the day, Clarke received fourteen shillings in pay—roughly $186 adjusted for inflation—and a job offer, "as very often happens in Canada if a man 'makes good' on temporary work." But he clearly saw that he could earn more by selling shares, including a 5 percent commission, simply by bringing clients into the office. Clarke applied to two companies and received job offers from both, and again Clarke succeeded in his new vocation. Clarke learned that companies increased their share prices over time, sometimes doubling them either after a certain length of time or after selling a predetermined amount of stock. Investors holding the cheaper stock then eagerly sold it back to reap the 100 percent profit, undercutting sales at the office as buyers and sellers turned to the "curb" market.[62]

For the third time in three days, Clarke changed careers to become a curb broker. In the reporter's estimation, being a broker was the easiest of the four jobs in Calgary. "This is all one had to do," wrote Clarke. "A man came up to you. 'Have you any so and so at so much?' You said, 'No, but I'll see if I can get you some.' You hustled around the chemists and clothiers and other places, all of them alive with men selling and buying, and found a man willing to sell at the price your buyer wanted." Insofar as Clarke could tell, the greatest difficulty of being a curb broker was that, at any given moment, there was no consensus about the share price of a given stock. Once, Clarke filled a buy order for 50 percent lower cost than what the buyer offered. "The buyer was so pleased that he gave me five percent and half the money I had saved him. On Friday morning I made nearly £9 in commission, in the afternoon £3.12 and on Saturday £7.00." In those two days, Clarke's commissions reached an astonishing total of $2,546, adjusted for inflation.[63]

For Clarke, his experience in Calgary proved that Canada was a land of opportunity. "Without experience of Canada, or of oil, or of stocks and shares, a man just ordinarily wide-awake could have come into Calgary as I did and made money." In fact, argued Clarke, if not for the fact that he liked his job as a journalist, and the lack of friends or influence in the city, he might have established himself permanently in Calgary as a stockbroker. "I had an offer. An Englishman with whom I did considerable business wanted me to take out a license and begin. He said I could have all his work and he would recommend me." While Clarke acknowledged that oil booms were the exception, not the rule, he concluded that "it is the immigrant who will tackle the unexpected that makes good in Canada. I get further proof of this every day I spend here."[64]

Some enterprising women emerged, determined to make their fortunes in the oil patch in a variety of ways, either by direct employment as secretaries or clerks in newly created companies, by becoming brokers, or investing directly in stock. Since average salaries for professional and tradeswomen working in Calgary were the highest in Canada, it made sense to try to and capture that market (see Table 5-3). Included in the proliferation of stock exchanges were at least four women-only exchanges as well as at least a half-dozen women working as independent agents or brokers, including at least one in Edmonton, Miss Edith McLachlan. The list of exchanges includes the Calgary Women's Oil Exchange, launched by Mrs. Blanche Mason and her partner Mrs. Annie Wolley-Dod; the Eureka Women's Oil Exchange, managed by Mrs. W.H. Ranlett; the Women's Oil Brokerage Company; and Woollard & Company, operating out of the same address as Miss A.A. Woollard's Lady's Wear Shop—1009, 1st Street West—which soon became the mailing address of the Hole-Woollard Oil Company. "A ladies' tailoring shop was dismantled in a jiffy," wrote the correspondent for the *Monetary Times*. "Its fair proprietress for the time being sells oil shares to her lady customers exclusively, instead of dresses."[65]

But by far the Calgary Women's Oil Exchange received the lion's share of publicity and, in many ways, became the public face of women's investing during the oil boom. Perhaps its notoriety is attributable to the fact that both Blanche Mason and Annie Wolley-Dod were prominent members of Calgary

Figure 5-10 "Men in cars and on sidewalk waiting to invest in oil stocks, Calgary, Alberta" Driller Joseph Brown (seated in the front passenger seat in car on the left) helped bring in the Dingman Well. By June 1914, Brown had left Calgary Petroleum Products to become a founding partner in Fidelity Oil and Gas. Brown poses with a large gathering outside Fidelity's head offices before visiting the company's first well site. (Glenbow Archives CU1137947)

society. Both were active members of several women's organizations in the city. However, the same could be said of the proprietor of the Eureka Women's Oil Exchange, Mrs. W.H. Ranlett, whose firm launched at approximately the same time as that of Mason and Wolley-Dod's. Active in the Local Council of Women, and two-term president of the American Woman's Club, Mrs. Ranlett travelled in the same circles and attended many of the same events as Mason and Wolley-Dod. However, as she was an American expatriate temporarily living in Calgary because of her husband's business concerns, it might be that the efforts of more permanent residents eclipsed Mrs. Ranlett's endeavours. After all, Annie and her husband, rancher Arthur G. Wolley-Dod, had settled in the area in the 1880s, cementing their stature as pillars of the community. Meanwhile, as the former society page writer for *The Western Standard*, Mrs. Mason had numerous contacts in the local press corps. The

Herald praised the two women's business sense and organizational abilities, proclaiming itself "proud that our women of Alberta are showing such foresight and shrewd business capabilities as there must be a great future for such an enterprise." The *Albertan* predicted that Mason and Wolley-Dod would "form a combination capable of producing results calculated to make the average male broker turn green with envy."⁶⁶

Like most women-run businesses of the time, these brokerages generally served other women. Given the built-in networks created by the large number of women's organizations and social connections, opportunities abounded for Mrs. Ranlett and Mrs. Wolley-Dod to find new clients. An ad for the Women's Oil Brokerage Company demonstrated how women expanded their networks beyond their immediate social circles. The ad informed readers that the firm offered information and advice "to women who are desirous of investing in oil stocks." To reassure potential investors that they need not worry about the hypermasculine atmosphere of the curb brokers, their ad noted that only women worked at the firm, and that their agents were "thoroughly informed in regard to all oil companies formed in Calgary." To make investing more convenient, the company also offered to send representatives to call on customers by appointment. "Do not hesitate," the ad implored. "This is the time to buy oil stocks if you wish to make some money. One dollar judiciously invested today may double and treble over night for you."⁶⁷

The participation of so many women in the oil boom as investors and brokers should not be surprising. Indeed, in 1913, *The Western Standard* noted that "self-supporting women of western Canada do not regard themselves as the unfortunate victims of unusual industrial conditions; they have come out here with the frank intention of making money, and finding happiness, and they assert, with considerable spirit those rights which should be the inalienable rights of womankind." Indeed, a quick examination of the 1920 shareholders list for Calgary Petroleum Products suggests that at least 20 percent of investors in the company were women. Out of 564 individual shareholder names on the register, 115 either used the prefix "Mrs." in front of the surname or had a distinctly female first name. This, however, likely undercounts the number of female investors in the company, as only initials identified most shareholders. Furthermore, in June 1914 at least one women's group, the Calgary Women's Press Club (CWPC), pooled funds to make a $50 investment in oil stocks. In another instance, a broker's wife not only brought her husband more business but brought in substantial commissions of her own by selling stock. It is likely that other groups made similar arrangements but received no press coverage. The *Herald's* story did not specify how many

Table 5-3 Average Professional & Tradeswomen's Salaries in Calgary, 1913

PROFESSION	SALARY RANGE	RATE
School Teacher	$750.00–$1,1000	Yearly
Nurses	$23.00–$35.00	Weekly
Milliners	$15.00–$40.00	Weekly
Stenographers	$15.00–$25.00	Weekly
Saleswomen	$7.00–$15.00	Weekly
Waitress	$7.00–$10.00	Weekly
Domestic	$4.00–$8.00	Weekly
Housekeepers	$30.00–$40.00	Monthly
Dressmakers	$2.00–$3.00	Daily
Reporters	$18.00–$30.00	Weekly
Clerks	$10.00–$18.00	Weekly
Cashiers	$12.00–$15.00	Weekly

Calgary's minimum cost of living estimated at seven to eight dollars per week in 1913. Two dozen eggs cost thirty-five cents while a package of breakfast cereal cost ten cents. Table adapted from "How Calgary Pays its Women," *The Western Standard*, June 12, 1913, 19.

women participated in the venture, the stocks bought, or the name of the individual who issued the stock certificate. Still, not everyone supported these developments, and older stereotypes about the propriety and morals of women who bought stock persisted. On June 13, 1914, the *Herald* reported that a "prominent Edmonton paper" disapprovingly reported that the women of Calgary were selling their jewelry to finance their new pastime.[68]

Convincing evidence suggests that attempts to maintain more "traditional" standards of investing for women, such as the pursuit of "safe" investments like real estate, endured. During Calgary's real estate boom between 1910 and 1913, ads in local papers encouraged both women and men to invest in property, but pitches to female investors emphasized more "feminine qualities" that real estate represented: long-term investment horizon, mitigated risk, preservation of capital, and possession of a tangible asset. Speculating on the market, especially in newly formed oil companies with their short-term outlook, and high-risk, high-reward qualities, was tantamount to gambling.

What is particularly striking is that most of the newspaper stories celebrating women making fortunes during the boom did so because of their success at managing mineral leases rather than speculating in stocks. While both were speculative activities, mineral leases were depicted as having parallels with real estate. Moreover, the fortunes made were directed toward improving marriage prospects or improving the family. For example, the *Day Book* (Chicago) highlighted Jennie Fitzgerald, who worked at the notion counter of a department store for eight dollars a week. Fitzgerald managed to secure a prize lease from the Dominion Land Office. During the subsequent boom "two strangers came in one morning and placed on the counter a marked check for $11,000 [$333,700 adjusted for inflation] as an offer for her holdings." Now Jennie Fitzgerald found herself on "a honeymoon trip down in North Dakota in a touring car."[69]

Four waitresses at the Rathskeller Restaurant, three Americans and one Swedish immigrant, pooled their money to buy mineral leases and received an offer of $92,000 ($2.78 million adjusted for inflation) for the leases. "We cannot say anything yet to the newspapers," said the group's spokesperson, who remained anonymous. "Of course, if we sell for what we expect, we shall not be obliged to work any longer." About a month later, Florence M. Hudson, a clerk in the Department of Natural Resources for the Canadian Pacific Railway, sold a 480-acre oil lease on an anticline for $54,000 cash ($1.6 million, adjusted for inflation) and "a dress suitcase full of stock" in the Montreal-based company that bought the lease. Hudson attributed her newfound fortune to her knowledge and skills rather than luck. "It is not necessary for me to tell you how I happened to pick out a lease right on the anticline and just north of the McDougall-Segur holdings," she told the *Albertan* when questioned. "I know all about anticlines and it was not all chance."[70]

Of course, any discussion of women investors making their fortune during the oil boom must include Jennie Earl of Black Diamond Oil Fields and the Coalinga Syndicate. In 1912, Earl was simply the stenographer in George Buck's office who overheard several conversations taking place. "Her imagination was stirred as she tapped the keys by stories she heard of 'expected' gushes and riches," wrote the *Day Book*. After learning that some government leases were set to lapse in August 1912, she went to the Dominion Land Office with Ida Fenner after work to file on some mineral rights. As there was already a lineup down the stairs of the land office across the street from the CPR station, Earl and Fenner took their place in line. The two women were still outside when the land office closed for the night, sending a good many of the other men in line home. "Armed with cushions and making themselves as comfortable as possible," the two women, according to the *Herald*, "waved aside all formality and gave an exhibition of gameness that is rarely displayed among the fairer sex."[71] As the night grew darker and cooler, one by one the men in front of Earl left until she and Fenner were at the front of the line. They waited outside all night for the land office to open. When it did, Earl placed a deposit of $160 and acquired one of the most valued sections of land in Turner Valley. In turn, she used the mineral rights to secure a one-quarter share in the Coalinga Syndicate and an appointment as one of the directors of Black Diamond Oil Fields. "She owns a quarter interest in a $1,000,000.00 company and occupies the post of secretary-treasurer," wrote the *Day Book*. "Miss Earl's bank account, in addition to her holdings, runs high into the tens of thousands."[72]

The lack of formal barriers, combined with Alberta's entrepreneurial ethos, comparatively low overhead costs, and their innate business sense facilitated women's entry into the brokerage business. Unlike today, where becoming a broker is a lengthy process that usually requires, at a minimum, a bachelor's degree (in either accounting, business, finance, or economics), completing a Canadian Securities Course, gaining a minimum of twelve months' experience in the field before completing a two-part Canadian Securities Course exam with a minimum score of 60 percent, at the start of the first oil boom in 1914, *The Natural Gas and Oil Record* noted that "a blackboard is all that is necessary to put one in business as an oil broker." Proving the *Record's* point was Leif Huseby of the First Unitarian church, who gave up his role as minister to become a broker, claiming that "the lure of building an empire was too much for me to resist" given that he descended from a family of financiers. "I do not say that I have abandoned the ministry permanently, but there was a division in my church over some trivial matter, and just about that time oil was struck in the Dingman well. The thing appealed to me as something tremendous."[73]

As the police chased the bucket shops off the streets, brokers rented every vacant store in the city or sought rental space in hotels, barber shops, and other business places. "The real estate boom in Western Canada a few years ago was nothing compared with this for local excitement" concluded the *Record*. The regulation of brokerages and the buying and selling of stock consisted only of municipal bylaws and the Province of Alberta's Companies Act (1911). In early 1914, the province amended the Companies Act, requiring companies selling stock to first file a prospectus with the government in Edmonton. Despite the long drilling time of Dingman #1, and the campaign by *the Herald* to strengthen regulation and oversight of stock speculation, it is clear that no one in a position of authority had given any serious or sustained attention to the issue despite months of anticipation. Belatedly, stockbrokers considered a variety of measures, including forming their own professional association, to establish industry standards.[74]

The selling of stock became so ubiquitous that when president of the Canadian Pacific Railway, Sir Thomas Shaughnessy, visited the city and approached a wicket to check his departure time, the clerk asked what oil stock he wanted to buy. Belatedly, on May 18, the City of Calgary amended Bylaw 1684, implementing a $50 fee for brokers over and above their $75 licence fee to operate as an intelligence office, and stipulated that the licence "shall not authorize any broker or agent to solicit" business outside the brokerage's place of business. Other provisions gave discretion to the licence inspector to ensure an applicant's "good character." At the last minute, a clause added a fifteen-dollar licence fee for any brokerage that decided to augment their business by employing a curb broker, with an additional ten dollar fee for every sub-agent employed thereafter. Most agreed the changes were necessary to maintain the city's character and commercial integrity. On May 21, the first day the new licences appeared at city hall, 104 applicants overwhelmed the two clerks on duty. Given the frenetic environment after the Dingman well and the proliferation of exchanges and bucket brokerages, enforcement proved both necessary and problematic. Long lineups across city sidewalks and spilling into traffic prompted the police to begin issuing tickets for loitering and obstructing traffic, as police chief Alfred Cuddy waged an all-out campaign to eliminate the curb brokers. Competition for sales, however, made brokers more aggressive. In one case before Police Magistrate's Court, Colonel Sanders complained that the brokers approached customers in a manner akin to an assault. "I thought," said Sanders before rendering his verdict, "that he was going to rob me instead of sell me oil shares."[75]

A spate of hiring since 1910 had resulted in the Calgary Police Force (CPF) deploying 1.8 policemen for every 1,000 citizens in 1914, nearly double the optimal ratio of one policeman per 1,000 citizens. Yet in the spring of 1914, the officers of the overworked CPF did their best to deter wildcatters, maintain the peace, keep the streets safe, and the sidewalks uncluttered.[76] Nevertheless, opportunistic thieves made off with thousands of dollars' worth of bills left unattended by overwhelmed brokers. On the streets, pickpockets operated in a target-rich environment with lots of distracted marks carrying plenty of cash. "Pickpockets cut one man's pocket clean from his clothes and took $53.00 and another man was either relieved of $40.00 or else lost it," Chief Cuddy told the *Albertan*. Police issued fines for loitering and broke up fist fights when investors grew frustrated while waiting in a queue to buy shares or leases. One particularly serious incident took place at the land office on June 5, 1914, when 362 ticket holders lost the right to select oil leases when an arrangement designed to keep the sidewalks clear by scheduling appointments did not work as planned. To cope with the crush of speculators flooding the land office, officials there had adopted a ticket system whereby prospective buyers were issued tickets and allotted half an hour to select leases. The system seemed straightforward and gave the appearance of creating appointments: the person with the first ticket would enter the building and have until 9:30, when the second person would be allowed in. But at nine a.m. on June 5, the holder of ticket 154 did not show up and the clerk continued to call numbers until C.E. Buell, a confectionary seller at the Pantages Theatre and the holder of ticket 516, called out when he heard his number. Buell selected 1,920 acres of land whose value *The Saskatoon Daily Star* confided was "conservatively" worth $100,000, and immediately turned down an offer of fifty dollars an acre.[77]

Police also coped with a dramatic increase in prostitution as the sex trade flourished alongside the boom. By mid-June, the CPF carried out a vigorous campaign to rid the city of undesirables—a euphemism for prostitutes. "Since the recent oil strike, the city has become overrun with them," complained Chief Cuddy. The June 14 edition of the *Herald* reported that new arrivals accounted for most morality cases appearing before Magistrate Sanders in Police Court, including one case where "the woman began soliciting within an hour of her arrival." Having promised upon his appointment as police chief in 1912 to eliminate prostitution, Cuddy succeeded in closing the brothels in South Coulee only to have them reappear in downtown Calgary. Determined to keep the city clean, Chief Cuddy and Magistrate Sanders also focused on "those depraved men who live by the proceeds of prostitution and the keeping of disorderly houses," threatening one sex worker's husband with a five-year sentence if he "knew what you were doing and was making money from it.[78] Raids on well-known brothels over the next few weeks resulted in a number of arrests, fines, and imprisonments, for both prostitution and selling liquor without a licence. One case involved William Wilkinson, the night clerk at the Arlington Temperance hotel, who faced a choice between paying cumulative fines of $250 for selling liquor without a licence and keeping a disorderly house or a three-month prison sentence.[79]

Cuddy's police force also vigorously enforced Alberta's Lord's Day Act, particularly against unwary brokers looking to make a buck on the Sabbath. Originally passed in 1888 and renewed in 1906 with the support of the Protestant churches, the moral reform movement, and the trade unions, the Lord's Day Act prohibited all businesses from operating on Sundays. Curb brokers quickly learned to operate six days a week, nearly twenty-four hours a day—apart from Sunday, after they learned that Police Chief Cuddy went undercover to enforce the law on unsuspecting brokers. As the boom evolved, bucket shops and curb brokers became more of a nuisance, prompting urgent pleas from the chief of police that city council adopt a $1,000 licensing fee for all oil brokers, both as individuals and exchanges, to clear the streets and impose order.[80] The business-friendly city council never implemented the proposed $1,000 licence fee but still had to fend off complaints about the more modest licence from pre-existing businesses.[81] One such firm, Robertson & Carlisle Limited, applied for a rebate, claiming that their city charter already permitted them to deal in buying and selling of stocks and bonds, immunizing them from the new fee. The city's solicitor agreed with Robertson & Carlisle that their act of incorporation covered the activities and recommended that the city only apply the amended licence fee to unchartered brokers. After the ruling, the city clerk wrote to the chief of police asking, "Will you kindly govern yourself in accordance with the above recommendation of the committee, and oblige?"[82]

Speculating in stocks neared the status of an all-consuming sacred duty beyond mere civic obligation. Eleanor Luxton writes that her grandparents David and Annie McDougall trekked out to the oil field every day, despite the mud roads, to check on progress at McDougall-Segur. Meanwhile, back in Calgary, Eleanor remembered that "the brokers were so busy in their offices they could not keep ahead of their work: everyone was buying and selling."[83] The *Albertan* reported that on the Calgary police force only the jailer, George Miller, held the "undesirable distinction" of holding no oil stocks. "His companions gather around him in excited groups and talk in restrained tones," said the *Albertan*. "They wonder whether he is Daniel Webster the Second or a candidate for Ponoka [Hospital for the Insane]. At any rate he is unique." The paper further claimed that Officer Joe Carruthers only possessed one complete set of clothes because he had pawned the rest of his personal effects to invest in leases and stocks. The mania bordered on an addiction; Officer Carruthers even contemplated mortgaging his home to raise more investment capital. "Anybody who is not 'in,'" wrote *The Natural Gas and Oil Record*, "is looked on as almost an outcast, one with whom conversation is almost an impossibility." Amid preparations for the visit of the Governor General, the Duke of Connaught, in mid-July, the *Albertan* suggested that, if the Duke and Duchess wanted to fully understand Calgary's oil boom, they should visit the oil exchanges. "Of course," added the paper with tongue planted firmly in cheek, "to do the thing right he would have to see them all, and as there are nine now, and doubtless will be twelve or fifteen before he arrives, some arrangement would have to be made to have the sessions at different times in the day."[84]

To demonstrate their civic pride, and attract attention, some businesses began thinking of ways to use the oil boom to their advantage. The Apparel Service Company, a cleaner, placed a special "Ladies Only" ad in the *Herald* offering women three free shares in the Erie Oil Company (with a par value of one dollar each) provided they brought a suit or dress to be French dry cleaned between June 15 and June 21.[85] The oil boom hit the entertainment sector hard, as people were too busy buying and selling oil stock with their savings to go to the theatre or play-houses. When asked how his business fared during the early weeks of the boom, the manager of the Orpheum said, "To be frank with you, it is rotten. In other words, extremely mellow or punk." Some creative thinkers began improvising solutions. The Regent Theatre's manager, Meyer Cohen, acquired (it is not clear if they were bought or given) 1,000 shares in Sunbeam Oil to give away to patrons purchasing either a fifteen-cent or twenty-five-cent ticket to see D.W. Griffith's *Judith of Bethulia* on June 8. Those buying a fifteen-cent afternoon ticket would receive one share while the twenty-five-cent evening fare would reap two shares. "The idea is an original one," wrote the editor of the *Herald's* Music and Drama section, "and the success is being watched with great interest by Manager Cohen and his associates."[86] However, outside the city, local officials adopted measures to contain speculation. Winnipeg, the largest urban centre on the prairies, forbade the sale of Calgary-based oil stocks unless a judge could be satisfied through documentation that the company was legitimate. Small-town police arrested Calgary brokers when they ventured south of the city to sell stocks over the weekend. Some men were taken into custody "by a typical constable with a huge star and chin whiskers, and carted off to the village pound, where they were cooped up with sundry stray horses, pigs and other unclaimed animals." When asked why he arrested the men, the constable replied, "I reckon you'd call it unscrupulous dealing in oil stocks. And they're going to stay locked up, too."[87]

Implicitly acknowledging the proclivity of would-be oil barons for fabulism, *The Natural Gas and Oil Record* reported there was "much confusion and trouble resulting from the lack of satisfactory regulations governing the drilling of wells in the lobby" of the King George Hotel. After holding "many hearings and conferring with the leading pioneers in the field," the hotel manager, W.V. Moran, produced a list of ten regulations to govern "drilling operations in the King George pool." Included were provisions that forbade the drilling of more than one well while occupying a leather chair and that drilling could not take place between three and six a.m.. If drilling in the lobby, "it is permissible to fire the vocal boilers with cigars, stogies, pipes or cigarettes." All wells "must be" 1,000 barrels or better and must "represent an outlay of at least $10,000.00."[88]

For a few delirious weeks in May 1914, much of southern and central Alberta threw itself headlong into the excitement of the boom and expected that good times and prosperity were right around the corner. Everyone with the courage to invest would be fabulously wealthy—provided the companies they invested in struck the oil they fervently believed lay waiting just beneath the surface. After all, it was not as if oil promoters were actively deceiving their investors, right?

6

Reign of the Charlatans

Everybody's nerves are tense. Every pulse beat of the Discovery well is carefully measured. When the oil "gushes," a responsive throb is felt all down the line. The boot-black sleeps with his ten-cent certificates under his pillow, and Mr. Wallingford smokes longer and blacker cigars.

And everybody dreams of an estate at Tarrytown [New York, home of Standard Oil's John D. Rockefeller] with a standing army to repel the IWW!

—A.G. Henderson
The Day Book (Chicago)
June 24, 1914[1]

That oil promotion was sheer anarchy [in 1914] can be judged by the fact that there were no blue-sky laws and nobody knew anything about the oil business, including what it might cost to drill a well. Water well drillers, who had never gone below a couple hundred feet, became oilwell drillers overnight. So there was no reason why Calgary fruit stores, laundries, barber shops, coal and wood dealers and pawn shops shouldn't blossom out as oil share brokers. They did, overnight.

—*Western Oil Examiner*
July 9, 1955

In June 1914, around the same time that Calgary's Regent Theatre offered paying customers free oil stock with movie tickets, the Bijou Theatre in Edmonton began screening *The Widow's Investment*, a film that could serve

189

as a cautionary tale for Calgary's would-be Rockefellers. Billed as a story of the California oil fields, the film's plot revolved around two confidence men, James Waldo and Henry Morgan, who hatch a get-rich-quick scheme by forming a fake oil company to bilk gullible investors out of their hard-earned money. Among the townsfolk victimized by the con is Widow Green, who is an easy target for charlatans and scoundrels. Widow Green uses all the money from her late husband's insurance settlement to buy shares in the fake company. For good measure, the death of her husband now means that her son Eben must leave the farm to support the family. Of course, however, Eben finds work as a rig hand with Waldo and Morgan's fake oil company, where he meets and falls in love with Marjorie, the daughter of the head driller. In a strange twist of fate, perhaps because the Hollywood story compelled the company to erect a rig and drill for oil instead of simply absconding with the townsfolks' funds, Waldo and Morgan strike oil, but a well-timed bribe to the head driller ensures his silence. Unaware that their investment has paid off and under pressure by the owners to divest, the shareholders decide to unload their stock for a fraction of its true value. Eben uncovers the details of this nefarious plot and secretly buys a majority of the stock, seizing control of the company from Waldo and Morgan when the stock's price rises, and marries Marjorie. The head driller learns that honesty is the best policy. The *Edmonton Journal* called the film "a delightful story of the oil country," noting its appeal "to the people of this district."[2]

Perhaps unsurprisingly given the film's plot, no record exists indicating that *The Widow's Investment* hit screens in Calgary that spring or summer. Art simply could not compete with the real-life drama and backroom shenanigans taking place in and around Calgary during the 1914 boom. The number and range of structural problems confronting the emerging petroleum industry were daunting, beginning with the lax regulatory environment, the considerable number of oil companies competing for scarce investment dollars, the flaws inherent in the self-regulated stock markets, and the overall lack of transparency. The dark side of high-risk, high-reward entrepreneurialism and unregulated laissez-faire capitalism came into full relief as it became clear there were few obstacles to deter mischief makers and plenty of incentives for companies to bend, break, or otherwise ignore whatever restraints existed on their behaviour in a cutthroat competition *before* drilling took place. By July 1914, over 450 companies representing half a billion dollars of capital investment on paper operated in the province.[3] However, given that local rather than national or international financing fuelled the 1914 boom—approximately half of the $4 million invested in stocks came from Calgary and Edmonton—there were too many companies competing for limited investment dollars. As *The Natural Gas and Oil Record* warned investors, "There is not enough money to be had to develop 450 Oil Companies at this time." At most, the industry journal estimated local investors could fund fewer than fifty companies and coldly assessed the daunting task ahead for entrepreneurs. Fifteen companies were already drilling; another twenty planned to drill within the next few weeks for a total of thirty-five companies with enough funds to launch a drilling program. According to the industry paper, that meant local investors could afford to fund perhaps as many as twelve or as few as ten companies out of the remaining 415. The competition to attract enough investment capital therefore would only become more intense and absolute.[4]

The second structural issue contributing to the chaos was related to the proliferation of stock exchanges and the short, sharp stock frenzy following the Dingman strike that provided ample cover for less-than-scrupulous promoters to concoct get-rich-quick schemes and starkly revealed the limits of self-regulation. Lax regulations and limited oversight enabled several types of transgressions to go unpunished for too long. For example, some promoters neglected their responsibility to issue stock certificates to investors in a timely fashion, ensuring that investors could not withdraw their cash provided they could find a buyer. Other promoters ensured they were paid first by issuing many more shares as promotion or vendor's stock rather than treasury stock. George Buck, though, raised the game to new levels with successive schemes to manipulate the stock market for personal gain. At some point in late 1913 or early 1914, it might be possible to believe Buck genuinely wanted to strike oil to realize his dreams. But that changed as Buck and his family flirted with financial disaster in the spring of 1914. Never a particularly wealthy company from the outset, Black Diamond Oil Fields limped along as a bottom-feeder compared to Calgary Petroleum Products and McDougall-Segur. Backed by Calgary's "old money," the latter never really worried about investors the way Buck and Black Diamond did. Without stock sales, the company could not sustain operations. For Black Diamond, stock sales were the lifeblood of the company. Without stock sales, they would not find oil and the company would die.

With the plan to salt the well, however, the means to an end became an end unto itself. Drilling for oil in Turner Valley was expensive and complicated. Buck's inexperience led him to create a chronically undercapitalized company that lived from hand to mouth, something Buck alluded to in interviews at the end of May, giving himself credit for sticking with the drilling program "when everything appeared dead in the search for oil" weeks earlier.[5] The plan had always been to drill more than one well, but Buck learned the hard way how thin his margin for error was and how close he came to personal financial ruin. But if the second company was much larger, Buck could raise even more money to sustain the operations of both. Capitalized at a robust $1 million, the new company would be a much more stable and reliable source of revenue—provided he could launch it. Before that could happen, though, the four partners of the Coalinga Oil Syndicate arranged to sell off their leasehold shares via an intermediary to hide the fact that they were, getting their cash out of the company.

According to Allan Clark, the plot began before the Dingman strike when Buck made a trip to Medicine Hat to talk with Martin and Phillips about his delinquent payments to the drilling company. Martin was in no mood to bargain and told Buck to make a substantial payment—about $5,000—or International Supply Company would pull its rig and personnel off the property. Now desperate to raise the cash and salvage what he could, Buck focused on how to sell more stock, and the notion of salting the well began to form. Clark was one of several salespeople in and out of Black Diamond's office in the spring of 1914, largely selling from the block of 1,000 United Oil shares Buck jointly owned (see Chapter 4). Aware that Buck and Black Diamond needed to raise some cash quickly, and likely complicit in the plot to salt the well, Clark approached Buck with a proposal on May 8—after salting the well but one day before the Cheely article appeared in the *Albertan*.[6] The deal would make Clark the exclusive seller for the remaining balance of 32,285 shares of treasury stock in Black Diamond Oil Fields in exchange for $2,000 in cash and healthy commissions (on a sliding scale determined by share price, from 62.5 cents for every share sold for one dollar rising to $1.50 for every share sold for five dollars). Buck did not insist on a time limit on Clark's term as exclusive seller, nor did he obtain a pledge from Clark regarding how much money would accrue to the company. According to Clark, Buck blanched at the commission rates but agreed to them when told the scheme would only work with highly motivated brokers. Buck agreed to the one-sided proposal but needed the approval of Black Diamond's board of directors because, according to the prospectus, 12.5 percent was the maximum commission the company could pay. Buck, however, remained confident that "we" would make up the difference; whether that was the Coalinga syndicate's partners or Black Diamond Oil Fields remained unclear. Clark's business partner, Fred Smith, recalled that it was difficult to tell when Buck spoke for himself, or as a representative of either Black Diamond Oil Fields or the

Coalinga Oil Syndicate. "He might speak for either one," said Smith months later when describing how the arrangement came together. "I did not ask him who he was representing." Regardless, officially the Coalinga Syndicate made up the balance by selling its leasehold stock. At a meeting on May 11, the Black Diamond board of directors agreed to the deal, and stipulated that the Coalinga Syndicate would reimburse the company fifty cents for every dollar of shares sold, to follow the prospectus's maximum commission provision.[7]

But Clark saw bigger profits if the volume of shares sold increased, and pressured Buck to increase the number of shares available. According to Buck, it was Clark who asked to sell some of Coalinga's Black Diamond leasehold stock. Seeing share prices take off in the aftermath of the salting, Buck needed little convincing. Urged on by Clark, who called it foolish to limit supplies when demand was so high, the conversation spread to include advertising manager Harry C. Beattie and Jennie Earl. Beattie supposedly urged Buck to "sell some of it if we had a chance." Presenting himself in depositions as a reluctant owner going along with the wishes of the majority, Buck maintained, "All I wanted to sell was enough to carry us along for the time being."[8] Clark claimed that on the night of May 13, 1914, he and Buck wrote up the terms of the agreement in longhand in the Black Diamond offices and were about to type them up when Smith burst in the door and blurted out that the Dingman well had struck oil. "Mr. Buck dropped everything and ran out to see about it and never came back." Although Clark and Smith claimed the parties finalized the deal the next day, he never obtained a written copy of the agreement from Buck.[9]

Matters now turned to trying to get the leasehold stock held by the Coalinga Syndicate in circulation. "We had to find some way of getting the stock onto the market without letting people know that it came direct from the office," testified Clark. Back in Black Diamond's offices, the staff focused on the logistics of selling the large volume of stock, including opening half a dozen offices around town to sell stock, employing a deferred payment option, or sending shares out to fifty or sixty different agents. Buck, however, approached the problem from a completely different direction, focusing his attention on constructing a backstory he could sell along with the stock. In discovery hearings for a subsequent lawsuit by Clark and Smith over unpaid commissions, Clark believed the impetus came from a conversation weeks before between Buck and himself regarding Clark's in-laws in California who were interested in buying a large block of Black Diamond stock—somewhere between $1,500 and $3,000 worth—at fifty cents a share. The sale never materialized, but something about the lure of California investors appealed to Buck. As the group brainstormed different ideas and approaches, Buck chimed in and pitched a backstory to hide the origin of the shares. What if a group of California capitalists, with an option on a large block of shares, suddenly made the stock available? When Buck's lawyer later questioned Clark about this plan, the salesman dismissed it as mere window dressing and deemed it immaterial to the subsequent sales of stock. But Clark overlooked the fundamental point. The backstory appealed to the anticipation and excitement investors already felt. It tapped into their hopes and dreams of rubbing shoulders with the Rockefellers, of financial security, and fame. Working with Black Diamond's advertising manager, H.C. Beattie, who initially opposed the plan but fell in line once it became clear that it was what Buck wanted, Clark paid for a series of ads in the *Albertan* and the *News Telegram*. As per Buck's wishes, Clark claimed he had acquired the option on a sizable block of Black Diamond stock from California capitalists and made them public starting at two dollars a share to cover drilling costs. "That was to be the public side of it," said Clark, rationalizing the decision. But Clark's partner, Fred Smith, who also worked in the advertising department of the *Albertan*, vehemently disagreed, mostly because it offended his sensibilities. Buck and Beattie's ad claimed the sale would help fund drilling the well, which Smith knew to not be true, prompting him to later claim "it had no business in the ad."[10]

Spurred by the ad's appearance on May 16 and the frenzy following the Dingman strike, the scheme to reintroduce Black Diamond stock to the market worked perfectly. Clark and Smith collected thousands of dollars from customers practically everywhere—some stopped them on the street, others pushed money into their hands in the stairwell to their office. In two weeks, approximately 56,000 shares of Black Diamond stock sold at an average price of three dollars per share, generating approximately $150,000 in sales. The two salesmen claimed the Syndicate sold enough shares to offset the losses incurred in offering the 25 percent commissions. Buck, for his part, claimed that, despite the sales, Black Diamond remained indebted to the Coalinga Syndicate and that Coalinga's partners sold their own stock to keep the two entities afloat. All proceeds from stock sales, insisted Buck, went to the company, but the question remained how much Black Diamond treasury stock Clark and Smith sold versus the leasehold stock provided by the partners in Coalinga. In his initial discovery hearing, Buck said he transferred at least 11,000 Black Diamond shares held by the Coalinga Syndicate to his mother-in-law, Elizabeth Beaty, as a gift and vigorously claimed she decided to sell them of her own volition. In a second hearing, where Buck testified as a member of the Coalinga Syndicate, Buck acknowledged a substantially larger transfer of 55,000–60,000 shares to his mother-in-law.[11] Jennie Earl, who wore many hats at Black Diamond, including the post of secretary-treasurer, stated Buck's mother-in-law received closer to 50,000 in shares for the sale. The larger block, she claimed, "made them easier to sell." When questioned what that meant, Earl did not elaborate. Still under oath, Jennie Earl steadfastly denied that the partners were cashing out by transferring shares to Beaty. Nevertheless, Earl could not offer a plausible alternative explanation for the transfer and sale of such a large block of shares to Beaty, especially after she claimed at the time of the deal with Clark that Black Diamond had enough money to cover all its expenses.[12]

For the five days of the sale, Clark ensured that the salespeople he employed received their commissions and constantly turned money over to Jennie Earl. On occasion, either Clark or Smith accompanied Earl as she made deposits at the bank. Both men noticed cheques and money from the sales campaign being deposited into the Coalinga Syndicate's bank account instead of Black Diamond's. Ledgers subpoenaed in connection to a civil action later showed Coalinga's net proceeds from the sale totalled $59,182.86—which happened to be the total amount turned over by Clark to Jennie Earl. Buck claimed the deposits reflected Coalinga's status as "bankers" for Black Diamond. Once the funds were in the possession of the syndicate, Buck admitted receiving a payout between $5,000 and 10,000 as share prices climbed to more than five dollars by the end of the campaign on May 20. Clark and Smith also noticed that members of the Coalinga Syndicate suddenly bought new automobiles while Black Diamond Oil Fields remained insolvent. Nevertheless, the *Albertan* reported Black Diamond took in $25,000 in an hour and a half on the final day of the campaign. "We have now enough for development purposes, and will offer no more," Buck claimed, before gratuitously adding that an investor in England had taken up all the remaining stock. In the next breath, Buck announced the launch of a second company, Black Diamond #2, and promised that company would begin drilling within thirty days. Clark found a seat on Black Diamond #2's board of directors when he transferred the petroleum rights for the location of Black Diamond #2—500 yards south of Black Diamond #1—to George Buck.[13]

Clark testified that Buck alone came up with the risky plan. After all, the company's salvation depended on inexperienced brokers, selling an indeterminate amount of stock at variable prices. At a deposition arising from a falling out between the partners, Buck's attorney asked Clark why Buck would be party to such a ridiculous and dangerous scheme. Clark offered a concise answer that hinted at the broader conspiracy to salt the well—Buck wanted to sell as much stock as possible. "They would do anything to sell their stock and raise the money." Although Clark's answer presented the attorneys the opportunity to probe deeper, no one followed up with the obvious question about what "anything" might entail. The conspiracy to salt Black Diamond #1 bound the two sides together in an uneasy alliance. Both knew revealing the plot would badly damage everyone, so it remained hidden for the time being. All told, the salesmen claimed they employed 100–150 agents selling an estimated 69,450 shares of Black Diamond. It took them five days to sell 11,000–37,165 shares of the lease stock issued to the Coalinga Oil Syndicate now held in trust by Buck's mother-in-law, Elizabeth Beaty. According to Clark the only reason he stopped selling was that Buck pulled the rest off the market. Even then, after May 20, 1914, Buck told Clark subsequent sales would have to take place "on the quiet." Indeed, Clark found Buck willing to sell leasehold stock "as long as he got the price that suited him."[14]

The burst of activity from Black Diamond immediately attracted the attention of the press. *The Natural Gas and Oil Record* openly wondered how many times the same company could take its own stock off the market again on May 21 and noted that "telephone crooks" were busy cold-calling people to drum up sales for "fake diamonds"—a euphemistic nickname for Buck's company. Nine days later, the *Record* again referred elliptically to Buck and Black Diamond's campaign, noting that one company reported four strikes at its well, took its stock off the market about once a week only to see it reappear somewhere else under a different name. "Those responsible for the rumor are inspired by various motives," noted the *Record,* "but chiefly by the desire to boost prices and realize profits on stock secured at low flotation figures."[15] In the meantime, Buck gave an extensive interview to the *Vancouver Daily World.* Less than a week after the Dingman discovery, the west coast newspaper dispatched a special correspondent to Calgary to follow the oil boom's progress. Despite pledging to its readers that it sought "authentic information as to the actual conditions in Calgary," the *World's* correspondent became one of the most effective conduits for Buck to get his message out to investors. This cozy relationship led to big sales of Black Diamond stock in Vancouver, prompting Buck to briefly consider opening an office on the lower mainland.[16]

Regardless, starting on May 23, the *World* published an uncritical write-up of Black Diamond Oil Fields, likely personally provided by Buck. The company's well lay in the Dakota sands, the report asserted, and "experts" agreed "that there is a big body of oil in the reservoir over which the company is working." Buck proclaimed his company "was first in the field" and came into being after he'd read Cunningham Craig's *Oil Finding*, wherein he intuitively understood and grasped the "value of scientific geology." The Black Diamond well, claimed Buck, tapped one of the largest oil fields in the world, extending from the southern boundary of the province to Athabasca. Oil was everywhere, but "the chosen areas will produce results at far lesser expense." Indeed, in several advertisements, Buck claimed without any basis that the oil under his lease sat 1,000 feet closer to the surface. Then, addressing himself to all Black Diamond stockholders, Buck implored them to hold on. "There is a good market for our shares and transfers are brisk, but those who hold will, I feel sure, not regret it." Despite the recession, the oil boom liberated capital in a remarkable way. "For the past twelve months or more people have been crying financial stringency," said the promoter, "but it was timidity more than anything else which kept over $50 million tied up in the saving banks in this city alone." Oil men had gained the confidence of the people, and "I trust it will not be abused," he intoned. Despite all the economic doom and gloom, Buck boasted stock sales of $26,600 in a day and a half plus an additional $25,000 in an hour the following day. But investors must be vigilant, warned Buck. "I venture to say that in one instance there has been over $500,000.00 invested in a company in this city that hasn't even a stick of timber on the ground." Whatever the intention, idle capital resulted. But Black Diamond, on the other hand, "is well advanced. If we strike a gusher, which may happen at any moment now, we have sufficient material at hand to construct a temporary reservoir in five days, provided our permanent reservoir is not completed at that time." Buck concluded the interview with a grand vision of development made possible by oil. The industry meant spending millions of dollars on labour, materials, and infrastructure projects. Who did not want such a future?[17]

For George Buck, media in the form of newspapers represented the best way to stoke investor interest and press forward with his pump-and-dump scheme. In many ways, Buck used the medium of advertisements the way later generations use social media to deliver his message unfiltered to his supporters without editorial comment. Bereft of pictures or illustrations, the advertisements developed in conjunction with H.C. Beattie, Black Diamond's advertising agent, served as extended conversations between the company and the public, and Buck used them to attract investors, settle scores, call people names, or simply infuriate his critics. But newspapers had standards about what they printed that served as a check on Buck's message. "We used to have to cut his ads down at the office," recalled Fred Smith, who worked in the *Albertan's* advertising department and sold Black Diamond stock on the side during the boom. "I would not run them at all, they were too wild."[18]

In the meantime, despite the cash flow problems with Black Diamond #1, Buck wanted to move quickly and lock in a drilling rig at Black Diamond #2, convincing Tiny Phillips and International Supply to work on the second site. The contract stipulated that work on the second well would begin after the completion of the first. Records show, however, that Martin and Phillips built a series of penalties into the contract because of their previous experience with Buck. The contract charged Black Diamond nine dollars "for each and every foot drilled" as well as a flat fee of seventy-five dollars plus replacement costs for every day the company did not furnish coal and water to run the boiler.[19]

Black Diamond #2 launched with an aggressive advertising campaign that used advertising space to speak directly to investors and address critics without having to formally speak to the press.[20] Ads for Black Diamond #2 shamelessly trumpeted the "success" of Black Diamond #1 as evidence that the new company's field would be as a profitable and that its corporate officers knew what they were doing.[21] But above all else, Buck used the opportunity to air grievances and settle scores. On May 25, an ad for Black Diamond #2 appeared to counter the aspersions heaped on Buck by announcing, "We drill for oil." This, claimed Buck, is what lay behind the smear campaign launched against himself and Black Diamond Oil Fields. Other promoters and companies could not compete with Black Diamond and that is what "arouses the envy, the jealousy, the animosity, the malice, and the last resort of the coward and defeated crook—the LIES he is busy circulating while we keep busy DEVELOPING." The ad intimated that Black Diamond might bring in a giant gusher "any day now" and promised Black Diamond #2 would have success "because ITS holdings comprise some of the choicest and most scientifically selected anticlinal oil land, enough for FIVE companies devoted to such active, energetic drilling and oil development." Black Diamond's ad the next day again claimed Black Diamond was "far in the lead to the big flow" and that Black Diamond was so busy with "real oil developments" that they did not have the time to even "enumerate the foolish falsehoods and the childish criticism concocted and circulated by the parasites of the business of genuine oil development." Once again, the ad claimed that Black Diamond alone was the "ONLY well in the Dakota Sands." Black Diamond, the ad further claimed, was "the centre of all intelligent OIL interest of the whole field from which all wise OIL calculations are NOW made." The company success "demonstrated that the DRILL is MUCH MIGHTIER than the puny hammers of the parasites."[22]

On May 27 unnamed brokers operating out of the King George Hotel claimed Black Diamond #1 had struck oil. The rumour lingered for hours, pushing sales of Black Diamond stock to lofty heights before reporters reached Buck for comment. The *Herald* claimed Buck shut down the report, but teased there was no truth to the rumour that the well had produced oil in "commercial quantities." The following day, the *Albertan* sent a reporter to the oil fields to provide a first-hand assessment of developments on the ground. Contrary to "Dame Rumor," the article claimed, there were no armed guards around the Black Diamond well and the visiting party arrived just in time to see the contents of the bailer dumped into the sluice box, producing sand and a black oily fluid. The reporter then picked up a piece of waste, lit it on fire and dropped it down the well, sending a fifteen-foot-high explosion of flame. The chief driller, James W. Hayes, his two assistants, and the watchman then claimed they had personally invested every cent they had in Black Diamond stock.[23]

Buck seemed to relish the role as showman, outspoken promoter, and iconoclast he found himself playing in the spring and summer of 1914. But his increasingly outrageous behaviour and brazen falsehoods offended the broader community and invited recriminations. One story making the rounds illustrated the increasingly low regard for Buck and Black Diamond. The rumour held that Buck went fishing with a priest on Sheep Creek near the Black Diamond well. Beforehand, however, allegedly Buck prepared the area with signs of oil and, while the priest fished, Buck went upstream and dumped oil in the creek. By the time Buck returned to the priest, the oil had made its way downstream to the two men. Seeing oil glistening on the water's surface, Buck made a huge demonstration, lamenting that oil seeps from his nearby well would ruin their day. The priest then dropped his fishing rod and went back to Calgary to buy as many shares as he could afford. As Buck expected, news of the seeps spread and the price of the stock rose temporarily. When it plateaued, the priest cashed out, supposedly making a small fortune in the process.[24] While the story might depict a dogged and determined promoter pursuing every investment dollar available to it, it also presents a stark, amoral tone with almost cartoon-like malevolence. A revival preacher actively "salting" the ground with signs of oil to defraud a priest? Who would do such a thing? Perhaps the only redemptive part of the rumour is that the priest made a profit—something that very few other investors in the boom could claim in 1914.

More serious was the response of George Thompson's *News Telegram*, which reached the decision to terminate coverage of Buck and Black Diamond Oil Fields. On May 28, 1914, Thompson's paper followed the lead of Tucker's

Natural Gas and Oil Record and omitted Black Diamond Oil Fields from its daily stock quotations and removed it from its daily update of "wells now drilling." Although Thompson did not directly address the decision, an editorial published that day took aim at "fake oil newsmongers," declaring the practice of issuing false reports "short-sighted and unprofitable." The paper suggested "various motives" for the practice but ranked "the desire to boost prices and realize profits on stocks" near the top of the list. While the paper acknowledged that finding the truth was sometimes difficult, it nonetheless declared that "there is little excuse for publishing reports for which there is not any foundation in fact." While the editorial avoided mentioning Buck or Black Diamond by name, the company's sudden disappearance from coverage of "legitimate" oil companies and a subsequent editorial decrying companies "made out of stock-selling campaigns" left little doubt regarding Thompson's feelings.[25]

In early June, the Coalinga Oil Syndicate circumvented this modicum of editorial oversight on its messaging by launching its own newspaper, *Black Diamond Press*, publishing its first issue on June 10, 1914. Former *Saskatoon Daily Star* reporter Vernon Knowles became the managing editor and B.J. Casey the business manager of the new paper. In retrospect, hiring Knowles seems a little surprising—a relatively young reporter with five years' experience under his belt. At the end of May, while working for the *Daily Star*, Knowles had published the first of three articles on Calgary's oil boom on May 28, 1914. Knowles's pieces encouraged oil development but were hardly uncritical, and earned some praise from business leaders in Saskatoon for their appeals to common sense.[26] Nevertheless, he was hired as the managing editor of the self-professed paper "containing the most authentic information and development notes on the Calgary oil fields"—if that information accorded with Buck's world view. The *Black Diamond Press* served as both sword and shield for Buck's company, promoting favourable stories while attacking critics. For example, the first issue targeted *The Regina Leader*, which effective June 1, 1914, refused to run ads from Calgary oil companies, citing difficulty in distinguishing legitimate businesses from fraudulent ones.[27] This decision earned the Regina paper the ire of the *Black Diamond Press*. Ironically, the *Leader* noted that the second issue of the *Black Diamond Press*, published on June 17, 1914, included an article titled "Oil Companies from Boundary to North Pole," claiming many Alberta oil companies were outright frauds that had no intention to drill, lacked leaseholds, or planned to let others take risks proving the field. The *Leader* expressed astonishment

Figure 6-1 "Birds of Prey" In a calculated dig at George Buck, *The Regina Leader's* editorial cartoon, "Birds of Prey," questioned how Buck could be both a newspaper publisher and an oilman simultaneously. The *Leader* published "Birds of Prey" on the front page of its June 11, 1914, edition, the day after *Black Diamond Press* published its first newspaper. The cartoon, with the additional editorial commentary about "knocking," was reprinted by *The Toronto Daily Star* four days later.

that a publication supposedly promoting oil investments would publish such criticisms, especially after attacking it for saying many of the same things.[28]

After two delirious weeks, the first spasm of excitement about Calgary Petroleum Product's oil strike began to die down. In a report dated June 8, *The Monetary Times* concluded that "oil is still paramount in the public interest, there is not so much doing in shares, or leases as there was a fortnight ago. Everyone is waiting for the next strike."[29] One Spokane-based broker, Mitchell Grostein, expressed some relief, noting that "the stock values are largely fictitious." More problematic was the fact that "it is impossible to sell shares at prices advertised" as investors now sought to cash in by asking for more than the market price. Indeed, the broker observed that shares of Calgary Petroleum Products sold for twenty dollars before the strike and reached $200 per share after the well came in before settling at eighty-eight dollars a share. But even this created another problem because it remained far too rich for the everyday investor to buy. The future of the Calgary field

Table 6-1 Selected Alberta Stock Prices, May 15–June 6, 1914, Published by the *Natural Gas and Oil Record*

	PAR VALUE ($)	STOCK ISSUED	COST ($)	PRESENT PRICE ($)	NOW WORTH ($)
United Oils	10.00	30,000	300,000	$18.50	550,000
Monarch Oil	1.00	100,000	100,000	$19.50	1,900,000
Calgary Petroleum Products	10.00	15,000	150,000	$30.00	1,350,000
Southern Alberta	1.00	35,000	35,000	9.00	315,000
Western Canada	1.00	71,000	71,000	5.00	355,000
Western Pacific	1.00	100,000	100,000	2.50	250,000
		351,000	756,000		4,720,000

Data adapted from *The Natural Gas and Oil Record*. Various dates.

depended on whether additional wells produced oil. Despite the heavy emphasis on the operations of the independent companies, Grostein detected an unmistakable shift in the direction of the boom that pointed to the ascendency of larger combinations and concentrated capital. Trading was "going on steadily, but it involves rather large amounts of capital and is no game for the small fry."[30] Almost as if to prove Grostein's point, on June 6, *The Natural Gas and Oil Record* claimed Alberta-based oil companies had made $4 million in oil since May 15 and published the above table (6-1) of stock prices. The Calgary Petroleum Products Company copied the information and then used it to feature prominently in its advertisements in Spokane newspapers.[31]

Careful readers, however, would note that, apart from Calgary Petroleum Products, none of the other companies produced any oil whatsoever. Their stock prices were largely fictitious and based largely on the success of other firms operating in the field rather than their own. To be sure, Monarch Oil's well near Olds showed some promise in early June, but striking oil was hardly guaranteed (see Chapter 11).

The boom, however, did not remain confined to Calgary and replayed itself throughout the month of June in communities across central Alberta. The press and investors eagerly awaited a second strike to confirm the extent of the field and, perhaps, the presence of crude oil in commercial quantities.

In Edmonton, as in Calgary, thousands of brokerages mushroomed, specializing in selling stock in firms seeking to develop the area delineated from Rocky Mountain House in the west to Athabasca in the north and as far east as Wainwright. In central Alberta near Red Deer, newspapers focused on Monarch's progress, especially after the *Albertan* reported the well struck wet gas on June 18. Red Deer newspapers published weekly rather than daily— *The Red Deer News* on Wednesdays and the *Red Deer Advocate* on Fridays, meaning that the two papers bracketed the Thursday, June 18, announcement made by the *Albertan* that injected a jolt of electricity into the boom. With most of the attention focused on the "Calgary district" and the horse race between Calgary Petroleum Products, McDougall-Segur, Black Diamond, and United Oils to produce crude first, hardly anyone paid close attention to developments in central Alberta, making events there deliciously unexpected. "The news has set a flame alight," wrote the *Vancouver Daily World*. "Calgary will never look back."[32]

While many around Red Deer predicted an oil find in the region, they were nonetheless surprised that crude oil showed at such a shallow depth—808 feet. Reports of the strike spread by word of mouth on the morning of June 18 and made their way to the land office to get a number to file on mineral rights. Rumours claimed swarms of Calgarians were on their way north by automobiles and via the morning train, prompting the *Red Deer Advocate* to report that one barber left a customer in the chair to go claim a number. The editor then made a friendly wager that the numbers currently sitting at 275 would not reach 500 by the end of the day, and lost.[33] By the time the train arrived at noon, over 500 people already had numbers, "including many ladies," noted *The Red Deer News*, "some of high social standing." Unaware that the local rush took place preceding their arrival, potential investors dashed off the train to Ross Street toward the land office. Some ran to their destination, arriving red-faced, winded by the exertion, and were "scarcely able to speak." "The look on the faces of some of them when they saw the number of their ticket was a study; disgust was expressed on every face." Another mad rush came with the arrival of the evening train. However, these visitors represented larger syndicates and they looked for people with lower numbers willing to sell their tickets and right to file. From seven to eleven p.m. the offices of local brokerages, Latimer & Botterill and Lionel Page, "were besieged with buyers and sellers, and many numbers changed hands from five dollars up to one hundred dollars." The impromptu sale of tickets produced other problems as many of the visitors now lacked funds for other expenses, like a hotel room, while they waited to file claims starting the next morning.

The CPR's telegraph office did brisk business as the visitors wired or phoned Calgary for money. In one case, one potential investor wired their partners in Calgary to send money to Red Deer for ten a.m. While their partners fulfilled the request, for some reason when the applicant went to the bank to withdraw the funds, the bank would not release the cash. Running out of time to make his claim at the land office, the man rushed around the streets looking for familiar faces to loan them some cash for half an hour. "They were successful in getting a part, but not all they wanted," noted the News.[34]

The Red Deer News proclaimed, "Great oil field in Red Deer District: Monarch, west of Olds, strikes heavy black oil." The extensive article that followed quickly claimed that the Monarch discovery was more significant than that of Dingman because it brought "black oil, long dreamed of by the Alberta oil operator, the mother fluid from which comes the lighter and more volatile oil, such as is produced by the Discovery well of the Calgary Petroleum Product company."[35] The luxury of producing a weekly paper enabled the editor of the News to contextualize the events of the previous week. "Discovery of oil west of Olds," wrote the News, "demonstrates beyond a doubt the claim of experts that the main body of oil would be found north of the Dingman well." Those same experts claimed oil-bearing formations covered a distance some 600 miles. If true, it meant the whole province sat upon a massive reservoir. "Every indication goes to show the Red Deer district ... is in the centre of the oil region, and that there is a great future in store for us." In the meantime, the editor urged every citizen to purchase "a few shares at least" in companies operating locally to "help along the good work."[36]

The Natural Gas and Oil Record claimed that Monarch's strike of wet gas produced a rush at the land office, where speculators filed leases on twenty sections of land close to Monarch's well. Monarch's success, noted the Record, "means an immense extension of the oil area, as this well is located many miles northwest of Calgary." The Record speculated that within three months, the number of wells in Alberta would be "almost countless," extending more than 150 miles northwest and southeast and fifty miles west and east of Calgary. The railroads would strain to handle the drilling equipment already ordered, let alone the equipment recently ordered.[37]

As Georgeson and Monarch stockholders celebrated their windfall, Buck continued to try and make a living from small investors as the directors of the Black Diamond attempted to rehabilitate Black Diamond's image. Perhaps Buck grew uneasy with the stories and rumours circulating around town or maybe he began to find it difficult to attract investment dollars when everyone assumed he was crooked. Or, for those less inclined to give Buck

Figure 6-2 "Picnic group at site of Dingman #1 well (Calgary Petroleum Products #1), Turner Valley, Alberta."
Picnics by members of the public at the oil wells, like this one at the Dingman well in 1914, sustained and nurtured public interest in the oil field and became standard practice. George Buck's picnic at the Black Diamond well in early June received extensive coverage from newspapers in Calgary and Vancouver. (Glenbow Archives CU1136172)

the benefit of the doubt, he just wanted another chance to fleece the public. Regardless of his motivation, Buck invited the press and the public to visit Black Diamond #1 for a picnic over the weekend of June 6–7 and followed up with open houses on June 8–9. Despite the announcement having been issued at the last minute in the Friday edition of the *Albertan,* press accounts and photographs reveal a successful, and well-attended, open house. One report noted that several ladies attended the picnic and played a game of pickup baseball. Jennie Earl oversaw the luncheon table and ensured "that all present were made to feel—what they really were—heartily welcome." L.D. Taylor, the managing editor of the *Vancouver Daily World,* visited the site and witnessed the explosion of natural gas when someone placed a piece of lit waste into the well. Afterward, Taylor announced that he "formed the impression that the prospects at the well were extremely bright."[38]

The *Albertan* sent a reporter, J.M.D. Ritchie, who promised to get to "the truth" about Black Diamond Oil Fields. Instead of a hard-hitting expose, the *Albertan* produced a puff piece that self-consciously tried to smooth over Buck's rough edges and depict the company, and its owner, as a misunderstood but hard-working man with a dream. Ritchie noted that by early June many Calgarians were well acquainted with George Buck and Black Diamond. Stories about the company were "about as numerous as the sands of the seashore" and obliquely referenced reports that the hole was between three and eight inches in diameter, and rumours that Buck had salted the well, by acknowledging that several stories circulated, "some of them of colossal absurdity."[39]

Ritchie reassured readers that he did not encounter flesh-eating dogs or armed guards when he entered the well site, but he did notice a gun "of patriarchal design" suspended on a hook in a building at the base of the derrick. Seeing that the gun caught the reporter's eye, someone said it was "the very one from which had been fired a bullet that had narrowly missed sending the great Napoleon to his death on the fatal field of Waterloo." Ritchie refused to venture an opinion about the story's accuracy but did suggest "it possesses the flavor and characteristic of the vast majority of the stories that have passed from mouth to mouth respecting the Black Diamond well." Whether Ritchie meant hard to disprove and mostly harmless or entirely fanciful and created out of whole cloth remained unstated. Ritchie then summarized where matters stood with Black Diamond as of early June. The well remained dry as it reached a depth of 1,625 feet, but Buck showed Ritchie "a large can containing black oil which had been skimmed from off the top of the contents of the bailer on various occasions since the Dakota sands were reached 1,380 feet below the surface." The reporter then said that neither the derrick nor the bailer operated during his visit but that he had no reason to doubt the honesty of Buck's statement. Admittedly, Black Diamond #1 had made little progress over the past few months but that was because "the Dakota sands form the hardest strata through which the drill has to pass." Several times during the weekend, burning waste dropped into the well produced an explosion of flame. Driller James Hayes told the reporter that "he thought considerable risk of serious damage to [the] derrick was involved by the dropping of waste into it." Yet the demonstrations continued. Ritchie then turned his attention to Hayes, whom he described as both "modest and sincere." Hayes had thirty years' experience in the oil fields of the United States and had literally drilled hundreds of wells. Hayes's informed opinion, noted Ritchie, is that "a body of crude oil would be struck at Black Diamond and that the strike would be made before the drill had penetrated a depth of 2,000 feet." The same sense of optimism pervaded the other five employees on the property, all of whom professed that they had invested their own funds in the well. Ritchie concluded the article by arguing that Buck and Black Diamond are "doing everything humanly possible to reach the oil, and their prospects of doing so are as fair and hopeful as looked the camp yesterday."[40]

Within a matter of days following the picnic at Black Diamond, rival United Oils announced that they expected to strike oil within a month, and the front page of the *Albertan* reported conditions at United's well mimicked those at Calgary Petroleum Products immediately before their strike. Buck's competitiveness compelled him to announce that conditions at Black Diamond #1 indicated the well would come in within the next four days. "The oil is increasing with every baler that comes out," Buck told the *Herald*. "The dumpings on the sluices are literally covered with black oil and the indications are so good that we think the shareholders should know." To the *Albertan*, Buck elaborated further, stating, "I believe that in four days' time one of the best wells on the continent will be brought in on this property." The announcement created a flurry of activity on June 12 on the Calgary Stock Exchange, which likely witnessed another kind of market manipulation known as "painting the tape" with successive small orders at increasing (or decreasing, depending on one's goals) values. On June 12, increased trade volumes brought the total value of Black Diamond stock traded to $80,000, including one block of 1,500 shares of Black Diamond for $25,000. The rally enabled Black Diamond to reach seven dollars, rising from three dollars over the previous two days, and drew the attention of Spokane newspapers.[41] But the *Albertan* reported that when sales fell below $4.75, Buck's own brokers, perhaps Clark and Smith, placed a floor under prices by buying shares liberally, enabling a close at five dollars. A few days later, Buck objected to the *Albertan's* story, claiming that "I have no brokers operating for me on the market, and I am not selling Black Diamond stock." The statement was technically true, as Clark and Smith sold Black Diamond stock held by the Coalinga Syndicate. Decades later, broker R.C. Carlile described another element to the explanation for the frenzy, claiming that, to stimulate interest in Black Diamond stock on the floor of the Calgary Stock Exchange, Buck sold shares directly to brokers with a fifty-cent discount. Now highly motivated by the search for an easy profit, the brokers did the rest of the work for Buck, pushing Black Diamond stock so they could capture higher commissions.[42]

George Buck's elaborate schemes started unravelling by mid-June and he began lashing out at enemies, both real and perceived. The Wolverton lawsuit drew his time and attention away from more serious matters, but he just would not admit defeat and move on. As the oil boom sputtered and flailed, Buck grew increasingly desperate to prolong it and inject more enthusiasm into investors by launching Black Diamond #2. However, on June 16, Wolverton's lawyer, Clifford Jones, secured an hour-long discovery hearing. The transcript of the hearing reveals either Buck's distractedness, irascibility, and belligerence or his stunning ignorance about his company. Asked at the outset by Jones if he took the time to prepare for the hearing by reviewing the plaintiff's complaint and reviewing documents subpoenaed from the Black Diamond company, Buck admitted, "I do not think I have." Worse, he failed to comply with the subpoena's request to provide any "books or documents" pertaining to the lawsuit. Things went downhill from there. A clearly preoccupied Buck could not recall basic information about the company, such as when it incorporated or the date the company filed the prospectus with the province, nor could he say when Wolverton obtained the share certificates. Buck's evasiveness and lack of recall created the impression he had something to hide. Questioned if he told Wolverton to keep the 2,000 shares for services already rendered, Buck snapped back that Wolverton never rendered any services to the company. "He was like the rest of the bunch," sniffed Buck, "and did all the knocking he could."[43] In all, it was a dreadful performance by a corporate officer in front of the court. Worse yet, Buck knew it too. Near the end of the hour, Buck's temper flashed after Jones questioned why Buck failed to sign the back of Black Diamond share certificates as required by the province.

Q: And you are the president?

A: Yes.

Q: And Campbell the secretary, is that your brother-in-law?

A: No, he is not my brother-in-law, that is one of the stunts you fellows have been shooting around town that makes me sick.

Q: I am not shooting anything.

A: Don't do that now any more or you might find something sticking into you sometime.

This was not the first whiff of violence around Buck. Certainly, some of his ads talked tough about his nemeses, and at the end of May, Lulu DeWitt accused Buck of assault, only to withdraw the complaint just before the arraignment.[44] But here, in front of a stenographer and court officials, Buck threatened an officer of the court. Moments later, the examination wrapped up with the clerk of the court making a pointed comment regarding Buck's lack of preparation and clearly stating the examination would resume after Buck refreshed his memory. Buck did his best to put off his return appearance by not showing at three consecutive scheduled hearings. Finally, Justice Stewart granted one final deferral, but issued a chamber summons to Buck, warning that another no-show might result in a summary judgment against him.[45]

What was so important that Buck would miss multiple court-appointed examinations? Buck was desperately trying to salvage his company. Despite all the schemes, picnics, and stock sold, Buck had yet to pay drillers Martin and Phillips for their services and now owed International Supply Company in excess of $12,000. Around the middle of the month, coinciding with Buck's discovery hearing, Martin and Phillips grew tired of subsidizing Black Diamond's drilling program and told Buck they would part ways, remove their rig and tools, and move on. International Supply Company had plenty of other drilling contracts to fulfil from paying customers. But if the rig left, it would shatter the illusion Buck had created of progress on the well and put an end to his attempts to raise money. Buck pleaded with the drillers to leave the derrick behind for one week and they finally relented, but Martin and Phillips took their tools with them and left behind the boiler, engine, and two men at camp waiting to start up again when Buck got some money in from selling stock.

Salting the well the first time had yielded quick returns; perhaps lightning could strike twice. To get around the messy fact that International Supply had pulled its equipment and people from the well site, Buck formed a drilling company, Earl Drilling (named after Jennie Earl), and bought a new cable before returning to Sheep Creek to run the tools down the hole. On June 18, Black Diamond announced that drilling had resumed at Black Diamond #1, and by June 20, fanned by reporting in *The Black Diamond Press*, multiple reports circulated in Vancouver, Edmonton, and Toronto of oil strikes at Black Diamond #1 and McDougall-Segur. Indeed, *The National Post* quoted George Buck's prediction that drillers would "pierce into the big body of oil at any moment."[46] Meanwhile, reached by the *News Telegram,* Black Diamond trustee E.H. Crandell said drillers had pulled very heavy black oil "in the bucketsful" out of the well. The *News Telegram* also received confirmation from Allan Clark, who reported that "it was probable that a large body of oil had been encountered."[47] That night, it is highly likely that Buck salted Black Diamond #1 for a second time. Two days later, on the evening of June 23—the very day Jones filed a request compelling Buck to appear or else forfeit the case—reporting likely published by *The Black Diamond Press* intimated that

Black Diamond #1 had struck oil and touched off what the *Albertan* called "the wildest, insanest, most exciting night yet."[48]

Perhaps the insanity owed at least part of its enthusiasm to the boldface headline of the June 24 edition of the *Albertan*—"**Persistent report that oil has been struck in well of Black Diamond**"—and the fact that the paper claimed having received confirmation of the strike "by an official in the Black Diamond company." The story also claimed an acquaintance of Buck's, Garnett Rice, "examined the oil in every conceivable manner, and was very enthusiastic over the discovery." At first, Buck refused to confirm or deny reports but later claimed "black oil had been encountered in the well" and said that it existed in "fair quantity."[49]

Not even the Dingman announcement of over a month before compared. People gathered on the street and hotel lobbies buzzed as if a large convention was taking place. Investors rushed to the various stock markets, which became so crowded it was impossible to move in or out for several hours. Black Diamond stock that traded for $4.78 before the rumour now sold for as much as sixteen dollars. One man waved a ten-share certificate in the air on 9th Avenue and declared he would sell it for ten dollars a share now but that it would surely reach twenty dollars a share the next day. Another man cried "take it" and "charged toward the vendor as though he intended to run him down." Black Diamond stock began to appear on the streets with eager sellers and buyers. "The more that was sold," wrote the *Albertan*, "the more stock seemed to fairly spring up from the ground . . . . It was as though a printing press somewhere was just grinding out certificates." By the time Buck authorized the *Albertan* to deny the story, both enthusiasm and the stock price dropped, with the stock settling at $5.50.[50]

In many ways, it did not matter if Black Diamond struck oil because other promoters used the rumours to sell their own stock. The Hartford Oil Company took a page from Buck's playbook and published a provocative advertisement in *The Saskatoon Daily Star*, complete with reprinted telegrams, claiming an oil strike. A week later, despite assurances from various quarters that oil existed, no one else could verify the report. With Buck maintaining his silence, the *Albertan* labelled him "the Sphinx of the Oil Field" even as he teased the paper with a provocative statement about a "gusher" at the well site. "Compared with him," grumbled the paper, "a deaf and dumb mute sounds like a militant suffragette at a meeting being addressed by [David] Lloyd George."[51]

Finally, on June 26, Buck gave an exclusive interview to the *Herald* that attempted to clean up many of the misstatements about Black Diamond #1 dating back to June 12—nearly two whole weeks—since Buck had issued a statement expecting an oil strike within four days. Buck then claimed a small well collapse delayed the discovery a few more days since the drill bit was more than 100 feet deeper than the casing. Driller James Hayes decided to under-ream (enlarge) the hole and lay down more casing. Then the under-reamer jammed and took twenty-two hours to dislodge. Nearly a week later, on June 18, Buck claimed drilling had barely resumed when cracks developed in the jars of the drilling tools, requiring another delay, this time for new parts to arrive. Drilling started again, according to Buck, but then the drill became stuck in the hole for twelve hours. Yet by this time, stories of an oil strike at Black Diamond #1 circulating in Calgary had reached Buck, who immediately dropped everything to travel out to the well with friend Garnett Rice. Allegedly, Buck told Rice that he could come to the well provided he would not make any statements about what he saw. The two men arrived just as the drillers were bailing out the well. When the emptied bailer revealed the oil, Buck claimed Rice became greatly excited. "It appears that when Rice got back to the city he was unable to withstand the importunities of those asking for information and told what he saw," suggesting that the reports of the strike at Black Diamond owed themselves to Rice's overactive imagination. Perhaps anticipating the question as to why he did not act to shut the story down earlier, Buck suddenly became the victim, claiming he did not wish to make any statement "because my statements are invariably misconstructed and this is the last time I am going to say anything for publication until we are ready to make an announcement."[52]

What Rice did not mention to reporters, and what Buck cleverly concealed, was that all drilling operations at Black Diamond #1 had ended more than a week earlier. Rumours of the strike at Black Diamond electrified Calgarians and made the front page of the *Spokane Daily Chronicle* under the headline "Oil-mad mobs in buying frenzy on Calgary streets."[53] In Edmonton, Tiny Phillips learned from a hotel switchboard operator that Black Diamond #1 had struck oil and promptly returned to Calgary. The next morning, a reporter stopped by his hotel room to ask if Phillips had any Black Diamond stock to sell. Phillips replied affirmatively—unusual for an oil company, Buck had given Martin and Phillips shares in the company as an incentive to keep drilling. But Phillips told the reporter the stock was worthless; the reporter responded it was not. Word around town was that Buck had drilled the hole a few feet deeper and struck oil, and Buck handed vials of oil-streaked water as proof. Phillips blurted that Buck was lying, explaining that International Supply had removed their tools and crew from the site, leaving only a driller and a tool dresser to watch over the derrick. Phillips doubted Buck possessed the wherewithal to drill the well any further. Phillips then went to Buck's office to confront him, only to find investors flooding the office, clamouring to buy Black Diamond #2 stock. Buck met Phillips at the door and hustled him into a back room. In the privacy of the office, Buck handed Phillips a cheque for $500 in partial payment on the $12,000 he owed and claimed that he had managed to drill a few feet further and struck oil, showing Phillips a bottle of oil allegedly from the well. Journalist and historian John Schmidt wrote that it was only at this moment that Tiny Phillips realized for the first time that Buck had salted the well and involved some of his employees in the process. After a heated exchange, Tiny Phillips severed all ties between International Supply Company and Black Diamond and left Buck's office to go to the well site to collect driller James Hayes. Once there, Phillips found the well site protected by armed guards. When questioned, driller Hayes told Phillips that Buck had brought a barrel of oil to the well and poured it in, "salting" the well. According to Phillips's account, he took Hayes to the railroad station and the driller left Calgary never to return. But court testimony later revealed that Hayes left International Supply Company when Phillips and Martin severed ties with Black Diamond Oil Fields on June 25. Instead of returning to the United States, Hayes was hired by Buck directly to continue drilling Black Diamond #1, with Buck sending him out of town to buy a string of tools to replace the ones removed by International Supply Company. Regardless, Phillips began telling anyone who would listen that it was impossible for Buck to strike oil. "However, my words did not seem to have any effect on the investing public," noted Phillips. "They were buying up stock like mad."[54]

The Natural Gas and Oil Record reported receiving private assurances that Black Diamond had struck oil but added that Buck would not confirm the same publicly, injecting a healthy dose of caution with its observation that "this is the Well of Mystery." Noting Buck's wild swings in transparency over the past month—from protecting the well with armed sentries to holding picnics on the property—the *Record* concluded, "It seems to us something like the old game—'Now you see it; now you don't.'" A week later, referencing a growing push by the attorney general's office cracking down on false advertisers, the *Record* suggested that "if the crown prosecutor will look over the advertising of a certain company and compare promises and statements with results that he will find plenty to keep him busy." The constant needling by the editor of the *Record* prompted Buck to promise he would swear out a warrant for the arrest of Tucker if given an opportunity.[55]

Growing unease with the frequency of stock market frenzies created by bogus rumours increasingly defined the emerging Alberta industry as brokers and investors both reacted violently to rumours. "It could take hours for a messenger to get from a telephone to a wellsite and back again," wrote the *Western Oil Examiner* decades later. "A rumor that would send the stock up in the afternoon might be exploded by the time the evening auctions got underway; or vice versa."[56] Reports of the rumoured strike at Black Diamond reached as far south as Spokane, where the *Chronicle* noted that Calgary newspapers were "anxious from the start to get true reports of the development work" and to disprove false alarms. In 1914, not only was Spokane the largest, and most proximate, US city to Calgary, it also had a distinguished history of providing capital for western Canadian mining ventures.[57] Contemporary estimates suggest Calgary oil promoters raised as much as $200,000 ($6.1 million adjusted for inflation) in Spokane alone. This compares favourably to the estimated $250,000 ($7.7 million adjusted for inflation) raised by Calgary oil companies in Vancouver.[58] The difficulty, noted the *Chronicle,* was that there were too many oil companies and corporate officials were too hard to reach, causing problems for potential investors seeking accurate information. "It often takes hours to get the facts after a rumor gets afloat," noted the Spokane paper. The reporter pointed out that, usually, "orgies of speculation" based on rumours started between editions of the newspapers. Calgary's southern neighbours sounded increasingly cautious and skeptical about the Calgary boom, pointing out that "the temper of the people and the method of the oil wildcatter" made investing increasingly risky and dubious. To prove its point, the paper pointed to Ira Segur's decision to drill a wildcat well in the Sweetgrass area near the international boundary and the frenzy that resulted of companies and investors rushing to snap up acreage. Then the market flooded with a deluge of shares based on nothing more than dubious holdings that informed opinion considered to be practically worthless. Slowly but surely, the boom became a caricature of itself where the phrase "Calgary oil" became the punchline. The Crescent Menswear store in Spokane pitched a new lightweight suit that "will add so much to your comfort it will prove a lot better investment than most of the Calgary oil stock."[59] The machinations of the rogues and charlatans had clearly left a mark.

7

Boycotts, Consumer Protection, and Private Detectives: Responses to the Boom, from Voluntary Associations to the Pinkertons

> *A provincial inspector should carefully scrutinize the capitalization and the initial assets of every company. He should formulate stringent regulations under which every company seeking a charter must operate and he should have no hesitation in cancelling a charter where these regulations have not been lived up to . . . . It is quite clear to the careful observer that, unless the government of Alberta comes forward and, by stringent regulations, places the stamp of governmental approval upon every legitimate company and assumes responsibility for the honest administration of organizations incorporated under the laws of this province, there will be legislation against Calgary oil stock in every province in the Dominion.*
>
> —Editorial
> *The Calgary News Telegram*
> June 6, 1914[1]

> *The* Post-Intelligencer *stands for all that is clean and decent and safe in financial affairs. Therefore it is opposed to all efforts to get Seattle money into stock-selling schemes, questionable on their face. To one experienced in financial matters a casual reading of the "literature" with which the United States mails hereabout are now being flooded is all that is necessary to reveal the real character of Calgary oil—that is, the part of Calgary oil that is getting into advertisements and circulars.*
>
> *The* Post-Intelligencer *will not print Calgary oil advertising either on the financial page or in any other part of the paper.*
>
> —"Beware of Calgary oils"
> *The Seattle Post-Intelligencer*
> June 12, 1914[2]

By early July 1914, the underhanded tactics of promoters had already irreparably harmed the reputation of Calgary oil as a sound investment and the province as a good place to do business, with dramatic repercussions. As early as May 29, 1914, Canadian trade journal *The Monetary Times* bluntly stated that "the Calgary oil boom is a very good thing for the investor—to leave alone."[3] Another British geologist, Dr. T.O. Bosworth, who arrived in Alberta in May 1914 on a prearranged contract for two businessmen interested in the petroleum potential of northwest Alberta, also weighed in on the Calgary field and found it wanting.[4] The subtitle of the May 1914 edition of *The Petroleum World* article called Bosworth's assessment "an unqualified condemnation of the Calgary district." While Bosworth found many positive and encouraging signs in the north around Fort McMurray, he remained unwavering in his belief that investors in Turner Valley would find nothing but grief. "Regarding the Calgary district—the Dingman or Black Diamond or Okotoks field—Dr. Bosworth's opinion remains entirely unfavourable, as it has been from the first." *The Petroleum World* noted that in every case where Bosworth was consulted "he has advised against the promotion of companies, against the acquisition of leases, and against the drilling of wells."[5] A few weeks later, *The Monetary Times* took notice of a story published by the *London Daily Chronicle* titled "Canadian Oil Dangers." The London paper pulled no punches, calling the volume and frequency of misrepresentation and fraud in Alberta's oil patch "appalling," detailing one instance where a company drilled two wells a few hundred yards apart and invited the public to inspect the well. At the designated hour, the well gushed pure gasoline, impressing the assembled guests and undoubtedly convincing a few to invest in the company. Few bothered to notice that the gasoline gusher resulted from the fuel being pumped down one boring and forced up the other. While the correspondent noted there was little reason to doubt that oil lay underground in Alberta's fields, not enough systematic prospecting had taken place to definitively conclude anything just yet. The article's closing must have sent shudders down the backs of Calgary's oil boosters: "It is dangerous to purchase shares in the present undeveloped stage."[6]

Given all the stories circulating about underhanded activities by several oil companies in the spring and early summer of 1914, it is fair to wonder what steps law enforcement took to protect investors. The short answer is not much. Despite having operated in Ontario since the mid-nineteenth century, the petroleum industry remained "new," small, and largely free from government oversight. Apart from generic provincial measures regarding the incorporation of new businesses via the Companies Ordinance, and the operation of US-based companies via the Foreign Companies Ordinance, regulation remained practically non-existent. No industry-specific laws existed regarding production quotas or health and safety, let alone conservation measures or environmental protection. Securities regulation was virtually non-existent. Meanwhile. lines of jurisdiction between the three levels of government were hazy at best. The Dominion government retained jurisdiction over the province's natural resources and mineral rights leases, but the province and city regulated businesses. While the federal government could rely on the Royal North West Mounted Police to execute its laws and the City of Calgary could do the same with the Calgary Police Force (CPF), the province lacked an independent enforcement body and relied either on the RNWMP or the CPF.

At the peak of the boom, the Sifton government thus proved unable or unwilling to restrict issuing corporate charters to fraudulent ventures and lacked the ability to adequately monitor company activities and protect consumers like other jurisdictions. In 1912, Manitoba passed "blue-sky" laws and appointed a public utilities commissioner to enforce legislation; in 1914, Alberta neither passed "blue-sky" laws nor employed a public utilities commissioner. Arguments about moral hazard—that it was not the government's responsibility to protect investors from the consequences of their foolish decisions because it could lead to even more reckless behaviour—ruled the day. However, with so many bad actors openly taking advantage of the lax regulatory environment, consumers could easily claim that moral hazard did not apply because government had abandoned its responsibility to ensure fair play by business. Instead, what investors found was a near-Hobbesian state of anarchy where no overriding authority governed relations between business and consumers and the only check on unruly behaviour was the conscience of individuals. For some, the newly emerging oil industry represented opportunity and the highest manifestation of the values and beliefs that made Alberta—conservative, entrepreneurial risk takers committed to freedom of opportunity—and therefore needed to be protected at all costs. For others, the process led them to distinguish between the characteristics of those in the oil industry and those who were not. For this latter group, while they agreed that the oil patch was conservative, wealthy, and entrepreneurial, they also saw those in it as arrogant, manipulative, dishonest, and "foreign." In this dynamic and fluid environment, people both inside and outside the petroleum industry—as well as people inside and outside Alberta—reconciled themselves to the new reality of Alberta oil by improvising a series of responses to make sense out of developments and reimpose order and predictability.

In the absence of pre-existing structures and institutions to provide protection to consumers, individuals and interest groups fashioned makeshift solutions from the creation of voluntary consumer associations to exercise oversight on the operations of companies and urge government investigations of rule breakers. In the meantime, despite the free market and laissez-faire ethos of the provincial government, both the provincial secretary and the attorney general's office did what they could to enforce existing legislation. When the volume of complaints threatened to overwhelm the system at the start of July 1914, the province retained a private company, the Pinkerton National Detective Agency, to help provide a modicum of protection for consumers by preventing fraud, conducting ad hoc investigations of the activities of individual oil companies, and gathering intelligence on developments in the industry for the attorney general's office. True to their corporate image of maintaining confidentiality, the role of the Pinkertons remained officially hidden even though information and intelligence gathered by Pinkerton operatives led to several criminal convictions of individuals as well as prosecutions of companies under the terms of the Companies Ordinance.

The enormous number of companies sprouting in spring 1914 raised alarm bells, particularly as stories circulated that some were selling shares before obtaining their provincial charters. "Such a procedure," predicted Archibald Dingman on May 20, "infinitely repeated, will give the whole district a bad reputation and do the new industry the greatest possible damage." A day later, the *News Telegram* reported preparations by provincial officials to target companies selling stock without provincial charters or leases as well as to enforce laws regarding the licensing of brokers. Brokers who did not deliver stock certificates risked criminal charges for obtaining money under false pretenses, but anecdotal evidence suggested enforcement of the law proved erratic and haphazard because it depended on the already strained resources of the Calgary Police Force.[7]

The proliferation of "wildcat" companies proved a greater concern to both provincial and municipal officials. Critically, however, an important distinction existed between the way the oil industry and governments defined "wildcats." Heavily influenced by the recent real estate boom, both levels of government defined "wildcatters" as companies operating like real estate speculators, buying and holding property as it appreciated in value, and then selling at a handsome profit. The petroleum industry, on the other hand, regarded wildcatting as a speculative drilling program (i.e., drilling for oil where no other previous drilling took place). The biggest difference is that oil industry wildcatters intended to develop and drill oil and gas properties. Wildcats described by the city and province generally possessed no assets beyond mineral leases but sold shares to investors on the premise that development—in this case, drilling for oil—would take place. As sales of shares increased, the directors recouped their initial investment plus a healthy profit in the process, pulling development capital out of the company treasury to pay themselves first. The crucial difference for would-be government regulators was the belief that wildcatters never intended to drill for oil. The definition, however, remained highly subjective and made enforcement incredibly difficult, especially because of the self-conscious pursuit of an independent oil boom. Could provincial officials reasonably infer malevolent corporate intent when avarice, inexperience, or plain incompetence remained equally plausible explanations for the same behaviour and results? With a finite amount of drilling rigs, tools, and equipment in the province, could law enforcement reasonably distinguish between a rank speculator and a genuine developer experiencing supply chain issues? More importantly, did Albertans want the province making that determination on their behalf? As the newspaper feud over the previous winter had revealed, reasonable people could disagree in their opinions about what constituted speculation.

Nevertheless, on May 21, 1914, the province announced that an official would soon arrive in Calgary to deal with those violating the Companies Ordinance by selling stock despite lacking either a provincial charter or possessing leases. Initially, the province relied on the CPF to try and make life a little more uncomfortable for would-be confidence men. Plainclothes police detectives fanned out over the oil district to check up on the oil companies and find out who had licences and identify the wildcatters. But Police Chief Cuddy made it abundantly clear that his officers would only intervene if oil companies operated without provincial letters of incorporation. On May 22, with Mayor Sinnott out of the city on a trip to Quebec, Acting Mayor Michael C. Costello placed dealing with wildcatters on the city commissioners' agenda for discussion. The most tangible result from municipal efforts was an appeal to the attorney-general's department in Edmonton to do something. The police chief agreed, and suggested the province simply ban wildcat companies because they were more likely to target the small investor, as if declaring the problem over would solve it. Cuddy's greater point, however, was that once companies obtained letters of incorporation from the province, the city had to let them operate. Ultimately, Cuddy believed wildcatters were "a matter for the provincial government and not for the city," leaving investors in jurisdictional purgatory with no one quite sure who was in charge.[8]

In the meantime, officials tried their best to warn investors to be cautious with their money and provide enough information to educate the public. The Dominion government's deputy minister of mines, R.W. Brock, suggested that, given the high production costs prevailing in Alberta, investors should only entrust their savings in companies with enough capital to sink several wells. This, Brock suggested, was one way to distinguish legitimate from illegitimate companies.[9] But the greater problem was a severe lack of transparency provided by some companies and the dearth of reliable information. The Geological Survey of Canada hurried publication of a map and field notes by Donaldson Bogart Dowling of the anticline along the Sheep River and made it available free of charge at all Mines Branch offices. The field notes provided a brief overview of the formation, comparing it to oil fields in Wyoming and Colorado. "The Sheep River anticline would seem to be a favourable situation for the concentration of any oil or gas in the rocks beneath," it stated, but warned of the need for deep drilling to access the producing horizons.[10] Vernon Knowles, while still with *The Saskatoon Daily Star*, advised investors to make use of the map and accompanying field notes to determine where on the anticline the company's property was but acknowledged that this information was difficult to come by. Companies used "inflated, robust, and florid wording" to hide precise locations, choosing instead to describe leases as being "near" some other location or well. "Unless locations are within the oil area, there is no chance of winning and every chance of losing," concluded

Knowles.[11] W.H. Berkinshaw, president of the Calgary Board of Trade, identified unfounded rumours caused by wildcatters to drive up share prices as another problem and feared they would inhibit the flow of investment capital to legitimate companies. Various ideas emerged from the discussion, including one that would adopt press censorship, but none proved practical in the short term.[12]

The provincial government moved slowly through the early stages of the growing oil boom in the province. More than ten days passed between the Dingman discovery and the arrival of provincial officials in Calgary to survey the situation. The promised investigation and elimination of wildcatters suffered from a sharply limited scope. Deputy Provincial Secretary E. Trowbridge arrived in Calgary and promptly consulted with Police Chief Cuddy. Created in 1906, the Provincial Secretary's Office handled incorporation and registration of companies under the Companies Ordinance. "The chief's man always checked on every company that opened for business," announced Trowbridge. This simply meant that a company possessed both a provincial charter and some leases. Trowbridge then pronounced his satisfaction that "everything was in lawful shape before consent was given to operate." However, despite the rapidly accelerated pace of development, specifically the formation of dozens of new companies on an hourly basis, the province refused to open a branch office in Calgary to expedite the incorporation of new companies. The interview concluded with Trowbridge declaring that there were no companies operating in Calgary "that had not complied with every letter of the law." While the statement was unquestionably accurate, insofar as it applied to the registration of companies under provincial laws, it also reflected the reality that regulation of the newly emerging petroleum industry remained poorly developed. Only on May 29, 1914, did the Attorney General's Office insist that companies issue a distinctive form of lithographed or printed receipt rather than a generic blank receipt form for stock purchases.[13]

Back in Edmonton, Trowbridge expressed his confidence in Cuddy's ability to handle the crush of business due to the latter's experience in previous mining booms, most notably as a member of the Toronto police. Realizing his role as the principal means of ensuring oil companies operated within the bounds of the law, Cuddy publicly, and politely, declined all attempts by oil interests to entice him to sit on various boards of directors. "I have no hankering either for oil honors or oil stock," said Cuddy. "At the same time, I wish all the drillers every success and hope that the biggest oil field in the world will be found in this district." The editorial page of the *Herald* marvelled that Cuddy managed to live "in the seething of the oil boom from its beginning, and still he declares he knows nothing about oil and has no opinions to offer on the subject. His is a position of splendid isolation."[14]

Tales of underhanded dealings extended well beyond a few bad actors, and the *Albertan* became concerned at the crush of new promotions and companies vying for attention. One scheme reported by Bob Edwards involved a well-known woman claiming to be a clairvoyant who convinced many that she had the gift of foresight. During the oil boom, people naturally began seeking investment advice. Crowds gathered at her house and people had to make appointments days, if not weeks, in advance. She was so popular that Bob Edwards believed the only person in town who failed to call on her was Police Chief Cuddy. It did not take long for a certain oil company "which bears the name of the emblem of the Hudson's Bay Company"—there are four beavers on the coat of arms for the Hudson's Bay Company—to join forces with the woman to hatch a get-rich-quick scheme. "The clairvoyant, with a mysterious, mystic air, would then proceed to foretell a tremendous gushing of oil at the well in question, earnestly advising her clients to lose no time in buying up all the shares they could get."[15] Founded in 1914 and capitalized at a robust $1.25 million, Beaver Oil Limited proposed to drill one of the first rotary rig wells in Alberta. After the company spudded in at a location in the Jumping Pound Field west of Calgary and set its surface casing, the derrick toppled over in a windstorm. Dr. J.T. Cox, Beaver Oil's managing partner, then announced the company would move the rig to a new location at Sweetgrass near Coutts along the international boundary, where it encountered some success in early 1915. But shortly thereafter, despite finding some oil traces in the well, the company abandoned the well and disappeared, presumably because investment capital dried up.[16]

Despite his roots in the city, the prevailing wisdom held that Premier Arthur Sifton was, at best, indifferent to Calgary's good fortune. At an appearance in Calgary, Premier Sifton's remarks made it clear that he remained informed about developments, expressing great delight at the flood of private sector investment in Alberta's petroleum industry. Sifton also placed clearly defined limits on what his government would do to encourage and regulate the new industry. Private sector development would proceed apace with little additional oversight, as Sifton readily acknowledged that "despite the fact that oil may be found in large commercial quantities," the boom would produce winners and losers. Obliquely referencing the concept of moral hazard, the premier reiterated that it was not his government's job to do anything that might influence those decisions. "There will be many companies that may not be fortunate enough to strike [oil] and many people will lose money.

But on the other hand, many will make money if the fields prove rich." The province, however, would remain at arm's length and allow the market to make decisions. From Sifton's perspective, there was little Edmonton could or should do; investors already provided enough capital "to assure an absolute test of every field in the province." A follow-up question touched on an area of clear provincial responsibility, the building of roads, that now loomed as particularly important to the development of the industry. Given the distance from navigable water, everything in western Canada depended on overland transportation to reach either processing facilities or markets. Since the costs were prohibitive to build railways everywhere, good roads loomed as essential for the development of provincial resources. The question put to Sifton was whether the machinery of government would directly or indirectly support development by embarking on a program of road building. Sifton issued a firm if somewhat circuitous statement that classified road building to the oil regions as speculative development.

> The province is not speculating and neither is it encouraging speculation such as the present. When there is positive assurance of oil in large quantities and the undertaking taken on more stability than an exploration venture, the province might develop some of the road allowance property. If there is oil and the territories where it lies are properly defined, I cannot see why the province itself should not benefit generally by developing in the proven field. But there will be no speculation nor encouragement of it.

Evidently, the premier needed more proof of the petroleum industry's sustainability before committing his government to undertake infrastructure projects.[17]

Sifton's concern regarding the economic viability of the oil boom was well founded. In late July 1914, *The Financial Post* published a primer for would-be oil investors describing what they received, and could expect, from an investment in a speculative oil venture. "A company," wrote the paper, "to be reasonably assured of seeing it through the expenses of exploitation, drilling a borehole, accidents, delays, etc., should have in its treasury $100,000.00 in cash." This would see the company through many anticipated and unanticipated delays. The paper suggested investors begin with an examination of the company's prospectus, particularly the ratio of share capital to the appraised value of the lease. "The lowest ratio at which a lease is usually turned into a company," advised the *Post*, was $501,000 for a company capitalized at

Figure 7-1 "J'Ever See Such Luck?" Premier Sifton (in back seat) wearily greets Calgary's continued good fortune. (University of Calgary Libraries and Cultural Resources CU1301447)

$1 million. Ideally, the company would hold $200,000 in its treasury while offering $299,000 equity in the company to the public. Share values set at fifty cents, less a 20 percent commission to brokers, would net a company $89,700 from the sale of shares. After paying expenses from incorporation and organization, the company capitalized for $1 million likely had $84,700 for drilling and operating expenses. With luck, after completing its sale of shares, the company would strike oil between three and six months later.[18]

But as Sifton remained all too aware, Alberta's oil wealth remained unproven. After all, in the summer of 1914, eighteen months had passed since Dingman started drilling, and the most promising well in the field had yet to strike crude oil. Supporters claimed oil was worth nine dollars per barrel in Calgary (roughly $238.37 per barrel, adjusted for inflation), but it was doubtful that local market price would hold if the field produced oil in any paying quantity. "If oil is struck in one percent of the quantity the oil brokers would have us believe," wrote *The Financial Post*, "the price would quickly drop to one dollar per barrel." This is what happened in the Bakersfield and Kern County fields in California despite pre-existing transportation facilities existing to haul the excess away. Calgary, on the other hand, only could rely on railroad tankers. "If the railroads become clogged with business and the market temporarily glutted, the price of oil might easily drop to fifty cents, and perhaps twenty-five cents per barrel." Assuming the average price of one dollar per barrel and assuming the company saved seventy-five cents per barrel for net earnings, to earn $120,000 the company would have to produce 160,000 barrels of oil for five years (438 barrels per day) simply to break even. The *Post*'s sobering assessment was that any company operating in the Calgary oil fields "must strike oil, and strike it in quantity, before it can get out its public shareholders even, and to make a profit out of operation for them, the company must make more than an ordinary strike." The paper quickly added that it based its assumptions on "companies offering shares in good faith," and left unanswered what would happen in instances "wherein fraud develops, or was there in its incipiency, where bad faith and incapacity are apparent."[19]

The challenge confronting provincial authorities was that persistent, and credible, reports of underhanded behaviour by several brokers, companies, and individuals threw into sharp relief both the province's inadequate regulatory regime and lack of an independent enforcement body. Section 92.14 of the British North America (BNA) Act authorized the provinces to create provincial police forces, but by 1914, such forces only existed in British Columbia, Ontario, and Quebec, while the prairie provinces relied on the Mounties to enforce provincial laws. Created by Prime Minister John A. Macdonald in 1873, the North West Mounted Police (NWMP) served as a cost-effective, but temporary, method for law enforcement in the West. But Macdonald and his successors found the NWMP both useful and effective. Even the Laurier government, which had planned to eliminate the NWMP after Alberta and Saskatchewan became provinces, reconsidered. Mounting public pressure in the West to retain the popular police force convinced Laurier to change his mind. Thus, a system emerged that enabled the provinces to "rent" a specific number of officers for an annual fee to circumvent the BNA Act's designation of policing a provincial responsibility while the Mounties were a federal agency.[20]

But the RNWMP (having been designated "Royal" by King Edward in 1904) only operated in the cities at the request of local police forces and, in 1914, sorely lacked an investigatory capacity capable of overseeing the boom. Given that Calgary served as the nexus of the oil boom, it meant that enforcement of what few provincial regulations there were fell on the already overstretched Calgary Police Force. Amid the rash of spurious oil strike reports in June 1914, Police Inspector William Nutt, who served as second in command to Chief Cuddy, joked to the *Albertan* that if someone were smart enough to salt a well using "unadulterated Calgary beer and announce a gusher" it would produce the biggest rush of investors in world history. "After we got them here, we could keep them till we struck oil which will only be a matter of a few days." Nutt's attempt at humour notwithstanding, the spate of unfounded rumours prompted the Calgary Board of Trade and the attorney general's office to act. Assistant Crown Prosecutor Joseph T. Shaw placed companies, promoters, and salesmen on notice: making knowingly false statements, verbally or in advertisements, to sell stock was illegal. Shaw also promised to vigorously pursue unregistered companies.[21]

Instead of finding financial security, some investors found only frustration as hasty decisions to invest in May unnecessarily tied up funds when brokers failed to complete sales or deliver stock certificates in a timely fashion, prompting a warning to investors by Acting Deputy Attorney General John Hunt on June 2, 1914, to make sure they secured their share certificates "without delay."[22] For some, it was already too late. Hugh Anderson of Calgary complained to the attorney general's office that they paid for 300 shares in British Canadian Oil Company on May 23, 1914, but only received 200 certificates. When Anderson contacted the company, he received assurances that the matter would be "straightened out" quickly. But when a month of back-and-forth between himself and the manager resulted in no action taken, Anderson contacted the attorney general. "I bought these shares in the first instances as a little investment against the present stagnation of trade," wrote Anderson. "I am now very poor. If I had these shares, I could turn them over and get about and look for a job." The involvement of the attorney general's office initially produced little traction, as the manager of British-Canadian Oil continued to disavow responsibility, claiming it was a matter between Anderson and the sales agent in Swift Current. "We have twice written our agent at Swift Current asking him to trace same for us, but so far he has not answered our letters." With a faint hint of condescension, the manager claimed, "We have explained all this to Mr. Anderson, & have assured him that he would receive his certificate in due course." Tiring of the game quickly, the acting attorney general, George Paget Owen Fenwick, tersely suggested "the proper thing for you to do is to deliver the stock and take it up with your agent afterwards," adding, "I should be glad if you would fix it up at once."[23]

As reports and complaints of criminal behaviour multiplied and with police forces in Edmonton and Calgary overwhelmed, the provincial government brought in Pinkerton detectives to serve as investigators and a security force preventing crime for the attorney general's department. Established by Allan Pinkerton in 1850, the US-based Pinkerton National Detective Agency evolved over the course of the nineteenth century from a masterful detective agency solving crimes to the premier private law enforcement organization of its era. Indeed, historian David Williams writes that by the 1890s, the name "Pinkerton" became synonymous with crime prevention and by 1910 "momentum towards security work gathered an irresistible force."[24] The attorney general's office files in the Provincial Archives of Alberta hold a total of seven reports labelled "Wild Cat Oil Company" from two Pinkerton operatives (never identified by name, per Pinkerton rules), P7 and P26. Operative P7 filed one report on events in Edmonton; Operative P26 filed the remaining six from Calgary via the Pinkerton office in Winnipeg. Reports specify that operatives took instructions directly from officials in the attorney general's office. In Edmonton, the Pinkertons reported to Arthur E. Popple, who served as the province's legal adviser to the RNWMP, while in Calgary they worked with Assistant Crown Prosecutor Joseph T. Shaw.[25]

Pinkerton operatives launched immediate investigations into several companies, brokers, and individuals with the intention of building criminal cases for provincial prosecutors when possible. Perhaps surprisingly, given its low reputation, no records exist of investigation into Black Diamond Oil Fields and George Buck, although one the Pinkertons' greatest successes tangentially involved Vernon Knowles, the managing editor of *The Black Diamond Press*. Lured away from Saskatoon by Buck to the frenzy of boomtown Calgary, Knowles received a telegram from his brother on June 19, asking him to buy fifteen dollars worth of shares (approximately $400, adjusted for inflation) in "a likely proposition." That evening, he sought confirmation of a rumoured oil strike at McDougall-Segur but his enquiries did not result in a definitive answer. Outside the People's Stock Exchange, speculation buzzed, but details were scarce. On 8th Avenue, Knowles saw a crowd gathered at Marceau Brothers Jewelry store, where a blackboard announced, "It is officially announced that McDougall-Segur has struck oil." Inside, Knowles questioned broker Frank Rose, determined to learn if the blackboard's announcement was accurate. According to Knowles's testimony, Rose allegedly responded, "You will see tomorrow when you are paying three dollars for Stokes-Stevens and two dollars for Piedmont," two companies with leases adjacent to McDougall-Segur. Although the day's trading saw both companies' shares trading between twenty and twenty-five cents per share, Rose offered Piedmont Petroleum shares for sale at seventy-five cents, claiming once again that the rumoured strike at McDougall-Segur was confirmed. Reassured by a clerk, Knowles bought twenty shares of Piedmont. By morning, however, company officials denied the strike, and Piedmont remained at twenty cents per share.[26]

Rather than report the incident to the police, Knowles published a piece in *The Black Diamond Press* detailing the incident, bringing himself to the attention of the Pinkerton investigation. Due to many brokers being willing to testify, the investigation soon identified Marceau Brothers as the origin of the rumour. Evidently, Rose was not particularly well liked by other brokers, who were only too eager to provide evidence against him. Within a week, the Pinkertons put Knowles in contact with Assistant Crown Prosecutor Joseph T. Shaw.[27] "We have a good strong case against [Rose]," noted Operative 26's report, "and expect a conviction." Publicly, credit for the investigation and the arrest went to CPF detective Tom Turner, as the *News Telegram* heaped praise on the provincial government in their efforts to "put to an end such rumors of oil strikes" rife in Calgary. The *Spokane Daily Chronicle* noted that despite numerous other examples of underhanded dealings, Rose was the first broker to have charges pressed against him. "The crown prosecutor declares this sort of thing will have to stop."[28]

The denouement of the Rose case, however, proved disappointing. At the preliminary hearing, Police Magistrate Colonel Sanders raised questions about the actions of the *Albertan* during Rose's questioning, noting that the newspaper played a pivotal role in creating the frenzied environment by publishing unverified rumours to scoop its competition. Assistant Crown Prosecutor Shaw readily agreed after conducting his own investigation in connection with the Rose case, accompanying Vernon Knowles to the Marceau Brothers Jewelry store on June 26 to question and charge Rose and Roberts. Allegedly, during their conversation, Rose told Knowles and Shaw that the brokerage business "was all done on rumors and that it was all a gamble."[29] Casting his net more broadly against the organizations and institutions that exploited the boom for their own purposes, Shaw urged newspapers to "keep within legitimate bounds in reporting the news of conditions at oil wells." Shaw also warned advertisers that they opened themselves to penalties "if they made untrue statements" while coaxing investments in their properties. While Shaw promised to prosecute "every dishonest advertiser against whom I can establish a case," he hoped he could count on the assistance of newspaper editors to keep oil advertising "clean and legitimate to the greatest possible extent."[30]

The rewards from spreading false rumours, however, far outweighed the potential punishment. At trial four months later in October, Rose estimated that on the night of June 19, the rumour led to between $7,000 and $8,000 (approximately $186,672 and $212,200, adjusted for inflation) worth of business at a time when the boom appeared dead on its feet. Indeed, examining bank clearings shows that the week prior to the wildcat rumour, Calgary bank clearings declined approximately 23 percent over the year before. But the week of the McDougall-Segur rumour, which also saw alleged strikes at Monarch and Black Diamond, enabled bank clearings to reach their highest total of the boom—nearly 38 percent larger than the year before (See Table 5-1). Assuming Rose took the standard 25 percent commission, stock sales alone netted him between $1,750 and $2,000 ($46,400–$53,000, adjusted for inflation). Although the court found him guilty, the punishment—a fifty-dollar fine plus court costs—still left him with a healthy profit and hardly served as a deterrent. Perhaps anticipating an outcry against his sentence, rendered in October 1914 after the collapse of the boom and the start of the Great War, Justice McCarthy observed that if he convicted everyone in Calgary who falsely claimed an oil strike there would be no one left to send to the Western Front.[31] The *Herald* used the judgment to argue for the importance of always telling the truth. "Had this rule been religiously observed by everyone connected with the oil game from its commencement, there would have been much less criticism of the oil boomers today, and generally the oil business here would stand on a much better footing than it does." For its part, *The Natural Gas and Oil Record* revelled in the irony that the Frank Rose case hinged on a connection to Black Diamond and stated that if the Crown prosecutor examined "the advertising of a certain company and compared promises and statements with results that he would find plenty to keep him busy."[32]

In addition to the Rose case, the Pinkertons pursued several other investigations, from companies working without a charter to further allegations of fraud. Investors who believed in the idea of an independent oil boom strenuously objected in July 1914 when seven companies proposed a merger to form Alberta Petroleum Consolidated—a conglomerate with an aggregate capital of $20 million ($606.7 million, adjusted for inflation) and approximately 100,000 acres of mineral rights.[33] Rallying other shareholders to oppose the move, the minority group belatedly realized the company's directors retained the controlling interest in the company despite the sales of thousands of shares. In some cases, companies issued hundreds of thousands of dollars worth of vendor's stock, diluting both the pool of shareholders and the influence of those holding treasury stock in the process. "We are informed," began one complaint lodged by B.W. Collison with the attorney general's office about Herron-Elder, "that this stock has been sold by the agents for the company's treasury stock and in nearly every instance a prospectus has been given to the purchaser, of vendor's stock, leading the purchaser to believe that the money paid by him was being paid into the treasury of the company for development purposes." More frustrating was that some certificates were unnumbered, making it "almost impossible to tell what stock was purchased from the vendor's stock and what stock was purchased from the treasury." Mr. Collison then implored the attorney-general's office to "send an Inspector to Calgary to investigate the affairs of the companies proposing to go into the merger." Unbeknownst to Collison, Pinkerton Operative 26 was already doing so.[34]

The Pinkertons' report observed that the proposed merger kicked up a substantial protest, as the operative and Shaw learned firsthand after attending a Herron-Elder shareholders' meeting on July 22. The minority shareholders learned that their voting power in the company's affairs was substantially less than what they imagined. Although 17,000 individuals held shares in the company, the company's directors still retained the controlling interest and pushed forward with plans to bring about a merger of several smaller concerns into a larger conglomerate. Disgruntled minority shareholders banded together and retained lawyer M.B. Peacock to block the move and file a lawsuit against the directors for $450,000 (roughly $13.5 million, adjusted for inflation). The plaintiffs alleged the requirements of the Companies Ordinance, including statutory meetings, reports of stock sales, and the numbering of shares, had gone unfulfilled.[35] Operative 26's investigation revealed the share certificates and books of the Herron-Elder company were "more or less in a muddled condition." Shaw's investigation found that vendors had returned 190,000 shares of vendor's stock to the treasury. Thus, when the company sold vendor's stock instead of treasury stock, the proceeds went to the vendor rather than to the treasury for development purposes. Shaw suspected that sloppy bookkeeping was far more common in 1914 than most investors realized. For most Herron-Elder shareholders, the issue only emerged as a source of friction in July 1914 when they found themselves dramatically outnumbered—200,000 voting shares versus 19,000 voting shares—and with little control over the direction of the company.[36]

Use of the Pinkertons hid the extent to which the provincial government exercised some oversight on the boom and spurred the use of self-help measures by groups, institutions, and organizations inside and outside the province to curb the wildcatters. Winnipeg's public utilities commissioner,

Judge H.A. Robson, invoked his responsibility toward consumers as his justification for prohibiting Calgary stockbrokers from selling oil shares in Manitoba. Classifying petroleum stock as mining stock meant Alberta-based petroleum companies were subject to Manitoba's Sale of Shares Act, exposing the companies to a modicum of oversight and preventing the advertisement of Calgary oil stocks in the province of Manitoba. Legislation required companies to keep current financial statements on file with the public utilities commissioner, demonstrating that businesses could carry out the operations they claimed to do. Robson also sent the federal postmaster general samples of circulars sent by oil companies to Manitobans. Not only did these circumvent Manitoba laws prohibiting the direct sale of stock, but many of the proposals they advertised were dodgy at best. Nova Scotia Conservative MP Fleming Blanchard McCurdy took up the issue in Parliament, asking the postmaster general to enforce more rigid standards "in view of the speculative excitement which is prevailing in the vicinity of these oil fields."[37] While critics complained that government action was too paternalistic, supporters replied that government "should err on the safe side when it comes to a question of protecting the people from the wiles of the oily promoter of questionable company flotations."[38]

Word of Manitoba's actions protecting consumers reached across the Atlantic, resulting in a renewed round of warnings from editors against investing in the Turner Valley boom, prompting one Canadian agency to urge that the Sifton government suspend the sale of shares "until development has proved or disproved the Calgary oil field."[39] Elsewhere, individual newspapers—like *The Victoria Colonist* and *The Regina Leader*—refused to run advertisements of oil stocks sent from outside brokers, for a few reasons. First was the question of the legitimacy of some of the companies. "We have not the least wish to interfere with the legitimate business carried on by legitimate brokers," announced the *Colonist*, "but it seems only right that we should advise readers to exercise great caution before buying oil stocks."[40]

Others questioned the legal status of Alberta-based petroleum companies selling stock within their jurisdictions. In Saskatchewan, no Alberta petroleum company filed incorporation papers with the provincial government, meaning that they were not subject to the terms of Saskatchewan's Companies Act. This mattered because it then meant companies were subject to Saskatchewan's Foreign Companies Act, section 3 of which dictated that "no foreign company having gain for its object or a part of its object shall carry on any part of its business unless it is duly registered under this Act."[41] *The Montreal Journal of Commerce* went even further in its criticism, calling Calgary's oil boom a danger to Canada and the worst wildcat proposition ever offered in the country's history. How did 400 companies raise so much money when scant evidence of oil existed? "The whole business smacks of quackery and fraud," harrumphed the paper.[42] Part of the answer to the *Journal of Commerce's* question came from the fact that investors in the boom were able to mobilize capital from across the country. While the boom started in Alberta with Alberta-based companies, by the middle of June 1914, eight different provinces were responsible for incorporating the 168 different oil companies representing approximately $84 million in capital investment.[43]

Campaigns against Calgary oil invited a series of ad hoc responses and retaliatory measures of varying sophistication, as Calgarians rallied to defend the city and its new industry. Some, like the Alberta Hotel's proprietor Charles D. Taprell, chalked up the "curious indifference" shown by outsiders to the province's good fortune to their jealousy and fears of what a strong and powerful Alberta would mean. Unable to "belittle the discovery of oil," Taprell claimed "they ignored it altogether," denying it existed in the process.[44] Others, like F. Leslie Sara, engaged in boosterism to hail the arrival of the industry. Sara's new "oil"-phabet, published in the pages of the *News Telegram*, included celebrations of Calgary and key figures of the oil boom ("H is for Herron, the plus eight millionaire"), and offered pointed responses to the industry's detractors: "O is for Opportunity, waiting for each; P is Possibilities, still within reach." Some were more whimsical, like "F is the Fool without stock—whom we pity;" others possessed an unmistakable edge—"K is the 'Knocker' whom Winnipeggers love; L is for Liar the same as above."[45]

Perhaps the most organized occurred after a visiting delegation from Winnipeg concluded that the Dingman well could not have produced oil and that the discovery was the result of a "doctored" well. After the *Albertan* carried the story on June 1, Acting Mayor Michael Costello sent a telegram to newspapers in Winnipeg, Vancouver, and Montreal defending the honour of both the city and Calgary Petroleum Products. The company, wrote Costello, "has on its board of directors some of the most prominent citizens of Calgary, and the board have afforded the opportunity to all the citizens of Calgary and visitors to the city as well to visit the property . . . . Any report to the effect that the well has been 'doctored' was too ridiculous to be given any serious consideration."[46]

Nevertheless, the Calgary Board of Trade, bankrolled by Montreal millionaire Sidney P. Howard, launched a campaign to "educate" Winnipeg about the Dingman well. City Councillor "Tappy" Frost pieced together a delegation that included Acting Mayor Costello, both the president and manager

Table 7-1 Distribution of Corporate Headquarters of 1914 Turner Valley Companies by Province

PROVINCE	NUMBER OF COMPANIES	CAPITALIZATION
Prince Edward Island	1	$90,000
New Brunswick	1	$150,000
Quebec	16	$1,758,600
Ontario	14	$6,750,000
Manitoba	6	$1,195,000
Saskatchewan	9	$710,000
Alberta	104	$71,309,000
British Columbia	17	$1,970,000
TOTAL	**168**	**$83,882,600**

Data from *The Monetary Times, Trade Review and Insurance Chronicle* 52, no. 24, June 12, 1914, 17.

of Calgary Petroleum Products—A.J. Sayer and Archibald Dingman, respectively—President of the Calgary Board of Trade W.H. Berkinshaw, and other luminaries. The group brought with them 200 gallons of oil in five barrels, thousands of glass vials to hand out with samples, testimonials from Calgary's leading citizens, a traction engine, and a high-powered motor car with signs and banners reading "This auto is being run on Dingman's oil" as it passed through the major thoroughfares of visited cities. Speaking with the *Herald* on the eve of his journey east, Frost said the campaign would not sell any stock or advertise for a particular company. His mission was "to prove beyond a shadow of a doubt that the first well to be sunk in Alberta oil fields is producing oil of a remarkable quality."[47]

Noting the zeal with which Frost threw himself into the mission, the *Albertan's* editorial page commented dryly, "Not since the time of the Crusades, we wot, has there been such a chivalrous spectacle as will be seen in Winnipeg soon when our own Tap Frost, with the rich gasoline dripping from his locks, goes right into the heart of the city of gilded skeptics and beards the liars in their den."[48] After two consecutive days of presentations at Winnipeg's Royal Alexandra Hotel, Frost wired back to Calgary that he believed his mission a success. "Winnipeg people very nice. Simply suffering from too much lime in the bone and too little iron in the blood." Frost's tour of central and eastern Canada included stops in Winnipeg, Toronto, Ottawa, and Montreal.[49]

Other responses invited self-help approaches. On June 5, 1914, *The Calgary News Telegram* reported the creation of the Oil Protective Association (also called the Oil Producers and Brokers' Protective Association) designed to thoroughly investigate all oil companies. Becoming a certified member of the OPA required an entry fee and providing answers to over thirty questions. The Oil Protective Association would conduct its own investigation into the company and, based on the results of that investigation, would either certify the company or not. "In short," noted the *News Telegram*, "the association is intended to perform the same function in the oil world as Bradstreets and Dun's do in the commercial with the further object of advertising the names of such companies as can be relied upon to deal honestly with the public." The association also planned an advertising campaign across Canada to highlight the trustworthy companies and avoid the wildcatters.[50] But under whose authority did the Oil Protective Association operate and what standards would they use to determine a good rating? After less than a month of operations, on July 10, 1914, Trowbridge suggested to Acting Attorney General G.P.O. Fenwick that the department launch an investigation into the association. Describing what seemed more like a shakedown than an attempt at self-regulation, Trowbridge reported, "I have been informed that they are asking $250.00 from companies to be labelled 'Honest.'" After reviewing the file, Fenwick informed the provincial secretary that he turned the matter over to Popple in Calgary with instructions to "have some of your sleuths look into this matter and take whatever action you think necessary," presumably meaning one of the Pinkertons.[51]

As industry attempts at self-regulation foundered, a consumer protection campaign labelling all Calgary oil companies "wildcat" operations unsafe for investors emerged among newspapers on the prairies and in the Pacific Northwest. As mentioned above, *The Regina Leader* refused to accept any advertising dollars from Calgary oil companies starting June 1, 1914. Meanwhile, the unofficial campaign in the Pacific Northwest started on June 12, 1914, when *The Seattle Post-Intelligencer* published a front page warning to small investors about investing in Calgary oil companies, before spreading to Tacoma, Spokane, and Portland. Participating newspapers pointed out that most companies, "probably 95 percent," were wildcatters and suggested an organized campaign existed among unscrupulous promoters to unload stock in bogus companies on unwitting Americans. While some legitimate companies existed, to date the province had produced petroleum condensates rather than crude oil. In any case, not all legitimate companies selling stock were likely to produce and small investors needed to proceed cautiously. *The*

Oregon Daily Journal went further and blasted both the oil companies and their sales agents for their "lurid" advertising targeting inexperienced investors "with wild tales of fortunes made overnight." Ultimately, the Portland-based paper labelled all Calgary oil stocks as being "of the usual wild cat variety and akin to fake mining promotion schemes."[52]

Newspapers as far east as Minneapolis reported details of the consumer protection campaign, but questions regarding the sustainability of the Calgary boom garnered much wider critical commentary throughout the United States.[53] In Custer, South Dakota, *The Custer Weekly Chronicle* noted that there were almost as many oil companies incorporated in Calgary as traded in Cobalt silver. But the Cobalt mine produced $53 million in dividends while Calgary only boasted a single well producing modest volumes of wet gas. This "slended base," the *Weekly Chronicle* noted, is "not for such a towering column of finance." Pointing squarely at George Buck's Black Diamond Oil Fields, the paper noted the incongruity of an oil company running its own newspaper "for the avowed purpose of keeping the public informed of the doings of a concern that today has not a speck of oil. They do not even pretend to have it." The problem, the paper surmised, is that "oil is new to the present generation in Canada, and being novel it is therefore more attractive." Bogus gold and silver schemes no longer fooled the public, but oil was a different matter.[54] By mid-July, the venerable *Chicago Tribune* tersely concluded that Calgary oil speculation "is based on a single producing well." While several companies were drilling, many more were just selling stock, prompting the paper to conclude "at present it would be a hazardous speculation to buy these shares."[55] Meanwhile, the *Minneapolis Journal* grumbled that "gambling is prohibited in Minnesota by state law. But the selling of Calgary oil and gas well shares does not come under the statute prohibiting gambling. There is no gamble about the purchase of them. The buyer doesn't have a gambling chance. He just gives his money away."[56]

Surprisingly, given the *Herald's* warnings to southern Alberta investors the previous autumn, the Calgary daily now dismissed similar complaints out of hand. On June 13, 1914, the editorial page declared Calgarians were perhaps too sensitive to outside criticism. After all, "it's delivering the goods that counts, and if we keep ourselves busy on that end of the contract we will not need to worry about what the knockers are saying about us."[57] Then, nearly ten days later, in reporting on the campaign in the Pacific Northwest, the paper concluded, "The Knockers' club, the anvil chorus and all the hammer boys out on the Pacific Coast are having the time of their lives rapping Calgary oil fields." Allan Clark, of Black Diamond Oil Fields fame, reported a frosty reception in Seattle and Portland upon return from a sales trip along the Pacific coast. "I never saw or heard the like of it in my life. They kidded me, tried to run me out of town, and eventually tried to get me in jail under the Oregon 'blue sky' law, but I was too smart for them and refused to sell them any of the stock I had." Not only did Clark find it difficult to convince people to invest, but he accused the Seattle and Portland chambers of commerce of buying up and destroying all the Calgary papers "to prevent news of the strike from spreading." In Oregon, Clark claimed the state's "blue-sky" law was so strict that "they won't even let you sell your own stock, let alone that of a company." In his hotel room where he entertained prospective investors, he admitted to having stock certificates lying around the room where anyone could see them. When people offered to buy some shares, Clark accused them of being police decoys looking to entrap him. "We wouldn't let you buy it, anyhow," said Clark. "We are selling all we want down east." Indeed, the *Herald* reported that Calgary oil companies were selling very well in Chicago, Minneapolis, and St. Paul.[58]

Meanwhile, William Davidson's growing concern about the boom's excesses yielded references to the ongoing revolution in Mexico. Davidson grimly concluded that Mexico "would have been very much better off at the present time if oil had never been discovered in that territory." More to the point, he concluded the Dominion government had failed to learn from the experience of other nations and ignored its own history. "The government should not have allowed the promiscuous development of the oil areas," charged Davidson. "It should have prevented the excessive filing, the wildcat organizing, and it could have done so by taking over the work of development itself. Then the oil wealth would have been of some value to [the] people of Canada." Even more striking is the public response to a letter sent by a Vancouver man to Acting Mayor Costello suggesting Calgarians set a day aside as thanksgiving to God for blessing the city with oil. The *Herald* editor summarily dismissed the suggestion out of hand, declaring, "What a farce it would be!" If the people of Calgary wanted to give thanks to the Almighty, the *Herald* suggested they do so "in deeds, not in empty word.... A few thousands in coin from the pockets of oil-enriched Calgarians for charity would indicate gratitude to Providence for favors bestowed much more effectively and acceptably than millions in meaningless words from their mouths."[59]

Ever sensitive to the shifts in public attitudes, especially following the week of false rumours at McDougall-Segur, Monarch, and Black Diamond, the June 27 edition of *The Eye Opener* turned toward pointed criticism, lampooning the proliferation of oil "experts" in the city, especially the geologists.

"An oil geologist's chief duty to his client is not so much to correctly locate an oil producing well as it is to prepare a Report that nobody can understand but which sounds devilish technical, don't you know."[60] Several civic leaders grew increasingly uneasy about the proliferation of fake oil rumours around Calgary. The *Herald* lamented that the rumours would persist "unless an example is made of someone." The reality, however, was that misinformation "serves a very useful, if unworthy, purpose with some people." Misinformation took on different forms, including misreporting the depth of wells, and inaccurate maps, particularly as drilling expanded south toward the Sweetgrass field near the international boundary. One geologist from California went so far as to propose that the provincial government should invite the US Geological Survey to the province to map the three buttes and adjacent territory.[61]

With so many people selling stock, bad actors gained an advantage, and generated larger profits, by inflating their stock prices. The problem, as the *Herald* expressed it, was that the practice harmed everyone, especially if investors lost trust in the honesty and integrity of the oil business in Alberta. "Individuals who are so poorly principled as to be willing to injure a legitimate enterprise of such possibilities as are to be found in oil investment deserve to be found out and punished severely when found" argued the *Herald*. Attuned to the growing concern, the Calgary Board of Trade's oil committee moved to curb the growing numbers of "wildcat extras"—the name given to false reports of oil strikes in Calgary newspapers—designed to artificially inflate stock prices. At the Board of Trade's June 24 meeting, officials suggested rumours would cease if companies made "immediate and direct reports of operations to the papers." The *Herald* readily agreed but doubted every oil company wanted such levels of transparency; indeed, the paper pointed out that the problem was more insidious because some made more trouble "by their suggestive silence . . . than the loudest-mouthed circulator of fake oil strike rumors." By early July, a private company, Baskins, Limited, brought greater transparency to the boom by installing wireless telegraph units to the main oil companies and maintaining a library of geological maps. The wireless service would always be at the disposal of the public and the newspapers, and a confident Baskins believed it would stop the spread of false rumours for stock manipulators. The company planned to have a floor operator on each of the stock exchanges operating in the city and promised to maintain a special department for women, "where the ladies may transact their business in absolute privacy."[62]

As speculating in stock grew more frenzied, the *News Telegram* continued advocating for greater government oversight in order to protect the public. Noting that "the oil game is a gamble at best," in view of the skepticism of outsiders "it is absolutely essential, in the interests of the local oil industry and in order to secure the capital necessary for its development, that we in Calgary should provide the most stringent regulations to protect the purchasers of oil stock." Failure to do so, the paper argued, would be a disaster, and continued reliance on the personal reputations and integrity of individual company owners was insufficient. Instead, the paper proposed that the province appoint an inspector given extraordinary powers to oversee the industry, from formulating "stringent regulations" to the enforcing them in order to ensure public trust. Absent government regulation, the *News Telegram* argued, "there will be legislation against Calgary oil stock in every province within the Dominion," making it impossible for Alberta to "attract that outside capital which is essential."[63] Colonel Woods's *Herald*, having warned against this very development nearly a year before, took no pleasure in pointing out the incredible hubris now on display. Months of self-interested boosting had made Calgarians "hysterical in regard to the oil situation." Hundreds of companies formed to offer stock to the public "which have not a scintilla of right to call themselves oil companies, and which have no reasonable prospect of ever striking a dollar's worth of oil." The editorial concluded by urging the public "to be slow and cautious in making alleged oil investments which are nothing but rank speculation."[64]

Inexorably, the wind fell out of the sails of the boom by mid-to-late June 1914, for several reasons. Public enthusiasm for oil stock perceptibly dipped as Albertans wearied of the constant state of heightened excitement and anticipation but unfulfilled expectations. Excitement soured into resentment as investors and Albertans gradually realized dreams of financial security did not immediately materialize from the first crush of investments made after the Dingman strike. Despite its omnipresence, the boom did not solve the problem of unemployment, nor did it transform the regional economy. Conspicuous by its absence were commercial quantities of crude oil. Instead, Calgarians encountered rogues, charlatans, and scoundrels in abundance. Letters to the editor complained that the boom brought immigrants, higher costs—for rent, taxes, groceries—but almost no new jobs. Unemployment remained mired in the doldrums of the previous winter, particularly amongst unskilled labor, artisans, and the skilled trades. Overall, the jobless rate increased from 9 percent of all adult males in January 1914 to more than 35 percent by autumn.[65]

The incongruence of free-flowing cash spent on an unproven oil sector uncomfortably co-existing with the ongoing economic hard times created a bifurcated social system in the process. People in the petroleum industry were seen as wealthy, aggressive, and somewhat arrogant entrepreneurs/specialists/interlopers who descended on the city and raised the cost or living for "true" Calgarians. More humiliating was that many of those "true" Calgarians now found themselves relegated to secondary roles, serving the newly rich and made to feel like outcasts in their own city. The excesses of 1914 therefore created a sharp divide between those who were involved in the emerging oil patch and those who were not. Looking at the ads that appeared illustrates the sharp divide between the two groups. People in the petroleum industry were adventuresome, risk-taking, free-spending entrepreneurs while those who were not were depicted as suffering from some kind of defect. An ad by the Magnet Oil Company called oil "the millionaire maker," and claimed that the opportunity existed for everyone to strike it rich, if only they had the courage to invest. "The discovery of crude oil in Alberta will revolutionize the world. You are in the midst of an opportunity such as comes once in a lifetime. Don't stand idly by and watch your neighbor make money—big money—in oil!"[66] A different Herron-Elder ad played on the same themes, arguing a "golden opportunity rests today in the hollow of your hand" and proclaiming, "Every man, woman and child who possesses Heron-Elder [sic] Oil Stock will have reason unqualified to feel proud of their discrimination."[67]

The result was the emergence of a sharp distinction between those who regarded themselves as "true" Calgarians and those who were not. Most interestingly, those who were identified primarily with the oil industry were increasingly regarded as being American immigrants. Surprisingly, one new Canadian oilman, Monarch Oil's William Georgeson (who, admittedly, built his fortune as a grocer and wholesaler before venturing into natural gas distribution and petroleum in the 1910s), nonetheless blamed Americans for the frenzied environment in Calgary. In an interview published in the *Spokane Chronicle*, Georgeson told the reporter, "It is you [Americans] who are responsible for this all prevailing idea here now to get rich quick—at once—by speculation in stocks, for this impatience of the public to wait for development to proceed before going wild over the discovery of an oil field which is not yet discovered." Georgeson reckoned he knew virtually every Calgarian by sight and charged that few familiar faces inhabited the broker's pits at the local oil exchanges. Local investors and capital no longer sustained Calgary's boom. "Our company was organized like a few others," said Georgeson, "by

Calgary people before the Americans flocked in to exploit the public with this boom."[68]

The conspicuous and sometimes ostentatious habits and behaviour of those involved in the petroleum industry summoned nativist impulses from the preponderantly white, Anglo-Saxon population. An ugly letter signed "F. Norris" on June 26, 1914, accused foreign-born workers of manifesting the worst kinds of racial stereotypes. Immigrants were "the laziest and most useless" workers he had ever encountered, who stole from their fellow workers, and only kept their jobs via graft and bribes. "There are foreigners working out there who have banking accounts and boast of them, and more than one of them, and yet there are Englishmen walking the streets practically starving, hundreds of them, and these foreigners . . . just laughing and thinking how easy the white man is."[69]

Norris's letter unleashed a howl of grievances from other whites and self-proclaimed native-borns, touching off a prolonged discussion in the editorial pages. On July 7, John Moore vociferously agreed with Norris and added that, as "a single white man," he could not find work but still needed to pay for the necessities of life but was constantly told to "get married[,] to get a job" and concluded his letter by stating, "It's about time the single white men were given some show in the city of Calgary."[70] Four days later, a *Herald* editorial pointed toward "a surplus of the wrong sort of population just now," and proposed the immediate deportation of recent arrivals who became charges of the state. "In the time of crisis it is our business to first provide for our own," wrote the paper. Immigrants would return to their place of origin "not because we didn't love them, but rather because we were not in a position to longer entertain non-paying guests."[71] A few columns over, a letter signed "Eastern Canadian" took up the complaint levelled by John Moore's letter about unemployed single men to point out that he was married but could not find a job as a carpenter because too many of them were already unemployed. "If a man can't make a living here let him move on to where he can. From present prospects the writer will be one of those who will have to move." Perhaps he would return when matters improved.[72]

As the boom began winding down in the midsummer of 1914, perhaps transitioning to more orderly development, Calgarians prepared for the most important event of the year. On July 28, 1914, the Governor General of Canada and members of the royal family, Prince Arthur, the Duke of Connaught, his wife, the Duchess of Connaught, and their daughter, Princess Patricia, would vacation in Alberta's mountain parks as part of the Duke's farewell to Canada tour before returning to England. The stop in Calgary would also afford the

Duke and the royal entourage the opportunity to inspect Dingman #1 in person. For the staunchly anglophile local community, the visit represented another opportunity to publicly manifest southern Alberta's loyalty and affection for both the Crown and Empire. For most oil promoters, it offered the opportunity to secure the support of a member of the royal family and the possibility of securing investment capital from England.

July 28, 1914, also loomed as the deadline for Serbia's response to the Austro-Hungarian ultimatum issued in the aftermath of Archduke Franz Ferdinand's murder by Bosnian nationalists. Across Europe, many were slow to appreciate the gravity of the unfolding crisis. Few believed it to be any more serious than a half-dozen or so previous crises, prompting present-day historian Margaret MacMillan to lament people's lack of imagination and the importance of contingency in human events.[73] Indeed, in early July, Calgary and Edmonton newspapers were more likely to predict a civil war in the United Kingdom over Irish Home Rule rather than the escalation of a regional conflict into a continental, and then global, war after the murder of the Archduke. Even as some papers declared the boom over before the Duke of Connaught's visit, many Albertans remained obsessed with the boom to the exclusion of all other events. *The Leduc Representative* declared the boom over, "but it is hardly fair to the holders of stock to deny them the fun of watching the quotation fluctuate for a while yet. The chance of a strike now and again will tend to keep things a little interesting at any rate."[74]

Looking back on the events of July 1914, Eleanor Luxton describes how Europe's problems barely penetrated people's conscious thoughts amidst the search for oil:

> The news went from day to day in the local field of oil and life of Calgary and its district. The people bought oil stocks recklessly and paid little heed to the headlines which told of unsettled conditions in Europe and of possibilities of war. Even David for once was quite unconscious of what was happening in the world at large. His whole time was taken by his beloved oil wells, and he and Annie spent much time at the field.[75]

Perhaps Albertans could be forgiven for their inattentiveness, as the July crisis unfolded behind the scenes in several European capitals, making it difficult to see the whole picture. The first hint of the broader dimensions of the crisis came on July 14 when the *Herald* warned in a brief front page article that the situation in Europe was critical. The next spark showed on July 21 as the

Edmonton Bulletin speculated the crisis could devolve into a regional war. Only on Friday, July 24, 1914, did Alberta newspapers grasp that the international implications of the crisis could devolve into a broader European war because of the involvement of at least three of the great powers.[76]

Local newspapers fretted that the Duke and Duchess would forever associate their visit to Calgary with the climax of the July Crisis.[77] Perhaps they should not have worried, because for George Buck, the vice regal visit brought an opportunity to impress visiting investors from Vancouver—with a plot to hijack the Duke and Duchess of Connaught and their daughter, Princess Patricia, as their motorcade travelled from Okotoks to the Dingman well on a dusty unpaved country road. Evidence of the half-baked scheme (it remains too farcical to call a plan) remains in a few stories carried in Vancouver and Calgary newspapers. Just one day before the Governor General's visit to Calgary, Buck took out an advertisement in the *Albertan* inviting Black Diamond #2 shareholders out to the well site to see the commencement of drilling on the site and planning for "about 20 motor cars" to ferry stockholders for lunch and entertainment. The ad ran again on the morning of July 28—one month to the day after the assassination of Archduke Franz Ferdinand.[78]

The ad did the trick, as Buck assembled thirty-two cars decorated with Canadian and British flags alongside the road. The front page story in the *Vancouver Daily World*, obviously planted by George Buck or one of his acolytes, carried the headline "Royal party sees crude oil at Black Diamond." When the royal party appeared, "motor horns and sirens, at a given signal, shrieked and honked, while the occupants of the cars vigorously cheered," wrote the *World*. "Immediately the royal party's cars had passed through the lines the Black Diamond cars took up the rear position, following to within a few hundred yards of Dingman well and, taking up a position on one of the hills overlooking the site, had a perfect view of the demonstration given at the Dingman well." The *World's* article proclaimed the Duke of Connaught was impressed by what he saw at Buck's well, including "sufficient oil to encourage any pessimist" that oil existed in Alberta. The piece then concluded with statements that echoed any one of a half-dozen or so Black Diamond ads. "There is not the slightest question that there is more oil in Black Diamond No. 1 (that is black crude) than in any other well at present operating in the Albertan fields, and Black Diamond stock at present day prices should not be overlooked." The piece concluded by praising both directors and shareholders of Black Diamond oil companies and singled out the "enterprising and energetic George Buck" for making the Duke's visit such a smashing success.[79]

Figure 7-2 "Caravan of automobiles en route to Turner Valley, Alberta"
Caravans of cars frequently travelled the narrow dirt road between Calgary and Turner Valley as people flocked to the valley to see the wells for themselves. (Glenbow Archives CU1928982)

The Natural Gas and Oil Record heaped well-deserved scorn on the *World* article after publishing it in full in its August 8 edition under the headline "Lies."[80] No other paper across Canada besides the *World* reported that the Duke had visited the Black Diamond well; the flip side of the coin is that no other paper besides the *Record* claimed Buck had attempted to hijack or otherwise interfere with the vice regal party. Nevertheless, the *World* claimed that the procession arrived at Black Diamond #1 for luncheon, while every other paper reported that the party arrived at the Dingman well. *The Natural Gas and Oil Record* reported a dramatically different story about the escort provided by Buck's improvised motorcade, depicting it in a much more aggressive light. While the *Record* did not identify Buck by name, and only referred to "another sightseeing party," surrounding the Governor General's car as it left Okotoks. "They were pocketed, in race horse parlance," wrote the *Record*. Even more recklessly, one of the vehicles in Buck's party manoeuvred at high speed so a photographer could capture an image of Buck's prey. "'Clear the way,' someone shouted," reported the *Record*, "and the big machines drove ahead—'Damn.'" Evidently, the Governor General's driver managed to steer the powerful 1914 Hudson touring car used especially for the royal party out of the pack and proceeded to the Dingman well site, where Tappy Frost drew a small glass of oil direct from the well.[81]

Figure 7-3 "Duke and Duchess of Connaught at Dingman number 1 well (Calgary Petroleum Products #1), Turner Valley, Alberta"
Tappy Frost, at left holding glass, is about to drink oil produced by the Dingman well in front of Princess Patricia, the Duchess of Connaught, the Duke of Connaught, Archibald Dingman, Martin Hovis, and unknown. (Glenbow Archives CU192442)

The looming war in Europe drove the final nails into the boom's coffin and brought what developments remained to an end as interest rates rose and the money supply contracted. The Bank of England raised their rate to 10 percent, signalling tightening European credit markets. By early August, as Britain delivered an ultimatum to Germany about the consequences of violating Belgian neutrality, at the request of the Board of Trade, several stock exchanges, including the CSE and the Calgary Oil and Stock Exchange, shut down effective August 3 until further notice. The shock of war depressed the petroleum industry in Alberta and cleared away most of the pretenders. After all, oil remained one of the greatest needs for modern industrial warfare, so *The Financial Post* heaved a sigh of relief on August 22, 1914, when it noted that companies with the financial wherewithal could go ahead with drilling but that "the floatation of new companies for oil development has practically ceased, fortunately so."[82]

It is easy enough to blame the outbreak of the Great War in August 1914 for breaking the back of the speculative boom and wounding the petroleum industry's development as the region shifted quickly to mobilize human and material resources for the war effort. This explanation, however, seems incomplete and counterintuitive given the important role played by petroleum for ships, airplanes, and motor vehicles in the coming struggle. As *The Natural Gas and Oil Record* pointed out in a full-page ad, the war presented both the circumstances and the opportunity for expansion of Canadian industry and trade, predicting "good times ahead."[83] But this did not happen, and it is fair to wonder why.

Any worthwhile explanation must begin with the observation that Alberta's petroleum production did not exceed that of Ontario until 1925. In the decade following the Dingman discovery, Tuner Valley produced approximately 66,000 barrels of oil in total—an average of less than twenty barrels per day. Compared to the mighty oil fields in Texas, where Spindletop blew in at 75,000 barrels *per day* in 1901, investing in Alberta oil was a much riskier proposition. In this and so many other ways, Alberta was not Texas and Turner Valley was not Spindletop, as other liabilities loomed. Circa 1914, Alberta lacked the transportation, refining, and distribution facilities to effectively exploit any petroleum find. While Texas could easily access the port facilities of the Gulf of Mexico, Alberta remained landlocked, far removed from tidewater and from major markets, refining, and transportation capacity. Britain and the Royal Navy turned to oil suppliers in Mexico, Venezuela, but above all Persia, to fuel their ships and motor cars. Starved of capital, the small independents soon closed as the oil boom petered out and companies struggled simply to hold on to their leaseholds.

A stronger case is that the boom burned hot and quick because several self-inflicted wounds and liabilities hindered the nascent Alberta oil patch. Few understood or appreciated the work and expense required to drill a hole sufficiently deep to prove or disprove the existence of an oil field in the province. Furthermore, a series of stock market manipulations and insider trading scandals plagued the Alberta industry and shocked outside investors. The lack of transparency or regulatory oversight made it difficult for investors to distinguish between legitimate operators and scam artists and resulted in very successful grassroots consumer protection campaigns against Calgary oil in nearby US and Canadian markets. Indeed, Edwin Selvin of *The Seattle Post-Intelligencer* later boasted that the paper's campaign against Calgary oil "succeeded in killing it here in Seattle."[84] Amid a growing economic depression that saw wages decline and skyrocketing unemployment, would-be investors grew increasingly cautious, less credulous, and more skeptical of the claims of oil promoters. The proliferation of self-help measures to protect consumer interests both in Canada and the United States also shrank the pool of investors enough to deny the Alberta the necessary capital to continue floating companies or sustain operations.

Perhaps the fatal flaw, however, resulted from attempts to keep large companies out of the field and favouring independents. At the outset of the boom, many small companies lacked development capital to meet the high drilling costs associated with Turner Valley, especially when drilling did not result in production to offset costs. Rotary rig technology, capable of drilling deeper, straighter holes more quickly and efficiently than standard cable tool rigs, were not widely used in Turner Valley in 1914 because of their higher costs and skill level required of crews. Other more mundane technological advances in the 1920s and 1930s would help improve the efficiency, lower production costs, and aid the search for oil in Turner Valley, in particular the introduction of trucks capable of transporting heavier drilling equipment and building better roads in the 1920s. During the boom, horses and wagons travelling across little more than dirt tracks of dubious durability placed limits on the quality of drilling equipment. Most entrepreneurs grew increasingly reluctant to shoulder the financial burden and uncertainty of drilling wells to depths of more than 3,000 feet with no guarantee that revenues could cover expenditures. Furthermore, the effusions of natural gas and scant amounts of naphtha were too modest to sustain the staggering volume of oil stocks on the market. Local investors, in the market for the short term, grew increasingly reluctant to advance any more capital. Indeed, financing for most companies came from private investors seeking quick returns. However, almost none of the companies broke even, let alone generated a profit.

J.L. Englehart, who made some of his fortune in Ontario's Petrolia oil fields and, in 1914, served as the chair for the Transportation Board of Toronto, seemingly offered the most elegant eulogy on the first oil boom, declaring somewhat paradoxically that 1914 proved there was "undiscovered oil" in Alberta. But Englehart identified the Peace River region north of Edmonton as the likely site of a future discovery. As for Calgary, Englehart predicted it would never be an oil centre and Turner Valley would never produce oil. "The one great obstacle in the way of oil—not gas, but crude oil—ever being produced in paying quantities is the formation of the country." For Englehart, the geology was all wrong. Fractured rock formations dominated southern Alberta along the foothills of the Rockies. "If the country were less fractured," said Englehart, "I would have more faith in it." Instead of oil, the field produced gas, and the people who invested in the Calgary oil boom became "excited about oil which has not been found." Englehart feared that investors were placing their money in companies that had less than one chance in a hundred of striking oil. "It Is most unfortunate that there should be so much dreaming of the possibility of finding oil. It is bad for the country. These dreamers are apt to lose their money."[85]

The legacy of 1914's frenzied orgy lingered and cast a long shadow. Many middle-class Calgarians who invested in oil stocks rather than paying off debt in June lost their savings and endured a very cold and grey winter. Real estate brokers who became stockbrokers during the boom found themselves unemployed once again. Some of the men who lined up to buy oil stock now did the same thing at the recruiting office, recalled Torchy Anderson on the fiftieth anniversary of the Dingman well. Women who emptied their sugar bowls that hid their savings to invest in oil stock now began to knit socks for soldiers. Anderson maintained that, while there were other oil booms, none of them could match the "whooping insanity" of May 1914.[86]

8

Reforming Self-Regulation: Taming the Brokers and the Calgary Stock Exchange

> *I am afraid that the history of all other oil fields is going to be repeated in Calgary, namely, that the small stockholder is going to get "cold feet" and lose out and the big interests will accumulate all the profits in the years that are to come.*
>
> —Anonymous Oil Company Official
> *The Calgary Daily Herald*
> May 29, 1915

> *The oil men are still as busy as bees, thus accounting for so many of us getting stung.*
>
> —Bob Edwards
> *Calgary Eye Opener*
> June 12, 1915

By autumn 1914, as the titanic battles on the frontiers unfolded between the great powers, a cold fear gripped many in Calgary that the Turner Valley field would languish, underdeveloped, given the growing weariness of investors with "Calgary field." Weeks before, *The Guardian* (London) complained that "only three classes of people are reaping a harvest" from Calgary's boom: geologists, earning extravagant fees for their expert opinion on the value of leases; promoters who sold stock; and the printers, who worked around the clock producing prospectuses and stock certificates.[1] Increasingly, informed opinion in London regarded Dingman's success as an aberration and made

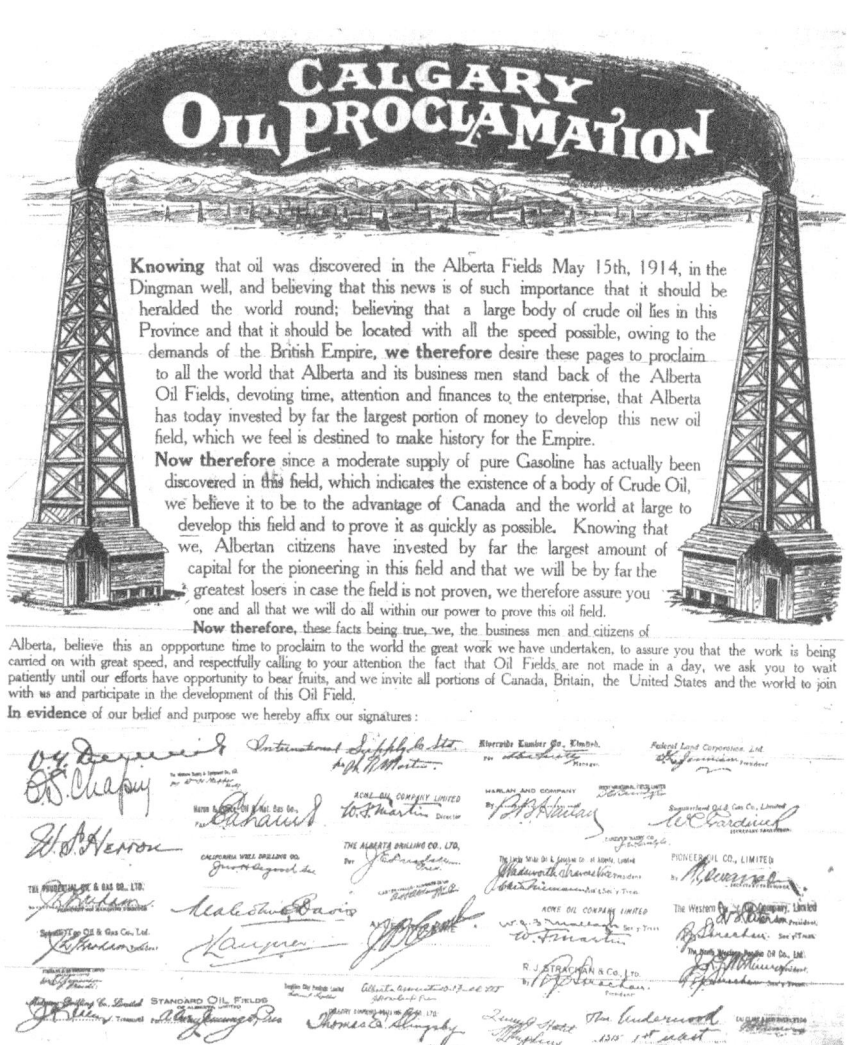

Figure 8-1 "Calgary Oil Proclamation"
Thirty-five signatures appear below the Calgary Oil Proclamation. Two noteworthy absences are any signatures from any level of government and that of George E. Buck of Black Diamond Oil Fields. (University of Calgary Libraries and Cultural Resources CU1702268)

their investment decisions accordingly. The realization prompted thirty-five leading figures in Calgary's oil patch—including Dingman, Herron, and Devenish—together with *The Morning Albertan*, which devoted an entire special section to a retrospective summary of developments in Turner Valley and the boom—to issue the Calgary Oil Proclamation. Written in the form of a resolution, the document declared that after the Dingman well discovered oil in Alberta on May 14, 1914, the people of Alberta joined together to spread the news of this epochal moment. Community and industry leaders "desire these pages to proclaim to all the world that Alberta and its businessmen stand back of the Alberta Oil Fields, devoting time, attention and finances to the enterprise." The proof of this commitment lay in the incredible allocation of resources, time, and capital that Albertans devoted to the effort. "Knowing that we, Albertan citizens have invested by far the largest amount of capital for the pioneering in this field and that we will be by far the greatest losers in case the field is not proven, we therefore assure you one and all that we will do all within our power to prove this oil field." The proclamation concluded that "Oil Fields are not made in a day," but invited "all portions of Canada, Britain, the United States and the world to join with us and participate in the development of this Oil Field."[2] Conspicuous by its absence from the proclamation's signers was representation of government at any level.

The political scientist Samuel Huntington observed that as a society becomes more complex, it requires more institutions to run it. The same could be said for the petroleum industry. Political scientist Keith Brownsey wrote that Alberta's multi-level regulatory system for its petroleum industry emerged out of the "constitutional, legal and political environment" that surrounds it. Shaped by competing federal and provincial visions and overlaid with rules, processes, and obligations established by municipal and international authorities, the result "is a multilevel regulatory structure which is complex and at times confusing and contradictory."[3] While the regulatory system of the early twentieth century lacked the robustness and sophistication of later iterations, industry promoters and government officials in 1914 would be able to easily relate to Brownsey's characterization of the problems and perils of a multi-level regulatory system that, in turn, created a new dynamic environment for petroleum development. In a 2006 article in *Foreign Affairs,* the eminent historian of the world petroleum industry and respected energy analyst, Daniel Yergin, suggested that development of petroleum supplies remain contingent on geology—is the oil there?—as well as assessments of "what happens above ground namely, international affairs, politics, decision-making by governments, and energy investment and new technological development,"⁴ Yergin's broader point that is that above-ground issues, such as regulatory environment, tax structure, royalties, availability of labour, and the presence of necessary infrastructure (refineries and transportation and distribution networks), exert a tremendous influence over which oil fields are developed and which are not. The repercussions of the "above-ground" problems created by the circus-like atmosphere of first Turner Valley boom lasted longer than the boom itself, tainting the province's reputation as a good place to invest money and prompting a reckoning of sorts regarding the private and public sectors' view of the proper roles of different levels of government and their roles and responsibilities for the regulation of the petroleum industry. In 1914, most Albertans necessarily believed that the government's role in the economy was sharply limited to upholding private property, preserving individual initiative, and facilitating economic growth. There were several ideological and structural reasons for this. A small population and limited tax base made the province dependent on outside investors. When combined with local boosterism, as historians Donald Wetherell and Irene Kmet concluded, this limited government as the means of facilitating natural resource development.⁵ This was reinforced by the courts. Time and again, in a number of early cases stemming from the abuses of 1914, judges adhered to the view that government power was sharply limited. Indeed, in 1915, in striking down legislation designed to give the provincial government a modest oversight role, the Alberta Court of Appeal explicitly ruled that the orders-in-council could "in no way" restrict "the expenses of management, investment of funds, nature of properties or claims held, the manner and cost of any stock sale or other disposal of stock, and other allied questions." It was plain to Justice Stewart that when provincial legislation "proposed to institute an 'investigation into the affairs' of a particular company, . . . the authority given by the statute is exceeded."⁶ But out of growing necessity this view slowly evolved because of the "other" development of 1914, the outbreak of the Great War. The experience of wartime mobilization and the government's massive intrusion into the lives of its citizens with policies related to conscription, internment, censorship, and labour relations helped change popular attitudes and altered expectations about what the public could expect from government.⁷

Despite the pressures generated by wartime mobilization and the financial constraints on spending, the provincial government knew it must confront the reality of rampant fraud and reckless stock market speculation, especially since most of the money spent by investors simply disappeared into the pockets of opportunists, rogues, and charlatans rather than developing the oil field. Unofficial estimates suggested during the brief boom of 1914, between $3 million and $4 million ($80–$106 million, adjusted for inflation) flowed into the province, ostensibly for exploration and development. But would-be oil promoters quickly grasped that it was far quicker to sell stock than drill for oil. The editors of the *Edmonton Journal* estimated that only one-third of the money invested developed the oilfield, either by securing acreage or drilling wells, although the paper allowed that this figure might prove overly optimistic.[8]

Developments in 1914–15 raised concerns for investors about both the geology of the Calgary field and its social, economic, political, and legal contexts. By early 1915, despite ongoing drilling by as many as twenty-six different outfits, the main body of oil remained untapped. From the very first show in October 1913, skeptics dismissed Dingman #1 as a "freak," and argued that the naphtha it produced came from a lateral seepage from a large body of crude oil lying further toward the mountains and was unlikely to be repeated.[9]

The field's erstwhile champion, E.H. Cunningham Craig, reluctantly acknowledged that long-time critics of Turner Valley's broken formation might have a point. Speaking before the Institution of Petroleum Technologists in London, on January 22, 1915, Cunningham Craig conceded that "there have been many criticisms levelled at [the Calgary field] by persons either ill-informed or 'wise after the event,'" "The wisest course," concluded Cunningham Craig, "is not to hasten or condemn the field, but to wait silently for each piece of authentic information that is brought to light."[10] To be sure, other wells continued drilling—forty-five derricks now dotted the landscape of Turner Valley—but only five (Dingman #1 and #2, Southern Alberta, Moose Mountain, and the Lineham) had encountered some modest success.[11] Far more common, however, were announcements like the one by Mowbray Berkeley, head of the British Alberta Oil Company (formerly the Mowbray Berkeley Syndicate) on May 6 that it was abandoning its well after reaching a depth of 3,145 feet and encountering "tremendous difficulties." Unlike many others, though, Berkeley stubbornly announced the company was not abandoning the Calgary field forever; it was, however, acting on the advice of its geological consultant, none other than E.H. Cunningham Craig, and temporarily suspending operations.[12]

If at all possible, assessments of the above-ground problems were more dire. The elephant in the room remained the parade of gluttony and excess of 1914. As the *Toronto Globe* pointed out, "the disgraceful and discreditable gamble in oil territory in Calgary" during the boom nearly destroyed all investor confidence in Alberta oil altogether. "Great sums of money which should have been devoted to sinking test wells never got beyond the pockets of the shrewd manipulators of the boom."[13] Never far behind, though, were pointed questions about the Sifton government's lax regulatory environment. One letter writer to the *Herald* complained that the provincial oil industry "is in a deplorable state, and I claim that the Alberta government is to blame for it all." Marked by confusion, contradiction, and laxity, provincial laws were, at best, inadequate. After detailing a litany of concessions granted to promoters (not all of which was entirely accurate), the writer concluded members the Alberta legislature were not governing "for the interest and protection of the people" but were, rather, looking out for "a few promoters and grafters." The Companies Act, they railed, "looks like a wilful and deliberate act to aid and abet unscrupulous promoters and grafters to prey on the public." As a result, oil stock prices were "ridiculously low" and the field did not "have the confidence and support of outside capital." Turner Valley languished as "a laughingstock."[14]

Indeed, the boom revealed several shortcomings in the province's regulatory regime. Two of the most prominent were the lackadaisical and haphazard regulation of brokers and stock exchanges and the lack of overt consumer protections. Provincial and municipal authorities shared responsibility for regulating the activities of stock exchanges and brokers. For example, as soon as it became clear that a few companies would not drill a well, the public expected either the city or province to act and shut down the company or prevent the sale of more stock. During the boom, city officials claimed their hands were tied; regulation of the operations of brokers fell under provincial jurisdiction. But the province relied on local police for enforcement, and the parlous state of provincial regulation and oversight meant the province lacked the capacity to enact changes even as it claimed the authority to do so. Furthermore, businesses adamantly refused to concede even the most basic reforms without a fight. As amply illustrated in 1915 when the City of Calgary altered licensing provisions for brokers and exchanges, it could not compel either the Calgary Stock Exchange or the unchartered exchanges to willingly adopt measures intended for the good of the whole industry. The exchanges fiercely defended their independence, maintaining that so long as they abided by the terms of their corporate charter and the standards established by the exchange, consumers had no further recourse.[15]

Meanwhile, as the effects of the economic downturn persisted into 1915, the provincial attorney general's office faced immense pressure from investors scalded by unscrupulous companies to "do something." The *Herald's* editorial page bitterly observed that after an October storm stranded several oil men out in the fields for a few days "they should now have some appreciation of the permanent situation of many hundreds of Calgary people who have invested in oil."[16] Surveying the wreckage, Eleanor Luxton remembered that the boom died out just as quickly as it appeared. But wells did not produce enough oil to sustain the industry. "Hundreds of people were poor overnight," she recalled. "Worthless oil stock was held for years, many firms failed."[17]

Letters and telegrams from across North America pleaded for the attorney general to get money back, revoke the provincial charters of disreputable companies, or prosecute offenders. Tempting as it might have been to blame all the boom's problems on the actions of a few bad actors and legal technicalities that enabled unscrupulous operators to escape without consequences, provincial authorities took a hard look at what happened. The Sifton government turned away, slowly, and incrementally, from self-regulation and difficult-to-enforce fraud statutes to exercise greater oversight on the emerging oil and gas industry. Part of the solution included passing new legislation in two stages that established greater transparency and affirmed the government's responsibility to protect consumers. In 1915, the Sifton government created the Public Utilities Commission. Similar commissions already existed in several Canadian provinces prior to 1914, including Ontario, Manitoba, and Saskatchewan. The next year, the province passed the "Act to Regulate the Sale of Shares, Bonds and Other Securities of Companies," better known as the Sale of Shares Act (1916). Taken together, these measures asserted the right of the provincial government to investigate fraudulent companies and established the means to assist authorities with the detection and prosecution of lawbreakers.

Just as the July Crisis reached its crescendo in the overlapping declarations of war at the end of that month and into early August 1914, participants in Alberta's oil boom began turning on one another. Speculators began to realize that the production of oil from Turner Valley remained far too modest to justify the amount of oil paper on the market, while the Calgary Stock Exchange tried to come to grips with mounting scandals, further discrediting the oil industry in the eyes of many. Meanwhile, *The Financial Post* noted geologist E.H. Cunningham Craig's growing exasperation with the damage wrought to Alberta's reputation by inexperienced oil companies. In October 1914 he noted that there were thirty-six companies engaged in drilling in Alberta and another twenty-five getting ready to drill. "Of the combined number less than half are likely to meet with any success, because they are drilling in the wrong places. As a matter of fact, oil has yet to be struck. There are three wells which have struck a high grade of gasoline, but this does not necessarily mean that oil will be found in that vicinity." Measuring his words carefully, Cunningham Craig concluded, "The future of the field is problematical, but in a few weeks more definite information may be forthcoming."[18]

Angry shareholders filed lawsuits against company officials who remained in Calgary, resulting in a sharp increase in the number of oil industry-related fraud cases. Prior to the boom, between 1909 and 1913, Calgary's Magistrate's Court saw an average of six fraud cases a year. But in 1914, the number climbed to forty-four, with an additional thirty-four filed in 1915. In one case heard in early January 1915, George E. Hayes, an engineer and geologist, received one hundred dollars from William Williams and other clients who believed the funds would cover expenses on a trip to England to secure investment capital for an oil company. But when Williams learned Hayes never made the voyage, he sought to recoup his money. In court, Hayes pointed to the fine print of his correspondence that revealed he received payment for examining certain oil leases and could, therefore, spend the money as he saw fit. There were other cases, too. Another broker used the terms of the CSE's charter to have criminal charges of theft against him dismissed after he failed to make an investment because he ran "short." But the broker claimed immunity from criminal charges because his actions were consistent with the terms of the CSE's charter. The case prompted Magistrate Sanders to grumble that brokers enjoyed the protection of the exchanges but nothing protected consumers. Sanders then expressed the wish that some arrangement or organization could provide the public better protection.[19]

Britain's imminent declaration of war prompted a request from the Calgary Board of Trade that Calgary's stock exchanges briefly suspend operations on August 3, 1914; eight of Calgary's thirteen stock exchanges complied.[20] The Calgary Stock Exchange resumed operations at eleven o'clock on the morning of August 19, 1914.[21] Over the next few months, a series of mergers winnowed the number of exchanges operating in the city from thirteen down to six. The first wave of mergers occurred by September 1914 when six oil stock exchanges representing approximately 200 brokers banded together to form the Calgary General Stock Exchange. Four larger exchanges—the Oil and Stock Exchange, the Standard Exchange, the Calgary Stock Exchange, and the General Stock Exchange—plus two smaller ones, the King George Exchange (run out of the King George hotel) and the Open Air Exchange. "This place of barter," wrote *The Vancouver Daily World*, "is one of the most unique exchanges in the business." Known for holding night session that attracted large crowds, the Open Air Exchange granted membership to all who attended their sessions.[22]

The Calgary Stock Exchange merged with some of the smaller exchanges operating in Calgary and coped with the growing pains of a new exchange in challenging circumstances. As investment capital grew scarce, the directors of the CSE addressed a string of "irregularities" in its operations, as brokers attempted to eke out a living in a tough economic environment, illustrating the difficulties of self-regulation when all members did not necessarily share the same incentive to abide by the rules. In one instance, the board of directors intervened in one questionable transaction when a broker immediately cashed the cheques of the purchasing party even though the sale fell through. When questioned by the board, the broker replied he simply wanted to collect his commission.[23] By December 1914, the directors had amended the exchange's bylaws, giving themselves the authority to cancel any transaction they suspected was "irregular, unprofessional, or fraudulent."[24]

Largely behind closed doors, the directors of the Calgary Stock Exchange wrestled with the thorny issue of enforcing its bylaws without damaging its public credibility. Occasionally, issues made their way into the public realm and caused some embarrassment to the CSE. One such instance became public early in 1915 when the *Herald* questioned fluctuations in the price of Moose Mountain and suggested that a small number of brokers were deliberately manipulating prices. "The chief people to profit by such unwarranted activity are the stockbrokers and one can imagine that if they had only two or three oil stocks to handle on the same basis, they might make quite a 'respectable' living out of the public." The paper asked pointed questions. Did the officers of the CSE "endorse and approve" the handling of stocks on the exchange? Did they approve of the "oil stock gambling" prevailing under current conditions? Were they ignorant of the "bull and bear movements" of Moose Mountain stock? Most importantly, "Do they seriously believe that it is in the interests of this city and country that gambling of the character recently carried on should be continued, and extended to the stocks of other oil companies under present business conditions?"[25]

Moose Mountain shares remained in the news for all the wrong reasons through the spring when a member of the CSE repurchased a certificate for ten shares of Moose Mountain only to find the certificate's value altered in the interim. When first purchased months earlier, the certificate represented one share, not the ten it now proclaimed. The CSE's board of directors first became aware of the problem on March 3, 1915, but by March 5, the *Albertan* revealed that "numerous" fraudulent Moose Mountain certificates circulated, so much so that "there are few members of the Calgary Stock Exchange who are not possessed of these bogus shares, and are out of pocket in consequence."[26]

Facing difficult questions regarding its integrity, the CSE's directors closed ranks and treated the problem as an internal matter. The directors passed a resolution placing responsibility for restitution with the member "who found the certificates in the clearing service on the day on which the raising was discovered . . . until such time as the certificates could be traced back to the member from whom they originally came and the responsibility fixed on him."[27] By the time of the next board meeting on March 17, 1915, with the identity of the perpetrator in hand, the directors gave the still unnamed broker of the fraud forty-eight hours to "make good" but made no mention of what would happen if he did not.[28]

Ever an accurate barometer of public attitudes, commentary in Bob Edward's *Eye Opener* reflected the seismic shifts in opinion regarding the oil boom and its acolytes—the associated promoters, boosters, and brokers. In May 1914, despite his well-known reticence about advertising products and services he could not vouch for, the *Eye Opener* published advertisements from oil companies like Black Diamond, Western Canada Oil Company, and Rocky Mountain Oil Fields. Edwards self-consciously referred to his idiosyncratic way of selecting the ads by including a "personal guarantee as to the soundness and integrity of every oil company whose ad we publish. Of course, we don't guarantee the oil, but simply the honesty and good faith of the company." A few columns over, Edwards predicted "the Alberta oil fields will probably equal if they do not eventually surpass, those of Pennsylvania and California."[29] But his optimism soon vanished and before the end of summer Edwards fully turned against the new industry as he watched the machinations of various groups—the oil companies, the stock exchanges, promoters, and other self-appointed experts—with growing disgust. Of all the groups involved in the boom, Edwards reserved a particular disdain for the role of the stockbrokers. In the early autumn of 1914, as the Imperial German Navy placed mines in the open sea without regard for the impact it would have on neutral merchant vessels, Edwards claimed that a lack of imagination rather than unwillingness explained why oil brokers refrained from selling shares in the mines now menacing international trade routes.[30]

Edwards's most savage piece about brokers appeared on July 3, 1915, when he wrote that the major figures and personalities from Alberta's oil boom could compel Kaiser Wilhelm II's atonement for the Dinant Massacre of 1914 that resulted in the deaths of 647 Belgian civilians, including women and children. Written as an open letter to the German Kaiser, Edwards began by saying that boiling him in oil was too merciful for the atrocities committed by Germany's armed forces. Instead, Edwards explained to the Kaiser that he could expect introductions to "groups of oil men, all of high business repute in the city, who will proceed to gnaw their way into the Hohenzollern fortune by selling you Monarch shares at $20.00, Alberta Petroleum Consolidated at $10.00, Dingman at $75.00, Black Diamond at $9.00 and so on." The punishment would continue on the floor of the Calgary Stock Exchange, where the Kaiser would "study the blackboard." At night, a "talkative oil expert (preferably [Clarence A.] Owens)" would "deliver a learned and involved disquisition on anticlines, Dakota sands, Claggett-Benton shale, faulty formations, broken bits, inadequate casing and wet gas. If this does not settle accounts for the Dinant atrocities, nothing will."[31]

The Companies Ordinances of the Northwest Territories (1901) served as the main piece of legislation regulating the operations of natural resource companies in Alberta during the boom. It facilitated the acquisition, management, development, and sale of mines, minerals, and petroleum properties in the province as well as claiming jurisdiction over the various stock exchanges operating within the province.[32] Responsibility for enforcement fell to the attorney general's office, which received and investigated complaints from customers and investors. Records in the attorney general's office reveal that it handled minor issues formally or informally, depending on the severity of the complaint. In some cases, it contacted the company by phone or letter to find a solution directly. More serious accusations that warranted formal investigation by the department to determine if criminal proceedings were necessary also included an assessment about the likelihood that departmental action would yield desirable outcomes. Acting Attorney General G.P.O. Fenwick provided the clearest expression of this policy in response to complaints lodged against Bonnie Brae Coal Company by Dr. Thomas Ritchie of Cochrane.[33]

After discovering a coal seam on his property, Ritchie sold the mineral rights to Arthur Phillips, who later formed the Bonnie Brae company to exploit the coal deposit. Shortly after Bonnie Brae began operations, Ritchie registered several complaints against the company with the attorney general's office, typical of most shareholder complaints levelled against oil companies, including failing to issue a prospectus, publication of misleading circulars to sell stock, and failure to obtain a company charter prior to beginning resource extraction. Deputy Attorney General J.D. Hunt initiated an investigation of Bonnie Brae. In a memorandum dated April 22, 1914, Fenwick agreed there were "undoubtedly irregularities and violations of the Companies Ordinance" but argued that the department should avoid acting for a variety of reasons and proceeded to lay them out in systematic fashion. First, the attorney general's office did not have unlimited funds, necessarily meaning that it selected cases carefully. Fenwick pointed out that, in this case, a mitigating factor was that the company "is still in pretty good shape." However, the auditor's report prepared in conjunction with the investigation concluded pursuing a case would likely result in Bonnie Brae's bankruptcy, harming investors further as "share-holders would not get a cent on the dollar now." On the other hand, allowing the company to reorganize as a new venture would protect both the rights and the capital put in the company by investors. Referencing Ritchie's original complaint, which argued the case could become a "cause celebre" among the public, thus facilitating a case, Fenwick disagreed. "The penalties under the Joint Stock Companies Ordinance are recoverable on a summary conviction and the case would, therefore, be tried before a Justice of the Peace." Fenwick advised that the attorney general's office would become involved in the matter "with the view of having the guilty parties settle up." The memorandum closed with the observation that the department might consider a prosecution "if there are poor people who have been defrauded of any considerable amount who will not benefit from the re-organization of the company." Otherwise, Fenwick advised "not to touch it."[34]

Fenwick's memo illustrates the fundamental dilemma the attorney general's office faced in responding to the challenge of the oil boom. The limited budget and finite capacity to conduct investigations necessitated a selective approach. In the case of the newly chartered oil companies, the department's greatest danger lay in miscalculating the short-term and long-term consequences of taking action. Acting too soon ran the risk of depriving investors and businesses of a chance of recouping some or all of their investment. Waiting too long, on the other hand, could result in nothing being salvageable. Furthermore, the attorney general's office dealt with myriad problems simultaneously, from companies operating without a charter to failing to provide share certificates to investors. This latter problem was particularly vexing during the boom because it left shareholders in a kind of investment purgatory with no means of getting their money out of the investment if their circumstances changed (e.g., unemployment) or if they wanted to pursue a different investment opportunity. Other propositions were outright scams designed to defraud unwary investors and fully deserving of prosecution.

Undoubtedly, the province's interest rested at establishing and nurturing the oil industry so that it could provide well-paying jobs for workers and revenues for government, and diversify the provincial economy. But it is equally true that, when the government faced voters to secure another mandate at the ballot box, they needed to prove they were good stewards of the public interest. After all, people, not industries, vote. Further complicating matters is the fact that the province was not wholly responsible for the laws and regulations governing petroleum development. Until 1930, all the mineral rights and leases in the province remained under the control and regulations established by the Dominion government. While the province could regulate businesses operating within its jurisdiction, federal regulations sometimes influenced what policy prescriptions were available to the provincial government. This certainly was the case in 1914 as the attorney general's office weighed its potential responses to reports of corporate malfeasance. Federal Orders in Council (1912) established regulations for petroleum and natural gas rights on Crown lands in effect at the time of the boom. Section 14 of the regulations stipulated that one year after acquiring the petroleum rights to a property, leaseholders had to prove they had "machinery and equipment suitable for carrying on prospecting operations." Lessees also had to provide evidence of "the character, quantity and value of the machinery installed." If the leaseholder did not install machinery or provide adequate evidence, "the lease shall be subject to cancellation."[35]

The intent of the policy was to stimulate development of the country's petroleum reserves as expeditiously as possible as well as preventing the holding of vast areas by a few wealthy landholders. In theory, the reasoning behind federal policies was unassailable and would likely provide for the timely development of petroleum resources. But they proved wanting in the reality of the provincial oil boom of 1913–14 and created a huge headache for the provincial government. By the early autumn of 1914, Canada was at war against the Central Powers in Europe and the first anniversary of the October 1913 strike of petroleum condensates at Dingman #1 approached. When William Elder brought word of a small quantity of white oil in the Dingman well, it had touched off the first speculative wave of lease and mineral rights purchases around the city of Calgary and led to the incorporation of several oil companies. Nearly a year later, rather than celebrate the anniversary of this discovery, its arrival provoked consternation as concerned investors, editorial writers, and businesses realized that investors who acquired acreage in October 1913 were only weeks away from losing their investments because they could not meet the development criteria outlined in section 14.

In some cases, the inability to prove that enough equipment was on the land was purely academic because the promoters of the so-called "oil company" only attempted to sell stock and never intended to drill for oil. But what about operators who could not secure adequate financing, a rig, or other equipment in the summer of 1914? Or companies run by people who were new to the petroleum industry and simply in over their heads? Should they have their provincial charters revoked? Compounding the problem for the provincial attorney general's office was that, as the use of Pinkerton operatives in the summer of 1914 revealed, given the large number of companies created, the province lacked a competent investigatory body of its own to distinguish fraudulent intent from incompetence.

Thus, while some consumers associated "doing something" with a vigorous prosecution of corporate offenders, for others, "doing something" meant recovering investments or intervening with the federal government via relaxed enforcement of section 14. Summarizing the issue, an editorial in the *Herald* on August 8, 1914, concluded that the scales between private sector interests and the public were dangerously out of balance. "It may well be that from the experience gained in the past six months, it would be advisable in some cases to strictly enforce the regulations and have the oil rights revert to the crown, not to be disposed of again except under revised regulation." On the other hand, there were "doubtless numerous instances" where enforcing the letter of the regulations would cause real hardship to people who had worked "honestly" toward complying with the terms. The most elegant solution to the problem, argued the *Herald*, was for the government to hold an inquiry to balance the interests of leaseholders and the public. Left unstated was the reality that investigating complaints too vigorously might inhibit further development if the Dominion government used the results to terminate leases. Faced with an unpalatable choice, the provincial attorney general's office kicked the can as far down the road as possible. Federal petroleum leases provided a full calendar year for leaseholders to develop their properties, and the Dominion government alone would determine what to do about extending the lease deadline. Any action taken before the leases expired would be premature.[36]

Part of the solution was the Sifton government's decision to put forward the Public Utilities Act in the legislature on March 22, 1915. The centerpiece of the act was the creation of a public utilities board with broad powers. While the specific details of the proposal remained known only to cabinet for the time being, many reporters assumed that the commission would have a broad mandate, including jurisdiction over public utilities and regulating the borrowing powers of urban and rural municipalities. "The act is the most far-reaching and the most important that has been under the consideration of the government for some time," reported the *Edmonton Bulletin*. The *Edmonton Journal*, on the other hand, speculated that the government had drafted the legislation on the Manitoba model wherein the commissioner,

Judge Robson, "exercises arbitrary powers."³⁷ Meanwhile, the *Albertan* observed that the government's signature piece of legislation for the upcoming session just barely scratched the surface with its possibilities. Pointing to the public utilities commissioner in Manitoba, the *Albertan* noted that Manitoba's Robson "prevented wide open, wild cat speculation in worthless oil stocks there," and "he keeps a guiding hand over the province in matters of that kind."³⁸ Noting the government's belated adoption of the institution, the Conservative-leaning *Herald* observed that "better late than never" is "about all one can say of most of the so-called 'advanced' legislation of the Sifton government."³⁹

Details about the proposed commission became public on March 30, 1915. The Public Utilities Act created a three-person Board of Public Utilities Commissioners appointed by the Lieutenant-Governor for a ten-year term unless removed by the Lieutenant-Governor or the legislative assembly. Conceived of as apolitical officeholders, commissioners, said MLA James R. Lowery, should be the most able people possible, "who would command the respect and confidence of all classes of people."⁴⁰ Expectations were that commissioners would devote all their time to the responsibilities of the board and were explicitly forbidden from being "financially interested in any public utility in the province, nor in any device or appliance used in the business of a public utility," which meant that they would instead be well compensated by the government. Commissioners could also be reappointed provided they did not exceed the mandatory retirement age of seventy. Meanwhile, the board's mandate included two broad areas of responsibility. First, supervisory jurisdiction over public utilities with the power to make orders "regarding equipment, appliances, safety devices, extension of works or systems as are necessary for the safety or convenience of the public." Second, "to inquire into the merits of any application of a local authority for permission to raise money by way of debenture or upon the security of stock, and to grant or refuse such permission." While the original Public Utilities Act did not say anything directly about regulating the petroleum industry or exercising oversight on the sale of shares, these were precisely the powers used by the Manitoba Public Utilities Commissioner to deny permission for the flotation of Calgary oil stocks in 1914. "The list of powers and responsibilities placed in the hands of the new board covered many areas," concluded Willie Grieve at the centennial celebration of public utility regulation in Alberta, "including functions that would not normally be included in any definition of a public utility but all of which were important at the time and shared the characteristics necessary for oversight independent from political influence and control."⁴¹ Significantly, the Act endowed the board with "the same powers and privileges as are vested in a judge as regards the attendance and examination of witnesses, the production of books and all other documents, and the ordering of costs to be paid by any party." The decision of the board on "any question of fact or law will be final." Appeals to the court of appeal could only permitted for "any question involving the jurisdiction of the board, but only by permission of a judge of the court of appeal."[42]

However, greater provincial regulation of companies under the auspices of the Public Utilities Commission remained a more theoretical than actual proposition in 1915, as the legislation did not include a role for the commission in the petroleum industry. Municipal efforts, on the other hand, grappled with the problem posed by the large number of exchanges operating in Calgary. The collapse of the boom and the beginning of the war thinned the ranks of exchanges and brokers. But in early 1915, multiple exchanges still operated under provincial charters, presenting seemingly endless opportunities for mischief as investment capital continued to shrink. The combination of the need to "do something" about the exchanges and the need for city council to raise revenues to continue funding poor relief spurred attempts by city officials to rein in the exchanges by taking advantage of the city's role in licensing brokerages. On May 10, 1915, the City of Calgary amended its earlier licensing bylaw for brokers by adopting a licence fee of $200 for all brokerage houses in addition to the fifty-dollar individual annual licence required of all brokers, whether they belonged to an exchange or not. The bylaw further stipulated that those exchanges keep membership lists and maintain accurate records of each transaction, including the number and description of stock certificates sold, the purchase price, and the names of the buyer and seller as well those of the agents, brokers, or other persons involved in the transaction.[43]

Even these modest measures drew organized resistance and court challenges from Calgary's brokerage community. One of the first cases testing the new bylaw involved J.T. Lovejoy, who claimed that he had bought out the Goldfields Oil Exchange and that the provincial charter transferred to him after the purchase. Police Chief Cuddy believed that under current laws, the exchange's charter would transfer to the new owner but that, at a minimum, Lovejoy should have obtained a new licence from the city. In Magistrate's Court, Lovejoy claimed he did not intend to evade the law, only to have Justice Sanders reply, "I don't see why these charters should be carried about in one's pocket." Turning to the City of Calgary's solicitor, Sanders asked, "Is there no way of limiting these oil exchanges?" The city solicitor replied that there was not. The best that the city could do was control them by means of the new bylaw. Sanders then summoned Robert Hood, the secretary of the Calgary Stock Exchange, to see if they had a licence. When Hood replied that the Calgary Stock Exchange and the city were still in discussions, Sanders remanded Lovejoy's case. Whatever city council decided to do for the Calgary Stock Exchange would also apply to Lovejoy.[44]

More formidable was the challenge mounted by the Calgary Stock Exchange to the bylaw. A delegation headed by Archibald Dingman made their case before city council. Dingman compared the CSE to similar exchanges in Toronto, Winnipeg, and Vancouver and argued oil stocks were a "sideline" for the CSE; selling war bonds now constituted the bulk of its transactions. Dingman returned to more solid ground when he argued that he knew of no other Canadian city that required chartered stock exchanges to purchase a licence, and called it an unfair tax. Of the ninety-seven brokers belonging to the CSE, only forty actively traded on the floor of the exchange. Dingman's delegation did not object to the remaining fifty-seven brokers dealing from offices paying the fifty-dollar fee but believed the ones who traded on the floor should be exempt because they paid both annual and monthly membership dues to the exchange. The province established the CSE for a specific purpose, argued Dingman. "There was a very loud public complaint that one man was buying a stock for one dollar at one place and another man was paying two dollars for the same stock at the same time at another place. The exchange was established to standardize values and save the reputation of the city of Calgary throughout Canada and the United States." More to the point, Dingman argued that without the CSE conditions would be much worse. "All these oil stocks that are being dealt in are stocks of purely speculative value. None of them have any intrinsic value, for the reason that none of the companies are paying dividends on them. Therefore, whatever sales are made are on a purely speculative basis." Dingman therefore argued that the CSE's provincial charter entitled it to separate treatment from the other, unchartered, "open call" exchanges.[45]

But City Councillor J.S. Arnold replied that businesspeople paid a tax on their stock of goods while the stock exchange did not. Besides which, licences were the only revenue source open to the city. Thus, city council proceeded with the dual fee partly for financial reasons—responsibility for poor relief fell to municipalities—but also to tame the stock exchanges. However, enforcement proved toothless because while the city collected licence fees from both the brokers and the exchanges it could not compel either of them to close if they did not comply with the regulations. Despite the warnings of

Dingman's delegation that the dual fee might force the CSE to suspend operations, city council's legislative committee stated it could not "make any alterations in the provisions of Bylaw 1794 for the current year" and instructed Police Chief Cuddy to "rigidly enforce" its provisions. The *Herald* noted that the recommendation specifically targeted the "open call" exchanges, which did not observe the same rules as the Calgary Stock Exchange. The oil brokers took the city to court and obtained a favourable ruling from Magistrate Sanders dismissing the additional fifty-dollar fee. Council reluctantly agreed to abide the ruling by a narrow vote of six to four.[46]

Shortly thereafter, the honesty and integrity of the Calgary Stock Exchange came into question due to two separate instances of market manipulation. The first came after Alberta Petroleum Consolidated conclusively demonstrated that its well in the Turner Valley field produced a high-grade crude oil at a rate of 100 barrels per day.[47] Despite a number of large "buy" orders from US investors (in the range of 5,000 to 200,000 shares of stock out of 800,000 issued,), Alberta Petroleum Consolidated lost more than half its value as share prices tumbled from 5.5 to 2.5 -cents per share. A company official told the *Herald* that a single broker was responsible for the stock losing value. Evidently, the broker's client issued a buy order for 200,000 shares at five cents but then the broker acted to drive share prices down to 2.5 -cents before processing his order, pocketing both the difference between the price the customer was willing to pay versus the sale price as well as the commission.[48] A far larger and more serious challenge arose when a plot by a "small clique" of brokers conspired to depress the market for Southern Alberta Oil Company to help others who sold short and scrambled when the Alberta Oil Company's stock value rose. The governing committee promised action against the clique for rigging the market but only if someone could provide names and dates to the committee. The public grew irate after the *Albertan* alleged that a midnight meeting between the conspirators was an open secret on the floor of the exchange.[49] A letter to the editor of *The Calgary Daily Herald* captured the urgency of the moment, suggesting that "nothing short of some drastic action will save the situation from the most serious consequences to the future development of an oilfield of so much promise." The crux of the problem was that the behaviour of a few bad actors "only tends to discourage the influx of funds necessary for development purposes."[50]

Thus, one of the government's responses to the boom was legislation designed to protect consumers from the worst excesses of stock market speculation. Government officials recognized the necessity of a modicum of government oversight and the beginnings of a regulatory framework capable of establishing standards, gathering information, conducting investigations, and ensuring transparency, especially over the actions of brokers. In a two-stage process, the Sifton government moved away from self-regulation of the stock exchanges to one where the province embraced a larger role in the regulatory regime for Alberta-chartered companies. Now all the province had to establish was that it had both the right, responsibility, and obligation to oversee the petroleum industry.

9

Public Interest Versus Private Rights: Judge Alexander A. Carpenter's Commission and the Big Boom's Big Hangover

I think there is a misunderstanding with regard to the intention of the directors of the company. Everybody was, about this time, wondering how they were going to get along and hold their leases. The whole atmosphere of the time you are investigating should be taken into consideration. I believe if that is done it will explain a large part of what was done, [and] was tolerated by the company.

—H.P. Carver
Director, Western Canada Oil Company
Testimony before the Carpenter Commission
August 19, 1915

How can it be said that the private affairs of a company is a public matter. It may well be that some members of the public are affected by them, but that does not make them a public matter.

—Alberta Chief Justice Horace Harvey
October 5, 1915

By the spring of 1915, the attorney general's department had arrived at a crossroads. Indeed, it seemed that hardly a week passed without the attorney general's office receiving complaints from defrauded investors across North America wondering what happened to their money. With dozens of ad hoc investigations under its belt, and jilted investors asking questions, the attorney general's office decided to tackle the issue head on and appoint a judicial commission to make a full and complete inquiry into the oil industry. Creating a commission was a bold move, serving as a tacit admission that the events of 1914 had created a crisis that required a more robust response from the government. The flagrant and open way in which some oil companies swindled investors demanded a public response to re-establish investor confidence in Calgary oil companies. A commission could address several imperatives simultaneously, including creating a public record of what happened; identifying areas of weakness in legislation; addressing the government's critics; spreading information quickly and efficiently to investors about criminal behaviour; and providing the justification for an expansion of provincial power over the regulation of industry.

Endowed with sweeping powers to call witnesses, gather evidence, and compel testimony, the commission, headed by Calgary judge Alexander A. Carpenter, raised uncomfortable questions about how far the provincial government could, or should, go to protect the public interest at the expense of individual initiative. While the commission's overall aim of establishing a common narrative of what happened during the boom was laudable and answered the demands of investors that the Sifton government "do something," some suggested the Carpenter Commission grossly overcorrected at the expense of individual rights. Complicating matters further, the commission revealed both the necessity and potential of government oversight with its investigation of Western Canada Oil Company (WCOC) and the actions of one of its board members, Julian Langner. Known to police before the boom as a convicted white-collar criminal, Langner established himself as a real estate broker and first secured a position with Stephen Beveridge's Rocky Mountain Oil Fields before joining WCOC as secretary and treasurer. Members of WCOC's board of directors claimed Langner took advantage of the chaotic and frenzied conditions created by the boom to hide his frequent and persistent raids of the company treasury, use of company funds to settle personal debts, and manipulation of Western Canada stock. Critics retorted that the board of directors failed to fulfill their fiduciary responsibilities to the shareholders and exercise proper oversight. Regardless, the meticulous way the Carpenter Commission laid out the various schemes, kickbacks, and bribes at the company shocked even the most jaded oil promoters. Was this how all oil companies operated?

Industry boosters like the *Albertan* responded quickly to the revelations by stoutly defending the industry and questioning the commission's motives. On the one hand, the *Albertan* argued that citizens succumbed to a mob mentality during the boom; everyone made poor choices in the spring of 1914 and the province should leave well enough alone. On the other hand, the editorial page waged a campaign to shut down the inquiry immediately by arguing its investigation was not in the public interest. Both responses indirectly absolved Langner and the board of directors of responsibility for their actions. While subsequent hearings failed to generate the same sensational headlines, they spooked George Buck, who feared what an investigation of Black Diamond might reveal. Just as Carpenter prepared to focus his attention on George Buck and Black Diamond, Buck's new attorney, Alexander A. McGillivray, secured a court injunction temporarily shutting down the commission by claiming its orders-in-council improperly allocated powers to the commission it did not have, setting up a fateful challenge before the Court of Appeal.[1]

The spring of 1915 saw the Sifton government pass the Public Utilities Act, which carved out a greater role for the province in the regulation of public utilities. At the time the legislation was passed, though, the government did not claim an oversight role for the petroleum industry for its new institution. But for months, the attorney general's office conducted a series of investigations stemming from public complaints about the actions of individual oil companies and now concluded that volume was sufficient to warrant a general inquiry. On June 22, 1915, Attorney General Charles Cross announced the creation of a commission to be chaired by Judge Arthur A. Carpenter of the District Court of Calgary and assisted by Edmonton lawyer Frank Ford, KC, and Calgary Barrister Gregory A. Trainor. The commission would hold hearings in both Calgary and Edmonton to investigate "all complaints regarding the operations, and failure to operate of oil companies in Alberta."[2]

Judicial commissions tend to limit their purpose—either to a policy review or a factual inquiry. Policy reviews provide policy recommendations to the government. Factual inquiries, on the other hand, seek to establish a collective understanding of what happened.[3] The Carpenter Commission clearly fell into the second category. However, the mandate of the inquiry was breathtaking; Carpenter claimed the authority to summon witnesses to give evidence and for companies under investigation to produce all documents he deemed necessary.⁴ The province determined it had the authority to do so under chapter 2, section 1 of the Public Inquiries Act of 1908, which enabled the cabinet to appoint a commission "to enquire into and concerning any matter within the jurisdiction of the legislative assembly and connected with the good government of the province or the conduct of public business thereof."⁵ On July 5, 1915, the Sifton government provided additional details about the scope of the commission's mandate, deeming it "expedient that Inquiry be made into the promotion, incorporation, management and operation of the various companies incorporated by and under the authority of the company ordinance," specifically, chapter 20 of the Ordinances of 1901.⁶ The commission enjoyed sweeping powers to examine the general history of the hundreds of oil companies created during the boom.⁷

In Carpenter and Ford, the commission boasted two of the best legal minds in the province. Originally from Hamilton, Ontario, Judge Arthur Allan Carpenter graduated from University of Toronto law school in 1894 at the age of twenty-one and then studied at Osgoode Hall and attained his law degree in 1897. After admission to the Law Society of Upper Canada, he practised law in Hamilton for six years before moving to Innisfail, Alberta, to establish his law practice. First appointed judge for the district of Macleod south of Calgary in 1907, Carpenter transferred in 1910 to the city, where he established himself as a pillar of the community. More recently, Carpenter had headed the provincial investigation into the June 1914 Hillcrest mine disaster that claimed the lives of 189 miners—Canada's worst mining accident. Lawyer Frank Ford hailed from Toronto and graduated from Trinity University before attending Osgoode Hall. Called to the Ontario bar in 1897, Ford served as secretary and solicitor to the premier, attorney general, and treasurer of the Province of Ontario from 1898 to 1903. Then, after moving west in 1904, Ford became deputy attorney general in Saskatchewan in 1906 and served in that position until 1910, when he moved to Edmonton and practised law with the firm Emery, Newell, Ford, Bolton, and Mount. His career was particularly distinguished, as Ontario, Saskatchewan, and Alberta all named Ford King's Counsel. In 1926 Ford joined the Alberta Supreme Court as a trial judge.⁸

Not surprisingly, given its stance toward the flotation of oil companies in late 1913, the *Herald* heartily approved the decision but thought it akin to "locking the stable door after the horse has been stolen." A year earlier, the commission might have prevented the "methods which have resulted in investors being separated from a great deal of hard-earned cash." Nonetheless the *Herald* believed the decision was a good one, especially considering the ongoing search for crude in the province. "Once the public learns just how its money has been spent it will perhaps be in a better position to decide what to do, should the temptations which were placed before it a year ago again be presented."[9] The *Edmonton Journal* welcomed the creation of the commission but lamented that the province had not adopted restrictions earlier. "One thing, however, may be accomplished by the commission," offered the *Journal*. "It should be the means of showing the necessity for restrictive legislation that will prove of value when future oil booms are launched."[10]

Other editorial opinions were more effusive. The *Red Deer Advocate* expressed its full confidence with the appointment of Carpenter and Ford. The latter selection drew much praise from the *Advocate* and served as "sufficient guarantee of the Government's desire to make the enquiry thorough."[11] The *Claresholm Review* wrote, "We understand it is the wish of the government that all assistance be given by the public . . . so that we may be able to purge this valuable industry from wrongdoing and improper manipulation." The *Western Standard* also applauded the move and argued that Calgary's reputation was at stake. "We do not want it said of us that, as a municipality, we have winked at the robbing of those who would put up money in the expectation that it would be spent in exploiting the Alberta oil field," wrote the editors. "The inquiry will be empowered to make sweeping recommendations and in the carrying out of these the city should be prepared to take part." A few weeks later, *The Weekly Standard* reasserted its position on the necessity of prosecuting those who broke the law but drew a careful distinction between law breakers and "reliable companies which started business and were obliged to stop for lack of sufficient funds even before they got very far." In those instances where investors drilled a dry well, they chalked their setbacks up to the vicissitudes of the market. But "it is the people who did nothing but sell certificates—worthless 'scraps of paper' that will probably have to give an account of their stewardships and it is time that they were brought to an account."[12] In Kingston, Ontario, the *Whig-Standard* reported that nothing less than "serious embezzlement charges will arise out of the investigation and that drastic action will be taken to clean up the whole oil situation."[13]

In addition to standard press coverage, the attorney general's office forwarded a memorandum on July 2, 1915, to all newspapers on its patronage list about the appointment of the commission and then watched papers to see if they used the information in a story. A week later, at least one newspaper, *The Alsask News* in Saskatchewan, received a follow-up letter from the acting deputy attorney general, G.P.O. Fenwick, asking if the paper used the memo's information in a story yet. "If you have not already published a news item in connection with this, would you be good enough to do so at once."[14] The memorandum carried out its intended aim, as publicity about the commission brought a flood of new complaints to the attention of the department as well as positive commentary from investors. One investor, J. Paton from Vernon, British Columbia, congratulated and thanked the attorney general for appointing the commission. "If you are satisfied that there was no fraud on the part of Mr. Macalister and his colleagues then no doubt the steps taken will be satisfactory. On the other hand, an example once made of such bad business methods would assist in preventing a recurrence in the future."[15] Others provided further details and complaints, like J.A. Ramage of Red Deer, who wrote that the Red Deer Oil and Gas Company only issued him a receipt for the fifteen dollars' worth of shares he bought. He later learned that "the Company does not intend to issue [shares.]" The previous fall, the company wrote to stockholders offering a refund if they so desired. After he informed the company that he would like his money returned, nothing happened for a few weeks until Mr. Ramage received a second letter offering him a cash settlement but only if he accepted fifty cents on the dollar. Ramage refused to settle on those terms. "All I want is a square deal and something to show for my money," he wrote the deputy attorney general, "and I think these people should be forced to either issue their shares or refund the stockholders their money."[16] Elizabeth Green of St. Vincent, Maine, wrote that she would follow the Carpenter Commission very closely as she had fifteen dollars "tied up" with the Premier Alberta Oil Company. While this might not be a lot to some, "it's a great deal to me in these strenuous times."[17] Brimming with confidence at the material already assembled by the attorney general's office, Judge Carpenter told a reporter, "There are plenty of written complaints to start work on."[18]

On the eve of the commission's opening, *The Toronto Globe* published an editorial, later reprinted in full by the *Edmonton Journal* and *The Red Deer News*, on the aftermath of the boom. Noting that only a year had passed since Alberta "was effervescing in all the excitement of an oil boom." Companies, and stock exchanges had formed quickly and floated their shares to willing investors. Some who got in early made a fortune on paper as the market took off. "This is the way with all such booms," observed the paper. "Everything soars along to the crest, and beyond that the drop is quick and complete." Now that a commission had been formed to investigate the oil companies the focus would be on complaints "in connection with exchange transactions or dealings with company officers," and the editorial subtly urged people not to forget that another party bore some blame. The government's attempt to "rescue ill-fated speculators is praiseworthy, but somewhat belated." The Toronto paper wondered why the government had continued issuing provincial charters to "patent frauds" the summer before and did not adequately monitor company activities. Officials in other jurisdictions on the prairies, namely Manitoba, had enacted "blue-sky" legislation and appointed public utility commissioners; why not Alberta? The Sifton government "let the oil boom overflow the channels of safety." Acknowledging the idea of moral hazard and arguments that "it is no duty of governments to protect foolish investors against the consequences of their folly," the piece also noted government's obligation "to ensure fair play in the disposition of their money." Canadian laws and regulations regarding resource extraction "have been far too lenient." But launching the investigation and "rounding up parasites who designedly fleece too-easy speculators would help in producing better future conditions."[19]

Weeks of anticipation culminated in the opening day of the Carpenter Commission, July 13, 1915. The *Albertan's* editorial page wondered if the oil probe would "'strike oil' at the very first go off, or must there be many weeks of patient drilling before anything substantial is reached? Or will the judge drill a 'duster?'"[20] At ten a.m., oil company lawyers filled Judge Carpenter's courtroom to the brim and a stack of letters a foot deep from disgruntled stockholders greeted the commissioners. Interestingly, most of the correspondence came from eastern Canada and the United States (with Philadelphia and Detroit being most prominent).[21] The letters alleged no crime, nor made specific allegations of criminal wrongdoing; many simply said that investors had paid good money for now worthless stock and wanted restitution. In his opening, Judge Carpenter began by tamping down public expectations, emphasizing that, while the provincial government had ordered the investigation, this did not necessarily mean investors would recoup lost investments. In some cases, Carpenter solemnly said, the money was long gone. In others, investors might be able to recover funds by initiating legal proceedings against the responsible company officers. Carpenter then got straight to the point. "The principal object of the investigation by the commission is to advise stockholders whether they have a civil or criminal action against officials of the erring oil companies."[22]

Carpenter's statement displayed few illusions about the daunting task ahead. Proving crimes was difficult due to the very lax regulatory environment. A company might claim capitalization of a million dollars and list a particular leasehold as an asset on its prospectus. When the company purchased the lease from the owner—usually a member of the board of directors, and usually at an inflated price, say $600,000—the company's directors divided the profits from that sale between them and left only $400,000 for the development of the field (securing a drill crew, building a derrick, drilling for oil). But another problem existed. As Carpenter explained, the 1911 Companies Act in force at the time of the stock market frenzy permitted companies to issue large volumes of promotion stock versus treasury stock. Companies would issue promotion stock to brokers as an incentive to sell their product. When brokers dumped the promotion stock into the market, it would compete against the smaller volume of treasury stock. Inevitably, with larger volumes of stock available, prices fell. Anticipating the question about the legality of the practice, Judge Carpenter demurred, citing the idea of moral hazard. "If a man had a prospectus in his hand and read it and in spite of the fact that it showed that the company was a very bad investment, he proceeded to put his money in, he would have himself to blame." In such a case, moral hazard declared it was not government's responsibility to nullify the poor decisions of the investor. However, Carpenter also identified two scenarios where the investor could seek some recourse. The first was when the company did not have the assets listed in their prospectus on hand when they applied for their provincial charter. The second was if a company sold stock before securing mineral leases from the Dominion Land Office or before receiving their charter from Edmonton. In either of those two instances, company officials would be potentially liable to possible civil or criminal action. Given the lengthy delays the Dominion Land Office experienced in processing applications and issuing leaseholds the winter of 1913/14, this latter scenario seemed very likely in some cases.[23]

Despite reams of letters sent to the attorney general's office, the investigations conducted by the Pinkertons, and Carpenter's own statement to the *Herald* the day before that there was plenty of work to do, Carpenter now claimed he was unable to begin the inquiry: public complaints failed to specify corporate wrongdoing. After weeks of preparation, it proved a shocking twist few had anticipated, and it was far from a good look. "People who kicked verbal holes in oil companies," wrote the *Albertan*, "complaining of inability to get value for money, had neglected to back up their complaints with any definite evidence."[24] No accusers were in the courtroom, just lawyers. In retrospect, the Carpenter Commission's apparent stumble left a poor first impression. Convinced that it would be an easy matter to prove wrongdoing by the oil companies, few investors had bothered to put in the necessary work of making a case.

Having created an inquiry that now sat twiddling its thumbs, the attorney general's office arranged to insert public notices in major Alberta newspapers advising that "anyone having complaints to make against any Oil Company can address their complaints to Judge Carpenter, or can personally consult G.A. Trainor."[25] A memo for Fenwick on August 5 pointed out that the justice department had failed to include similar notices in *The Medicine Hat News* and the *Lethbridge Herald* in cities where investors bought large quantities of stock. "The public," advised the official from the provincial treasurer's office, "should have notice through the local papers." Fenwick promptly forwarded the message directly to Judge Carpenter.[26] In the meantime, less than a week before the inquiry resumed, Calgary-based barrister Gregory Trainor asked the attorney general's office for a $100 advance to cover disbursements for witnesses to appear, raising the question of which department or entity was covering the costs of the investigation. Fenwick forwarded the request directly to Attorney General Charles Cross along with a request to have an order-in-council put through "making the expense of the investigation payable out of general revenue, or at least a part of the expenses." Fenwick noted that the investigation would be one that benefited the entire government and, to date, all the revenue had gone to the provincial secretary's department. The commission "is liable to be quite expensive," and Fenwick reported the attorney general's office "is not in a position to stand it."[27]

After a month-long delay, on August 16, the commission laid charges against eight oil companies—Western Canada Oil Company, the Canada Crude Oil Company, Herron-Elder, Monarch Oil Company, Alberta Petroleum, Phillips-Elliott, Union Oil Company, and Black Diamond. Shareholders levelled complaints against another twenty-five companies, mostly hoping to recoup their investments. In the debate between the public interest and private rights, one local paper left little doubt where its loyalties lay. "Let us hope that this oil probe will do its full duty," commented *The Calgary News Telegram* as it exhorted witnesses to embrace their responsibility "of giving evidence on someone else." The *News Telegram* argued that only a thorough housecleaning would restore investor confidence in Alberta, and the paper seemed to question whether the attorney general's office had gone far enough. "A government audit of the books of all the oil companies whether under suspicion or not would help in the purging process."[28]

Aware that the opening investigation would set the tone for the rest of the inquiry, Judge Carpenter personally selected Western Canada Oil Company (WCOC) to be the first company examined when the hearings reopened on August 18, 1915.[29] Back in the heady days of May 1914, WCOC was both eager and desperate to start drilling to cash in on the boom. But, undercapitalized from the start—the firm's prospectus showed it only had $75,000 in its treasury before acquiring four sections (2,560 acres of leases) from John F. Eastwood (who was also a company vice president) for $25,000 in stock and $7,500 in cash—the company compounded the error by making a series of questionable decisions. Determined to sell as much stock as they could quickly, the directors announced they would pay brokers a 25 percent commission on the sale of the remaining $50,000 of stock. The decision sold more stock but hurt the firm's bottom line. After paying the sky-high commissions, only $30,000 remained in the treasury for development of the leaseholds—$10,000 short of the average cost required to drill a single well. Land-rich, but short on cash, the directors were determined to spud in a well with outside financing to either develop or retain their eleven leaseholds.[30] That's when Julian Langner, WCOC's twenty-five-year-old fiscal agent, began his machinations.

A quasi-reformed white-collar criminal originally from London, England, Langner had a history of separating unwary investors and inattentive corporate directors from their cash. Arriving in Calgary in October 1911 near the end of the real estate boom, Langner billed himself as an estate agent and land surveyor by profession and landed a position with the Co-Operative Small Investor's Company, a small investment firm capitalized at $10,000. That company folded in early 1912 after Langner's arrest on four charges of obtaining money under false pretenses. Placed on trial before Judge Carpenter, Langner convinced the judge to be lenient because of his inexperience and sincerity. Left unsupervised by a lackadaisical board of directors, Langner claimed to be doing his best but made mistakes along the way and found himself accused of diverting company resources to his personal use. After finding Langner not guilty on all charges, Judge Carpenter addressed Langner directly, saying, "I hope that this will be a salutary lesson to you and teach you for the future not to indulge in any fantastic flights of high finance."[31]

Langner's brush with the law did not prevent Western Canada Oil Company's directors from retaining him as their secretary and treasurer shortly after the company formed in September 1913.[32] In this capacity, Langner approached banker H.P. Carver of the Dominion Trust, who also served on Western Canada's board of directors, to secure outside development capital. Carver knew Langner well, having done business with him in the past, and in the heady days of May 1914, plenty of outside investors eager to get into the oil fields arrived daily, including H.W. Leyens from Vancouver. With previous experience in civic and bank bonds, Leyens wanted to broaden his portfolio to include Alberta oil. With the city in the grip of a frenzy,

Leyens became intoxicated by the promise of a quick and easy fortune. Leyens later told *The Vancouver Sun* that he was impressed by the degree to which Calgarians offered moral and financial support to the companies struggling to get off the ground; Calgary's solicitors were so overwhelmed, he reported, that they took meetings late into the night and recalled that one solicitor scheduled a meeting at three a.m.. Carver arranged to introduce Leyens and Langner in exchange for a 10 percent commission or $2,000.[33] Carver then introduced Leyens to the WCOC's directors and the two parties struck a deal that created a new company, Lion Oil. Lion Oil purchased eight quarter sections from WCOC for half a million dollars on paper—the actual financing was $200,000 in cash and 600,000 shares in Lion Oil valued at one dollar each. Leyens received half the shares as his commission for bringing the deal together, leaving the rest—300,000 shares—for Western Canada.[34]

The deal temporarily transformed Western Canada Oil Company into one of the early darlings of the oil boom. After the deal was announced on May 23, 1914, Western Canada's stock value increased 400 percent, establishing Langner's reputation as a big-time promoter in the process. Within weeks, Langner was a flurry of activity, emerging as secretary and treasurer of three other companies—Lion Oil, the Pittsburg Oil Company [sic], and the Peerless Oil Company—as well as forming a syndicate with seven other associates to drill near the Monarch well in the Olds district. A circular sent out to shareholders in Western Canada urged them to invest in Peerless Oil. Claiming "a large number of the shareholders who have made considerable money as a result of their getting in 'right' in the Western Canada," Langner also claimed that Peerless had acquired certain lands "which have been FAVORABLY REPORTED UPON BY MR. E.H. CUNNINGHAM CRAIG" and assured investors that drilling on the site would begin as quickly as possible.[35] To the press, Langner claimed the situation looked promising. "We are going to put our own money into it and take a chance."[36] In an advertisement in the *Spokane Chronicle,* Langner launched his appeal to investors in his new venture, the Peerless Oil Works, by claiming the new company was organized along the same "strong, conservative basis" and "sound financial backing" as Western Canada Oil Company.[37] Behind the scenes, though, Langner was far from confident. When Carver came to collect his $2,000 commission from Langner for helping to put together the Lion deal, he found the promoter exceedingly reluctant to pay up. Langner tried to briefly back out of the agreement before giving way. Over a year later in front of the Carpenter Commission, Carver testified he knew Langner was in some kind of financial trouble. After he encouraged Langner to keep paying his debts, Langner complained to Carver that every solution to his money problems was "blocked."[38]

In the meantime, Western Canada Oil Company signed a contract with Janse Drilling and activity began on the company's lease. Janse Drilling built the bunkhouses and hauled equipment and machinery out to the drill site. However, despite the recent sale to Lion Oil, Western Canada experienced a cash crunch, and shareholders, who believed the deal would provide the funds necessary to drill, were furious and angrily demanded to know what had happened to the money from the sale. Backed into a corner, Western Canada's directors sent a letter to shareholders on July 15, 1914, clarifying the terms of the deal.[39] The fine print signed with Leyens and Lion Oil revealed the Vancouver money man secured half of Western Canada's assets with no cash changing hands. The contract stipulated that Western Canada's $200,000 would come out of the proceeds from the first stock sold *after* Lion Oil secured $50,000 for the development of leases. By August 1914, WCOC had yet to file a financial statement and activity on the company's leasehold ceased as the derrick packed up and disappeared. A letter to the editor of the *Herald* wondered loudly what had happened to the money investors placed in the company and whether Lion Oil could retain the former WCOC leases without paying any money.[40] By April 1915, a preliminary investigation by shareholders in the Western Canada Oil Company strongly urged the province's attorney general "to undertake a complete investigation of the affairs of the company with a view to taking criminal proceedings against the former secretary treasurer, Julian Langner," who promptly left Calgary for California along with $22,660 (approximately $710,500, adjusted for inflation) from Western Canada's treasury.[41]

Despite his unassuming title of fiscal agent and secretary, Julian Langner effectively served as the most powerful person in Western Canada Oil Company, in part because of the lackadaisical oversight provided by the board of directors. As fiscal agent, Langner controlled and set prices for the company's stock. "Today they were to be at par $1," complained the *Butte Miner*, "tomorrow $2, next day $3, then $2.50, then $3, and so on, up and down to $10."[42] Unfortunately for investors, Langner treated the company like his own personal bank, literally giving away 10,000 shares of treasury stock instead of vendor's stock to friends and acquaintances in exchange for loans or as repayment for past favours. In other instances, Langner gave bonus shares to people without seeking payment. He advanced $600 out of the treasury to Leyens to pay for the incorporation of Lion Oils and then, when Western Canada's share price sat at five dollars a share, Langner sold 1,000 shares of

Western Canada at two dollars a share to Leyens. The company's auditor later found that Leyens received the shares in exchange for a promissory note that remained outstanding. Langner even arranged to put through a $700 loan to one of the directors from the company's treasury with no expectation of repayment.[43]

The Carpenter Commission's first witness, Western Canada's auditor William Ireland, painted a damning portrait of corporate malfeasance and near-criminal incompetence. Despite the litany of other mistakes, one decision by Western Canada's board of directors looms as an exception—hiring accountant William Ireland to audit the company's books. He performed his first audit in October 1913 and found everything in order, but during the second audit on December 30, 1914, Ireland could not make sense of the company's finances at all. Missing invoices and sketchy entries in the ledgers raised alarm bells for the accountant, who then sought out the company secretary treasurer. Questioned about the books, Langner became evasive, avoided giving direct answers to questions, or equivocated, prompting Ireland to ask Langner for all the original contracts with sales agents. Langner produced some but not all of them, forcing the auditor to do some more digging on his own. Ireland expressed shock at what he found. One sales agent received an option from Langner to sell shares the ledgers indicated were already sold, but at neither time did the company receive any money for those sales. When Ireland questioned the sales agent further, he learned that Langner practically gave the agent 2,029 shares as a present because "Langner wanted certain shares he had to sell handed back to him." The 2,029 shares of company stock were to "compensate any loss he might realize in the transaction." Alerted to what could generously be termed an accounting irregularity, Ireland dug deeper into the company's records. After going through the register of stocks, Ireland told Langner he had found a discrepancy he wanted Langner to explain. Langner promptly left for California, never to return.[44]

To the Carpenter Commission, Ireland testified that he discovered the books poorly kept and the records in shambles. Langner lumped all stock, both treasury stock and promotion stock, together; so too for the proceeds of stock sales. Only after months of patient work—consulting and cross-referencing the cash book and certificate stubs—did Ireland piece together Western Canada Oil Company's finances. Ireland found records for 23,417 of the 39,711 shares sold for cash. The books of the Dominion Trust company, who served as transfer agents for Western Canada, showed they issued 26,194 shares for prices between $1.00 and $8.66 per share. Altogether, records indicated that the total amount of money paid to WCOC for shares sold should have been $76,654. But Ireland discovered a discrepancy between the books, the company's statements, and the records of Dominion Trust—5,629 shares were unaccounted for, along with $28,393 in cash. Ireland could not explain the shortage except by pointing to the sale of a block of 3,000 shares that supposedly sold for $25,500.00; a receipt was issued for the sale, but no corresponding deposit showed in the company's bank account. "I knew this money had gone from the company," said Ireland, "and I came to the conclusion that Secretary Langner still has it."[45]

Testimony before the commission also revealed that days before the Dingman strike, on May 12, 1914, Langner signed a new contract with Western Canada that, among other provisions, authorized him to sell 40,000 shares at one dollar. A second signed contract provided Langner an option to pay 10 percent on 28,000 shares with the balance due in fifteen days. According to the terms, the company received the first dollar, Langner the second dollar, and the company the balance on any price over that. But "by some remarkable bookkeeping and crossing of cheques" the company did not receive any payment at all for these two contracts. As far as Ireland could tell, Langner made no attempt to carry out the contract as shown in the books. Furthermore, records kept for 14,000 stock certificates sold at the peak of the boom in May 1914 did not list the sale price. Western Canada's premium account should have recorded stock sales worth $36,943 instead of the $14,274 listed, leaving a hole of approximately $22,660 in the company's books. Ireland also revealed that various corporate directors received an estimated 1,270 shares, representing $85,000 worth of stock, as gifts. All told, it appeared that Langner managed to embezzle at least $22,660 from the company's treasury, although the strong intimation was that the total was much higher—$55,053 ($1.7 million adjusted for inflation)—if the missing $28,383 in stock sales was included in the total. This total does not include the unknown amount Langner sold the 68,000 share options for.[46]

The day's session concluded with the testimony of company director John F. Eastwood, who carefully explained that he was a director when the company launched, took a step back in early 1914 before Langner's reign, and resumed control of the company in the spring of 1915. The commission wanted to know if Eastwood ever spoke to the other directors about the company. Eastwood replied that he had, "but they did not seem to bother much about it." Then Eastwood acknowledged several deals "very carelessly" carried out, including seven transactions Langner authorized, transferring $8,500 worth of shares as gifts to members of the board of directors. When the company attempted to collect payment, only one, Dominion Trust's H.P. Carver, made payment. But Eastwood admitted the road ahead would be difficult. Many important transactions never found their way into the company minutes, making it difficult to determine if any more surprises were on the way.[47]

Commenting on the first day of hearings, the *Albertan* noted that "the revelations made caused the band of hardened oil speculators who formed most spectators to almost gasp. Every offense on the limited company calendar seems to have been committed, speculation, slipshod methods, lax directors, handing over stock promiscuously for nothing, taking cash without accounting for it—no contravention of the legal or moral canons seemed to have been overlooked."[48] After hearing the evidence laid out by Ireland, Judge Carpenter muttered aloud, "I don't believe anybody had much show in this company except the directors." The *Edmonton Journal* pointed its finger elsewhere, suggesting "such looseness would not have been possible if the government had taken any reasonable steps whatever for the protection of the public."[49]

In many ways, Judge Carpenter accomplished what he wanted to with the selection of Western Canada Oil as the first case. The conduct of Langner and the other directors shocked the public and seemingly illustrated the necessity of broader oversight of the industry in the interests of the public at large. Tempting as it was to blame the entire Western Canada fiasco on Langner, other directors were directly or indirectly complicit in his poor behaviour by their failure to exercise any oversight over Langner's actions. Could businesses really be trusted to conduct themselves in the public interest? By the end of the first day's worth of testimony, the proposition seemed to be very much in doubt.

The second day of testimony focused on the activities of other directors, including those of former bank manager H.R. MacMicking, who arranged the drilling contract with Janse Drilling in June 1914, and H.P. Carver, who helped put Langner and Leyens together for the ill-fated partnership with Lion Oil. Perhaps unsurprising, MacMicking had money problems of his own in the spring of 1914 and the Dingman strike provided the means to resolve it. After interviewing three companies, MacMicking awarded a $10,000 contract to Janse Drilling, claiming to the other directors that Janse's offer was the lowest. However, when auditor Ireland compared the books of Janse Drilling and Western Canada, other irregularities appeared, as one of the conditions in the contract required Janse Drilling to pay $1,000 directly to MacMicking. A second condition that raised red flags with the accountant was a second payment for $26,000 from WCOC to Janse Drilling three weeks later, for a grand total of $36,000 for a 3,000-foot well. Under oath, MacMicking acknowledged he received a loan from Janse about the same time he awarded the drilling contract and thereafter continued to borrow money from Janse, leaving the impression that MacMicking's decision might not have reflected purely business concerns. But MacMicking was hardly alone in placing his own interests above those of the company. Regarding the partnership with Lion Oil, Langner obscured the actual terms of the deal with Leyens so thoroughly that the other members of the board were completely unaware that no cash changed hands. Thus, when MacMicking signed the contract with Janse Drilling, Western Canada had less than $10,000 on hand and could not afford to make the additional $26,000 payment three weeks later to start drilling, so Janse packed up its equipment and left. Testimony also revealed Langner provided a $700 loan to MacMicking in the form of shares. Asked whether he paid for the shares, MacMicking responded that he understood these shares were a gift from Langner not requiring payment.[50]

Realizing they hardly presented a picture of sound decision making and entrepreneurial acumen, the directors quickly changed tack, pointing a finger at the supercharged atmosphere of the boom. Western Canada Oil Company's directors argued it was unfair to criticize their actions and decisions in isolation; the Carpenter Commission needed to account for and consider the boom's frantic environment—the crush of investors, the number of competitors hustling for the same client, lease, or capital, the need to satisfy shareholders, all the while making the best decision possible with incomplete or imperfect information under incredibly fluid and dynamic circumstances. Not to mention the fact that most corporate directors simultaneously attended to other businesses making demands on their time. Indeed, very few people in Calgary made their living off the oil industry in 1914. Oil was a business they merely dabbled in, some more seriously than others. MacMicking argued his other responsibilities were more pressing, leaving him unable and unwilling to spend all his time around the Western Canada offices "watching things and people." When the examiner alluded to a director's duty of care to gather and assess information, as well as a director's fiduciary responsibilities beyond self-interest, MacMicking declared that during the boom, the directors did their best to obtain accurate information. Despite the board's constant efforts, "they could not find out how many shares were sold."[51]

Other directors of Western Canada, particularly former president A.B. Fielden, were content to let Langner operate on his own. Fielden claimed business was so pressing in May 1914 that he had no time to keep track of Langner's activities because he could barely keep up with the paperwork of signing checks and stock certificates. Questioned by Ford as to why Langner transferred 1,000 shares to him, Fielden said he believed Langner was simply thanking him for all his hard work. Asked if he ever considered the possibility that Langner intended the shares as a bribe for Fielden's passivity while Langner fleeced the company, Fielden snapped back, "Never for a second." Left lingering in the air was the uncomfortable question as to why Fielden still refused to return or reimburse the company for those shares after the scope of Langner's graft became clear.[52]

Despite stumbling out of the gate, with the Western Canada case the Carpenter Commission established a formidable reputation for thoroughness that sent a shock wave through the oil industry and highlighted two problems for the oil companies to address. The first was the disproportionate profits made by leaseholders in nearly every transaction. In many cases, leaseholders were the first, and sometimes only, people who saw any profit from their activities in 1914. Second was the related issue of the cozy relationship between the companies and their fiscal agents.

Although it had been known since the *Herald's* "flotations" articles in 1913 (see Chapter 2), leaseholders enjoyed disproportionate benefits and profits from the possession and sale of mineral rights to oil companies that were, frankly, little better than lottery tickets. Possession of an oil lease did not guarantee oil existed under that property. Yet this did not stop leaseholders from realizing huge returns—from one hundred to 4,000 times greater than their original investment—by the sale of mineral rights to an oil company. Having "invested" in mineral rights, the oil company then needed to sell treasury stock to the public to finance development. Public expectations were that promoters assumed the same risk as investors; both would only profit if the company struck oil. Furthermore, many investors naively assumed that, since they provided the development capital to drill wells, they would be the first ones to profit. But as *The Western Standard* pointed out, for leaseholders, "it was not a case of 'heads I win, tails I lose.' Heads or tails, oil or no oil, it was a win." As part of the terms of the initial sale of mineral rights to an oil company, the lease vendor also became a director of the company who was the first person paid. In short, the risks of investment were disproportionate, with investors bearing more and directors shouldering less.

The second issue raised by Western Canada related to those instances when an individual, like Julian Langner, served as a director and fiscal agent. Fiscal agents are generally third-party organizations, like a bank or trust company, that handle financial and administrative responsibilities on behalf of another company or organization. However, in many cases in 1914, the fiscal agent was not a third party at all but, like Langner, served as a director of the company as well, practically inviting a conflict of interest. In his capacity as a fiscal agent, Langner received bonus stock (sometimes referred to as vendor's shares) in Western Canada to dispose of as he saw fit as an incentive to promote the company. Langner could hold onto the bonus stock and profit if the company struck oil; alternatively, Langner could sell the bonus shares for whatever price he could and keep the profits himself. Furthermore, not only did Langner profit by selling the bonus stock, he also double dipped by collecting commissions from Western Canada of anywhere between 15 and 50 percent on all shares he sold. Therefore, when Langner flooded the market with vendor's stock, he undercut sales of the company's treasury stock by selling vendor's stock for less. Western Canada's shares would sell, but if the investor bought the cheaper vendor's stock, their money would not provide any cash toward development of the field, just profits for Langner.[53]

Judge Carpenter and his assistants, Ford and Trainor, embraced their investigatory role with zeal. After speaking with the Carpenter Commission attorney Gregory Trainor, the *News Telegram* promised the probe into the oil companies would continue "to be hot and interesting" based on the headlines generated by the Western Canada investigation.[54] *The Butte Miner* added its voice to those heaping praise on Carpenter, writing that "as the investigation proceeds, it may be possible to introduce more system into the method of examination and thus the maximum ground may be covered in the minimum time; but still it does not appear possible that the investigation can be completed within the next few weeks,"[55] While the *News Telegram* and *The Butte Miner* eagerly anticipated subsequent investigations, the *Albertan* did not. In fact, after the end of the second day of hearings, the *Albertan's* editorial page called for an immediate end to the commission. "There is no need of pointing the finger with 'I told you so.'" Taking up the explanation offered by MacMicking and Fielden that the boom had created a super-charged atmosphere non-conducive to rational decision making, the *Albertan* argued that a collective mania gripped the city for a few weeks in the spring of 1914 and everyone took leave of their senses. "We have learned a lot since then," concluded the editorial with a dismissive shrug.[56]

But the *Albertan's* attempt to exonerate company officials and explain the excesses of the boom as the product of a collective failure obscures more than it illuminates. Not every company employed a Julian Langner, whose questionable practices invited previous legal scrutiny. Nor did every board of directors treat their responsibilities as cavalierly as MacMicking and Fielden. Indeed, subsequent investigations by the commission into Phillips-Elliott, Herron-Elder, and Oils Limited revealed companies competently led and on solid financial and business ground. The only difficulty these companies encountered stemmed from the war disrupting their operations.[57]

On the other hand, Carpenter's supporters replied that, far from being a kangaroo court bent on smearing the oil industry, the Carpenter Commission carried out its mandate professionally and competently, guided by the facts, not emotion. Perhaps the *Albertan's* editorial opinion on this issue represented a genuine desire to move on from 1914; alternatively, it could reflect more political concerns that revelations from the hearings would harm Sifton's Liberal government for its failure to adequately regulate business or adopt the basic features of consumer protections offered by "blue-sky" laws. Regardless, the *Albertan* downplayed the first month of hearings, claiming the oil probe "is not bringing out anything sensational and, since the initial case, nothing that savors of wrongdoing. There were some foolish things done, to be sure, but who of us is guiltless of that impeachment in connection with the oil excitement of last year?"[58]

Carpenter scheduled George Buck and Black Diamond Oil Fields to give their testimony starting on Monday, September 27. Eagerly anticipated as this testimony was—no other company's stock value had fluctuated as widely and as much as Black Diamond—it was also clear that Buck was determined to prevent investigation of his company. Unsurprisingly, Buck and Black Diamond already faced several lawsuits involving thousands of dollars related to Black's Diamond's corporate practices, record keeping, and attempted stock market manipulation. The litigation had begun a year earlier on August 15, 1914, when Edward Kolb, Amos W. Scott, Frederick C. Smith, and Allan Clark sued Buck on behalf of Black Diamond shareholders. The suit alleged the partners in the Coalinga Syndicate used Black Diamond Oil Fields as a cash cow to enrich themselves and charged them with theft, misrepresentation, and failure to account for funds.[59] Buck's arraignment before Police Magistrate Sanders on September 4, 1914, turned into a spectacle. As Buck and his party prepared to leave the courtroom, H.C. Beattie placed his cap on his head before reaching the door. The court officer, Constable Patrick Dorrian, who enforced Judge Sanders's strict instructions regarding head coverings, forcibly removed Beattie's hat, only to have Beattie strike Dorrian with his hat in return. For that, Beattie was immediately charged with assaulting a police officer.[60]

Another round of lawsuits began, in December 1914, when Martin and Phillips of International Supply Company filing two lawsuits against Buck and Black Diamond for unpaid bills totalling $25,052 in relation to Black Diamond #1 and Black Diamond #2. Filing on December 21, 1914, Martin and Phillips claimed the sum of $4,423.36 for rental of equipment, cost of materials, and penalties for failing to provide a drilling location. The second suit against Black Diamond #2 company, filed on December 24, 1914, alleged Buck broke the contract with International Supply to the tune of $20,700. Despite drilling Black Diamond #2 to a depth of 1,208 feet, Buck failed to adhere to the terms of the contract requiring $8,000 upon execution of the agreement and balloon payments of $3,000 and $2,000 for drilling the well 500 and 1,000 feet, respectively. "The drilling of the Black Diamond wells," writes the *Herald*, "seems destined to be the subject of considerable litigation." As if to prove the *Herald's* point, Buck countersued for $22,700.[61] Finally, in January 1915, Allan Clark and Fred Smith sued Buck for $30,000 over unpaid commissions for selling Black Diamond oil stock.[62]

Despite the blizzard of lawsuits against him and his company, Buck continued defying the odds, winning ruling after ruling in the courts, prompting him to become even more brazen as he tiptoed through the raindrops. For example, as the Kolb, Scott, Smith, and Clark lawsuit progressed through early November, lawyers for the plaintiffs obtained a court order directing Buck to produce documents that Buck refused to obey, even going so far as to skip out of a scheduled discovery hearing. Acquainted with Buck's tricks from their earlier work on his behalf, the plaintiff's law firm, Lougheed, Bennett, McLaws, obtained a summons for Buck and Jennie Earl to appear at a discovery hearing, only to encounter extreme difficulty in serving the papers. Told that Buck was at the well site, Calgary sheriff F.H. Graham contacted Okotoks bailiff D. McKay Murray with strict instructions that the papers be served on or before November 20, 1914. "I have reason to believe," Murray later swore in an affidavit, "that the said George E. Buck purposely evaded service." On November 20, Murray arrived at the well only to be informed Buck was at his coal mine. By sheer coincidence, a teamster arrived from the mine and Murray asked if Buck was at the mine, only to be told by the teamster that Buck was not there. Murray waited until six o'clock that night before leaving. The next day, Murray wrote to Calgary's sheriff that he believed Buck and Earl "sufficiently kept away" to avoid being served.[63] Murray returned to the well on December 14 and again heard that Buck was not there. This time, however, two of Buck's employees—H.C. Beattie and one identified only as Lawson—barred Murray from entering the derrick. Lawson went a step further, claiming to be a provincial constable and threatening to arrest the bailiff if he tried to serve the papers. "I will make another attempt today," wrote Murray to Graham, "but look for no success under these circumstances."[64] Indeed, the only blemish on Buck's string of favourable rulings came in the

Wolverton suit, when Justice Walsh ruled in favour of Wolverton, ordered Buck to return the contested stock certificates to the plaintiff, and awarded Wolverton an additional $250 in damages.[65]

Part of the reason for Buck's confidence was that he had found one of the most gifted young lawyers in Alberta as his representative. After burning through several law firms in 1914, Buck finally settled on Alexander McGillivray as his preferred counsel. Born in 1884 at London, Ontario, Alexander McGillivray cut an imposing figure in Alberta's legal and political communities. A graduate of St. Francis College in Richmond, Quebec, and Dalhousie University's law school, McGillivray came out west in 1907 and practised law in Stettler, Alberta, until 1910, when he moved to Calgary to form the firm Tweedie and McGillivray. Named King's Counsel in 1919, McGillivray became the Crown prosecutor for several famous trials in the 1920s. McGillivray, noted historian James Gray, personified the public's perception of the eminence of a King's Counsel, working in "striped trousers, morning coats, grey vests, and winged collars, the very personification of unbending formality." A staunch Conservative, McGillivray campaigned in the 1911 federal election for the Red Deer seat but lost. Appointed leader of the provincial Conservative Party in 1925, McGillivray won election as an MLA for Calgary a year later, where he served as party leader before stepping down in 1929. Two years later, at age forty-seven, McGillivray became one of the youngest provincial Supreme Court appellate justices in Canada after joining the Appellate Division of the Alberta Supreme Court. As legal historians Knafla and Klumpenhouwer conclude, McGillivray "was acknowledged as a distinguished litigator with a vast knowledge of legal lore." In 1938, the Province of Alberta named him commissioner for the Royal Commission of Inquiry into the Alberta Oil Industry that produced the "McGillivray Report" in 1940, just months before his sudden death of a heart attack at age fifty-six in December 1940.[66]

While Buck seemed little bothered by the prospect of endless lawsuits, Alexander McGillivray worried a great deal now that the Carpenter Commission appeared to have his client firmly in its sights. At the Black Diamond's statutory shareholders meeting on April 9, 1915, the company disclosed $32,573.75 from the sale of 500,000 shares plus an additional $3,050 loan from the Coalinga Oil Syndicate, giving receipts totalling $35,623.75. From that amount, only $15,196.93—less than forty-three cents of every dollar—went into drilling the well. After paying salaries and expenses, the company reported only $143.38 in cash on hand.[67] Fearing that a public investigation of Buck and Black Diamond would reveal details that could harm his client's interests in several pending civil actions, McGillivray made a virtue out of necessity by claiming the civil lawsuits precluded investigation by the Carpenter Commission because information that the public hearings might reveal were prejudicial to his client's interests. On that basis, McGillivray asked and received an injunction to prevent Carpenter from compelling the attendance of witnesses and gathering evidence. It was a masterful, and well-executed piece of legal jiu-jitsu that transformed Buck's greatest liability into a strength.[68]

According to the *News Telegram*, McGillivray's request for an emergency injunction on September 22 caught the Carpenter Commission by surprise. Understanding that the court's ruling would directly affect the subsequent operation of the commission, Justice Stewart granted a temporary injunction to McGillivray and turned matters over to the Appellate Division of the Alberta Supreme Court. A banner headline in the *Herald* on September 24, 1915, warned, "Alberta oil probe may be declared illegal."[69]

Before the Appellate Division in Edmonton, McGillivray contended that the orders-in-council underpinning Carpenter's investigation of Black Diamond did not fall under the terms of the Public Inquiries Act that served as the basis for the Carpenter Commission. The legislation delineated provisions for the appointment of provincial officials, such as inspectors, sheriffs, and registration clerks in the public realm. A private company was clearly a different entity than the ones specified within the terms of the ordinance. Furthermore, McGillivray argued that the ability to compel the company to produce evidence against itself would be prejudicial considering outstanding lawsuits pending against Black Diamond and would harm shareholder interests. Judge Carpenter did not have the authority under the orders in council to make an investigation and lacked the authority to either summon witnesses or to compel them to produce documents. McGillivray's appeal sought injunctions restraining Carpenter and the commission from investigating the company or summoning company officers as witnesses to either testify or produce documents.

Frank Ford responded for the commission and argued that the Act intended to provide the government with the power to make enquiries "into and concerning any matter within the jurisdiction of the legislative assembly and connected with the good government of the province or the conduct of the public business." Ford's test, essentially, was that the Act granted authority sufficient to cover inquiries "into any matter which may be the subject of legislation by the legislature." The Carpenter Commission's mandate related to the good government of the province; the court could not restrict the definition of the term "good government." This prompted a discussion between the lawyers and the justices about the meaning of the word "government;" whether it referred to the administration or operation of the law or the governing of the province.[70]

On October 5, the ruling of the Appellate Division found in favour of Buck and Black Diamond and delivered a scathing rebuke to the government in the process. "A number of objections were taken to the validity of the commission," noted Chief Justice Horace Harvey, "but I do not find it necessary to consider more than one, which appears to me to be fatal." The Appellate Division declared that the Public Inquiries Act provided for a general inquiry, but the commission issued by the executive—the Lieutenant-Governor-in-Council—administering the laws would generate information for the legislative branch. The information collected, admonished the court, "is not for the use of the legislature, but for the use of the executive." The problem lay in the fact that the terms of the Act were too broad. This, argued the court, "and other considerations require them to be restricted." Chief Justice Harvey argued that a reading of the order-in-council "furnishes not the slightest suggestion that the information to be gained from the inquiry is to be used for any legislative or any other public purpose." Furthermore, the order-in council also revealed that "the inquiry is limited almost entirely to the private affairs of the companies and stock exchanges, and the commissioner is given the power to compel the production of evidence even by fine and imprisonment." This raised particular problems for the Appellate Division because the justices believed "statutes should be interpreted, if possible, so as to respect private rights." Presumably, the Act did not intend to "confiscate the property or to encroach upon the rights of persons." More to the point, section 125 of the Companies Ordinance made allowances for an investigation into the private affairs of a provincial company but only "upon the application of some shareholders—that is to say, upon the application of some of those whose private affairs are to be investigated."[71]

Justice Charles Stuart's opinion proclaimed that if the legislature intended to grant the commission those powers "it was necessary for the legislature to say so specifically." Like Chief Justice Harvey, Stuart held that the affairs of Black Diamond Oil Fields were a private matter between the shareholders and the company's officers and did not constitute a matter affecting the "public business of this province." If the attorney general's office needed a silver lining, they could find it in Justice Nicholas D. Beck's separate opinion. While Justice Beck concurred with the majority regarding the commission's misinterpretation of the Public Inquiries Act—"the defendant company was notified that on a certain date an investigation would be made 'into affairs' ... the statute does not authorize such an inquiry"—he nonetheless believed the commission could fulfill its mandate without extending the term "good government" to include an investigation of a single company.[72] Nevertheless, the court's decision effectively shut down the Carpenter Commission and sent Sifton's government back to cobble together a new piece of legislation to continue the inquiry.[73]

The *Herald* urged the government to learn its lesson and frame the new order-in-council to withstand all legal attacks and "give the widest possible scope to the investigator." The editorial noted that "it was the will of the people that the oil business of Alberta should be investigated. That is still the people's will and at the worst this knockout blow should mean no more than a setback of a temporary nature." Later, the editorial page dismissed arguments of "there being too much law in this province" and insisted the real problem was political: "too few people in the legislature seem to understand and be able to interpret the law."[74] Bob Edwards responded to the court's ruling with scarcely concealed outrage and expressed growing public displeasure. As Edwards revealed, public anger turned away from the oil companies and began to point an accusing finger at the government and its institutions for failing to protect the public interest. "Those wonderful judges of ours granted the injunction asked for by the Black Diamond Oil company ... restraining Judge Carpenter from investigating the affairs of that (!!!!!???!!!) company," began Edwards in a tour de force piece that is worthwhile quoting at length because it reveals exactly how far public attitudes had shifted against the oil industry since the heady days of the 1914 boom.

> To the ordinary mind it would seem to be eminently logical that the Attorney General's Department cause investigation to be made into alleged wholesale frauds upon the public. We thought that this was one of the things that the Attorney General was paid to watch out for—frauds upon the public. But it appears that we are wrong. Our Supreme Court judges have decided that alleged frauds—no matter on how large a scale—cannot be investigated.
>
> This is an appalling state of affairs.
>
> These judges claim that the statute does not authorize such an investigation. Yet there is a lot of bunk in the statute about "**any matter connected with the good government of the province or the conduct of the public business thereof.**"

The fact of the matter is that this province is cursed with too much lawyer.

Another thing. This province is cursed with too many small fry in high places. What we lack is big men to take hold of big problems and handle them in a really big fashion, regardless of the precedents and immature statutes. Here we have the public of Alberta, as a matter of common knowledge, victims of a system of colossal frauds in oil stock, and yet the crooks connected therewith are deliberately protected by Supreme Court judges!

Next thing we know, some murderer will be getting acquitted because of a Statute dug up from somewhere is shown to prove that murders are permissible. Hereabouts, subject to certain limitations, and that, anyway, when Moses broke the tablets of stone he automatically nullified the terms of the Ten Commandments.

Too much lawyer. *Trop d'avocat* and too much d_____d ingenuity on McGillivray's part.

There was not one of those judges sitting in the appellate court that was big enough to lean forward from the bunch and say, "See here, the public has been swindled right and left by these oil sharks and has a perfect right to the investigation it demands. Let us therefore ignore this Statute, which was obviously framed by some cheap guy of our own profession, and allow this oil probe to be carried out to a finish."

No. Lawyer-like, these judges clung to the letter of the stupid little Statute and declined to consider its spirit.

And the public who got stung? Oh, to hell with the public. Lawyers and judges must live.[75]

Edwards's column served as the funeral oration for the Carpenter Commission. The ruling left the status of further inquiries in jeopardy. "No government official can be found who will make a definite statement for publication," wrote the *Herald*, before noting that the prevailing belief was that the ruling "put an end to all inquiries being made by the Royal Commission appointed to investigate the operation of oil companies in the province." The paper took note that the court declared that an inquiry was possible provided the government received the consent of certain stockholders possessing a significant amount of stock. That meant consent for inquiries had to lie with "those actually running the company, the big holders."[76] As Judge Carpenter surmised, the injunction prevented him from producing a formal report on his commission. Later, after the commission ceased its operations, Carpenter wrote Deputy Attorney General Fenwick that it was only in connection with the Western Canada Oil Company that "there appear[s] to be anything radically wrong."[77] Less than a month later, Judge Carpenter received a new appointment on October 20, 1915, as a board member of the newly created Alberta Utilities Commission along with George H.V. Bulyea, and Chairman James E. Reilly.[78]

In the meantime, several companies investigated by Carpenter found themselves embroiled in lawsuits in the aftermath of the injunction; the commission, noted one paper, created "unusually knotty complications in litigation."[79] The Western Canada Oil Company never really recovered, despite a new board of directors, and the company dissolved in July 1916.[80] The court ruling placed individual rights at the centre of the public policy debate, and now the attorney general's office had an opportunity to respond.

10

"I am Not Going Back to Canada:" The Law Comes for Buck

> *Every day or two rumors are wildly circulated about strikes of oil in the different wells. These rumors are sometimes followed by fluctuation in the prices of stock which would profit if the rumors were true. The result is that people are made victims of designing people. If the police could get a case against one of these sharpers and make an example of him, they would do a public service.*
>
> —Editorial
> *The Calgary Morning Albertan*
> June 20, 1914

> *The Black Diamond Oilfields, Limited takes exception to [the Carpenter Commission], arguing that if the investigation is legal, the commission appointed has no authority to summon witnesses or compel them to give evidence. Straws usually show how the wind blows. To the man on the street, it looks as if there is something wrong in the state of Denmark.*
>
> —*The Western Standard*
> October 24, 1915

Challenging the authority of the Carpenter Commission did not stop the provincial attorney general's investigation into George Buck's oil company. The commission had already generated enough evidence to justify bringing a criminal case against him. By late 1915, Buck's litigious and confrontational nature was well established. Lawsuits filed against him by sales agents and drillers provided ample evidence that Buck's lack of attention to detail as a corporate officer had created many problems for his company. When combined with the persistent rumours and creditable accusations of stock price manipulation, including salting Black Diamond #1, Buck's brazenness made him the poster child for the excesses of 1914. Likely tipped off about an imminent arrest warrant, Buck disappeared for a few weeks but then returned equally abruptly, claiming he wanted to defend himself. However, before the trial began in January 1916, Buck fled Calgary despite $20,000 worth of bail bonds (approximately $530,490 adjusted for inflation) provided by friends, family, and business acquaintances. The province faced a choice, in that it could simply let Buck go or attempt to locate and return him to face trial. Some in Calgary's oil and gas community assumed that provincial officials got what they wanted most—Buck's immediate departure from the city. They reasoned, given the philosophy and ideology of limited government prevailing in the province, that there would be no attempt to pursue Buck. But both the provincial government and the City of Calgary still smarted from the spectacle of an unrealized oil boom. Civic leaders bemoaned the bumps and bruises to the city's reputation because of the actions of unscrupulous promoters. Others criticized the inability or unwillingness of provincial officials to either prevent abuses in the first place or to stop them after it became clear what was taking place. Several companies—not just Black Diamond—made announcements of oil finds in June 1914 that were, at best, unsubstantiated. At worst, they were outright lies.

In earlier mining booms, federal and provincial officials proved reluctant to resort to extradition of promoters facing fraud charges from angry investors for several reasons. First and foremost, the chances that prosecution would succeed were doubtful. This dilemma became more acute when provincial governments considered the expense associated with extradition plus the possibility that a criminal lawsuit might be triggered by every stockholder who lost money in an investment.[1] However, in 1915, both elected officials and the civil service made repeated references to public expectations that the Province of Alberta would pursue George Buck and bring him back for trial. Indeed, it is significant that the same provincial government that, a year before, claimed it did not want to regulate the industry now spent tens of thousands of dollars and hundreds of thousands of work hours bringing a single offender to justice. Despite the rhetoric of limited government and laissez-faire, Deputy Attorney General A.G. Browning presided over a three-month manhunt that mobilized people and resources from Canada to Mexico. Although provincial officials eventually secured Buck's extradition from Wichita, Kansas, after a lengthy legal battle, the process proved a bruising, humiliating, and humbling ordeal for the province and gave added urgency to reform efforts.

In the early autumn of 1915, McGillivray's legal challenge to the Carpenter Commission effectively stopped all work as the matter pended before the court. The investigation would not rest for long. On October 11, 1915, Frank Ford reached out to James Short, KC, a Crown prosecutor in Calgary, and his assistant on the Carpenter Commission, Gregory Trainor, to assemble a criminal case against George Buck and Black Diamond. Born in Pilkington, Ontario, in 1862, Short graduated from the University of Toronto with a Bachelor of Arts degree. Hired as a teacher in the town's only school, he moved to Calgary in November 1889. Arriving in town at four a.m. on a frosty morning, he vividly remembered the sight of the Rocky Mountains from his hotel room window and that just across the street on the top of a one-storey building stood a mountain goat "ready to do battle to all comers." Short discovered the town of 1,200 residents had no sidewalks, and the boys all wore cowboy hats and rode horses to school. He was recruited to serve as the principal of Central School in 1891, and historian Harry Sanders concludes that Short "essentially created Calgary's public high school program" and served as its sole teacher until 1892, when he left teaching as the result of a dispute with the school board over teacher compensation.[2]

Short moved from education to the law in 1892, articling with a law firm for a few years before entering practice in 1897. The next year, Short joined future provincial chief justice and premier Arthur M. Sifton and Charles Stewart to found the firm of Sifton, Short, and Stewart. As his original law partners retired from the firm to become members of the bench, Short formed a new partnership with George H. Ross and F.S. Selwood that produced another high-powered law firm with ambitious partners, Short, Ross and Selwood, in 1907. Four years later, Joseph T. Shaw, whom Short had taught years earlier, joined the firm. In 1901, Short became a Crown prosecutor and held the post until 1926. Despite future controversy over Short's actions and views, few at the time questioned Short's reputation as one of Calgary's foremost lawyers and prosecutors, especially with his having handled several high-profile cases.[3] Indeed, in a trial that drew international attention, Short served as prosecutor for Arthur Pelkey's manslaughter charge after his opponent, Luther McCarty, died in the ring in 1913.[4] If anyone could handle the pressure of a prosecuting a high-profile case, Short certainly could.

In the meantime, Ford asked Trainor to assist Short any way he could. Eager to start, Trainor tracked down Short on the steps of the courthouse. The two men were discussing Ford's instructions when Alexander McGillivray left the courthouse and passed by. Unprompted, McGillivray said he hoped they were not talking about the Black Diamond company and its proprietor, George Buck. The remark seemed odd to Trainor, who immediately became suspicious and wired Ford in the attorney general's office in Edmonton to seek an immediate warrant for Buck's arrest. "Accused's Solicitor appears suspicious," warned Trainor. "There is a possibility of the accused skipping out." Ford quickly agreed. "If any danger tell Mr. Short to go ahead without waiting." Again, Short demurred and insisted the case belonged to Shaw who, in turn, dismissed Trainor's concerns. Shaw believed there was no danger Buck would escape as he had already notified the Calgary police to keep track of Buck's movements. Trainor warned Shaw that Calgarians would blame him if Buck got away, so Shaw called Chief Cuddy again in Trainor's presence, asking him to tail Buck. Three days later, as Trainor went about his business, a reporter for *The Calgary News Telegram* appeared, seeking a comment regarding Buck's impending arrest. Shocked that word had leaked so quickly, Trainor appealed to the editor of the *News Telegram* to withhold publication of the story until Buck was in custody.[5]

On October 15, 1915, Assistant Crown Prosecutor Joseph Shaw laid three charges against Buck and H.C. Beattie under section 414 of the Criminal Code: defrauding the public; conspiracy to defraud the public; and "making, circulating or publishing a statement known to be false . . . with intent to induce persons to become shareholders" in Black Diamond Oil Fields in local newspapers as well as in Buck's own press organ, *The Black Diamond Press* while serving as a director and manager of Black Diamond Oil Fields. If convicted on the conspiracy charge, Buck faced up to seven years in prison. But when the Royal North-West Mounted Police went to serve the warrant on Buck out at the well, they were unable to locate him despite the surveillance requested by the attorney general's office. Trainor contacted a trusted detective on the Calgary Police Force, Tom Turner. The detective claimed October 11 as the date of the last reliable report of Buck's whereabouts, the day Shaw asked the police to track his movements. Trainor suspected, but could never prove, that someone tipped Buck off. The *Herald* reported that the arrest warrant and charges sought by the attorney general were politically motivated—payback, they speculated, for the embarrassment caused by McGillivray's successful challenge to the Carpenter Commission. The police prepared wanted circulars and notified the RNWMP. Meanwhile, Trainor received a tip that Buck was in Graybold, Montana, had shaved his mustache, and travelled under the name "Hugh Johnston," but some reports still placed Buck in southern Alberta. A week after his disappearance, Trainor confided to Acting Deputy Attorney General G.P. Owen Fenwick that "the public appear to be almost satisfied to be rid of him." Trainor overlooked the comment on the *Herald's* editorial page suggesting Buck's "little game" ensured police "are not going to 'pass the buck.'" Bob Edwards, however, took a different tack, arguing that Buck clearly had an informant working on the inside of the investigation. "This always happens when too many crooks are fussing around the pot where the broth is being prepared. Buck's vanishing act only goes to show how very rarely one catches a weasel asleep." Furthermore, Edwards wondered why Trainor and the attorney general's office focused on Buck. "There are other oil crooks in this town just as bad as Buck ever was," wrote Edwards. "One company in particular, so far as misrepresentation and fraud goes had Black Diamond skinned 47 different ways."[6]

After evading law enforcement for three weeks, Buck suddenly reappeared and arranged with his lawyers to turn himself in to the police. Upon his return, *The Calgary Daily Herald* fawned over Buck, reporting that the oil man appeared at the police station "clad in a black broadcloth overcoat, wore a dark soft hat and was smoking a cigar that gave evidence of class." The report took special delight in highlighting that Buck "had no difficulty whatever in keeping out of the toils of the authorities until he chose to give himself up." This latter observation prompted some of Buck's acquaintances to speculate that the "real hope of the prosecution was that Mr. Buck would hop over the line and stay there [in the United States]." Returning to Calgary by train from Spokane on October 31, Buck's unmistakable form sauntered up Centre Street to 8th Avenue, casually visiting several hotels and calling on friends, among them the prosecution's chief witness Norman Fletcher. Nevertheless, as Buck continued conspicuously making the rounds, he remained unmolested by law enforcement. "There was no recognition from the police," noted the *Herald*. "Not a wink." The next morning, Buck presented himself to Chief Cuddy in advance of an appearance before police magistrate Davidson. Buck posted $10,000 for bail—$5,000 personally, the other $5,000 from his wife.[7]

With the date of the preliminary hearing set, Buck turned his attention toward his defence. Trainor and the attorney general's office began receiving reports that Buck had approached prosecution witnesses, starting with Norman Fletcher, to buy them off or otherwise compel their silence. Buck also settled various pending civil actions against Black Diamond Oil Fields to lift the freeze on the company's remaining assets, estimated to be between

$6,000 and $12,000. Whether this was to pay for his defence, or for use as bribes for witnesses, it is clear that Buck desperately tried get his hands on as much cash as he could. Trainor suspected Buck would attempt to escape once again, and enlisted Reuben James Bolt to file a civil action against Black Diamond to keep the company's assets frozen on behalf of shareholders. One of the statements of claim read, "I am informed and verily believe that the defendant company's manager, G.E. Buck, deals with the money as if it were his private property and should settlements of the actions now pending be effected there will be nothing to prevent him from drawing the balance of the money and paying it to who[m] he pleases."[8]

The preliminary hearing quickly established a damning case against Buck as it became public for the first time that Black Diamond had "salted" its well to sell more stock, confirming what was already long suspected about Buck and Black Diamond. Guided by Trainor, Crown witness Norman Fletcher calmly testified that in March 1914 the company was hard pressed financially and described the evolution of Buck's scheme to raise stock prices to pay the drillers. "The International Supply Company had threatened to stop the work and take possession when 1,500-foot depth was reached," testified Fletcher. "It was said that oil could be placed in the well and that the shares would sell." The *News Telegram* noted that Buck "sat almost unmoved, serious of attitude and listening intently" as Fletcher testified. Under rigorous cross-examination by Buck's lawyer, Fletcher told the court that several employees of Black Diamond had prepared sworn statements "in case Buck should take any proceedings" against them. Fearing that Buck was "too shrewd," Fletcher avoided going to court with only his word against Buck's. Four other employees joined Fletcher, signing declarations of facts to protect themselves from "a bad, dangerous man" who had promised to "get" Fletcher, casting Buck's visit with Fletcher upon returning to Calgary in a more sinister light.[9]

Fletcher's dramatic and compelling testimony took the bulk of the first three days of the hearing and generated national headlines when he revealed the details about the salting of the well.[10] During a cross-examination on November 10, 1915, Fletcher testified that, in the spring of 1914, Buck instructed him to "untangle" some things. The tasks included going incognito to the King George Hotel to determine whether the driller was revealing secrets about the Black Diamond well and making certain inquiries to Devenish and Beveridge. When Fletcher made a sarcastic reference to "the lawyer," Buck's counsel, Tweedie, took exception and angrily accused him of being "a spy" who did "sneaking tricks." The clash might have spiralled further if not for the judge's intervention to restore a sense of decorum between the two parties.[11]

On the second day of the hearing, two other witnesses, Roy Minue and Major Gillespie, buttressed Fletcher's testimony. Tweedie challenged Gillespie, asking why he did not tell company director and city alderman E.H. Crandell about the salting when he came to measure the well. "It is one thing to say a thing and another to prove it," replied Gillespie. "I'm not afraid to tell the public now. I've been wanting to get this thing off my chest for a long time."[12] When court recessed for lunch on the second day, it became clear to Trainor that Buck's bail was too low given the strength of evidence presented against Buck and the growing list of charges the oil man might face, especially after Fletcher revealed that Buck ordered Ray Minue to fire several shots from a rifle over the heads of potential investors scheduled to visit the well. According to Fletcher's testimony, Buck wanted to scare the investors and "to give them a good impression of the progress of the well." Trainor believed few ties held Buck to the city and the incentive to flee again would be overwhelming. Thus, Trainor broached the subject of a bail increase with Shaw, who dismissed it out of hand by insisting the bond was sufficient. But later in the afternoon, Shaw relented and asked for a further bond of $1,000 from a third party. After a slight delay, Buck found a third party to pay the bond.

Two days later, as the case against Buck grew still stronger, Trainor again recommended that Shaw seek an increase in the bond to discourage Buck from skipping town. This time, Shaw responded angrily, saying he "had a great deal more experience in matters of this kind than I had had and that it appeared to him that he should know at what the bonds should be placed." Trainor disagreed and countered that, not only was the bail too low, but Shaw had accepted as surety property from Mrs. Buck already pledged as collateral in another case. Owen Fenwick, the acting deputy attorney general, agreed with Trainor and wired instructions down for Shaw insisting, "You must insist on proper bail at once. Suggest Ten Thousand Dollars." Trainor, in turn, notified Police Magistrate Davidson that a request to increase the bail would be forthcoming. Judge Davidson agreed, telling Trainor "he had absolutely no faith in Buck [sticking around to face trial], and especially as the evidence was so damaging against him." At a two p.m. meeting in the judge's chambers, Davidson insisted that he would not set bail below $10,000 (approximately $300,000 adjusted for inflation). According to Trainor, Shaw then became "nasty," stating "that as far as he was concerned, he would not 'persecute' Buck for the Attorney General or for anyone else." Told to contact his office for the attorney general's instructions, Shaw listened as Short read the telegram. Back in front of Buck and his attorney, Shaw stated that "he was speaking as the mouth-piece of the Department and that he had received a telegram from the Department stating that the bail be placed at $20,000 and that he was very sorry to have to inform Buck and his Solicitor that he could not be admitted to bail in any other way." With that, the bailiff placed Buck in jail until the next day, when he again seemed to have little difficulty posting a $10,000 bond for himself while the other $10,000 came from other sources. While Shaw informed the attorney general's office that Buck had posted bonds, he did not convey that information to Trainor.[13]

While unfortunate, the bickering between Trainor and Shaw clearly did not affect the results of the preliminary hearing. On November 16, Justice Davidson committed Buck for trial on three charges—two of conspiracy to defraud and one of publishing false statements with intent to induce persons to become shareholders in Black Diamond Oil Fields. At the very least, though, the infighting over bail bonds revealed a deeper problem regarding strategy in the attorney general's office that led to costly mistakes. Shaw's petulant statement that he was a mere "mouthpiece" for the department surely sent signals to Buck that a division existed between the prosecuting attorneys. Furthermore, although Trainor's memo never explicitly accused Shaw of tipping Buck off in October about his impending arrest, it is reasonable to infer that Trainor said as much to Fenwick in a letter that accompanied his report. "There are a great many things which I have read between the lines in this case, in connection with Mr. Shaw and in regard to the bonds and his connections with Crandell, etc. that I have not expressed an opinion on. These matters are of course, as well known to you as they are to me as we have talked them over together." Other matters mentioned by Trainor included questions regarding Shaw's decision about the testimony of witnesses, particularly Alderman E. H. Crandell, whom Trainor believed Shaw protected, with the decision resulting in a slightly weaker case.[14]

With Buck's trial scheduled to begin on January 11, 1916, in front of Chief Justice Horace Harvey, both parties gathered evidence and interviewed witnesses. In early December, Gregory Trainor applied to Justice Stuart to travel to Ohio to collect evidence from former Black Diamond driller James M. Hayes and rig hand Lafe Terrill against Buck. Earlier, driller Hayes told the Crown he would not return to Calgary for the trial. Trainor insisted to the judge that there were exigent circumstances: the two witnesses were likely to be "induced to disappear" if the court waited much longer. Stuart gave Trainor until January 10, 1916, to return with the statements. In the meantime, at the annual meeting of Black Diamond shareholders on December

6, 1915, Buck received a confidence vote and unanimous re-election to the board of directors. In a brief statement, Buck announced that the company would not resume drilling "until such time as the crooks who are after us" quit. To a shareholder who requested more reports, Buck claimed he had provided several official reports to the newspapers but the press misconstrued his statements so he would make no more. Furthermore, printing and mailing reports every two weeks was too expensive, costing about $150 per report.[15]

After dispensing with the shareholders meeting, Buck turned attention back to his pending court cases and crumbling empire as a series of costly decisions mounted against him. A few weeks earlier, as Buck's preliminary hearing revealed that he salted Black Diamond #1, International Supply Company secured settlements of $9,000 and $23,000 against Black Diamond Oil Fields for breach of contract and moneys due under contract.[16] Buck asked the court to withhold $1,300 from International Supply on the grounds that it was not earned, and the court agreed pending a resolution. Other looming lawsuits, including one for $256 in past due office rent filed by landlord David McDougall, proved more problematic when McDougall sought, and received, a court order freezing all of Buck's company and personal bank accounts.

According to Buck's later statements, around this time he secretly decided to flee Canada. Claiming business to attend to in Ohio, namely gathering of evidence from the two former Black Diamond employees, Buck left the city promising to return in time to defend himself in the criminal case. Apart from his accountant, Hugh Miller, who accompanied him, and his cousin, Jennie Earl, whom he left in charge of his business interests, few knew his plans. When Buck did not appear for the start of his trial on January 11, 1916, Chief Justice Harvey issued a bench warrant for his arrest. Within a matter of days, the court moved to file caveats on the property of Ada Buck and J. Herchmer Poyniz, a salesman for Black Diamond who was also listed as the head of Black Diamond's Vancouver office, both of whom had guaranteed Buck's bonds.[17]

Meanwhile, as the most public-facing member of the attorney general's office in Calgary and connected with both the Carpenter Commission and the criminal case against Buck, Gregory Trainor felt the sting of public dissatisfaction. On January 20, he wrote to the deputy attorney general that the prevailing consensus was that Calgarians were "not very anxious whether Buck appeared or not" but wanted Buck held to account for something. Indeed, within weeks of his departure, the editor of *The Alberta Oil Review and Industrial Record*, E.M. Robertson, suggested that since "the absconding president of the two Black Diamond Oil companies . . . is still in parts unknown," the province should use the forfeited sum to do something useful like improve the road between Okotoks and the oil field. "Unless," added Robertson, "the government intends to spend the money in bringing him to justice and prosecuting him." Considering the public temperature, Trainor advised the newly appointed deputy attorney general, A.G. Browning, KC, that "the Department should use every endeavor to locate Buck" and asked to be assigned to lead the effort.[18]

Born in Yale, British Columbia, in 1851, Arthur George Browning received his education at the Orillia high school and the University of Toronto, graduating with academic distinction by winning prestigious Governor General's Silver Medal for philosophy and the astronomy prize. After graduating from Osgoode Hall, in 1888, Browning became North Bay, Ontario's, first Crown attorney and, after 1893, Crown prosecutor. In addition to his busy law practice, Browning devoted considerable time to community-building efforts, serving as chair of the newly formed high school board of trustees and editor of the local paper, *The North Bay Nugget*. A brief visit to Alberta in 1914 sufficiently impressed Browning that he moved to Edmonton to join the law firm of Browning and MacDonald. In short order, Browning earned an appointment as a police magistrate before securing the post of Alberta's deputy attorney general in 1915. Browning remained for eight years until he resigned and returned to Ontario in 1923.[19]

Despite Trainor's plea, Browning turned to Alberta's chief of detectives, John D. Nicholson, to spearhead provincial efforts. Alberta's chief of detectives since 1911, Nicholson was already a living legend in provincial law enforcement circles. The son of parents born in Nova Scotia, Nicholson left home as a teenager, serving as a cook on a ship. Only later did Nicholson learn it was a rum-runner operating out of the island of St. Pierre along the Atlantic seaboard. For the next few years, Nicholson sailed across the globe until the age of twenty-two, when he abruptly changed careers and joined the North-West Mounted Police. Stationed in Edmonton after training, Nicholson fought in the North-West Rebellion against the Metis and their Indigenous allies before injuries sustained in the line of duty made it painful for him to ride a horse. Then, stricken by a bout of appendicitis in February 1896, Nicholson required a lengthy convalescence. By the time he recovered in February 1900 and could resume his duties, he discovered the NWMP had struck him off the rolls two years earlier. At age thirty-five, he then volunteered to serve with the 1st Battalion, Canadian Mounted Rifles in the Boer War. Wounded during the fighting, and catching enteric fever during another lengthy convalescence, he re-enlisted, but the fighting ended two days before he returned to

South Africa. After the war, he rejoined the NWMP, working in the Hudson Bay area before returning to Alberta in 1907 and becoming the Province of Alberta's chief detective in 1911. In that capacity, Nicholson would log over 13,000 miles across North American in pursuit of Buck.[20]

As rumours multiplied regarding Buck's whereabouts, the attorney general's office launched several different efforts to track him down. In Montreal, the province retained the Thiel Detective Service to follow up leads. Closer to home, the attorney general's office placed Buck's family and known associates under surveillance in case Buck tried to contact them. By early February, friends and associates who posted bonds for Buck's bail received notification that the province would move to seize the assets used as collateral. E.H. Crandell asked Crown prosecutor Joseph Shaw to intercede on his behalf with the attorney general's office as he suddenly found himself short on cash and pleaded for special consideration.[21]

Days before Crandell's letter arrived, Browning received a report from Gregory Trainor outlining the cozy relationship between Buck and the former city council member. Trainor reminded Browning that back in 1914, Crandell had served as a director on Black Diamond's board, and rumours held that Crandell profited handsomely from his association with Buck, making close to $25,000 ($750,000 adjusted for inflation) on the sale of Black Diamond stock alone. The report also intimated that a close friendship between Shaw and Crandell might explain the prosecutor's actions at Buck's preliminary hearing. Trainor placed Crandell on the witness list because Crandell visited the well on May 7, 1914, along with Alderman Freeze and reporter Tryon. But when the clerk called for Crandell to testify, Shaw "told the magistrate that he had talked with the witness Crandell and that as his evidence was not material" he had sent Crandell home.[22]

Whatever the reason, Browning answered Crandell's letter in an unforgiving mood. "When the bond was entered into, he must have understood its effect and the position in which it might place him," replied Browning. "You are, therefore, instructed to proceed at once for the enforcement of the bond and I will be glad to be advised of the result at your earliest convenience."[23] James Short duly went before the court to remove the stay of execution for the seizure of collateral placed up by Crandell, but the chief justice blocked the move as premature. Nevertheless, Crandell was sufficiently worried that he wrote Attorney General C.W. Cross directly to plead for special consideration, adding that if Browning were looking for political cover "there are precedents along this line."[24]

In the meantime, Nicholson tracked Buck's favourite auto—the red, eighty-horsepower McFarlan Six. Like so much else about Buck, the luxury automobile was both big and conspicuous, attracting attention wherever it went. Buck drove the vehicle to Montana and arranged for delivery to the factory at Connorsville, Indiana, to overhaul the engine. To Nicholson, Buck later claimed he crossed the border at Detroit, where his brother lived and worked as a mortuary attendant, to pick up his car.[25] While chasing down another lead in Toledo, Ohio, Nicholson learned that Buck had loaded up with fuel and headed due south, for Mexico. Buck did, indeed, arrive in Mexico, but the ongoing civil war made conditions too dangerous, prompting him to leave for New Orleans, where Nicholson picked up Buck's trail again. Nicholson thought Buck would make his stand against extradition in Louisiana, where state laws differed by making the governor's duty to extradite a fugitive discretionary rather than mandatory. Article 160 of the Louisiana Code of Criminal Procedure stipulated the governor could deny extradition in cases where the wanted person completed a "complete self-rehabilitation" and established themselves as a worthwhile member of the community.[26] Indeed, while in Louisiana, Buck consulted a lawyer about his case who told the fugitive the charges against him were not extraditable. Armed with this information, Buck briefly considered staying in Louisiana and establishing another business. However, Buck picked up stakes once again, disappearing into Texas. With the trail getting cold, Nicholson returned to Edmonton.[27]

Shortly thereafter, in early April 1916 the province offered a reward of $1,000 for Buck's arrest—$25,000 adjusted for inflation. As part of the dragnet, Nicholson prepared a circular offering a reward "for information leading to the arrest" of Buck. Browning suggested that Nicholson remove "information" from the reward description and Nicholson drew a line through it with a pencil. The printer overlooked the edit and initially the circular offered a reward for "information," although subsequent printings corrected the mistake. Regardless, the attorney general's office sent out circulars to the RNWMP as well as to police departments and the major detective agencies in every American city.[28]

In the meantime, after leaving New Orleans, Buck travelled to New Mexico and doubled back to El Paso, Texas, and Oklahoma before finally settling in Wichita, Kansas, at the start of February under the assumed name Joe Barnes. According to Buck, he settled in Wichita "as this city has the name of being a refuge for criminals." Indeed, after spending a month in Wichita, Nicholson believed it the best place for Buck to stage his defence. Crime seemed abundant; hardly a day passed without the newspapers reporting

Figure 10-1 "George E. Buck Wanted Circular"

Securing the $1,000 reward for information leading to Buck's arrest would become a central preoccupation of the McWain and Miller Detective Agency in Wichita, Kansas. (Provincial Archives of Alberta, GR1972.0026)

killings, lynchings, or some other violent incident. To be sure, some crime stemmed from the state's decision to go "bone dry" with the prohibition of alcohol in 1880, which created opportunities for bootleggers and organized crime to flourish, particularly with "wet" Missouri so close by. More than one public official or member of local law enforcement developed malleable ethics and profited from kickbacks or bribes from illicit activities. With the rich and powerful observing laws and norms with a winking smirk, perceptions that lawbreakers could buy their way out of trouble proliferated. To Nicholson's disbelief, the people of Wichita treated Buck as just another businessperson and closed ranks around him as one of their own. Buck advanced that narrative by highlighting his family's roots in Pennsylvania and allowing some press reports to claim that he was really an American.[29]

Wichita also suited Buck because the discovery of the Augusta and El Dorado oil pools in 1914 and 1915, respectively, had touched off an oil boom in Kansas. Between 1914 and 1918, Kansas's oil production grew from three million barrels per year to eight million barrels in 1916 before reaching forty-five million barrels in 1918.[30] Upon arrival in Wichita, Buck concocted a backstory in which he was "Joe Barnes," an oil developer from Texas starting a new company, the Miller Oil Syndicate. The syndicate was named after Hugh Miller, the accountant who had fled Calgary with Buck. Locals could not help but notice "Barnes" driving about town in a conspicuously big, red McFarlan Six with wire wheels. For weeks, he surveyed the land between Central Avenue and the Butler County line, chatting with folks and making connections. Finally, at a series of meetings with landowners and financial backers in Oklahoma and Wichita, Buck purchased leases on approximately 2,000 acres around Augusta, eighteen miles east of Wichita and announced the company would commence drilling soon.[31]

What happened next is not entirely clear, as the accounts of Buck's arrest vary. One telegram in the Alberta Provincial Archives indicates that the attorney general's office received reliable information that Buck settled in Wichita as early as February 29, 1916. On that date, Browning notified the US commissioner of immigration of Buck's location and Canadian citizenship. On a different occasion, Browning also claimed that the province notified authorities in Wichita of Buck's presence in their city.[32] A separate account in Kansas papers relates that one of the provincial "wanted" posters tipped off State Marshal "Dad" Cheatum of Kingman, Kansas, located forty-three miles west of Wichita. Marshal Cheatum apparently immediately recognized Buck's picture as the person he knew as Joe Barnes. The Kansas marshal claimed that he telegraphed the attorney general's office in Edmonton on April 12 but received no acknowledgement of his message. No record of a telegram from Cheatum exists in the material released by the Alberta Provincial Archives.[33] However, on April 12, for reasons that are not entirely clear from the documentary record, Browning wired Jack Hays, Wichita's chief of police, that Buck "is reported to be in your city" and asked him to detain Buck and wire back immediately. According to historian John Schmidt, Hays began plotting to collect a portion of the $1,000 reward, but his status as chief of police made him ineligible to claim the reward. The same rules, however, did not apply to private detectives. Instead of arresting and detaining Buck himself, Hays tipped off his former detectives, W.A. McWain and John W. "Long John" Miller of the McWain and Miller Detective Agency.[34]

Founded a year earlier from the ashes of the Gilleland Detective Bureau, the McWain and Miller Detective Agency described itself as "a modernized Secret Service" protecting businesses and individuals from "theft, robbers, bad checks and burglaries." As former police officers in Wichita, they enjoyed a cozy relationship with the police chief, Jack Hay, something their agency's predecessor, W.S. Gilleland, had lost in 1915 after five years in the business, allegedly because of his "misconduct as an officer and public criticism of his superior officers." Gilleland's real offence, however, stemmed from his effort to reform and regulate the city's private detectives and their agencies in the aftermath of a two-month partnership that went sour and jeopardized both his and the agency's reputation. After publicly severing ties with his former partner, Gilleland spearheaded community efforts urging the police commission to adopt changes leading to the increased professionalization of detectives, such as having all private detectives post a $1,000 bond and paying a licensing fee. If adopted, the proposal would have made detectives and their agencies liable for fraud committed by the agency or detectives in the course of their business operations. Gilleland's proposal encountered stiff opposition from other private investigators and produced an increasingly bitter rift with the chief of police, O.K. Stewart. In this feud, however, Stewart held the upper hand because Gilleland required his permission to operate as a licensed private investigator in the city. The dispute between the two boiled over in December 1914 when Gilleland called Stewart incompetent and threatened to file a $5,000 lawsuit after Stewart refused to sign Gilleland's detective licence. Wichita's mayor, William J. Babb, then revoked the agency's commission and with it, Gilleland's power to make arrests. Whatever else it may have accomplished, the move amply illustrated the power that the chief of police exerted over Wichita's private detectives. Within five months, Gilleland sold what remained of the business to McWain and Miller, who were abruptly relieved of their responsibilities as police officers by the new mayor, Bentley, with no explanation. Stewart's triumph over Gilleland proved temporary. A federal grand jury indicted Stewart for bootlegging liquor out of city hall in November 1915, forcing him to resign as chief of police.

To the press, McWain and Miller claimed they began investigating Buck on April 8, two weeks before his arrest, as part of a routine check in connection with a large stock deal. Claiming that something about Barnes prompted them to probe deeper, they suddenly remembered information contained in the provincial circular that said Buck had a habit of putting his thumbs in the armpits of his vest and that he constantly and vigorously smoked or chewed gum. They recalled that when they originally approached him, "Barnes" put his thumbs in his armpits and when questioned, Barnes smoked vigorously. It was either a remarkable display of sleuthing or an incredible coincidence that McWain and Miller detained the right person on such remarkably thin evidence. But before closing in to detain Buck, the Wichita detectives telegraphed Browning in Edmonton requesting a certified copy of the arrest warrant on April 20. Two days later, McWain and Miller tapped Buck on the shoulder and arrested him.[35]

Once McWain and Miller notified Canadian authorities, the detectives reached an agreement with Buck. For twelve dollars a day, McWain and Miller allowed Buck a fair degree of freedom to go about his business, including attending baseball games, provided at least one of the detectives accompanied him. They also allowed Buck to cover the expenses of a guard at night. Buck used his liberty to tend to his business interests and launch a public relations offensive against the government of Alberta in interviews with local papers. "I am not going back to Canada," said Buck hours after his detention became public. "My solicitors assured me that I cannot be extradited on the offense charged. Were it not an unjust charge, I would return." In another interview, Buck proclaimed his innocence, alleging that blackmailers and an unfriendly attorney general framed him for a crime he did not commit. Going back to Alberta to face charges "would be to again suffer such unfair treatment as I have already suffered." Pulling out a letter from one of his daughters, Buck wept as he said his family suffered more than he had. He also confessed that he had not told his wife, Ada, his plans before fleeing Calgary, lest she become an accomplice. Buck expected to make his home in Wichita and planned to send for his wife and children—after he developed his business, of course. Buck retained George McGill, Wichita's well-connected former county attorney, of McGill, Hudson, and Hudson, to defend him against extradition. In short order, McGill proclaimed his client's innocence in the press, alleging that Buck had incurred the wrath and enmity of certain unnamed high-ranking officials in the province because of his political activities. These shadowy men conspired with Buck's employees to salt an oil well and then framed Buck for the crime, making Buck's prosecution politically motivated. If this were the case, it would trigger the "political offences" exception recognized in international law against politically motivated extradition requests.[36]

To *The Wichita Beacon*, Buck presented himself as an honest businessman struggling to overcome the weight of the government's oppressive hand. "I left Canada in December after the dirtiest treatment a person under persecution ever had to undergo. I simply couldn't stand the gaff any longer." The charges against him were untrue, he claimed, and suggested politics played a part. "In the first place, I am a conservative of some strength and the attorney general's department includes Liberals." Buck then fudged the facts, claiming the attorney general's Royal Commission targeted his company first. "We were then in the midst of the big stock sale and an investigation with or without foundation would be damaging in the extreme." According to Buck, he bent over backward to accommodate the commission, "but nothing would do but a public investigation and a lot of noise." Forced into a corner, Buck claimed there was little alternative but to fight back in the courts, bringing about the end of the Royal Commission. "Then the attorney general's department opened a direct attack upon us using a man named Clark and another named Fletcher." Both were disgruntled ex-employees looking to hurt him by alleging fraud. According to Buck, "the field proved a dry one, but we are able to show that we gave all of our personal holdings, even $37,000 in cash, to push the drilling in an effort to save our stockholders loss." Regarding the many lawsuits pending against him, the promoter claimed they were all opportunistic and unfounded. Remarkably, while discussing the Clark lawsuit, Buck admitted to some nefarious dealings. "I had holes bored in the wall between two of our offices," permitting him to overhear conversations that he attempted to use in court. However, even Buck allowed that admitting "such evidence might cost the gown of a leading counsel and there were other reasons why it was not admitted." He also revealed a stunning lack of self-awareness or empathy while complaining about his troubles obtaining a bond by presenting another family's tragedy as incidental to his own travails: "No sooner had we made bond than we were again required to make $20,000 bond for my cousin, a young woman, who when driving my car accidentally ran over a child and when the child died, she was held for manslaughter."[37]

Buck's callous statement referred to a tragic accident in Calgary on April 19, 1915, that claimed the life of eighteen-year-old Elinor Griffiths as she crossed the street. Eyewitness accounts claimed that Buck's McFarlan, driven by Jennie Earl, failed to sound a warning that she was turning (by blowing the horn), cut the corner at a high rate of speed, and wound up on the wrong side of the road when she knocked Griffiths down, passed over her head and torso, and dragged her for fifteen feet. Remarkably, Griffiths survived the initial crash but suffered a fractured skull and internal injuries and died the following morning.[38] According to Buck, the province only charged Earl with manslaughter to "get back" at him, not because the accident claimed the life of Elinor Griffiths. The interview closed with Buck's declaration that he was the real victim and accused the attorney general's office of passing on pursuing cases against other "notedly lawless" oil companies in the pursuit of its vendetta against him.[39]

Little did Provincial Detective J.D. Nicholson know the firestorm he was walking straight into. Buck's interviews were published just as Nicholson started the 1,785-mile, three-day train trip from Edmonton, arriving in Wichita early in the morning of April 27. His first stop was an eight a.m. meeting with Chief Of Police Hays where Nicholson planned to present a handful of documents, take custody of the prisoner, and arrange to return to Calgary. Upon meeting Hays, however, Nicholson discovered that returning Buck to Calgary would be far from the straightforward process he imagined. Unaware of the arrangement between Hays and detectives McWain and Miller, Nicholson presented Hays with his copy of the bench warrant only to have the Kansas sheriff refuse to lift a finger. Hays replied that Kansas law dictated Buck would remain in the custody of detectives McWain and Miller until they received the reward. When Nicholson protested and suggested Buck's safety meant a city or county jail would be more appropriate, Hays simply replied that McWain and Miller were reliable. Nicholson then visited the offices of the detectives to verify Buck's identity and to make a direct plea that they transfer Buck to police custody. The detectives refused and insisted they required full payment of the $1,000 reward before turning the prisoner over. Despite Nicholson's personal assurances that they would receive the reward, the detectives would not budge. Buck's sharp lawyer would file a writ of habeas corpus and spring Buck from custody if they tried transferring the prisoner. Seeing that he was getting nowhere, Nicholson asked to speak to Buck. Nicholson asked whether Buck would waive extradition and return to Calgary voluntarily or if he intended to fight the charge. Rather than wasting his time and money in Wichita, Nicholson told Buck he could stage his defence more effectively in Calgary. Confident, however, that none of the offences charged by Canadian authorities were extraditable, Buck said he would go with Nicholson if he could show him which charge was extraditable. Nicholson immediately pointed to the fraud charge on the bench warrant. Buck remained unconvinced and boasted that not only would he fight extradition but that he would win. But it seemed as if Buck was fishing for information and Nicholson ended the conversation. Nicholson returned to detectives McWain and Miller to see if there was a mutually agreeable solution that would result in, at a minimum, placing Buck in police custody, but the detectives again refused and claimed that they would take all necessary precautions.[40]

Nicholson's final visit on May 27 took him to the office of the county attorney, Ross McCormick. To the county's chief lawyer, Nicholson reiterated his belief that Buck was not in proper custody. Earlier conversations with Chief Hays and the private detectives prompted Nicholson to adopt a softer tone, as Nicholson informed the county attorney that "I did not wish to curtail Buck's liberty in the daytime to clear up his business under proper supervision" but had to insist "on him being locked up at night." McCormick agreed to investigate the matter but warned Nicholson that if he attempted to remove Buck from McWain's custody it would prompt a writ of habeas corpus from Buck's lawyer resulting in Buck's freedom. Speaking to the press a brief time later, Nicholson said the papers in his possession "will convince his attorneys that the charge is extraditable. If he does decide to fight, I am confident that any judge would deny his claim on the strength of the complaints against him." The provincial detective also dismissed Buck's claim of political motivation behind the prosecution. Nicholson, however, misstated the reason for the Carpenter Commission's dissolution, claiming that it disbanded with its inquiries complete. The detective also expressed surprise at learning Jennie Earl and Buck were cousins. Soon after, Nicholson telegraphed Browning of Buck's intent to fight extradition and McWain's demand for immediate payment of the bounty. A second message asked permission to retain counsel because Nicholson did not know if he could testify in court.[41]

Nicholson's brief interview with the two Wichita dailies brought forth a furious public letter from Buck published in the April 28, 1916, edition of the *Beacon*. Buck seized on Nicholson's statement that the Carpenter Commission had retired automatically upon completion of its work. This simply was not true, and Buck delighted in pointing out that the court had dissolved the commission as the result of his lawsuit. The promoter also alleged Attorney General Charles Cross held a personal vendetta against him. As for the salting of the well, Buck wrote that "the King's star witness, Norman Fletcher, admitted on the stand that he poured the oil in the sump of the well, and I defy any man to make the statement that any one ever said on the witness stand or that I was ever charged with putting a drop of oil into the well, neither is there a particle of evidence in which it was said I had done the same." Regardless, Buck returned to his defence that sales of Black Diamond shares "were withdrawn from the market a week before the alleged salting of the well." To the claims that he defrauded thousands of shareholders, Buck pointed to the endorsement given to him at the shareholder's meeting. How could there be disgruntled shareholders when they unanimously passed a vote of confidence? What cut Buck to the quick, however, were the "bumps" delivered to his family and relatives by the province. He could withstand whatever the province threw at him, but when the province attempted to "get" at him "through his relatives," presumably referring to Jennie Earl's manslaughter case, "then it touches him in tender places." He further claimed he did everything possible to bring in the well, including loaning the company $35,000 and putting up his own property as security to drill the wells. In fact, Buck claimed "the King's star witness, Norman R. Fletcher" was the only dissatisfied shareholder. Before closing his letter, Buck delivered a bouquet to the people of Wichita:

> I feel perfectly satisfied that the Province of Alberta is not as anxious to get me back to Canada as it is to knock my business in Wichita, which, by the way, is not the selling of oil stock in the Augusta field, but we are developers of property. It is my intention to remain a citizen of Wichita and all I ask is the fairness which I am assured always goes with American citizenship, which my forefathers boasted of, in years gone by.[42]

Buck's letter threw Nicholson on the defensive. To the *Beacon*, Nicholson said that the provincial attorney general's office "did not stoop to the tactics" described by Buck and dismissed claims that the province's pursuit of Buck tried to hurt his new business venture as "ridiculous." The attorney general, said Nicholson, "is noted for his fairness. He has never permitted politics to be mixed with the affairs of the department in any way. I think he may not know Mr. Buck personally, and that his deputy has preferred the charges. I am sure Mr. Cross does not concern himself with personal attacks on Mr. Buck." Back in Calgary, the *Herald* grumbled, "Buck revels in publicity of poor sort." While Nicholson and the province waited for additional papers to secure Buck's extradition, the oil man "has attended three ball games, written a thousand words [of] attack upon Charles Cross, attorney general, and Mr. Nicholson, and has been spending the evenings driving about the city in his 80 horse-power car."[43]

The contents of Nicholson's first telegram and press reports of Buck's relative comfort brought forth expressions of irritation from Browning at the turn of events in Wichita. The detectives' intransigence "is something for which we will not stand, and I am sure that the American authorities will refuse to countenance conduct of that kind." The request to retain a lawyer for the province, however, puzzled Browning, who thought it unnecessary but approved it nonetheless. "You understand we are going to bring Buck back and nothing must be spared to that end." In a rash decision, Browning retained the Wichita county attorney, McCormick, on behalf of the province and notified him by telegram that his fee for completing Buck's extradition should not exceed one hundred dollars.[44]

Little did Browning appreciate how complicated securing Buck's release would become. The arrest set in motion a blizzard of communications between officials in the United States and Canada. The Alberta attorney general's office notified the secretary of state in Ottawa and asked them to arrange for Buck's detention pending arrival of formal documentation. The missive brought a prompt reply from Thomas Mulvey, the undersecretary of state, seeking additional information. Was the province seeking Buck's extradition or his deportation as an undesirable citizen? Furthermore, had the province, via Nicholson, already initiated one process or the other? Some at state believed pursuing one precluded the other.[45]

While deportation and extradition are similar, some notable differences and nuances distinguished them from one another. Section 2 of the 1903 US Immigration Act in force when Buck entered the United States excluded "undesirable" foreign nationals from the United States or subjected them to deportation. The Immigration Act (1903) defined the classes of undesirables as including:

> All idiots, insane persons, epileptics, and persons who have been insane within five years previous; persons who have had two or more attacks of insanity at any time previously; paupers; person likely to become a public charge; professional beggars; persons afflicted with a loathsome or with a dangerous contagious disease; persons who have been convicted of a felony or other crime or misdemeanour involving moral turpitude; polygamists, anarchists, or persons who believe in, or advocate the overthrow by force or violence of the Government of the United States, all government or of all forms of law, or the assassination of public officials.

However, exceptions existed for "persons convicted of an offense purely political."[46] Deportation proceedings were shorter, unappealable, and immediately enforced. Indeed, by May 1, 1916, the province had already secured the necessary paperwork from Ottawa and Washington, including evidence of Buck's Canadian citizenship, to initiate deportation proceedings. "Deportation [of] George Buck [now a] matter for United States Government," telegraphed W.D. Scott, the Canadian superintendent of immigration, on the afternoon of May 1. "I have issued letter authorizing his return to Canada if they wish to deport him."[47]

Extradition, on the other hand, could be a much lengthier process by which a person, regardless of citizenship, accused or suspected of engaging in criminal activity returns to face charges. In 1916, Canada did not have an extradition treaty with the United States; as a Dominion within the British Empire, Canada relied on Anglo-American treaties. The Webster-Ashburton Treaty (1842) established extradition arrangements between the United States and the British Empire after a prolonged period of uncertainty following the lapsing of Jay's Treaty in 1806. Known more for the settlement of boundaries, according to legal historian Gary Botting, Webster-Ashburn is "arguably one of the most influential documents in the development of extradition law" between Britain and the United States and remained in force until superseded by the Canada–United States Extradition Treaty in 1976.[48] Article X of the Webster-Ashburton Treaty included provisions for extradition for the crimes of murder, assault with intent to commit murder, piracy, forgery, arson, and robbery, provided these were also crimes where the fugitive was found. Significantly, the Webster-Ashburton Treaty initiated a custom wherein the two governments agreed to extradite persons for specific, but oftentimes undefined, offences. In this regard, the Blaine-Pauncefote Convention (1889) reached two notable decisions. First, it included the "specialty principle"—the assumption that a person can only face trial for the offence(s) charged in extradition proceedings. Thus, a suspect extradited for committing murder could not face additional charges, for example, of robbery, unless specified in the extradition order. The Blaine-Pauncefote Convention also expanded the list of extraditable offences by ten, including various white-collar crimes, and specified two broadly defined categories of fraud. The first category specified that extradition for fraud could occur in cases where the crime involved "receiving any money, valuable security, or other property, knowing the same to have been embezzled, stolen or fraudulently obtained." The second category addressed "fraud by a bailee, banker, agent, factor, trustee, or director, or member or officer of any company, made criminal by the laws of both countries."[49] Supplementary conventions expanded the range of crimes from time to time. In 1900, a supplementary convention expanded the crime of fraud to include "obtaining money, valuable securities or other property by false pretenses." Anglo-American extradition laws expanded again in 1905 but did not alter provisions covering fraud. Thus, in 1916, extradition treaties covered the three broad categories of fraud: knowingly receiving fraudulently obtained property; fraud committed by a company officer; and obtaining money, securities, or property by false pretences.

In the Canadian system, individuals and provinces cannot file extradition requests—only the federal government can. In practical terms, this meant that in 1916, the provincial attorney general, Charles W. Cross, applied to the province's Lieutenant-Governor, Robert Brett, to have Buck extradited from the United States. Lieutenant-Governor Brett then notified the Dominion's secretary of state in Ottawa of the request. Although the establishment of the Department of External Relations in 1909 enabled Canada to quietly assume some control over its foreign policy, officially speaking, in 1916, London, not Ottawa, still made most of the real decisions regarding Canadian foreign affairs. Thus, the secretary of state transmitted the application under the signature of the Governor General of Canada to the British Foreign Office. This additional layer of complexity resulted from Canada's status as a British Dominion because Canada did not formally establish diplomatic relations with the United States until 1927. Instead, official requests to the US government regarding the Buck case needed to flow through the British Foreign Office and were delivered to the US government via the British Embassy in Washington, DC.[50]

Distinct from the logistics of returning Buck, the situation on the ground in Wichita hardly improved. In fact, things appeared worse. McCormick slow-walked Nicholson's request that he investigate Buck's custody status with respect to detectives McWain and Miller. Expressing his disappointment, Nicholson told McCormick that he depended on him to act as the proper legal authority. Furthermore, if McCormick continued to sandbag him, Nicholson threatened to go to the state attorney general in Topeka. McCormick seemed unbothered. Nicholson remained free to check with the state attorney general if he wanted, but McCormick believed the state would not interfere. McCormick reassured Nicholson he would look after his interests but believed it better to leave Buck in the hands of the private detectives. Both were reliable men and McCormick believed they ensured Buck's appearance wherever required. McCormick then suggested Nicholson contact Deputy Attorney General Browning to get "his personal assurance as to the payment of the reward." The comment cut Nicholson to the quick. Having provided his personal assurances about the reward's payment, Nicholson announced, "I must take it as an insult to myself and my employer to doubt for a minute that the reward would not be paid in the regular way."[51] Over Nicholson's objection, McCormick asked for Browning's personal assurances that McWain and Miller would receive the whole reward and suggested the deputy attorney general "grant me authority over your signature that you will personally see that when prisoner is turned over to Mr. Nicholson the full reward will be paid to arresting detective." After sending the wire, McCormick impertinently asked Nicholson when he could expect a reply.[52]

McCormick's message prompted Browning to contact Thomas Mulvey, the Canadian undersecretary of state, and J. Bruce Walker, the US commissioner of immigration in Winnipeg. To Mulvey, he requested the state department intercede with US federal authorities. "Am informed that certain private detectives in the United States are holding up matters in regard to extradition and refuse to give assistance in handing over [Buck] without reward being paid in advance," wrote Browning. "Kindly advise American Authorities to render assistance to have accused handed over to the Sheriff or Chief of Police." Mulvey replied with confusion, "I do not see how the detectives could stand in the way. It appears to me that the proceedings in this case have been somewhat irregular." To Immigration Commissioner Walker, Browning emphasized that "the Department is very anxious to have him returned for trial" and inquired if "you will have him deported," which read more like an instruction than a question. Walker's reply, sent later that same day, informed Browning that Buck's case lay "entirely in the hands of US Commissioner Immigration Montreal . . . provided Buck is a Canadian citizen this department will have no objection to his return to Canada."[53]

Back in Wichita, Nicholson wrote Browning a nine-page, single-spaced summary of his first days in Kansas that gave a sense as to the obstacles and irregularities he had already encountered. Nicholson kept track of Buck (and his car) during the daytime and hired a detective for three dollars per night to continue the watch while he rested. In addition to tracking Buck's whereabouts, Nicholson arranged a response with the sheriff in case Buck tried anything, and devoted some energy to gathering information on the people in Kansas and peppered his letters and reports with brief sketches and opinions on each to the deputy attorney general. George McGill, a very well-connected Democrat and former county attorney, represented Buck. McGill had entered private practice after a failed attempt to become state attorney general in 1914. As for detectives McWain and Miller, Nicholson reported that they were the two best men on Chief Hays's force before "political influence" cost them their jobs. Hays still took care of his former officers by "giving them all the important cases and is no doubt in with them in this one." County Attorney Ross McCormick merited Nicholson's most critical comments. McCormick served as McGill's deputy for four years and earned McGill's endorsement in the 1914 election. With another campaign looming in November, Nicholson reported that McCormick "is afraid of [McGill]," fearing that McGill would challenge him for the nomination to reclaim his old job. The province's newly retained representative was "afraid of them all and is standing in with them." Nicholson clearly believed that a conspiracy existed between the principal players in Wichita over the province's reward, telling Browning:

> I am informed if there is money in it that Buck could be got out on Habeas Corpus writ and decided to let matters rest till I have the proper authority and then I expect to have a fight if they are not satisfied about the Reward as [I] feel sure that his lawyers would drop his case if the detectives wanted them to. They are all in [it] together and I can do nothing but wait.[54]

In a separate telegram to G.P.O. Fenwick, Nicholson explicitly stated, "Believe the real obstacle is doubt as to payment of reward [and] am up against a political combination here [that I] can't explain in [a] wire."[55]

In all, Nicholson's correspondence revealed much for the attorney general's office to be concerned about. Their fugitive remained in the custody of two detectives who, to all appearances, behaved more like bullies and mercenaries than law enforcement. The local constabulary not only lent its implicit support to the scheme but appeared to be in on it, too. Meanwhile, the local newspapers seemed well informed about Nicholson's communications with Edmonton, in some cases quoting verbatim instructions and statements in their reports. On May 3, Nicholson travelled to Topeka and arranged to visit State Attorney General S.W. Brewster, who provided him with "some good information" regarding the situation in Wichita that Nicholson carefully parcelled out over time. Upon his return to Wichita, Nicholson finally explained in greater detail his request to retain a lawyer. Unfamiliar with Kansas state law, Nicholson wanted someone to advise him on its idiosyncrasies. "Mr. McCormick," confided Nicholson after his trip to Topeka, "is not considered strong as an attorney and I found I was up against a strong political combination." In any case, McCormick became immersed in a murder trial that he claimed required his full time and attention. The detective also advised circumspection to the attorney general's office in its correspondence to him in Wichita; "nothing is kept confidential." Alluding to the detectives' fixation on the reward, Nicholson revealed they suggested they could convince Buck to accept returning to Canada—for a price. But revealing their underhandedness in such a cavalier manner cut both ways. If the detectives offered an under-the-table deal to Nicholson, what deal had they promised

Buck? In closing his letter, Nicholson admitted to going to the courthouse to observe McCormick at work and to teach himself about Wichita legal customs. His visit prompted him to reach two pessimistic conclusions. First, that McCormick was out of his depth as a courtroom lawyer. Secondly, that Wichita courts kept "things very lax in regarding prisoners."[56]

Some of the difficulties the province encountered in Wichita were the product of rash and incomplete decision making by the attorney general's office. Failing to notify the federal government, specifically the Canadian state department, or consult with Ottawa prior to Nicholson's arrival in Wichita, for example, looms large in this respect because it violated established diplomatic protocol and created unnecessary confusion that needed a few days to untangle. Furthermore, the difficulties of making informed decisions when confronted by incomplete information and hampered by poor communication between Edmonton and Wichita partially explains Browning's rash decision to retain McCormick. Unquestionably, however, the gravest mistake made by the attorney general's office was the $1,000 bounty offered for Buck. The documentary record reveals little about its provenance, who proposed it, or even how or why the final figure of $1,000 gained approval. Regardless, the size of the reward reflected the importance of Buck's case as well as the scale of resources devoted to cleaning up the mess of 1914. However, in attempting to solve one problem, the attorney general's office inadvertently created another. The generous and elastic terms—"information leading to the arrest"— meant pursuit of the reward became an end for some treasure seekers. Only after McWain and Miller advanced a claim did the province attempt to clean this up by insisting payment would follow Buck's return to Canada, much to the irritation of McWain and Miller.

Officially, if belatedly, the department of the secretary of state mobilized the Governor General's office and then applied to detain Buck through Sir Cecil Spring Rice, the British ambassador to the United States.[57] Efforts to remove Buck from the United States henceforth moved simultaneously on two tracks: the first sought his deportation as an undesirable citizen and the second required provincial officials to file an extradition claim, raising questions about what Buck could be formally charged with from the existing warrants that would comply with the terms of the Anglo-American extradition treaty. However, by May 4, the possibility of mounting an extradition case appeared dead in the water as the federal justice ministry notified Browning that the treaty did not recognize conspiracy as an extraditable offence. To be sure, some individual states did, but in 1916 Kansas did not. Acting Deputy Attorney General Fenwick questioned whether the charge of fraud "by a director, member or officer of a Company" would suffice. With that, on May 5, 1916, the Governor General informed the British ambassador that the charge of "fraud by a director or officer of a company" justified Buck's extradition.[58]

Little appreciated at the time, the decision to file for Buck's extradition on the single charge of fraud by a director carried tremendous implications, especially considering the "specialty principle" preventing additional charges to the accused after extradition. Back in Calgary, until the moment Buck absconded from Canada, the Crown had planned to base its case against Buck on the two separate counts of conspiracy because Crown Prosecutor James Short believed they were the easiest to prove and the attorney general's office would not pay the expenses to bring in witnesses to prove a fraud charge. Even before Buck fled, Short worried that too few witnesses remained in Calgary to make the fraud charge stick. Compounding the error was the fact that no one from the attorney general's office informed Short about this decision until September 1916. In retrospect, it is easy to see how this happened. Given the difficulties Nicholson encountered in Wichita and the growing perception that McWain and Miller were at best unreliable and at worst motivated solely by the money, provincial authorities grew increasingly concerned that they might "lose" Buck altogether. Better to have Buck back on Canadian soil and then let the chips fall where they may.[59]

One other hope remained. Concurrent to extradition, the provincial attorney general's office contacted the US Department of Labor Immigration Service in Kansas City requesting Buck's deportation as an undesirable citizen because of his outstanding warrants. With fewer strings attached, namely the "specialty principle" that would limit the prosecutor's options, the attorney general's office prioritized deportation. "The matter is one of great public concern," wrote Fenwick, "and the Alberta Government is very anxious to have Buck brought back." Immigration Inspector M. Arthur Coykendall replied in short order, promising his full cooperation. Immediately upon receiving Coykendall's telegram, Fenwick issued instructions to send all materials requested by Coykendall to Kansas City and notified Nicholson in Wichita.[60]

With two levels of government simultaneously pursuing two different avenues to secure Buck's release from the United States, the need to coordinate the flow of information became apparent. Belatedly, to impose order and to ensure the delivery and return of official court documents, the Dominion's deputy minister of justice outlined how communication on the Buck case would proceed to the undersecretary of state. After the documents arrived from the province to the Department of Justice for authentication, the undersecretary of state who would then submit the authenticated documents to the

US consul general in Ottawa for certification before mailing the now certified and authenticated documents to the British ambassador in Washington for presentation to the US government. Finally, it fell to Nicholson to return all original court documents for trial.[61]

In the meantime, Buck continued to build public sympathy in Kansas when his wife, Ada, arrived in Wichita at 2:10 a.m. on May 3, 1916. Her husband, his guards, and some members of the press witnessed the reunion. Described by *The Wichita Eagle* as "a small motherly Canadian woman," Mrs. Buck wept while the two embraced. Addressing the press, Mrs. Buck said she arrived to help her husband fight extradition and to make their home in Wichita. Plans were in the works for their five children and Buck's mother-in-law to join them "as soon as this trouble is settled." Buck used the opportunity to rehash his story of a conspiracy by the provincial government to prosecute him. The Carpenter Commission called no witnesses against him and collected not a single word of evidence against Black Diamond Oil Fields. He also claimed his lawyer filed for an injunction to restrain the commission because it would not wait to examine the company's executives until after a civil lawsuit concluded. Black Diamond Oil Fields had nothing to hide; Buck agreed to produce "books, documents, and all the evidence the commission desired if a continuance was granted," but the court dissolved the commission before it could investigate the company. Buck insisted the record reflected "the king's star witness admitted under oath that he poured the oil in the well and I was never charged with the act." Besides which, Buck withdrew the company's stock from the market when the salting took place "and no stock was offered or sold at that time."[62]

Presenting Buck as a father and family man persecuted by the Alberta provincial government, the article labelled Nicholson as an unscrupulous outsider. Egged on by Buck and the two detectives, *The Wichita Beacon* reported that Nicholson had attempted to kidnap Buck, allegedly enlisting the support of a third party, J. Clarence Smith, to approach Buck's nighttime guard Ed Stiger, another former Wichita police officer, with a bribe. The newspaper claimed Nicholson attempted to pay Stiger fifty dollars to look the other way so Nicholson could abscond back to Canada with his quarry. But with only eighteen dollars in his wallet, Nicholson lowballed Smith, giving him one Canadian dollar and two two-dollar US bank notes. In this recounting, Smith promptly turned the notes over to McWain.[63] The paper remained silent about how Nicholson intended to turn his remaining thirteen dollars into fifty dollars to bribe Stiger. The inconsistencies of the kidnapping story are due to the fact that they originated with Buck acting in league with the

McWain and Miller Detective Agency both to embarrass Nicholson and to shame the Province of Alberta as they continued to bleat loudly and often about the unpaid $1,000 bounty. "We only want to do the fair thing by every one concerned," said McWain to the press on May 3.

> We are entitled to the reward and to get that is our only interest in the affair since we took Mr. Buck into custody. When I talked to Mr. Nicholson on the morning of his arrival here, he said we would not get all of the reward as certain Canadian officials wanted part of it. I showed him that they had nothing to do with locating the oil man and were entitled to no reward.... Mr. Nicholson's plan is to get Mr. Buck out of our custody to beat us out of the reward. He has been trying to get Chief Hay and the county attorney to take him away from us.

Conveniently omitted from McWain's press statement were details of an attempt by Buck to bribe his way out of captivity by offering McWain ownership of his prized red McFarlan and $600. McWain turned down the offer. Hearing the story prompted Nicholson to learn Buck transferred ownership of it on April 29, 1916 to his business partner, Hugh Miller, who in turn used the title to the vehicle a partial retainer for Buck's attorney, Charles B. Hudson.[64]

Wichita newspapers filled with rumours by Buck's friends claiming that Alberta's deputy attorney general, A.G. Browning, had arrived in Wichita "incognito" to take Buck back to Canada. "A mysterious stranger has called on various public officials," confided *The Wichita Eagle* to its readers. The stranger managed to keep his identity a secret while inquiring about the Buck case. McWain and Miller chimed in that the official intended to cheat them out of the $1,000 bounty. In the meantime, Buck took to antagonizing Nicholson by calling him twice to demand that the detective file charges against him. "They have no right to keep me sitting around here unable to attend to business without preferring a charge," said Buck. Shortly thereafter, the case of George Buck garnered the attention of the Dominion's justice and state departments. In the meantime, Gregory Trainor, the chief investigator for the Carpenter Commission, told the *Herald* on May 3 that if American officials refused to hand over Buck, it would establish a precedent. Still, Trainor assured the reporter that in other instances, US officials immediately deported wanted fugitives after a preliminary hearing established a prima facie case. In all, Trainor expected Buck to be back in Canada within twenty days.[65]

At seven a.m. on the morning of May 12, US Immigration Inspector M. Arthur Coykendall arrived in Wichita from Kansas City. Since his appointment to the Buck case, the province had sent material and documents directly to Coykendall. Nicholson's meeting was the first in-person contact and the two spoke for about an hour as the Alberta detective provided all the information he could about the case. Nicholson fully expected those documents would provide "all the evidence required to prove a prima facie case here." Coykendall informed Nicholson that the US consul in Ottawa needed to authenticate all the sworn statements, depositions, and documents sent by the province. The court would ignore all unauthenticated documents. Moments later, accompanied by Deputy US Marshal Sam Hill, the party arrived at the McWain and Miller Detective Agency and arrested Buck on a deportation warrant charging him with entering the United States while evading a felony indictment in Canada. *The Wichita Beacon* reported that the sudden deportation hearing caught Buck off guard.[66]

Contradictory accounts of Buck's deportation hearing exist in the newspapers, likely because federal regulations barred reporters from the proceedings. At the request of Buck's lawyers, Coykendall also barred Nicholson from sitting in the hearing, only allowing him in to testify in the afternoon. *The Wichita Eagle* reported that Buck's criminal record listed a conviction of an undisclosed felony in Canada, a guilty plea on a misdemeanour charge involving moral turpitude, and an accusation of being a man likely to become a public charge. According to the Kansas newspaper, Canadian officials, and Detective Nicholson in particular, "fell down" and were unable to prove their case against Buck. Nicholson later stated that the "neglect and incompetence" of Coykendall stacked the outcome in Buck's favour. Nicholson complained that "there was ample evidence available if they took it." However, with copies of depositions, warrants, and transcripts from Buck's preliminary hearing excluded, Coykendall accepted Buck's written statement minimizing his criminal history to a single speeding ticket—insufficient grounds for deportation. That afternoon, as Nicholson waited outside the chamber to give his evidence, he heard McWain testify that Buck "was as fine a gentleman as he had ever met when he knows different."[67]

At the conclusion of the hearing, Nicholson spoke briefly with Coykendall and reported back to Edmonton reasons to be optimistic about the outcome. The case seemed straightforward to Coykendall, who said that he would recommend Buck's immediate deportation. For good measure, Coykendall obliquely suggested Nicholson should initiate extradition proceedings as well. Buck drew a completely distinct set of conclusions regarding the hearing. To

Wichita's newspapers, Buck said Canadian officials should hurry up and show their hand. He was a busy oil man and drilling operations east of Wichita required his full attention. After all, he taunted, drilling a dry hole was the only reason he got in trouble back in Calgary.[68]

Buck's confidence reflected faith in his well-connected lawyers, who behaved as though the hearing was less than half of the battle. As soon as they wrapped up their courtroom duties, Charles Hudson, one of Buck's lawyers, went to St. Louis, while McGill travelled to Washington, DC, to lobby federal officials on their client's behalf. Furthermore, just before the deportation hearing, on May 11, McWain and Miller raised the stakes in their showdown with the province and tried to force Nicholson to pay the reward immediately. Buck's legal team prepared a writ of habeas corpus for the courts to free the oil man from their custody following the deportation hearing. McWain and Miller, in turn, informed Nicholson about the plot and again promised to release Buck into Nicholson's custody if he simply paid them the reward, raising the question as to how far Nicholson and his prisoner would get before someone else interfered. During the deportation hearing, Coykendall granted Buck's release pending the posting of a $1,000 bond. The next day, just after Buck posted his bail, Nicholson filed the extradition claim based on a single charge of fraud, for knowingly making false statements to induce investors to purchase stock in a company, before Immigration Commissioner Paul J. Wall. Wall, in turn, issued a warrant for Buck's arrest to the US Marshall's Service, causing Buck's re-arrest on May 13. At the arraignment before Wall, Nicholson spoke on behalf of the Province of Alberta. The provincial detective asked that Wall deny bail; after all, $20,000 in bonds had failed to keep him in Calgary. Hudson insisted that it be set much lower. The discussion between the two men grew heated, and at one point Hudson turned to Nicholson and demanded to know if he had brought a gun into the courtroom. "I don't see where that is any of your business," replied Nicholson. "Well," answered Hudson, "I'm going to make it some of my business. I don't believe that you have a right to pack a gun around Wichita!" With that, Wichita detective John T. Young arrived to search Nicholson, who, in turn, demanded to see a warrant before submitting to a search. When temperatures cooled between the parties thereafter, Wall set Buck's bail at $1,000, leaving him in the custody of McWain and Miller and making them personally responsible for ensuring Buck's presence at the hearing. Wall granted Nicholson a continuance until May 23. As Nicholson telegraphed the attorney general's office in Edmonton, "Can do nothing further without papers authenticated by American consul."[69]

In the meantime, Coykendall's original deadline for a decision—May 22, ten days following the hearing—came and went without word from the Department of Labor in Washington. The only report from Washington about the Buck case arrived on May 26, when *The Wichita Eagle* reported that McGill had just returned from a productive trip lobbying lawmakers on behalf of his client. In Washington, McGill met with Kansas Representative William A. Ayers, visited with members of Congress and the Senate, and called on President Woodrow Wilson at the White House. Returning to Wichita, McGill confidently predicted, "Mr. Buck will never be deported under the law and evidence produced at the hearing. He is a good citizen, whose ancestors were respected citizens of Pennsylvania, and he shouldn't be deported."[70]

Nicholson clipped the article out of the paper and sent it to the attorney general's office in Edmonton because it reflected his growing unease over the deportation process and his sense that Buck might slip away. Earlier in the week, Nicholson issued a warning about the deportation hearing and urged the department to take the extradition case more seriously. "I don't believe you quite understand how I am fixed here so I will try and explain." Nicholson described the deportation hearing in greater detail, reminding Arthur Popple that all the orders, indictments, and depositions brought from Edmonton should have been sufficient evidence to compel Buck's immediate deportation as a wanted fugitive. "As you know, they were not authenticated by the American consul so I could not use them in any proceedings here." Of growing concern to Nicholson was the fact that documents sent to Ottawa for authentication seemed to disappear into a black hole. Nonetheless, Nicholson made headway, managing, in his words, to "bull through" an attempt by Buck's attorneys to have the case dismissed. By the time of the hearing, Nicholson still did not have the certified documents in his possession and Buck's attorneys had put forward three separate grounds for dismissal: that the facts alleged in Nicholson's complaint did not constitute fraud; that the province's complaint and warrant were "too indefinite and uncertain" to permit Buck to know why Canada sought his extradition; and finally, that the warrant did not specify an extraditable offence covered by the Anglo-US extradition treaty. Over the objections of the defence team, Nicholson secured a continuance until June 2.[71]

While staying hopeful that the province would prevail in the deportation case, Nicholson nonetheless recommended that the department focus on building the strongest possible case for Buck's extradition by asking the attorney general's office to provide him with all the original documents related to the Buck case, including warrants, depositions of witnesses, and all available evidence. In his explanation, Nicholson referred explicitly to Buck's well-connected defence team and his growing doubts about the impartiality of the deportation process. "[Buck] has three lawyers working for him and they are trying political influence as well as other means to block the deportation. I don't know where he is getting his money. I believe the firm of lawyers are in with him in the oil syndicate he had founded here." Buck's team of lawyers, he noted, are "used to winning all cases in the newspapers," while he refused to talk to reporters. Unsurprisingly, then, Nicholson thought the extradition process would be better for the province. He judged the extradition commissioner, Paul Wall, to be "fair-minded" and expected he would do justice to the province's case. In a much briefer telegram sent the next morning, Nicholson said he needed the authenticated documents to prove the fraud charges. "I must have something to show for my [request for] further adjournment."[72]

In response, Browning let Nicholson know that Arthur E. Popple, the department's legal adviser to the RNWMP, now served as his principal point of contact. The new lines of communication streamlined the flow of information and provided faster responses to Nicholson's requests. In the meantime, Browning sympathized with Nicholson and shared his frustrations regarding the delays in Kansas, writing, "It is difficult to understand at this end why the matter is dragging on so long and though I feel sure you are doing all that can be done to bring this matter to a speedy conclusion, do not hesitate to let us know if there's anything we can do at this end in the way of communication with Washington that will assist you." Alluding to the public pressure building on the attorney general's office, Browning exclaimed, "Buck has to be brought back and it will never do for us to fall down now." To queries from the attorney general's office urging him to check in with Coykendall, Nicholson reported that several attempts to reach Coykendall by wire and by telephone had elicited no response. Now the deputy attorney general of Alberta sent a tersely worded telegram to Coykendall practically demanding an explanation for the "delay in connection with deportation proceedings, which does not permit Buck being immediately deported" and threatening to go over Coykendall's head. Coykendall responded that he could not help Browning as the matter was in the hands of the Department of Labor in Washington.[73]

Messages, letters, and telegrams fanned out to Calgary, Edmonton, Ottawa, and Wichita trying to collect and coordinate the delivery of authenticated documents to Nicholson before the extradition hearing on June 2. Browning contacted Gregory Trainor in Calgary to rework affidavits from crucial witnesses that would conform to extradition regulations as well as obtaining three original copies of the arrest warrant from the office of Police Magistrate Walter S. Davidson. In response to Coykendall's ruling that conspiracy to commit fraud was not a deportable offence, but that actual fraud was, Trainor "drew the affidavits so as to show as much fraud as possible on the part of Buck" without leaving the evidence given at the preliminary hearing too far behind. After reworking the affidavits, Trainor described the importance of the Buck case for the people of Calgary. "This matter is very, very important," wrote Trainor, "and nothing should be left undone with regard to bringing the accused here to Calgary, even if it were necessary to lay a further charge against him to bring him here. The feeling against him in Calgary is very strong and that is the reason I refer to the matter in this way." After a couple of long days and late nights, a courier hand delivered the affidavits to Browning in Edmonton on the morning of May 29. Browning thanked Trainor for his efforts and personally assured him that "the Department is taking every step possible towards having [Buck] brought here for trial."[74]

However, unless Browning could clear the bureaucratic logjam in Ottawa inhibiting the prompt delivery of authenticated documents to Nicholson, all this effort would go for naught. To Undersecretary of State Thomas Mulvey in Ottawa, Browning wrote that delay in document authentication "is causing expense and inconvenience" and asked if British authorities could nudge the US State Department along. The acting undersecretary of state responded later that day, assuring Browning the Buck case received "immediate attention."[75]

In the meantime, both Browning and Nicholson also contended with the growing impatience of detectives McWain and Miller about the still unpaid bounty. On May 22, McWain sent a blunt telegram to Attorney General Cross stating that thirty-two days had passed since they detained Buck and demanded to know when the province would pay. Browning replied that the $1,000 reward would be "paid to the parties entitled at the proper time" and that the detectives "need have no apprehension that you will not be treated fairly." McWain claimed the detectives had helped Nicholson's efforts, causing an eruption from the normally even-tempered Nicholson. "This man has not assisted me in any way whatever in this case and had it not been for him I am satisfied I would have had no difficulty." Particularly galling was that the Wichita detective did not treat Buck as a wanted criminal as much as he did a paycheque. "Nothing can be got in the way of information without paying for it," Nicholson grumbled. Speculation in Wichita held June 15 as the day for a decision in the deportation case. "I believe," he wrote Browning, "we should be prepared to go on with the fraud [extradition] case in any event." Even though Wall was friends with Buck's lawyers, Nicholson optimistically believed Wall would be fair and just. Warming to the idea of appearing before Wall, Nicholson saw the hearing as an opportunity to convince the people of Wichita that "Buck is not such a good citizen as they think he is. He is certainly a smart criminal and I have no doubt but what he is doing crooked work here but have had no chance to find out so far." With each passing day, Nicholson's skepticism about Buck's deportation increased.[76]

Three days before the fraud case before Wall resumed, Nicholson inquired once more about the whereabouts of the authenticated documents. The matter served as a source of consternation and anxiety in Edmonton as well as Wichita. Browning had originally sent the documents for authentication on April 27. Over a month later, they still had not arrived in Kansas. The delay took a toll on Nicholson, who, in the face of immense provocations from Buck and McWain, bit his tongue and bided his time. "I have had to take more insults from [Buck] and McWain than I thought I could ever stand from anyone," admitted Nicholson. Nicholson hoped that the authenticated documents would enable him to make his case, sweep aside the obstructions put in place by lawyers and bureaucrats, and result in Buck's return to Calgary. Belatedly, on May 30, Nicholson learned from the newspapers that the documents had arrived the day before and were in the possession of Ross McCormick, but the latter had not bothered to tell Nicholson of their arrival. "I am going to wake them up from now till the 2nd June," wrote Nicholson to Popple, "and let them know that we intend [to] take this man back."[77] Then, on June 1, Coykendall notified the lawyers that the immigration department had cancelled Buck's warrant for insufficient evidence and dismissed the province's attempt to deport him. With deportation no longer on the table, the entire case against Buck now hinged on proceedings before immigration commissioner Paul J. Wall.[78]

The first question taken up by Wall on June 2 was whether the province had charged Buck with an extraditable offence covered by the Anglo-American extradition treaty. It took an hour for lawyers on both sides to make their case, but Wall ruled the fraud charge laid by the province valid. Then Wall placed the onus on the province to prove Black Diamond Oil Fields had broken the law. Essentially, before granting extradition, Wall decided that the lawyers must prove that Buck had done what he stood accused of in Calgary, while Nicholson and McCormick objected, and argued extradition should follow because Wall found the Canadian charges extraditable offences. But Wall still expressed concerns about the documentation provided by the province, ruling that the depositions from Calgary and the crucial one from driller J.W. Hayes in Ohio were inadmissible for two reasons. First, the documents remained unauthenticated by US authorities in Ottawa. Second, Buck's lawyers did not attend the Hayes deposition, denying Buck the right to face his accuser. Wall insisted on seeing the "original evidence taken at the Preliminary and signed and certified by the Police magistrate [Davidson]." He also requested the stenographer's certificate and any documents filed by "the complainant in the way of evidence to show a crime was committed." Wall gave the parties until June 16 and said clearly there would be no further continuances. Writing back to Popple after the hearing, Nicholson warned that Wall "will not admit anything that is not authenticated by the US authorities at Ottawa."[79]

The challenge before Nicholson and the province lay in gathering original documents scattered between Calgary, Edmonton, and Ottawa, and arranging to have them authenticated by US officials and then delivered to Wichita. In an era before the internet and nearly instantaneous electronic communication, the only way to do so was by hand. Nicholson proposed that he personally travel the nearly 1,500 miles to Ottawa and meet with the deputy minister of justice. This would ensure the US consul authenticated all the necessary papers. All he needed from Browning now was to approve payment of a sixty-dollar return train fare from Wichita to Ottawa. After proposing the plan, Nicholson confided to Popple that he never expected to have such a difficult case again in his career. The particulars of Buck's crimes were uncomplicated; what generated the greatest friction and unease was the feeling that Kansas officials were actively working against Nicholson. Repeatedly, Alberta's chief detective commented about the unscrupulous motives and outright greed of people in Buck's orbit. At the top of this list was the private detective McWain, who surely knew Buck was crooked but with visions of the $1,000 bounty in his head, nevertheless testified to his "good character" before Inspector Coykendall at the deportation hearing. "There is a strong political and personal interests working in Buck's favor," wrote Nicholson. "I have impressed on Mr. McCormick and Mr. Wall that this man must go back for trial and that I will get anything in reason that he wants if he will give me the time to get it here." Still, having spent a month in Wichita so far, Nicholson pessimistically observed that "a man with money can evade justice in this city."[80]

Nicholson arrived in Ottawa and immediately set to work on having the documents certified and authenticated. "I had the certificate of the Secretary of state with seal attached to one side of the papers and the certificates with the seal of the US Consul General attached to the other side and the ribbons of both through each document." Nicholson also bought an official Criminal

Code from the government printing office to replace his copy of *Snow's Criminal Code*. Official copies of the documents arrived back in Wichita with Nicholson on June 11, with additional material arriving from Edmonton after Nicholson's departure from Ottawa via registered mail.[81] Back in Calgary, Attorney General Charles Cross, who largely embraced a hands-off approach to the case, nonetheless told the *Herald* that "you can tell the people that Mr. Buck is coming back."[82] Another delay pushed the start of hearing to the morning of June 16. This time, the walls closed in on Buck as Nicholson presented all his evidence. "I was in the witness box all day and was the only witness called," wrote Nicholson. Despite near-continuous objections from Buck's attorney, McGill, Nicholson managed to establish himself as the attorney general's representative in Wichita and finally present the certified documents. Depositions from Charles E. Tryon of the *News Telegram*, and Black Diamond employees Ray Minue and Norman Fletcher, painted a clear picture of fraud, particularly the deposition of the reporter. After a recess until 1:30 in the afternoon, the defence attorney Dierks immediately objected to the introduction of the materials, "each and every one of them," on the fourteen separate grounds. Perhaps the most serious objection was the defence's contention that the prosecution must prove that any crime committed by Buck in Canada "is made criminal" by laws in the State of Kansas. In response, Ross McCormick cited sections 2584 and 2585 of the General Statutes of Kansas (1909), Chapter 2 of the Session Laws of 1915.[83]

In making his decision, commissioner Wall said that he would not consider the statements of the men who salted the well, noting that they were co-conspirators in the crime if they were telling the truth. Since J.D. Nicholson asked for Buck's extradition for fraud based on the Tryon article, Wall paid particular attention to Tryon's affidavit that described the circumstances around the May 7, 1914, visit to the Black Diamond well and Buck's attempt to encourage the reporter to put out a special edition of the paper. On this basis, Extradition Commissioner Paul J. Wall committed Buck to extradition on a charge of fraud and confined the prisoner to the county jail. According to Nicholson, Buck took the ruling "very hard." All Nicholson sent to Edmonton, though, was a brief message. "Buck committed today. He is taking case to a higher court on habeas corpus proceedings will write particulars tomorrow. Please have my check forwarded to me here."[84]

Wall's ruling sent Buck's defence team grumbling. "There was absolutely nothing in the evidence to hold Mr. Buck," said George McGill. "The deposition of the reporter [Tryon] on which he was held, did not state what Buck asked the reporter to publish. There was no newspaper article shown and all that was shown was that Buck had asked him what he was going to publish, what it would cost to get out an extra, and that he agreed to pay for an extra. The extra was not issued and what was contained in a report published by the paper was not shown." Although Buck would have fifteen days to appeal, Buck's old habits, namely an inability to pay bills on time, came back to haunt him. As McGill prepared to leave for Kansas City to apply for a writ of habeas corpus in front of Federal Judge John C. Pollock, the law firm asked Buck for $1,000 in fees. Nicholson estimated that Buck's legal defence cost approximately $3,000. Unable to clear his debt with his lawyers, McGill notified *The Wichita Beacon* that his firm no longer represented Buck, leaving him without legal representation for most of the window to file an appeal.[85] In the meantime, Calgary newspapers celebrated the news. "George E. Buck is coming back despite all the efforts that have been made to keep him away," crowed the editorial page of *The Morning Albertan* before getting in a shot at the *Herald* for doubting the provincial government's effort.[86]

With Buck's financial reserves exhausted, Hugh Miller and Ada Buck tried to raise the money by liquidating assets and asking friends and family to cover Buck's legal bills. "It is practically hopeless," Miller told the Wichita press before giving up the last room of the suite of offices occupied by the Miller Oil Syndicate. Wichitan lawyers contacted by newspapers said they were doubtful they would take the case. On that front, Nicholson notified his superiors that the province had narrowly avoided a complete disaster. As Buck scrambled to put two dimes together for his defence, the Augusta field where the Miller Oil Syndicate planned to drill brought in a 1,700-barrel gusher and, as Nicholson described to A.E. Popple, drillers continued to strike flowing wells all around the field. "If Buck had been loose a few more days he would have cleaned up $30,000." Lingering in the air was the question of what kind of defence Buck could mount against the province with virtually unlimited funds. In a postscript, Nicholson informed the attorney general's office that Buck threatened to kill himself rather than face charges in Calgary. The detective wanted Popple to know this "in case anything happens later." Buck's large size and state of mind concerned Nicholson, but he also acknowledged that he could "size things up better when I am ready to leave."[87]

With Buck now having no lawyer, his time limit to file an appeal of Wall's ruling slipped away. Nicholson dryly observed to Popple that lawyers "won't work for nothing, so nothing has been done up to date in the habeas corpus proceedings." The *Herald* counselled patience but pessimistically predicted American lawyers would delay Buck's return "until they have bled him dry." Eventually, Judge Jesse Newton Haymaker agreed to serve as his representative in a hearing before Federal Judge John C. Pollock on June 28. After a promising start for Buck where Judge Pollock doubted that a fraud charge would sustain extradition, the situation abruptly changed. Judge Pollock proclaimed that Buck "should have been charged here on all three charges as laid out in the Bench Warrant issued by Chief Justice Harvey." Pollock directed Nicholson to go back before Extradition Commissioner Paul J. Wall at Wichita and add two more charges of conspiracy to defraud.[88]

Suddenly, Pollock's instruction and ruling changed the entire narrative about the conspiracy charges. District Attorney Robertson told *The Kansas City Globe* there was no significant difference between the conspiracy statutes of the United States and Canada. "Under the terms of the conspiracy statute of the United States it has to be shown that the commission of an act of conspiracy, such as mailing a forbidden letter, has actually been carried out. In Canada, the conspiracy statute is more strict, and the wording of the Canadian complaint against Buck simply states he is charged with conspiracy in connection with the alleged oil field deal." Robertson said a new complaint making more specific charges against Buck would conform with the conspiracy provisions of the treaty. The new charges prompted Buck's attorney, Judge Haymaker, to file a second writ of habeas corpus back in Kansas City on the grounds that the Canadian government had only applied for extradition on the fraud charge as well as submitting that conspiracy was not extraditable under the laws of Kansas. On June 30, Wall committed Buck to surrender on the three original charges of conspiracy to defraud the public, conspiracy to affect the market price of shares in a body corporate, and fraud by a director and officer of a company. The very next day, Judge Pollock dismissed Haymaker's argument and committed Buck to the custody of the US marshalls without bail to await the order of surrender from Washington. "Appeal Judge decided in our favor," Nicholson informed the Alberta attorney general's office. "No order for surrender from Washington here yet that is only delay. Can you hurry them?"[89]

Pollock did, however, grant Haymaker sixty days to appeal the ruling that the conspiracy charges were extraditable offences to the Court of Appeals in either St. Louis or St. Paul, imposing a deadline of September 1, 1916.[90] Additional reasons for concern emerged. Buck signed an oil lease over to his lawyers and now had "lots of funds" for his defence. While Nicholson remained convinced the province would prevail, in a second letter two days later he acknowledged that "the cost would be immense." After debating whether he should stay in Kansas or leave and return in September, Nicholson decided that if the surrender order arrived from Washington, he would leave with Buck at once. The prolonged standoff invited more attention, particularly Browning's increasingly stubborn refusal to pay the $1,000 reward to McWain and Miller. By early July, Nicholson practically pleaded with the attorney general's office to simply pay the reward. To Nicholson, there was little doubt that "the reward will have to be paid in full to McWain & Miller . . . if only for the prestige of the province." Nicholson intimated this gesture might soothe ruffled feathers, as Wichita newspapers mentioned the reward in every article about the Buck case. Moreover, the two detectives now "have given me all the assistance they can."[91]

But Browning refused to listen—vanity and pride precluded compromise. US Senator William H. Thompson wrote Alberta Attorney General Charles Cross about the outstanding bounty. Senator Thompson observed that McWain and Miller "wired you, asking if Buck was still wanted and that you answered to arrest him at once which they did." Senator Thompson further alleged that McWain and Miller contacted Browning several times without reply. The letter from Thompson brought a curt summons from Browning to speak with Cross at once. While no record exists in the Provincial Archives of that meeting, Cross evidently reached a decision about the payment of the bounty. That same day, Browning wrote James Short in Calgary about the high costs and significant effort the province had incurred to return Buck for trial. Browning directed Short to "at once proceed as vigorously as possible" to protect the department by collecting outstanding balances owed on Buck's bonds. As for Nicholson's suggestion to simply pay McWain and Miller, Browning tackled the detective's concerns directly in a subsequent letter. "I do not think the prestige of the province will suffer by the non-payment of this until Buck is on this side," wrote Browning, indicating that he considered the matter closed pending Nicholson's return to Edmonton. But Browning could not resist complaining about the rather "discourteous way" Wichita Police Chief Hays acted in turning the matter over to a private detective "when he well knew that Buck was doing business openly in that city. The whole matter seems to be a desire on the part of some one to make easy money."[92]

Indeed, Buck always seemed to attract attention seekers. On June 30, *The Wichita Eagle* alerted readers to a last-minute attempt by Reverend Guy L. Brown, pastor of Wichita's First Baptist Church, to save a temporary resident of Wichita in trouble with the law. Formerly a chaplain in Trenton, New Jersey, as well as chaplain for the New Jersey Senate when Governor Woodrow Wilson occupied the state house, Reverend Brown had moved a year earlier to Wichita, where his personal friendship with the now president of the United States enhanced his stature and leavened his sermons. According to

Brown, attorneys for the condemned man had convinced him of the man's innocence. Now the lawyers hoped to use Brown's influence to secure their client's release by prevailing on the president to issue a pardon. Despite ongoing international crises in Mexico and Europe that prevented him from seeing members of his own cabinet for weeks at a time, the president gladly made time for Reverend Brown. Before leaving for Washington, Brown held a press conference and declared to the press that "the mission is purely a business matter. It has no connection with Kansas or national politics."[93]

The pastor pointedly refused to name the person on whose behalf he would speak to the president, only saying that a prominent, but temporary, resident of Wichita "is in trouble." Given that the president's pardon power only applied to federal offences, the *Eagle* narrowed the list of potential subjects for Brown's mission of mercy to George Buck and two others—Professor Henry Samuels, a sixty-five-year-old patent medicine vendor, and George S. Badders, a former Topeka clothier who now sold cars in Wichita.[94] Both the paper and Brown, however, presented timelines and thinly veiled references to developments in Buck's case. Another tip-off came when the reporter asked Brown if the president was interested in oil. "He may be," answered Brown.[95] Brown travelled to Washington. DC, where, on July 5, accompanied by Congressman W.A. Ayers, Brown met with President Wilson for a couple of hours, talking about the details of the mystery man's case. According to the *Eagle*, President Wilson tread carefully, promising to do what he could but also explaining that he seldom interfered in such matters. The newspaper reported that Brown's intervention secured a temporary respite for the still unnamed prisoner until September 1, which just happened to be the date scheduled for Buck's appeal, when Brown believed the man would be set free.[96]

In the meantime, spurred along by the attorney general's office in Edmonton, Canadian officials grew increasingly concerned about the delay in processing and serving the warrant of surrender for Buck. On July 4, 1916, H.M. Cate, the deputy minister of justice, wrote to Thomas Mulvey suggesting that the state department should nudge the British ambassador. "Proceedings are being delayed awaiting the United States warrant," observed Cate. Perhaps the ambassador "should take such steps as may be proper to expedite the matter." Meanwhile, the prolonged and expensive stay in Kansas began to wear on Chief Detective Nicholson. Wiring A.E. Popple that Buck planned to appeal, Nicholson advised he would leave Kansas as soon as the order of surrender arrived. In the meantime, he asked Wall to write to Secretary of State Lansing to inquire about the status of the warrant of surrender and learned that Lansing had sent it to the British ambassador on July 5, but nothing had arrived in Wichita. In a separate letter to Popple, Nicholson confided that he intended to take Buck "the quickest way I can" the minute the order for surrender arrived. To "prevent any interference and overcome any resistance made by [the] prisoner," Nicholson planned to take Deputy US Marshal Sam Hill with him at least to the state border.[97]

Growing concerned about the financial costs and believing that Buck's appeal could delay delivery of the warrant of surrender, Nicholson contacted Browning on July 12 and offered to make a return trip in September. Fortunately for Nicholson, though, the Canadian Department of State issued instructions that day to forward the warrant of surrender directly to him. Finally, on July 17, the surrender order signed by Secretary of State Robert Lansing two weeks earlier arrived around two p.m. Based on a single charge of "fraud by a director and officer of a company," the US government returned George Edward Buck to Canadian authorities.[98] Rather than wait another forty-four days for Buck's appeal, which could have expanded the charges to include conspiracy, Nicholson decided to get his prisoner north of the border. The implications were significant. If Nicholson returned Buck based on the current surrender order, it only covered the fraud charge; waiting until September 1 for Buck's appeal hearing would enable the province to continue with all three charges, provided the appeal failed. Although Nicholson believed the province would prevail in Buck's final appeal, the lure of returning Buck at once proved overwhelming. *The Calgary Daily Herald's* editorial page gloated at Buck's imminent return. With tongue in cheek, the paper proclaimed, "Our esteemed fellow-townsman, George E. Buck, is returning after a pleasant holiday spent with his friend, the sheriff of Wichita, Kansas. Mr. Buck is leaving his touring car in Wichita and returns by train."[99]

The *Herald's* stringer in Kansas filed one more colourful story, making Buck's departure seem like an epic kidnapping. According to the reporter, Nicholson and Deputy US Marshal Sam Hill appeared at the jail minutes before their train's scheduled departure. However, Buck had befriended several prisoners, enlisting the support of six of the burliest men to help him resist transfer to Nicholson's custody by alleging a fantastic plot to kidnap him—the very story that Hugh Miller, Buck's business associate and bookkeeper, kept telling any reporter who would listen. Regardless, six prisoners vowed they would stand by him at all costs. When Nicholson and Hill entered the holding area, Buck stood in the centre of the cell, dressed only in his underwear, and surrounded by the other prisoners. Summoned by the undersheriff to come forward, Buck ignored the request and continued talking to his companions in hushed tones. Sensing trouble brewing, the undersheriff requested help from Sam Hill. At six feet tall and a powerfully built 200 pounds, Hill entered the cell and walked toward the protective ring of prisoners that formed around Buck. "Boys," he announced, "we are going to take Buck because the secretary of state has ordered it. If you don't want trouble, get out of the way."

Reports of the ensuing confrontation read like the script of a Hollywood blockbuster and almost seem too fantastical to believe. A big, strong harvest hand by the name of James P. Reavis stood between Buck and Hill. According to accounts in Wichita papers, Reavis's original arrest of drunk and disorderly three weeks earlier became a matter of life and death when Reavis slashed the arresting officer with a straight-edge razor four times across the back and arms before the wounded policeman subdued him. Apparently, the sight of the officer's slashed and bloodied coat was all the judge needed to deny Reavis bail pending trial. Having left one officer permanently disfigured, Reavis now intended to protect Buck from Hill come what may. Without warning, Hill's "right fist shot out with the suddenness and force of a cannon ball, knocking Reavis over on a bench some feet away and stunning him. He lay there where he fell and the courage of the other prisoners suddenly vanished. 'Put on those clothes, Buck,' said Hill, 'and quit stalling.'" When Buck muttered something under his breath, Hill moved toward him, bringing a yelp from Buck, who quickly dressed. With Buck finally in Nicholson's custody, Nicholson and Hill shoved him into a cab, where he continued to dress and "abused" the provincial policeman with "rough language." Back in Alberta, Nicholson heard the story as reported and categorically denied to the *Albertan* that any of the prisoners stood up for Buck before his departure, although Nicholson did confirm that Buck was in his underwear. The *Albertan* published an extensive account of Nicholson's pursuit of Buck across North America, and its editorial page lauded both the provincial government and Chief Detective Nicholson for their dogged determination to bring Buck to face justice.[100]

Buck's extradition left at least two people in Kansas disappointed. The McWain and Miller Detective Agency complained that Buck stiffed them $500 in back pay for the guards they employed to watch Buck as he tended to his affairs. To recoup some of their losses, the detectives tried to charge the Province of Alberta eight dollars a day for Buck's room and board, conveniently ignoring the obstacles and objections they had mounted along the way. Most of all, an increasingly bitter exchange between Wichita and Edmonton took place as McWain and Miller advanced their claim to the $1,000 reward from the attorney general's office.[101] The detectives eventually wrote a letter to the editor of the *Herald* claiming sole credit for the arrest of George Buck and complained that Deputy Attorney General Browning remained delinquent on promises to pay the $1,000 reward. "If they wanted to be just in the matter," wrote McWain and Miller, "they would pay this reward without writing us a lot of letters telling us that someone in Canada was claiming this reward and that we would have to take whatever the other parties did not want. I would like very much for you to see some of the letters he has written us in the matter." When reached by the *Herald* for comment by long distance telephone, Browning retorted, "And I wish you could see some of the letters they have written me. These letters are simply the last word in abusiveness." Less than a week later, McWain and Miller finally received their cheque for $1,000 from the Government of Alberta.[102]

Although little appreciated at the time, the fate of Buck's prized red McFarlan provided an apt coda for both the province and George Buck. Mere weeks following Buck's return to Calgary, the McFarlan's new owner got into a wreck on August 6, 1916, when it totalled a government vehicle, a US Post Office Ford Model T. "No one was hurt," reported *The Wichita Eagle*, "but the Ford sustained considerable damage. One wheel was smashed, and all the wheels lost their tires."[103] Buck's Kansas interlude resulted in long-lasting repercussions. At the very least, fleeing Canada left an overwhelming impression of guilt. At the same time, however, wrangling over the precise charges for Buck's extradition unwittingly forced the province to make choices the implications of which the prosecution did not immediately grasp. Extradition removed the possibility of charging Buck with conspiracy, by far the easiest crime to prove given the evidence prosecutors already collected. Far more ambiguous were the fraud charges that remained. Could the province repurpose its evidence to make a fraud case stick, or would Buck's stout defences cause the wheels to come off the province's case?

11

"A Matter of Public Concern:" The Lees Commission and Monarch Oil

> *As a Shareholder in the Monarch Oil Company, Limited, I want to inquire if the investigation into the acts, etc., of the Officers of this Company at the time of the Oil Boom here is completed. . . . When this is completed it will be easier for the Shareholders to see that Criminal Action is taken against the guilty parties (if Any) and that they receive their just punishment.*
>
> —Letter, George P. Ovans to
> Attorney General Charles W. Cross
> January 13, 1916[1]

> *The oil probe will be put to work again. Among the accomplishments of our townsman, George E. Buck, was to delay the oil probe for several months. In the meantime, the task of driving the probe home has increased very greatly.*
>
> —Editorial,
> *The Calgary Morning Albertan*
> July 25, 1916

As provincial officials wrestled with the international dimensions of securing George Buck's return from the United States, efforts to buttress provincial oversight of the emerging petroleum sector continued apace. The disappointing appellate court ruling that brought a swift end to the Carpenter Commission in October 1915 did not mean the end of public complaints to the attorney general's office, nor of attempts by the provincial government to oversee the petroleum sector. If anything, the ruling strengthened the resolve of the attorney general's office to hold lawbreakers responsible for the excesses of 1914. John D. Nicholson's dogged pursuit of George Buck to Wichita and back offers a particularly compelling example of the perseverance of Charles W. Cross's department. Another appeared early in 1916, when the province amended its orders-in-council, paving the way for the creation of a second oil commission with Judge William Andrew Dickson Lees replacing Judge Carpenter. Commencing its inquiries just as the struggle over Buck's extradition from Kansas reached its climax, the Lees Commission's investigation created other problems for Buck's prosecution as witnesses in the Monarch Oils case raised pointed questions about the reliability of newspaper statements during the 1914 boom.

Crucially, given the appellate court's decision that the original orders-in-council establishing the Carpenter Commission violated the rights of individuals, the provincial government amended the Public Inquiries Act in 1916, giving it far greater powers than it had before. More to the point, the province also moved a second piece of legislation, the first "blue sky" law to address the lack of oversight and transparency revealed by the Carpenter Commission's inquiry into 1914 boom (see Chapter 9). Despite this newfound provincial government assertiveness, the Lees Commission proved much less ambitious and successful than Carpenter's inquiry a year earlier. Some of this is because fewer companies and witnesses remained in Alberta for commissioners to investigate. Furthermore, with the return of prosperity due to rising grain prices and the stabilization of the economy following wartime mobilization, the desperate pursuit of lost funds of 1915 gave way to resignation by 1916. Indeed, a year before, with events still fresh in mind amidst economic misery, Albertans were keenly interested in finding out what happened. Carpenter's truncated investigation revealed enough unsavoury behaviour to enable some to reach their own conclusions about what took place, so the appetite for further inquiries was not nearly as voracious. With fewer witnesses and companies to draw on for material, the commission struggled to find a rhythm and abruptly ended its hearings after only a few weeks after it became impossible to find anyone to testify.

Nevertheless, the Lees Commission generated another legal challenge to the province's ability to regulate the oil industry when William A. Georgeson of Monarch Oil sued his former business partner, James Moodie, for slander for testifying that a sample of oil produced by the Monarch well was "faked." Moodie's defence team claimed the statements were delivered under oath by a witness compelled to appear before a judicial inquiry under subpoena, granting Moodie immunity. Like Buck in 1915, Georgeson claimed the orders-in-council creating the Lees Commission were ultra vires (outside the law), meaning the commission lacked the authority to subpoena witnesses and compel testimony from witnesses under oath. If the appellate court found the commission ultra vires, not only was Moodie liable for his statements, allowing Georgeson to sue him for $50,000 in damages, but the courts would again declare that the province lacked the power to oversee the petroleum industry's operations.

Although Buck and Georgeson had joined the search for oil at approximately the same time, differences in temperament, experience, and background distinguished the two. In fact, William A. Georgeson and Monarch Oils seemed the opposite of Buck and his company. Blessed with generous backers and deep pockets, Georgeson and Monarch Oils had every advantage that economies of scale and capital could provide: a geologist on staff to consult and select the company's first drill site, enough cash to drill a handful of wells, and a dominant position in the field around Olds in central Alberta that practically oozed success; expectations for Monarch were sky high. Where Buck craved the limelight, Georgeson shunned it, preferring to do his business with little fanfare. "There is a certain impersonality about the Monarch that made it peculiar among the major companies," wrote the *Albertan* in late 1914, "not a gulf dividing it from any of them, but a subtle, distinguishing difference."[2]

Their approaches to the oil business were radically different, yet both independently and on their separate paths arrived at the same place—where "salting" their wells to drive up stock prices was a rational alternative.[3] On the eve of a corporate restructuring that would see the company expand its capital from $200,000 to $5 million, the company's drillers buried news that they had struck a small seepage of crude oil until the window for original stockholders to expand their holdings closed. The next morning, the company announced the strike, sending its stock prices through the roof, making instant fortunes for those who had held on, or even expanded their holdings, during the transfer period. Company president Georgeson repeated the confident predictions of his chief geologist that the bit would pierce the main oil-bearing strata within the next 400 feet. Over the following weeks, though, the company wound up drilling an additional 3,000 feet and never struck oil. Even before the end of summer, rumours contended that the June 18 announcement was fake and an orchestrated move to drive up stock prices. A year later, officials with the Carpenter Commission prepared an investigation into Monarch left untested due to Buck's successful challenge of the commission's authority. At approximately the same time, Monarch Oil slid into receivership as the company went bankrupt by 1916. The two largest claimants on Monarch's assets when the company folded were International Supply Company, which claimed they were not paid $4,900 for their work, and geologist Bird W. Dunn, who claimed $4,800 in back wages.

Chartered by William Georgeson, Monarch Oils was not supposed to end in ignominious failure and disgrace. Born in Quebec City in 1859, Georgeson worked for Thompson-Codville, a wholesale grocer with operations in both Canada and the United States, and arrived in Calgary as manager of that concern in the early 1900s. By 1907, Georgeson bought out the business and relaunched it as Georgeson and Company, emerging as a pillar of the community, regularly dining with future prime minister Richard Bennett and other local luminaries at the "Bennett Table"—a separate table with a drawn curtain at the back of the dining room in the Alberta Hotel. His businesses touched on nearly every industry in the city, from wholesales of tea, coffee, and spices to selling coal through the Rosedale Coal and Clay Products Company. In 1912, Georgeson added oil and gas to his portfolio and formed a syndicate to pipe gas from Medicine Hat to Winnipeg, all the while servicing points along the line. Alberta's producers and provincial government both opposed the plan, fearing that exporting natural gas to other provinces would impede deliveries to Albertan communities, but Georgeson never fully gave up on the idea. An active member of the Conservative party, Georgeson earned a stellar reputation for public service and philanthropy as well as a desire to remain out of the spotlight. A brief list of his activities during 1913 alone reveals that Georgeson served on the Calgary School Board, spearheaded efforts to build an electric railway, led a program encouraging local consumers to "buy in Calgary," and served as president of the Imperial Home Reunion Association (formed to encourage immigration by families from England to Alberta).[4]

Georgeson founded the Monarch Oil syndicate following the October 1913 Dingman discovery and a bitter competition with Eugene Coste to secure the right to supply natural gas to Moose Jaw, Saskatchewan. During those negotiations, Coste flaunted his natural gas assets from Bow Island, Alberta, and taunted Georgeson with the fact that he lacked any source of supply. Within a matter of weeks, Georgeson sold off the wholesale grocer business to Minneapolis investors and launched Monarch Oil,[5] capitalized at $200,000, with the first tranche of 100,000 shares issued to investors with a par value of one dollar per share. Monarch Oil claimed a few well-heeled luminaries on its board of directors, including Winnipeg capitalist William Beach and O.S. Chapin, who also served on the board of directors for Dingman's Calgary Petroleum Products. Unlike the penny pinching at Black Diamond, Monarch Oil seemed determined to do things bigger and better than everyone else. For starters, the company's prospectus revealed that directors and other officers, except for the secretary, former City Councillor George W. Morfitt, would not draw a salary until the company struck oil. Georgeson made a further splash on November 28, 1913, acquiring 56,000 acres of leases (the equivalent of four townships) on the Red Deer River west of Olds in central Alberta. The move gambled that the oil field extended further north than previously thought. At the time, the $14,000 Monarch paid for the leases was the largest sum ever received in a single day by the Calgary land office. Georgeson then hired geologist Bird W. Dunn, formerly of Standard Oil, to oversee its operations. A graduate of the Michigan Mining School in Houghton, Michigan (the precursor to Michigan Technological University), Dunn could claim an impressive run of success—seventy-five consecutive producing wells without a dry hole—in addition to his experience in the Tampico fields of Mexico prior to arriving in Alberta.[6]

After surveying Monarch's holdings, Dunn selected a drill site west of Sundre for the location of Monarch's first well and believed so much in the field that he invested $4,900 of his own money in the company. In February, Monarch generated province-wide attention when it signed a contract with Phillips and Martin's International Supply Company to drill eleven wells on its properties. With a minimum expenditure of $150,000, the contract represented the greatest single attempt to develop the Alberta oil fields to date. When this was combined with Mowbray-Berkeley's announcement that they would install the machinery and plant to drill two wells on their properties, a bolt of excitement surged into Alberta's seemingly moribund search for oil that cold and grey winter of 1913/14. The *Herald's* editorial page believed that the resources committed to exploration by Monarch and the British-backed Mowbray-Berkley "should let us know whether or not we are on the oil map within a few months at the latest." The *Edmonton Journal* concurred, arguing that "these well-financed companies" proved that "plenty of money" remained available to finance promising developments. Drilling on the Monarch well began in early April and struck a flow of wet gas at 633 feet in sufficient quantities that it could now supply the boilers. The reports caused an increase in Monarch share prices on the curb from $3.00 to $8.50.[7]

Just over a week following the Dingman strike, on May 25, 1914, Dunn allegedly reported to Monarch's directors that the well now produced a heavy flow of wet gas and signs of crude oil, prompting the *Albertan* to pronounce the directors "jubilant." The paper even claimed the drilling contractors trooped from Olds to Calgary to buy Monarch shares. One director, company vice president Robert L. Shimmin, told the paper that an unnamed Vancouver syndicate made cash offers for a few sections held by Monarch but could not secure an acre. The directors, he assured the paper, remained confident in their position that the oil field reached central Alberta.[8] However, considering the future lawsuit filed by William Georgeson against another director, James F. Moodie, it is important to note there was a significant dispute about the provenance of this alleged report and references to it in Cheely's paper, *The Morning Albertan*. Georgeson later claimed as part of a libel suit against Moodie that "a report was made to the officers of the . . . Monarch Oil Company, Limited that oil had been discovered in the course of the said boring operations." Moodie, however, emphatically maintained that "no report worthy of reliance, was ever made" to the directors.[9]

The context and timing of the Monarch's alleged discovery is crucial and reveals some possible motivation for a false report. As the first spasm of excitement after the Dingman strike died down, by early June, several oil companies sought to stimulate investor interest in developing Calgary oil from outside Alberta because of a growing belief that local capital was exhausted (see Chapter 6.) On June 4, 1914, Monarch's directors moved to increase the company's capitalization by releasing the second tranche of 100,000 shares.[10] A public notice in all major Calgary papers indicated that original shareholders could exercise the first option on the new shares and that the company would, in effect, allow shareholders to buy on credit by allowing them to pay the balance owing over the coming weeks. In the meantime, the transfer books and register for members of Monarch Oil Company would close at six p.m. on June 15 until ten a.m. June 18 to enable all holders of the original stock to purchase additional shares in installments at a par value of one dollar. The release of the second set of shares pushed Monarch's share prices from between fifteen and seventeen dollars to a high around twenty-one dollars before June 18, prompting a sizable number of shareholders to sell. Then, on the afternoon of June 16, Dunn summoned company officials to the well site to inform them that he expected the well to strike oil sometime after midnight.

According to the account of the Monarch discovery published in the *Albertan* under Bill Cheely's byline on June 18, 1914, a few company officials, including Georgeson, vice president Robert Shimmin, secretary George Morfitt, and director William Beach, camped out at the well to be on hand when it struck oil. Almost as if on cue, at 3:45 a.m. on June 17 at a depth of 808 feet, the night shift driller reported finding traces of black oil in the well. Geologist Dunn took the first sample from the sluice box and said to the excited and eager men around him, "It is the real stuff. It is what the oil operators of Alberta have been looking for all these years. It is black petroleum."[11]

Cheely wrote that the assembled directors, drillers, and rig hands immediately recognized the significance of the moment. "In the presence of the fluid that has proven the northern field, [they] shook hands with each other in congratulations." Dunn also predicted there were three oil zones in the Monarch well and the bit had just pierced the one closest to the surface, with the remaining two at depths of approximately 1,000 and 1,200 feet. Dunn remained confident that even if this pocket did not contain large holdings of oil, drilling another 400 feet would certainly do the trick.[12] But Cheely then reported that Dunn noticed the well's gas pressure was too high, and feared it might produce a gusher that the company lacked the equipment and tools to handle. Out of an abundance of caution, Dunn ordered a halt to drilling operations until "a special appliance which will permit the drilling to be continued with the well capped" arrived.[13] Cheely conceded that "it may have to be made to order in the [International Supply] machine shop at Medicine Hat." With a ready-made explanation to account for why no oil would appear despite the driller's recent success, the rest of the article reassured even the most jaded of investors. Then Dunn said something that does not quite make sense. According to Cheely, Dunn told directors that Monarch had found a "considerable" body of oil and suggested to Georgeson that "shooting" the well with a 600-pound "shot" of nitroglycerine would likely be sufficient to "bring a gusher of sufficient strength to blow down the derrick" anytime they wanted.[14]

Oil well shooting began as a rudimentary form of enhanced oil recovery in 1864 when Civil War veteran Colonel E.A.L. Roberts exploded an iron tube (called a torpedo) filled with gunpowder and ignited by a weight dropped by a suspension wire onto percussion caps. In the oil fields of Pennsylvania, the resulting explosion usually improved the flow of oil from paraffin-clogged wells. By 1867, Roberts obtained exclusive rights from Alfred Nobel to replace gunpowder with nitroglycerine, a notoriously sensitive and violent substance, as the explosive of choice. Thirteen times more destructive than gunpowder and capable of blasting twenty-five times quicker, it proved an effective, if dangerous and inexact, method of enhanced oil recovery. No formal training existed for well shooting—it was an art rather than a science, requiring a great deal of courage (or maybe just a smidgen of insanity) to become a "nitro shooter" because the price of making a mistake with this volatile substance was often fatal. Because of the inexact nature of shooting, there was also the risk that the explosion might accidentally close off the formation, transforming a producing well into a duster. Nevertheless, the popularity of oil well shooting persisted mostly because of its ability to revive production from declining wells in limestone and sandstone formations.[15]

Given that Dunn ordered drilling stop on the well because it was supposedly on the verge of becoming uncontrollable until special equipment arrived, why would it be necessary to shoot the well with nitroglycerine? The Monarch well was not clogged with paraffin or asphaltene deposits. Dunn's suggestion to shoot the well is therefore either incredibly premature, ill-informed and reckless, or coldly calculated—an all-or-nothing shot, as it were, that would either produced a duster or a gusher.

With the transfer books closed for another thirty hours, later allegations suggested some directors used that time and insider knowledge to buy additional stock from shareholders who were unaware of the discovery. Several small containers with samples arrived in Monarch's offices in Calgary. One Monarch director, O.S. Chapin, later claimed he examined the samples in the afternoon of June 17, 1914, and began phoning Monarch shareholders urging them not to sell their stock and encouraging them to exercise their options to buy additional ones. Meanwhile, another strange event occurred when George Morfitt arranged to transfer, rather than sell, Monarch stock to the drillers.[16] Later, allegations emerged that some of Monarch's directors used their knowledge of an impending announcement to buy additional stock from other shareholders who were unaware of the supposed strike.

With the transfer books scheduled to open in less than twelve hours, the company issued a brief announcement to the press confirming the strike on the night of June 17. Cheely ran the full story on the morning of June 18, 1914, under the banner headline CRUDE OIL IS FOUND AT LAST, which came complete with self-congratulatory statements from a number of Monarch directors.[17] Georgeson underscored the significance of the strike for the province. "Our company is a modest concern and I do not care to say too much about our good luck, further than that a discovery has been made which is of vast importance to the petroleum industry of Alberta." Director O.S. Chapin echoed Georgeson's claim about the significance, arguing that the combination of the Dingman well's production of high-grade gasoline and black oil in the Monarch well to the north of Calgary all but proved "that this is the largest oil field in the world." Analysis of oil samples taken from the Monarch well, according to Chapin, revealed "a crude oil absolutely different from anything

Figure 11-1 "Charles Stalnaker pouring nitroglycerine down torpedo tube inside oil rig, possibly Montana, United States"
Shooting an oil well with nitroglycerine to fracture formations was a standard practice in the petroleum industry back to the nineteenth century. Charles Stalnaker (above) made a career out of shooting oil wells in Alberta and Saskatchewan, based from his home in Shelby, Montana. Unlike most of his contemporaries working with explosives in the oil patch, he lived into old age. (Glenbow Archive CU12117942)

that has been found so far in the oil fields of Alberta."[18] Furthermore, the paper claimed the field "has already been covered pretty well by some of the foremost geologists and oil experts in the world and they are practically unanimous in their opinion." Even the normally staid *Toronto Globe* reported that the Monarch discovery "is more convincing than even the remarkably fine product of the Dingman well." Meanwhile, in Spokane, the Monarch strike made the front page of the *Chronicle,* in part because Spokane investors held several thousand shares in Monarch but also because the paper speculated that "the entire Calgary region is underlaid with oil producing strata."[19]

That afternoon's edition of the *News Telegram* quoted Georgeson boldly claiming that the Monarch well had struck black oil. For good measure, an unattributed photo titled "A gusher caught in the act" accompanied the headline and story. Few who saw the front page could be blamed for believing the photograph was of the Monarch.[20]

In the aftermath of the announced discovery, share prices reached forty to fifty dollars a share among curb traders. The *Albertan* reported one financier presented his brokers with $20,000 in one hundred dollar bills to buy Monarch stock but could not find any available.[21] Some Monarch shareholders, like Calgary lawyer McKinley Cameron, decided to cash out at least some of their holdings. Not all trading took place in bucket shops or the exchanges. On June 22, Cameron arranged a private sale of ten shares for $500—a return of 49,900 percent in four days. By the terms of the sale, Cameron allowed the buyer to cancel their offer until June 27 without penalty. Thereafter the buyer had thirty days to meet the terms.[22]

Among those caught up in the buying frenzy was Monarch's fiscal agent, James Francis Melville "Frank" Moodie. Born in Chesterville, Ontario, in 1878, James F. Moodie came to Calgary in 1901 after graduating with a degree from the Massachusetts Institute of Technology, launching a jewellery/watch repair business. When that business stalled, he and his older brother, Kenneth Moodie, turned to ranching and, eventually, mining. As an avid outdoorsman, tramping through the backcountry of British Columbia and Alberta, Moodie became, by all accounts, a very good amateur geologist, with his insights leading to the discovery of a major coal deposit near Drumheller in 1911. As discoverer, developer, and part owner of the Rosedale Coal and Clay Products' mine (with the Canadian Northern Railway and William Georgeson as partners), Moody emerged as one of Calgary's leading capitalists and entrepreneurs. Indeed, Moodie, like so many others during the boom, had several overlapping business concerns with regular partners, few more important in the summer of 1914 than William Georgeson. Georgeson played an important role in the success of Rosedale Coal and Clay Products and Moodie, arranging for sales of coal through his retail businesses while Moodie reciprocated by serving as fiscal agent for Monarch Oil stocks.[23]

Moodie and Georgeson met regarding a different matter on June 18, but It did not take long before their conversation turned to Monarch's oil strike. Moodie asked to see a sample of Monarch's oil. Georgeson readily agreed to supply one, and the two men found themselves in front of George Morfitt at Monarch's offices, where the latter kept the samples under lock and key. Told by Georgeson that Moodie wanted to examine an oil sample, Morfitt reacted defensively, refusing at first, and vigorously objected to the request. The company, he claimed, did not have enough samples to give away to everyone who asked, even if Moodie was a director. Georgeson waved away Morfitt's objections, saying, "We can let Frank have a sample." Three small oval-shaped bottles containing samples sat in the office, so Moodie helped himself to one and brought it back to his office, where it sat in his desk, unexamined, for about a year.[24]

In the meantime, the noise and fury around Monarch continued. Cheely attempted to add Dunn to the Alberta oil patch's growing pantheon of heroes, hailing Dunn as the "petroleum genius who created a new oil district in the north." After inspecting an oil sample from the well, Dunn told Cheely, "If this well is not a producer, a flowing well, with a little more development, either by drilling or by shooting the well, there is nothing in geological indications by which men experienced in such matters judge these things." The geologist reiterated his belief that the Monarch field around Olds contained three pay zones before emphasizing his main point: Alberta had crude oil. "This will have a greater effect on outside capital than anything else that could occur. It means that oil men all over the world will have sufficient confidence in the future of the petroleum industry of Alberta to put their millions into it for the necessary development. It has demonstrated beyond the slightest doubt that there exists in this section a definite, well-defined zone of crude petroleum." To the *News Telegram*, Dunn estimated the Olds district field at ten miles long and four miles wide and believed Monarch could "drill at least twelve wells" on the level ground around the Monarch well.[25]

The company adopted strict measures to limit access of the press and public to the well site, posting a sentry to protect the property. In fact, the *News Telegram* maintained no one could be within 100 yards of the well; Dunn informed the press that these orders would remain until the company could "show the public the oil flowing out of the well in commercial quantities." Drilling at Monarch resumed on June 23, 1914, with the company president, Georgeson, one of the directors, and Treasurer George Morfitt at the camp outside of Olds. "The road from Olds to the camp consists of alternate stretches of corduroy and muskeg," noted the *Albertan*, "and it is a journey that is many degrees short of a joy ride." Yet the VIP's made the trip, at least in part because of the belief that "the next few days will be productive of most important disclosures."[26] The *Albertan* published an unverified report on June 24, 1914, that the Monarch well had struck a flow of oil at a rate of 300–500 barrels per day. Although he made no secret of his continuing attempts to urge Georgeson and the directors to shoot the well with nitroglycerine, Dunn confidently predicted to reporters that he expected "a strike at any moment." The bit made rapid progress, drilling 470 feet in less than a week, passing both the 1,000- and 1,200-foot markers without so much as a trickle of oil, let alone a gusher.[27]

As more time passed and the depth of the well plunged deeper without a crude strike, the bloom came off Monarch and Dunn's golden reputation. The bit having passed Dunn's two predicted depths (1,000 and 1,200 feet) without encountering oil in paying quantities raised suspicions about the legitimacy of the Monarch strike, and by early July share prices softened substantially, tumbling from twenty dollars on July 1 to six dollars by July 10. This, in turn, forced Dunn into a defensive crouch. "Every time the bailer goes past the zone where we struck oil the first time," Dunn reminded reporters, "it comes up with its sides dripping with oil." At a board of directors meeting on July 3, Dunn recommended that the directors return to 800 feet and shoot the well with nitroglycerine.[28] However, the same risk remained. While it might transform the well into a gusher by fracturing the formation and liberating more oil, it might just as easily seal up the seepage and turn the well into a duster. "From the best advice that we are able to obtain," commented *The Natural Gas and Oil Record*, "the shooting proposition was a bad one."[29]

Supposedly, Georgeson and the directors overruled Dunn and insisted that drilling continue to 1,500 feet. After all, the contract with the driller obliged them to pay for a hole 1,500 feet deep anyway. If the worst came to pass, they could always backtrack and follow Dunn's suggestion to "shoot" the well at 808 feet if need be. As the well hit 1,470 feet, Dunn reported encountering a sandstone formation. "With the present conditions as developed in the hole," wrote Dunn in a supposedly secret report to Georgeson that almost immediately leaked to the *Herald*, "I am most certain that we have a producing well either by shooting or by drilling."[30]

However, at the same time, Monarch's board of directors approved a second recapitalization plan for the company. If it was approved by most existing shareholders, the company would reissue stock at a ratio of twenty-four to one—twenty-four shares in the new company for every share in the old company. The sale of existing holdings—approximately one-third, 200,000 acres of Monarch's leaseholds—would finance the capitalization. *The Toronto Daily Star* reported that shareholders pushed the board of directors to increase the company's capitalization from $200,000 to $5 million because of complaints that the high price of Monarch shares precluded speculation by the average investor. Small buyers, insisted shareholders, should have a chance to deal in the stock. Cumulatively, the board claimed the moves projected confidence that oil in the Olds district existed in commercial quantities.[31]

However, *The Natural Gas and Oil Record* considered Monarch's recent statements and actions puzzling. Why had directors approved plans to keep drilling when Dunn claimed the well could bring in crude oil "any time" by shooting it with nitroglycerine? Furthermore, why did directors approve a second plan to recapitalize so soon after the first? "We cannot quite understand this move," concluded the *Record*, "because the insiders held most of the stock and if they had a big thing it would make no difference to them what the capital stock was." Monarch could make money one of two ways—"by having big oil deposits" or by selling $5 million worth of shares. The *Record* stopped just short of accusing Monarch's directors of manipulating the market but made their doubts about the veracity of Dunn's statements plain. "Mr. Dunn does not claim to be a geologist, but he does claim to be an engineer. We understand that his work around Calgary heretofore was a position as checker in the Riverside Lumber Yards."[32] As the *Record* reported on the front page of its next issue, the remarks brought a terse response from Monarch's solicitor objecting to the tone and none-too-subtle direction of the article. However, J. Tucker, the editor of the *Record,* feigned surprise. "We cannot imagine just how he arrives at these conclusions unless it enters his mind that Monarch officials would do all that he states we intimate they might do." Tucker then took the offensive, asking the solicitor about his client's own statements on June 17 about an oil strike. "The best advice that he can give his clients is for them to show a few spoonfuls of oil."[33]

Just as suddenly as the second plan to recapitalize the company appeared, the directors shelved it in the aftermath of the attention drawn to it by *The Natural Gas and Oil Record*.[34] To be sure, the market shifted and Monarch's stock price already sat well below the fifty dollar a share level reported as the justification for the recapitalization effort in the *Star's* story. Perhaps more alarmingly, evidence abounded that no one wanted to buy Monarch. Just sixteen days after arranging a private sale for $500 for ten shares, McKinley Cameron wrote the buyer of his shares and offered to cancel the deal. When the sale closed, the well was at 800 feet and Georgeson and Dunn confidently predicted an oil strike by 1,200 feet at the latest. But on July 13, the well reached 1,510 feet with no sign of oil. "I think it would be extremely foolish for you to pay the five hundred dollars for these shares when they are selling on the open market at ten dollars per share," wrote Cameron, "and it is quite possible they may go down still lower."[35]

By the end of July, International Supply Company drillers continued to push the Monarch well deeper. On August 1, 1914, Georgeson provided a terse reply to a reporter's question about conditions at the well upon his return from Olds. All signs seemed favourable, maintained Georgeson. The drill reached 2,250 feet and continued to make satisfactory progress. The flow of wet gas remained strong but, apart from small seepages, the well remained "all prospects, no oil."[36] By the time of the annual shareholders meeting on September 3, 1914, Monarch had the deepest well in Alberta at 3,147 feet, a heavy flow of wet gas, but still no commercial supply of oil. To the shareholders, Dunn reported that the petroleum shows grew stronger as the well drilled further down. Indeed, the strongest show of petroleum occurred between 1,775 and 1,832 feet, and Dunn again urged the company to "shoot" the well. "It is my opinion that if any of these three zones be 'shot,' oil in commercial quantities—from one hundred barrels per day and up—can be obtained."[37] Despite continued drilling, however, much like Calgary Petroleum Products #1, the Monarch produced wet gas and condensates but scant traces of oil. Soon the company began falling into arrears with its creditors as well as the drillers, but Georgeson insisted that the well keep drilling as stock prices continued to fall well below fifty cents per share. Monarch Oil eventually declared bankruptcy in 1916.

As the province ramped up its investigations into the oil companies in anticipation of the appointment of the Carpenter Commission in the summer of 1915, Monarch was a conspicuous target because of the spike in share prices and the fact that subsequent events did not corroborate the seemingly definitive reports of an earlier oil strike in the *Albertan* on June 23, 1914. As provincial investigators gathered information about Monarch, rumours spread that a detective investigating the company's activities learned that James F. Moodie suspected that something underhanded had taken place at Monarch. It fell to provincial attorney Gregory Trainor to follow up with an interview of James Moodie in June 1915 about events of the previous year. During the interview, Moodie allegedly said, "William Georgeson, president of the Monarch Oil Company, limited, gave me what he represented to be a sample of oil taken from the well. I had this sample analyzed and I was told by the analyst that the sample was 'faked.'"[38]

Moodie later claimed he only entertained doubts regarding the authenticity of the sample once—in April 1915, when he saw a second sample from the well, long after more drilling had pushed the well "quite a little further" down. To quell his suspicions, Moodie took the sample to Calgary chemist Edward G. Voss for analysis. Voss reported back to Moodie that the sample consisted mostly of mud and water with a strong smell and was "not a natural product" but rather more closely resembled refined crude. Based on that report, Moodie later told prosecutors he believed that the "mixture had been prepared, faked." In the meantime, however, Moodie remained uncertain about how to proceed. Moodie sat on Voss's report and claimed he did not tell anyone, least of all William Georgeson, of the results until his interview with Trainor.[39]

Thus, largely because of Moodie's statement, Monarch became one of the initial eight companies targeted by the Carpenter Commission for further investigation. But company officials did not appear before Judge Carpenter prior to the injunction shutting the commission down. Even as commission staff wound up their inquiries, they clearly expected that another commission would soon resume their efforts. Indeed, even before the injunction became permanent, attorney Frank Ford wrote one investor that "the inquiry cannot go on until after the next session of the legislature when it is probable an amendment will be passed to permit a further commission being issued."[40]

If the courts expected average Albertans to be pleased with their ruling in favour of individual rights, they were sadly mistaken. As the provincial legislature prepared for a new session in March 1916, the *News Telegram* reported rumours that the oil investigations would continue once legislative reforms passed. But the editorial went a step further to argue for a more proactive stance by government—essentially arguing in favour of even more power to the government to dissuade wrongdoers. "It was a favorite saying of Robert Ingersoll that everything in this world has progressed but the law. Truly, that is the case if one were to judge by the laws affecting corporations and their almost all-powerful directorates, who often 'skin' the widow and the orphan of their hard-earned savings. Why not have laws to prohibit as well as laws to punish?"[41] Meanwhile, J.M. Murdoch of Stettler, Alberta, wrote to the attorney general's office about the status of the investigation. "A movement was on foot about a year ago to prosecute the directors of this Company and that is the last I have heard or can hear of the matter. Most of the funds have been fooled away by Criminal mismanagement. What is your department doing in the matter?"[42]

As public questions mounted about the state of investigations in late March 1916, Deputy Attorney General Arthur G. Browning wrote Frank Ford asking about the status of the province's oil inquiry. Ford explained that the appellate court ruling "held that there was no authority under the statute as it stands" for the commissioner to exercise the powers granted by the orders-in-council, resulting in the injunction becoming permanent. Ford then relayed that in his conversations with Attorney General Charles Cross, "instructions have been given to make provision by an amendment either to the Companies Ordinance or in some other way to permit a commission" with the same terms issued to Judge Carpenter. "I have reason to believe," reported Ford, "that Mr. Fenwick has the matter in hand now." Ford therefore advised Browning that if he felt "certain that the amendment will be introduced and passed and that a new commission will subsequently issue, I would suggest that you write your correspondents telling them of the position of the matter." Ford then alluded to the importance of the province resuming the commission as soon as possible. This would be the only explanation most investors would ever receive of what happened to their money, and the only time most promoters would have to account for their actions. Certainly, individual investors could launch civil actions to recover their investment, but as Ford pointed out, "very few" oil companies still existed let alone had "anything to make it worth while bringing actions against."[43]

Rather than the Companies Ordinance, the necessary changes were incorporated into the Public Inquiries Act. The Appellate Division's ruling in *Black Diamond v. Carpenter* declared that the commission had exceeded the limits of the legislation by designating Black Diamond's private concerns a public matter. Amendments to the Public Inquiries Act conferred on the Lieutenant-Governor the power to appoint an inquiry "when ever he deems it expedient and in the public interest." Inquiries could "be made into and concerning any matter within the jurisdiction of the Legislative Assembly either connected with the good government of the province or the conduct of the public business thereof, *or which he shall by his commission declare to be a matter of public concern*," and to "appoint a commissioner or commissioners to make such inquiry and to report thereon."[44]

On June 8, 1916, the *Herald* broke the news that the government would resume investigating the oil companies. "At the last session of the legislature the provincial statutes were so amended that the powers of the commission were broadened sufficiently and now investigation can proceed more satisfactorily to the government."[45] Finally, on July 15, 1916, the Lieutenant-Governor approved the orders-in-council appointing Judge Lees commissioner of a new inquiry "into and concerning the promotion, incorporation, management and operation of the various companies incorporated under the authority of the Companies Ordinance." Similar to the Carpenter Commission, the orders-in-council declared the issue "*a matter of public concern*" and claimed powers authorized under Chapter 2 of the Statutes of Alberta (1908) granting the commissioner "the power of summoning witnesses before him and or requiring such witnesses to give evidence on oath, orally or in writing ... and to produce such documents and things as the said William A.D. Lees may deem requisite to the full investigation." Lees also had the power "to enforce the attendance of witnesses, and to compel them to give evidence, as is vested in any court of record in civil cases."[46]

However, the prospect of another investigation did not fire Albertans' imaginations the way it used to. "Interest in the majority of these companies has considerably subsided," wrote the News Telegram. It is doubtful if there will now be developments of a very sensational nature."[47] On August 4, 1916, Trainor announced to the Herald that Judge Lees would oversee investigations of perhaps as many as a half dozen companies, vastly different from the Carpenter Commission's more ambitious agenda. The paper noted that the attorney general encountered "considerable difficulty" in gathering evidence because so many witnesses had left the province, either as part of the armed forces (as in the case of Monarch's George W. Morfitt, now serving overseas as Lieutenant-Colonel George Morfitt of the 137th Calgary Infantry Battalion), or simply moving on to other professions.[48]

In the meantime, the Sifton government moved to formalize and institutionalize its oversight role by creating a permanent home in the bureaucracy, completing the task begun with the creation of the Public Utilities Commission a year earlier by promulgating the first "blue sky" law, or transparency laws, for the province. Proposed by former Attorney General and current Provincial Treasurer C.R. Mitchell, the "Act to Regulate the Sale of Shares, Bonds and Other Securities of Companies," better known as the Sale of Shares Act, established the right of the government to regulate securities transactions and protect consumers. The Act drew its inspiration from "blue-sky" laws first established in Kansas in 1911 that targeted so-called "blue-sky merchants" who sold securities backed by nothing more than the "blue skies of Kansas." Similar legislation migrated north to Manitoba in 1912 and Saskatchewan in 1914. Alberta's bill simultaneously addressed several issues identified by the Carpenter inquiry and various court cases filed in connection to the 1914 boom, such as the responsibility of advertisers and the press to ensure accurate information, the licensing of stockbrokers, consumer protection, and reserving a regulatory role for the state.[49]

The Sale of Shares Act explicitly carved out a new bailiwick for the Public Utilities Board by extending its mandate to oversee the sale of municipal bonds to include "a mandate to detect and prevent stock market abuses" by vetting the sale of all stocks, shares, bonds, and securities within the province and carefully regulating who could sell what to whom and when.[50] Henceforth, individuals could not act as sales agents on their own behalf or that of a company. To eliminate the unregulated curb or bucket brokers believed responsible for much of the rampant speculation in 1914, the Act dictated that only licensed brokers could sell shares, stocks, bonds, or other securities directly or indirectly. Furthermore, the express permission of the Board of Public Utility Commissioners was necessary before businesses could sell securities. The Act also made it illegal for newspapers or publishers to print any advertisement for the sale of securities without first obtaining proof that the company had received authorization for sales from the Public Utility Commission. Legislation also compelled all companies selling securities to file copies of all contracts, bonds, or securities and to file a statement showing the name and location of the company, and an itemized accounting of the company's financial condition, including its properties and liabilities as well as "other information touching its affairs as the Board of Public Utility Commissioners may require." If the company did not incorporate in the province or maintained its headquarters elsewhere, the board required companies to file copies of the laws of incorporation, its corporate charter, articles of incorporation, constitution, and current bylaws. Furthermore, the province insisted that the filing include the company's written consent "irrevocable, that [legal] actions may be commenced against it" in provincial court.[51]

The Sale of Shares Act passed with barely a second glance by most Alberta newspapers despite the low-standing reputation of Alberta's oil industry in the spring of 1916. In Butte, Montana, just to the south of Alberta, a grand jury investigation of that state's "blue sky" laws declared them defective because they did not seem to discourage "sidewalk operators" from Calgary. The final report of the investigation contained several unflattering references to Alberta oil companies. "Much of the worthless stuff peddled around the county consists of Canadian oil and coal land stocks and bonds. Canada apparently has no blue-sky law, and during the past few years has turned out a tremendous amount of fake stocks and bonds."[52]

While it was one thing for a Montana grand jury to remain ill-informed about the state of Alberta's regulator legislation, it is stunning to note that the pro-Liberal *Albertan* seemed oblivious to its passage as well. Months after the Sale of Shares Act passed, the *Albertan* published an editorial on August 25, 1916, complaining that the "resources of the province are lying dormant because of lack of capital. Wildcat enterprises vigorously but improperly exploited, have made capital suspicious." Thus, the paper proposed that the provincial government should "investigate and report on any propositions for development that may be offered." Government's findings would carry "more weight with the public, with the big money, or with any other organization than the finding of a private company." The *Albertan* acknowledged that this was far more progressive and/or intrusive than anything the paper had advocated before, "but conditions are changed now, and many a program which was regarded as red radicalism a few months ago must be regarded as sane and reasonable at the present time."[53] One letter to the editor of the *Herald* pointed out that the rival paper's proposals were completely in line with the Sale of Shares Act passed by the legislature during the previous session but noted that its oversight by the morning paper "is not at all surprising, for the matter has not received the publicity that it deserved."[54]

If the *Albertan* did not register the effects of the Sale of Shares Act, the Public Utilities Commission immediately noticed the changes wrought on its workload. "This Act renders it necessary for all companies selling, or offering for sale, their shares within the province, to obtain the permission of the Board before so doing," noted the board's first annual report in 1916. The board also embraced educating both the public and private sectors about best practices as part of its official functions. While the board believed the Sale of Shares Act did not authorize "giving publicity" to companies denied certification, they published eight failed applications from a variety of industries—three in mining, two in finance, and one each in ranching, real estate, and manufacturing—illustrating the reasons for rejection.[55] The annual report filed by the agency after 1916 observed that "administration of the Sale of Shares Act has increasingly occupied the attention of the Board." During its first full year of enforcement, the Public Utilities Commission estimated the Act prevented the sale of $3.5 million worth of questionable securities to the public, either because the commission denied companies a certificate or because the board specified the terms promoters failed to meet. With some self-satisfaction, the board concluded its actions "prevented the offer to the public of much stock in companies, doomed from the very outset to failure, there can be no doubt."[56]

Building on the successful passage of legislation formalizing an oversight role, the start of hearings before the Lees Commission seemingly affirmed the government's regulatory prerogatives. Although a couple of other companies received scrutiny from investigators in public hearings, the Monarch hearings were arguably the most important and consequential because of the level of detail extracted by the commission, and especially because of Georgeson's subsequent challenge to the legal basis of the commission. At bottom, Lees Commission investigators believed a plot at Monarch Oils unfolded differently from Buck's Black Diamond scheme though both sought the same outcome—to defraud investors and driving up share prices after false claims of an oil strike. Whereas testimony before the Carpenter Commission produced a smoking gun, with Fletcher's testimony directly implicating Buck in the plot to salt the well, the Lees Commission's working hypothesis—that Monarch's board of directors knowingly issued false statements on June 18, 1914, to drive up share prices—remained, at best, ambiguous and unproven.

Monarch's time before the Lees Commission began on the morning of August 22, 1916, and featured testimony by company president William Georgeson and Director O.S. Chapin. Both men denied that the directors launched an organized attempt to boost stock prices with a false report of an oil strike. Georgeson stated he genuinely believed the well had struck oil and maintained "every confidence in the ability and integrity of geologist Dunn." Georgeson explained that Dunn's statements to him served as the basis of his statements to the press. Under questioning by his own solicitor, H.E. Forrester, Georgeson emphatically stated that he did not sell any of his shares between June 18 and June 20, 1914, and that "I made the statements on the information of Geologist Dunn, and protected myself by quoting him." After all, Dunn's predictions about the formation beneath the Monarch well proved uncannily accurate; so too did his predictions to Georgeson about the Dingman and McDougall-Segur wells.[57]

The next witness, stockbroker John Ballintyne, testified that he broke larger blocks of Monarch shares into smaller increments following the supposed strike. This enabled him to sell the shares under his name rather than that of the original stockholder. Ballintyne denied selling any stock for Monarch's directors when questioned directly but revealed under cross-examination that George Morfitt transferred some shares to the drillers at their request. Although newspapers refrained from speculating on the reasons for the transfer, considering the suspicion that the well was salted, transferring shares to people who knew what was going on at the well appears less benign and more like an attempt to contain a potential problem. The biggest sparks of the day came when O.S. Chapin took the stand and revealed he did not trust geologist Dunn after visiting the well in the spring of 1915. "We were reading accounts in the paper of big strikes in gas then," recalled Chapin. Prodded further by Trainor, Chapin said there were signs of both oil and gas at the well. Trainor then segued to the status of Chapin's holdings of Monarch stock. As one of the original backers of Monarch, Chapin received 500 shares from the company for his efforts to secure financing, as well as a seat on the board of directors. Then the probe turned to Cheely's article in the *Albertan* on June 18, which quoted Chapin as declaring Alberta's oil field the biggest in the world. Chapin denied speaking to the paper but added he believed the statement nonetheless. Regardless, Chapin then argued that Cheely made the statements up himself and was too hurried to wait to speak to Georgeson. The answer did not satisfy George Trainor, who then asked why Chapin did not contradict them if they were false. "I did not think it worth while," responded Chapin, prompting Judge Lees to restate the question, eliciting the same answer from the witness. Prosecutor Frank Ford pointed out that Chapin also gave interviews to the afternoon papers on the 18th and confirmed the oil strike for them. "I don't remember," said Chapin. "I was called up three or four times a day by the papers at that time and cannot remember what I said to all of them." Essentially, Chapin argued he might have spoken to some papers, or he might not have. Regardless, his name kept appearing in the paper for the next week attributing some remark or another to him even though he gave no further interviews. While Chapin stood his ground in asserting that he did not recall making any specific statements to the press, he did admit to doubling his holdings to 1,000 shares and recalled seeing an oil sample in Morfitt's office on June 17, 1914. Trainor then asked if there was an effort to boost Monarch stock prices by the directors making "fake purchases." Chapin's response—"not to my knowledge"—seemed evasive.[58]

To a large degree, Georgeson and Chapin succeeded in stonewalling the inquiry and shifting blame for the false reports onto William Cheely, whom they rationally calculated would not appear before the commission. Not all directors, however, were willing to cover things up. George P. Adams's testimony raised doubts about the reliability of Dunn and Morfitt. Adams described visiting the well as early press reports indicated a heavy flow of gas had appeared at the well. Once there, Adams testified, he saw no evidence of a gas strike and said so to George Morfitt. Morfitt allegedly told Adams to stay quiet and say nothing about it.[59] Summarizing the first day of testimony, the *Vancouver Daily World* declared "a state of affairs nothing short of rotten has been shown to exist" in the affairs of Monarch Oil. "The directors and president of the Monarch Oil Company ... allowed a report to be published in the press which they deny being responsible for but did not take the trouble to have the correction issued."[60]

The commission recalled both Georgeson and Chapin on August 23, 1916, to clarify and expand on their previous testimony. Frank Ford challenged Georgeson's assertions that responsibility for false reports lay with the *Albertan*. If he knew the statements about an oil strike were false, why did he allow them to stand? "I was not paying much attention to the paper then," replied Georgeson. Besides which, Georgeson claimed, the newspapers "were boosting things to make money for themselves." Presumably, he meant that the newspapers' sensational approach to the oil boom drove circulation numbers, but perhaps he was referring to Cheely's sudden financial windfall because of his investments. Georgeson then denied meeting William Cheely or giving an interview at all on the night of June 17, 1914, challenging the authenticity of Cheely's extensive article published on the morning of June 18, 1914. The Monarch president claimed he was at the well site and unavailable to the press for comment, apart from the statement issued to the press by Morfitt over his signature. Ford was unconvinced by the explanation. Surely Georgeson could have corrected the paper upon his return to Calgary? Georgeson responded that "I did not think it necessary." Georgeson's solicitor, H.E. Forester, asked if Georgeson had any reason to believe that the oil strike did not occur. The Monarch president declared he did not; he had faith in Dunn's abilities. Follow-up questions concerning the statements issued in his name on June 18 elicited from Georgeson that they represented a good faith effort to keep the public informed, not to deceive investors. Judge Lees inquired about the transfer of stock to the drillers by George Morfitt. "Did I understand you to say that the drillers had asked Mr. Morfitt to purchase stock for them?" When Georgeson affirmed they had, Lees wondered if Morfitt had "any obligation" to the drillers, at least hinting that they might have been paid to stay silent. Georgeson replied Morfitt did not, explaining that the drillers "were enthusiastic about prospects, and were not able to get in from the well to buy it." Besides which, answered Georgeson, International Supply Company provided the drillers, and that company was unaffiliated with Monarch Oil. When Chapin returned to the stand, his solicitor J.E.A. MacLeod returned to the alleged interview given by Chapin to Cheely. Chapin now remembered it would have been impossible for him to speak to Cheely because he had left Calgary for Columbus, Ohio, on or about June 18 and even saw a baseball game in Chicago. Frank Ford asked if Chapin saw Georgeson before departing, but Chapin could not recall any particular conversation with him, bringing that portion of the inquiry to an end for the day.[61]

Tangible differences already distinguished the Carpenter and Lees commissions, particularly with relation to the way witnesses behaved before the inquiry. For the Monarch case, the Lees Commission called witnesses, some of whom (like Chapin) arrived late, if at all. Oscar Chapin, wrote the *News Telegram*, "did not appear for a time," while four others called—Andrew Rutherford, Joseph Kerby, Archie Fowler, and B. Martin—failed to respond to the commission at all. Another witness and company director, R.L. Shimmin, claimed an illness prevented him from testifying and received a leave from the Judge to appear later, although the Lees Commission shut down before he could appear.[62]

If the responses of witnesses differed from those in the Carpenter Commission, the attitude of the *Albertan* remained consistent. Much as it had with the Carpenter Commission the year before, the *Albertan's* editorial page downplayed the significance of the testimony, again referring to collective responsibility for the intense emotions of the boom and absolving everyone else in the process. Now, with Cheely's journalistic integrity called into question by two separate witnesses, both of whom alleged that the former *Albertan* reporter had made up entire portions of his stories, it must have raised uncomfortable questions for the *Albertan's* publisher, William Davidson, as to whether the *Albertan* had become part of the story itself. These revelations must also have stirred some unease in the attorney-general's office, where Cheely loomed as a crucial witness in the department's case against George E. Buck. If Cheely "made up" quotations for his stories about Monarch Oil, did he do the same in his stories about Black Diamond? (See Chapter 12.) On the morning of August 24, the *Albertan* sniffed that "the stories told by witnesses at the oil probe investigation bring back memories of an intense, overheated mad month or more a couple of years ago, when one entire city and the people beyond lost their senses for the time being. They have had a long time to think it all over since then."[63] Meanwhile, the *Edmonton Bulletin* concluded that "the fundamental idea in this oil company probe is to find out why the stock market gushed so much more than the wells."[64]

After Georgeson and Chapin's testimony, the inquiry briefly turned to the affairs of Rocky Mountain Oil Fields before resuming the Monarch investigation with the testimony of James F. Moodie on August 24. Moodie was a reluctant witness. After receiving a letter from Gregory Trainor seeking information about his acquisition of the oil sample, Moodie appeared at Trainor's office on the afternoon of August 23. Trainor asked Moodie to testify about how he secured a sample of oil from the Monarch well, leading up to his decision to have the sample analyzed and the results of the chemical analysis that concluded it was not a "natural product." Moodie refused, claiming what happened at Monarch Oil had nothing to do with him. Part of Moodie's reluctance stemmed from the fact that he and Georgeson had since had a falling out. While he insisted there was no ill will between the two of them, Moodie said he would prefer to go his own separate way. Notwithstanding Moodie's reluctance, Trainor replied that if he did not testify willingly, the commission would issue a summons compelling his appearance.[65]

Moodie's testimony before the commission on August 24 began with Trainor walking Moodie through his association with Monarch Oil. Trainor asked if Moodie met with Georgeson in the spring of 1914 and obtained a "bottle of oil" from the Monarch well. Moodie confirmed he had, explaining as well that the sample remained in his desk for "some time" before he took it to Edward Voss for analysis. According to Moodie, Voss's analysis concluded the sample was not crude oil at all; rather, it was refined product. Based on that information, Moodie stated the sample from the Monarch well was "faked."[66] Trainor inquired about subsequent samples brought back to Calgary from further down the hole. What opinion did Moodie have of these? "It was not a natural product in my opinion," stated Moodie. "I tried to get a sample and couldn't get it." Judge Lees evidently misheard Moodie's testimony and asked him to clarify where he obtained the second sample from and Moodie reiterated he did not secure a second sample, leading to the following exchange:

> A: I am satisfied in my own mind that the oil I saw the second time was not a natural proposition; I have Voss' analysis of this [first sample]; he had not much to work on as he says but I know of no reasons why that should be necessary.
>
> Q: Does Mr. Voss suggest in his report to you that that is a fake proposition?
>
> A: He made the statement to me verbally that it was.
>
> Q: He did?
>
> A: Yes. . . .
>
> Q: Have you any reason to believe yourself, with your own knowledge of oil, that that [second sample] was a fake mixture of oil?
>
> A: I have.[67]

During the cross-examination, Georgeson's lawyer, H.E. Forrester, zeroed in on Moodie's motives, claiming that the only reason Moodie raised the issue was to strike back at Georgeson for the failure of their business arrangement, producing what the *Albertan* called "a lively interchange of repartee." Moodie admitted that he bought some Monarch stock following the strike and Forrester suggested that he had been influenced to do so by the oil sample. "No, that was not the reason," Moodie snapped back. "I just bought the stock to call one of Georgeson's bluffs." Exactly what bluff Moodie called remained unexplained.[68] Forrester then changed tack and asked Moodie if he had any training as a geologist. Forrester's greater point was that Moodie lacked the scientific background and training to determine on his own if the Monarch sample was crude oil or not. When Judge Lees suggested that Moodie could express his opinion about the depth of the Dakota sands at the Monarch well, Moodie replied somewhere between 4,000 and 5,000 feet. Forrester jumped up to his feet to challenge Moodie's assertion by pointing out he was not a geologist. Georgeson's solicitor then asked, "Would you know the Dakota sands if you saw them?" Moodie replied firmly, "Yes, I would," before taunting, "Bring them here and I will point them out to you."[69]

After Moodie's testimony, Chapin phoned his erstwhile partner and asked if he could come by for a chat. At the appointed hour, Moodie arrived at Chapin's office. Chapin wondered why Moodie had testified before the commission and Moodie replied that he had not wanted to, but Trainor's subpoena compelled him to do so. Chapin told Moodie that "he had been badly misled by men that he considered friends." While Chapin sold off most of his holdings in Monarch, he still held some shares. The conversation then turned to Georgeson, with Moodie telling Chapin he "thought the old man was unbalanced." Moodie's concern stemmed from a series of statements made by Georgeson on matters unrelated to Monarch Oil (the bankruptcy of Rosedale Coal and Clay as well as a pending lawsuit against Georgeson and Moodie).[70]

After granting a continuance to give Trainor time to find witnesses, the investigation resumed on August 29 with O.S. Chapin recalled a second time to clarify his earlier testimony. Previously, Chapin claimed Georgeson gave him approximately 1,500 shares of Monarch Oil for helping establish the company. After consulting his records, though, Chapin amended the total to 10,375 shares. He gave 900 shares to Devenish and others were "similarly disposed of." By the time Monarch ceased operations, his portfolio contained 1,325 shares. Following Chapin on the stand were a pair of witnesses—L.B. Martin and A.L. Smith—who worked for Chapin in various capacities and verified they received shares from Chapin in Monarch Oil. The highlight of the morning session came when chemist Edward G. Voss testified about the analysis performed on the oil sample provided by Moodie. The sample consisted "chiefly of mud and water with a strong smell." Voss determined that the small volume of oil in the sample caused the smell. When asked what he reported to Moodie, Voss stated that the sample did not contain natural petroleum, but he was not yet prepared to conclude what it did contain.[71]

Cross-examination of Voss by Georgeson's lawyer did not seek to discredit Voss, but rather raised questions about Moodie. "Mr. Moodie implied in no uncertain terms that you gave him a statement that the sample was a hatched-up mixture," began Forrester. "Did you make such a statement?"

Voss replied he had not. Voss also desperately sought to correct the impression left by Moodie that he had tested the sample "immediately after the strike," pointing out that his analysis took place in April 1916. Asked what the potential effects of waiting two years could have on an oil sample, Voss stated that it would result in the evaporation of the lighter fractions within the crude oil and give the sample the appearance of being a refined product. "Then in your opinion," asked Forrester, "it was not a fair test for the oil?" "No," replied Voss, "it was not a fair test." After hearing a few more witnesses who added little of substance to the issue, Judge Lees adjourned the commission until the following week as he had other business to attend to outside the city, but it was also clear that the inquiry's lack of witnesses also played a factor. Further conflicts in Judge Lees's schedule compelled postponement until September 19.[72]

The Monarch investigation had reached an unsatisfactory equilibrium. Unlike the Black Diamond case, where Buck openly plotted the deception of shareholders with his employees, the Monarch case remained ambiguous. Was the well salted or not? Even among those who suspected something untoward, there were too many suspects and unanswered questions to state definitively what took place. Some questioned the authenticity of Bill Cheely's story printed in the *Albertan* on the morning of June 18, 1914, announcing that Monarch had struck oil. Such was Cheely's reputation by then that others wondered if Cheely was in on the scam, or an unwilling dupe. Did B.W. Dunn salt the well? Was Georgeson in on the plot? If so, why did he allow Moodie to take a sample? Even better, why did Georgeson continue drilling until bankrupting the company? What should investigators make of the decision to transfer shares in the company to the drillers? Was this an attempt to buy their silence? Or was all this simply what happens when inexperienced people get together and form an oil company?

Before the investigation resumed, though, Trainor noted the uncomfortable reality that after a few weeks of hearings, the commission had already reached the end of its tether and run out of witnesses. In a memo to Ford, Trainor clearly felt hamstrung by public expectations that "three or four companies" needed investigation and highlighted the department's difficulty in securing witnesses to testify before the inquiry. Frank Ford agreed with Trainor regarding the difficulty of convincing witnesses but thought the inquiry had already succeeded at establishing the principle of oversight. Differing from Trainor on the issues of public expectations, Ford then suggested the indefinite postponement of the inquiry due to "the almost entire lack of interest which is being taken in the matter at the present time."[73]

If public interest waned, however, the oil companies took notice of provincial exertions. Some companies now proactively sought to make amends and comply with provincial legislation. In one case, the directors of Western Land appealed to Deputy Attorney General A.G. Browning to allow them to have charges against them for violating the Companies Ordinances dropped provided they took steps to rectify the situation. As Browning explained to the prosecutor of the case, "I do not think the application is likely to be granted," and reiterated that his office would not influence the decision one way or the other. Upon the resolution of the case, the defendant's lawyers suggested the directors were ignorant of the law but were, overall, "decent men although not very competent."[74]

Instead of the commission resuming on September 19, a brief announcement appeared in the *Albertan* stating that the oil inquiry would cease operating because of a lack of witnesses. As with the Carpenter Commission before it, the Lees Commission would not issue a formal report. The ambiguous ending of the inquiry prompted one letter writer to the *Herald* to wonder what the point of it all was. "It seems hardly worth while going to the trouble and expense of having this inquiry if it was simply to wash somebody's dirty linen in public and let the offenders off scot free."[75] Despite the criticisms, the Lees Commission succeeded in establishing the provincial government's right and responsibility to oversee and regulate the oil industry.

A year later in 1917, William Georgeson mounted a legal challenge to the provincial government's right to hold a public inquiry, albeit indirectly, via a slander suit pursued against James Moodie. The alleged slanderous statements occurred when Moodie answered questions put to him as a witness before the Lees Commission. Claiming no specific loss of income and unable to prove any diminution in his reputation, Georgeson sought $50,000 ($1.5 million, adjusted for inflation) for the damage inflicted to his "credit and reputation." The crux of Georgeson's lawsuit, filed by his attorney A. MacLeod Sinclair, however, was not the alleged slanderous statements as much as Sinclair's claim that the Lees Commission lacked the authority to summon witnesses and conduct the inquiry despite the amendment to the Public Inquiries Act. In this respect, Georgeson's attorney made two claims. First was that, as McGillivray argued in 1915, the Public Inquiries Act could not authorize an inquiry of the scope and scale of the Lees Commission, making it ultra vires (outside the law). Second, based on the precedent established in *Black Diamond v. Carpenter* (1915), the Public Inquiries Act "does not authorize the holding of the enquiry in question." Even if the plaintiff granted that the amendment passed by the legislature in April 1916 meant the inquiry was intra vires (within the law), Sinclair's suit claimed "no commission was ever issued. There was no declaration that the matter was of 'public concern.'"[76]

After the initiation of legal action against Moodie, some mildly critical press coverage—reporters pointed out a connection between the publication of Georgeson's official statement on June 18, 1914, and the rise of Monarch share prices—revealed a surprisingly thin-skinned Georgeson, who believed such stories suggested some underhanded behaviour or nefarious motives. Speaking with the *Albertan* a couple of days later, Georgeson stated that he wished to emphasize that he issued his statement on June 18, 1914 "in the interests of the shareholders, and by the instructions of the board of directors, who acted on the report of our geologist, Mr. Dunn." Although Georgeson attempted to foist responsibility on others for the statement, he nonetheless also reiterated he had "every faith in the report." As proof, he pointed toward the large block of Monarch stock he purchased on the open market. The curious press conference concluded with Georgeson referring to the fact that all this had been "brought out at the government's investigation of oil companies" whose very provenance Georgeson questioned. Despite it all, Georgeson still believed in the promise of Alberta oil fields. "The majority of Albertans have forgotten the fact that Alberta wells, very few of them completed, showed the greatest oil seepage in the world, outside of fields producing gushers of crude oil."[77]

Moodie's defence claimed that the commission subpoenaed him to give evidence under oath to Judge Lees, duly appointed under the authority of the Public Inquiries Act and, as such, Moodie's testimony was privileged and not subject to sanction.[78] On September 11, 1917, before the master in chambers, Georgeson's legal team, headed by Sinclair, claimed the statute ultra vires—"beyond the law"—of the legislature to delegate to the commission and requested an immediate hearing before the Appellate Division in Edmonton.[79] If Georgeson's claim held, it meant that Moodie's testimony was not privileged speech, leaving him liable if the court found his statements slanderous.[80]

Citing the precedent established in *Black Diamond v. Carpenter* (1916), Sinclair called into question the wording of the orders-in-council and caused no end of consternation among Moodie's defence team, who immediately appealed to the attorney general's office for help on September 6, 1917. "We think there is some statute or rule under which the attorney general may intervene where a defence is set up that any statute of this province is *ultra vires*," wrote Moodie's lawyer, James Muir, to the attorney general's department. "Would you let us know whether we are right in this and whether or not the attorney general desires to intervene to support the statutes referred to." The deputy attorney general received a memo the same day arguing that no such statute or rule existed and further suggested that the department really had no interest in the case "unless the Court holds that the Statute referred to is *ultra vires*, in which case the question of a reference might be considered." The department's legal council revised its opinion slightly on September 8 by acknowledging that chapter 9 of the Statutes of 1908 enabled the Lieutenant-Governor in Council to provide a reference on "any constitutional or other legal question." Still, however, the department counsel insisted the attorney general's office had no interest in the case unless the court ruled the statute ultra vires. Browning delivered the news to Muir on September 8.[81]

Through it all, the attorney general's office publicly retained confidence in the amended terms to the Public Inquiries Act even as they warily fielded requests for assistance from Moodie's team. Arguably, the most serious part of Georgeson's lawsuit stemmed from Sinclair's claim that, even if the amended Public Inquiries Act was within the law, the Lieutenant-Governor had failed to issue a commission properly declaring the inquiry "a matter of public concern," thereby voiding Moodie's claim of privilege.[82] Muir worried that the attorney general's office had missed something and that his client would be left holding the bag. "The solicitor for the plaintiff objects that no order was made under this commission appointing Judge Lees commissioner," wrote the attorney. Reminding Browning that Moodie faced the prospect of paying $50,000 in damages in a case where the "principal charge is the evidence he gave before this commission," Muir again pleaded for greater assistance from the attorney general's office.[83]

Muir's correspondence betrayed the gnawing fear that the courts would uphold the precedent distinguishing personal rights from the public interest established by *Black Diamond v. Carpenter*. Part of the problem may have been a misunderstanding between Muir and the attorney general's office. Muir asked for, and received, a copy of the June 13, 1916, orders-in-council appointing the commission. In that document, the Executive Council advised Judge Lees to "declare the matter referred to him to be a matter of public concern."[84] The formal commission, signed by the Lieutenant-Governor on July 15, 1916, and printed in the *Alberta Gazette*, contained the formal statement "We Do Hereby Declare the matter above referred to Our said Commissioner to be a matter of public concern."[85]

It is unclear from the existing records why the attorney general's office did not point to the July 15 commission and seemed to rely exclusively on the orders-in-council. Regardless, Muir's growing agitation became apparent in a second letter sent the very next day. While he agreed the orders-in-council expressly appointed Judge Lees and granted him the power to summon witnesses, compel testimony, and enforce its rulings, Muir also argued that "there are some other parts of the order which would appear to require a further order." Muir pointed specifically to the plaintiff's argument that an inquiry must declare the issue "a matter of public concern." Georgeson's lawyer claimed that this required "some further commission" to be valid. "The plaintiff seems determined to have the proceedings under the commission invalidated so that the defendant may not be able to succeed on his plea of privilege." Lingering in the air was Muir's implicit challenge: his client would endure the most pain of another misstep by the provincial attorney general's office. Was Browning prepared to do anything to prevent another humiliating setback for the provincial attorney general in court?[86]

Evidently, Muir's second letter struck a nerve, as Browning became sufficiently concerned that he asked E.R. Gording in the attorney general's legal department for its opinion on the plaintiff's interpretation of the statute. According to Gording's subsequent report to Browning, the biggest challenge Georgeson's lawyers might make was a semantic one. "The commission issued by the Lieutenant Governor in Council [on July 15] follows the wording of the recommendation without changing the verbs to the present tense," wrote Gording matter-of-factly. In any case, the point was rather moot: no subsequent commission was issued. The department could not change anything even if it wanted too. "If the commission, a copy of which was forwarded to Messrs. Muir & Co., is not valid nothing can now be done."[87]

When the hearing opened on November 21, 1917, James Muir based Moodie's defence around two main points: that Georgeson could not point to any tangible losses of money or status because of Moodie's statements, nor were the words capable of bearing the meaning alleged by Georgeson. "The only alleged ground on which, as the defendant submits, the words referred to are actionable," argued Muir, "is that the plaintiff was thereby charged with an indictable offence." Since Georgeson remained unindicted as of September 25, 1917, Georgeson had no case to pursue. As for Moodie's statements before the Lees Commission, Muir asserted that they were privileged under the auspices of chapter 3, section 24 of An Act respecting Inquiries Concerning Public Matters. "The presumption that the commissioner was duly appointed existed when the defendant gave the evidence in question and under that presumption . . . he was protected and the privilege remained." As for Georgeson's claim that the commission was ultra vires, Muir pointed to the orders-in-council and argued Moodie had no reason to suspect anything untoward took place with Lees's appointment. Then Muir pointed out the obvious—if a witness refused to testify before an appointed commissioner and insisted on verifying the "proper appointment of the official... he would almost certainly run the serious risk of being committed for contempt."[88]

Georgeson's lawyer, A. MacLeod Sinclair, however, claimed "no commission was issued by the Lieutenant Governor," and Moodie's statements were actionable because they alleged Georgeson committed a crime while performing his duties as "a director of the Monarch Oil Company." Regarding Moodie's defence that the statements were privileged, Sinclair maintained that the statute did not authorize holding the inquiry, citing the precedent of *Black Diamond v. Carpenter* (1915). "Even if the amending Statute be *intra vires*," stated Sinclair, "the inquiry is not one which is authorized because no commission was ever issued. There was no declaration that the matter was of 'public concern.'"[89]

The Appellate Division's ruling came down on December 4. The seven-page unanimous opinion, written by Chief Justice Horace Harvey, identified two questions for the court to resolve. The first question related to the defendant's claim of privilege because the alleged slanderous statements "were made by the defendant when giving evidence before a commissioner appointed by the Lieutenant Governor in Council under Chapter 2 of 1908 and the question is whether that fact gives the defendant the protection that is afforded to a witness giving evidence in a Court of Justice." The plaintiff claimed that the privilege "does not extend to such an inquiry." The second issue related to the legality of the Lees Commission and whether the appointment of the commissioner was valid. Chief Justice Harvey found that the Act authorized any inquiry "made into and concerning any matter within the jurisdiction of the Legislative Assembly" and that the Lieutenant Governor could appoint a commissioner with the power of taking evidence under oath.

Chief Justice Harvey dealt first with the question of immunity. Harvey's opinion began by stating the legal grounds establishing the Lees Commission contained in the Public Inquires Act. Then he cited legal precedent that "no action will lie for defamatory statements" made during the course of a judicial proceeding and that everything said "by a Judge on the bench, a witness in the box, the parties, or their advocates in the conduct of a case, is absolutely privileged so long as it is in any way connected with the case." Such immunity rests on "obvious grounds of public policy and convenience." For Harvey, the critical distinction in this case was that the immunity granted to witnesses was "founded upon a rule of law declared by the Courts and is based upon grounds of public policy and convenience." The rule should be applied to any witness appearing before a commissioner provided their evidence be relevant. Since there was no question about the relevance of Moodie's evidence, the real issue was the questions raised regarding the authority of the commission itself.[90]

Chief Justice Harvey referred to the provisions of the Public Inquiries Act requiring the appointment of a commission by the Lieutenant Governor in Council and the orders-in-council to be produced in order for the commission to be valid. The plaintiff claimed that a strict reading of the statute required an order in council authorizing the appointment followed by a commission by the Lieutenant Governor in Council. Harvey found that instead of this two-step process, the Lieutenant Governor had combined the two. The order-in-council made the appointment directly and therefore served as the commission as well. Did condensing the process in this way negate the legality of the commission and the defendant's claim to privilege? On this point of law, Harvey found it unreasonable to expect a layman, like Moodie, to determine if authorities had followed the proper procedure establishing the commission. Applying a firm dose of common sense, and citing the precedent established in *Dawkins v. Lord Rokeby* that stated "witnesses may feel free to give their testimony without fear of being harassed" after the fact by lawsuits, Harvey ruled that Moodie's statements before the Lees Commission were protected. "It appears to me that the principle upon which the rule is founded demands its extension to such a case as this even if the legal objections which are taken are sound as to which I have formed no opinion." With that, Harvey dismissed Georgeson's lawsuit with costs.[91]

In the aftermath, few noticed that Harvey had sidestepped the question as to whether the Lees Commission was ultra vires, but the point was moot considering that the commission had already terminated its proceedings and never filed an official report. Nevertheless, the attorney general's office scored a major victory with the Lees Commission. Less than a year after the appellate court ruling shut the Carpenter Commission down for exceeding the bounds of what the province could investigate, the resulting amendment to legislation dramatically expanded its powers. In the process, it resolved the dilemma raised by the Carpenter Commission of distinguishing between public and private concerns by effectively stating that investigating a private concern could become the subject worthy of an inquiry if declared to be in the public interest.

In a short amount of time, the Sifton government had come quite far from where it began in 1913–14 regarding its willingness to intervene in the lives of its citizens, especially upon consideration of its earlier inability to properly execute oversight of the emerging petroleum industry. Having established a minimum standard of consumer protection, the question remained how far the government would move to safeguard the public interest. Even as the Lees Commission slipped quietly below the horizon in September 1916, another manifestation of the willingness to use expanded government power—the trial of George Buck—was prepared to begin.

12

"The Most Important that has Ever Been Tried in the Province:" The Trial of George Buck

> *Whenever Calgary oil is mentioned, it seems that the decorative name of George E. Buck must come up and mingle with the matter under observation.*
>
> —*The Calgary News Telegram*
> July 24, 1915[1]

As Chief Detective Nicholson returned to Calgary with George Buck, Deputy Attorney General A.G. Browning wrote to Crown Prosecutor James Short that Buck would be back in Calgary by the end of the week. Undoubtedly, however, the province's dogged pursuit of George Buck, the most visible—and notorious—promoter of the 1914 boom also signalled its intentions. At every step along the way, Buck stretched the law beyond the breaking point. Now the province had to act against Buck lest he ruin Alberta's reputation as a safe place for people to do business. Browning told James Short that the pressure was on. Attorney General Charles Cross "is very anxious that we secure a conviction in this case, as he thinks that it is the most important that has ever been tried in the province." Browning did not need to elaborate further. To further underscore the importance of the case, Browning offered to visit Calgary and spend a day with Short going over the evidence. "I trust you will not resent my suggesting this." Short readily accepted the offer.[2] In the meantime, the attorney general's office also kept a close eye on the affairs of Black Diamond Oil Fields, notifying the provincial secretary's office that they had received information that the company's assets would be liquidated "for the purpose of supplying funds to Mr. Buck."[3]

The attorney general's office began preparations for the trial, which now included going through all the paperwork from Kansas. Because Buck's case remained on appeal in Kansas, it took until August 9 for all the province's original documents to return to Calgary. Once the judicial process of extradition was complete, the executive process of extradition would presumably be straightforward. As with Sir Isaac Newton's Third Law—for every action there is an equal and opposite reaction—the process is routine, predictable, and yields very few surprises. US Secretary of State Robert Lansing issued a warrant of surrender listing fraud by a director of a company as the sole charge for Buck's extradition. In return, the Canadian government issued a warrant of recipias (loosely translated as "recapture," or "take back"), acknowledging the charge(s) and naming John Nicholson as the person taking custody of Buck to return him to Calgary. On July 5, 1916, Nicholson served the warrant of recipias to US Marshal Sam Hill. Simple, straightforward, and routine. But among the papers returned to Alberta, officials discovered two copies of the US state department's warrant of surrender for Buck. The first listed a single charge of fraud, but the second contained three charges: the original charge of fraud by a director of a company plus two combined charges of fraud and conspiracy. American officials had included the second warrant in the file even though, officially speaking, it was not executed.

The inclusion of the second warrant created a dilemma for Deputy Attorney General Browning, who now saw an opportunity to resurrect the Crown's strongest case against Buck. Strategizing with James Short by mail, Browning outlined a plan to write the Canadian undersecretary of state, Thomas Mulvey, asking the Canadian government for a second warrant of recipias citing three charges contained in the second order of commitment. "So far as the jurisdiction of this province is concerned," wrote Browning, obtaining the second warrant would be "conclusive evidence that George E. Buck was committed on the three charges." Short liked the idea and urged Browning to "use every endeavor to get Warrants of Surrender on the two 'Conspiracy' charges duly issued if they have not already been issued."[4]

But the provincial attorney general's need to prosecute Buck did not necessarily align with federal imperatives, and asking the Canadian state department to issue a second warrant of surrender after the fact would involve the Dominion government in an attempt to falsify the official record. In his letter to Mulvey, Browning acknowledged that Nicholson served the original warrant of recipias on July 5 and that "Nicholson did not wait for the second warrant of surrender on the two charges of conspiracy which also included a charge of fraud." Browning did not offer Mulvey any explanation for Nicholson's departure before receiving the second warrant. Nevertheless, Browning acknowledged that Buck's lawyers would certainly object to any additional charges beyond fraud, meaning "it will be necessary to produce evidence that George E. Buck was surrendered on three charges;" hence the request to the state department for a second warrant of recipias. On August 31, the acting undersecretary of state advised that it was impossible for the state department to comply with Browning's request. Officially, the second warrant of surrender did not exist. Nicholson served the first warrant on July 5 and brought Buck over the border on that basis. But the acting secretary of state then chided Browning for even suggesting that the department issue a second warrant of recipias it knew contained charges that were "not included in our extradition treaties with the United States." To drive the point home, he reminded Browning that "you were advised in this sense in telegrams on the 4th and 5th May last."[5]

Although it might not have seemed like it at the time, the state department's stance likely saved Browning and Short from considerable grief. For unknown reasons, McGillivray was aware that the attorney general's office might attempt to include more charges against Buck. Short reported that Buck, via his lawyers, had already requested that the attorney general produce an original copy of the writ of surrender issued by the US state department. Nicholson, however, gave the original document to US Marshal Sam Hill upon Buck's surrender, meaning that the writ of surrender remained in the United States. In the meantime, Buck's lawyers contacted the US state department on August 23, requesting a copy of the warrant of surrender "showing the charge or charges" justifying Buck's extradition. The lawyers' initial telegram brought a speedy reply from Robert Lansing, and by August 28 Buck's lawyers had their own copy of the July 5 warrant of surrender. Once he learned that Buck's lawyers had written to Robert Lansing for a copy of his ruling on the matter, Browning advised Short not to challenge the defence's copy.[6]

Judge W. Roland Winter presided over Buck's arraignment on September 8, 1916. After serving six years on the district court of Lethbridge, Winter joined the district court of Calgary in December 1913. Born in 1850 in Messina, Italy, to English parents and educated in England and France, Winter practised law in England until emigrating to Calgary in 1893. He served as a police magistrate and then as registrar of land titles until appointed to the district court in Lethbridge. Years later, one colleague stated Winter "possessed in no uncertain degree, the first two qualities of a gentleman—kindliness and courtesy." An avid cello player with an extensive art collection, Judge Winter and his wife, Lydia, were patrons of Calgary's growing arts community. As a member of the bench, Justice Horace Harvey said Winter was "thoroughly conscientious, a hard worker, and an able jurist."[7]

At Buck's arraignment, Crown Prosecutor Short charged Buck with three offences: that Buck did "concur in making, circulating, or publishing a statement as a director of a company" known to be false on or about May 7, 1914 "at Calgary;" a second count of "making, circulating, or publishing a statement as a director of a company" known to be false on or about May 7, 1914 "at or near the City of Calgary;" and a third charge that Buck did "concur in making, circulating, or publishing a statement as a director of a company" known to be false on or about May 17, 1914 "at or near Calgary." When Short mentioned that other charges might be forthcoming, Judge Winter reminded him that, due to Buck's extradition, the rule of specialty permitted no added charges.[8]

Reluctantly, James Short realized the conspiracy charges were likely to drop from the indictment, throwing a wrench into his plans. Most of the evidence gathered by the province supported the conspiracy charges, and Short had originally planned to build his case on proving the conspiracy elements rather than fraud. The Crown prosecutor also entertained doubts that the attorney general's office would pay for a fraud conviction, as it would require a larger budget to bring in witnesses to testify. Although the Crown relied on affidavits and depositions in the preliminary hearing and Nicholson had used some to secure Buck's extradition from the United States, Short knew that the defence would object strenuously to their use in a trial. Indeed, at a preliminary hearing on August 28, 1916, Buck's lawyers had already filed motions to throw out the depositions and dismiss the charges against Buck. With the trial scheduled to start September 26, 1916, and perhaps seeing how easily William Georgeson and O.S. Chapin had cast doubt on the accuracy of Cheely's reports before the Lees Commission, Short now deemed it "absolutely necessary" that William Cheely testify.[9]

The attorney general's office and James Short spent the rest of September preparing for the trial. Chief Detective Nicholson arrived in Calgary on September 19—one week before the scheduled start date of the trial and the same day the Lees Commission wrapped up—and began tracking down witnesses, serving subpoenas on those who were in Calgary, and planning for the Royal North-West Mounted Police to serve others. Short's most important witness, former *Albertan* reporter W.W. Cheely, had moved to Great Falls, Montana, following the oil boom. Reached by Nicholson on the morning of September 21, Cheely indicated he would not return to Calgary until at least October 15, by which time Nicholson expected the trial would be over. Nicholson travelled to Great Falls to convince the reporter to return for the trial. Failing that, Short instructed Nicholson to find out if "Buck inspired the report in [the] daily *Albertan* of May 8, 1914, describing oil strike and to whom Buck gave information whether to Cheely or someone else." Reached by Nicholson, the reporter relayed that Buck asked William Davidson to send a reporter with him to the Black Diamond well, where he saw that the contents of the bailer showed evidence of of oil and reported this in the *Albertan* on the morning May 8, 1914. At Short's direction, Nicholson arranged for a commissioner to collect an affidavit from Cheely, but neither side could agree on a commissioner. The dispute dragged on until September 26, when Judge Winter pushed the trial back to October 19 to give the commissioner time.[10]

More than two years had passed since those events, and Cheely reacted cagily to efforts to secure his statement before refreshing his memory by reading a copy of his story. The Crown prosecutor's office sent a copy of the *Albertan* by mail on September 21, but it did not arrive in Montana until October 2. But Cheely did not recognize the article, for good reason; J.D.M Ritchie was the author of the May 8, 1914, article. Cheely insisted that his article had occupied the same position on the front page of the *Albertan* but appeared before Ritchie's story. In fact, Cheely's story appeared a day later. Nevertheless, the prosecutor's office moved to secure a copy of the article before the commission taking Cheely's statement met at ten a.m. on October 4. But with Short busy on another case, his office could not find Cheely's article and attributed their misfortune to the fact that the *Albertan*'s files were incomplete, and they would now go through the *Herald*'s files. They remained empty-handed when the commission gathered in Great Falls to take Cheely's evidence. As the search through the files continued back in Calgary, Short instructed Nicholson to take into evidence any statements Buck made to Cheely about boosting sales of stock. Nicholson, however, expressed concern because Cheely now "can't swear to any date or statement made by Buck without seeing paper." Although Short had not asked for Nicholson's opinion, the provincial detective offered one regardless. "Not safe to call [Cheely]," reported Nicholson. In the meantime, Nicholson reported that Buck's lawyer in Montana, no one less than McGillivray's partner and future Justice of the Supreme Court of Alberta Thomas M. Tweedie, "objects strongly to further adjournment" to continue the search for the missing article. Finally, another law partner found the piece, and at eight p.m., Short frantically wired, "Forwarding *Morning Albertan* May 9, 1914. Ask adjournment of Cheely Commission till paper arrives." By the time Short's telegram arrived, it was already too late. The judge presiding over the commission, J.B. Leslie, had sustained Tweedie's objection six hours earlier at two p.m. to any further adjournment. A second commission would have to collect Cheely's testimony later in the month.[11]

As the trial drew closer, pressure mounted on Short. An internal memo dated October 10, 1916, revealed the attorney general's office had already spent a substantial sum—$4,287.26 ($113,312 adjusted for inflation)—on incidental payments since November 12, 1915, on the Buck case. After a series of delays requested by the defence, Buck's trial began on October 25, 1916. From the beginning, the trial attracted a great deal of press coverage and the extra attention of the provincial attorney general's office. Reporters noted Buck arrived in court wearing a new suit, looking "very jaunty and smiling as he took his seat in the dock when court opened." With his famous moustache returned and "waxed in the old style," Buck confidently greeted old friends and acquaintances, seemingly without a care in the world. After the clerk read, and corrected, the three charges, Buck's attorney, Alexander McGillivray, quickly moved to quash the indictments on four separate grounds. The first charge, fraud by a corporate officer, "disclose[s] no offence known to the law in Canada." McGillivray allowed that the second and third charges of conspiracy were crimes in Canada, but the warrant of surrender signed by Secretary of State Robert Lansing did not specify them, violating the speciality provision of the Anglo-US extradition treaty. Third, McGillivray argued that the court could not prosecute Buck in Canada for these latter two crimes until providing Buck with the "opportunity of returning to the United States." Finally, Buck's indictment contained three charges while the extradition order specified only one.[12]

To prove his point that the charges pursued by the prosecution were fundamentally different from those pursued at the extradition, McGillivray introduced two affidavits to show that James Short had continued to build the prosecution's case against his client after extradition. Taken together, the sworn statements proved that, back in Kansas, the province made its case to Commissioner Paul J. Wall on the conversation between George Buck and Charles Tryon on May 7, 1914. The other affidavit, from James Short, no less, secured William Cheely's testimony a few weeks earlier. This, accused McGillivray, violated the speciality provision contained in the third section of the Anglo-US extradition treaty. "The Crown, in its zeal in the prosecution of this man, has laid two other charges in the face of the express provision in the treaty arrangement between the United States of America and Great Britain that a man was not to be charged except in respect of the offense in connection with which he was extradited." If convicted, McGillivray pointed out, Buck would be liable to serve fifteen years in the penitentiary instead of a maximum five years if convicted on the one charge. Judge Winter, however, disagreed. "This is one offense, and I should like if you can to differentiate. The indictment lays two others, on the 7th and on the 17th of May, and Calgary is charged in one place and near Calgary in the other. Can you say he was not extradited on the charge which laid an offense of the sort without going into the others? It is all one offense." McGillivray disagreed. "You cannot charge a man twice with doing the same thing with a view to giving him twice the punishment."[13]

McGillivray then turned to the question as to whether "fraud by a director" constituted a crime in Canada. McGillivray conceded the crime existed in the United States, but not that it did in Canada. "There is no difference between fraud of a director, fraud of a lawyer, fraud of a Judge, fraud of a policeman and fraud of anyone else," Judge Winter responded, by referring to sections 412 to 414 of the Criminal Code dealing with fraud and property. Section 414, argued Winter, "says that every one [sic] is guilty of an indictable offense and liable for five years imprisonment [who] being a director issued a statement which he knows to be false, and intended to induce persons to become shareholders. I think that is conclusive, showing what is intended by the offense which is entitled there that is coming within the term fraud." Judge Winter believed this "is an offence known to the law of Canada upon which the accused can be tried."[14]

When called upon to defend the charges, James Short granted that there might be some question with regards to the "offense of fraud as the director of a company," but in his mind there was no issue about the other two charges specifying "at Calgary and the other near Calgary." These were equivalent counts in one charge. "It was a continuous matter," explained Short. "It was about 7 May, that charge alone would be sufficient to permit the introduction of evidence covering on the seventh, and other days in the immediate neighbourhood of the seventh, even so far as up to the end of the month of May 1914, and what I assert is that it was a continuous action." Judge Winter cut to the heart of the matter. "If these charges were allowed to go as they stand, the accused [could serve up] to three terms of imprisonment for the same offence." Short countered that the United States "delivered up" George Buck for the crime of fraud by a director and officer of a company. "I can lay any charge that comes within the purview of those terms, provided it comes also within the purview of the evidence which is given on the extradition proceedings." Short acknowledged that Buck's extradition on a charge of fraud meant he could not also face charges of murder or theft. "But I am not prevented from multiplying, giving fifty charges on the crime of fraud by a director or officer of the company, so long as they have any relation to the evidence which was adduced in the extradition proceedings." Furthermore, Short contended that extradition proceedings only had a limited purpose—to satisfy the commissioner that a prima facie case exists. "They are not intended to be an absolute proof of the charge which is laid against the accused in the foreign country." With the morning session ending, Judge Winter adjourned to consider McGillivray's objections more fully. The *Herald*, which published in the afternoon, considered the session a smashing success for Buck, saying "the former oil promoter may be walking the streets of Calgary before nightfall a free man."[15]

When court resumed for the afternoon session, Judge Winter asked Short whether the extradition commissioner had heard any evidence for offences committed on May 17, 1914. When Short replied in the negative, Winter dismissed the second charge. "My own view is that there are two distinct offences as distinguished from crimes brought before this Court and only one has been brought before the Extradition Commissioner," reasoned Winter. "I can only assume that the Extradition Commissioner extradited the accused in respect of a charge laid at or near Calgary on the 7th of May, 1914, and I think the accused should be tried on that."[16] With that, the judge dismissed the second of three charges against Buck, leaving only the charge of being a director of the Black Diamond Oil Fields where he caused publication of a false statement with the object of getting people to invest in the stock of the company.

With the procedural questions out of the way, the afternoon session turned to collecting evidence from three witnesses. Short first called Roy Cleveland Lee, Buck's mechanic, who secured the distillate used to salt the well. Lee testified that Buck left his cars at his garage during the oil boom and that all the supplies of gasoline for running Buck's vehicles came from his garage. Furthermore, Lee testified that on one occasion in 1914 Buck bought two gallons of distillate from him. Following Lee on the stand was W.R. Martin, the president of International Supply Company, the drillers contracted by Buck to drill Black Diamond #1. Martin's testimony proved that Buck's company quickly fell into arrears with its payments under the terms of the contract. Martin testified that he and his partner, "Tiny" Phillips, brought pressure to get payment before May 6, 1914, culminating with the threat of removing the rig unless Buck cleared his debt. But, as the *Albertan* noted, Martin's memory of events and Buck's debt with the company appeared "uncertain, and he was finally told to stand down and refresh his memory by looking over his books."[17]

The Crown's final witness, Major William G. Gillespie, closed out the day's testimony. Originally hired as an illustrator for Black Diamond's advertisements, Gillespie became a trusted hand around the office, serving as Buck's occasional chauffeur and regular troubleshooter. Gillespie's testimony established that around May 6, 1914, Buck invited himself, advertising manager H.C. Beattie, Norman L. Fletcher, and others into his private office, where he alleged Buck said, "I have a little scheme." However, Gillespie could not say what that was because he left the office without hearing the details of the scheme; later that afternoon, Buck sent Gillespie on some errands that included picking up a picnic lunch that Mrs. Buck prepared, as well as stopping by his garage on 12th Avenue, where, on Buck's instructions, Gillespie collected two five-gallon tins of gasoline and brought them back to the office. Back at the office, Buck asked Gillespie to go with him to the well. Before leaving, Gillespie testified that Norman Fletcher came out and told him something that, as the *Albertan* salaciously wrote, "excited dark suspicions in the major's bosom that all was not well." McGillivray objected before he could repeat the remark, but Gillespie made it clear that Fletcher's statement and Buck's subsequent behaviour aroused his suspicions. When asked to provide examples, Gillespie noted that, instead of taking the usual route to Okotoks, he took a more circuitous route to the well east of the cemetery. Before leaving the city limits, Buck and Gillespie met stock promoter Allan Clark, who then was in discussions with Buck to exclusively sell the company's remaining treasury stock (see Chapter 6). Clark gave them something in a sack Gillespie could not identify apart from saying that it might have been a pail or a can.[18]

After stopping to have a picnic lunch, Gillespie and Buck continued their trip to Okotoks and reached the Black Diamond well somewhere between nine and ten o'clock that night. Instead of parking at the camp, the car stopped near the boiler house, where William E. Budge, the night watchman, patrolled. Buck asked Gillespie and Budge to take the cans of gasoline and the sack to the derrick house. Buck let himself into the derrick and brought out a lantern and a note from driller James W. Hayes. Buck said he was going to the camp to see Hayes, and while he was gone, Budge and Gillespie took the cans in the sack into the derrick. Gillespie knew what was going to happen next because he and Buck had talked about it on the way out from Calgary. "I was pretty well aware what was going to happen," said Gillespie. "From what I was told by Fletcher. I knew something was going to happen." McGillivray objected and had the remark stricken from the record. Gillespie then testified he begged Buck not to get anyone in trouble and carry out his intentions. "Did you deliver a little moral lecture on his iniquity," asked Judge Winter, "or did

Buck begin it?" Gillespie could not remember but did recall that Buck "told me that he was going to carry out what he intended to. He told me he was going to go through with it." Buck then told Budge go to the Black diamond post office next day and telephone him at the Calgary office and to use a certain word, "Paul," that he assumed was a code. Gillespie visited the well site on two more occasions. First, taking Mr. Crandell to measure the depth of the hole, where they saw oil covering the bits and the drill. Gillespie made another trip with William Cheely on May 8. With that, Short turned the witness over to McGillivray. Somewhat to the surprise of many in the court, McGillivray had no questions for Gillespie, and the court adjourned until the next day. As the *Albertan* concluded, "It took a whole lot of questioning to elucidate his story. The witness was constantly 'presuming' that things were thus and so, and Mr. McGillivray was on his feet objecting half the time."[19]

When the trial resumed on the afternoon of October 27, much to the surprise of McGillivray, William Cheely arrived back in Calgary from Great Falls, Montana, to give his testimony in person despite previous claims to the contrary. As Cheely revealed later, his attendance became mandatory when Attorney General Charles W. Cross personally requested his presence. When asked what changed his mind, the former *Albertan* reporter shrugged, Cross made "a personal matter of it and I came." Cheely being a crucial prosecution witness to establish that Buck had made fraudulent statements, Short zeroed in on Cheely's May 9, 1914, story published in *The Morning Albertan* about the reported oil strike at Black Diamond #1 as well as the conversations he had with Buck on May 8, 1914, to prepare the article. McGillivray objected that the substance of the witness's testimony "was not in any way before the Extradition Commissioner in the United States" and the judge should strike it from the record. Short countered that Judge Winter had already ruled on this matter the day before, and Winter concurred, stating, "I think anything in the way of additional evidence, pertaining to the same charge, is admissible." Cheely then described the invitation from Buck and the series of hand signals at the gate blocking the entrance to the well site, bringing forth another objection from McGillivray, who demanded to know how Cheely could possibly know if these were a password or not. Undaunted, Cheely described going into the derrick house and hearing Buck say, "We will show you what we have here," before ordering the driller to bail out the well. The driller sent the bailer down the hole and brought it back up, dumping the contents into a sluice box where it ran off down into Sheep Creek. "There was a thick sheen of oil on top of the drillings. There was a very perceptible coal oil odor, and over the stream, Sheep Creek, below where the drillings were dumped it was colored for a considerable distance." Cheely then described Buck dropping a match or a piece of burning waste into the well, causing the gas to explode and send a flame ten feet high out of the well. The reporter said he stayed at the well for about an hour or so, talking with Buck and the driller, watched the bailer rise from the well a second time and emptied into the sluice box. Again, producing traces of crude oil. After Cheely described the process by which he researched, wrote, and prepared the story for publication in the May 9, 1914, edition of the *Albertan*, Short introduced the article into evidence over McGillivray's objection. The Crown prosecutor noted that the article used a lot of geological terms, like "Dakota sands" and "Claggett shales" and asked if Cheely were an expert in geology. The *Albertan* noted that Cheely smiled as he admitted he was not. McGillivray then injected some levity in proceedings by noting that "lots of people used those words in Calgary who were not geologists," causing many in the courtroom to burst out laughing. Short's point, however, remained. Cheely was no geologist; Buck had provided the geological information used in the article.[20]

Upon cross-examination, McGillivray endeavoured to raise doubts about the extent of Buck's culpability and alluded to the testimony before the Lees Commission revealing that Cheely sometimes took liberties with the facts. "You are a live newspaper man and you were looking for a good story," began McGillivray before drawing from the witness an admission that he could not remember any specific statements made by Buck, and that he spoke to three or four men, including the driller at the well. "You did not go down [to the well] to have talks; you were going down to see," said McGillivray, "so that any doubting Thomases, through the medium of the press, would get some information." Cheely agreed. McGillivray stated that reporters "write stories up attractively.... And is it not an uncommon newspaper custom, is it, when you are giving what you consider a gist of anything, to put it in quotations? You do not pretend by that that the words you are employing in an article are the exact words used by anybody?" The reporter agreed that he tried "to conform as generally as you can" to the practice of attributing exact quotations where possible. Sensing doubt, McGillivray boxed Cheely in and secured an admission that "it would not be a verbatim report." On the redirect, Short asked if Cheely would, or did, "put into [Buck's] mouth words of the driller, Mr. Hayes, or anyone else?" Cheely stated he did not. Judge Winter followed up, asking whose quotations they were. The reporter answered quickly and unequivocally, "Mr. Buck's, as nearly as I could write them from my notes." Short then called James Kelso of Kelso Laboratories, who provided the technical report quoted liberally by Cheely in the May 9 edition of the *Albertan*.

Kelso described receiving a sample of oil mixed with fine sand from Buck delivered in a beer bottle on May 8, 1914, and the analysis he performed. Kelso could not recall if he mailed or delivered his analysis to Buck's office after writing up the report, leaving a loose end in the prosecution's case about how the details of the technical report wound up in the *Albertan*. Short contended Buck gave the material to Cheely, but McGillivray's cross-examination prevented the prosecution from definitively placing the report in Buck's possession. After this exchange, court adjourned for the day.[21]

As the trial began its third day, McGillivray attempted to extract a statement from prosecutor Short that "the facts deposed to by Mr. Cheely in his evidence given at this trial were not deposed to before the Extradition Commissioner in the United States." Initially, Short believed McGillivray simply intended for him to acknowledge that Cheely neither testified directly nor presented an affidavit before the extradition commissioner. But Short balked when McGillivray asked for a more sweeping statement negating the entirety of Cheely's testimony. The defence attorney wanted Short to definitively state that no other witness could confirm Cheely's evidence, and Short emphatically refused to do so, prompting a rare outburst from McGillivray that cast a pall over proceedings for the rest of the day.[22] The *Herald* noted "several sharp clashes between the solicitors for the prosecution and defence" before describing one of several testy exchanges between McGillivray and Short. "One little eruption after another kept breaking out all morning," summarized the newspaper. Short called two witnesses, Jennie L. Earl, Buck's cousin, stenographer, secretary, and a director of Black Diamond Oil Fields, and Van Gordon Gosnell, chief clerk of the provincial secretary's office. Both established George Buck's status as managing director of Black Diamond Oil Fields. Earl testified that Black Diamond sold little stock prior to the strike of oil at the Dingman well. She also established that Buck continued to make payments to International Supply Company by selling his own oil leases and stocks. All told, McGillivray generated the biggest headlines of the day by promising to file an immediate appeal in the event of a guilty verdict. To Judge Winter, McGillivray said that he desired a short trial so the appeal book would be as small as possible.[23]

When court resumed on Monday, a more workmanlike approach prevailed. Short called several witnesses to testify about the salting of the well, including Ray Minue, who claimed he poured about five gallons of a mixture of oil and distillate down the well at the behest of driller Hayes. Minue also testified that Buck brought the cans to the site. Meanwhile, Buck's longtime chauffeur, Harold Hodgson, stated that Buck asked him to procure some crude oil in early May 1914. Then, on the night of May 6, 1914, Buck instructed Hodgson and Norman Fletcher to bring the can down to the Black Diamond well.[24]

Short devoted part of the afternoon to establishing the effect that salting the well had on individual investors, like John Young, who worked as a janitor in the McDougall Block where Buck established his first offices in Calgary. Young testified that he read the *Albertan* daily, invested in Black Diamond Oil Fields, and recalled that "it was in the Black Diamond where I made the first investment of any company in connection with the oil properties." When shown a copy of the May 9, 1914, edition of the *Albertan,* Young vividly remembered the paper as the one that first reported seepages at Black Diamond. McGillivray objected on the grounds that it was not relevant evidence. Judge Winter overruled. "He says he remembers seeing that," responded Winter, before pointing out that the testimony related to the charge that Buck knowingly made false statements. When Short resumed questioning, he asked Young if he ever purchased Black Diamond shares. "Yes," came the answer, "I purchased it after reading that. It might've been a week or so afterwards. Me and a son-in-law of mine went down to the Black Diamond office and made the purchase, I don't know what date it was, but I know it was some little time after reading the report in the paper." When asked to describe what effect the report had on his mind, Young unequivocally stated that it was decisive. "It was by the good reports in the papers which induced me to buy stock." Frank Sydenham provided similar testimony but, unlike with Young, McGillivray cross-examined the witness. Buck's solicitor attempted to poke holes in the prosecution's case that Cheely's article influenced investors to buy Black Diamond stock. When McGillivray asked the witness if another event, say, perhaps the Dingman strike, prompted him to invest, Sydenham emphatically said it did not and estimated he acquired at least 30 percent of his investments before the Dingman strike. McGillivray then tried a different tack, trying to insert some distance between his client and the stock sales. Even through the dry transcript, it is clear that McGillivray's brief cross did not go as planned:

McGillivray: .... You didn't buy from Mr. Buck?

A: Yes sir.

Q: Where?

A: At his office.

Q: Was he there himself?

A: Yes sir.

Q: And when did you register your shares?

A: Oh, not for a considerable time after I bought them.

Q: Not for a considerable time. Well, the records would show. You say, for a considerable time later?

A: Those records would show when I bought them.

Q: All right, that is all.[25]

Most of the afternoon's session focused on McGillivray's attempts to have Norman Fletcher's testimony taken at the preliminary hearing excluded from consideration as well as throwing out the evidence of J.W. Hayes taken by commission in Lima, Ohio. Along with the testimony of William Cheely, the prosecution and defence both regarded Fletcher's evidence as crucial to establish the fraud charge against Buck. Initially, both witnesses had informed Short they would be unable to testify in person; Cheely moved to Montana and no longer resided in the city, but Attorney General Cross's personal intervention ensured the newspaper man testified in open court. The same would not be true for Fletcher, whose health had begun to fail due to tuberculosis. On doctor's orders, Fletcher sought treatment for the condition in Kamloops in the summer of 1916. Unbeknownst to Short, Nicholson, or the police, Fletcher moved out of the city just weeks before Buck's trial started. In a letter to Browning, Short recalled his shock when he discovered two days before the trial that Fletcher had moved to Ontario. Short immediately "set the wires going" to locate Fletcher and found him in Port Huron, Michigan. The prosecutor obtained statements from Fletcher and summoned his physician in Calgary, Dr. William E. Graham, to testify about the danger to Fletcher's health if called as a witness. "Any great excitement," said Graham, "such as would be involved in a severe cross-examination might produce a return of his trouble in its acute form." Graham further explained that anything that would increase Fletcher's heart rate could produce a pulmonary hemorrhage or a fever with potentially fatal consequences.[26]

Short tried to solve his dilemma by petitioning the court to include Fletcher's testimony from the preliminary hearing in the record. To McGillivray's objection that he would be unable to cross-examine Fletcher,

Short pointed out that McGillivray's law partner, Thomas Tweedie, handled those responsibilities at the preliminary hearing and that it constituted 134 out of the 151 pages of evidence given by Fletcher. Judge Winter concurred, estimating that reading the cross-examination into the record would take nine hours. Nonetheless, McGillivray doggedly fought to exclude the testimony, for reasons including that it was irrelevant in that the preliminary hearing primarily focused on the two conspiracy charges since thrown out. For good measure, McGillivray added objections touching on Fletcher's exact whereabouts and the severity of his illness, pointing out that Fletcher had only recently started travelling after J.D. Nicholson served a subpoena. Ultimately, Winter declared he must accept the commission. "I mean the same thing arose when Mr. Cheely was being examined quite recently on commission, they came to the conclusion that it was better to take everything there was, even if it was not strictly allowable as evidence, and if it is not evidence. It would be left out," said Winter. McGillivray remained wary. "It seems to me I am to entitled to know exactly what words, what sentences are evidence in this case," he argued, "and the only way that can be arrived at is by going through that evidence line by line determining it." At a bare minimum, McGillivray wanted all mentions of conspiracy excluded if Judge Winter thought it feasible. "You may think it is a hard thing to do to mentally throw out, but it isn't." The two sides arrived at a compromise: prior to Judge Winter reading the commissioned testimony, the two solicitors would go through the document noting their objections to any parts of it before Winter issued a final ruling. The same solution applied to the deposition of driller James Hayes.[27]

The marathon of witnesses concluded with Charles E. Tryon, the manager of *The Calgary News Telegram*. As with Cheely, Tryon's trip to the Black Diamond well in May 1914 served as the basis for a newspaper article, although Buck did not find Tryon's submission sufficient for his purposes. Tryon testified that in May 1914, George Buck possessed an advertising account with the newspaper that Tryon attended to personally; since December 1913, Buck had bought plenty of ad space in the paper on behalf of Black Diamond Oil Fields. Tryon recalled speaking with Buck on several occasions about progress on the well and the oil business but admitted he did not always understand what Buck said. Then, on May 7, 1914, Buck called the paper and invited Tryon to visit the well. Five people, including Tryon and City Councillors Crandell and Freeze, arrived at the well shortly after eleven o'clock. The party entered the derrick, where Buck introduced Mr. Hayes, the driller, and then put on a demonstration. "We were shown a barrel of oil, at least a barrel of something that was sitting on the floor," testified Tryon. Someone—Tryon could not identify who precisely—asked when it came out of the well. The reply was the night before. Tryon then vividly recalled Buck skimming oil off the top of the barrel, throwing it on top of the grass and setting it on fire. As Buck took the councillors out on the bank of the creek to see the oil seepages, Tryon remained behind to speak to Mr. Hayes but did not receive very much information. In his earlier sworn statements, Tryon had detailed Hayes's reluctance to speak with him and the impression this left on him. Short did not attempt to draw out this point now, allowing Tryon to wrap up his testimony. On the drive back to Calgary, Tryon found himself in the front seat with Buck when the promoter urged him to send the news into the office. "He wanted me to phone from Black Diamond, I think, or Okotoks," said Tryon. The reporter refused to do so, stating that it was too late to make the regular edition. Buck urged Tryon to get out an extra, but Tryon said it would cost too much to do so. Buck became insistent, asking what it would cost. "I told him from $50–$500, depending on what we put into it. He said 'get out the extra,' and he will give me stock for it." When Tryon refused, the two spent the rest of the trip in silence. Short then asked Tryon whether Buck said anything to him subsequently about the article Tryon produced from his trip. The manager replied that Buck made his displeasure with it widely known, as Buck threatened to pull all his advertising from Tryon's paper to give it to the *Albertan*. With that, the day's testimony concluded. The lawyers gathered with Judge Winter briefly to discuss the next day's schedule before adjourning at four p.m. The day proved an important one for the prosecutor, James Short. "A number of witnesses were put on by the crown," summarized the *Albertan*, "each one adding a link to the chain of evidence which the crown prosecutor is endeavoring to forge around the former oil promoter."[28]

October 31, 1916, proved to be the final day of testimony in the Buck case. Less than twenty-four hours after deferring rulings on Hayes's sworn statement and Fletcher's testimony at the preliminary hearing, Judge Winter inquired if the defence still objected to Hayes's evidence taken on commission. "After reading it," replied McGillivray, "I am the more confirmed in my view that it should not be admitted in evidence." The commission, pointed out McGillivray, placed greater emphasis on the conspiracy charges. "Consequently," argued McGillivray, "there is no part of it which, to my mind, is properly admissible here." Crown Prosecutor Short countered that the testimony related "to precisely the same particulars that are alleged in the charge now before the court—that the evidence that was taken was on the same set of facts." Judge Winter reviewed the commissioner's order, noting that it required the commissioner to gather evidence on all three charges, including fraud. "On looking at it," said Winter, "there will be evidence common to all three counts, applicable to all three counts, therefore, it seems to me it should be admitted." Regarding Fletcher's testimony, Judge Winter announced he found that "with a certain degree of hesitancy, that it should be admitted." The affidavits provided by Fletcher's doctor proved decisive for Winter, making it reasonable to infer that Fletcher's illness made it dangerous to his health and life to give evidence in person.[29]

The logistics of entering the statements now took centre stage as no one seemed quite certain how to proceed. James Short knew that for a trial by jury, the court would read Hayes's testimony out loud for the jurors. Judge Winter proposed he could read it on his own to save everyone's time, but the real question was what the court should do with Fletcher's testimony. With Hayes's evidence, Short correctly pointed toward Buck's right to hear the testimony read aloud as "he has not heard the Commission evidence." The same did not hold for Fletcher's testimony at the preliminary hearing, however. The prosecutor now proposed reading the entire 200 pages, noting Buck's right to hear them read aloud as "he has not heard the Commission evidence." McGillivray offered a compromise to help end the trial expeditiously. Since Fletcher's testimony corroborated that of Minue, Budge, and Hayes, McGillivray proposed that if Short did not "weary the rest of us with the reading of those 200 pages, or whatever it may be, that I would not call any witness in contradiction of the Minue, Budge outfit." At first, Short refused to take McGillivray's offer and started reading Fletcher's testimony from the preliminary hearing. McGillivray appealed to Short's common sense. At 134 pages, the cross-examination alone would take hours to read into the record. Sensing a compromise that might end the case sooner, Judge Winter asked McGillivray if the defence would allow Short to read just his direct examination of Fletcher, omitting the cross-examination. "Yes," said McGillivray plainly. "Surely that is fair." Winter readily agreed. Uncertain, Short asked for time to read over the cross-examination again to "see if there are any parts that I wish to put in." McGillivray countered that he would not permit Short to cherry-pick lines from the cross-examination. If the prosecutor wanted any part of it in the record, he must enter it all. Again, Winter commented on the reasonableness of McGillivray's proposal before reminding Short that "on the direct examination, as a rule, you are supposed to have extracted all the good you can out of your witness. You don't expect the cross-examining counsel to bring out facts which you could not get yourself?" Short protested: "But they often do, and in this case where there is 117 pages . . . ." Judge Winter interrupted, "Well, Mr. Short would like to read it." Moments later, court adjourned until two p.m.[30]

When court reconvened, Short read driller James Hayes's testimony of the events surrounding the salting of the well into the record. Hayes admitted that he, not Buck, ordered Terrill and Minue to salt the well. "[I] just told [Terrill] Mr. Buck wanted it put in and they could go ahead and put it in." Following Hayes's testimony, Short inserted Fletcher's direct testimony in the record. Originally hired as an auditor, Fletcher established Black Diamond's financial difficulties, particularly an inability to finance the well. "It was a matter of general discussion around the office every day," said Fletcher, who managed to raise $4,000 for the company. But that was not enough. Fletcher described how International Supply Company could take all of Buck's property if the well reached 1,500 feet. "Mr. McLaws had charge of the affairs of the International Supply Company, and if the money was not forthcoming. He would take the whole of the Black Diamond outfit, that was his property and his home property, which I understand he had in escrow for this debt." According to Fletcher, Buck suggested several different ways to finance the debt, including enticing an outside investor to buy stock, and when that fell through "the proposition was to create a boom" by creating an oil discovery. "It got very urgent at the last around about the third, fourth and fifth of May, and on May 6, Mr. Buck got down to the concrete proposition that something had to be done right quick." During that week before May 6, 1914, Fletcher asked Mr. Hayes to delay the drilling for ten days at Buck's request to avoid the payment $9,800. But delaying drilling did not tackle the main problem of the lack of money, and on May 6, Buck "outlined a proposition. He thought the money could be raised easily. If oil was to be put in the well." Fletcher described how "things were looking suspicious" the week before. "Crude oil had been coming into the office and gasoline, and things were working to appoint a person, I did not know where I was at." As for his role in the proposition, Fletcher testified that, at Buck's instruction, he spoke to Hayes to see if there would be any problem or danger in salting the well. Fletcher claimed he told Buck, "I would have nothing to do with it. It was too serious an offense. It came to the point, I would quit." Buck replied that he was going to go through with it even if he had to do the job himself. Fletcher then said he did not hear anything more about the salting of the well until May 12, 1914, when he met Buck in Medicine Hat. "He told me they got along all right, but Hayes backed out from the former arrangements, but they accomplished it." Buck then claimed that Tryon's visit to the well was unproductive so "they had to get the *Albertan*" to provide a good write-up. According to Fletcher, though, it still did not produce the expected results.[31]

After reading Fletcher's direct testimony, Short asked the court to consider inserting three pages of Fletcher's cross-examination. McGillivray reiterated his earlier objection. "My friend is not at liberty to put in any cross-examination. What he is entitled to put in is preliminary evidence." Asked directly by Short if he would consent to adding the page, McGillivray refused, ending the prosecution's case. McGillivray announced the defence would not call any witnesses, bringing the case to a rapid denouement. All that remained was the summation of the prosecution's case. The *Herald* concluded that the prosecution "characterized Buck as one not fit to be at large, and asked for a conviction." Short summarized that the Crown charged Buck under section 414 of the Criminal Code. The prosecution showed that Buck "was a director and manager of a body corporate," and that Buck "concurred in making, circulating or publishing a statement . . . that oil was found in the well of the company of which he was president." The oil, argued Short, "was not there naturally, but was put their artificially and for a set purpose." McGillivray objected when Short used Tryon's testimony to show that Buck "did concur in making, or circulating a statement." To the court, McGillivray pointed out that "Mr. Tryon said he could not remember who did phone him." Short countered that the prosecution presented much more damning evidence, most prominent of which was Buck's attempt to induce Tryon to publish a special edition of the *News Telegram*. "If that was not concurring in the publication of a statement, I do not know what would be concurring." After some bickering between Short and McGillivray over whether Tryon said Buck "had," "could," or "would" go to the *Albertan* to publish a favourable statement, Short returned to his main point—that Buck took several people, including Tryon, and City Councillors Freeze and Crandall, out to the well.

> What possible object had he in taking those men out there, knowing as he did how the oil had come into that well, if we believe the evidence of the witnesses in this case, what possible object had he except getting them to publish the statement that oil had been found in the Black Diamond well? By his very conduct, which was calculated beforehand with a great deal of skill and knowledge of human nature, and I think in this case with a great amount of knowledge of human nature, he was calculating the means, which I submit was the best calculated of all, to mislead the public as to the state of oil in that well.[32]

Short then turned to the events surrounding Cheely. The very next day, summarized Short, a reporter for the paper that Buck said he "would" or "could" get a favourable story from arrives at the well. Cheely's story on May 9, 1914, quoted Buck as saying, "This is only a seepage." That, declared Short, "was an absolute fabrication—it was not a seepage." Buck brought Cheely to the well, made false statements about finding oil, and showed him evidence of the strike in order to generate publicity that would result in greater stock sales. Cumulatively, these facts "clearly show that he has brought himself within the section, which says, that he concurred in making, circulating, or publishing" statements intending to defraud. Anticipating defence claims that Buck did not read Cheely's article, the prosecutor argued Buck could not claim innocence. What other conclusion could Cheely draw from this performance? Buck clearly knew the statements were false, especially since the testimony of Fletcher, Gillespie, Minue, and Hayes established that Buck was fully aware of his actions. Short concluded, "I say, in this case, the facts are some of the most astounding circumstances that, I think, have ever come to the attention of any court in the Dominion of Canada."[33]

As Judge Winter retired to review the evidence, the prosecution team took stock of its case. Over the course of the three-day trial, the Crown had called twenty-one witnesses, inserted Hayes's evidence on commission, and succeeded at including Fletcher's direct testimony from the preliminary hearing. Although he believed Winter would find Buck guilty, Short had few illusions about the case. Altogether, the testimony painted a convincing, but nonetheless circumstantial, picture of Buck's involvement and direction of the scheme to salt Black Diamond #1 on the night of May 6, 1914, and made it easy to see how a conviction for conspiracy would be far easier for the prosecution to secure. Proving fraud, however, was a different proposition. Testimony and evidence presented by the prosecution established Black Diamond Oil Fields' financial difficulties and that Buck spoke openly about salting the well to several people. However, none of the witnesses could definitively state that Buck poured oil into the well, as Buck always placed another individual between himself and the activity. A guilty verdict for fraud therefore likely hinged on how Judge Winter evaluated the testimony of William Cheely and the story published under his byline on May 9. Still, had McGillivray created enough doubt by eliciting from Cheely the admission that he spoke to several individuals, not just Buck, and could not say definitively that Buck specifically said anything directly to Cheely? Nor could Short definitively place Kelso's report attesting to the characteristics of the oil found at Black Diamond #1 in Buck's hands before it arrived at the offices of the *Albertan*.

Finally, as Short also contended with the procedural question raised by the defence arising from the speciality principle, "McGillivray objected to the evidence of Cheely on the ground that there was no mention made of it in the Extradition Proceedings, nor of the facts deposed to by Mr. Cheely." If Buck were convicted, Short believed McGillivray's objection to Cheely's testimony would feature prominently in any appeal. Popple, who assisted Short with the case, predicted Buck would appeal regardless. In the meantime, Browning wrote Short that the department was "very well satisfied" with the case he presented and pre-emptively absolved Short from blame "if the result is not as we expect." According to Browning, "The public must feel that everything possible has been done by this Department and the Crown Agent to bring the case to a successful conclusion."[34]

Less than a week later, Judge Winter arrived at a verdict. Newspaper accounts said Buck entered the courtroom on November 7 confidently wearing a "radiant smile." Judge Winter got quickly down to business. The Crown charged Buck with two offences. The first of "making, circulating, or publishing a statement as a director of the company, such statement to his knowledge being false. And that he made this statement on or about May 7, 1914, at the city of Calgary." The prosecutor levelled a second count of the same offence but alleged it "was committed at or near the city of Calgary." Winter decided to lay out "certain facts" that the Supreme Court could easily take up on appeal; namely, that George E. Buck served as managing director of Black Diamond Oil Fields in May 1914, and that Black diamond "had been in great want of funds." In debt to International Supply Company, Black Diamond Oil Fields had no source of income except by the sale of treasury stock that Buck now desperately needed to sell for as much as possible. The evidence showed that George Buck had a meeting where he stated "that he had a proposition, and he hinted at the proposition, and then finally revealed the latter when he stated that he would take oil to the well and pour it down." Winter paused to clearly state Buck did not face charges of salting the well, despite how reprehensible Winter found it, because "it is not possible to try him under our laws and under our arrangement with the United States of America from which country he was extradited." Rather, Buck "is being tried for concurring in a publication" of false statements to defraud investors. After detailing the plot that unfolded between Fletcher, Hayes, Gillespie, and Budge, Winter arrived at the crucial events of May 8 when *Albertan* reporter Bill Cheely appeared at the well. "Under the instructions of the driller the bailer was sent down into the well. On being drawn up, it showed oil on it, and a mixture of sand, and there was a very perceptible odour of natural oil." Everything done at the well had one purpose—"to impress Mr. Cheely with the genuineness of the discovery."[35]

After Cheely's report appeared on May 9, Buck made no attempt to correct the record. Directors, argued Judge Winter, had a responsibility to correct false reports made by optimistic reporters. "As far as the evidence goes," stated Winter, "the only oil that that well produced was the oil that was put into it, and the natural supposition in publishing a statement that they had oil meant that they had oil produced from its natural source." A false pretence, argued Winter, "can be made just as well by action as by words. In this case, the publication was not done by action, the statement was not done entirely, but the statement was made that oil was there, and was a seepage. Buck never contradicted this report at all." There was no doubt in Judge Winter's mind that Buck "doctored" the well and arranged to have stories published about it. Recalling the spring of 1914, Winter said "certain statements were made in the papers, by perhaps some too optimistic reporters." Newspapers printed retractions that included statements by "some official on behalf of the company in the same paper." But no such statement existed in this case. Considering the careful stage Buck and his co-conspirators prepared for Cheely that included a bucket filled with oil and water, and the oily fluid running down into the creek, covering the sluice box with oil, Winter said, "I cannot help feeling that he had, by his acts, shown what he wanted." All these things, argued Winter, "show that the intention of the man was that the so-called discovery should be published, because it was not intended that these reporters should keep this information to themselves." Winter therefore declared Buck guilty as charged. As a practical matter, Winter said the two charges pressed against Buck were the same "as far as I am concerned."[36]

In pronouncing his sentence, Winter suggested that, perhaps, "it does not sound quite so badly" to take away a person's money "by means of publications which were made" as it did to steal directly from someone's pocket. But "the result is practically the same—just as if you had taken it out of their pockets." Calgarians, Winter concluded, "have been really preyed upon by all sorts of similar schemes." Buck was hardly the only one, but he was the one standing in front of the court. With that, Winter sentenced him to serve four years, at hard labour, in the Edmonton penitentiary.[37]

Buck left the scene in the custody of two policemen with his head hanging "and a general air of dejection." Two days after the verdict, Buck boarded a train to Edmonton for incarceration at the penitentiary. Buck chatted with those around him about his future. "I am rather glib with my tongue," Buck supposedly said. "The fact that I have served time in the 'pen' will add greater publicity, so I figure that I can make a fine showing as an evangelist." The *Herald* noted this could be a homecoming of sorts for Buck, who had arrived in Calgary nearly a decade earlier as a revival preacher for the Church of Christ. Buck claimed that he would make a success of his new venture, pointing to the recent example of Percy Hagel. Regarded as a young up-and-coming lawyer in Winnipeg, Hagel assisted his client, "Bloody" Jack Krafchenko, to escape from prison. The case generated national headlines as Hagel delivered a smuggled pistol and rope to Krafchenko, who was serving time for a murder he committed in connection with a bank robbery gone wrong. His role in the jailbreak got Hagel disbarred (temporarily) and earned him a prison sentence of his own. After release, Hagel briefly became an itinerant evangelist in great demand. Evidently, the public, by the hundreds, wanted to hear the former "silver-tongued" barrister speak about sin and redemption on the temperance circuit.[38]

Even though Cross billed the case as "the most important" in the young province's history, press reaction remained muted. *The Wichita Beacon* carried news of Buck's conviction in a small article on page thirteen. James Short reported Buck's conviction to the attorney general's office in sombre tones.[39] Although gratified by the verdict, Short quickly transitioned to preparations for the appeal promised by McGillivray even before the trial ended. To Browning, Short claimed he was not worried by the prospect but nevertheless wanted to preserve "the fruits of our victory." Browning's response remained equally subdued, consisting of a brief letter of congratulations to Short and perfunctory telegram to the attorney general, Charles E. Cross, in Victoria informing him of the sentence.[40] Now, in the face of a determined appeal, the attorney general's office had to ensure the conviction remained.

13

"It is to be Regretted that Such a Scoundrel Should Escape Punishment:" Buck's Appeals

The defendant is certainly not entitled to any sympathy. That he committed a gross criminal fraud was overwhelmingly proved. He fully deserved the term of imprisonment to which he was sentenced. But much as it is to be regretted that such a scoundrel should escape punishment, it is of vastly greater moment that the good faith of this country shall be scrupulously maintained and a strict observance of its treaty obligations insisted upon.

For these reasons I would allow the appeal.
    —Supreme Court Justice Francis Alexander Anglin
        Rex v. Buck[1]

Before Buck's trial ended, McGillivray knew exactly the grounds on which he intended to launch an appeal and did everything possible to have the case before the appellate court during its current seating. To facilitate transcription of evidence, McGillivray approached Short about omitting the evidence of ten witnesses to keep the appeal book as small as possible in exchange for a lengthier admission of facts. Short agreed, but insisted that James Hayes's affidavit remain in its entirety.[2] Ultimately the two sides reached an agreement that included the following stipulations:

- Buck served as managing director of Black Diamond Oil Fields in 1914

- Black Diamond Oil Fields owed $9,800 to International Supply Company on May 7, 1914
- George Buck furnished "a quantity of fluid, a mixture of oil and gasoline resembling crude oil" to pour into the Black Diamond Oil Fields' well
- The well produced no oil "outside of the oil thus put into the well"
- Buck instructed William Budge to send a coded message to Calgary meaning "oil is found."[3]

On November 28, 1916, four weeks after Winter's guilty verdict, Alexander McGillivray filed Buck's appeal to the Appellate Division of the Alberta Supreme Court. In all, McGillivray listed twenty-six grounds for the appeal and Judge Winter forwarded fifteen, including McGillivray's three core objections that the charges disclosed no offence known to the law in Canada, that the United States did not extradite Buck on the offences charged by the prosecution, and that fraud by a corporate director was not a crime under Canadian law. Judge Winter also wanted the appeal court to rule on his decision to amalgamate two separate charges into one; the legality of admitting Norman Fletcher's preliminary hearing testimony; and convicting Buck based on Cheely's May 9, 1916 article despite its exclusion from the case before Extradition Commissioner Paul J. Wall in the United States.[4]

Starting on December 12, 1916, the four judges on the appellate court—Chief Justice Horace Harvey, Justice Charles A. Stewart, Justice Nicholas D. Beck, and Justice Maitland S. McCarthy—heard Buck's appeal. McGillivray believed he had a strong case and condensed the appeal down to three essential points. First, McGillivray argued that Crown Prosecutor Short failed to establish a connection between Buck's statements to *Albertan* reporter Bill Cheely's 1914 article and the subsequent rise in the price of Black Diamond shares. Furthermore, the prosecution did not try Buck for the same offence that prompted his extradition from the United States. Staying with that same point, McGillivray wondered how the United States could extradite Buck on one charge, but Judge Winter combined them into two. This, he argued, directly contravened the terms of the Anglo-American extradition treaty.[5]

The hearing for Buck's appeal took about a day and a half to complete, wrapping up on the afternoon of December 13. At the end of the hearing, Crown Prosecutor James Short gloomily wrote Browning that, by the end of the first day of the hearing, he believed the court would overturn the conviction. Short based this conclusion on the fact that Paul J. Wall did not read Cheely's May 9, 1914, article at the extradition hearing. Short reported that the justices "intimated that they thought under the circumstances the charge as to concurring with W.W. Cheely having been thoroughly proved they should order a new trial." By the morning of December 13, however, the court "seemed to take the ground that there was more evidence of concurring with W.W. Cheely than there was with W. Tryon." Short wrapped up his letter to Browning claiming he could not predict which way it would land. "It looks as though there might be a division of the court." To A.E. Popple, Short proved even more pessimistic, stating that the justices would order a new trial "on the grounds that the chief evidence which convicted him here was not before the Extradition Court in the States." If that happened, Short doubted the province could detain Buck on another charge, and the oil promoter would, once again, be in the wind. This latter observation prompted a concerned memo from Popple to Charles Cross regarding the prospect of Buck's appeal being sustained.[6]

Short's nightmare scenario did not come to pass. Instead, the Appellate Division upheld Buck's conviction ten days later in a split decision—two concurring with the trial verdict and two opposed. Short's old law partner, Justice Stuart, penned the dissenting opinion with Justice Maitland S. McCarthy concurring. Stuart found McGillivray's argument that Buck was "not extradited for the offence of which he was convicted" compelling. In every instance when the province pressed charges against Buck—from the original charge before Police Magistrate Davidson back in 1915 to the hearings before the extradition commissioner, Paul J. Wall, right up to the Crown formally laying charges in front of Judge Winter in September 1916—no prosecutor even cited Cheely's May 9, 1914, article. Yet Short wanted the appellate court to believe Cheely's article nonetheless contributed to Buck's extradition. "For my part," wrote Stuart, "I cannot believe it." In fact, Stuart pointed to Short's affidavit on October 4, 1916, requesting the appointment of a special commission to gather Cheely's testimony "a few weeks before the trial and long after the extradition" as being when the prosecutor first learned of Cheely's article. Furthermore, Stuart found the charge laid before Judge Winter too vague, alleging that "on or about the 1st day of May 1914 the accused . . . concurred in the publication of a false statement." As Stuart pointed out, the charge did not specify any statement and the accused had a right to know what statement brought the charge. "It was a general and therefore a defective charge and I think the consequence is that it was not a charge with respect to the Cheely statement." Stuart interpreted the word "offence" contained in Article III of the Anglo-US Extradition Treaty to mean "the particular offence and not the general kind of offence." He then pointed to the trial transcript, where the prosecutor admitted that "if an accused has been extradited for the murder of A he cannot be tried after extradition for the murder of B committed before the extradition." Summing up his ruling, Stuart concluded, "There was not sufficient evidence in my opinion to support any other charge than that for which he was convicted." For good measure, Stuart added that the "statement" required to fulfill Section 414 of the Criminal Code "means necessarily a written statement" rather than an interview published in the paper.[7]

Justice Beck's opinion, with Chief Justice Harvey concurring, upheld the conviction. Beck wrote that the court found Buck guilty because of Cheely's testimony regarding the visit to the Black Diamond well on May 8, 1914, where Buck "made statements which were false, intending and expecting that Cheely would publish them in the *Albertan*." Regarding the two charges, Justice Beck wrote, "There is no difference between them except the statement of the place; one at Calgary and one at or near Calgary." For Beck, this amounted to a distinction without a difference, as "the facts justify a conviction under both or either or the charges." Beck then dismissed McGillivray's grounds for the appeal and turned his attention to Justice Stuart's opinion that the extradition treaty required the enumeration of a specific offence. Justice Beck argued that Buck was aware of the charges against him. After all, at Buck's arraignment on November 10, 1915, James Short devoted most of his time and attention to the conspiracy charges. However, Buck's illegal act (fleeing Canada for the United States) negated these two charges because they were not part of any Canada-USA treaty. Justice Beck wondered why, on July 3, 1916, US Secretary of State Robert Lansing signed an instrument of surrender directing Buck's extradition so that he could "be tried for the crime of which he is so accused." Beck took issue with Justice Stuart's opinion that the extradition treaty required the enumeration of a specific offence. Beck disagreed. The warrant of the extradition magistrate "may describe the offence in the generic words of the Extradition Treaty." While the accused "is entitled when brought before the Extradition Magistrate to have the offence particularized so as to fairly apprise him of the particular offence with which he is charged and to enable the magistrate to judge whether or not it is in truth an offence covered by the treaty," the trial court, argued Beck, "has nothing to do with this." While McGillivray argued this point "with a great sense of personal conviction," in practical terms "the evidence before the Extradition Magistrate was that taken by the Police magistrate at Calgary." While Justice Winter dismissed Tryon's evidence in rendering a verdict, McGillivray, argued Beck, asked too much of the court by seeking to overturn the conviction because the statements given to Tryon by Buck "turned out to be unobjectionable." Furthermore, Beck disagreed with McGillivray's claim that the Tryon article provided the sole grounds for Buck's extradition, arguing that the cumulative evidence presented accomplished the feat. To prove his point, Beck pointed out that Fletcher's testimony placed before the extradition commissioner contained this exchange between Fletcher and Tweedie on cross-examination:

Q: Was there a strike of oil there?

A: According to the *Albertan*.

Q: The *Albertan* is a pretty reliable journal?

A: They are when they get reliable information.

Q: Were you present when the *Albertan* ever got any information?

A: No sir.

Q: You don't know anything about it?

A: I know Mr. Buck told me he put (it?) over them—that is all I know—and could not over the *News-Telegram*.

Q: When did Mr. Buck tell you that?

A: In Medicine Hat, on the 12th day of May.

Q: And where were you when he told you?

A: I don't know which street.

Q: What day was the big strike?

A: The 7th of May was the supposed strike.

Beck then quoted from Fletcher's direct testimony about the conversation on May 12, 1914 with Buck:

A: [Buck] said Tryon of the *News Telegram* was taken out [to the well] but they did not take the matter seriously and they had to get *The*

Albertan and he had got a good write up from them, but they had not obtained the monetary results they expected.

Q: From the talking?

A: From putting the oil in.

Because Fletcher specifically cited Cheely's May 9, 1914, article, Beck suggested that "there is the highest probability that it was on all events, in fact, at least in part upon the evidence relating to the Cheely article that the surrender was directed." Thus, "the prisoner could properly be convicted on evidence relating to that article, as in fact was what happened, without contravention of Section 32 of the Extradition Act." As for McGillivray's contention that Cheely's article did not go before either the police magistrate or the extradition magistrate, Beck dismissed it as "a matter of no consequence." According to the Criminal Code, section 690, there is a difference between the amount and completeness of evidence "sufficient to put the accused on his trial and that which is sufficient to justify conviction." Beck concluded that, clearly, Buck "induced Cheely to publish material. In the *Albertan* with the intent alleged. Surely that was sufficient on a preliminary inquiry, though upon a trial, it would be improper not to insist upon more particularity."[8]

As *The Calgary Daily Herald* noted, the split decision meant "it is very probable that the appeal will now be carried to the Supreme Court of Canada," making it, potentially, the first criminal appeal from Calgary before the court. On January 4, 1917, notice arrived from McGillivray of Buck's appeal to the Supreme Court. The chances of a successful appeal were slim. Under the Chief Justiceship of Sir Charles Fitzpatrick, between his appointment on June 4, 1906, and October 21, 1918, when he resigned to become the Lieutenant- Governor of Quebec, an average of 68.2 percent of appeals heard by the court failed.[9] Despite James Short's evident interest in representing the province (he had previously appeared before the Supreme Court in 1914), the attorney general's office looked to retain legal counsel closer to Ottawa. Hearings regarding a second case from Calgary might appear during the same session and the department believed it could save money by hiring a single attorney to handle both.

In the meantime, the pressure of the case and the appeals took a toll on Browning, who increasingly regarded developments in the Buck case personally. The deputy attorney general's frustration soon fixed on how long the court took to schedule the date of the proposed hearing, bringing forth two grumpy messages to Short on the subject. On January 31, 1917, Browning lashed out, urging Short to recoup some department expenses by going after the property of those who posted bail bonds for Buck. "Buck is putting us to all the trouble possible and I do not know of any reason why his bondsmen should be given further consideration," wrote Browning. The next day, Browning fired off a terse, single-sentence letter to McGillivray. "I would appreciate your advising me as to the probable date on which [the Buck case] will be heard at Ottawa, so that I may be in a position to decide as to counsel." Ignoring Browning's evident frustration, and the reality that McGillivray did not set the court's calendar, McGillivray responded that he suspected the case would not appear before February 19, 1917, but then again "it might very well come on at an earlier date." In any case, McGillivray requested the name of the province's solicitor in Ottawa in case matters arose requiring immediate communication with opposing counsel.[10]

McGillivray's question touched a sore spot in the attorney general's office because the department proved unable to reach Browning's desired counsel, Eugene Lafleur of Montreal. Little wonder. As both a practising lawyer and a professor of international law at McGill University, Lafleur established an illustrious career that included more than 300 appearances before the Supreme Court of Canada. Even prosecutor James Short seemed a little star struck at the potential of working with Lafleur, writing Browning that one of his law partners, George Ross, heard Lafleur argue a Crown case on a recent trip to Ottawa and said "he never heard anything finer in his life."[11] However, Lafleur's schedule would not permit taking on the Buck case. Instead, Browning retained the Ottawa firm of Lewis and Smellie to serve as Crown agents in the matter, with Robert C. Smith, KC, as counsel. To Smith, Browning confessed the province had spent a lot of time and energy in pursuit of the case, adding, "It is very important that conviction should be maintained."[12]

Until the mid-twentieth century, the Canadian Supreme Court remained "a modest affair" that only became the final court of appeal in 1949. In the words of legal historians James G. Snell and Frederick Vaughan, inconsistent support from the government and questionable partisan appointments ensured that the Fitzpatrick Court (1906–1918) would overcome neither its weak public reputation nor its partisan flavour. Indeed, as a political appointee himself, Charles Fitzpatrick stepped down as Wilfrid Laurier's justice minister in order to, for all intents, appoint himself chief justice. Although an experienced defence lawyer who acted as chief counsel for Louis Riel in 1885, Fitzpatrick is the only chief justice of the Supreme Court who never served on the bench prior to his appointment in 1906.[13]

Before the Supreme Court, McGillivray zeroed in on the Cheely article's importance to the prosecution's case. Indeed, the agreed statement of facts between the attorneys did not dispute that Buck served as director of the company, nor did it dispute that Buck conspired with others to salt the well, nor that "some people may have been influenced to buy shares" in Black Diamond because of Cheely's article in the *Albertan*. Nevertheless, McGillivray considered Buck's conviction "strange" because the prosecution failed to establish a basic connection between Buck and Cheely. Buck's trial presented no evidence that Buck "knew who Cheely was," nor did the prosecution establish that Buck invited Cheely "or anyone from the *Albertan* office to go to the well." For all Buck knew, "Cheely went as any ordinary passenger desiring a ride to the oil fields." Nor did the prosecution prove that Buck "knew why Cheely had come [to the well,]" or that he "asked Cheely to write one word." McGillivray claimed, "There is no evidence that the defendant knew that [Cheely] was making notes of what he saw or heard." Furthermore, McGillivray argued that no one could prove that Buck "either suggested that the article be written or that the defendant knew that any article was to be written." In fact, McGillivray pointed out that Cheely testified that he did not speak to Buck after publishing the article at all.[14]

McGillivray contended a discrepancy existed between the charge of "making, circulating or publishing a statement" known to be false and the grounds for Buck's conviction. Two key questions stood out for the defence attorney: What statement did Buck make that broke the law and where was it published? In delivering his verdict, Judge Winter answered both questions by pointing to Cheely's May 9 article. However, before Extradition Commissioner Paul J. Wall, the circumstances around Tryon's visit to the well on May 7, 1914, and subsequent article in the *News Telegram* on May 8 provided the grounds for Buck's extradition. Yet in his written opinion upholding the verdict, Justice Beck referred to the Cheely article and the testimony of Norman Fletcher, not to Tryon. Furthermore, McGillivray argued Beck's opinion erred in linking Fletcher's statement that Buck "put it over" on the *Albertan* to the Cheely article when it "might equally well refer to any one of the number of similar articles written by the *Albertan* concerning defendant's alleged oil strike." Indeed, prosecutor James Short mistook Ritchie's article of May 8, 1914, for one authored by Cheely and admitted to first learning of the piece on October 4, 1916. As a final point, McGillivray reiterated that neither Cheely nor any other member of the *Albertan* provided evidence before the extradition commissioner.[15]

McGillivray then concluded the appeal by returning to his core argument—that the charge against the defendant at the extradition hearing was defective because it did not specify the statement that he allegedly concurred with, nor with whom he allegedly concurred. "It surely follows," argued McGillivray, "if the Crown proposes to convict a man of concurring with someone else in doing something, that that other person must be named, or, it must be said that he is unknown." Inasmuch as the prosecutor chose not to amend the charges as soon as the defence raised this issue, McGillivray urged the Supreme Court to overturn the conviction. McGillivray turned to his argument that an interview with a newspaper reporter did not constitute a "statement" as contemplated by section 414 of the Criminal Code. Certainly, Buck "may be said to have made a false verbal statement as to the oil in the well." But McGillivray contended that the law confined the term "statement" to mean "formal statements of the affairs of the Company in the nature of a prospectus or account." Section 414, argued McGillivray, "is not directed to the punishment of people who merely tell lies, whether for their own amusement or in the hope of gains, simply because they are directors."[16]

James Short prepared the Crown's response and quickly dispensed with McGillivray's argument that the charge did not disclose an indictable offense because it did not furnish particulars. "Particulars were not asked," wrote Short. "Nevertheless, at the opening of the trial herein they were given." Furthermore, the particulars addressed McGillivray's objection that the person with whom Buck allegedly concurred remain unnamed. On the contrary, argued Short, the particulars provided "the time, the place, and the occasion" of the false statement. "The person to whom the statement was made is not only described by his occupation but is further identified in the account of his journey to the oil well in the same motor .... His name, W. W. Cheely, appears at the beginning of the article containing the particulars."[17]

The prosecutor dealt with McGillivray's contention of a different charge at trial from the extradition hearing. The extradition warrant charged Buck with one count of fraud as a director and manager of the company. Short contended the particulars of the offence were not necessary to the validity of the extradition warrant. "It is the rule, not to do so. It is sufficient if it names the offense in the words of the Extradition Act." If the defendant faced different charges at trial, they could seek remedy by pointing to the evidence brought before the extradition commissioner. "He does so in this case and says nowhere is Cheely's name mentioned, and any references to the statement made by him are fragmentary." Short conceded this point and readily suggested there was a reasonable explanation. "The evidence before the Commissioner is the evidence taken before the magistrate in the preliminary enquiry at Calgary" that resulted in Buck being committed for trial. The inquiry began with the charge of conspiracy to defraud under Section 414 of the criminal code. At the conclusion of the preliminary hearing, "the evidence of taken was applied by agreement between the Crown and the Appellant on the charge under Section 414." Thus, extradition proceedings began on all three charges, with the conspiracy charges removed when it became known that they were not extraditable. As for McGillivray's contention that Cheely's evidence never appeared before the extradition commissioner, Short countered that "ample" references existed because of Fletcher's testimony from both the affidavit and transcript of the preliminary hearing placed before Wall. Citing section 18B of the Extradition Act, Short argued the Act established the amount of proof required for extradition as the same amount of evidence required by law to "justify his committal for trial." Furthermore, the prosecution needed only establish a prima facie case to secure a trial, not present its full case.[18]

The Crown's factum then raised the question of what constituted a statement under Section 414 of the Criminal Code. Short argued that this section of the code extended back to 1869's Larceny Act. In its various iterations, the law originally referred to "any written statement or account;" only in 1892 did the words "promoter" and "prospectus" appear. Short then referred to the legal principle of *ejusdem generis*—the notion that when a law provides a specific list of items followed by a general term, the law interprets the general term to include items like the ones specifically listed. Citing the Alberta Companies Ordinance (1901) definition of a prospectus as including "any prospectus, notice, circular, advertisement, or other invitation offering to the public for subscription or purchase any shares, stock, or debentures of a company," Short suggested Buck's words were not a prospectus "but they were a statement of like nature." Buck's statement to Cheely intended "to deceive and mislead the community and induce the public to purchase the stock of the corporation." Concurring, on the other hand, noted Short, "is evidenced by the acts of the Appellant more even than by his words." Buck's actions went "far beyond concurring. He arranged the whole matter of publication beforehand by a clearly devised plan." Namely, he got the well ready for inspection, invited Charles Tryon, and two city councillors to the site specifically to "use the oil strike with their own eyes." After completing the visit, Buck urged Tryon to get out a special edition of the *News Telegram*, which Tryon refused to do. The next day, Buck arrived at the well with William Cheely and repeated the demonstration and secured a favourable article published on May 9, 1914. Short then neatly summarized the prosecution's case by contending that

Cheely's visit, the interview given by Buck, and the *Albertan's* story "were not accidental but were part of a premeditated plan" to induce people to become shareholders in Black Diamond Oil Fields as proven by Fletcher's testimony. With that, Short wrapped up the Crown's response.[19]

The five justices of the Supreme Court heard Buck's case on February 23, 1917, and reserved its opinion. Despite the growing partisan flavour of the court under Fitzpatrick, it nonetheless displayed a more collegial atmosphere than previous iterations. The practice of circulating draft judgments among the justices for comment became more common under Fitzpatrick, helping to catch errors or inconsistencies, and making rulings more robust before they become official. Nevertheless, a conservative view prevailed of the court's proper place as an intermediary body, subordinate to the Judicial Committee of the Privy Council in London. Knowing that decisions were likely reviewed in London prompted even gifted legal minds to strictly adhere to the principle of stare decisis lest their rulings be overturned. Rulings typically placed a heavy emphasis on precedent.[20] These factors likely combined to produce a decision overturning Buck's conviction as Chief Justice Fitzsimmons changed his mind between the hearing and delivering the verdict on June 22, 1917.

In a split decision of three-two, Fitzsimmons, Duff, and Anglin upheld Buck's appeal, with Idington and Brodeur dissenting. In writing the majority opinion, the chief justice reaffirmed the principles contained in the extradition treaty that a fugitive could not be committed for extradition except in cases where the crime was the same and that the person surrendered would only face trial for the crime specified during the extradition hearing. The charge leading to Buck's extradition "must therefore be gathered from the warrant and the depositions filed before the extradition commissioner." The chief justice confessed that he initially believed that "it was impossible to say that [Buck] was tried for an offence different from that for which he was extradited." But after examining the precedent of *Regina v. Balfour*, Fitzsimmons arrived at a different conclusion. The ruling in that case "would appear to be that there is no jurisdiction to try a fugitive criminal in England for any offence not disclosed by the depositions etc., on which his extradition was obtained." The reason for this ruling is that "the demand for extradition is a criminal proceeding and the accused has a right not only to cross-examine but to adduce evidence before the magistrate." To do this effectively, the defendant "is entitled to be informed of the specific offence with which he is charged." Furthermore, regarding the prosecution's claim that Buck's statements to Tryon and Cheely were one and the same, the chief justice ruled that "the publication of a statement on one day in a newspaper cannot be said to constitute the same offence as the publication in another newspaper on another day of a statement which may or may not be to the same effect or identical with the first." The Tryon article served as the only evidence placed before the extradition commissioner, while Cheely's article served as the basis for the trial. Cheely's article "was not before the extradition commissioner and it cannot therefore be said that he was extradited for having concurred in the publication of that statement." Therefore, Fitzsimmons ruled in Buck's favour on the grounds that "it cannot be said that this indictment corresponds as it should with the depositions and information used for the application in extradition."[21]

Justice John Idington's dissent dismissed McGillivray's argument that Buck's trial charged a different offence than the one for which the United States surrendered him. He pointed to the fact that, perhaps, the court did not have the same information before it that the US extradition commission did, leaving the justices to infer its contents. This constituted a problem for Buck, "who has been convicted in a prosecution under and pursuant to the terms of a warrant of surrender." Justice Idington argued that warrant of surrender issued by Secretary Of State Lansing is "founded upon and follows in its terms the charge as laid before the Commissioner, and that we have not the right to impute to the Commissioner a neglect of duty in that regard." Evidence given by Fletcher proved Buck's admission relating to the interview given to Cheely resulting in the May 9 *Albertan* article "is in general terms and seems wide enough to cover any statement put forth by that newspaper at or about the time in question." Furthermore, Extradition Commissioner Paul J. Wall's inquiry did not seem limited in any way. Cheely's trip to the well on May 8 "was testified to by at least one witness whose evidence as well as that of Fletcher appears in the deposition submitted to that officer." When pressed about the nature of Cheely's trip to the well, Fletcher "did not think Cheely had gone merely for the ride. I agree." Idington found that the charges levelled by Short were clearly in evidence before Commissioner Wall. The commissioner and the Department of State "had before it a copy of the entire evidence" used to issue the original warrant. "The fact that there were several other charges of a like kind alleged to have taken place about the same time by another issue of falsehood, does not help the accused it seems to me, but rather tends to justify the surrender as related to any or all of them." Furthermore, Idington ruled too much "has been made of an error in relation to these other charges." The test "is not by such informations as laid before magistrates in this country," argued Idington, "but that which appears on the whole case before the Commissioner as containing evidence upon which such a warrant could issue." Information presented at preliminary hearings "are but a means for getting evidence in a judicial proceeding" taken under oath and "constitute but a part of the entire evidence upon which the commissioner may act." Idington believed the US surrender of Buck both covered and intended to cover Buck's numerous offences "as would justify one of our own magistrates committing for trial." According to Idington, Buck's conviction fell firmly "within the grounds upon which he was surrendered and upon evidence thereof disclosed in the material laid before the Commissioner as expressive of the purpose of those demanding his surrender."[22]

Lest anyone think the court found Buck innocent, Justice Francis Alexander Anglin's opinion overturning the conviction would thoroughly disabuse them of the thought. Anglin shed no tears for George Buck. "That he committed a gross criminal fraud was overwhelmingly proved," argued Anglin, and Buck "fully deserved the term of imprisonment to which he was sentenced." Unfortunately, the court had larger questions to consider, such as Canada's standing and international reputation, than Buck's guilt or innocence. "But much as it is to be regretted that such a scoundrel should escape punishment, it is of vastly greater moment that the good faith of this country shall be scrupulously maintained and a strict observance of its treaty obligations insisted upon."[23]

The attorney general's office in Edmonton and the Crown prosecutor in Calgary waited patiently for the telegram delivering the news of Buck's verdict. Anticipation turned to disappointment that unfolded slowly over several days as initial wire reports carried only the verdict and little more. The *Albertan* reported that word of the "oil manipulator's" ruling arrived but could add little beyond that; the same held true for the *Herald*, which published a generic article providing a thumbnail sketch of the progress of the Buck case to the appeal to round out the piece. In the meantime, Popple wired back to Ottawa the following day to see if the judgment provided for a new trial, and a negative answer came two days later. An official copy of the ruling arrived on July 4, 1917.[24]

In the aftermath of the Supreme Court's decision, reporters asked whether the attorney general's office would hold Buck until he paid the balance of his bail money. Somewhat disingenuously, Popple replied the matter was still under advisement.[25] In fact, the attorney general's office had prepared for the Supreme Court to grant Buck's appeal, making plans to ensure Buck's life became decidedly more uncomfortable in the process by holding him for jumping his bail. Between the February hearing in front of the Supreme Court and the delivery of the verdict in June, the attorney general's office collected or obtained adequate security for roughly a quarter of the $20,000 in bonds used to secure Buck's bail in 1915. Buck provided $10,000 of his own in securities, and bondspeople E.H. Crandell, John H. Poyntz, and his wife Ada Buck furnished the balance. Buck's $10,000 worth of securities disappeared like mist before the sun as property prices continued to soften because of the war, limiting the amount the province could recover. In several cases, property valuations provided for bail proved hopelessly optimistic at auction. To try and limit provincial losses on March 15, 1917, James Short suggested delaying property sales until June 23. Browning agreed and suggested that "in case Buck's appeal is successful, proceedings may be taken under Bond."[26]

The record is clear that the attorney general's office only intended to pursue a low-level harassment operation against Buck if the Supreme Court ruled in his favour. Since the province could not hold Buck on new criminal charges unless he voluntarily returned to Canada from abroad first, they decided to hold him on a civil charge for not paying his bail on the original two charges. Short reasoned that the collection of the bail debt was a civil matter and therefore was not subject to the terms of the extradition treaty. The plan reeked of pettiness and more than a whiff of spite but came together very quickly after March 15. By March 24, Short obtained conditional writs of *fieri facias* and *capias* and issued instructions to the Provincial Police. The writ of *fieri facias* gave the province the right to seize and sell Buck's property to satisfy the bond he forfeited by dint of fleeing to Kansas. On the other hand, the writ of *capias* compelled law enforcement to arrest Buck and bring him before the court. This latter writ seemed dubious in light of the specialty provisions of the extradition treaty. Nevertheless, Short assured Browning that the instructions provided to the superintendent of the Provincial Police and the sheriff of the Calgary Judicial District dictated "no action whatever will be taken unless the appeal in this case, which is now pending at Ottawa, results in favour of quashing the conviction." The orders were highly unusual and prompted a letter from McDonell, the superintendent of the new Alberta Provincial Police, to the deputy attorney general. Noting that "it is very unsatisfactory to receive a warrant with a string attached to it;" the superintendent specifically requested written confirmation of his instructions from Browning.[27]

In the meantime, some of the bondholders pleaded with Short to reduce their obligations. Short, however, remained unprepared to grant any leniency whatsoever. One letter in particular captures the frustration of the attorney general's office and the Crown prosecutor and the seething resentment they felt toward the bondholders. In 1915, John H. Poyntz put up some of his property, including his house, as collateral for $2,500 worth of the bond. Now, as the province moved to collect on the bond, Poyntz lay hospitalized with tuberculosis. His wife, Ruby, called on James Short to plead with him not to claim her house. Short proved unrelenting. Her husband's actions had made it possible for Buck to escape. Short said that "had her husband not given the Crown the assurance that Buck would remain for his trial the Crown would have been enabled to keep Buck in prison until his trial came on." His actions cost the Crown "over $15,000 in expenses"—nearly half a million dollars, adjusted for inflation—plus the expenses of two additional appeals. Even worse from Short's perspective was that the actions prevented him from charging Buck with two conspiracy charges that were easier to prove. "In all probability, if the easier charges had been proceeded with there would have been no grounds for appeal and the crown would have been saved the further expense of two appeals." Given the circumstances, no matter how much he sympathized with her plight, forgiving some or all of the debt "would still be a bad example to set to other bondsmen."[28]

With Buck set for release from the Edmonton penitentiary on July 4, Browning set in motion the plan for Alberta Provincial Police to arrest Buck "immediately" and return to him to Calgary. Although the press caught wind of the story, they speculated Buck "would have an option of returning to the United States" and declared it "improbable that Canada would be able to place hands on him unless he could be deported from the States at the boundary as an undesirable citizen." Yet on July 4, 1917, Browning issued instructions to McDonell to "execute the warrant in your hands arising out of the order of estreatment of bail in this case," Provincial Police duly rearrested Buck on a bench warrant signed by F.M. Graham, the sheriff of the Calgary Judicial District. The *Herald* reported the sheriff "failed to find either real or personal property of Buck" equivalent to $10,000 and issued the writ so that Buck could answer to the court. "In legal circles a good deal of surprise is expressed at the action of the attorney-general's department," wrote the *Herald* the next day. "The next move by either side is awaited with considerable interest." Asked by the *Albertan* if the province would take Buck to the border if he paid his bail, Short bluntly said no. "We would set him free here. He would then be allowed a reasonable time to get back to the [United] States, and if he did not do so he would be rearrested and tried on the other two charges."[29]

Despite the dubious legality of the attorney general's moves, negotiations began between James Short and Alexander McGillivray to find a mutually acceptable solution, and by July 13 the framework of a deal emerged. In exchange for serving a modest prison sentence to satisfy his outstanding debt, Buck agreed to leave the country. Short wired A.E. Popple to determine "the least term" Buck should serve. In a handwritten note on the back of the telegram, Popple specified that he would be satisfied with a term of two months or less but added the caveat that McGillivray would not take any further action. The message—minus the warning prohibiting future action by McGillivray—arrived back in Calgary via night letter. As negotiations continued, Buck's prison term contracted to one month, but the attorney general's office insisted that this would become conditional upon Buck's other bondsmen—Crandell, Poyntz, and Ada Buck—remaining responsible for payment of their bonds. Although Alexander McGillivray did not believe that the province's actions were entirely legal, he was "very anxious" to settle the matter expeditiously. Indeed, McGillivray told Short's law partner, Maynard Mayhood, that "it is a matter of indifference to him" if the immunity provision promised by prosecutors was in writing "so long as he has it definitely stated that such is the understanding." Browning pushed back and drew a line at granting Buck any kind of immunity. "If this is not agreeable to Mr. Buck's counsel then he is at liberty to take any proceedings he may deem advisable." The final deal between the two sides stipulated that Buck's one month in prison would "constitute full satisfaction of the indebtedness of the said George E. Buck." Upon completion of the month-long incarceration, Buck's "freedom and immunity" would "continue for a period of not less than ten days" to enable him to return to the United States.[30]

On July 23, 1917, Buck appeared before Justice William C. Ives of the Alberta Supreme Court and agreed to the deal worked out between McGillivray and Short. As Short reminded Browning, the Crown secured its right to recover the bonds from the other bondholders. "This," wrote Short, "was merely a measure of caution." More to the point, Short wrote that the deal "completes the matter, which has claimed our attention for a long period." At best, it seemed an anticlimactic end. "The sale of the lands of Mrs. Buck and Mr. Poyntz is to take place on Saturday, [July] 28[, 1917]. There does not seem to be much prospect of a sale as nobody seems anxious to buy."[31]

Starting on August 15, 1917, following Buck's release from prison, the attorney general's office gave Buck ten days' grace to settle his affairs and get out of the country. The press expressed some concern over Buck's plight, with the *Albertan* worrying whether he could obtain a passport in time and if the US government would consider him a desirable citizen. Considering recent events, "his chances of getting by are slim," predicted the newspaper. A different reporter phoned the Buck residence to see if he remained in the city but could not get a statement from the person who answered the phone.[32] Nevertheless, Buck and his family crossed the border without incident and relocated to Spokane, Washington. Unwilling as he likely was to test the resolve of the attorney general's office, there is no evidence that Buck ever returned to Alberta.

George Buck and his family adjusted quickly to life in the United States after their relocation to Spokane following exile from Canada in 1917. The first mention of the Bucks occurred in the Society pages of the *Spokane Chronicle* as daughter, Kathleen, married Ralph Burnett in June 1920.[33] As for George, old habits die hard. Following the Great War, fears abounded that existing oil supplies were insufficient to meet growing consumption, producing a rush of investments into exploration and development across North America. Surface oil seepages near Chewelah (45 miles northwest of Spokane) periodically attracted the attention of oil prospectors Gus Fritchie and Fred R. Burdette after 1905. Digging a hole by hand, they abandoned their first well because oil and gas odours proved too strong. Periodically, Fritchie and Burdette revived their efforts, and by 1920 they reported digging a second well to 52 feet with pick and shovel when gas odours again forced them to stop. Still, the prospectors reported digging through 15 feet of "solid oil shale."[34] Efforts ramped up in February 1921, when *The Colville Examiner* reported that the Chewelah Valley Oil Company filed eight oil leases with the county auditor. In late August 1921, George E. Buck and his partner, George L. Fisher, incorporated a new joint stock oil company, the Chewelah Basin Oil Company, to drill for oil in the Inland Northwest.[35]

Based out of Spokane, the Chewelah Basin Oil Company filed a prospectus claiming $400,000 of treasury stock with a par value of twenty-five cents a share. In many respects, Buck remained the same bundle of frenetic energy and hype, peppering reporters with word of his experience as an oil promoter, although careful observers noticed details remained sparse. A few weeks later, Buck opened local offices for the company at the Yale hotel in Colville, Washington.[36] Within two months, Buck announced that Chewelah Basin's drilling rig "will be set up complete for drilling within 30 days." Investors looking for a wonderful opportunity could buy shares starting in a few days at ten cents a share. "We have had geologists report on our holdings," Buck told the *Spokane Press* on October 22, 1921, "and feel confident that we are located on one of the greatest structures in eastern Washington." Days later, Buck claimed state geologists had completed two surveys and their reports would guide the company's activities. "The existence of a perfect formation is reported," noted *The Spokane Spokesman-Review*. Four days later, at a meeting of the Chewelah Chamber of Commerce, Buck asked the chamber to help finance the drilling of the first well. The chamber responded enthusiastically, and many of the fifty attendees pledged personal support.[37]

Investors in Black Diamond Oil Fields would likely recognize a well-worn formula. The old oil promoter claimed operations based according to "scientifically-based" principles would be the standard. Geological experts attested to the certainty of an oil strike on the company's land. References to similar success and expertise abounded. Frequent announcements flooded newspapers, conveying the appearance of action. But more than anything else, the absence of capital to finance drilling would be all too familiar. Admittedly, without the support of a larger boom taking place to help sustain it, Buck's act in 1921 proved too threadbare and the Chewelah Basin Oil Company collapsed within a couple of months. Two weeks after the October 25, 1921, announcement that the company would begin drilling within thirty days came another announcement that the acquisition of 5,000 acres of land pushed back the original timeline to December.[38] Predictably, the company's demise triggered at least one lawsuit as Buck sued the drilling company to recover drilling costs. That proved to be the last mention of the Chewelah Basin Oil Company. It is also the final connection of George Buck with oil and gas promotion. Only in retrospect does it become obvious how little the company accomplished. The State of Washington's Department of Natural Resources recorded no drilling information from the company and a 1930 newspaper article noted three previous attempts to drill for oil in Colville county all at the same location. None, prior to the Indian Foot Oil Company, including Buck's Chewelah Basin Oil Company, moved beyond selecting the well site.[39]

Fleeting glimpses of George Buck's life after backing out of the oil industry dot the public record. By the mid-1920s, Buck's marriage to Ada unravelled when daughter Kathleen filed for divorce from Ralph Burnett.[40] The dissolution of the daughter's marriage, in turn, caused strains between George and Ada Buck. "I thought the trouble was my daughter's fault and wanted her to go back to her husband," testified George Buck, who now identified his profession as a car salesperson rather than an oil promoter. "But my wife thought she should get a divorce and trouble resulted. We then separated." Asked why he wanted a divorce, Buck responded that "I do not want to be married to woman who does not care for me. In fact, I believe she never cared for me." Harsh words, indeed, for the mother of his five children and the woman who endured so much in the service of Buck's various schemes. The attorney pronounced to the presiding judge that the case represented "the saddest kind of divorce. Here is an old couple seeking a divorce after 30 years of married life."[41] Within six months of the divorce from Ada, in December

1925, Buck remarried a Spokane pioneer, the widow Clara Carr. Ada never remarried and lived to be ninety-two years old, passing away in California in 1958.[42]

Occasionally, word of the old promoter surfaced, usually in connection with lawsuits filed over unpaid commissions as Buck turned his full attention to auto sales.[43] Buck's last big splash occurred during the Depression, when he became a vocal supporter of retired California doctor Francis E. Townsend, who briefly became a populist icon during the Depression. One morning while shaving in 1933, Townsend claimed he glanced out his window to see three old women rummaging through his garbage cans for something to eat. Outraged that the women were reduced to such circumstances, Townsend vowed to do something about it. In the pages of the Long Beach *Free Telegram*, he first advanced the Townsend Recovery Plan, which advocated the development of an old-age pension plan that would see the federal government institute a 2 percent sales tax to pay $200 a month to every American over the age of sixty who agreed to stop working. The sole caveat was that the recipient must spend the full amount every month, recirculating the money and reviving the economy in the process. The plan appealed to middle America, embraced traditional values, and promised to save capitalism from collectivism, socialism, and communism. Critics who investigated the plan estimated that, with ten to twenty million eligible Americans, the benefits would accrue to 9 percent of the population, consume half the national income to fund, and require a police state to enforce. Nevertheless, at a time when caring for the elderly typically fell on family and relatives, the idea of establishing some kind of national pension proved incredibly popular. An estimated twenty million people signed petitions in support of the plan and thousands of Townsend Clubs sprang up across the United States, including in Washington state, where a sixty-six-year-old George Buck served as president of Townsend Club No. 10, the largest in Spokane. Historian Robert Dallek compared Townsend club meetings to old-time religious revivals complete with "prayers, hymns, and shouts of 'amen.'" Exhorted with evangelical fervour by Townsend, now referred to as "the Founder," supporters lobbied Congress and the Senate to adopt the scheme. The movement, according to Townsend, embraced people "who believe in the Bible, believe in God, cheer when the flag passes by, the Bible Belt solid Americans."[44]

As a lifelong Democrat, Buck supported the incumbent president, Franklin D. Roosevelt and the New Deal through the summer of 1936 but abruptly changed allegiances as the November presidential election drew closer. In late October 1936, much to the consternation of local Townsend

Club officials, Buck urged Townsendites to vote for the Republican candidate, Governor Alf Landon, warning, "You can kiss the Townsend Plan goodbye forever if Roosevelt is re-elected." Briefly, Buck returned to his element as iconoclast and prognosticator, able to see what others could not. Denouncing FDR and the New Deal as failures, Buck further declared that the Townsend Plan was the only viable option to save the United States from the alternatives of fascism or communism. With Landon in the White House and New Dealers in control of Congress, Buck argued a Republican president must form a political coalition with Townsendites to enact his agenda. The price would be making the Townsend Plan a reality.[45]

Involvement with the Townsend clubs returned Buck to more familiar trappings at the centre of a larger movement, this time political rather than commercial, where his ability to attract attention garnered favourable notice. However, Buck's political acumen proved no better than his ability to drill a producing oil well. Despite Buck's best efforts, Franklin Roosevelt won the 1936 election over Landon in a landslide that remade US politics for the next thirty years with the creation of the New Deal coalition. With this new majority, Roosevelt passed his signature reform, the Social Security Act.

When he passed away at the age of seventy-six in January 1944, Buck's obituary claimed he was a retired automobile insurance salesman and included no mention of his origins in Canada, nor his time as an oil promoter in Turner Valley, Kansas, or just outside Spokane. Perhaps the family simply wanted to forget, or preferred just tacitly acknowledging with silence that, as an oil promoter, George Buck never produced a barrel of oil apart from that which he poured down Black Diamond #1 in 1914. As it turned out, that would be the only oil that well site ever produced.

The second Turner Valley era (1924–1936) that began when Royalite drilled into the Madison limestone, deeper than any other well in western Canada, revived interest in Turner Valley as a natural gas producer. It also led to the renaissance of both the Black Diamond Oil company and interest in the original Black Diamond well site. At approximately the same time that George Buck divorced his first wife in June 1925, new investors revived the Black Diamond moniker under a federal charter after buying the assets of Buck's old company. Calling themselves the New Black Diamond Oil Company, the new owners announced plans to extend the original well much deeper—to 8,000 feet—with rotary rig technology. As the *Calgary Herald* pointedly reminded investors, "the old company was wiped out long ago" and therefore this constituted a new enterprise. Consciously or not, however, the New Black Diamond Oil Company borrowed Buck's faith in the location, emphasizing the quality of their leasehold as the best in the field. The new company also hinted that they would work out a deal with stockholders of the old company, but the details remained fuzzy. The New Black Diamond enjoyed some success as a natural gas producer, surviving the Great Depression and the Second World War before winding up corporate operations in 1961. But the success they did have came because of production from other wells; like Buck they, too, had little success at the original well site.[46]

Black Diamond #1's last kick at the can happened in 1950. During the Second World War, Shell expanded into Alberta with the creation of Shell Exploration, eager to acquire new production to offset losses of traditional supplies in Asia. Included in the 450,000 acres of mineral rights bought by the company were those to the original Black Diamond site. Despite the pressure to find alternative sources of supply, Shell limited exploration efforts to seismic surveying of the region.[47] Only after Imperial Oil's Leduc discovery in 1947 in the much deeper Devonian limestone revived interest in the eastern half of the Turner Valley field did Shell begin a serious drilling program. In early 1948, Anglo-Canadian Oil, then one of Canada's largest independents, announced it would extend the old Black Diamond #1 down 10,500 feet, with Shell paying the exploration costs.[48] Labelling the well "Anglo-Black Diamond #1," the company bored down to 9,309 feet before trying to stimulate oil production with acidization with no success. When a second acidization treatment failed, Anglo-Black Diamond declared the formation too tight and abandoned the well in March 1949. Despite another deep test a year later, this time below 10,000 feet, Shell abandoned the well again, this time for good. In the late 1970s, one long-time resident of Black Diamond, familiar at least in passing with George Buck and his various schemes, provided one final update on Black Diamond #1: "the well never amounted to much although it did produce a little coal oil."[49]

14

Conclusion: Buck and the Boom

> *Calgary was quite some place on the map of Canada once. They used to find oil wells there, and there are, as 'Spider' says in the third act, plenty of get-rich-quick land schemes in Calgary and considerable luck in the name . . . . I've got to knock my home town. Gosh, how I hate it, but the playwright says I must, and he ought to know.*
> —Calgary Actor Gus A. Forbes discussing the role of "Pat," in the Broadway play "The Dummy"
> *Edmonton Journal*
> April 27, 1916

Philosophers of history point out the paradox that every act of remembrance also serves as an act of forgetting—that by choosing to memorialize one thing, we neglect another. In practical terms, Alberta's collective memory of 1914 celebrates William Stewart Herron and Archibald Dingman at the expense of George Buck. The consequences of this collective amnesia about the events of the 1913–14 boom are quite significant. Forgetting Buck also means forgetting the thousands of investors stripped of their savings amidst a worsening depression. The irreparable harm done to legitimate businesses and the demand that government "do something" to protect consumers. It means forgetting the origins of the first "blue-sky" legislation the province ultimately was forced to adopt because of the steps others—both consumers and industry—adopted to make sure Buck's swindles could not be replicated.

Buck's legacy in Alberta is somewhat ambiguous, if only for the fact that for several years after his departure, Buck became shorthand for the excesses of 1914—a caricature whose actions seemed more buffoonish than harmful. The details of the conspiracy to salt the well and defraud investors became background noise as Calgarians and southern Albertans meekly shrugged off

419

the stories of the boom as another manifestation of the city's willingness to have a good time, like the eleven days of the Stampede every July or, in today's context, when the beloved Calgary Flames go on an extended playoff run. As Buck receded into the background, other developers, most notably William S. Herron, Archibald Dingman, Edward H. Crandell, and even William Georgeson ascended to the pantheon of the petroleum industry's local heroes and visionaries.

Periodic reminders of Buck's infamy appeared, but rarely, if ever, within the context of the broader boom. William Davidson, the editor of *The Morning Albertan*, printed reminders over the next few decades marking the anniversaries of Buck's arrest and trial for fraud; he also published some of Bob Edwards's columns about Buck as well. As time passed, reminders of Buck appeared less frequently, especially after Davidson sold the *Albertan* in the 1930s, and the details became hazy. Carl O. Nickle, Jr., the publisher and proprietor of *Nickle's Daily Oil Bulletin* since 1937, who likely forgot more history about Alberta's petroleum industry than most people ever knew, nevertheless made mistakes in retelling the story to Jack Peach of *The Calgary Herald*. Nickle inaccurately claimed Buck was an American oil promoter who came to Calgary during the boom to defraud investors by salting his well, not a middle-aged itinerant preacher from Ontario desperate to use petrodollars to create God's kingdom of heaven on Earth. In 1978, Fred Kennedy—who arrived in Calgary in 1912 and sold oil stock out of his newspaper bag in the lobby of the Palliser Hotel during the boom—published the last mention of George Edward Buck in *The Calgary Albertan* but made a few mistakes in the process. The article correctly pointed out that Buck "salted" the well, but it made mistakes on other details, claiming that the well was only 100 feet and that a newspaper reporter discovered the fraud by accident when he stumbled across the "'drilling crew' replenishing the oil."[1]

Given enough time, memories of the exploits of Buck and his contemporaries, Julian Langner, Bird W. Dunn, and William Georgeson faded, but they nonetheless bequeathed a challenging legacy for Calgary—and Alberta—to resolve. In many ways, these four figures embodied notions of the ethos of limited government, bootstrap independence, and the entrepreneurial spirit that established the province's oil culture and animated the boom. Advertisements for oil shares in 1913–14 established the belief that oil could provide personal freedom and financial security. Debates in the public square—letters to the editor, cartoons, opinion pieces in newspapers, and conversations between individuals—fostered the dream of an "independent" boom with particular characteristics: freedom from domination by a large integrated company like Standard Oil; investment capital raised by private investors, preferably local ones, so that the province would benefit the most from development; and finally, one where companies operating in the field focused on exploration and production of oil. Buck embodied these ideals and went to extreme lengths to realize them.

At the height of the oil boom in 1914, the Province of Alberta lacked the institutions and administrative capacity to regulate the sale of stock and the actions of promoters and brokers, enabling Buck and his confederates to run roughshod over consumers. Facing the unforgiving side of laissez-faire capitalism, bilked consumers resorted to self-help measures—consumer boycotts, information campaigns, and ultimately resort to the courts—to find some form of protection and relief. Convinced that the Sifton government lacked both the intent and capacity to ensure fair dealing by Alberta-based companies and brokers, consumers in nearby markets—both in Canada and the United States—mounted "anti-Calgary oil" campaigns that forbade the selling shares of all Alberta oil companies within their jurisdictions because of the actions of a decided minority. Painting all producers and brokers with the same brush seemed excessive but justified, considering provincial helplessness, and provided an object lesson in collective responsibility. That other jurisdictions evaluated the new-found industry on the actions of its weakest members was a hard and bitter lesson for provincial officials to absorb. Given that southern Alberta investors lacked sufficient capital to finance development of all the companies operating in the province, inhibiting outside capital posed a substantial obstacle to timely and efficient development.

Consumers were not the only constituency caught unprepared for the emergence of a new industry; so too were all levels of government. Hampered by muddied lines of jurisdiction and an incomplete multi-level regulatory regime, officials often responded haltingly, if at all, to problems. Indeed, although the province claimed the right under the Companies Act to investigate the activities of all companies with a provincial charter, they largely remained dependent on the overworked Calgary police to conduct investigations. In turn, the Calgary police punted the ball back to the provincial government when it came to investigating "wildcat" companies. Ultimately, the province squared the circle by employing Pinkerton agents on an ad hoc basis but realized this was not a permanent solution.

In the aftermath of the boom, the process of regaining public trust and investor confidence in Alberta oil caught the attention of the Sifton government and Charles Cross's attorney general's office as they worked to strengthen the province's hand by creating institutions and precedents for future development. Certainly, the events of the boom dictated that the province could not continue its hands-off approach, but it would be impossible to imagine the province sustaining laissez-faire following the outbreak of the Great War in August 1914. As the radical writer Randolph Bourne observed in 1918, "War is the health of the state," and the dramatic expansion of government power to reach into the lives of its citizens following the opening of hostilities represented a difference of kind rather than degree over everything that transpired before 1914. The War Measures Act (1914) reserved wide-ranging powers for the Dominion government, including the ability to suspend civil rights, censor the press, intervene in the economy, allocate resources, levy an income tax, and even change what Canadians could eat or drink. Along the way, the war decisively changed public attitudes toward the state, transforming it into, in the estimation of historian John Thompson, "an organization capable of vigorous, positive activities." In this, the character of the Great War and the sweeping universalist tone of British war aims—securing democracy and freedom from German militarism and tyranny—only strengthened the hand of reformers.[2]

Repeatedly, government officials drummed into Canadians the notion that efficiency was a prerequisite for victory over Germany. Perhaps more significantly, the war briefly challenged the primacy of bootstrap individualism. With 61,000 Canadian soldiers making the ultimate sacrifice for freedom and liberty, the war demonstrated the importance of subordinating individual desires to the good of the many. Unquestionably, the creation of the Public Utilities Board in 1915 and the expansion of its powers a year later with the Sale of Shares Act were important watersheds for businesses operating in the province. Sandwiched between these two pieces of legislation, the Sifton government launched the Carpenter Commission. Given the broad mandate granted by the orders-in-council—enabling Judge Carpenter to summon witnesses and compel testimony and evidence—the Carpenter Commission attempted to establish the provincial right and responsibility of overseeing practically any matter that took place within the province. Although the commission did not survive a legal challenge to its authority mounted by Buck and Alexander McGillivray, amending the Public Inquiries Act finished what the Carpenter Commission started. Furthermore, the Carpenter Commission gathered enough information to influence the details of Alberta's first "blue-sky" legislation, the 1916 Sale of Shares Act, as well as its enforcement.

Only a handful of companies maintained sufficient capital flow to continue drilling in Turner Valley after 1914. Ominous signs of a struggling industry accumulated. The number of stock exchanges in Calgary continued to dwindle, some through mergers with the CSE, while others simply ceased operations as exploration of the field declined. As the provincial government moved to exercise greater control over the sale of securities, the number of members working on the Calgary Stock Exchange dropped to eight. Shortly thereafter, the CSE suspended operations for the next nine years.[3]

Perhaps no one experienced these developments more acutely than William Stewart Herron. On the cusp of becoming the wealthiest person in Alberta's nascent oil patch by dint of his extensive leaseholds, Herron instead found himself struggling to keep his head above water. As the war ramped up, investment capital shrank. What little exploration activity remained did so because individual drillers and crews from the United States continued working the field. However, when the United States declared war on Germany in April 1917 and began mobilizing, nearly all interest—and investment capital—for Alberta's oil development vanished. Between 1911 and 1915 Herron estimated he spent approximately $225,000 ($6.9 million adjusted for inflation) developing the Turner Valley field.[4] During the wartime emergency, however, he needed to raise capital simply to hang on to what he had. "His aggressive strategy had become a money trap," writes biographer Frank Dabbs. By early 1918, rental payments for some of Herron's leases were at least three years in arrears and Herron stood to lose everything. Herron pleaded with officials at the Department of the Interior for special consideration. "I [have] perhaps done more than any other individual towards the development of Alberta's oil resources, and for that reason I think that my leases should be the last leases that would be cancelled by your department," wrote Herron in January 1917.[5] Only after he sold off some personal assets, including his Calgary home in September 1919—at one-third the price he bought it for in 1914— were Herron's payments brought up to date.

Others were luckier. Hotelier William J. Stokes, who accumulated plenty of stock certificates both in his own and other companies, eventually faced the unenviable reality of what to do with these now worthless pieces of paper. Rather than destroy them, Stokes decided to use them to wallpaper the lobby of his hotel. But then one day in 1926, shortly after the start of the second Turner Valley boom, Stokes examined the certificates again and discovered some companies had resumed operations, making his "wallpaper" more valuable than he thought.[6] The final accounting of the first Turner Valley era (1912–24) shows an estimated $4 million ($124,500,000 adjusted for inflation) invested and approximately 500 oil companies formed. Drill crews spudded in nineteen wells, seven of which were abandoned. Only four wells from the frenzy of 1914 still operated by 1920, with Calgary Petroleum Products running three of them—Dingman #1, #2, and #3. Faced with mounting debt in the aftermath of a fire that destroyed CPP's uninsured extraction plant, Herron and his partners faced another agonizing choice whether to rebuild. At the urging of R.B. Bennett, Herron sold the company's remaining assets to Standard Oil of New Jersey's Canadian subsidiary, Imperial Oil. Since Imperial marketed its kerosene under the brand name Royalite, the newly acquired Calgary Petroleum Products was rebranded as the Royalite Oil Company.[7]

In certain ways, the first Turner Valley era prepared the province for much of what followed, leading up to the Leduc discovery. It established Calgary, rather than Edmonton, as the corporate and financial capital of the petroleum industry in Alberta. Activity in Turner Valley revived in 1924 when Royalite #4 blew into production with a naphtha flow of 24 million cubic feet per day. As the industry revived, some echoes of the first boom a decade before resonated as specific institutions and practices revived, like the Calgary Stock Exchange. When the CSE resumed operations in March 1926, Calgary had 116 brokers, including seven women, and five licensed exchanges. The city's licence fee for brokers remained at fifty dollars, provided brokers resided in the city; perhaps reflecting the suspicion that the crush of outsiders was responsible for the troubles of 1914, the city's fee for out-of-town brokers spiked to $5,000.[8]

On the other hand, the legacy of George Buck's bootstrap entrepreneurialism and wildcat Christianity remained alive and well in the province. Albertans did not fully appreciate in 1914 the degree to which their vision of an idealized "independent" boom already conflicted with the reality of an increasingly global petroleum industry. The single-minded determination to produce every possible barrel of oil regardless of economic reality established by the first boom in 1914 produced a bitter harvest in later decades. Oil companies found ways around the modest oversight and regulatory framework established by the province by moving their charters to the federal government rather than operating under a provincial one. The drive to produce as much petroleum as possible meant that many of these companies engaged in positively reckless behaviour in the 1920s and early 1930s.

Enabled by federal regulations that placed an emphasis on production rather than conservation, and pursuing their own self-interest, producers stripped the naphtha out of the gas and set the much more voluminous natural gas they encountered ablaze, in a process known as flaring, to burn off the "excess"—that is, gas produced without a market—as industrial waste.[9] "It was quite a show place for tourists," recalled geologist J. Grant Spratt. "Almost

Figure 14-1 "Flare at Turner Valley oil field, Alberta"
Flaring the natural gas produced by Turner Valley wells in the 1920s and 1930s could be seen as far away as Calgary (ninety kilometres, or forty miles), especially since the flares provided enough light to enable people to read a newspaper at night. The practice consumed as much as 90 percent of the field's natural gas cap and earned Turner Valley the nickname "Hell's Half Acre." (Glenbow Archives CU1153082)

every night there was that great red glare in the skies. People would go out visiting it from Calgary and eastern Canada and the United States." Spratt recalled that the flares enabled pilots to get their bearings for the first airplanes through southern Alberta. As far away as Medicine Hat, 367 kilometres (approximately 167 miles) from Calgary, one could see the red reflection of the fires in the sky.[10]

British newspapers compared it to Dante's Inferno, claiming "men have gone mad gazing into its heart."[11] No single answer adequately explains why flaring became the industry standard. Several factors—the economics of natural gas (limited demand, abundant supplies, prohibitive transportation costs, and limited technology,); the law of capture; and laissez faire capitalism that rewarded the bold and punished the cautious—governed production, and ensured that natural gas markets remained small and local rather than regional or national in size. By the 1920s, Calgary's population plateaued at approximately 65,000, with average daily natural gas consumption remaining static at 20 million cubic feet per day. On cold days, natural gas consumption reached 70 million cubic feet per day—less than one-tenth of the estimated

500–600 million cubic feet of natural gas flared every day in Turner Valley. Stated another way, producers in Turner Valley regularly burned ten dollars' worth of natural gas to produce a dollar's worth of gasoline.[12]

Cumulatively, between 1924 and 1937, flaring consumed an estimated 1.8 trillion cubic feet of "sour" gas—approximately 90 percent of the commercially recoverable natural gas, worth several hundred billion dollars today. Even at current rates of consumption, Turner Valley flares consumed enough "waste" to supply all of Canada's natural gas demand for the next 417 years.[13] This constitutes one of the worst man-made environmental disasters in provincial history. Flaring depressurized the field, squandering the gas cap capable of lifting the crude oil beneath Turner Valley to the surface. Thus, despite being a prolific oil field, as Robert "Streetcar" Brown, Sr., finally proved in 1936, Turner Valley produced far less oil than it could have. Of the one billion barrels of crude estimated to be in Turner Valley, only around 140 million barrels were recovered.[14] Arguments by the province that producers were hurting the environment and harming the oil field did not stop the practice. It continued to draw negative attention from international commentators and forced the provincial government to step in and expand the regulatory regime over the extreme objections of independent producers. Even still, the backlash against government intervention, in favour of bootstrap individualism and the free market, proved so fierce that Turner Valley producers sued the province, challenging the premise that the provincial government had the right and responsibility to regulate the petroleum industry operating within its borders.

But that's a different story altogether.

Acknowledgements

This is not the book I set out to write. *The Boom* began as a COVID project—to pass the time and make the most of a year-long research and scholarship leave in 2022–23. I had originally planned to work on a different topic, but like so many things upended by the pandemic, I had to improvise and adjust on the fly. As the world slowly began reopening, I calculated that I was more likely to gain access to local archives before national or international ones—and that gamble paid off as travel restrictions gradually loosened. Even then, my research had a different focus before I concluded that I needed to cover the first Turner Valley boom. While going through the digitized newspaper collection at the University of Calgary Libraries, I stumbled across a few ads for Black Diamond Oil Fields that stood out from the flurry of advertisements in Alberta newspapers in 1913–14. As I dug deeper, the stories became increasingly colorful, and it didn't take long for me to realize there was a compelling story worth telling.

Historians always accumulate debts to archivists and librarians who unfailingly lend their help and expertise. Nadine Hoffman, the History Department's librarian—and one of my late sister Ann-Marie's friends—kept me updated on when archives would reopen. Finally, in the spring of 2023, I was back at the Glenbow Western Research Centre, and the project really took off.

At many steps along the way, I have received excellent advice and guidance. At the Provincial Archives in Edmonton, I had the good fortune to work with Michael Gourlie, Kathy Epp, Elizabeth Johnson, and Kari Cartwright. At Library and Archives Canada in Ottawa, Michel Brideau and Alexandra McEwen were invaluable in helping me navigate their collections; Wade Popp at the National Archives in Kansas City; and Lynn Bullock at the City of Calgary Archives. I'm also grateful to all the staff and archivists at the Glenbow Western Research Centre. With its fabulous reading room and helpful staff—especially Allison Wagner and Maggie Hunter—I am only partially joking when I tell people it is my summer home. This project benefited enormously from the expertise and generosity of all these individuals.

This book owes a great deal to the hard work and skill of the exceptional team at the University of Calgary Press—Brian Scrivener, Helen Hajnoczky, Alison Cobra, Melina Cusano, and Peter Enman, who has now edited two of my books. I'm also grateful to the two anonymous reviewers who offered insightful feedback and suggestions for improving the manuscript. As always, any remaining errors are mine alone.

For a historian, writing a book is an exercise in delayed gratification—but it's hardly a solitary pursuit. I'm more grateful than I can say to the friends, family, and colleagues who offered encouragement, advice, suggestions, or simply listened patiently as I launched into yet another story about the Turner Valley boom. Many thanks to my departmental colleagues, past and present, at the University of Calgary, beginning with our outgoing department head, Jewel Spangler. I'm grateful to George Colpitts, Petra Dolata, Warren Elofson, John Ferris, Betsy Jameson, Nancy Janovicek, Hendrik Kraay, Mark Konnert, Courtnay Konshuh, David Marshall, Amie Kiddle, Frank Towers, and Tim Stapleton—all of whom patiently and politely indulged me or offered suggestions. Special thanks to my departmental neighbor and colleague Lyndsay Campbell, who went above and beyond to patiently answer my many questions about Alberta's laws and legal history.

I've been fortunate to meet and occasionally work with many talented and generous people—and to form lasting friendships along the way. My thanks to Mark Baron, Scott Beekman, Dave Chin, Sarah Jarvis Deschamps, Darren Dochuk, Alfred E. Eckes, Jr., Tim Glowa, Richard Hawkins, Rob Huebert, Jim Keeley, Kim Little, Dominique Perron, Francine G. Smith, Justyna Sarna, and David Wachal. Each of you contributed to this project in your own ways—through encouragement, guidance, or by helping me navigate life's problems. Often, you did all three. Everyone carries a sack of hammers, but it's generous, kind people like you who help lighten the load or offer comfort. My life is a better place because you are in it.

Families experience the writing of a book more intimately than anyone else, becoming part of the process in too many ways to count. My two boys, William and Jack, had front-row seats as the story of George Buck took shape. They listened intently over dinner conversations and came to accept that their dad might vanish into pre-war Turner Valley for long stretches. Thanks to Jack for always checking in on my progress and for helping to choose which pictures to use; and to William, for his Photoshop skills. You both keep me grounded—and made sure I took breaks for video games and table hockey.

My mother, Audrey, was the manuscript's first proofreader and welcomed our conversations being overtaken by Turner Valley's stories. She never hesitated to tell me when things didn't make sense and—true to form—didn't even blink when I told her one night that there might be a book in the tale of George Buck.

This book holds special meaning because of two people who helped inspire it—my dad, Tony Chastko, and my late uncle, George Glowa—neither of whom got to see it completed. They taught me the importance of a great story at countless family dinners. Unlike a historian, however, they might have played fast and loose with the details—but always in service of the story.

My dad arrived in Calgary during a later boom in 1968, a newcomer to the oil patch, and launched himself fully into the life of a Calgarian until his passing in 2009. As I wrote certain sections, I could hear his laugh and see his smile. I think he would have loved this book.

My uncle George saw the early stages of this project. One late summer evening, he asked what I was working on. I gave him a quick sketch of George Buck and Turner Valley in 1914, and he instantly knew it was a helluva story. Every few months, he'd ask for updates. Just before he passed, I sent him four chapters—but I don't know if he got to read them. Maybe, as my cousins—Tim Glowa, Jackie Kane, and Michelle Wilks—read this book, they'll remember the stories our dads used to tell at countless family dinners.

Finally, to my partner, wife, and ride-or-die—Michelle—what more can I say than I'm having the time of my life, fighting dragons with you. Yes, I just quoted a Taylor Swift song in the acknowledgements. There's nothing I can't do with you by my side—except for a true crime podcast. Unless, of course, it's about George Buck . . .

Bibliography

Archival Sources
City of Calgary Archives (CCA)
    Board of Commissioners fonds
    City Clerk's Department fonds
        Correspondence with other Municipalities
        Memoranda to City Officials, Aldermen and Employees
        Miscellaneous Out of Town Correspondence
Glenbow Western Research Centre, Calgary (GWRC)
    Alberta Stock Exchange Fonds
    Bob Edwards Fonds
    Calgary Chamber of Commerce Fonds
    Charles Stalnacker Fonds
    Dingman Family Fonds
    Elizabeth Price Fonds
    Herron Fonds
    Petroleum Industry Oral History Project
    Hugh Dempsey Fonds
    James Gray Fonds
    John Schmidt Fonds
    McKinley Cameron Fonds
    Percival Timms Fonds
    Tiny Phillips Fonds
Library and Archives Canada, Ottawa (LAC)
Provincial Archives of Alberta, Edmonton (PAA)
    Attorney General Central Files
        Companies Ordinances General Files
    Calgary Civil Court Files
    Calgary District Court Files
    Provincial Secretary Files
Supreme Court of Calgary Trial Division
National Archives at Kansas City

Newspapers/Journals

Anaconda Standard (Montana)
Bellevue Times
Butte Daily Post
Calgary Eye Opener
Calgary Herald (CH)
Calgary Morning Albertan (CMA)
Calgary News Telegram (CNT)
Canadian Mining Journal
Cascade Courier (Montana)
Chicago Tribune
Colville Examiner
Courier-Reporter (Waterloo, IA)
Custer Weekly Chronicle (South Dakota)
Day Book (Chicago)
Daily Mail (London, UK)
Detroit Free Press
Edmonton Bulletin (EB)
Edmonton Capital
Edmonton Journal (EJ)
Financial Post
Hutchinson Gazette (Kansas)
Idaho Daily Statesman (Boise)
Indianapolis Star
Kansas City Globe
Kingston Whig-Standard
Leavenworth Times
Lethbridge Daily Herald
Los Angeles Times
Manitoba Free Press
Miles City Star (Montana)
Minneapolis Star-Tribune
Minneapolis Journal
Monetary Times, Trade and Insurance Chronicle
Montana Record-Herald
Montreal Gazette
Natural Gas and Oil Record (Calgary)
National Post
North Bay Nugget
Omaha Daily Bee
Oregon Daily Journal (Portland)

Ottawa Citizen
Ottawa Journal
Petroleum Gazette
Petroleum World (London)
Quebec Telegraph
Red Deer Advocate
Red Deer News
Regina Leader
Rochester Democrat and Chronicle
Salina Evening Journal (Kansas)
Saskatoon Star-Phoenix
Seattle Post-Intelligencer
Spokane Chronicle
Spokane Spokesman-Review
Star Press (Muncie, IN)
Topeka Daily Capital
Topeka State Journal
Toronto Globe
Toronto Star
Wall Street Journal
Washington Standard (Olympia)
Western Oil Examiner
Western Standard
Wichita Beacon
Wichita Eagle
Windsor Star
Valley News (Van Nuys, CA)
Vancouver Daily World
Vancouver Sun
Victoria Colonist
Victoria Daily Times

Government Documents

Alberta. An Act to regulate the Sale of Shares, Bonds and other Securities of Companies, *Statutes of Alberta, 1916.*

Alberta Board of Public Utilities Commissioners, *First Annual Report, 1916.* Edmonton: Government Printer, 1917.

Alberta Board of Public Utilities Commissioners, *Second Annual Report, 1917.* Edmonton: Government Printer, 1918.

Cairnes, DeLorme Donaldson. "Moose Mountain District of Southern Alberta." Geological Survey of Canada, Report 968. 1907.

Canada. Dominion Bureau of Statistics. Department of Railways and Canals, Sessional Paper 20b. "Railway statistics of the Dominion of Canada for the year ended June 30, 1915." Ottawa: King' Printer, 1916.

Dawson, G.M. "Preliminary Report on the Geology of the Bow and Belly River Region, North West Territory, with Special Reference to Coal Deposits." Geological Survey of Canada, Report 1880–81–82, B, 1–23. 1883.

Dominion of Canada. Regulations for the Disposal of Petroleum and Natural Gas Rights, the Property of the Crown in Manitoba, Saskatchewan, Alberta, and the Northwest Territories, the Yukon Territory, the Railway Belt in the Province of British Columbia and Within the Tract Containing Three and One-Half Million Acres of Land Acquired by the Dominion Government from the Province of British Columbia, and Referred to in Sub-Section (b) of Section 3 of the Dominion Land Act. Ottawa: Government Printing Bureau, 1912.

Dowling, Donaldson B. "Geological Notes to Accompany Map of Sheep River Gas and Oil Field, Alberta." Geological Survey of Canada, Report S2-1357. 1914.

Hayes, C.W., and William Kennedy. "Oil Fields of the Texas-Louisiana Gulf Coastal Plain." United States Geological Survey. Washington: Government Printing Office, 1903.

Government of the North West Territories. "An Ordinance respecting Companies," in *Ordinances of the North West Territories*. Regina: Government Printer, 1901.

Livingston, Vaughn E., Jr. "Oil and Gas exploration in Washington, 1900–1957." Washington State Division of Mines and Geology. Information Circular No. 29. Olympia: SPO, 1958.

Malcolm, Wyatt. "Oil and Gas Prospects of the Northwest Provinces of Canada." Geological Survey of Canada, Memoir 29-E. 1913.

United States Congress. *U.S. Statutes at Large, Volume 32 –1903, 57th Congress*. United States, – 1903, 1902.

Secondary Sources

Anderson, Allan. *Roughnecks and Wildcatters*. Toronto: Macmillan, 1981.

Anderson, Benedict. *Imagined Communities: Reflections on the Origins and Spread of Nationalism*. 2nd ed. London: Verso, 2016.

Armstrong, Chris. *Blue Skies and Boiler Rooms: Buying and Selling Securities in Canada, 1870–1940*. Toronto: University of Toronto Press, 2016.

Banack, Clark. *God's Province: Evangelical Christianity, Political Thought, and Conservatism in Alberta*. Montreal: McGill-Queen's University Press, 2016.

Barrett, Ross, Daniel Worden, and Allan Stoekl. *Oil Culture*. Minneapolis: University of Minnesota Press, 2014.

Beeby-Thompson, Arthur. *Oil Pioneer: Selected Experiences and Incidents Associated with Sixty Years of World Wide Petroleum Exploration and Oilfield Development*. London: Sidgwick & Jackson, 1961.

Black, Brian. *Crude Reality: Petroleum in World History*. Lanham: Rowman & Littlefield, 2012.

Black, Brian. *Petrolia: The Landscape of America's First Oil Boom*. Baltimore: Johns Hopkins University Press, 2000.

Bliss, Michael. *Northern Enterprise: Five Centuries of Canadian Business*. Toronto: McClelland & Stewart: 1987.

Bloomfield, Arthur I. *Patterns of Fluctuation in International Investment Before 1914*. Princeton: Princeton University, 1968.

Botting, Gary Norman Arthur. *Extradition Between Canada and the United States*. Ardsley, NY: Transnational, 2005.

Brands, H.W. *"A Traitor to His Class:" The Privileged Life and Radical Presidency of Franklin Delano Roosevelt*. New York: Doubleday, 2008.

Breen, David H. *Alberta's Petroleum Industry and the Conservation Board*. Edmonton: University of Alberta Press, 1993.

Breen, David H. *William Stewart Herron: Father of the Petroleum Industry in Alberta*. Calgary: Historical Society of Alberta, 1984.

Breen, David H. "Anglo-American Rivalry and the Evolution of Canadian Petroleum Policy to 1930." *Canadian Historical Review* 62 (1981): 283–303.

Bright, David. *The Limits of Labour: Class Formation and the Labour Movement in Calgary, 1883–1929*. Vancouver: UBC Press, 1998.

Bright, David. "Technology and Law Enforcement: The Transformation of the Calgary Police Force, 1900–1940." *Urban History* 33, no. 2 (2005): 30–44.

Brinkley, Alan. *Voices of Protest: Huey Long, Father Coughlin and the Great Depression.* New York: Vintage, 1982.

Brownsey, Keith. "The Alberta Oilpatch: Multilevel Regulation Transformed." In *Rules, Rules, Rules: Multilevel Governance*, edited by G. Bruce Doern and Robert Johnson. Toronto: University of Toronto Press, 2006.

Buell, Frederick. "A Short History of Oil Cultures, or The Marriage of Catastrophe and Exuberance." In *Oil Culture*, edited by Ross Barrett, Daniel Worden, and Allan Stoekl. Minneapolis: University of Minnesota Press, 2014.

Burrough, Bryan. *The Big Rich: The Rise and Fall of the Greatest Texas Oil Fortunes.* New York: Penguin, 2009.

Cameron, Harvey. *The Law Society of Manitoba, 1877–1977.* Peguis: Winnipeg, 1977.

Cass, Douglas. "Investment in the Alberta Petroleum Industry, 1912–1930." MA thesis, University of Calgary, 1984.

Cavanaugh, Catherine Anne, Michael Payne, and Donald Grant Wetherell, eds. *Alberta Formed, Alberta Transformed.* Vol. 2. Edmonton: University of Alberta Press; Calgary: University of Calgary Press, 2006.

Chancellor, Edward. *Devil Take the Hindmost: A History of Financial Speculation.* New York: Farrar, Straus and Giroux, 1999.

Chernow, Ron. *Titan: The Life of John D. Rockefeller, Sr.* New York: Random House, 1998.

Colpitts, George. *Game in the Garden: A Human History of Wildlife in Western Canada to 1940.* Vancouver: UBC Press, 2002.

Corley, Thomas Anthony Buchanan. *A History of the Burmah Oil Company, 1886–1924.* London: Heinemann, 1983.

Cunningham Craig, Edward Hubert. *Oil Finding: An Introduction to the Geological Study of Petroleum.* London: Edward Arnold, 1913.

Dabbs, Frank. *Branded by the Wind: The Life and Times of Bill Herron.* Calgary: Marjorie A. Herron, 2001.

Daintith, Terence. *"Finders Keepers?" How the Law of Capture Shaped the World Oil Industry.* New York: Taylor & Francis, 2010.

Dallek, Robert. *Franklin D. Roosevelt: A Political Life.* New York: Viking, 2017.

Danforth, June. "Shady Deals." In *In the Light of the Flares: History of the Turner Valley Oil Fields*, edited by Turner Valley Historical Society. Turner Valley: Turner Valley Historical Society, 1979.

Davis, Kenneth S. *FDR: The New Deal Years, 1933–1937*. New York: Random House, 1986.

De Mille, George. *Oil in Canada West: The Early Years*. Calgary: Northwest Printing, 1969.

Dempsey, Hugh A. "Robert Chambers Edwards." *Dictionary of Canadian Biography*. Vol. 15. University of Toronto/Université Laval, 2003–, accessed November 26, 2022, http://www.biographi.ca/en/bio/edwards_robert_chambers_15E.html.

Dempsey, Hugh A. *Calgary, Spirit of the West: A History*. Saskatoon: Fifth House, 1994.

Dochuk, Darren. *Anointed with Oil: How Christianity and Crude Made Modern America*. New York: Basic Books, 2019.

Dochuk, Darren. *From Bible Belt to Sun Belt: Plain-Folk Religion, Grassroots Politics, and the Rise of Evangelical Conservatism*. New York: W.W. Norton, 2011.

Downey, Morgan. *Oil 101*. Albany: Wooden Table Press, 2009.

Dumenil, Lynn. *Modern Temper: American Culture and Society in the 1920s*. New York: Hill and Wang, 1995.

Elofson, Warren. *So Far Yet So Close: Frontier Cattle Ranching in Western Prairie Canada and the Northern Territory of Australia*. Calgary: University of Calgary Press, 2015.

Emery, J.C. Herbert, and Ronald D. Kneebone. "Socialists, Populists, Resources, and the Divergent Development of Alberta and Saskatchewan." *Canadian Public Policy* 34, no. 4 (2008): 419–40.

Feldberg, John, and Warren Elofson. "Financing the Palliser Triangle." *Great Plains Quarterly* 18, no. 3 (1998): 257–68.

Finch, David. *Hell's Half Acre: Early Days in the Great Canadian Oil Patch*. Surrey: Heritage House, 2005.

Finch, David, and Gordon Jaremko. *Fields of Fire: An Illustrated History of Canadian Petroleum*. Calgary: Detselig, 1994.

Francis, R. Douglas. "Turner Versus Innis: Bridging the Gap." *American Review of Canadian Studies* 33, no. 4 (2003): 473–85.

Frehner, Brian. *Finding Oil: The Nature of Petroleum Geology.* Lincoln: University of Nebraska Press, 2011.

Friesen, Gerald. *The Canadian Prairies: A History.* Toronto: University of Toronto Press, 1984.

Gallup, W.B. "Geology of Turner Valley Oil and Gas Field, Alberta, Canada." *AAPG Bulletin* 35, no. 4 (1951): 797–821. doi: 10.1306/3D9341ED-16B1-11D7-8645000102C1865D.

Gerali, Francesco. *Torpedoes (Well shooting),* Engineering and Technology History Wiki. (2019): https://ethw.org/Torpedoes_(Well_shooting).

Gow, Sandy. *Roughnecks, Rock Bits and Rigs: The Evolution of Oil Well Drilling Technology in Alberta, 1883–1970.* Calgary: University of Calgary Press, 2005.

Grant, Hugh M. "The Petroleum Industry and Canadian Economic Development: An Economic History, 1900–1961." PhD diss., University of Toronto, 1986.

Grant, Hugh M., and Henry Thille. "Tariffs, Strategy, and Structure: Competition and Collusion in the Ontario Petroleum Industry, 1870–1880." *Journal of Economic History* 61, no. 2 (2001): 390–413.

Gray, Earle. *The Great Canadian Oil Patch.* 2nd ed. Edmonton: JuneWarren, 2005.

Gray, James H. *Talk to My Lawyer. Great Stories of Southern Alberta's Bar and Bench.* Edmonton: Hurtig, 1987.

Gray, James H. *Troublemaker! A Personal History.* Toronto: Macmillan, 1978.

Gray, James H. *Red Lights on the Prairies.* Toronto: Macmillan, 1971.

Grieve, Willie. "One Hundred Years of Public Utility Regulation in Alberta." *Energy Regulation Quarterly* (September 2015). https://energyregulationquarterly.ca/articles/one-hundred-years-of-public-utility-regulation-in-alberta#sthash.uVK946Hg.dpbs.

Hanson, Eric J. *Dynamic Decade: The Evolution and Effects of the Oil Industry in Alberta.* Toronto: McClelland & Stewart, 1958.

Hanson, Eric J. *Eric J. Hanson's Financial History of Alberta.* Edited by Paul Booth & Heather Edwards Calgary: University of Calgary Press, 2004.

Harrison, Trevor W. "Petroleum, Politics, and the Limits of Left Progressivism in Alberta." In *Alberta Oil and the Decline of Democracy in Canada,* edited by Meenal Shrivastava and Lorna Stefanick. Edmonton: Athabasca University Press, 2015.

Hidy, Ralph W., and Muriel E. Hidy. *Pioneering in Big Business, 1882–1911*. Vol. 1: *History of Standard Oil Company (New Jersey)*. New York: Harper & Brothers, 1955.

Hilborn, James D., ed. *Dusters and Gushers: The Canadian Oil and Gas Industry*. Toronto: Pitt Publishing, 1968.

Hinton, Diana Davids, and Roger M. Olien. *Easy Money: Oil Promoters and Investors in the Jazz Age*. Chapel Hill: University of North Carolina Press, 1990.

Hinton, Diana Davids, and Roger M. Olien. *Oil in Texas: The Gusher Age, 1895–1945*. Austin: University of Texas Press, 2002.

Horan, John William. *On the Side of the Law: A Biography of J.D. Nicholson*. Edmonton: Institute of Applied Art, 1944.

Hume, G.S. "Fault Structures in the Foothills and Eastern Rocky Mountains of Southern Alberta." *Bulletin of the Geological Society of America* 68, no. 4 (1957): 395–412.

Hutchinson, Brian. "As the Bust Paralyzes Calgary One Word Reignites the City: Oil." In Ted Byfield, *Alberta in the 20th Century: A Journalistic History of the Province in Twelve Volumes*. Vol. 3: *The Boom and the Bust*. Edmonton: United Western Communications, 1994.

Hutchinson, Brian. "Blowouts, Fires and Injuries Were All Part of the Job on Those First Cable Rigs." In Ted Byfield, *The Boom and the Bust, 1910–1914*. Edmonton: United Western Communications, 1994.

Hutchinson, Brian. "The Cigar-Chomping Pastor and his Oilfield Scam." In Ted Byfield, *The Boom and the Bust, 1910-1914*. Edmonton: United Western Communications, 1994.

Inkpen, Andrew, & Michael H. Moffett. *The Global Oil and Gas Industry: Management, Strategy and Finance*. Tulsa: PennWell, 2011.

Janigan, Mary. *"Let the Eastern Bastards Freeze in the Dark!" The West Versus the Rest Since Confederation*. Toronto: Vintage, 2013.

Jaremko, Gordon. *Steward: 75 Years of Alberta Energy Regulation*. Edmonton: Energy Resources Conservation Board, 2013.

Jaremko, Gordon. "Turner Valley: The Beginning of a Long Apprenticeship." *Alberta History* 62, no. 2 (Spring 2014): 8. https://go.gale.com/ps/i.do?p=AONE&u=googlescholar&id=GALE%7CA365891752&v=2.1&it=r&sid=AONE&asid=a0060098.

Johnston, Russell T. *Selling Themselves: The Emergence of Canadian Advertising*. Toronto: University of Toronto Press, 2001.

Jones, David C. "The Dance of the Grizzly Bear: Boom to Bust, 1912–13." In *Alberta Formed, Alberta Transformed*, edited by Catherine Anne Cavanaugh, Michael Payne, and Donald Grant Wetherell. Vol. 2. Edmonton: University of Alberta Press; Calgary: University of Calgary Press, 2006.

Kerr, Aubrey. *Corridors of Time*. Calgary: S.A. Kerr, 1988.

Kerr, Aubrey. *Corridors of Time II*. Calgary: S.A. Kerr, 2000.

Kerr, Aubrey. *Corridors of Time III*. Calgary: S.A. Kerr, 2004.

Klassen, Henry. *Eye on the Future: Business People in Calgary and the Bow Valley, 1870–1900*. Calgary: University of Calgary Press, 2002.

Knafla, Louis, and Richard Klumpenhouwer. *Lords of the Western Bench: A Biographical History of the Supreme and District Courts of Alberta, 1876–1990*. Legal Archives Society of Alberta, 1997.

Laycock, David. "Populism in Alberta: Then and Now." *Alberta Views*, January 1, 2023.

Langdon, M. Elizabeth. "Female Crime in Calgary." In *Law and Justice in a New Land: Essays in Western Canadian Legal History*, edited by Louis A. Knafla. Calgary: Carswell, 1986.

Lebel, Daniel. "Reading the Rocks Reloaded: A Celebration of the Geological Survey of Canada 175th Anniversary with a View to the Future." *Geoscience Canada* 45, nos. 3–4 (2019): 151–62.

Link, Theodore A., and P.D. Moore. "Structure of Turner Valley Gas and Oil Field, Alberta." *AAPG Bulletin* 18, no. 11 (1934): 1417–53. https://doi.org/10.1306/3D932C80-16B1-11D7-8645000102C1865D.

Lonn, George. "Canadian Oil Pioneers." In *Dusters and Gushers: The Canadian Oil and Gas Industry*, edited by James D. Hilborn. Toronto: Pitt, 1968.

Luxton, Eleanor. *Latch String Out: Annie McDougall, A Woman's Pioneer West*. Edited by George Colpitts. Banff: Summerthought, 2015.

MacEwen, Grant. *Eye Opener Bob: The Story of Bob Edwards*. Edmonton: Brindle & Glass, 2004.

MacEwen, Grant. *Fifty Mighty Men*. Saskatoon: Modern Press, 1958.

MacKay, Paul Andrew. "A Geometric, Kinematic and Dynamic Analysis of the Structural Geology at Turner Valley, Alberta." PhD diss., University of Calgary, 1991.

MacLeod, R.C. *The North-West Mounted Police and Law Enforcement, 1873–1905*. Toronto: University of Toronto Press, 1976.

Macmillan, Margaret. *The War that Ended Peace: The Road to 1914*. Toronto: Allen Lane, 2013.

Massey, Lesley McIntaggart. "'Alberta's Own:' The Provincial Police." MA thesis, University of Calgary, 1995.

McCormick, Peter, and Suzanne Maisey. "A Tale of Two Courts II: Appeals from the Manitoba Court of Appeals to the Supreme Court of Canada, 1906–1990." *Manitoba Law Journal* 21, no. 1 (1990): 1–23.

McFeely, Tim. "The Discovery Defied the Geological Wisdom of 1914." In *Alberta in the 20th Century: A Journalistic History of the Province in Twelve Volumes*. Vol. 3: *The Boom and the Bust*, edited by Ted Byfield. Edmonton: United Western Communications, 1994.

McKenzie-Brown, Peter. "The Bosworth Expedition: An Early Petroleum Survey." In *The Frontier of Patriotism: Alberta and the First World War*, edited by Adriana A. Davies and Jeff Keshen. Calgary: University of Calgary Press, 2016.

McKenzie-Brown, Peter, Gordon Jaremko, and David Finch. *The Great Oil Age*. Calgary: Detselig, 1993.

McNeill, Leishman. *Calgary Herald's Tales of the Old Town*. Calgary: Calgary Herald, 1966.

Michie, Ranald C. "The Canadian Securities Market, 1850–1914." *Business History Review* 62, no. 1 (1988): 35–73.

Miller, Bradley. *Borderline Crime: Fugitive Criminals and the Challenge of the Border, 1819–1914*. Toronto: University of Toronto Press, 2018.

Millman, Brock. *Polarity, Patriotism and Dissent in Great War Canada, 1914–1919*. Toronto: University of Toronto Press, 2018.

Mittelstadt, David. *The MacLeod Dixon Century: 1912–2012*. Calgary: Legal Archives Society, 2012.

Moir, Sean. "The Alberta Provincial Police, 1917–1932." MA thesis, University of Alberta, 1992.

Mossop, G.D., and I. Shetsen, eds. *Geological Atlas of the Western Canada Sedimentary Basin*. Canadian Society of Petroleum Geologists and Alberta Research Council, 1994. https://ags.aer.ca/reports/atlas-western-canada-sedimentary-basin.

Mottram, R.H. *A History of Financial Speculation*. Boston: Little, Brown, 1929.

Nickle, Carl O. "Valley of Wonders: The Turner Valley Story." Calgary: The Oil Bulletin, n.d.

Nixon, Earl K. "The Petroleum Industry of Kansas." *Transactions of the Kansas Academy of Science* 51, no. 4 (December 1948): 369–424.

Norrie, Kenneth H., Doug Owram, and John Charles Herbert Emery. *A History of the Canadian Economy*. 4th ed. Toronto: Thomson Nelson, 2008.

O'Hearn, W.J. "Extradition." *Canadian Bar Review* 8, no. 3 (March 1930): 175–83. https://cbr.cba.org/index.php/cbr/article/view/3839/3832.

Olien, Roger M., and Diana Davids Hinton. *Oil Booms: Social Change in Five Texas Towns*. University of Nebraska Press, 1982.

Olien, Roger M., and Diana Davids Hinton. *Wildcatters: Texas Independent Oilmen*. College Station: Texas A & M University Press, 2007.

Palmer, Howard. *Alberta: A New History*. Edmonton: Hurtig, 1990.

Paterson, Donald G. *British Direct Investment in Canada, 1890–1914: Estimates and Determinants*. Toronto: University of Toronto Press, 1976.

Peach, Jack. *Thanks for the Memories: More Stories from Calgary's Past*. Saskatoon: Fifth House, 1994.

Phillips, Jim, Philip Girard, and R. Blake Brown. *A History of Law in Canada*. Vol. 2. Toronto: University of Toronto Press, 2022.

Poitras, Geoffrey. "Fleecing the Lambs? The Founding and Early Years of the Vancouver Stock Exchange." *BC Studies* no. 201 (Spring 2019): 37–66. https://ojs.library.ubc.ca/index.php/bcstudies/article/view/189777.

Porter, Dilwyn. "'Speciousness is the Bucketeers' Watchword and Outrageous Effrontery His Capital:' Financial Bucket Shops in the City of London, c. 1880–1939." In *Perspectives on Consumption and Society since 1700*, edited by John Benson and Laura Ugolini. London: Routledge, 2006.

Richards, John, and Larry Pratt. *Prairie Capitalism: Power and Influence in the New West*. Toronto: McClelland & Stewart, 1979.

Rodgers, Daniel T. *Atlantic Crossings: Social Politics in a Progressive Age*. Cambridge: Belknap Press of Harvard University Press, 1998.

Sanders, Harry. "A Bit of Space Between: Chinatown and the Former James Short Park and James Short Parkade." Calgary: City of Calgary, 2022.

Schmidt, John. *Growing Up in the Oil Patch*. Toronto: Dundurn, 1989.

Shiels, Bob. *Calgary: A Not Too Solemn Look at Calgary's First 100 Years*. Calgary: *Calgary Herald*, 1974.

Shrivastava, Meenal, and Lorna Stefanick, eds. *Alberta Oil and the Decline of Democracy in Canada*. Edmonton: Athabasca University Press, 2015. https://www.aupress.ca/books/120251-alberta-oil-and-the-decline-of-democracy-in-canada/.

Smil, Vaclav. *Energy and Civilization: A History*. Cambridge: MIT Press, 2017.

Smith, Catherine Munn. "J. Frank Moodie: The Man and the Mine." *Alberta History* 48, no. 2 (2000): 2–9. http://peel.library.ualberta.ca/bibliography/9021.48.2.html.

Smith, Jean Edward. *FDR*. New York: Random House, 2007.

Smith, Philip. *The Treasure-Seekers: The Men Who Built Home Oil*. Toronto: Macmillan, 1978.

Snell, James G., and Frederick Vaughan. *The Supreme Court of Canada: History of the Institution*. Toronto: Osgoode Society and University of Toronto Press, 1985.

Stacey, C.P. *Canada and the Age of Conflict. Vol. 1: 1867–1921*. Toronto: University of Toronto Press, 1984.

Supreme Court of Canada. *The Supreme Court of Canada and Its Justices, 1875–2000*. Toronto: Dundurn, 2000.

Sur, F. John. "Method of Drilling for Oil in the Calgary-Alberta District." *Mining and Engineering World* 40 (June 27, 1914): 1234.

Taylor, Graham D. *Imperial Standard: Imperial Oil, Exxon, and the Canadian Oil Industry from 1880*. Calgary: University of Calgary Press, 2019.

Thomas, L.G. *The Liberal Party in Alberta: A History of Politics in the Province of Alberta, 1905–1921*. Toronto: University of Toronto Press, 1959.

Thompson, A.R. "Sovereignty and Natural Resources – A Study of Canadian Petroleum Legislation." *Valparaiso University Law Review* 1, no. 2 (Spring 1967): 284–319.

Thompson, John Herd. *The Harvests of War: The Prairie West, 1914–1918*. Toronto: Oxford University Press, 1978.

Thorner, Thomas, and Neil B. Watson. "Keeper of the King's Peace: Colonel GE Sanders and the Calgary Police Magistrate's Court, 1911–1932." *Urban History Review* 12, no. 3 (1984): 45–55.

Turner, Frederick Jackson. *The Significance of the Frontier in American History*. Ann Arbor: University of Michigan Microfilms, 1966.

Turner Valley Historical Society, eds. *In the Light of the Flares: History of the Turner Valley Oil Fields.* Turner Valley: Turner Valley Historical Society, 1979.

van Herk, Aritha. *Mavericks: An Incorrigible History of Alberta.* Toronto: Penguin Canada, 2001.

Ward, Tony. "The Origins of the Canadian Wheat Boom, 1880–1910." *Canadian Journal of Economics* 27, no. 4 (November 1994): 865–83.

Wetherell, Donald G., and Irene R.A. Kmet. *Town Life: Main Street and the Evolution of Small Town Alberta.* Edmonton: University of Alberta Press, 1995.

Williams, David Ricardo. *Call in Pinkerton's: American Detectives at Work for Canada.* Toronto: Dundurn, 1998.

Williamson, Harold F., and Arnold R. Daum. *The American Petroleum Industry.* Vol. 1: *The Age of Illumination, 1859–1899.* Chicago: Northwestern University Press, 1959.

Williamson, Harold F., and Arnold R. Daum. *The American Petroleum Industry.* Vol. 2: *The Age of Energy, 1899–1958.* Chicago: Northwestern University Press, 1959.

Willoughby, Hector Charlesworth. *A Cyclopaedia of Canadian Biography.* Toronto: The Hunter-Rose Company, 1919.

Winegard, Timothy C. *The First World Oil War.* Toronto: University of Toronto Press, 2016.

Yergin, Daniel. *The Prize: The Epic Quest for Oil, Money and Power.* New York: Simon & Schuster, 1991.

Yergin, Daniel. "Ensuring Energy Security," *Foreign Affairs* 85, no. 2. (2006): 69–82. https://doi.org/10.2307/20031912.

Young, Walter D. *Democracy and Discontent: Progressivism, Socialism and Social Credit in the Canadian West.* Toronto: McGraw-Hill, 1978.

Zaslow, Morris. *Reading the Rocks: The Story of the Geological Survey of Canada, 1842–1972.* Toronto: Macmillan, 1975.

Notes

NOTES TO INTRODUCTION

1   John Schmidt, *Growing up in the Oil Patch* (Toronto: Dundurn, 1989), 104–5.
2   "Disciples invite all followers to unite," *Calgary Morning Albertan* (hereafter cited as *CMA*), July 13, 1909, 5.
3   Contemporary newspaper coverage and court documents occasionally spelled Jennie Earl's last name as "Earle." However, examination of various documents shows that she signed her surname without the second "e"; therefore, the text will reflect her preference unless referring to the title of a specific newspaper article.
4   PAA, GR1979.0285, file 7056, reel 132, Calgary District Court, *Allan Clark et al. v. Black Diamond Oil Fields et al.*, Examination for Discovery, Ada Buck, Calgary, January 15, 1915, 4.
5   June Danforth, "Shady Deals," in *In the Light of the Flares: History of the Turner Valley Oil Fields*, ed. Turner Valley Historical Society (Turner Valley: Turner Valley Historical Society, 1979), 74.
6   Library and Archives Canada (hereafter LAC), R927, RG125-A, vol. 398, file 3906, part 1, Supreme Court of Canada, *The King v. George Buck* (1916), Appeal from the Judgment of the Supreme Court of Alberta, Appellate Division, "Deposition of J.W. Hayes," Lima, Ohio, December 27, 1915, 307–11.
7   "Many outfits are busy in oil fields," *Calgary Herald* (hereafter cited as *CH*), March 24, 1914, 5.
8   PAA, GR1979.0285, file 6342, reel 118, Calgary District Court, *Grant S. Wolverton v. Black Diamond Oil Fields et al.* (1914), Statement of Claim, Calgary, April 24, 1914; Letter, George E. Buck to Grant Wolverton, Calgary, March 25, 1914; Letter, Jennie Earl to Grant Wolverton. Calgary, March 30, 1914.
9   "Action over oil claim," *CH*, April 25, 1914, 1; "Wolverton suit in Black Diamond case under way," *CH*, November 14, 1914, 9.
10 *Natural Gas and Oil Record*, April 25, 1914, 3.
11 LAC, R927, RG125-A, vol. 398, file 3906, part 1, Supreme Court of Canada, *The King v. George Buck*, Appeal from the Judgment of the Supreme Court of Alberta, Appellate Division, "Deposition of Norman R. Fletcher," Preliminary Inquiry, Calgary, 332; "Black Diamond Foreman tells of salting well," *CH*, November 12, 1915, 11.
12 LAC, R927, RG125-A, vol. 398, file 3906, part 1, Supreme Court of Canada, *The King v. George Buck*, Appeal from the Judgment of the Supreme Court of Alberta, Appellate Division, "Deposition of J.W. Hayes," Lima, Ohio, December 27, 1915, 306; "More oil litigation," *CH*, May 5, 1914, 8.
13 "Impressions of Calgary before and just after," *Vancouver Daily World*, May 30, 1914, 19.
14 Vaclav Smil, *Energy and Civilization: A History* (Cambridge: MIT Press, 2017), 246–48.
15 Mahan's writings spurred major naval building campaigns in Britain, France, Germany, and the United States and contributed to the flurry of colonial expansion in the late nineteenth century. Arguably, they also produced a naval arms race between Imperial Germany and Great Britain that served as one of the long-term causes of the Great War. Although Germany was a traditional land power, Kaiser Wilhelm II's infatuation with Mahan's writings and Germany's sudden foray into shipbuilding in the late 1890s and early 1900s alarmed the British, prompting the Royal Navy to commission a new class of battleship, the HMS *Dreadnought*, which, among other technological innovations, included oil-fired turbine engines. Despite indications that Britain intended to preserve its naval supremacy, the Germans persisted, seemingly determined to scare the British into signing an alliance with them. Finally, eighteen months before the outbreak of the Great War in August 1914, First Lord of the Admiralty Winston Spencer Churchill ordered the Royal Navy to convert its ships from solid fuel (coal) to liquid (petroleum) because of the innumerable advantages oil provided, including a greater steaming radius, the ability to refuel at sea and travel further and faster than coal-powered ships, and the simplification of a ship's architecture. See Daniel Yergin, *The Prize: The Epic Quest for Oil, Money and Power* (New York: Simon & Schuster, 1991), 153–58.

16   Brian Black, *Crude Reality: Petroleum in World History* (Lanham: Rowman & Littlefield, 2012), 59–60; Yergin, *The Prize*, 150.

17   Harold F. Williamson & Arnold R. Daum, *The American Petroleum Industry, vol. 1: The Age of Illumination, 1859-1899* (Chicago: Northwestern University Press, 1959), 255; Timothy C. Winegard, *The First World Oil War* (Toronto: University of Toronto Press, 2016), 50.

18   *Oil and Gas Journal*, August 28, 1913, 1.

19   David H. Breen, "Anglo-American Rivalry and the Evolution of Canadian Petroleum Policy to 1930," *Canadian Historical Review* 62 (1981): 284; "Mother country watches with interest development of oil prospects in the northwest," *CMA*, October 2, 1913, 12; "Naval use of fuel oil a most vital question: United States rests secure while Great Britain and others look for a supply," *Wall Street Journal*, May 15, 1914, 1.

20   Earle Gray, *The Great Canadian Oil Patch*, 2nd ed. (Edmonton: JuneWarren, 2005), 66–67.

21   GWRC, M6745, John Schmidt Fonds, Manuscript re oil well drillers, Frosty Martin and Tiny Phillips, "George E. Buck," n.d., box 1.

22   David Laycock, "Populism in Alberta: Then and Now," *Alberta Views*, January 1, 2023.

23   James H. Gray, *Troublemaker! A Personal History* (Toronto: MacMillan, 1978), 36–37.

24   David H. Breen, *Alberta's Petroleum Industry and the Conservation Board* (Edmonton: University of Alberta Press, 1993), 16.

25   "Four years in jail oil man's penalty," *Great Falls Leader*, November 26, 1916, 2.

26   "The gaudy failures get lost in the shuffle," *Western Oil Examiner*, July 9, 1955, 6.

NOTES TO CHAPTER 1

1   Theodore A. Link and P.D. Moore, "Structure of Turner Valley Gas and Oil Field, Alberta," *AAPG Bulletin* 18, no. 11 (1934): 1417, https://doi.org/10.1306/3D932C80-16B1-11D7-8645000102C1865D.

2   David Finch and Gordon Jaremko, *Fields of Fire: An Illustrated History of Canadian Petroleum* (Calgary: Detselig, 1994), 26.

3   Paul Andrew MacKay, "A Geometric, Kinematic and Dynamic Analysis of the Structural Geology at Turner Valley, Alberta" (PhD diss., University of Calgary, 1991), 12, 18–19.

4   Aritha van Herk, *Mavericks: An Incorrigible History of Alberta* (Toronto: Penguin Canada, 2001), 16–21; Peter McKenzie-Brown, Gordon Jaremko, and David Finch, *The Great Oil Age* (Calgary: Detselig, 1993), 22–23;*Canadian Encyclopedia*, "Geography of Alberta," published June 18, 2020, last edited March 15, 2023, https://www.thecanadianencyclopedia.ca/en/article/geography-of-alberta; *Imperial Oil Review* (June–July 1937): 28.

5   R.A. Price, "Cordilleran Tectonics and the Evolution of the Western Canada Sedimentary Basin," in G.D. Mossop and I. Shetsen (eds.), *Atlas of the Western Canadian Sedimentary Basin* (Edmonton: Canadian Society of Petroleum Geologists and Alberta Research Council, 1994), 1.

6   G.D. Mossop and I. Shetsen, "Introduction to the Geological Atlas of the Western Canada Sedimentary Basin," in Mossop and Shetsen, *Atlas of the Western Canadian Sedimentary Basin*, 1.

7   G.S. Hume, "Fault Structures in the Foothills and Eastern Rocky Mountains of Southern Alberta," *Bulletin of the Geological Society of America* 68, no. 4 (1957): 397; Gray, *Great Canadian Oil Patch*, 85; Sandy Gow, *Roughnecks, Rock Bits and Rigs: The Evolution of Oil Well Drilling Technology in Alberta, 1883-1970* (Calgary: University of Calgary Press, 2005), 30.

8   Daniel Lebel, "Reading the Rocks Reloaded: A Celebration of The Geological Survey of Canada 175th Anniversary with a View to the Future," *Geoscience Canada* 45, nos. 3–4 (2019): 152.

9   Morris Zaslow, *Reading the Rocks: The Story of the Geological Survey of Canada, 1842-1972* (Toronto: Macmillan, 1975), 3.

10 Aubrey Kerr, *Corridors of Time* (Calgary: S.A. Kerr, 1988), 2.

11 Hugh M. Grant and Henry Thille, "Tariffs, Strategy, and Structure: Competition and Collusion in the Ontario Petroleum Industry, 1870-1880," *Journal of Economic History* 61, no. 2 (2001): 391; Graham D. Taylor, *Imperial Standard: Imperial Oil, Exxon, and the Canadian Oil Industry from 1880* (Calgary: University of Calgary Press, 2019), 26.

12 Taylor, *Imperial Standard*, 26–27.

13 The well produced natural gas continuously until 1954. Philip Smith, *The Treasure-Seekers: The Men Who Built Home Oil* (Toronto: Macmillan, 1978), 7; George De Mille, *Oil in Canada West: The Early Years* (Calgary: Northwest Printing, 1969), 63–64.

14 G.M. Dawson, "Preliminary Report on the Geology of the Bow and Belly River Region, North West Territory, with Special Reference to Coal Deposits," Geological Survey of Canada, Report 1880-81-82, B, 1-23 (1883).
15 Wyatt Malcolm, "Oil and Gas Prospects of the Northwest Provinces of Canada," Geological Survey of Canada, Memoir 29-E (1913), 56-62.
16 GWRC, 4545, Hugh Dempsey Fonds, box 1, file 1, Interview with Harold F. Herron by Hugh Dempsey, June 6, 1956 (Calgary); David H. Breen, *William Stewart Herron: Father of the Petroleum Industry in Alberta* (Calgary: Historical Society of Alberta, 1984), xxiii-xxiv; "Discovery oil well and story of how it was exploited," *CH*, October 25, 1913, 16; Frank Dabbs, *Branded by the Wind: The Life and Times of Bill Herron* (Calgary: Marjorie A. Herron, 2001), 7-10.
17 There appears to be a dispute as to how much time Herron spent in the Pennsylvania oil fields. One feature article from 1914 claimed Herron spent approximately three years in Pennsylvania before moving back to Cobalt. Herron's son, on the other hand, maintained that he only "visited" Pennsylvania briefly before travelling out west. GWRC, RCT-890-1, Interview with W.S. Herron by Jack Peach, 1987, Tape 1, Side A; "How the great oil boom in Calgary commenced," *Vancouver Daily World*, May 26, 1914, 14.
18 Smith, *The Treasure-Seekers*, 17-18; Breen, *William Stewart Herron*, xxiv; De Mille, *Oil in Canada West*, 118-25; "Natural gas discovered on Sheep Creek," *CH*, August 3, 1904, 1; "Pioneers of oil-search see Turner Valley rise to Dominion's greatest," *CMA*, January 25, 1929, 26; "City fathers failed to file," *CH*, May 21, 1964, 2.
19 "W.S. Herron, pioneer of Alberta oil field, is very optimistic," *CH*, October 25, 1913, 16; The report Herron referred to is DeLorme Donaldson Cairnes, "Moose Mountain District of Southern Alberta," Geological Survey of Canada, Report 968 (Ottawa: GPO, 1907).
20 GWRC, RCT-890-1, Interview with W.S. Herron by Jack Peach, 1987, Tape 1, Side B; Petroleum Industry Oral History (hereafter cited as PIOH), William Herron II, 1981, 4, 5; Breen, *William Stewart Herron*, xxv; Gray, *Great Canadian Oil Patch*, 66-69; Diana Davids Hinton and Roger M. Olien, *Oil in Texas: The Gusher Age, 1895-1945* (Austin: University of Texas Press, 2002), 17; Brian Frehner, *Finding Oil: The Nature of Petroleum Geology* (Lincoln: University of Nebraska Press, 2011), 40-41, 71-73.
21 GWRC, 4545, Hugh Dempsey Fonds, box 1, file 3, Arthur Graves, "McDougall-Segur," June 11, 1956 (Calgary); Gray, *Great Canadian Oil Patch*, 76; Statistics Canada, *The Canada Year Book, 1927/1928*, available at https://www65.statcan.gc.ca/acyb02/1927/acyb02_19270777005a-eng.htm (accessed September 24, 2022).
22 Gray, *Great Canadian Oil Patch*, 66-67; Dabbs, *Branded by the Wind*, 34-35.
23 GWRC, M6840, McKinley Cameron Fonds, box 87, file 920, "To the Shareholders of the McDougall-Segur Exploration Company, Limited," March 23, 1929.
24 Henry Klassen, *Eye on the Future: Business People in Calgary and the Bow Valley, 1870-1900* (Calgary: University of Calgary Press, 2002), 113. van Herk, *Mavericks*, 291.
25 "David McDougall, one of Confederation pioneers, still Calgary Resident," *CH*, June 30, 1927, 29; "Pioneer fur trader of north dies at the ripe old age of 82," *CMA*, December 7, 1927, 2; Grant MacEwan, *Fifty Mighty Men* (Saskatoon: Modern Press, 1958), 330. One of David McDougall's granddaughters, Eleanor Luxton, posthumously published a vernacular history of her grandparents' life in the pioneer west: Eleanor Luxton, *Latch String Out: Annie McDougall, A Woman's Pioneer West*, ed. George Colpitts (Banff: Summerthought, 2015), 280.
26 "At the oil fields," *CH*, December 16, 1912, 18; Douglas Cass, "Investment in the Alberta Petroleum Industry, 1912-1930" (MA thesis, University of Calgary, 1984), 56-57; Gray, *Great Canadian Oil Patch*, 71.
27 GWRC, 4545, Hugh Dempsey Fonds, box 1, file 1, Interview with Floyd K. Beach by Hugh Dempsey, June 6, 1956 (Calgary); Gray, *Great Canadian Oil Patch*, 61; "Pioneers of oil," *Calgary Albertan*, January 24, 1929, 26.
28 GWRC, M330, Dingman Family Fonds, box 1, file 6, Claude Dingman, "Highlights of the 'Pioneer Days' of the Gas and Oil industry in Alberta," 1956, 1-2; *CH*, July 24, 1905, 8; *CH*, October 23, 1911, 3; Gray, *Great Canadian Oil Patch*, 59-63.
29 GWRC, M6840, McKinley Cameron Fonds, box 88, file 936, Legislative Assembly of Alberta, Agricultural Committee Turner Valley Hearings, Part II, William Stewart Herron Testimony, March 19, 1932, M70-M71; Breen, *Alberta's Petroleum Industry*, 12-15; "How the great oil boom in Calgary commenced," *Vancouver Daily World*, May 26, 1914, 14.
30 Ralph Armstrong, "Dingman well 50 years old," *Calgary Herald Magazine*, May 2, 1964, 1; Jim Armstrong, "Dingman success 50 years ago launched Alberta's oil industry," *Calgary Herald*, May 21, 1964.
31 Brian Black, *Petrolia: The Landscape of America's First Oil Boom* (Baltimore: Johns Hopkins University Press, 2000), 64-65.

32 Like many oil patch myths, the story varies greatly in its details with the telling. Versions differ over who Herron brought (Dingman, Lougheed, and Bennett, alone or in some combination), what meal was prepared (lunch or dinner), and the food Herron cooked (eggs and bacon are the most common; ham has also been mentioned, as has boiling water for coffee). PIOHP, William Herron interview by Jack Peach, Calgary, July 1981. 5; Eric J. Hanson, *Dynamic Decade: The Evolution and Effects of the Oil Industry in Alberta* (Toronto: McClelland & Stewart, 1958), 43; "Discovery oil well and story of how it was exploited," *CH*, October 25, 1913, 16; Canadian Western Natural Gas Company ad, *CH*, June 14, 1956, 38.

33 GWRC, M6119, Memorandum of Agreement, William Stewart Herron and James A. Lougheed, Alfred E. Cross, Isaac Kendell Ker, Richard Bedford Bennett, William Pearce, Thomas J.S. Skinner, William Henry McLaws, A. Judson Sayre, A.W. Dingman, July 16, 1912; Contract, Dingman and Herron, July 1, 1912; GWRC, 4545, Hugh Dempsey Fonds, box 1, file 1, Interview with Floyd K. Beach by Hugh Dempsey, June 6, 1956 (Calgary); David Breen, *William Stewart Herron*, xxvi; "How the great oil boom in Calgary commenced," *Vancouver Daily World*. May 26, 1914, 14. Brian Hutchinson, "As the Bust Paralyzes Calgary One Word Reignites the City: Oil," in *Alberta in the 20th Century: A Journalistic History of the Province in Twelve Volumes*, vol. 3: *The Boom and the Bust*, ed. Ted Byfield (Edmonton: United Western Communications, 1994), 360.

34 GWRC, M330, Dingman Family Fonds, box 1, file 4, C.L. Dingman; "A.W. Dingman the soapman turned wildcatter," *Western Oil Examiner*, July 9, 1955, 33; Jack Peach, "Rumors of oil deposits lured adventurers west," *CH*, June 15, 1965, G7; "Calgary to be an oil center," *Rochester Democrat and Chronicle*, August 20, 1913, 3.

35 GWRC, M968, A.P. "Tiny" Phillips Fonds, box 1, file 1, Blue Scribbler.

36 "Discovery oil well and story of how it was exploited," *CH*, October 25, 1913, 16; Claude Dingman, "Natural gas brought prosperity to Calgary," *Calgary Herald Magazine*, August 30, 1958, 3; Torchy Anderson, *Calgary Herald*, May 21, 1964, 55; Chester Bloom, "Reporter recalls 'mud and mosquitos,'" *Calgary Herald*, May 21, 1964, 67.

37 F. John Sur, "Method of Drilling for Oil in the Calgary-Alberta District," *Mining and Engineering World* 40 (June 27, 1914): 1234; Carl O. Nickle, "Valley of Wonders: The Turner Valley Story" (Calgary: The Oil Bulletin, n.d.), 2; Gow, *Roughnecks, Rock Bits and Rigs*, 5, 103, 275; James H. Gray, *Talk to My Lawyer: Great Stories of Southern Alberta's Bar and Bench* (Edmonton: Hurtig, 1987), 141.

38 Aubrey Kerr, *Corridors of Time II* (Calgary: S.A. Kerr, 2000), 122; Smith, *The Treasure-Seekers*, 75–76, 81; Roger M. Olien and Diana Davids Hinton, *Oil Booms: Social Change in Five Texas Towns* (University of Nebraska Press, 1982), 6.

39 Breen, *Alberta's Petroleum Industry*, 6.

40 Terence Daintith, *Finders Keepers?: How the Law of Capture Shaped the World Oil Industry* (New York: Taylor & Francis, 2010), 429–30.

41 Gray, *Great Canadian Oil Patch*, 56.

42 Hinton and Olien, *Oil in Texas*, 18–19.

43 Schmidt, *Growing up in the Oil Patch*, 88.

44 Brian Hutchinson, "Blowouts, fires and injuries were all part of the job on those first cable rigs," in *Alberta in the 20th Century: A Journalistic History of the Province in Twelve Volumes*, vol. 3: *The Boom and the Bust*, ed. Ted Byfield (Edmonton: United Western Communications, 1994), 364–65; Schmidt, *Growing Up in the Oil Patch*, 14–15.

45 David Finch, *Hell's Half Acre: Early Days in the Great Canadian Oil Patch* (Surrey: Heritage House, 2005), 13.

46 "Says Calgary oil is on sounder basis," *Manitoba Free Press*, February 2, 1915, 10.

47 Herron's claim about drilling time to completion in GWRC, M8160, Herron Fonds, box 4, file 102, Letter, Herron to J.I. McFarland, January 15, 1927; Gow, *Roughnecks, Rock Bits and Rigs*, 5; Breen, *Alberta's Petroleum Industry*, 15–16; Aubrey Kerr, *Corridors of Time III* (Calgary: S.A. Kerr, 2004), 22; "The gaudy failures get lost in the shuffle," *Western Oil Examiner*, July 9, 1955, 6.

48 "Standard Oil Co. sends man here to investigate," *CH*, March 22, 1913, 1; "Promise of early discovery made by promoters," *CMA*, March 24, 1913, 8; A.W. Dingman, Open Letter, *CH*, May 21, 1913, 1; "Manager Dingman not booster of oilfield," *CMA*, May 22, 1913, 1, 8; Prospectus, Calgary Petroleum Products Limited, Calgary, December 1914; "Drillers say oil will be struck soon," *CH*, August 4, 1913, 1, 11; "Discovery oil well and story of how it was exploited," *CH*, October 25, 1913, 16; Finch, *Hell's Half Acre*, 20; "The Royalite story starts before Dingman," *Western Oil Examiner*, July 9, 1955, 22.

49 GWRC, M4540, J. McKinley Cameron Fonds, box 87, file 918, McDougall-Segur, Minutes – Directors, October 11, 1913; Minutes – Directors October 30, 1913; Minutes – Directors, May 4, 1914; Minutes – Directors, May 15, 1914.

50 By way of comparison, in 2017, the Canadian Association of Petroleum Producers estimated the costs of drilling a conventional well in Alberta at between C$0.6 million and C$4.8 million. "Predicted costs for drilling and completing a well in the Cardium this summer," *Daily Oil Bulletin*, June 15, 2017.

51 Donald G. Paterson, *British Direct Investment in Canada, 1890–1914: Estimates and Determinants* (Toronto: University of Toronto Press, 1976), 63; Ranald C. Michie, "The Canadian Securities Market, 1850–1914," *Business History Review* 62, no. 1 (1988): 44, 50.

52 Daniel T. Rodgers, *Atlantic Crossings: Social Politics in a Progressive Age* (Cambridge: Belknap Press of Harvard University Press, 1998), 79; Lynn Dumenil, *Modern Temper: American Culture and Society in the 1920s* (New York: Hill and Wang, 1995), 18.

53 "Newspaper men get leases," *Kingston Daily Standard*, August 4, 1913, 4. The original eight businesspeople were William Toole, Archibald Dingman, Louis P. Strong, Oscar Grant Devenish, Thomas J.S. Skinner, Edmund Taylor, Hugh MacLean, and J. Edward A. MacLeod. "Finally decided to form stock exchange," *CH*, August 26, 1913, 12; Dabbs, *Branded by the Wind*, 34; GWRC, M5769, Alberta Stock Exchange Fonds, box 1 file 2; Bill No 23 of 1913 (Second Session), An Act to Incorporate Calgary Stock Exchange, assented to October 25, 1913; GWRC, M5769, Alberta Stock Exchange Fonds, file 36, "History and Review of the Calgary Stock Exchange," July 25, 1951.

54 Michie, "The Canadian Securities Market, 1850–1914," 44, 50.

55 A.R. Thompson, "Sovereignty and Natural Resources – A Study of Canadian Petroleum Legislation," *Valparaiso University Law Review* 1, no. 2 (Spring 1967): 291.

56 Michie, "The Canadian Securities Market, 1850–1914," 50.

57 Cass, "Investment in the Alberta Petroleum Industry," 9; "Reported oil discovery precipitates rush to file on land," *CH*, October 10, 1913, 1, 22.

58 LAC, "Bulletin XVIII. Fifth Census of Canada. Ages of the People for the year 1911 as Enumerated Under Date First June," Ottawa, Officer of the Census and Statistics Office, January 7, 1914; LAC, Census of the Prairie Provinces, 1916; "Table XXVI Per cent distribution of population of Prairie Provinces according to country of birth by provinces, 1916 and 1911" (Ottawa: Census and Statistics Office, 1918), 223; Clark Banack, *God's Province: Evangelical Christianity, Political Thought, and Conservatism in Alberta* (Montreal: McGill-Queen's University Press, 2016), 56, 59–60.

59 "Oil strike reported to have been made this week at the Dingman well," *CH*, October 9, 1913, 1; "Dingman statement of oil discovery electrifies city," *CMA*, October 10, 1913, 1, 8; "Authoritative statement on extent of oil strike given to public today," *CH*, October 10, 1913, 1; "Oil strike near Calgary probable," *Edmonton Journal* (hereafter cited as *EJ*), October 10, 1913, 1.

60 "New report says well is full of oil," *CH*, October 11, 1913, 1, 13; "Gasoline from Dingman well on the market," *Calgary News Telegram* (hereafter *CNT*), October 16, 1913, 10; "Dingman well is highest grade recorded," *CNT*, October 18, 1913, 21, 25; "Oil from Alberta fields is phenomenal in value," *CNT*, October 23, 1913, 16.

61 "Dingman strike is more consequential than first thought," *CMA*, October 13, 1913, 1, 8; "Automobile was run from well to Calgary on product of the discovery well," *CMA*, October 13, 1913, 1; "Epidemic of oil fever is more pronounced," *CNT*, October 13, 1913, 1; "Discovery oil well and story of how it was exploited," *CH*, October 25, 1913, 16; Editorial, *CMA*, January 7, 1914, 3.

62 Recall that Cunningham Craig also served as a consultant for Ira Segur's company, McDougall-Segur, and picked that company's well site, too.

63 "Tremendous oil possibilities about Calgary," *EJ*, October 15, 1913, 1; "Cunningham Craig says prospect is good one," *CMA*, October 17, 1913, 1, 8; "Ex-alderman tried to file oil claim in centre of city," *CH*, October 17, 1913, 26; "Vice president Bury arrives to inquire into oil situation," *CH*, October 18, 1913, 1; "Calgary oil fields attract investors," *Vancouver Sun*, November 3, 1913, 7.

64 Smith, *The Treasure-Seekers*, 19; "Oil discovery causes flurry of excitement," *CNT*, October 10, 1913, 1; "Oil has been struck at the Dingman well," *CNT*, October 10, 1913, 20; "Reported oil discovery precipitates great rush to file on land in region," *CH*, October 10, 1913, 1; "Would-be O.K.'s (oil kings) besiege land offices to lay basis of fortune," *CNT*, October 21, 1913, 13.

65 Harold F. Williamson and Arnold Daum, *The American Petroleum Industry*, vol. 2: *The Age of Energy, 1899–1958* (Chicago: Northwestern University Press, 1959), 16–17, 34; Hinton and Olien, *Oil Booms*, 21; Hugh M. Grant, "The Petroleum Industry and Canadian Economic Development: An Economic History, 1900–1961" (PhD diss., University of Toronto, 1986), 212; *Oil and Gas Journal*, June 12, 1913, 6.

66 Kerr, *Corridors of Time III*, 21–25.

67 "Wildcatting in Calgary real estate as told by C.A. Owens," *CMA*, October 1, 1913, 1; "Record rush at Calgary land office," *CNT*, October 13, 1913, 1; "Great rush for lease in the oil field continues," *CNT*,

October 16, 1913, 1; "Frost testifies that Dingman well is worth $1,250,000; Owens organizes New York company," *CMA*, October 20, 1913, 1.

68   Yergin, *The Prize*, 81–88.

NOTES TO CHAPTER 2

1. In many ways, different meanings of the word "speculation" reveal a great deal about the underlying assumptions of Davidson and Woods toward the boom. Davidson was more apt to equate speculation to investment because there are more similarities than differences between the two terms. Both deploy capital in the pursuit of profits. A simple definition is that the goal of investment is to preserve wealth while speculation aims to increase wealth. But as historian Edward Chancellor observed, such a definition means the line separating speculation from investment is razor thin—perhaps to the point where successful speculation can be regarded as an investment and failed investments are speculation. A more sophisticated argument acknowledges that investing is usually regarded as a wealth-preserving activity that typically takes fewer risks, involves careful consideration and analysis by the investor, produces modest returns, in part because investors tend to mitigate risk by diversification, seeks modest returns, and tends to have longer terms. On the other hand, speculation involves greater short-term risk and offers higher rewards, leaving greater room separating the two terms. Woods tended to favour the latter definition and defined speculation as a reckless, and fraught, activity. See Edward Chancellor, *Devil Take the Hindmost: A History of Financial Speculation* (New York: Farrar, Straus and GIroux, 1999), xi.
2. Ralph W. Hidy and Muriel E. Hidy, *Pioneering in Big Business, 1882-1911*, vol. 1: *History of Standard Oil Company (New Jersey)* (New York: Harper & Brothers, 1955), 9–23; Yergin, *The Prize*, 35–55; Ron Chernow, *Titan: The Life of John D. Rockefeller, Sr.* (New York: Random House, 1998).
3. R.H. Mottram, *A History of Financial Speculation* (Boston: Little, Brown, 1929), 20.
4. See Adam Smith, *An Inquiry into the Nature and Causes of the Wealth of Nations*.
5. Pierre Berton, "Papers, Pickets and Profits," *MacLean's*, July 15, 1950, available at https://archive.macleans.ca/article/1950/7/15/papers-pickets-and-profits (accessed July 15, 2022).
6. Howard Palmer, *Alberta: A New History* (Edmonton: Hurtig, 1990), 57; *CH*, May 14, 1940, 2; Jessica Potter, "Southam Inc.," *The Canadian Encyclopedia*, published July 20, 2009, last edited December 16, 2013, https://www.thecanadianencyclopedia.ca/en/article/southam-inc; *CH*, May 21, 1941, 10.
7. "Davidson, William McCarney, M.P.P" in Hector Willoughby Charlesworth, *A Cyclopaedia of Canadian Biography* (Toronto: The Hunter-Rose Company, 1919), 225–26; Jack Peach, *Thanks for the Memories: More Stories from Calgary's Past* (Saskatoon: Fifth House, 1994), 45."Loss in *CMA* fire estimated at $200,000," *Edmonton Bulletin* (hereafter *EB*), April 19, 1913, 11; W.M. Davidson, "Yesterday, Today and Tomorrow," *CMA*, August 23, 1941; "W.M. Davidson, pioneer editor, dies at coast," *CH*, March 24, 1942, 9; "The Albertan: 1902-1980," *Calgary Albertan Magazine*, July 27, 1980, 3.
8. "Cecil Armstrong visits hub city," *Saskatoon Star-Phoenix*, June 16, 1933, 3; "S-P founder dies at coast," *Saskatoon Star-Phoenix*, February 11, 1971, 3.
9. *Saskatoon Phoenix*, June 21, 1912, 4.
10. Peach, *Thanks for the Memories*, 44–45.
11. L.G. Thomas, *The Liberal Party in Alberta: A History of Politics in the Province of Alberta, 1905-1921* (Toronto: University of Toronto Press, 1959), 10; *Saskatoon Star-Phoenix*. August 15, 1908, 4; *Saskatoon Phoenix*, June 21, 1912, 4; *Windsor Star*, August 9, 1912, 5; "Secretary of Tories insists Riley will be a candidate," *CMA*, March 25, 1913, 1; *CMA*, October 20, 1916, 3; "George M. Thompson announces pending plans of re-organization," *Saskatoon Daily Star*, October 25, 1917, 2; "Newsman dies, founded paper," *Windsor Star*, December 20, 1949, 10; "G. Thompson Star-Phoenix founder dies," *Kingston Whig-Standard*, December 20, 1949, 15; "Mrs. George Thompson obituary," *Kingston Whig-Standard*, September 20, 1963, 9; "S-P founder dies at coast," *Saskatoon Star-Phoenix*, February 12, 1971, 3.
12. Bob Shiels, *Calgary: A Not Too Solemn Look at Calgary's First 100 Years* (Calgary: Calgary Herald, 1974), 77.
13. Hugh A. Dempsey, "Robert Chambers Edwards," *Dictionary of Canadian Biography*, vol. 15, University of Toronto/Université Laval, 2003–, accessed November 26, 2022, http://www.biographi.ca/en/bio/edwards_robert_chambers_15E.html.
14. GWRC, M353, Bob Edwards Fonds, Letter, Edwards to Jessie McCauley Ross, February 7, 1915.
15. van Herk, *Mavericks*, 313; Grant MacEwan, *Eye Opener Bob: The Story of Bob Edwards* (Calgary: Brindle & Glass, 2004), 3.

16 Chris Armstrong, *Blue Skies and Boiler Rooms: Buying and Selling Securities in Canada, 1870–1940* (Toronto: University of Toronto Press, 2016), 39–40.
17 "Official warning in regard to oil strike is issued," *CH*, October 24, 1913, 1.
18 Michie, "The Canadian Securities Market, 1850–1914," 35.
19 John Feldberg and Warren Elofson, "Financing the Palliser Triangle," *Great Plains Quarterly* 18, no. 3 (1998): 259.
20 David Bright, *The Limits of Labour: Class Formation and the Labour Movement in Calgary, 1883–1929* (Vancouver: UBC Press, 1998), 99.
21 Palmer, *Alberta: A New History*, 153–56.
22 Tony Ward, "The Origins of the Canadian Wheat Boom, 1880–1910," *Canadian Journal of Economics* 27, no. 4 (1994): 873–74; Palmer, *Alberta: A New History*, 51, 106–7; Kenneth H. Norrie, Doug Owram, and John Charles Herbert Emery, *A History of the Canadian Economy*, 4th ed. (Toronto: Thomson Nelson, 2008), 203–10. Eric J. Hanson, *Eric J. Hanson's Financial History of Alberta*, eds. Paul Booth and Heather Edwards (Calgary: University of Calgary Press, 2004), 7, 32, 87.
23 Warren Elofson, *So Far Yet So Close: Frontier Cattle Ranching In Western Prairie Canada and the Northern Territory of Australia* (Calgary: University Calgary Press, 2015), 143–44; Palmer, *Alberta: A New History*, 51–58.
24 "Year's total for building is $4,000,000," *CH*, December 11, 1914, 1.
25 Bright, *The Limits of Labour*, 101.
26 "Unemployed request relief measures," *CH*, December 31, 1913, 12.
27 Arthur I. Bloomfield, *Patterns of Fluctuation in International Investment Before 1914* (Princeton: Princeton University, 1968), 1–2; C.P. Stacey, *Canada and the Age of Conflict, vol. 1: 1867–1921* (Toronto: University of Toronto Press, 1984), 169. John Feldberg and Warren Elofson, "Financing the Palliser Triangle," *Great Plains Quarterly* 18, no. 3 (1998): 259; Hutchinson, "As the bust paralyzes Calgary" 358; David C. Jones, "The Dance of the Grizzly Bear: Boom to Bust, 1912–13," in *Alberta Formed, Alberta Transformed*, ed. Catherine Anne Cavanaugh, Michael Payne, and Donald Grant Wetherell, vol. 2 (Edmonton: University of Alberta Press; Calgary: University of Calgary Press, 2006), 380; Palmer, *Alberta: A New History*, 166.
28 "George Bury advises people to go slow in oil speculation," *CH*, October 21, 1913, 18.
29 Dilwyn Porter, "'Speciousness is the Bucketeers' Watchword and Outrageous Effrontery his Capital:' Financial Bucket Shops in the City of London, c. 1880–1939," in *Perspectives on Consumption and Society since 1700*, eds. John Benson and Laura Ugolini (London: Routledge, 2006); *CH*, December 29, 1913, 1.
30 "Official warning in regard to oil strike is issued," *CH*, October 24, 1913, 1; "The floatation of oil companies," *CH*, October 25, 1913, 1.
31 "The floatation of oil companies," *CH*, October 25, 1913, 1
32 "The floatation of oil companies," *CH*, October 27, 1913, 1.
33 GWRC, M4545, Hugh Dempsey Fonds, file 2, "T.A.P. 'Tappy' Frost"; *CH*, June 11, 1915, 6; "'Tappy' Frost is taken by death," *EJ*, October 5, 1927, 1; "'Tappy' Frost passes after years of service," *CH*, October 7, 1927, 10; "'Tappy' Frost laid to rest Saturday," *CH*, October 6, 1927, 25.
34 "Tappy Frost on oil," *CMA*, October 29, 1913, 8; "The Floatation of oil companies," *CH*, October 29, 1913, 1; for further context and discussion of Cunningham Craig's comments, see below.
35 Historian Chris Armstrong writes that the buying and selling of securities in Canada became commonplace and mining stocks in particular became the favoured investment of people previously uninvolved in securities. Between 1901 and 1914 individual buyers purchased $446.2 million worth of stocks and bonds. See Armstrong, *Blue Skies and Boiler Rooms*, 20–22.
36 "Concerned Citizen," Letter to the Editor, *CH*, October 30, 1913, 1.
37 "The floatation of oil companies," *CH*, October 28, 1913, 1; "The floatation of oil companies," *CH*, October 29, 1913, 1; "The floatation of oil companies," *CH*, October 30, 1913, 1; Archibald W. Dingman, Letter to the Editor, *CH*, November 1, 1913, 1; "A word of advice," *CH*, November 1, 1913, 1.
38 *Calgary Eye Opener*, December 20, 1913, 2.
39 "Wildcat schemes," *Ottawa Journal*, December 5, 1913, 9; "Object and effect," *CMA*, October 30, 1913, 3; *CNT*, October 30, 1913, 1; "Local oil flotations: an unbiased analysis," *CMA*, October 31, 1913, 1; *Natural Gas and Oil Record*, November 1, 1913, 3.
40 Editorial, "The question of 'oil,'" *CNT*, November 5, 1913, 4.
41 Editorial, "The question of 'oil,'" *CNT*, November 5, 1913, 4.

42 Editorial, "The question of 'oil,'" *CNT*, November 5, 1913, 4.
43 "True every word," Rocky Mountain Oil Fields Ad, *CNT*, November 6, 1913, 5; "Alberta oil and asphalt," *Financial Post*, November 22, 1913, 8; "Exaggerated Canadian reports," *Petroleum Gazette*, November 1913, 12.
44 "The floatation of oil companies," *CH*, October 31, 1913, 1.
45 "The Oil Record's position," *Natural Gas and Oil Record*, November 21, 1913, 6.
46 Henderson's Calgary Directory, 1914, 712; "At the hotels," *CH*, November 7, 1913, 5; *Natural Gas and Oil Record*, November 8, 1913, 2, 3.
47 PAA, GR1979.0285, reel 5, file 280, Calgary District Court, *S.E. Beveridge v. James H. Woods*, Testimony of Charles Pohl, December 5, 1913, 39.
48 Ad, "Cause and Effect," *Natural Gas and Oil Record*, November 7, 1913, 8; "The floatation of oil companies," *CH*, November 4, 1913, 1; "Regarding the black spot," *Natural Gas and Oil Record*, November 14, 1913, 1.
49 "Interesting comment on the oil situation by a Chicago Man," *CH*, November 7, 1913, 22.
50 "Oil optimist discusses the present Alberta situation," *CNT*, November 15, 1913, 29.
51 "Oil optimist discusses the present Alberta situation," *CNT*, November 15, 1913, 29.
52 GWRC, M4540, J. McKinley Cameron Fonds, box 87, file 918, McDougall-Segur, Minutes – Directors, October 11, 1913; Minutes – Directors October 30, 1913; "Better to have 'chanced' and lost than never had a chance at all," *CNT*, November 24, 1913, 4.
53 "A duty of the government to protect the oil industry," *CNT*, November 28, 1913, 4.
54 *CMA*, November 19, 1913, 11; "Alberta oil possibilities," *Victoria Daily Times*, November 20, 1913, 11.
55 The *Toronto Globe*, *Ottawa Journal*, *Quebec Telegraph*, and *Montreal Gazette*, among others, published articles/editorials endorsing the *Herald's* campaign.
56 Editorial, *CMA*, November 20, 1913, 3; "Oil stock promoters and their methods," *CH*, November 20, 1913, 1.
57 "Banded for protection," *Lead Daily Call* (South Dakota), December 3, 1913, 2.
58 "Oil men at meeting form organization for self protection," *CH*, November 24, 1913, 1, 11.
59 "Oil men at meeting form organization for self protection," *CH*, November 24, 1913, 1, 11.
60 "Will sane men control?" *CH*, November 25, 1913, 11; *Petroleum Gazette*, December 1913, 5.
61 Editorial, *CMA*, November 26, 1913, 1.
62 Editorial, *CMA*, November 27, 1913, 1.
63 Editorial, *CMA*, November 28, 1913, 1.
64 "Oil development association perfects organization," *CMA*, November 27, 1913, 1, 8.
65 PAA, GR1979.0285, reel 5, file 280, Calgary District Court, *S.E. Beveridge v. James H. Woods*, Complaint, November 27, 1913.
66 GWRC, M6745, John Schmidt Fonds, Manuscript "George E. Buck," 12–13.
67 Gray, *Talk to My Lawyer*, 11–14.
68 PAA, GR1979.0285, reel 5, file 280, Calgary District Court, *S.E. Beveridge v. James H. Woods*, Testimony of Stephen E. Beveridge, December 5, 1913. 2.
69 Editorial, "Clean them out!" *CH*, April 20, 1895, 2; "Editor charged in court with criminal libel," *CNT*, November 28, 1913, 1; "Facts about floatation of oil companies are brought out in court," *CH*, December 3, 1913, 1, 14; "An anonymous telegram," *CH*, December 10, 1913, 1.
70 "The oil wealth," *CMA*, December 10, 1913, 3.
71 "Publicity is slogan of oil association," *CMA*, December 11, 1913, 1, 8; "Oil men discuss anonymous wire," *CH*, December 11, 1913, 1, 11; "Oil Association news," *Natural Gas and Oil Record*, December 12, 1913, 1.
72 "Oil development association may secure organizer," *CNT*, December 11, 1913, 1; "Oil Association news," *Natural Gas and Oil Record*, December 12, 1913, 1.
73 "Oil secretary resigns," *CH*, December 12, 1913, 1, 30; Editorial, *CMA*, December 13, 1913, 3; "Oil association raises #2,000 to exploit the petroleum fields of southern Alberta," *CMA*, December 17, 1913, 1; "Oil association officials resign, then reconsider," *CH*, December 17, 1913, 11; "Alberta oil association executive decides upon sweeping campaign of publicity," *CMA*, December 19, 1913, 1, 5; "Oil association in suspended condition," *CH*, January 6, 1914, 1; "Calgary oil association to meet in near future," *CMA*, February 19, 1914, 1.
74 Between December 25, 1913, and January 5, 1914, similar ads appeared in *The Minneapolis Star-Tribune*, *The Ottawa Citizen*, *The North Bay Daily Nugget*, *The Idaho Daily Statesman* (Boise), *The Detroit Free Press*, *The Los Angeles Times*, *The Indianapolis Star*, *The Star Press* (Muncie, IN), and *The Omaha Daily Bee*.

NOTES TO CHAPTER 3

1   The metropolis-hinterland thesis assumes there are two kinds of regions: metropoles (sometimes called heartlands) that serve as the core of the economy and exert dominance over its hinterlands; and peripheral areas that are subservient to the core. As cities evolve outward, so too does the pattern of development, replicating and expanding into new regions. For western Canada, this meant control by the metropolitan centres of Montreal and Toronto. J.M.S. Careless advanced the thesis by arguing that the growth of cities in the West, like Calgary, meant these new metropolitan areas would dominate the surrounding hinterland of southern Alberta. But as historian R. Douglas Francis observed, the fundamental relationship between western and central Canada remained unaffected, as the Prairie West is consistently depicted "as a hinterland to metropolitan centers outside its borders." Where Innis describes a series of subordinate, dependent relationships evolving from these arrangements, Turner sees successive waves of settlers on the frontier replacing European norms with American values of freedom, independence, individualism, democracy, egalitarianism, inventiveness, coarseness, idealism, and progress.

Contrary to US historian Frederick Jackson Turner's conception of the frontier as the "true America," successive Canadian historians working in the tradition of Harold Innis, particularly Donald Creighton and J.M.S. Careless, developed the metropolitan-hinterland school to describe the Canadian frontier. Influenced by geography, climate, and communications, the frontier regions of Canada and the United States emerged differently. In the United States, the frontier, broadly defined, extended from the Midwest to the Pacific coast and contained seemingly endless waves of arable land and favourable climates, Where Turner sees the frontier as the cradle of uniquely American values and beliefs separate from Europe, Innis concluded unequivocally that, due to transportation and communication networks along the St. Lawrence River, European influences still prevailed in Canada, where "the civilization of North America is the civilization of Europe." The corollary of this argument is that while cities in the United States were eventually linked together by railroads and canals, the development of transportation and communications infrastructure took time, providing a period of isolation on the American frontier that, Turner argued, left a mark. Frederick Jackson Turner, *The Significance of the Frontier in American History* (Ann Arbor: University of Michigan Microfilms, 1966), 200–201; R. Douglas Francis, "Turner Versus Innis: Bridging the Gap," *American Review of Canadian Studies* 33, no. 4 (2003): 474–75; Walter D. Young, *Democracy and Discontent: Progressivism, Socialism and Social Credit in the Canadian West* (Toronto: McGraw-Hill, 1978), 2–3; John Richards and Larry Pratt, *Prairie Capitalism: Power and Influence in the New West* (Toronto: McClelland & Stewart, 1979), 15; Gerald Friesen, *The Canadian Prairies: A History* (Toronto: University of Toronto Press, 1984), 162–63; Michael Bliss, *Northern Enterprise: Five Centuries of Canadian Business* (Toronto: McClelland and Stewart, 1987), 293; J.C. Herbert Emery and Ronald D. Kneebone, "Socialists, Populists, Resources, and the Divergent Development of Alberta and Saskatchewan," *Canadian Public Policy* 34, no. 4 (2008): 419–40.

2   After reaching a peak of an average price of $1.07 in 1900, crude prices fluctuated between a low of $0.61 and a high of $2.21 per barrel of crude in 1919: Williamson and Daum, *The American Petroleum Industry*, vol. 2, 40.

3   Scholars John Richards and Larry Pratt observed that, prior to 1947, oil and gas development "provoked a populist response in Alberta" which held that the people should benefit economically, politically, and socially from development rather than some large industrial combination: Richards and Pratt, *Prairie Capitalism*, 24, 91.

4   John D. Rockefeller Sr. and Standard Oil's preferred strategy for dealing with all inquiries into their business was to say as little as possible, but this strategy proved wanting as public attitudes toward trusts more generally changed by the late 1880s. Hinton and Olien argue Standard Oil's greatest weakness was political because its opponents "perfected political infighting" to offset Standard's strengths. Using rhetoric that equated monopoly with conspiracy and corruption, independent oil men mobilized political power against Standard's economic strengths by bringing it before investigating committees and the courts. The Republic of Texas's 1836 constitution enshrined the state's anti-monopoly sentiment by barring grants of exclusive privilege by the state, and the provision found its way into subsequent iterations of the constitution. By 1893 twenty-one states and two territories had either constitutional or statutory measures opposing the operation of monopolies or trusts within their borders. Hidy and Hidy, *Pioneering in Big Business*, 208, 306–9; Chernow, *Titan*, 294–95; Hinton and Olien, *Oil in Texas*, 20–23; Bryan Burrough, *The Big Rich: The Rise and Fall of the Greatest Texas Oil Fortunes* (New York: Penguin, 2009), 11–12.

5   Diana Davids Hinton and Roger Olien, *Easy Money: Oil Promoters and Investors in the Jazz Age* (Chapel Hill: University of North Carolina Press, 1990), x.

6   In various sources he is referred to by surname as Craig, Cunningham-Craig, or Cunningham Craig. For the sake of consistency, we will use Cunningham Craig throughout.

7   George Colpitts, *Game in the Garden: A Human History of Wildlife in Western Canada to 1940* (Vancouver: UBC Press, 2002), 104, and especially Chapter 4.
8   Black, *Petrolia*, 8; Gordon Jaremko, "Turner Valley: The Beginning of a Long Apprenticeship," *Alberta History* 62 (Spring 2014): 8, available at https://go.gale.com/ps/i.do?p=AONE&u=googlescholar&id=GALE%7CA365891752&v=2.1&it=r&sid=AONE&asid=a0060098.
9   "The Standard Oil's gigantic spider web of pipes," *CH*, October 9, 1911, 13.
10 "U.S. Supreme Court orders the dissolution of Standard Oil Co.," *CMA*, May 16, 1911, 1; "Standard Oil will still grip Canada," *EJ*, May 17, 1911, 1.
11 "May investigate Standard Oil's operations in the dominion," *EB*, May 17, 1911, 1; "Judgement is not taken seriously," *CMA*, May 17, 1911, 7; A.W.N. Gogay, Letter to the Editor, *CH*, June 28, 1911, 10.
12 Roger Olien and Diana Davids Hinton argued that the petroleum industry applied a very elastic definition of the term. At various times, the term "independent" was applied to "wildcatters, mail order promoters, lease brokers, producers, stripper well operators, royalty owners, refiners, and retailers, and to giant corporations with production in many countries as well as to one-man operators working in shared offices." Meanwhile, leading petroleum business authors Andrew Inkpen and Michael Moffett apply a much narrower definition that describes an independent as a non-integrated company that generates nearly all its revenue from oil and gas production or downstream (transportation, refining, and marketing) operations, although they allow that some only apply the term to oil and gas producers. See Roger M. Olien and Diana Davids Hinton, *Wildcatters: Texas Independent Oilmen* (College Station: Texas A&M University Press, 2007), 2–5; Andrew Inkpen and Michael H. Moffett, *The Global Oil and Gas Industry: Management, Strategy and Finance* (Tulsa: PennWell, 2011), 11–12; Morgan Downey, *Oil 101* (Albany: Wooden Table Press, 2009), 4.
13 "Oil men complete their organization at further meeting," *CH*, November 27, 1913, 1.
14 "Standard Oil Co. sends man here to investigate," *CH*, March 22, 1913, 1; "When oil is discovered," *CMA*, October 13, 1913, 3; "A petrol railway projected," *CNT*, October 17, 1913, 20; "Drilling at the Dingman well started again," *CNT*, October 17, 1913, 20–21.
15 Editorial, "The millionaire and Canadian resources," *CNT*, October 27, 1913, 4.
16 Prospectus, Rocky Mountain Oil Fields, Limited.
17 "Pessimists and Otherwise," Rocky Mountain Oil Fields Limited ad, *CMA* October 23, 1913, 8; "Are You Playing the Long Shot?" Rocky Mountain Oil Fields Limited ad, *CMA*, November 1, 1913, 15.
18 "The Okotoks Oil Fields," Rocky Mountain Oil Fields Limited ad, *CMA*, October 20, 1913, 9; "The Future," Rocky Mountain Oil Fields Limited ad, *CMA* November 10, 1913, 11; "A Great Future," Rocky Mountain Oil Fields Limited ad, *Natural Gas and Oil Record*, November 21, 1913, 6; *Chicago Tribune*, January 13, 1914, 23.
19 D. Austin Lane, "Difficulties getting cash," *Calgary Albertan*, June 15, 1956, 18.
20 Thomas Anthony Buchanan Corley, *A History of the Burmah Oil Company, 1886–1924* (London: Heinemann, 1983), 131.
21 Arthur Beeby-Thompson, *Oil Pioneer: Selected Experiences and Incidents Associated with Sixty Years of World Wide Petroleum Exploration and Oilfield Development* (London: Sidgwick & Jackson, 1961), 116.
22 "Noted geologist makes inspection of Mitford mine," *CH*, October 1, 1912.
23 E.H. Cunningham Craig, *Oil Finding: An Introduction to the Geological Study of Petroleum* (London: Edward Arnold, 1913), ix.
24 Boverton Redwood, "Introduction," in Craig, *Oil Finding*, ix.
25 United States Geological Survey, C.W. Hayes and William Kennedy, "Oil Fields of the Texas-Louisiana Gulf Coastal Plain" (Washington: Government Printing Office, 1903), 137.
26 Craig, *Oil Finding*, 1, 4.
27 Craig, *Oil Finding*, 189.
28 Craig, *Oil Finding*, 151.
29 Craig, *Oil Finding*, 190.
30 "At the oil fields," *CH*, December 16, 1912, 18.
31 "Calgary oil may be used for the navy," *CH*, October 15, 1913, 1; "Ex-alderman tried to file oil claim in centre of city," *CH*, October 17, 1913, 26.
32 "Cunningham Craig may not make statement regarding oil fields until he returns to England," *CMA*, October 29, 1913, 1.
33 "Alberta can supply fuel oil for navy," *Victoria Daily Times*, November 14, 1913, 15.

34 "Warning against oil boomsters," *Montreal Gazette*, November 13, 1913, 22.
35 PAA, GR1986.0166/235g, Attorney General Central Files, Companies' Ordinance General File, Letter, Julian Langner, Calgary, June 1914.
36 "Extensive development campaign said to be contemplated by the petroleum company and others," *CMA*, November 6, 1913, 1.
37 "Craig tells of oil find in Alberta," *CH*, December 2, 1913, 1.
38 Herron-Elder ad, *CMA*, December 4, 1913, 9.
39 "Interest in oil," *CH*, January 13, 1914, 1.
40 Cunningham Craig, "The New Oil Fields of Canada," in *The Petroleum World*, February 1914, 60.
41 Cunningham Craig, "The New Oil Fields of Canada," 60.
42 Cunningham Craig, "The New Oil Fields of Canada," 62–63.
43 Malcolm, "Oil and Gas Prospects of the Northwest Provinces of Canada," 5; Cunningham Craig, "The New Oil Fields of Canada," 63.
44 Cunningham Craig, "The New Oil Fields of Canada," 63
45 Cunningham Craig, "The New Oil Fields of Canada," 63, 65.
46 Cunningham Craig, "The New Oil Fields of Canada," 65.
47 Editorial, "An authority speaks," *CH*, January 22, 1914, 6.
48 "Chancellor and First Lord appear in public together," *Vancouver Daily World*, January 21, 1914, 1; "Calgary oil boom is doing much mischief," *Toronto Star*, January 21, 1914, 1.
49 Editorial, *EJ*, January 24, 1914, 4.
50 Editorial, *CMA*, January 22, 1914, 3.
51 Editorial, *CMA*, February 7, 1914, 3.
52 Bliss, *Northern Enterprise*, 316–17.
53 "Seven drills are at work in Calgary oil fields," *Weekly Albertan*, March 1, 1914, 6; Piedmont Petroleum Products Company ad, *CMA*, May 12, 1914, 7; Piedmont Petroleum Products Company ad, *CMA*, May 13, 1914, 9.
54 Frederick Buell, "A Short History of Oil Cultures, or The Marriage of Catastrophe and Exuberance," in Ross Barrett, Daniel Worden, and Allan Stoekl, *Oil Culture* (Minneapolis: University of Minnesota Press, 2014), 74–75.
55 *Wall Street Journal*, April 27, 1914, 2; Herron-Elder ad, *CMA*, May 16, 1914, 9.
56 Breen, *Herron*, Section II, Document 15, "W.S. Herron statement regarding dispute with A.W. Dingman, April 10, 1919 and attachment of February 3, 1914," 52–54.
57 Breen, *Herron*, xxvi; "No controversy over location of second well," *CH*, February 4, 1914, 14; "Calgary oil men in warring factions," *EB*, February 5, 1914, 7; "Litigation started over valuable oil lease in proximity to No. 1 well," *CH*, February 7, 1914, 1, 13; "Fight starts over valuable oil land," *CMA*, February 9, 1914, 8.
58 "Rapid developments are taking place in oil circles," *CH*, May 20, 1914, 1.
59 Leishman McNeill, *Calgary Herald's Tales of the Old Town* (Calgary Herald, 1966), 26.
60 Hinton and Olien, *Easy Money*, 25.

NOTES TO CHAPTER 4

1 Gray, *Troublemaker*, 38.
2 Darren Dochuk, *Anointed with Oil: How Christianity and Crude Made Modern America* (New York: Basic Books, 2019), 39. Several scholars note the influence of US-style evangelism in Alberta politics and culture. See, for example, Trevor W. Harrison, "Petroleum, Politics, and the Limits of Left Progressivism in Alberta," in *Alberta Oil and the Decline of Democracy in Canada*, ed. Meenal Shrivastava and Lorna Stefanick (Edmonton: Athabasca University Press, 2015), available at https://www.aupress.ca/books/120251-alberta-oil-and-the-decline-of-democracy-in-canada/.
3 Bright, *The Limits of Labour*, 18–30.
4 Will Ferguson, "Introduction," in MacEwan, *Eye Opener Bob*, viii; Hugh A. Dempsey, *Calgary, Spirit of the West: A History* (Saskatoon: Fifth House, 1994), 81.
5 Friesen, *The Canadian Prairies: A History*, 390.
6 James H. Gray, *Red Lights on the Prairies* (Toronto: Macmillan, 1971), 125.

7   van Herk, *Mavericks*, 359; Gray, *Red Lights on the Prairies*, 105, 125–27; Dempsey, *Calgary: Spirit of the West*, 101.
8   "Woman testifies she believes there were three to four hundred houses of ill-fame in the city during March last," *Edmonton Capital*, June 12, 1914, 1; "Mayor M'Namara denies evidence given by Lancey," *EB*, June 27, 1914, 11.
9   "Ex-chief Carpenter causes sensation," *CH*, June 19, 1914, 5.
10 "Statement from Evangelist [J.A.L.] Romig of Christian Church," *CH*, May 27, 1909, 2.
11 Derren Dochuk, *From Bible Belt to Sun Belt: Plain-Folk Religion, Grassroots Politics, and the Rise of Evangelical Conservatism* (New York: W.W. Norton, 2011), 213; Banack, *God's Province*, 70–71; *CH*, November 5, 1910, 7; *CH*, November 12, 1910, 11; *CH*, November 19, 1910, 11; *CMA*, November 19, 1910, 11.
12 McNeil, *Tales of the Old Town*, 68. McNeil misidentifies George Buck as "George Brick."
13 John Schmidt, *Growing Up in the Oil Patch*, 105–6; Luxton, *Latch String Out*, 279; "More gifts of land to the university," *CH*, February 3, 1913, 1; "Feature event of auto races to be run in two heats," *CH*, September 17, 1913, 9.
14 "Financial stringency gives way to oil fever throughout Alberta," *Vancouver Daily World*, May 23, 1914, 10, 12.
15 PAA, GR1979.0285, file 7056, reel 132, Calgary District Court, *Allan Clark et al. v. Black Diamond Oil Fields et al.* (1915), Examination for Discovery, Jennie L. Earl, Calgary, January 9, 1915, 3–8.
16 PAA, GR1979.0285, file #7056, reel 132, Calgary District Court, *Allan Clark et al. v. Black Diamond Oil Fields et al.* (1915), Affidavit, George E. Buck, Calgary, January 8, 1915, 3; PAA, GR1979.0285, file 8673, reel 145, Calgary District Court, *International Supply Company v. Black Diamond Oil Fields*, Statement of Claim, Calgary, December 18, 1914; GWRC, M1232, Percival Timms Fonds, box 1, file 5, Prospectus: The Black Diamond Oil Fields, Limited. (1913); "Two Calgary girls file on oil leases," *CH*, August 12, 1912, 1; "Mineral claims near city are filed on," *CH*, August 23, 1912, 20; "Many filings on copper and coal claims in Sheep Creek and Highwood districts," *CMA*, August 23, 1912, 1; "The floatation of oil companies," *CH*, October 28, 1913, 1; "Calgary oil flotations: an unbiased analysis," *CMA*, November 1, 1913, 1, 12; "Martin will drill for Black Diamond Oil Fields," *CMA*, December 11, 1913, 1; "Financial stringency gives way to oil fever throughout Alberta," *Vancouver Daily World*, May 23, 1914, 10, 12; Hutchinson, "As the Bust Paralyzes Calgary One Word Reignites the City: Oil," 372. Schmidt, *Growing Up in the Oil Patch*, 104–7; GWRC, M968, A.P. "Tiny" Phillips Fonds, box 1. file 1, Blue Scribbler. Tiny Phillips left two handwritten accounts of his career in the oil patch and dealings with George Buck—a short one in a receipt book, and another longer one in a blue scribbler. The accounts both contain the same basic story, but the blue scribbler contains greater detail. For ease of reference, they will be referred to as "Receipt Book" and "Blue Scribbler." J.M.D. Ritchie, "The truth about the Black Diamond well," *CMA*, June 8, 1914, 1, 5.
17 PAA, GR1979.0285, file 8673, reel 145, Calgary District Court, *International Supply Company v. Black Diamond Oil Fields* (1915), Statement of Claim, Calgary, December 23, 1914.
18 "Oil strike is expected soon at Black Diamond," *CH*, June 13, 1914, 13.
19 Examination of Discovery, George Buck, Calgary, January 9, 1915, 35.
20 "Brick and stone for Calgary," *CMA*, January 4, 1906, 5; "Red Cross home to be opened Wednesday," *CMA*, July 13, 1920, 3; "City pioneer Crandell dies," *Albertan*, June 5, 1944, 7; Ken Liddell, "Brick plant area rests in pieces." *CH*, October 9, 1953, 3; Jack Peach, "Crandell homes characterized by solid workmanship," *CH*, July 11, 1981, F14; Susan Scott, "Preserving the brickwork," *CH*, July 14, 1994, *Neighbors*, 1; "Then and now," *CH*, December 30, 2003, B2.
21 "Drilling is started on Black Diamond," *CMA*, January 31, 1914, 1; "A square deal in oil, for you" ad, *CMA*, February 2, 1914, 7; "Autoists travel to Black Diamond field derrick," *CMA*, February 2, 1914, 7, 12.
22 "Everybody enthusiastic about Black Diamond" ad, *CMA*, February 3, 1914, 7.
23 George Buck, "Important Announcement on Oil," *CMA*, February 3, 1914, 9; "Look out for wet gas at 200 feet" ad, *CMA*, February 6, 1914, 7; "Caveat out on Black Diamond property," *CMA*, February 16, 1914, 3.
24 Black, *Petrolia*, 39–42.
25 "Oil strike is expected soon at Black Diamond," *CH*, June 13, 1914, 13.
26 PAA, GR1979.0285, reel 128, file 6873, Calgary District Court, *Taxation of the costs of Lougheed, Bennett, McLaws & Company against George E. Buck & Black Diamond Oil Fields, Limited* (1914).
27 PAA, GR1987.0246, box 8, Case 222, Appellate Division, *Grant S. Wolverton v. Black Diamond Oil Fields et al.* (1914), Appeal Book, Testimony of Carlton M.S. Kipling, 8; Testimony of Grant S. Wolverton, 9, 17.
28 "Devenish company to be launched Monday," *CMA*, November 15, 1913, 1.
29 PAA, GR1979.0285, file 6342, reel 118, Calgary District Court, *Grant S. Wolverton v. Black Diamond Oil Fields et al.* (1914), Examination of Discovery, Grant S. Wolverton, Calgary, November 13, 1914, 4, 8; PAA,

GR1987.0246, box 8, Case 222, Appellate Division, *Grant S. Wolverton v. Black Diamond Oil Fields et al.* (1914), Testimony of Grant S. Wolverton, 10.

30 PAA, GR1987.0246, box 8, Case 222, Appellate Division, *Grant S. Wolverton v. Black Diamond Oil Fields et al.* (1914), Testimony of George E. Buck, 33, 35.

31 "Good morning, Baron! Are your surface rights all right?" *CMA*, February 18, 1914, 5; "Buck's friends say he is being persecuted," *CMA*, February 18, 1914, 8; "Charge against George E. Buck not substantiated," *CMA*, February 19, 1914, 1; "Injunction against G.W. [sic] Buck is dissolved," *CMA*, February 21, 1914, 1; George Buck ad, *CMA*, February 21, 1914, 8.

32 *Natural Gas and Oil Record*, March 7, 1914, 3.

33 "Caveat on the Black Diamond withdrawn," *CMA*, March 18, 1914, 1, 7; "New caveat filed on Black Diamond," *CH*, March 21, 1914, 1.

34 Ad, Canadian Press Association, "The Poor Man's University," *CH*, January 15, 1914, 15; Russell T. Johnston, *Selling Themselves: The Emergence of Canadian Advertising* (Toronto: University of Toronto Press, 2001), 145–47.

35 LAC, R927, RG125-A, vol. 398, file 3906, part 1, Supreme Court of Canada, *The King v. George Buck* (1916), Appeal from the Judgment of the Supreme Court of Alberta, Appellate Division, "Deposition of J.W. Hayes," Lima, Ohio, December 27, 1915, 307–11; "Deposition of Norman R. Fletcher," Preliminary Inquiry, Calgary, 311–12. GWRC, M968, A.P. "Tiny" Phillips Fonds, box 1, file 1.

36 PAA, GR1979.0285, file 7056, reel 132, Calgary District Court, *Allan Clark et al. v. Black Diamond Oil Fields et al.* (1915), Examination of Discovery, George E. Buck, Calgary, January 8, 1915, 39–45; Examination of Discovery, John A. Campbell, Calgary, February 9, 1915, 4–5; GWRC, M1232, Percival Timms Fonds, box 1, file 5, Prospectus: The Black Diamond Oil Fields, Limited.

37 *Natural Gas and Oil Record*, May 2, 1914, 1.

38 LAC R927, RG125-A, vol. 398, file 3906, part 1, Supreme Court of Canada, *The King v. George Buck*, Appeal from the Judgment of the Supreme Court of Alberta, Appellate Division, "Deposition of Norman R. Fletcher," Preliminary Inquiry, Calgary, 332; "Black Diamond Foreman tells of salting well," *CH*, November 12, 1915, 11.

39 LAC, R927, RG125-A, vol. 398, file 3906, part 1, Supreme Court of Canada, *The King v. George Buck*, "Deposition of Norman R. Fletcher," Preliminary Inquiry, Calgary, 332.

40 LAC, R927, RG125-A, vol. 398, file 3906, part 1, Supreme Court of Canada, *The King v. George Buck*, Appeal from the Judgment of the Supreme Court of Alberta, Appellate Division, "Deposition of J.W. Hayes," Lima, Ohio. December 27, 1915, 283.

41 LAC, R927, RG125-A, vol. 398, file 3906, part 1, Supreme Court of Canada, *Buck v. Rex*, "The Crown's Factum," 1917, 1–3; Supreme Court of Alberta, Rex v. Buck, "Appellant's Factum," 1917, 8–11.

42 LAC, R927, RG125-A, vol. 398, file 3906, part 1, Supreme Court of Canada, *The King v. George Buck*, Appeal from the Judgment of the Supreme Court of Alberta, Appellate Division, "Charles E. Tryon, Direct Examination," 236–50; "Deposition of J.W. Hayes," Lima, Ohio, December 27, 1915, 305.

43 "Crude oil found in Black Diamond oil well," *CMA*, May 8, 1914, 1, 8.

44 "Death overtakes W.W. Cheely, one of Montana's most widely known citizens and newspaper man," *Miles City Star*, April 4, 1939, 8.

45 "William W. Cheely," *Montana Standard*, April 2, 1939, 4.

46 "W.W. Cheely has leap year birthday fete," *Great Falls Tribune*, March 1, 1936, 19.

47 *CMA*, April 28, 1939, 4.

48 "Montana loses widely beloved editor in death of William W. 'Bill' Cheely," *Cascade Courier*, April 19, 1939, 7.

49 "Cheely a millionaire strike in oil did it," *Anaconda Standard*, June 2, 1914, 9; "William Cheely rites to be in Great Falls," *Butte Daily Post*, April 1, 1939, 3; "William W. Cheely writes '30' on last copy," *Miles City Star*, April 4, 1939, 4.

50 LAC, R927, RG125-A, vol. 398, file 3906, part 1, Supreme Court of Canada, *The King v. George Buck* (1916), Appeal from the Judgment of the Supreme Court of Alberta, Appellate Division, "Wm. Winbourne Cheely, Direct Examination," 88–98; GWRC, Tiny Phillips Fonds, box 1, file 1, W.W. Cheely, "Black Diamond find gives promise of petroleum values," *CMA*, May 9, 1914, 1, 8; "Cheely testifies in the Buck case," *CH*, October 28, 1916, 4; "Buck before court," *Western Standard*, November 14, 1915, 7; Brian Hutchinson, "The cigar-chomping pastor and his oilfield scam," in *Alberta in the 20th Century: A Journalistic History of the Province in Twelve Volumes*, vol. 3: *The Boom and the Bust*, ed. Ted Byfield (Edmonton: United Western Communications, 1994), 372.

NOTES TO CHAPTER 5

1. The truce between Dingman and Herron proved temporary and reignited in 1919 when Herron filed a countersuit against Dingman. See Breen, *Herron*, 52–61;"Fight starts over valuable oil land," *CMA*, February 9, 1914, 8; "Rumors of strike are discredited in city today," *CH*, April 8, 1914, 1; *Natural Gas and Oil Record*, April 11, 1914, 3.
   Luke 6:24–30 (King James Version) reads: "But woe unto you that are rich! for ye have received your consolation. Woe unto you that are full! for ye shall hunger. Woe unto you that laugh now! for ye shall mourn and weep. Woe unto you, when all men shall speak well of you! for so did their fathers to the false prophets. But I say unto you which hear, Love your enemies, do good to them which hate you, Bless them that curse you, and pray for them which despitefully use you. And unto him that smiteth thee on the one cheek offer also the other; and him that taketh away thy cloak forbid not to take thy coat also. Give every man that asketh of thee; and of him that taketh away thy goods ask them not again."

2. W.S. Herron to A.W. Dingman, December 11, 1912, in Breen, *William Stewart Herron*, 25; "Sprays from the derrick," *Natural Gas and Oil Record*, November 21, 1913, 3; "Drilling at Dingman well discontinued," *CNT*, November 21, 1913, 1; "Eyes of men of oil world are on the Calgary fields," *CMA*, February 19, 1914, 1; "Directors of the Dingman company believe drill is working in capping just above oil deposit," *CMA*, April 13, 1914, 1; "Fate of fortunes is hanging in balance: feeling is tense," *CMA*, April 14, 1914, 1; "Oil within the next 100 feet is idea of Dingman," *CMA*, April 17, 1914, 1.

3. GWRC, M4540, J. McKinley Cameron Fonds, box 87, file 918, McDougall-Segur, Minutes – Directors, May 4, 1914; Minutes – Directors, May 15, 1914; "Segur now trying to interest Standard Oil in local field," *CH*, March 6, 1914, 1; *CH*, March 12, 1914, 1; "Ira E. Segur Back," *CH*, March 23, 1914, 1; Taylor, *Imperial Standard*, 119; Cass, "Investment in the Alberta Petroleum Industry," 57; Gray, *Great Canadian Oil Patch*, 63; Breen, *Alberta's Petroleum Industry*, 17.

4. GWRC, M330, Dingman Family Fonds, box 1, file 6, Claude Dingman, "Highlights of the 'Pioneer Days' of the Gas and Oil industry in Alberta," 1956, 3; De Mille, *Oil in Canada West*, 117.

5. W.W. Cheely, "1,000 feet of oil in Dingman Well," *CMA*, May 15, 1914, 1.

6. "Oil strike is food for thought to W.S. Herron," *CH*, May 16, 1914, 1.

7. "How the great oil boom in Calgary commenced," *Vancouver Daily World*, May 26, 1914, 14.

8. "Bill Cheely is sure discovery is 'real thing,'" *CNT*, May 15, 1914, 11; "Oil discovery will mean that problem of unemployment is solved," *CH*, May 16, 1914, 1; Editorial, *CMA*, May 16, 1914, 6; "The discovery of oil will be of incalculable benefit to Calgary and Alberta," *CNT*, May 15, 1914, 1; "Calgary is oil mad stocks are booming," *Victoria Daily Times*, May 16, 1914, 3; "The new Calgary," *Natural Gas and Oil Record*, May 18, 1914, 1; "Oil strike may end stringency," *CNT*, May 21, 1914, 1.

9. *CMA*, May 16, 1914, 1.

10. "Fourteen drilling outfits for the Calgary district," *CMA*, May 19, 1914, 1.

11. "The discovery of oil will be of incalculable benefit to Calgary and Alberta," *CNT*, May 15, 1914, 1; "Calgary is oil mad stocks are booming," *Victoria Daily Times*, May 16, 1914, 3; "The new Calgary," *Natural Gas and Oil Record*, May 18, 1914, 1; "Oil strike may end stringency," *CNT*, May 21, 1914, 1.

12. "The discovery of oil in Alberta; What it is and what it promises," *Western Standard*, June 20, 1914, 19–20.

13. "Mackie boys rich strike," *Ottawa Citizen*, May 27, 1914, 7; *Natural Gas and Oil Record*, May 23, 1914, 23.

14. The council meeting loomed as a potential bloodbath between the mayor and his detractors over the issue of the tender of municipal contracts. Before his departure, Mayor McNamara issued an inflammatory statement alleging that he alone protected the city "against a gang of wolves," including some on city council who received bribes, kickbacks, or otherwise profited from the awarding of city contracts. "Oil fever here," *EJ*, May 16, 1914, 1; "Many visit oil fields near Okotoks," *EB*, May 18, 1914, 1; "Mayor stricken with an attack of 'Oilitiritis,'" *EJ*, May 19, 1914, 1; "Aldermen to know who are gang of wolves to whom mayor referred," *EB*, May 20, 1914, 1.

15. Statistics Canada, "Average wages of farm help in Canada, by province, 1909, 1910 and 1914 to 1916," available online at https://www65.statcan.gc.ca/acyb02/1917/acyb02_191702028-eng.htm (accessed May 27, 2022); "Putting savings into holes," *National Post*, January 2, 1915, 25.

16. The number of Alberta-based CPR employees is inferred from a few different pieces of data. Dominion government data places the average monthly salary for all Canadian railroad workers in 1915 at $60.56. Contemporary newspaper reports suggested that the CPR's monthly payroll of $6 million required the company to issue 120,000 cheques. Further analysis of Dominion data suggests the average railroad worker across Canada worked approximately 305.8 days a year, with the number of days worked for hourly employees based on a ten-hour workday. This results in an average daily salary of $2.58. In October 1914, the CPR reported that its Alberta division donated $15,000 to the Patriotic Fund, a private initiative that

took donations to support soldiers and their dependents during and after the Great War. The donations were part of a campaign inaugurated by CPR president T.G. Shaughnessy to donate a day's salary. See Canada, Dominion Bureau of Statistics, Department of Railways and Canals, Sessional Paper 20b, "Railway statistics of the Dominion of Canada for the year ended June 30, 1915" (Ottawa: King' Printer, 1916), lviii–lx; "A wage bill of $6,000,000," *Brantford Daily Expositor*, July 4, 1914, 7; "When pay day comes," *Bassano Mail*, August 13, 1914, 1; "New York sentiment is unanimously in favor of allies," *CMA*, October 14, 1914, 8.

17   "Calgary is oil mad, stocks are booming," *Victoria Daily Times*, May 16, 1914, 3.
18   GWRC, M5769, Alberta Stock Exchange Fonds, series 9, file 47, "A 'Share' of the Business," n.d.; *CH*, May 21, 1964, 55; Breen, *Alberta's Petroleum Industry*, 16; "Throwing money in for oil shares," *Vancouver Province*, May 18, 1914, 22.
19   GWRC, M330, Dingman Family Fonds, box 1, file 6, Claude Dingman, "Highlights of the 'Pioneer Days' of the Gas and Oil industry in Alberta," 1956, 7–8.
20   "Oil in Alberta Reported," *Christian Science Monitor*, May 18, 1914, 9; "Canadian oil boom," *Manchester Guardian*, May 20, 1914, 9; "Western Canada depressed before the war broke out," *Wall Street Journal*, September 15, 1914, 5; "People and capital are pouring into Calgary from all parts of the continent," *CH*, May 21, 1914, 15; "Dingman well on holiday yesterday but brokers busy," *CMA*, May 26, 1914, 1.
21   "Oil is plentiful but clams scarce," *Tacoma News Tribune*, May 19, 1914, 13.
22   *Calgary Eye Opener*, May 23, 1914, 1.
23   Shiels, *Calgary*, 191.
24   Adjusted for inflation, that works out to an average of $50.55 per square foot of retail space, nearly double the 2023 price for prime real estate in Calgary. "Impressions of Calgary before and just after," *Vancouver Daily World*, May 30, 1914, 19; E.T. Smith, "Sudden riches in oil discoveries," *Spokane Spokesman-Review*, June 1, 1914, 5; "The interesting phases of Calgary oil boom," *Toronto Star*, May 28, 1914, 18.
25   "100 drilling plants will be in operation within three months," *CMA*, May 22, 1914, 1.
26   *Financial Post*, May 30, 1914, 3.
27   "The brokers are still here, but they are a colorless lot now," *Western Oil Examiner*, July 9, 1955, 34; *CNT*, May 20, 1914; *Calgary Herald*, May 21, 1964, 55; "All wells will probably strike oil; some will do better than others," *Vancouver Daily World*, May 23, 1914, 1, 14.
28   *Day Book* (Chicago), June 24, 1914, 1.
29   "Impressions of Calgary before and just after," *Vancouver Daily World*, May 30, 1914, 19.
30   "Rescued sobbing young investor from vale of woe," *CMA*, May 21, 1914, 1.
31   "Impressions of Calgary before and just after," 19.
32   "Impressions of Calgary before and just after," 19.
33   PAA, GR1979.0285, file 8496, reel 142, Calgary District Court, *Herbert Strong Company v. Black Diamond Oil Fields*, Discovery of Herbert Strong, Calgary, April 1, 1915, 12.
34   "The oil excitement in Alberta field," *Vancouver Sun*, June 6, 1914, 3.
35   *EJ*, August 1, 1913, 1; *CH*, August 7, 1913, 1; *CH*, August 14, 1913, 1; *CH*, January 6, 1914, 12; *CH*, January 9, 1914, 19; *CH*, January 16, 1914, 19; *CH*, January 23, 1914, 17; *CH*, January 30, 1914, 9; *CH*, February 2, 1914, 11; *CH*, February 6, 1914, 13; *National Post*, February 14, 1914, 16; *CH*, February 20, 1914, 15; *CH*, February 27, 1914, 14; *CH*, March 2, 1914, 11; *CH*, March 6, 1914, 15; *National Post*, March 7, 1914, 23; *CH*, March 13, 1914, 19; *National Post*, March 21, 1914, 16; *CH*, March 27, 1914, 19; *CH*, April 3, 1914, 23; *National Post*, April 4, 1914, 12; *National Post*, April 11, 1914, 25; *National Post*, April 18, 1914, 16; *CH*, April 24, 1914, 17; *National Post*, April 25, 1914, 18; *National Post*, May 2, 1914, 16; *CH*, May 8, 1914, 17; *National Post*, May 9, 1914, 16; *National Post*, May 16, 1914, 16; *National Post*, May 23, 1914, 16; *CH*, May 29, 1914, 25; *National Post*, May 30, 1914, 16; *CH*, June 5, 1914, 23; *CH*, June 12, 1914, 13; *National Post*, June 13, 1914, 16; *CH*, June 19, 1914, 29; *National Post*, June 27, 1914, 16; *CH*, July 3, 1914, 23; *National Post*, July 4, 1914, 16; *CH*, July 10, 1914, 20; *National Post*, July 11, 1914, 16; *National Post*, July 18, 1914, 16; *CH*, July 24, 1914, 19; *National Post*, July 25, 1914, 1; *CH*, July 31, 1913, 17; *National Post*, August 1, 1914, 16; *CH*, August 7, 1914, 14; *National Post*, August 8, 1914, 16; *CH*, August 14, 1914, 13; *National Post*, August 15, 1914, 12; *CH*, August 21, 1914, 11; *National Post*, August 22, 1914, 12; *CH*, August 28, 1914, 15; *National Post*, August 29, 1914, 1.
36   "The interesting phases of Calgary oil boom," *Toronto Star*, May 28, 1914, 18.
37   Advertisement, Calgary Furniture Store, Limited, *CNT*, May 16, 1914, 13; "Peculiar effect of the spectacular oil boom on different businesses," *Natural Gas and Oil Record*, May 20, 1914, 2; "To oil advertisers," *CMA*, May 23, 1914, 1; *Natural Gas and Oil Record*, May 23, 1914, 2.

38 The Standard Oil Fields of Alberta, Limited ad, *CMA*, November 8, 1913, 15.
39 "Oil fever at MacLeod," *Lethbridge Daily Herald*, May 18, 1914, 1; "Leases at Lethbridge," *EJ*, May 20, 1914, 3; "Oil excitement reaches locations north and north-west of Edmonton," *EJ*, May 22, 1914, 1; "Forty oil companies incorporated in Edmonton," *CMA*, May 26, 1914, 5; Athabasca Petroleum Company ad, *EJ*, May 27, 1914, 3; "Rush for oil fields," *CH*, May 28, 1914, 1; *Natural Gas and Oil Record*, May 30, 1914, 3.
40 "The oil fever," *Red Deer Advocate*, June 22, 1914, 1.
41 Hartford Oil Corporation ad, *Saskatoon Daily Star*, June 18, 1914, 12.
42 "Oil in western Canada," *Vancouver Sun*, May 19, 1914, 8–9; "Oil companies have big capitalization," *Vancouver Sun*, July 14, 1914, 9.
43 "London not aroused," *EJ*, May 22, 1914, 1; "Calgary oil 'boom,'" *Scotsman* [Edinburgh], May 21, 1914, 5.
44 "The Flame and the Moth," *Toronto Star*, May 30, 1914, 30.
45 "Toronto broker sizes up the Calgary oil boom," *Toronto Star*, June 16, 1914, 14.
46 *Financial Post*, June 6, 1914, 12; "Calgary Oil Flotations," *Canadian Mining Journal* 35, no. 14 (July 15, 1914): 1.
47 *Montreal Gazette*, May 29, 1914, 10.
48 "Henshaw writes on Calgary conditions," *Natural Gas and Oil Record*, July 18, 1914, 9.
49 William W. Cheely, "Oil strike sets gold flowing," *Spokane Spokesman-Review*, May 31, 1914, 34.
50 "Says oil excitement grows," *Spokane Spokesman-Review*, May 31, 1914, 7; *Spokane Chronicle*, June 2, 1914, 8.
51 "Calgary strikes oil" ad, *Courier-Reporter* (Waterloo, IA), September 12, 1914, 3.
52 "Calgary oil," *Toronto Star*, June 11, 1914, 6.
53 Athabasca Petroleum Company ad, *EJ*, May 27, 1914, 3.
54 "Outside capital now flocking in to develop oil," *CH*, May 20, 1914, 1.
55 GWRC, M5769, Alberta Stock Exchange Fonds, box 1, file 1, Committee of Management Minutes, May 25, 1914; Minutes, May 28, 1914; Minutes, June 19, 1914; Minutes, June 22, 1914; *CH*, May 25, 1914, 1; "Prices of stocks are variable," *CMA*, May 26, 1914, 1; "Men who will direct Calgary's stock exchange," *CMA*, May 26, 1914, 1; "Oil stock exchange forms at Calgary," *Vancouver Daily World*, May 26, 1914, 14; Advertisement, "Calgary Stock Exchange," *CH*, May 29, 1914, 25.
56 "Oil exchange will be opened in city," *Vancouver Sun*, July 9, 1914, 11.
57 Armstrong, *Blue Skies and Boiler Rooms*, 53; "Oil stocks are stronger," *Vancouver Province*, May 19, 1914, 18; "Manitoba bars agents of Calgary oil stock," *CNT*, May 21, 1914, 13; "'Peg business men pleased by outlook," *CNT*, May 21, 1914, 13; "Brokers asleep," *Natural Gas and Oil Record*, July 25, 1914, 1.
58 GWRC, M5769, Alberta Stock Exchange Fonds, box 4, file 35, Letter, R.C. Carlile to A.E. Graves, June 16, 1955.
59 "Calgary oil stocks on two exchanges," *Natural Gas and Oil Record*, May 30, 1914, 7; "Oil brokers are having very busy time these days," *CH*, June 13, 1914, 1; "Lively trading continues in oil stocks in Calgary," *Toronto Star*, June 18, 1914, 20.
60 Basil Clarke, "Oil madness," *Daily Mail* (London), June 8, 1914, 6.
61 Clarke, "Oil madness," 6.
62 Clarke, "Oil madness," 6.
63 Historical exchange rates for the dollar into British pound sterling places the pre–First World War pound at roughly $5 per £1. Clarke, "Oil madness," 6.
64 Clarke, "Oil madness," 6.
65 "From conservative trading to oil," *The Monetary Times: Trade Review and Insurance Chronicle* 52, no. 24 (June 12, 1914): 20.
66 In 1917 Mrs. W.H. Ranlett left Calgary for Spokane for a few years before settling in California. Mrs. Annie Wolley-Dod remained an active member of Calgary society and women's groups during the Great War and into the Great Depression. She died in November 1945 at the age of eighty-one. Perhaps somewhat ironically, Mrs. Blanche Mason is the most difficult person to trace following the summer of 1914. C.A. Owens ad, *CH*, April 2, 1912, 13; Eureka Women's Oil Exchange ad, *CH*, May 25, 1914, 14; "Calgary Woman's Oil Exchange," *CH*, May 25, 1914, 16; "First lady broker to enter the oil-stock business in Calgary," *CMA*, May 27, 1914, 1; *Toronto Globe*, June 6, 1914, 11; "Member of EWPC goes into 'oils,'" *EJ*, June 12, 1914, 10.
67 Calgary Women's Oil Exchange ad, *CH*, May 20, 1914, 3.

68   PAA, GR1979.0285, file 7056, reel 132, Calgary District Court, *Allan Clark et al. v. Black Diamond Oil Fields et al.*, Examination of Discovery, Allan Clark, Calgary, January 7, 1915, 126–28; GWRC, M330, Dingman Family Fonds, box 1, file 3, Calgary Petroleum Products List of Shareholders, 1920; Klassen, *Eye on the Future*, 299; Mabel Hutton, "Three Thousand Club Women," *Western Standard*, June 12, 1913, 9; "Women's press club to invest in oil," *CH*, June 8, 1914, 14; *CH*, June 13, 1914, 16.

69   *Day Book* (Chicago), June 24, 1914, 2.

70   "Calgary girls make some lucky oil deals," *CMA*, May 19, 1914, 4; "Lease brings fortune to CPR lady clerk," *CMA*, June 18, 1914, 1.

71   "Two Calgary girls file on oil lands," *CH*, August 12, 1912, 1.

72   *Day Book* (Chicago), June 24, 1914, 2.

73   "No abatement in oil fever is yet reported," *Natural Gas and Oil Record*, May 20, 1914, 5; "Minister becomes an oil broker," *CMA*, June 22, 1914, 1.

74   "No abatement in oil fever is yet reported," *Natural Gas and Oil Record*, May 20, 1914, 5; "Oil brokers may form an association," *CNT*, May 20, 1914, 11.

75   Allan Anderson, *Roughnecks and Wildcatters* (Toronto: Macmillan, 1981), 69; Calgary City Council Minutes, May 18, 1914, 3–4 (hereafter cited as CCC); "Fifty-dollar fee for brokers is finally passed," *CH*, May 20, 1914, 5; "Curb brokers in oil stock are mulcted," *CNT*, May 20, 1914, 11; "Over a hundred oil brokers have already taken out licenses," *CH*, May 21, 1914, 1; *Natural Gas and Oil Record*, May 23, 1914, 3, 13, 21; "Oil brokers locked up by village cops," *CH*, May 25, 1914, 1; "Another rumor about Monarch nipped in bud," *CH*, July 9, 1914, 1; "We should give duke a good time," *CMA*, July 15, 1914, 3; CCC, Legislative Committee Report, July 15, 1914, 1; CCC, Finance Committee Report, October 23, 1914, 2.

76   The term "policeman" is used advisedly, as the CPF under Alfred Cuddy pointedly refused to hire female officers. David Bright, "Technology and Law Enforcement: The Transformation of the Calgary Police Force, 1900–1940," *Urban History* 33, no. 2 (2005): 31, 32.

77   "Keep away crook is Cuddy's advice," *CMA*, May 22, 1914, 1; "Near riot started in Calgary office," *Saskatoon Phoenix*. June 6, 1914, 1.

78   M. Elizabeth Langdon, "Female Crime in Calgary," in Louis A. Knafla (ed.), *Law and Justice in a New Land: Essays in Western Canadian Legal History* (Calgary: Carswell, 1986), 301–2; "Police trying to rid Calgary of flood of undesirables," *CNT*, June 18, 1914.

79   "Police will not let loose women roam this city," *CH*, June 19, 1914, 7; "Are pushing crusade against undesirables," *CH*, June 24, 1914, 12.

80   City of Calgary Archives, City Clerk's Department Fonds, City Clerk's Correspondence, box 73, file 564, Letter, Chief Constable A. Cuddy to Mayor and commissioners, Calgary, June 29, 1914.

81   The cozy partnership between business and municipal government was a feature of early Alberta. Across the province, it was believed that business owners made the best mayors and councillors and that this "meant that business interests were promoted." See Donald G. Wetherell and Irene R.A. Kmet, *Town Life: Main Street and the Evolution of Small Town Alberta* (Edmonton: University of Alberta Press, 1995), 36–37.

82   City of Calgary Archives, City Clerk's Department Fonds, City Clerk's Correspondence, box 73, file 564, Letter, City Clerk to Chief Constable A. Cuddy, Calgary, November 24, 1914; CCC, Legislative Committee Report, July 15, 1914, 1; CCC, Finance Committee Report, October 23, 1914, 2; "Wouldn't sell stock on the sabbath," *CMA*, May 18, 1914, 10; "Chief on trail of Sunday stocksellers," *CH*, May 18, 1914, 9; Gray, *Talk To My Lawyer*, 15.

83   Luxton, *Latch String Out*, 286.

84   "Future millionaires are now pounding police beats," *CMA*, June 15, 1914, 1; "No abatement in oil fever is yet reported," *Natural Gas and Oil Record*, May 20, 1914, 5; "We should give duke a good time," *CMA*, July 15, 1914, 3.

85   The Apparel Service Company ad, *CH*, June 13, 1914, 16.

86   The Regent ad, *CH*, June 8, 1914, 12.

87   "Peculiar effect of the spectacular oil boom on different businesses," *Natural Gas and Oil Record*, May 20, 1914, 2; "Oil brokers locked up by village cops," *CMA*, May 25, 1914, 1.

88   *Natural Gas and Oil Record*, May 23, 1914, 8.

NOTES TO CHAPTER 6

1 *Day Book* (Chicago), June 24, 1914, 3.
2 *EJ*, June 16, 1914, 2; plot summary of *The Widow's Investment* (1914), IMDB.com, https://www.imdb.com/title/tt0437562/ (accessed July 5, 2022).
3 "Oil companies have big capitalization," *Vancouver Sun*, July 14, 1914, 9.
4 "To the public," *Natural Gas and Oil Record*, July 25, 1914, 1.
5 "Companies all getting enough money to drill," *CH*, May 25, 1914, 23.
6 Norman Fletcher, perhaps the most reliable witness regarding the plot to salt the well, testified on November 11, 1915, that Allan Clark helped secure a case of oil shipped from Vancouver to salt the well but could not recall whether Clark asked Buck to pay the freight for it or if Buck volunteered to do so himself.
7 PAA, GR1979.0285, file 7056, reel 132, Calgary District Court, *Allan Clark et al. v. Black Diamond Oil Fields et al.*, Affidavit, George Buck, Calgary, January 8, 1915; Examination of Discovery, George Buck, Calgary, January 9, 1915, 49–50; Examination of Discovery, Allan Clark, Calgary, January 7, 1915, 22–24, 61, 76–77; Examination of Discovery, Fred C. Smith, Calgary, January 7, 1915, 11–14; Examination of Discovery, Jennie L. Earl, Calgary, January 12, 1915, 5–16; GWRC, M1232, Percival Timms Fonds, box 1, file 5, Prospectus: The Black Diamond Oil Fields, Limited.
8 PAA, GR1979.0285, file 7056, reel 132, Calgary District Court, *Allan Clark et al. v. Black Diamond Oil Fields et al.* (1915), Examination of Discovery, George Buck, Calgary, January 9, 1915, 16; Examination of Discovery, Allan Clark, Calgary, January 7, 1915, 62; Examination of Discovery, Allan Clark, Calgary, January 7, 1915, 10–11.
9 PAA, GR1979.0285, file 7056, reel 132, Calgary District Court, *Allan Clark et al. v. Black Diamond Oil Fields et al.* (1915), Examination of Discovery, Allan Clark, Calgary, January 7, 1915, 22.
10 PAA, GR1979.0285, file 7056, reel 132, Calgary District Court, *Allan Clark et al. v. Black Diamond Oil Fields et al.* (1915), Examination of Discovery, Fred C. Smith, Calgary, January 7, 1915, 19.
11 Mother and daughter both shared the same name—Elizabeth Ada. While she was married to George Buck, all references to her use the name "Ada." Later in life, she used the name "Elizabeth." PAA, GR1979.0285, file 7056, reel 132, Calgary District Court, *Allan Clark et al. v. Black Diamond Oil Fields et al.* (1915), Examination of Discovery, George Buck, Calgary, January 9, 1915, 12, 16; Examination of Discovery, George Buck, member of Coalinga Syndicate, Calgary, January 8, 1915, 13–15.
12 There is a significant difference in the testimonies of Buck and Earl regarding the leasehold shares allocated to the Coalinga Oil Syndicate. Earl claims the shares were the property of the syndicate and were not distributed to individual members. Buck, on the other hand, clearly differentiates between shares he considered "his" and those of the other partners. PAA, GR1979.0285, file 7056, reel 132, Calgary District Court, *Allan Clark et al. v. Black Diamond Oil Fields et al.* (1915), Statement of Claim, Calgary, January 9, 1915; Examination of Discovery, George Buck, Calgary, January 9, 1915, 9–12; Examination of Discovery, Jennie Earl, Calgary, January 9, 1915, 10–13, 27, 29.
13 PAA, GR1986.0166/235j, Attorney General Central Files, Companies' Ordinance General File, Letter, Alex Hannah to G.P.O. Fenwick, Calgary, June 24, 1914; PAA, GR1979.0285, file 7056, reel 132, Calgary District Court, *Allan Clark et al. v. Black Diamond Oil Fields et al.* (1915), Examination of Discovery, Allan Clark, Calgary, January 7, 1915, 25–26, 56–60; Examination of Discovery, Fred C. Smith, Calgary, January 7, 1915, 5, 21–22; Examination of Discovery, George Buck, Calgary, January 9, 1915, 32; Examination of Discovery, George Buck, member of Coalinga Syndicate, Calgary, January 8, 1915, 33–34; PAA, GR1979.0285, file 7055, reel 132, Calgary District Court, *Kolb et al. v. Buck et al.*, Affidavit, Allan Clark, Calgary, August 25, 1914; Affidavit, Frederick C. Smith, Calgary, August 25, 1914; Examination of Discovery, Allan Clark, Calgary, March 4, 1915, 16, 20–23, 27; Examination of Discovery, Amos Scott, Calgary, March 3, 1915, 26–31, 32, 33–34; Black Diamond ad, *CMA*, May 16, 1914, 16; Black Diamond ad, *CH*, May 25, 1914, 5; "Nothing definite from Buck," *CMA*, May 21, 1914, 1; "People and capital are pouring into Calgary from all parts of the continent," *CH*, May 21, 1914, 15; "100 drilling plants will be in operation within three months," *CMA*, May 22, 1914, 1.
14 Recall that on January 30, 1914, the Black Diamond Board of Directors had reduced the original public offering from 75,000 shares to 50,000, meaning more lease-shares would have to sell if the figure of 69,450 shares sold by Clark and Smith is accurate. PAA, GR1979.0285, file 7056, reel 132, Calgary District Court, *Allan Clark et al. v. Black Diamond Oil Fields et al.* (1915), Examination of Discovery, Allan Clark, Calgary, January 7, 1915, 27–28, 51, 91, 116–23; Examination of Discovery, Fred C. Smith, Calgary, January 7, 1915, 8.
15 *Natural Gas and Oil Record*, May 23, 1914, 18; "Fake oil news-mongers should be discouraged," *Natural Gas and Oil Record*, May 30, 1914, 16.

16 "Investors urged to look into promotions carefully," *Vancouver Daily World*, May 21, 1914, 1; "Black Diamond Co. to open office in Vancouver," *Vancouver Daily World*, June 17, 1914, 10.
17 "Financial stringency gives way to oil fever," *Vancouver Daily World*, May 23, 1914, 10, 12.
18 PAA, GR1979.0285, file 7056, reel 132, Calgary District Court, *Allan Clark et al. v. Black Diamond Oil Fields et al.* (1915), Examination of Discovery, Fred C. Smith, Calgary, January 7, 1915, 19.
19 PAA, GR1979.0285, file 8673, reel 145, Calgary District Court, *International Supply Company v. Black Diamond Oil Fields*, Statement of Claim, Calgary, December 23, 1914.
20 "Nothing definite from Buck," *CMA*, May 21, 1914, 1; "Some scepticism in Saskatoon," *CMA*, May 28, 1914, 1.
21 "Nothing definite from Buck," *CMA*, May 21, 1914, 1; "Some scepticism in Saskatoon," *CMA*, May 28, 1914, 1.
22 "We drill for oil" ad, *CMA*, May 25, 1914, 20; "Far in the lead" ad, *CMA*, May 26, 1914, 7.
23 "Was not a strike," *CMA*, May 28, 1914, 1; "Dingman spouted yesterday; some oil in Black Diamond," *CMA*, May 29, 1914, 1; George Lonn, "Canadian Oil Pioneers," in *Dusters and Gushers: The Canadian Oil and Gas Industry*, ed. James D. Hilborn (Toronto: Pitt, 1968), 35.
24 George Lonn, "Canadian Oil Pioneers," in Hilborn, *Dusters and Gushers*, 35.
25 "Fake oil newsmongers should be discouraged," *CNT*, May 28, 1914, 4; "'Wildcatters' are outside the pale of decency," *CNT*, May 29, 1914, 4.
26 Vernon Knowles, "Scores of oil companies but few boring; Star man's first view of the oil mad town," *Saskatoon Daily Star*, May 28, 1914, 3; Vernon Knowles, "Star Man after visiting oil fields in quest of facts, believes Calgary's boom has real substantial basis," *Saskatoon Daily Star*, May 29, 1914, 13; Vernon Knowles, "Many uncertain propositions mixed with the sound in Calgary fields; be sure of promoters before buying," *Saskatoon Daily Star*, May 30, 1914, 7.
27 "An announcement," *Regina Leader*, June 1, 1914, 1.
28 Editorial, "The Calgary oil craze," *Regina Leader*, June 23, 1914, 4; The *Leader* also reprinted the *Black Diamond Press*'s story under the title "The oil madness" in the same issue.
29 "Crops in Alberta," *Monetary Times, Trade Review and Insurance Chronicle* 52, no. 24 (June 12, 1914): 61.
30 "Calgary oil boom is quieting down," *Spokane Chronicle*, May 29, 1914, 8.
31 Advertisement, Calgary Alberta Petroleum Company, *Spokane Spokesman-Review*, June 20, 1914, 3.
32 "Calgary goes wild when news arrives," *Vancouver Daily World*, June 18, 1.
33 "What's your number?" *Red Deer Advocate*, June 19, 1914, 1.
34 "Great oil field in Red Deer District," *Red Deer News*, June 24, 1914, 6.
35 "Great oil field in Red Deer District," *Red Deer News*, June 24, 1914, 6.
36 "The oil situation," *Red Deer News*, June 24, 1914, 4.
37 *Natural Gas and Oil Record*, May 20, 1914, 4, 9.
38 Ritchie, "The truth about the Black Diamond Well," *CMA*, June 8, 1914, 1, 5; "Terrific flow of oil and gas at the Dingman well," *CMA*, June 8, 1914, 1; Black Diamond Announcement, *CH*, June 8, 1914, 5.
39 Stories about the width of the well reached *The Saskatoon Daily Star* and were debunked by Vernon Knowles a few weeks earlier. "Star Man after visiting oil fields in quest of facts, believes Calgary's boom has real substantial basis," *Saskatoon Daily Star*, May 29, 1914, 13.
40 Ritchie, "The truth about the Black Diamond Well," *CMA*, June 8, 1914, 1, 5.
41 "Black Diamond soon to produce," *Spokane Spokesman-Review*, June 16, 1914, 11.
42 GWRC, M5769, Alberta Stock Exchange Fonds, box 4, file 35, Letter, R.C. Carlile to A.E. Graves, June 16, 1955. The letter misidentifies George Buck as "Tim." "Latest oil development news," *CH*, June 12, 1914, 1; "G.E. Buck thinks Black Diamond is nearing oil," *CMA*, June 12, 1914, 1; "Conditions at United well similar to Dingman's 200 feet before striking oil," *CMA*, June 13, 1914, 1; "Sold shares valued at $80,000 on oil exchange," *CMA*, June 13, 1914, 1; "Calgary exchange is excited over published report," *EJ*, June 13, 1914, 1; "To resume drilling at Black Diamond," *CMA*, June 17, 1914, 1; "Monarch Oil Company issues prospectus," *CH*, March 7, 1914, 19.
43 PAA, GR1979.0285, file 6342, reel 118, Calgary District Court, *Grant S. Wolverton v. Black Diamond Oil Fields et al.* (1914), Examination of Discovery, George E. Buck, Calgary, June 16, 1914, 2, 13.
44 "A girl's charge against George Buck dropped," *CNT*, May 29, 1914, 11; "A girl's charge against George Buck dropped," *Natural Gas and Oil Record*, May 30, 1914, 6.
45 PAA, GR1979.0285, file 6342, reel 118, Calgary District Court, *Grant S. Wolverton v. Black Diamond Oil Fields et al.* (1914), Examination of Discovery, George E. Buck, Calgary, June 16, 1914, 21, 23–24; Clifford

Tisdale Jones, Affidavit for further examination of George E. Buck, Calgary, June 23, 1914; Justice Charles Stewart, Chamber Summons, Calgary, June 24, 1914; Chamber Summons, Calgary, June 18, 1914.

46 "Drilling again at Black Diamond," *CMA*, June 19, 1914, 1; "Oil share pushing still flourishes," *National Post* (Toronto), June 20, 1914, 9; "Reports of oil strike causes flurry in city," *EB*, June 20, 1914, 1.

47 "Ald. Crandell has faith in oil report," *CNT*, June 21, 1914.

48 "Deposition of J.W. Hayes," Lima, Ohio, December 27, 1915, 287, 306; "Report of strike at Black Diamond sets the city crazy," *CMA*, June 24, 1914, 1.

49 "Persistent report that oil has been struck at Black Diamond well," *CMA*, June 24, 1914, 1; "Report of strike at Black Diamond sets all Calgary buzzing again," *Vancouver Daily World*, June 24, 1914, 1; "Black Diamond said to have struck oil at depth of 1900 ft," *Vancouver Sun*, June 24, 1914, 1, 4.

50 "Report of strike at Black Diamond sets the city crazy," *CMA*, July 24, 1914, 1.

51 "'I see we have a gusher,'" *CMA*, June 26, 1914, 1.

52 "Real facts about Black Diamond well are told by Buck," *CH*, June 26, 1914, 1, 22.

53 O.S. Morris, "Oil-mad mobs in buying frenzy on Calgary streets," *Spokane Chronicle*, June 27, 1914, 1.

54 PAA, GR1979.0285, file 8673, reel 145, Calgary District Court, *International Supply Company v. Black Diamond Oil Fields* (1914), Statement of Claim, Calgary, December 18, 1914; GWRC, M6745, John Schmidt Fonds, Manuscript re oil well drillers, Frosty Martin and Tiny Phillips, "George E. Buck," n.d., box 1, "Deposition of J.W. Hayes," Lima, Ohio, December 27, 1915, 306.

55 "The local situation," *Natural Gas and Oil Record*, June 27, 1914, 1; "Making statements," *Natural Gas and Oil Record*, July 4, 1914, 1; "Buck tells the truth!" *Natural Gas and Oil Record*, July 4, 1914, 8.

56 *Western Oil Examiner*, July 9, 1955, 35.

57 Geoffrey Poitras, "Fleecing the Lambs? The Founding and Early Years of the Vancouver Stock Exchange," *BC Studies* no. 201 (Spring 2019): 37–66, available at https://ojs.library.ubc.ca/index.php/bcstudies/article/view/189777.

58 *Financial Post*, July 25, 1914, 2; *Financial Post*, January 2, 1915, 25.

59 Crescent Menswear ad, *Spokane Spokesman-Review*, June 13, 1914, 11; "Oil-mad mobs in buying frenzy on Calgary streets," *Spokane Chronicle*, June 27, 1914, 1, 2; "Interest is keen in Calgary's oil," *Spokane Spokesman-Review*, July 9, 1914, 5.

NOTES TO CHAPTER 7

1 *CNT*, June 5, 1914, 3.

2 "Beware of Calgary oils," *Seattle Post Intelligencer*, June 12, 1914.

3 *Monetary Times, Trade Review and Insurance Chronicle* 52, no. 22 (May 29, 1914): 15.

4 On Bosworth's expedition to Northern Alberta, see Peter McKenzie-Brown, "The Bosworth Expedition: An Early Petroleum Survey," in *The Frontier of Patriotism: Alberta and the First World War*, ed. Adriana A. Davies and Jeff Keshen (Calgary: University of Calgary Press, 2016). "Dr. T.O. Bosworth and the Oil Fields of Northwest Canada," *The Petroleum World*, May 1914, 92.

5 "Dr. T.O. Bosworth and the Oil Fields of Northwest Canada," 93.

6 "Calgary oil and misrepresentation," *Monetary Times, Trade Review and Insurance Chronicle* 53, no. 3 (July 17, 1914): 9.

7 "Wildcats in the zoo," *CNT*, May 20, 1914, 1; "May prosecute wildcats," *CNT*, May 21, 1914, 1.

8 "Wildcats in the zoo," *CNT*, May 20, 1914, 1; "May prosecute wildcats," *CNT*, May 21, 1914, 1; "City will help tame wildcats," *CNT*, May 22, 1914, 21; "Police sleuths will check up oil companies," *CNT*, May 22, 1914, 20; "Will try to stop fake oil rumors," *CH*, June 24, 1914, 1.

9 "Deputy minister of mines issues warning on oil," *CH*, May 28, 1914, 1, 11; "Oil prospecting very speculative," *Financial Post*, June 6, 1914, 12.

10 D.B. Dowling, "Geological Notes to Accompany Map of Sheep River Gas and Oil Field, Alberta," Report S2-13577, Geological Survey of Canada (Ottawa: GPO, 1914), 3.

11 Vernon Knowles, "Many uncertain propositions mixed with the sound in Calgary fields; be sure of promoters before buying," *Saskatoon Daily Star*, May 30, 1914, 7.

12 "Board of trade discusses fake 'strike' rumors," *CH*, June 25, 1914, 20; "A sample wildcat," *Bellevue Times*, June 26, 1914, 4; "Would make game of oil resemble whist more than poker," *CMA*, June 27, 1914, 1; "Number of companies not alarming," *CMA*, July 11, 1914, 7.

13 "Says must use receipts that are different," *CNT*, May 29, 1914, 21; "Oil share receipts must now be distinctive," *CNT*, May 30, 1914, 16.
14 "Official is satisfied with Calgary companies," *CMA*, May 25, 1914, 1; "No abatement in oil fever at Calgary," *EB*, May 26, 1914, 1; "18 new oil companies secure incorporation," *EB*, May 27, 1914, 5; "Cuddy is not after oil honors," *CMA*, May 28, 1914, 12; Editorial, *CH*, May 28, 1914, 6.
15 *Calgary Eye Opener*, October 23, 1915, 2.
16 "Rotary drills soon to be more generally used," *CH*, June 25, 1914, 4; "Company to ship derrick to the Sweetgrass field," *CH*, August 26, 1914, 4; "Showing of oil at well of Beaver Co.," *CH*, April 30, 1915, 3; "Notes on oil," *CH*, May 18, 1915, 10; Captain W.B. Layock, "Potential oil fields of Canada reviewed, Ft. Norman to border," *Calgary Herald Magazine*, July 5, 1924, 7; Gow, *Roughnecks, Rock Bits and Rigs*, 52; Breen, *Alberta's Petroleum Industry*, 16.
17 "Premier Sifton refuses to join any oil company," *CH*, June 19, 1914, 1; *Financial Post*, July 11, 1914, 8.
18 *Financial Post*, July 25, 1914, 2.
19 *Financial Post*, July 25, 1914, 2.
20 R.C. Macleod, *The North-West Mounted Police and Law Enforcement, 1873–1905* (Toronto: University of Toronto Press, 1976), 57–58; Friesen, *The Canadian Prairies: A History*, 163–68; Lesley McIntaggart Massey, "'Alberta's Own:' The Provincial Police" (MA thesis, University of Calgary 1995), 6–9; Sean Moir, "The Alberta Provincial Police" (MA thesis, University of Alberta 1992), 38–39.
21 "May prosecute wildcatters," *CNT*, May 21, 1914, 1; "Future millionaires are now pounding police beats," *CMA*, June 15, 1914, 1; "Companies making false statement will be prosecuted," *CMA*, June 16, 1914, 1; "Thieves made raids on oil offices," *CMA*, June 19, 1914, 1.
22 "Warning issued to stock buyers by government," *CNT*, June 2, 1914.
23 PAA, GR1986.0166/235g, Attorney General Central Files, Companies' Ordinance General File, Letter, H. Anderson to C.W. Cross, Calgary, July 9, 1914; Letter, G.P.O. Fenwick (acting deputy attorney general) to H. Anderson, Edmonton, July 10, 1914; Letter, G.P.O. Fenwick to British Canadian Oil Company, Edmonton, July 10, 1914; Letter, British Canadian Oil Company to G.P.O. Fenwick, Calgary, July 13, 1914; Letter, G.P.O. Fenwick to British Canadian Oil Company, Edmonton, July 14, 1914.
24 David Ricardo Williams, *Call in Pinkerton's: American Detectives at Work for Canada* (Toronto: Dundurn, 1998), 25–26.
25 PAA, GR1986.0166/235i, Attorney General Central Files, Companies' Ordinance General File, Operative P26, Report, "Wild Cat Oil Company," Winnipeg, June 29, 1914.
26 PAA, GR1979.0285, reel 7, Case 365, Calgary District Court, *Rex v. Rose and Roberts* (1914), Evidence of Vernon Knowles, June 30, 1914, 1–3.
27 "Oil broker pinched as speculator was stung," *Toronto Star*, July 3, 1914, 18.
28 PAA, GR1986.0166/235i, Attorney General Central Files, Companies' Ordinance General File, Operative P26, Report, "Re: Wild Cat Oil Company's," Winnipeg, June 29, 1914; PAA, GR1979.0285, reel 7, Case 365, Calgary District Court, *Rex v. Rose and Roberts* (1914); "Sequel to McDougall-Segur strike is the arrest of man on charge of false pretences," *CNT*, June 29, 1914; "Oil broker pinched as speculator stung," *Toronto Star*, July 3, 1914, 17. Rose and his clerk, Fred Roberts, went to trial in *Rex v. Rose and Roberts* in October 1914. Press coverage of the trial did not identify the Pinkertons' role in the case, instead crediting Calgary Police Force Detective Tom Turner with conducting the investigation and consulting prosecutor Shaw before pressing charges. "Two oil brokers taken in custody," *Spokane Chronicle*, June 29, 1914, 6; "Frank Rose on trial charged with spreading a false oil rumor," *CH*, October 19, 1914, 1.
29 PAA, GR1979.0285, reel 7, Case 365, Calgary District Court, *Rex v. Rose and Roberts*, Evidence of Vernon Knowles, June 30, 1914, 13.
30 "Authorities are to go after fake advertisers," *CMA*, June 29, 1914, 1; "Two oil brokers taken in custody," *Spokane Chronicle*, June 29, 1914, 6; "Fraudulent oil representations," *EB*, July 9, 1914, 11.
31 "Oil rumor case is continued in Supreme Court," *CH*, October 20, 1914, 13; "Frank Rose is fined $50 and costs," *CMA*, October 21, 1914, 6.
32 "Truth as an investment," *CH*, October 21, 1914, 6; *Natural Gas and Oil Record*, July 4, 1914, 1.
33 "Big oil merger," *Natural Gas and Oil Record*, July 18, 1914, 1; "Herron-Elder, Calgary-Alberta Petroleum, Alberta Petroleum and Okotoks join," *Natural Gas and Oil Record*, July 18, 1914, 6.
34 PAA, GR1986.0166/235g, Attorney General Central Files, Companies' Ordinance General File, Letter, B.W. Collison to C.W. Cross, Calgary, July 22, 1914.

35   PAA, GR1986.0166/235g, Attorney General Central Files, Companies' Ordinance General File, Operative 26 Memo, "Re: Wild Cat Oil Co.'s., Winnipeg, July 25, 1914"; "Action started by shareholders of Herron-Elder," *CH*, July 24, 1914, 1.

36   PAA, GR1986.0166/235g, Attorney General Central Files, Companies' Ordinance General File, Letter, J.T. Shaw to G.P.O. Fenwick, Calgary, July 29, 1914; "Effort to enjoin the Herron-Elder fails," *CMA*, September 29, 1914, 1; "Supreme Court has refused to grant injunction," *CH*, September 29, 1914, 11.

37   F.B. McCurdy (May 26, 1914), "Censorship of Mails," Canada, Parliament, House of Commons, *Edited Hansard*, 12th Parliament, 3rd session, Retrieved from LiPaD: The Linked Parliamentary Data Project website: https://www.lipad.ca/full/permalink/403828/; "Censor oil matter in mails," *Winnipeg Tribune*, May 26, 1914, 1; "Mails may be closed," *Edmonton Journal*, May 29, 1914, 17.

38   "Oil stocks and the mails," *Regina Leader*, June 2, 1914, 4.

39   "Warn against oil shares," *Toronto Star*, June 3, 1914, 15.

40   Editorial, *Victoria Colonist*, June 2, 1914; "RE" Editorial, *Regina Leader*, June 17, 1914, 7.

41   "Should oil co's be registered in Saskatchewan?" *Regina Leader*, June 3, 1914, 8.

42   Quoted in *The Regina Leader*, July 16, 1914, 4.

43   "Alberta's Oilfields Attract Company Promoters," *Monetary Times, Trade Review and Insurance Chronicle* 52, no. 24 (June 12, 1914): 18.

44   "Oil brokers putting money in mail sacks," *Vancouver Daily World*, May 22, 1914, 28.

45   F. Leslie Sara, "The new 'oil-phebet,'" *CNT*, June 10, 1914.

46   "Armed with barrels of oil, Ald. Frost will visit 'peg," *CMA*, June 2, 1914, 1, 4.

47   "Two hundred gallons of Dingman oil will be taken to Winnipeg," *CH*, June 3, 1914, 1; "Sealed oil for those who doubt," *CNT*, June 5, 1914, 20.

48   Editorial, *CMA*, June 3, 1914, 3.

49   "Did Winnipeg party even get to the Dingman well?" *CMA*, June 6, 1914, 1, 11; "Big men watch oil in Alberta," *Vancouver Daily Province*, June 6, 1914, 15; "Near riot started in Calgary office," *Saskatoon Phoenix*, June 6, 1914, 1; "Tappy Frost talks plainly in Winnipeg," *CNT*, June 10, 1914; "Frost furnishes oil proof to 'peg skeptics," *CNT*, June 11, 1914; "Ald. Frost diagnoses tough case," *CNT*, June 11, 1914; "Tractor men were delighted with Dingman oil," *CMA*, June 12, 1914, 1; "'Tappy' Frost's oil delayed in freight," *CMA*, June 29, 1914, 2.

50   "Oil protective association is formed here," *CNT*, June 5, 1914; "Joe Brown has been engaged by the Fidelity Co.," *CMA*, July 13, 1914, 7.

51   PAA, GR1986.0166/253i, Attorney General Central Files, Companies' Ordinance General File, Letter, E.T. Trowbridge to G.P.O. Fenwick, Edmonton, July 10, 1914; Letter, G.P.O. Fenwick to E.T. Trowbridge, Edmonton, July 13, 1914; Letter, G.P.O. Fenwick to A.E. Popple, Edmonton, July 13, 1914.

52   "Calgary oil stocks declared as a rule wildcat scheme," *Oregon Daily Journal*, June 16, 1914, 18.

53   "'Calgary Oils; fall flat in Seattle," *Minneapolis Journal*, June 18, 1914, 22.

54   "Calgary oil," *Custer Weekly Chronicle* (South Dakota), August 15, 1914, 3.

55   "Calgary oil speculation," *Chicago Tribune*, July 15, 1914, 16.

56   "Oil stocks offered in Minneapolis," *Minneapolis Journal*, August 3, 1914, 16.

57   "Do we worry too much," Editorial, *CH*, June 13, 1914, 6.

58   "Pacific coast is very dubious on Calgary oilfield," *CH*, June 22, 1914, 11.

59   CCA, Board of Commissioners, series 1, box 52, Letter, G.Y. Burnett to the Mayor of Calgary, Vancouver, June 12, 1914; Editorial, "Government and oil," *CMA*, June 23, 1914, 3; "Speaking of thanksgiving," *CH*, June 26, 1914, 6.

60   *Calgary Eye Opener*, June 27, 1914.

61   Earl E. Smith, "Interest is keen in Calgary's oil," *Spokane Spokesman-Review*, July 9, 1914, 5.

62   Editorial, "Those fake oil rumors," *CH*, June 22, 1914, 6; Editorial, *CH*, June 25, 1914, 6; Editorial, *CH*, June 26, 1914, 6; "Wireless will soon put stop to fake rumors," *CH*, July 7, 1914, 16; "Baskins LTD open sale of Atlantic & Pacific Oil Company," *Natural Gas and Oil Record*, July 11, 1914, 10.

63   "To protect the oil industry," *CNT*, June 6, 1914, 14.

64   "When thieves fall out," *CH*, July 29, 1914, 6; "Is government lax?" *Natural Gas and Oil Record*, July 25, 1914, 1.

65   Bright, *The Limits of Labour*, 101; "Conditions in the south," *EJ*, July 13, 1914, 4.

66   "Oil! Oil! Oil! The Millionaire Maker," Magnet Oil Company Ad, *CMA*, June 20, 1914, 17.

67 "Golden opportunity rests today in the palm of your hand," *Natural Gas and Oil Record*, May 20, 1914, 2.
68 Oliver S. Morris, "Pays big dividend," *Spokane Chronicle*, July 4, 1914, 3.
69 Letter to the Editor, F. Norris, *CH*, June 26, 1914, 6.
70 Letter to the Editor, John Moore, *CH*, July 7, 1914, 6.
71 Editorial, "Deporting the surplus," *CH*, July 11, 1914, 6.
72 Letter to the Editor by "Eastern Canadian," *CH*, July 11, 1914, 6.
73 Margaret MacMillan, *The War that Ended Peace: The Road to 1914* (Toronto: Allen Lane, 2013), xxix.
74 Editorial, *Leduc Representative*, July 24, 1914, 3.
75 Luxton, *Latch String Out*, 288.
76 "Critical situation," *CH*, July 14, 1914, 1; "Relations of Austria and Servia strained," *EB*, July 21, 1914, 3; "Situation over Austrian note is realized," *EJ*, July 24, 1914, 1; "If supported Servians will declare war," *CH*, July 24, 1914, 11.
77 Editorial page, CH, July 29, 1914, 6.
78 "Royal party sees crude oil at Black Diamond," *Vancouver Daily World*, July 29, 1914, 1, 2; Black Diamond #2 ad, *CMA*, July 27, 1914, 11.
79 "Royal party sees crude oil at Black Diamond," *Vancouver Daily World*, July 29, 1914, 1, 2.
80 *Natural Gas and Oil Record*, August 15, 1914, 1.
81 "Royal party sees crude oil at Black Diamond," *Vancouver Daily World*, July 29, 1914, 1, 2.
82 *Financial Post*, August 22, 1914, 5; *Natural Gas and Oil Record*, August 29, 1914, 1.
83 "Good Times Ahead," *Natural Gas and Oil Record*, August 29, 1914, 6.
84 *Financial Post*, January 2, 1915, 25.
85 "Mr. Englehart has doubts as to Calgary oil fields," *Toronto Star*, July 2, 1914, 18; "Opinions on Calgary," *Petroleum Gazette*, August 1914, 31–32.
86 Torchy Anderson, *CH*, May 21, 1964, 55.

NOTES TO CHAPTER 8

1 "The Calgary oil boom," *Guardian* (London), July 22, 1914, 6.
2 "Alberta oil proclamation," *CMA*, October 14, 1914, 9.
3 Keith Brownsey, "The Alberta Oilpatch: Multilevel Regulation Transformed," in *Rules, Rules, Rules, Rules: Multilevel Governance*, ed. G. Bruce Doern and Robert Johnson (Toronto: University of Toronto Press, 2006), 284.
4 Daniel Yergin, "Ensuring Energy Security," *Foreign Affairs*. 85, no. 2 (2006): 69-82, https://doi.org/10.2307/20031912.
5 Wetherell and Kmet, *Town Life*, 289.
6 *Black Diamond Oil Fields Ltd. v. Carpenter*, 1915 CanLII 770 (AB CA), https://canlii.ca/t/g9hrc, 126, 127.
7 On the expansion of state powers, see Brock Millman, *Polarity, Patriotism, and Dissent in Great War Canada, 1914-1919* (Toronto: University of Toronto Press, 2018).
8 "$4,000,000 is invested in Alberta oil," *CMA*, October 14, 1914, 13, 15; Editorial, "The oil commission," *EJ*, June 24, 1915, 4.
9 "Extraordinary well in western Canada," *The Petroleum World*, May 1914, 275.
10 "Cunningham Craig delivers address on the oilfield," *CH*, March 5, 1915, 6.
11 "Oil is discovered in new Calgary well," *Toronto Globe*, March 5, 1915, 6; "Boom days over for Alberta oil wells," *Toronto Globe*, April 3, 1915, 15; "Big strike of oil at Southern Alberta Monday midnight," *CMA*, June 9, 1915, 1, 5.
12 "Drilling operations are discontinued at Mowbray Berkeley," *CH*, May 6, 1915, 1.
13 "The Alberta oil field," *Toronto Globe*, March 23, 1915, 4.
14 "Disgusts him," *CH*, June 26. 1915, 6.
15 "$4,000,000 is invested in Alberta oil," *CMA*, October 14, 1914, 13, 15; Editorial, "The oil commission," *EJ*, June 24, 1915, 4; *Western Standard*, June 27, 1915, 4.
16 *CH*, October 13, 1914, 6.
17 Luxton, *Latch String Out*, 288.

18   "Craig says oil not yet struck," *Financial Post*, October 10, 1914, 6.
19   "G.E. Hayes dismissed," *CH*, January 16, 1915, 12.
20   "All except one exchange favors closing up now," *CH*, August 3, 1914, 14.
21   GWRC, M5769, file 1, Alberta Stock Exchange Fonds, Board of Directors Minutes, August 14, 1914.
22   The Calgary General Stock Exchange resulted from the merger of the Public Exchange, the People's Stock Exchange, the Dominion Exchange, and the Consolidated and Majestic Exchanges. "Oil exchanges at Calgary merge," *National Post*, September 5, 1914, 2.
23   GWRC, M5769, file 1, Alberta Stock Exchange Fonds, Board of Directors Minutes, November 28, 1914, 89.
24   GWRC, M5769, file 1, Alberta Stock Exchange Fonds, Board of Directors Minutes, December 16, 1914, 121.
25   "Irregularities on oil exchange to be inquired into," *CH*, January 8, 1915, 1; "Those Moose Mountain stock deals," *CH*, January 11, 1915, 1, 8.
26   "Bogus certificates of oil stocks in circulation," *CMA*, March 5, 1915, 1, 5.
27   GWRC, M5769, file 1, Alberta Stock Exchange Fonds, Board of Directors Minutes, March 3, 1915, 165–66.
28   GWRC, M5769, file 1, Alberta Stock Exchange Fonds, Board of Directors Minutes, March 17, 1915, 167.
29   *Calgary Eye Opener*, May 23, 1914, 1.
30   *Calgary Eye Opener*, November 21, 1914, 3.
31   *Calgary Eye Opener*, May 22, 1915, 1; *Calgary Eye Opener*, June 12, 1915, 1; *Calgary Eye Opener*, July 3, 1915, 3.
32   Government of the North West Territories, "An Ordinance respecting Companies," in *Ordinances of the North West Territories* (Regina: Government Printer, 1901), 63–123.
33   Although it was not an oil company, records associated with Bonnie Brae Coal Company are among the most complete in the Attorney General's Companies Ordinance general files, as no trace remains of the files created in relation to the oil investigations. This is possibly because after George Buck obtained an injunction halting the operations of the Carpenter Commission, the Appellate Division deemed the commission illegal.
34   The attorney general's office proved unable to placate Ritchie with the results of its investigation, as he continued to lodge complaints against the company and demanded a public forum to air his grievances. Ultimately, Ritchie's persistence prompted Bonnie Brae's inclusion as part of the Carpenter Commission's activities, making it the only non-petroleum related company investigated in 1915. PAA, GR1986.0166/235i, Attorney General Central Files, Companies Ordinance General File, Memo, G.P.O. Fenwick to J.D. Hunt, Edmonton, April 22, 1914; "Bonnie Brae Coal Co. investigation has opened," *CMA*, August 24, 1915, 2; "Much testimony offered at Bonnie Brae coal probe," *CH*, August 25, 1915, 3.
35   Regulations for the Disposal of Petroleum and Natural Gas Rights, the Property of the Crown in Manitoba, Saskatchewan, Alberta, and the Northwest Territories, the Yukon Territory, the Railway Belt in the Province of British Columbia and Within the Tract Containing Three and One-Half Million Acres of Land Acquired by the Dominion Government from the Province of British Columbia and Referred to in Sub-Section (b) of Section 3 of the Dominion Land Act (Ottawa: Government Printing Bureau, 1912).
36   Editorial, "Lapsing oil leases," *CH*, August 8, 1914, 16.
37   "Public Utilities Commission for Alberta is to be established," *EB*, March 23, 1915, 8; "Budget debate closes; house to do some work," *EJ*, March 26, 1915, 13; "Division in legislature over supply," *CH*, March 26, 1915, 6.
38   "Provincial utilities commission," *CMA*, March 24, 1915, 3.
39   Editorial, *CH*, March 23, 1915, 6.
40   "Millions wasted on phone system through political manipulation," *EJ*, April 16, 1915, 7.
41   Willie Grieve, QC, "One Hundred Years of Public Utility Regulation in Alberta," *Energy Regulation Quarterly*, September 2015, available at https://energyregulationquarterly.ca/articles/one-hundred-years-of-public-utility-regulation-in-alberta#sthash.VxNiol3x.dpbs.
42   "Wide powers will be invested in public utilities commission," *EB*, March 30, 1915, 4.
43   CCC, Legislative Committee Report, March 17, 1915; CCC, Legislative Committee Report, April 21, 1915; Legislative Committee Report, May 5, 1915; CCC Minutes, May 10, 1915, 5.
44   "Too many oil exchanges, say Colonel Sanders," *CH*, May 26, 1915, 10.
45   "Exchange pleads for remission of brokers' licenses," *CH*, June 14, 1915, 10; "Calgary Stock Exchange," *Western Standard*, June 20, 1915, 7.

46 CCC, Legislative Committee Report, June 14, 1915; CCC, Legislative Committee Report, July 14, 1915; CCC Minutes, July 9, 1915, 3; "Members of oil exchange needn't pay license fee," *CH*, July 6, 1915, 11.

47 "Real green crude struck within half-a-mile of Dingman discovery well," CH. March 15, 1915, 1. "Oil has risen to one thousand foot level now," *CH*. March 16, 1915, 1. "Financial position of A.P. Consolidated is explained by pres." *CH*. 3 April 1915, 1, 15. "Volume of oil at A.P.C. makes drilling difficult," *CH*. April 14, 1915, 1. "Consolidated well is producing at rate of over 100 barrels daily," *CH*. May 20, 1915, 1.

48 "Should oil exchanges be closed down in the interest of industry?" *CH*. May 29, 1915, 1.

49 "A midnight meeting plots manipulation of stock market," *CMA*. June 30, 1915: 1, 5. "'Jugglers' subdued; Southern steady on stock market," *CMA*. 1 July 1915, 8.

50 Letter to the editor, *CH*, June 23, 1915, 6.

NOTES TO CHAPTER 9

1 Judge Carpenter believed the ruling precluded him from writing a formal report about the commission's activities. To date, no formal records—transcripts, investigatory files, company records, or memoranda—gathered or produced by the Carpenter Commission are in the Provincial Archives of Alberta, meaning that newspaper accounts are the most complete source regarding the day-to-day operations of the commission. The Companies Ordinances General File does, however, contain general documents, letters, memos, and correspondence about both the Carpenter and Lees commissions.

2 "Judge Carpenter to investigate oil business," *CH*, June 22, 1915. 1.

3 The Honourable Associate Chief Justice Dennis R. O'Connor, Freya Kristjanson, and Borden Ladner Gervais, "Some Observations on Public Inquiries," *Canadian Institute for the Administration of Justice [Conference]*, Halifax, NS, October 10, 2007, available at https://www.ontariocourts.ca/coa/about-the-court/archives/publicinquiries/.

4 PAA, GR1986.0166/235e, Attorney General Central Files, Companies Ordinance General File, Order, C.W. Cross to Bulyea, Edmonton, June 22, 1915.

5 "Appointing commission to go into complaints regarding operations of oil companies in the province," *EJ*, June 22, 1915, 1; "Echo of oil boom in this province," *EB*, June 23, 1915, 3.

6 Province of Alberta, "Commission," Edmonton, July 5, 1915, in *The Alberta Gazette*, vol. 11. no. 13 (July 15, 1915), 493–94.

7 "Oil judgment by full supreme court bench stops commission inquiry," *Western Standard*, October 10, 1915, 7-8.

8 Louis Knafla and Richard Klumpenhouwer, *Lords of the Western Bench: A Biographical History of the Supreme and District Courts of Alberta, 1876-1990* (Legal Archives Society of Alberta, 1997), 25, 45.

9 "The oil inquiry," *CH*, June 23, 1915, 6.

10 Editorial, "The oil commission," *EJ*, June 24, 1915, 4.

11 "Investigating oil companies," *Red Deer Advocate*, July 16, 1915, 4.

12 "The oil companies' investigation to start this week," *Weekly Standard*, July 11, 1915, 8; "Public are not protected, says Col. Sanders," *Weekly Standard*, July 11, 1915, 8; Thomas Thorner and Neil B. Watson, "Keeper of the King's Peace: Colonel GE Sanders and the Calgary Police Magistrate's Court, 1911-1932," *Urban History Review* 12, no. 3 (1984): 52.

13 "Oil investigations," *Claresholm Review*, July 8, 1915, 5; "Investigate oil companies," *Kingston Whig-Standard*, July 2, 1915, 12.

14 PAA, GR1986.0166/235h, Attorney General Central Files, Companies Ordinance General File, Letter, G.P.O. Fenwick to Editor *Alsask News*, Edmonton, July 9, 1915.

15 PAA, GR1986.0166/235h, Attorney General Central Files, Companies Ordinance General File, Letter, J. Paton to C.W. Cross, Vernon, BC, July 11, 1915.

16 PAA, GR1986.0166/235h, Attorney General Central Files, Companies Ordinance General File, Letter, J.A. Ramage to A.G. Browning, Red Deer, July 10, 1915.

17 PAA, GR1986.0166/235h, Attorney General Central Files, Companies Ordinance General File, Letter, Elizabeth Green to G.P.O. Fenwick, St. Vincent, Maine, July 17, 1915.

18 "Oil probe tomorrow," *CH*, July 12, 1915, 9.

19 *EJ*, July 9, 1915, 4; *Red Deer News*, July 9, 1915, 4.

20 *CMA*, July 13, 1915, 3.

21 "Fail to furnish detail; oil probe suddenly halts," *EB*, July 13, 1915, 3.

22 "Oil company probe opens and adjourns till August 18 next," *CH*, July 13, 1915, 9; "Fail to furnish detail; oil probe suddenly halts," *EJ*, July 13, 1915, 3.
23 "Oil company probe opens and adjourns till August 18 next," *CH*, July 13, 1915, 9; "Definite charges made against eight oil companies," *CMA*, August 16, 1915, 6.
24 "Oil probe opens, but goes over until August 18," *CMA*, July 14, 1915, 8.
25 Public notice, *CMA*, August 3, 1915, 5.
26 PAA, GR1986.0166/235g, Attorney General Central Files, Companies Ordinance General File, Provincial Treasurer's Office memo for G.P.O. Fenwick, Edmonton, August 5, 1915; Letter, G.P.O. Fenwick to Judge Carpenter, Edmonton, August 7, 1915.
27 PAA, GR1986.0166/235g, Attorney General Central Files, Companies Ordinance General File, Memo, G.P.O. Fenwick to C.W. Cross, Edmonton, August 10, 1915.
28 "Purging the oil situation," *CNT*, August 17, 1915, 4.
29 "Thousands of dollars of oil company's money disappear," *CNT*, August 18, 1915, 3, 7.
30 "Local oil flotations: an unbiased analysis," *CMA*, November 4, 1913, 1.
31 "Manager of local company arrested; depositors paid," *CH*, February 12, 1912, 16; "Langner arraigned," *CH*, February 13, 1912, 20; "Remains in cells," *CMA*, February 14, 1912, 2; "Langner case is before court now," *CH*, February 16, 1912, 1; "Later manager of Small Investors Co. is on trial," *CH*, March 29, 1912, 6; "All losses went into the assets," *CH*, March 30, 1912, 1; "Julian Langner gives evidence on stand," *CH* April 1, 1912, 3; "Langner is found not guilty by Judge Carpenter," *CH*, April 2, 1912, 22.
32 "New appointments," *CH*, September 20, 1913, 12.
33 "Carelessness is revealed at oil company investigation," *CNT*, August 19, 1915, 3, 7.
34 "Vancouver man buys heavily in Calgary," *Vancouver Sun*, June 1, 1914, 4; Western Canada Oil Company Notice to Shareholders, *CH*, June 13, 1914, 17.
35 PAA, GR1986.0166/235c, Attorney General Central Files, Companies Ordinance General File, Julian Langner Circular, Peerless Oil Works, Calgary, June 5, 1914.
36 "The signing up of drilling contracts still continues," *CH*, June 24, 1914, 10.
37 "Four hundred per cent profit in fifteen days," Peerless Oil Works advertisement, *Spokane Chronicle*, June 18, 1914, 9.
38 "Thousands of dollars of shareholders cash has gone somewhere," *CH*, August 18, 1915, 1, 9; "Discrepancies in oil company found; money is missing," *EJ*, August 18, 1915, 1; "Business of Western Canada Oil Company left to Langner," *CH*, August 19, 1915, 1, 9; "Western Canada affairs take up a lot of time," *CH*, August 19, 1915, 7.
39 "Western Canada did not receive $200,000 in cash," *CH*, July 14, 1914, 16.
40 Letter to the Editor, *CH*, August 22, 1914, 11.
41 "Western Canada Co.'s good fortune is well founded," *CMA*, May 27, 1914, 1; "Attorney General asked to bring J. Langner back," *CH*, April 13, 1915, 12.
42 "Trickery shown by the oil concern," *Butte Miner*, September 28, 1915, 9.
43 "How money took wings in some oil companies," *CMA*, August 19, 1915, 1, 5; "Just signing checks; thought everything was all right," *CMA*, August 20, 1915, 1.
44 "Thousands of dollars of oil company's money disappear," *CNT*, August 18, 1915, 3, 10.
45 "Thousands of dollars of shareholders' cash has gone somewhere," *CH*, August 18, 1915, 1, 9; "How money took wings in some oil companies," *CMA*, August 19, 1915, 1, 5.
46 "Thousands of dollars of shareholders' cash has gone somewhere," *CH*, August 18, 1915, 1, 9.
47 "Thousands of dollars of oil company's money disappear," *CNT*, August 18, 1915, 3, 10.
48 "How money took wings in some oil companies," *CMA*, August 19, 1915, 1, 5.
49 "Thousands of dollars of shareholders cash has gone somewhere," *CH*, August 18, 1915, 1, 9; "Discrepancies in oil company found; money is missing," *EJ*, August 18, 1915, 1; "Business of Western Canada Oil Company left to Langner," *CH*, August 19, 1915, 1, 9; "Western Canada affairs take up a lot of time," *CH*, August 19, 1915, 7; Editorial, "The oil enquiry," *EJ*, August 21, 1915, 4; "Oil investigation is likely to be lengthy; many companies listed," *CH*, August 21, 1915, 1.
50 "Langner is being made scapegoat at oil inquiry," *CNT*, August 19, 1915, 10.
51 "How money took wings in some oil companies," *CMA*, August 19, 1915, 1, 5.

52 "Business of Western Canada Oil Company left to Langner," *CH*, August 19, 1915, 1, 9; "Just signing checks; thought everything was all right," *CMA*, August 20, 1915, 1.
53 "Clamping on the lid in the oil investigation," *Western Standard*, October 24, 1915, 8.
54 "Probe into oil companies will be thrust deep," *CNT*, August 20, 1915, 3.
55 "Trickery shown by the oil concern," *Butte Miner*, September 28, 1915, 9.
56 *CMA*, August 20, 1915, 3.
57 "Phillips-Elliott Oil Company is under inquiry," *CH*, September 2, 1915, 10; "Probing of the Phillips-Elliott Company started," *CNT*, September 2, 3; "Evidence closes at inquiry into Phillips-Elliott," *CH*, September 3, 1915, 5; "Herron-Elder gas company investigated," *CNT*, September 7, 1915, 3.
58 *CMA*, September 16, 1915, 3.
59 PAA, GR1979.0285, file 7055, reel 132, Calgary District Court, *Kolb et al. v. Buck et al.*, Affidavit, Allan Clark, Calgary, August 25, 1914; Affidavit, Frederick C. Smith, Calgary, August 25, 1914; Discovery of Allan Clark, March 4, 1915, 16, 20-23, 27; Discovery of Amos Scott, Calgary, March 3, 1915, 26-31, 32, 33-34; "Oil company brought into court," *CH*, August 25, 1914, 1, 11; "Injunction asked against Buck et al.," *CH*, September 1, 1914, 1; "Legal probe of the affairs of Black Diamond deferred," *CMA*, September 2, 1914, 5.
60 McGillivray had the charge reduced to disorderly conduct, for which Beattie paid a five-dollar fine. "H.C. Beattie Arrested," *CMA*, September 4, 1914, 5; "Pays five spot for privilege of striking officer," *CH*, September 9, 1914, 13.
61 PAA, GR1979.0285, file 8673, reel 145, Calgary District Court, *International Supply Company v. Black Diamond Oil Fields*, Statement of Claim, Calgary, December 23, 1914; Statement of Defense, Calgary, February 19, 1915; "Black Diamond is sued by drilling co. for $4,400," *CH*, December 21, 1914, 4; "Another writ faces Black Diamond head," *CH*, December 24, 1914, 1.
62 "Allen Clark claims big sum from Buck," *CH*, January 8, 1915, 5; "Garnishee against Black Diamond for $30,000," *CMA*, January 9, 1915, 8.
63 PAA, GR1979.0285, file 7056, reel 132, *Allan Clark et al. v. Black Diamond Oil Fields et al.*, Letter, Sheriff F.H. Graham to Bailiff D. McKay Murray, Calgary, November 18, 1914; Letter, Bailiff D. McKay Murray to Sheriff Graham, Okotoks, November 21, 1914; Affidavit, D. McKay Murray, Okotoks. December 17, 1914.
64 PAA, GR1979.0285, file 7056, reel 132, Calgary District Court, *Allan Clark et al. v. Black Diamond Oil Fields et al.*, Letter, Bailiff D. McKay Murray to Sheriff F.H. Graham, Okotoks, December 15, 1914.
65 "G.E. Buck of Black Diamond fame, is defendant," *CMA*, November 14, 1914, 7; "G.E. Buck is assessed $250 damages in oil case," *CMA*, November 16, 1914, 5; "Wolverton wins case against oil company," *CH*, November 16, 1914, 4.
66 Knafla and Klumpenhouwer, *Lords of the Western Bench*, 120-21; Gray, *Talk To My Lawyer*, 61-62; "A.A. McGillivray, Justice, is dead," *EJ*, December 12, 1940, 1, 7.
67 "Black Diamond Oil," *National Post*, May 8, 1915, 11.
68 "Injunction to prevent probe of Black Diamond," *CNT*, September 22, 1915, 3.
69 "Injunction to prevent probe of Black Diamond," *CNT*, September 22, 1915, 3; "He attacks authority of oil commission to force any witnesses," *CH*, September 24, 1915, 1; "Oil probe is halted," *EJ*, September 24, 1915, 13; "Appeals to court to halt oil probe," *EB*, September 24, 1915, 4; "Counsel argues that oil probe prejudices sits," *CH*, September 25, 1915, 6.
70 *Black Diamond Oil Fields Ltd. v. Carpenter*, 1915 CanLII 770 (AB CA), https://canlii.ca/t/g9hrc.
71 *Black Diamond Oil Fields Ltd. v. Carpenter*, 125-26.
72 *Black Diamond Oil Fields Ltd. v. Carpenter*, 127-28.
73 "Alberta oil probe has been declared illegal by appellate judges," *CH*, October 5, 1915, 1, 9; "Black Diamond probe enjoined by full court," *CNT*, October 6, 1915, 6; "Decision of the Supreme Court will stop oil companies probe," *EB*, October 6, 1915, 2.
74 *CH*, October 6, 1915, 6.
75 *Calgary Eye Opener*, October 23, 1915, 3.
76 "Outlook for any further inquiry is problematic," *CH*, October 8, 1915, 1.
77 PAA, GR1986.0166/235g, Attorney General Central Files, Companies Ordinance General File, Memo, Judge A.A. Carpenter to G.P.O. Fenwick, Edmonton, November 1, 1915.

78 "Bulyea, Stocks and Carpenter appointed as members of first Alberta Utilities Board," *CMA*, October 21, 1915, 1, 5.
79 "Many legal actions will likely follow stopping of inquiry," *Vancouver Sun*, October 12, 1915, 8.
80 "Western Canada Oil Co. to be wound up," *CH*, June 18, 1916, 8.

NOTES TO CHAPTER 10

1   Armstrong, *Blue Skies and Boiler Rooms*, 39.
2   Short retained an abiding interest in education, serving as a secretary-treasurer of the school board from 1892 to 1904; thereafter, Short served as an elected school board trustee between 1904 and 1914, where he acted as the board's chair in addition to serving three years as board chair (1908-10, and 1914). He was also intimately involved in the establishment of the first private boy's school in Calgary, Western Canada College (1903) and sat on the board of governors for Calgary's anticipated university, Calgary College, until it closed in 1915. Furthermore, Short served on a delegation that lobbied the provincial government to establish the Provincial Institute of Technology and Art—the forerunner of the Southern Alberta Institute of Technology. Harry Sanders, "A Bit of Space Between: Chinatown and the Former James Short Park and James Short Parkade" (City of Calgary, 2022), 10-11; "Successful man or woman does not stop studying, James Short tells pupils," *CH*, December 3, 1938, 20; "Short recalls pioneer schools," *CMA*, December 3, 1938, 13; "Early teacher, lawyer, James Short, K.C., dies," *CMA*, May 11, 1942, 1, 2; "James Short dies at 80," *CH*, May 11, 1942, 9, 15; "Pioneer lawyer James Short dies," *EJ*, May 11, 1942, 5.
3   Reflecting the community's gratitude for years of public service, in December 1938, the Calgary school board renamed the Commercial High School, which served as the same location for the original brick schoolhouse Short taught at in 1889, as James Short Junior High School. Former editor of the *Albertan*, William Davidson, confided to his readers that Short had resisted previous attempts by the city to honour him. The city demolished the school, with the exception of the cupula, in 1968, and thirteen years later, the city named both the park and underground parkade built on the site after Short.
    However, like many others of his era, James Short held several prejudices and assumptions regarding race that eventually became glaringly outdated in an increasingly multicultural country. In the same 1938 speech dedicating the new James Short Junior High, where Short urged students to be lifelong learners, Short used the term "half-breed" to refer to the Metis of Calgary. More controversial, however, is Short's opposition to the establishment of Chinatown in Calgary, as well as efforts to segregate Chinese residents. A front-page story in the *Calgary Herald* on October 4, 1910, quoted Short as saying, "When [Chinese] come to reside in a place [they] ought to be treated much the same as an infectious disease or an isolation hospital. They live like rabbits in a warren and 30 of them crowd into where five white people would ordinarily reside. have not the first idea of cleanliness or sanitation. Everywhere they go they are undesirable citizens and furnish a problem to the municipality." On the Chinatown controversy, see Dempsey, *Calgary: Spirit of the West*, 93-97; Sanders, "A Bit of Space Between"; "Withdraw Chinese permit," *CH*, October 4, 1910, 1, 3; "The Chinese question," *CMA*, October 15, 1910, 3; "Chinese can get permits," *CH*, October 20, 1910, 1; "To check Chinese," *CH*, October 25, 1910, 1; "Council turned down petition of residents," *CMA*, October 28, 1910, 1; Editorial, *CH*, October 28, 1910, 6; W.M. Davidson, "Today, Tomorrow, and Yesterday," *CMA*, December 14, 1938, 4.
4   David Mittelstadt, *The MacLeod Dixon Century: 1912-2012* (Calgary: Legal Archives Society, 2012), 42-43, 46-47.
5   PAA, GR1972.0026, box 1, file 1C, Report, G.A. Trainor, February 5, 1916.
6   PAA, GR1972.0026, box 1, file 1C, Letter, G.A. Trainor to A.G. Browning, Calgary, October 23, 1915; Report, G.A. Trainor, February 5, 1916; "Three warrants out for the arrest of George E. Buck," *CMA*, October 16, 1915, 6; "President Buck, of Black Diamond Co. is still at large," *CH*, October 16, 1915, 6; "George E. Buck is still among missing," *CH*, October 20, 1915, 9; "Warrant issued for oil magnate," *EB*, October 16, 1915, 1; "George E. Buck cannot be located," *CMA*, October 18, 1915, 1; "George E. Buck is still among missing," *CH*, October 20, 1915, 9; Editorial, *CH*, October 21, 1915, 6; *Calgary Eye Opener*, October 23, 1915, 2.
7   PAA, GR1972.0026, box 1, file 1C, Telegram, G.F. Owen Fenwick to J.T. Shaw., Edmonton, November 12, 1915; Letter, J.T. Shaw to G.P.O. Fenwick, Calgary, November 12, 1915; Letter, J.T. Shaw to G.P.O. Fenwick, Calgary, November 13, 1915; Letter, J.C. Duguid to G.F. Owen Fenwick, Calgary, November 16, 1915; Report, G.A. Trainor, February 5, 1916; "Geo. E. Buck gives himself up to police," *CH*, November 1, 1915, 1; "George E. Buck gives himself up to police," *CNT*, November 1, 1915, 1; "George E. Buck is released by police on $10,000 bail," *CMA*, November 2, 1915, 1, 2.
8   "Action is taken by shareholders against G.E. Buck," *CH*, November 6, 1915, 9.

9 LAC, R927, RG125-A, vol. 398, file 3906, pt. 1, Supreme Court of Canada *The King v. Buck – Alberta* (1917), "Appeal Book" (hereafter cited as "Appeal Book"), 204; "'Salting' of Black Diamond well is charged in court," *CNT*, November 10, 1915, 3, 10.

10 "N.A. Fletcher tells of alleged preparations of Buck to salt well," *CH*, November 10, 1915, 1, 11; "Say he 'salted' an oil well," *Toronto Star*, November 2, 1915, 12; "President of Black Diamond Oil Co. Surrenders to Calgary police," *Vancouver Daily World*, November 2, 1915, 6; "Says crude oil was bought in Vancouver," *Victoria Daily Times*, November 11, 1915, 12; "Oil well salted, witness declares," *Vancouver Province*, November 11, 1915, 1; "Committed for trial," *Saskatoon Daily Star*, November 16, 1915, 7; "Oil company head sent up for trial," *Free Press Prairie Farmer* (Winnipeg), November 7, 1915, 1; "Declare oil well 'salted,'" *Montreal Gazette*, November 7, 1915, 9.

11 "Says Buck offered to pay freight on oil from coast," *CMA*, November 11, 1915, 6.

12 "Black Diamond employees say they helped to 'salt' well," *CNT*, November 2, 1915, 3.

13 PAA, GR1972.0026, box 1, file 1C, Telegram, G.P. Owen Fenwick to J.T. Shaw, Edmonton, November 12, 1915; Letter, J.T. Shaw to G.P. Owen Fenwick, Calgary, November 12, 1915; Letter, J.T. Shaw to G.P. Owen Fenwick, Calgary, November 13, 1915; Report, G.A. Trainor, February 5, 1916; Letter, G.A. Trainor to G.P. Owen Fenwick, Calgary, February 9, 1916; "Fletcher admits he put oil in sluice, but not down bore," *CH*, November 11, 1915, 1, 11; "Buck still in jail," *CH*, November 13, 1915, 14.

14 PAA, GR1972.0026, box 1, file 1C, Letter, G.A. Trainor to G.P. Owen Fenwick, Calgary, February 9, 1916.

15 "Black Diamond re-elects George Buck president," *CH*, December 6, 1915, 1.

16 "Big Black Diamond suit now settled," *CH*, November 16, 1915, 1; "Another suit is settled by consent," *CH*, November 29, 1915, 10.

17 PAA, GR1972.0026, box 1, file 1C, Letter, G.A. Trainor to A.G. Browning, Calgary, January 19, 1916; "Black Diamond re-elects George Buck President," *CH*, December 6, 1915, 1; "Evidence against Geo. Buck to be taken in States," *CH*, December 6, 1915, 12; "They called Buck's name but George failed to appear," *CH*, January 11, 1916, 1; "George E. Buck of Calgary oil fame, missing," *EB*, January 12, 1916, 5; "Application to estreat bail is made by counsel," *CH*, January 14, 1916, 14; "Prosecution drove him away; weeps when telling of flight," *Wichita Beacon*, April 24, 1916, 4.

18 PAA, GR1972.0026, box 1, file 1C, Letter, G.A. Trainor to A.G. Browning, Calgary, January 19, 1916; Letter, G.A. Trainor to A.G. Browning, Calgary, January 20, 1916; GWRC, M5769, Alberta Stock Exchange Fonds, box 5, file 60, *Alberta Oil Review and Industrial Record* (April 1916): 3.

19 "New law partnership," *EJ*, September 24, 1915, 13; "Deputy attorney general leaving Alberta shortly," *EJ*, April 30, 1923, 3; "Former official Law Branch dies," *EJ*, July 8, 1941, 11; "Former North Bay pioneer Arthur G. Browning dead," *North Bay Nugget*, July 8, 1941, 3; "N. Bay's 1905 phone book had 2 Smiths, no Browns," *North Bay Nugget*, March 25, 1966, 11; "North Bay lawyer, George E. Wallace, QC, chronicles District of Nipissing judiciary," *North Bay Nugget*, August 2, 1975, 35; Hartley Trussler, "Reflections," *North Bay Nugget*, April 21, 1979, 4; "Legal presence felt in 1886," *North Bay Nugget*, August 7, 1982, 31.

20 John William Horan, *On the Side of the Law: A Biography of J.D. Nicholson* (Edmonton: Institute of Applied Art, 1944), 30, 208.

21 PAA, GR1972.0026, box 1, file 1C, Letter, J.T. Shaw to A.G. Browning, Calgary, February 9, 1916.

22 PAA, GR1972.0026, box 1, file 1C, Report, G.A. Trainor, February 5, 1916.

23 PAA, GR1972.0026 box 1, File 1C, Letter, A.G. Browning to J.T. Shaw, Edmonton, February 11, 1916.

24 PAA, GR1972.0026, box 1, file 1C, Letter, James Short to A.G. Browning, Calgary, February 14, 1916; Letter, James Short to A.G. Browning, Calgary, February 15, 1916; Letter, A.G. Browning to R.R. Carrington, Edmonton, February 29, 1916; Letter, E.H. Crandell to C.W. Cross, Calgary, March 31, 1916.

25 One version of the story has Buck crossing into the United States in Montana. Nicholson's report to the attorney general has him crossing in Detroit. PAA, GR1972.0026, box 1, file 1C, J.D. Nicholson Crime Report, Wichita, Kansas, June 1916.

26 Dale E. Bennett, "Extradition – A Comparison of Louisiana Law and the Uniform Act," 20 *Louisiana Law Review* (1959): 32–33, available at https://digitalcommons.law.lsu.edu/lalrev/vol20/iss1/14.

27 J.E. Pember, "Buck caught in drag net that spread continent wide," *CMA*, July 22, 1916, 1, 7; Horan, *On the Side of the Law*, 212–13; "Prosecution drove him away; weeps when telling of flight," *Wichita Beacon*, April 24, 1916, 4.

28 PAA, GR1972.0026, box 1, file 1C, Letter, A.G. Browning to Superintendent Horrigan, Edmonton, April 6, 1916.

29 PAA, GR1972.0026, box 1, file 1C, Letter, J.D. Nicholson to A.E. Popple, Wichita, May 27, 1916; J.D. Nicholson, Crime Report, Wichita, Kansas, June 1916.

30 Earl K. Nixon, "The Petroleum Industry of Kansas," *Transactions of the Kansas Academy of Science* 51, no. 4 (December 1948): 386–87, 406.

31 PAA, GR1972.0026, box 1, file 1C, J.D. Nicholson, Crime Report, Wichita, Kansas, June 1916; "Wichita oil man is arrested as a fugitive from Canada," *Wichita Beacon*, April 22, 1916, 6; "Buck weeps bitter tears when telling of wife and family," *CH*, April 24, 1916, 1.

32 PAA, GR1972.0026, box 1, file 1C, Telegram, A.G. Browning to John K. Clark, Edmonton, February 29, 1916; Letter, A.G. Browning to McWain and Miller Detective Agency, Edmonton, July 18, 1916.

33 Portions of the attorney-general's file on Buck that were either police records or records subject to solicitor-client privilege remain classified under Alberta's Freedom of Information and Protection of Privacy Act (FOIP). It is possible that such a telegram might be in files still protected by FOIP.

34 PAA, GR1972.0026, box 1, file 1C, Telegram, A.G. Browning to Jack Hays, Edmonton, April 12, 1916; "Printer's mistake may place reward," *Hutchinson Gazette*, May 5, 1916, 2.

35 PAA, GR1972.0026, box 1, file 1C, Telegram, McWain & Miller Detective Company to A.G. Browning, Wichita, April 20, 1916; "Wichita oil man is arrested as a fugitive from Canada," *Wichita Beacon*, April 22, 1916, 6; "Buck weeps bitter tears when telling of wife and family," *CH*, April 24, 1916, 1.

36 PAA, GR1972.0026, box 1, file 1C, Letter, J.D. Nicholson to A.G. Browning, Wichita, May 1, 1916; J.D. Nicholson, Crime Report, Wichita, Kansas, June 1916; "Claims arrest spite," *Wichita Eagle*, 23 April 1916, 10; "George Buck under arrest at Wichita," *EB*; April 24, 1916, 1; "Buck weeps bitter tears when telling of wife and family," *CH*, April 24, 1916, 1.

37 "Claims arrest spite," *Wichita Eagle*, April 23, 1916, 10; "Prosecution drove him away; weeps when telling of flight," *Wichita Beacon*, April 24, 1916, 4; "George Buck under arrest at Wichita," *EB*, April 24, 1916, 1; "Buck weeps bitter tears when telling of wife and family," *CH*, April 24, 1916, 1.

38 "Griffiths girl dead; Miss Earle held by police," *CH*, April 20, 1915, 9; "Coroner Costello opens inquest on motor fatality," *CH*, April 21, 1915, 6; "Miss Earle on wrong side of street when fatality occurred," *CH*, April 21, 1915, 6; "Miss Earle appears," *CH*, April 22, 1915, 1; "Soldiers on stand at Miss Earle's trial," *CMA*, April 28, 1915, 5; "Miss Earle held for trial," *CMA*, April 30, 1915, 5; "Jennie Earle charge goes over to next criminal session," *CMA*, October 27, 1915, 1; "Jennie Earl now on trial on charge of manslaughter," *CH*, January 23, 1916, 7; "Miss Earl tells of tragic motor accident," *CMA*, January 26, 1916, 1; "Miss Earl guilty; sentence was suspended," *CMA*, January 27, 1916, 1; "Judge suspends sentence in case of Jennie Earl," *CH*, January 27, 1916, 9.

39 "Prosecution drove him away; weeps when telling of flight," *Wichita Beacon*, April 24, 1916, 4. On Buck's claim that the province attempted to use his extended family to lash out at him, see also the letter to the editor published by *The Wichita Beacon*, April 28, 1916, 14.

40 PAA, GR1972.0026, box 1, file 1C, Letter, J.D. Nicholson to A.G. Browning, Wichita, May 1, 1916; J.D. Nicholson, Crime Report, Wichita, June 1916.

41 PAA, GR1972.0026, box 1, file 1C, Telegram, J.D. Nicholson to A.G. Browning, Wichita, April 27, 1916; Telegram, J.D. Nicholson to A.G. Browning, Wichita, April 27, 1916; "George Buck, Calgary oil man, arrested in Wichita, Kan.," *CMA*, April 24, 1916, 1; "Canadian detective takes Wichita prisoner," *Leavenworth Times*, April 28, 1916, 6; "Buck poured oil in the dry well," *Wichita Beacon*, April 27, 1916, 9; "Here to get oil operator," *Wichita Eagle*, April 28, 1916, 2; "Canada officer comes to get Buck in Wichita," *Topeka Daily Capital*, April 28, 1916, 2; "Geo. Buck will resist extradition to Alberta," *CMA*, April 29, 1916, 1.

42 "Accused oil man presents defense," *Wichita Beacon*, April 28, 1916, 14.

43 "Accused oil man presents defense," *Wichita Beacon*, April 28, 1916, 14; "Buck revels in publicity of poor sort," *CH*, April 29, 1916, 1.

44 PAA, GR1972.0026, box 1, file 1C, Telegram, A.G. Browning to Ross McCormick, Edmonton, April 29, 1916.

45 PAA, GR1972.0026, box 1, file 1C, Telegram, A.G. Browning to Secretary of State, Edmonton, April 27, 1916; Letter, A.G. Browning to Secretary of State, Edmonton, April 27, 1916; Telegram, Thomas Mulvey to A.G. Browning, Ottawa, April 28, 1916.

46 US Congress, *U.S. Statutes at Large, Volume 32 – 1903, 57th Congress*. United States, – 1903, 1902. Periodical. https://www.loc.gov/item/llsl-v32/.

47 PAA, GR1972.0026, box 1, file 1C, Telegram, W.D. Scott to A.G. Browning, Montreal, May 1, 1916; Telegram, W.I. Dick to G.P. Owen Fenwick, Milton, ON, May 1, 1916; Telegram, G.P. Owen Fenwick to W.D. Scott, Edmonton, May 1, 1916; Telegram, G.P. Owen Fenwick to W.I. Dick, Edmonton, May 1, 1916; Telegram, W.D. Scott to G.P. Owen Fenwick, Ottawa, May 1, 1916.

48 Gary Norman Arthur Botting, *Extradition Between Canada and the United States* (Ardsley, NY: Transnational Publishers, 2005), 75–76; Bradley Miller, *Borderline Crime: Fugitive Criminals and the Challenge of the Border, 1819-1914* (Toronto: University of Toronto Press, 2018), 112–13.
49 Botting, *Extradition Between Canada and the United States*, 110–11.
50 W.J. O'Hearn, "Extradition," *Canadian Bar Review* 8, no. 3 (March 1930): 178–79.
51 PAA, GR1972.0026, box 1, file 1C, Letter, J.D. Nicholson to A.G. Browning, Wichita, May 1, 1916.
52 PAA, GR1972.0026, box 1, file 1C, Telegram, Ross McCormick to A.G. Browning, Wichita, April 29, 1916; Telegram, A.G. Browning to Ross McCormick, Edmonton, April 29, 1916; Letter, J.D. Nicholson to A.G. Browning, Wichita, May 1, 1916.
53 PAA, GR1972.0026, box 1, file 1C, Telegram, A.G. Browning to Thomas Mulvey, Edmonton, April 29, 1916; Telegram, A.G. Browning to J. Bruce Walker, Edmonton, April 29, 1916; Telegram, J. Bruce Walker to A.G. Nicholson, Winnipeg, April 29, 1916; Letter, Thomas Mulvey to A.G. Browning, Ottawa, May 2, 1916.
54 PAA, GR1972.0026, box 1, file 1C, Letter, J.D. Nicholson to A.G. Browning, Wichita, May 1, 1916.
55 PAA, GR1972.0026, box 1, file 1C, Telegram, J.D. Nicholson to G.P. Owen Fenwick, Wichita, May 1, 1916.
56 PAA, GR1972.0026, box 1, file 1C, Letter, J.D. Nicholson to A.G. Browning, Wichita, May 3, 1916; J.D. Nicholson Crime Report, Wichita, Kansas, June 1916.
57 LAC, RG 7, G21, vol. 246, file 350, part 9b, Letter, Thomas Mulvey to the Governor General, Ottawa, April 29, 1916; Telegram, Governor General to Sir Cecil Spring Rice, British Ambassador to the US, Ottawa, April 29, 1916; Letter, Sir Cecil Spring Rice to Governor General, Washington, DC, May 4, 1916; PAA, GR1972.0026, box 1, file 1C, Telegram, Canadian Consul General (New York) to G. Owen Fenwick, New York, May 4, 1916; Letter, Thomas Mulvey to A.G. Browning, Ottawa, May 6, 1916.
58 PAA, GR1972.0026, box 1, file 1C, Telegram, E.L. Newcombe to A.G. Browning, Ottawa, May 4, 1916; Telegram, G.P. Owen Fenwick to E.L. Newcombe, Edmonton, May 4, 1916; LAC, RG 7, G21, vol. 246, file 350, part 9b, Telegram, Governor General to Sir Cecil Spring Rice, Ottawa, May 5, 1916; Letter, Undersecretary of state to the Governor General, Ottawa, May 5, 1916.
59 LAC, R927, RG125-A, vol. 398, file 3906, part 1, Supreme Court of Canada, *The King v. George Buck*, Affidavit, James Short, Calgary, October 7, 1916.
60 PAA, GR1972.0026, box 1, file 1C, Letter, G.P. Owen Fenwick to US Department of Labor (Kansas City), Edmonton, May 5, 1916; Telegram, M.A. Coykendall to G.P. Owen Fenwick, Kansas City, May 6, 1916; Telegram, G.P. Owen Fenwick to M.A. Coykendall, Edmonton, May 6, 1916; Letter, G.P. Owen Fenwick to M.A. Coykendall, Edmonton, May 6, 1916; Telegram, G.P. Owen Fenwick to J.D. Nicholson, Edmonton, May 6, 1916.
61 LAC, RG 7, G21, vol. 246, file 350, part 9b, Telegram, Governor General to Sir Cecil Spring Rice, Ottawa, May 5, 1916; Letter, Undersecretary of state to the Governor General, Ottawa, May 5, 1916; RG 13-A-2, vol. 215, file 1917-1530, Letter, Deputy Minister of Justice to Under Secretary of State, Ottawa, May 5, 1916.
62 "They make the fur fly," *Wichita Eagle*, May 4, 1916, 9.
63 "Hint at kidnapping in the Buck case," *Wichita Beacon*, May 3, 1916, 3; "Detectives are afraid Buck may be kidnapped; will he be deported?" *CH*, May 3, 1916, 1.
64 PAA, GR1972.0026, box 1, file 1C, J.D. Nicholson, Crime Report, Wichita, Kansas, June 1916; "Here to get oil operator," *Wichita Eagle*, April 28, 1916, 2; "Hint at kidnapping in the Buck case," *Wichita Beacon*, May 3, 1916, 3; "They make the fur fly," *Wichita Eagle*, May 43, 1916, 9; "Detectives are afraid Buck may be kidnapped; will he be deported?" *CH*, May 3, 1916, 1; "Oil man goes to prison," *Wichita Eagle*, November 10, 1916, 5.
65 "Detectives are afraid Buck may be kidnapped; will he be deported?" *CH*, May 3, 1916, 1; "A new warrant in the Buck case," *Wichita Beacon*, May 12, 1916, 16; "What's in air bothers," *Wichita Eagle*, May 12, 1916, 2.
66 PAA, GR1972.0026, box 1, file 1C, Letter, A.G. Browning to M.A. Coykendall, Edmonton, May 9, 1916; Letter, W.W. Scott to G.F. Owen Fenwick, Ottawa, May 10, 1916; Letter, A.G. Browning to M.A. Coykendall, Edmonton, May 11, 1916; "A new immigration officer," *Kansas City Times*, 1 July 1915, 4; "H.C. Allen quits federal service," *Kansas City Star*, July 16, 1915, 5; "Canada to lose oil man?" *Wichita Eagle*, May 13, 1916, 12.
67 "Canada to lose oil man?" *Wichita Eagle*, May 13, 1916, 12; Horan, *On the Side of the Law*, 215.
68 PAA, GR1972.0026, box 1, file 1C, J.D. Nicholson, Crime Report, Wichita, Kansas, June 20, 1916; Telegram, J.D. Nicholson to A.G. Browning, Wichita, May 12, 1916; J.D. Nicholson to A.G. Browning, Wichita, May 13, 1916; Letter, J.D. Nicholson to A.E. Popple, Wichita, June 2, 1916.
69 PAA, GR1972.0026, box 1, file 1C, Telegram, J.D. Nicholson to A.G. Browning, Wichita, May 15, 1916; Request for Writ of Habeas Corpus, May 13, 1916; Case File 109, Law Cases (1891–1938), Records of the

U.S. District Court of the District of Kansas, Second Division, Record Group 21, National Archives and Records Administration – Wichita, Kansas; "Canada changes charge," *Wichita Eagle*, May 14, 1916, 24.

70   PAA, GR1972.0026, box 1, file 1C, J.D. Nicholson, Crime Report, Wichita, Kansas, June 20, 1916; "Thinks Buck will remain," *Wichita Eagle*, May 26, 1916, 2.

71   Demurrer, May 23, 1916, Case File 109, Law Cases (1891–1938), Records of the U. S. District Court of the District of Kansas, Second Division, Record Group 21, National Archives and Records Administration – Wichita, Kansas.

72   PAA, GR1972.0026, box 1, file 1C, Letter, J.D. Nicholson to A.E. Popple, Wichita, May 23, 1916; Telegram, J.D. Nicholson to A.G. Browning, Wichita, May 24, 1916; "Services held in Victoria for former city prosecutor," *EJ*, September 13, 1966, 22.

73   PAA, GR1972.0026, box 1, file 1C, Telegram, A.G Browning to Coykendall, Edmonton, May 25, 1916; Letter, A.G. Browning to J.D. Nicholson, Edmonton, May 25, 1916; Telegram, Coykendall to A.G. Browning, Kansas City, May 27, 1916.

74   PAA, GR1972.0026, box 1, file 1C, Letter, A.G. Browning to G.A. Trainor, Edmonton, May 26. 1916; Letter, G.A. Trainor to A.G. Browning, Calgary, May 26, 1916; Letter, A.G. Browning to Office of the Police Magistrate, Edmonton, May 27, 1916; Letter, G.A. Trainor to A.G. Browning, Calgary, May 28, 1916; Letter, Office of the Police Magistrate to A.G. Browning, Calgary, May 29, 1916; Letter, A.G. Browning to G.A. Trainor, Edmonton, May 29, 1916.

75   PAA, GR1972.0026, box 1, file 1C, Telegram, A.G. Browning to Thomas Mulvey, Edmonton, May 27, 1916; Telegram, Phillip Pelletier to A.G. Browning, Ottawa, May 27, 1916.

76   PAA, GR1972.0026, box 1, file 1C, Letter, J.D. Nicholson to A.G. Browning, Wichita, May 27, 1916.

77   PAA, GR1972.0026, box 1, file 1C, Letter, J.D. Nicholson to A.E. Popple, Wichita, May 30, 1916.

78   LAC, RG 13-A-2, file 715/16, Telegram to A.G. Browning, Ottawa, May 30, 1916; PAA, GR1972.0026, box 1, file 1C, Letter, J.D. Nicholson to A.E. Popple, Wichita, June 2, 1916; J.D. Nicholson Crime Report, Wichita, Kansas, June 20, 1916; "Refuse deportation of George E. Buck," *Wichita Beacon*, June 1, 1916, 10; "George Buck wins out and will not be deported; now for the extradition case," *CMA*, June 2, 1916, 1; "Oil promoter was winner in the first case," *CH*, June 2, 1916, 7; "This time Canada wins the round," *Wichita Beacon*, June 2, 1916, 8; "Canada to try oil man," *Wichita Eagle*, June 29, 1916, 2.

79   PAA, GR1972.0026, box 1, file 1C, Letter, J.D. Nicholson to A.E. Popple, Wichita, June 2, 1916; "Must bring more proof of offence," *CH*, June 2, 1916, 1.

80   PAA, GR1972.0026, box 1, file 1C, Telegram, J.D. Nicholson to A.G. Browning, Wichita, June 2, 2016; Telegram, J.D. Nicholson to A.E. Popple, Wichita, June 2, 1916; Letter, J.D. Nicholson to A.E. Popple, Wichita, June 2, 1916; J.D. Nicholson Crime Report, Wichita, Kansas, June 1916.

81   LAC, RG 13-A-2, vol. 215, file 1917–1530, Letter, A.E. Popple to H.M. Cate, Edmonton, June 7, 1916; Letter, H.M. Cate to A.E. Popple, Ottawa, June 12, 1916; Telegram, J.D. Nicholson to J.E. Norraway, Wichita, June 14, 1916; Telegram, J.E. Norraway to J.D. Nicholson, Ottawa, June 15, 1916.

82   "Buck is coming back says hon. C.W. Cross," *CH*, June 9, 1916, 8.

83   Direct Examination of John D. Nicholson, June 16, 1916, Case File 109, Law Cases (1891–1938), Records of the U.S. District Court of the District of Kansas, Second Division, Record Group 21, National Archives and Records Administration – Wichita, Kansas.

84   In extradition cases, all judges on habeas corpus proceedings can rule on is whether the charged offence falls within the existing extradition treaty and whether the extradition judge has jurisdiction. See W.J. O'Hearn, "Extradition," 182; PAA, GR1972.0026, box 1, file 1C, Telegram, J.D. Nicholson to A.G. Browning, Wichita, June 16, 1916; Crime Report, Wichita, Kansas June 1916; Letter, J.D. Nicholson to A.E. Popple, Kansas City, July 5, 1916.

85   PAA, GR1972.0026, box 1, file 1C, Letter, J.D. Nicholson to A.E. Popple, Wichita, June 20, 1916; "'Salted' well to get cash," *Wichita Eagle*, June 17, 1916, 2; "Buck confined to jail; bail not allowed," *EJ*, June 17, 1916, 3; "His fifteen days are fleeting away," *Wichita Beacon*, June 20, 1916, 3; "He needs $1,000; fight nears end," *Wichita Beacon*, June 24, 1916, 12; "A dark outlook for George in the Wichita courts," *CH*, June 23, 1916, 1.

86   *CMA*, June 19, 1916, 3.

87   PAA, GR1972.0026, box 1, file 1C, Letter, J.D. Nicholson to A.E. Popple, Wichita, June 20, 1916.

88   PAA, GR1972.0026, box 1, file 1C, Letter, J.D. Nicholson to A.E. Popple, Wichita, July 1, 1916; "His fifteen days are fleeting away," *Wichita Beacon*, June 23, 1916, 3; "He needs $1,000; fight nears end," *Wichita Beacon*, June 24, 1916, 12; "Fighting against extradition," *Kansas City Globe*, June 27, 1916, 1; *CH*, June 29, 1916, 6; "Buck wins first round of fight for his liberty," *CH*, June 28, 1916, 1.

89 PAA, GR1972.0026, box 1, file 1C, Telegram, J.D. Nicholson to A.E. Popple, Wichita, June 30, 1916; Letter, J.D. Nicholson to A.E. Popple, Wichita, July 1, 1916; "Canada to extradite Buck," *Kansas City Globe*, June 29, 1916; "Canada to try oil man," *Wichita Eagle*, June 29, 1916, 2; "Ordered Buck to Canada," *Kansas City Globe*, July 2, 1916, 1; "Buck loses his second appeal before U.S. judge," *CH*, July 3, 1916, 5.

90 *CH*, July 4, 1916, 6.

91 PAA, GR1972.0026, box 1, file 1C, Letter, J.D. Nicholson to A.E. Popple, Wichita, July 1, 1916; Letter, J.D. Nicholson to A.E. Popple, Kansas City, July 3, 1916.

92 PAA, GR1972.0026, box 1, file 1C, Letter, Senator Wm. H. Thompson to C.W. Cross, Washington, DC, June 6, 1916; Memo, C.W. Cross to A.G. Browning, Edmonton, July 3, 1916; Letter, C.W. Cross to Wm. H. Thompson, Edmonton, July 3, 1916; Letter, A.G. Browning to James Short, Edmonton, July 3, 1916; Letter, A.G. Browning to J.D. Nicholson, Edmonton, July 7, 1916.

93 "Wichitan to visit Wilson," *Wichita Eagle*, June 30, 1916, 5.

94 Convicted in 1914 of fraud, Samuels was sentenced by Judge Pollock to one year plus a day in Leavenworth for using the mails to amass a small fortune selling eye drops to sick people that he claimed could cure any ailment. At trial, the prosecution presented evidence that Dr. Samuels sold his eye drops to "cure" a man with one leg shorter than the other. Laboratory analysis, however, revealed the drops only contained sugar, salt, and rainwater. A federal court found Badders guilty on seven counts of using the mails to defraud creditors after ordering an estimated $70,000 worth of clothing and furnishings from suppliers and then selling the items for less than half their cost. Sentenced to five years in Leavenworth and fined $7,000, the young businessman began serving his sentence on May 19, 1916. "Samuels loses; sentence stands," *Wichita Eagle*, February 29, 1916, 1; "Samuels' sentence affirmed," *Wichita Beacon*, February 29, 1916, 1; "Must surrender in thirty days," *Wichita Beacon*, May 9, 1916, 6; "His friends are working," *Wichita Eagle*, May 11, 1916, 2; "Wilson won't pardon prof. Henry Samuels," *Wichita Beacon*, June 7, 1916, 6; "Samuels to pen; must serve year," *Wichita Beacon*, June 9, 1916, 3; "Debate Samuels issues," *Wichita Eagle*, June 11, 1916, 3; "Another Badders trial today," *Kansas City Globe*, January 20, 1916, 1; "Case of Badders," *Topeka State Journal*, January 21, 1916, 6; "Badders loses in high court," *Wichita Eagle*, March 8, 1916, 8; "His conviction is affirmed," *Leavenworth Times*, March 8, 1916, 1; "Badders denied rehearing," *Wichita Eagle*, April 21, 1916, 9.

95 "Wichitan to visit Wilson," *Wichita Eagle*, June 30, 1916, 5.

96 Not all the details provided by Brown coincide with the particulars of Buck's case, and there are some statements that are flat-out fabrications. Brown, for instance, referred to the machinations of a pre-emptive "pardon board" with the power to review court-imposed sentences prior to their imposition on a prisoner. Where Brown's story begins to fall apart is in its explanation of what Wilson could do to help. In early September, Brown suggested Wilson's intervention gave the prisoner "immunity" until October 4. Typically, however, only prosecutors or the court have the power to grant immunity from incarceration, and there is no explicit provision in the Constitution that permits a temporary pardon. Then in October, Brown claimed a letter from the president extended the reprieve until "the president has time to go over the voluminous report of the board of pardons and decide whether or not liberty shall be granted." However, the president of the United States does not have the powers described by Brown to grant temporary immunity from a prison sentence. After Wilson's victory in the November 1916 presidential election, Brown did not speak of the mystery prisoner again. "Repentant jury tires president," *Wichita Eagle*, August 8, 1916, 2; "Not telling," *Wichita Eagle*, August 11, 1916, 10; "Put it off," *Wichita Eagle*, September 8, 1916, 5; "Hope for Wichitan," *Wichita Eagle*, October 31, 1916, 2.

97 LAC, RG 13-A-2, vol. 215, file 1917–1530, Memorandum, H.M. Cate to Thomas Mulvey, Ottawa, July 4, 1916; PAA, GR1972.0026, box 1, file 1C, Telegram, J.D. Nicholson to A.E. Popple, Wichita, July 6, 1916; Letter, J.D. Nicholson to A.E. Popple, Wichita, July 7, 1916.

98 LAC, RG 13-A-2, vol. 215, file 1917–1530, Memorandum, H.M. Cate to Thomas Mulvey, Ottawa, July 12, 1916; PAA, GR1972.0026, box 1, file 1C, Telegram, J.D. Nicholson to A.G. Browning, Wichita, July 12, 1916; US Department of State, Extradition Order for George Edward Buck, Washington, July 3, 1916.

99 *CH*, July 18, 1916, 6.

100 "Officer terribly slashed," *Wichita Eagle*, June 30, 1916, 2; "Slashed an officer while under arrest," *Wichita Beacon*, June 30, 1916, 8; "Slashed coat was enough," *Wichita Eagle*, July 12, 1916, 5; "Buck started for Canada in custody today," *CH*, July 7, 1916, 1; "Swoop down on Buck and carried him away," *CMA*, July 18, 1916, 3; "Buck worked up sympathy for himself," *CH*, July 20, 1916, 1; "Say Buck kidnapped," *Wichita Eagle*, July 18, 1916, 2; Editorial, "A fine piece of work," *CMA*, July 22, 1916, 3.

101 Hill expressly denied making such a claim in a letter to Browning on August 16. PAA, GR1972.0026, box 1, file 1C, Letter, Sam P. Hill to A.G. Browning, Wichita, August 16, 1916.

102 PAA, GR1972.0026, box 1, file 1C, Letter, McWain & Miller Detective Agency to A.G. Browning, Wichita, August 15, 1916; Letter, A.G. Browning to McWain & Miller Detective Agency, Edmonton, August 19, 1916; Letter, A.G. Browning to James Short, Edmonton, August 21, 1916; Letter, A.G. Browning to McWain & Miller Detective Agency, Edmonton, August 25, 1916; "Want reward for arresting George E. Buck," *CH*, August 19, 1916, 22; "Gossip about town," *Wichita Eagle*. September 6, 1916, 7.

103 "Smashes mail motor," *Wichita Eagle*, August 8, 1916, 5.

NOTES TO CHAPTER 11

1 PAA, GR1986.0166/235a, Attorney General Central Files, Companies Ordinance General File, Letter, G.P. Ovans to C.W. Cross, Calgary, January 18, 1916.

2 *CMA*, October 14, 1914, 12.

3 Historian John Schmidt categorically states the Monarch well was "salted."

4 "Would pipe gas to Winnipeg from Bow Island," *CMA*, January 9, 1913, 1; "Elbow River suburban railroad ambitious project to tap rich Springbank district," *CMA*, March 1, 1913, 1; "Buying elsewhere is disloyal to Calgary – Buy at home," *CH*, March 22, 1913, 6; "City may buy its coal by carload from local mines," *CH*, April 24, 1913, 16; "Calgary reunion society has done a splendid work," *CH*, May 1, 1913, 11; *CH*, September 3, 1913, 1; *CH*, Apri 18, 1929, 1; "W.A. Georgeson," *CMA*, October 14, 1914, 12.

5 "Rival Calgary gas men have a wordy row at Moose Jaw," *CH*, January 9, 1914, 18; "Mark Drumm makes fight for Georgeson people," *CMA*, January 14, 1914, 3; "Gas for Calgary at seven and a half cents per 1,000," *CMA*, January 22, 1914, 2; "Coste explains gas offer to Regina," *CMA*, January 23, 1914, 1, 8; "Will try for gas in Saskatchewan," *Bow Island Review*, January 23, 1914, 1; "Firm of Minneapolis wholesalers take over Georgeson's," *CH*, February 12, 1914, 1.

6 *Natural Gas and Oil Record*, April 25, 1914, 1; W.W. Cheely, "Crude oil is found at last," *CMA*, June 18, 1914, 1.

7 *CH*, October 31, 1913, 1; "Contract let by the Monarch Oil Company for the drilling of eleven wells west of Olds," *CMA*, February 18, 1914, 1; "Big drilling contract," *CH*, February 18, 1914, 11; "Eleven oil wells to be drilled in the Olds district," *EB*, February 18, 1914, 1; Editorial, *CH*, February 19, 1914, 6; Editorial, *EJ*, February 21, 1914, 4; "Monarch Oil Company issues prospectus," *CH*, March 7, 1914, 19; "Drilling to commence west of Olds next week," *CH*, April 4, 1914, 1; *CH*, May 18, 1914, 9; W.W. Cheely, "Crude oil is found at last," *CMA*, June 18, 1914, 1.

8 "More wet gas and oil globules at Monarch well," *CMA*, May 25, 1914, 1.

9 PAA, GR1979.0285, reel 214, file 12695, Calgary District Court, *William Georgeson v. James F.M. Moodie* (1917), Statement of Claim, Calgary, July 12, 1917; Statement of Defense, Calgary, September 1, 1917.

10 "Monarch stock said to be in demand," *CNT*, June 5, 1914; "What the Monarch Oil Co. have accomplished on a capital of $5,000,000," *Natural Gas and Oil Record*, July 11, 1914, 1.

11 "Drowsy ones sell stock; lose money," *CNT*, June 18, 1914, 1.

12 "More wet gas and oil globules at Monarch well," *CMA*, May 25, 1914, 1; "Crude oil is found at last," *CMA*, June 18, 1914, 1; "Drillers at Monarch Oil cut into heavy black oil," *CH*, June 18, 1914, 1; "Monarch strike of black oil now confirmed," *EJ*, June 18, 1914, 1, 17; "Monarch oil seems to have both asphalt and paraffin base," *CH*, June 18, 1914, 1.

13 Perhaps Dunn referred to the need for a control head. Prior to the Second World War, control heads were a heavy fitting that screwed on the top of the innermost string of casing. The control head could open to allow tools in and out of the hole or be closed to fit around the drilling line as a way of eliminating the waste associated with uncontrolled gushers. See Gow, *Roughnecks, Rock Bits and Rigs*, 123.

14 "Crude oil is found at last," *CMA*, June 18, 1914, 1.

15 See Williamson and Daum, *The American Petroleum Industry, vol. 1*, 151–56; Gow, *Roughnecks, Rock Bits and Rigs*, 125–28; Francesco Gerali, *Torpedoes (Well shooting)*, Engineering and Technology History Wiki (2019), https://ethw.org/Torpedoes_(Well_shooting).

16 "Dunn's report of oil at well was believed by Monarch officials," *CH*, August 22, 1916, 5.

17 Historian and reporter John Schmidt believed it highly likely that William Cheely knew the details of Monarch's plot and played an integral part in its execution by whipping up public enthusiasm with some over-the-top coverage. "Cheely," concluded Schmidt, "became part of this story and others, in which he [helped] promoters fly kites and kept the whole city in ferment and frenzy for some months." See Schmidt, *Growing up in the Oil Patch*, 99.

18 "Crude oil is found at last," *CMA*, June 18, 1914, 1.

19 "Largest oilfield in the world, says O.S. Chapin," *CMA*, June 18, 1914, 1; "Big commercial oil field is undoubtedly opened in Alberta," *CH*, June 18, 1914, 1; "Crude black oil struck at Monarch," *Toronto Globe*, June 20, 1914, 18; "New oil strike in Calgary field," *Spokane Chronicle*, June 18, 1914, 1.
20 "'We have struck the real black oil,' says president Georgeson of Monarch," *CNT*, June 18, 1914, 1.
21 Monarch Oil Co. Ltd. "Notice to Shareholders," *CMA*, June 4, 1914, 9; "Thirty barrels of oil blown into Dingman tank in quarter hour," *CH*, June 4, 1914, 11, 18; "Wanted to buy $20,000 worth of Monarch stock," *CMA*, June 18, 1914, 5.
22 GWRC, M6840, McKinley Cameron Fonds, box 3, file 33, Letter, McKinley Cameron to William Armstrong, July 13, 1914.
23 Catherine Munn Smith, "J. Frank Moodie: The Man and the Mine," *Alberta History* 48, no. 2 (2000): 2–9, available at http://peel.library.ualberta.ca/bibliography/9021.48.2.html; Jack Peach, "Pioneer jeweller alert to Calgary's growth," *CH*, January 2, 1982, C6.
24 PAA, GR1979.0285, reel 214, file 12695, Calgary District Court, *William Georgeson v. James F.M. Moodie* (1917), Examination for Discovery, James F.M. Moodie, Calgary, October 22, 1917.
25 W.W. Cheely, "Development may astound the world," *CMA*, June 19, 1914, 1; "Second stratum 1,000 feet deep, third 1,200, opinion of Monarch well expert," *CNT*, June 19, 1914, 1.
26 "May be memorable day in history of oilfield," *CMA*, June 22, 1914, 1.
27 "Report of strike at Black Diamond sets the city crazy," *CMA*, June 24, 1914, 1; "Should be on sands now, says geologist Dunn," *CH*, June 29, 1914, 1, 20.
28 "Will they drill deeper or plug the hole back for a shot at 800 ft?" *CH*, July 3, 1914, 22.
29 "What the Monarch Oil Co. have accomplished on a capital of $5,000,000," *Natural Gas and Oil Record*, July 11, 1914, 1.
30 "Geologist Dunn makes report on Monarch again," *CH*, July 7, 1914, 11.
31 "Stock exchanges will be numerous in Calgary," *Toronto Star*, July 7, 1914, 14; "The Monarch capital will be increased," *Natural Gas and Oil Record*, July 4, 1914, 10.
32 "What the Monarch Oil Co. have accomplished on a capital of $5,000,000," *Natural Gas and Oil Record*, July 11, 1914, 1.
33 "Friendly advice," *Natural Gas and Oil Record*, July 18, 1914, 1.
34 "Reorganization of Monarch has been postponed," *CH*, July 14, 1914, 1; "Reorganization postponed," *Toronto Star*, July 21, 1914, 12; "Monarch Oil stock drops," *Kingston Whig-Standard*, July 23, 1914, 2.
35 GWRC, M6840, McKinley Cameron Fonds, box 3, file 33, Letter, McKinley Cameron to William Armstrong, July 13, 1914.
36 "Everything favorable at the Monarch well," *CH*, August 1, 1914, 26.
37 "Statutory meeting of Monarch Oil Co. held in Paget Hall," *CH*, September 3, 1914, 13.
38 PAA, GR1979.0285, reel 214, file 12695, Calgary District Court, *William Georgeson v. James F.M. Moodie* (1917), Amended Statement of Claim, Calgary, September 25, 1917.
39 PAA, GR1979.0285, reel 214, file 12695, Calgary District Court, *William Georgeson v. James F.M. Moodie* (1917), Examination for Discovery, James F.M. Moodie, Calgary, October 22, 1917; "Monarch Oil was mud and water with strong smell to it," *CH*, August 29, 1916, 1, 4.
40 PAA, GR1986.0166/235f, Attorney General Central Files, Companies Ordinance General File, Letter, Frank Ford to Marian Gill, Edmonton, October 13, 1915.
41 *CNT*, March 15, 1916, 4.
42 PAA, GR1986.0166/235f, Attorney General Central Files, Companies Ordinance General File, Letter, J.M. Murdoch to C.W. Cross, Stettler, March 18, 1916.
43 PAA, GR1986.0166/235e, Attorney General Central Files, Companies Ordinance General File, Letter, A.G. Browning to Frank Ford, Edmonton, March 22, 1916; Letter, Frank Ford to A.G. Browning, Edmonton, March 25, 1916.
44 Emphasis mine. Alberta, "An Act to amend The Statute Law, SA 1916, c 3, s 34," in *Alberta Annual Statutes* (Edmonton: Government Printing Office, 1916), https://canlii.ca/t/54213.
45 "New oil probe to be started in near future," *CH*, June 8, 1916, 5.
46 Emphasis mine. PAA, GR1987.0246, box 17A, file 512, *William Georgeson v. James F.M. Moodie* (1917), Government of Alberta, *The Alberta Gazette*, vol. 12. no. 13, Edmonton, July 15, 1916, 403–4.
47 PAA, GR1986.0166/235d, Attorney General Central Files, Companies Ordinance General File, Letter, Judge J.D.C. Lees to A.G. Browning, Red Deer, June 22, 1916; Letter, A.G. Browning to Judge Lees, Edmonton, June 27, 1916; Letter, G.A. Trainor to A.G. Browning, Calgary, June 29, 1916; Letter, A.G.

Browning to G.A. Trainor, Edmonton, June 30, 1916; Letter, Frank Ford to A.G. Browning, Edmonton, July 14, 1916; Editorial, *CNT*, July 25, 1916, 6.

48 "Col. Morfitt testifies at oil probe today," *CH*, July 29, 1916, 18; "Monarch Oil Co., is likely to be probed at start," *CH*, August 4, 1916, 12.

49 An Act to regulate the Sale of Shares, Bonds and other Securities of Companies, S.A. 1916, c. 8, https://canlii.ca/t/54219; "Stock salesmen must be licensed to sell securities," *EJ*, March 16, 1916, 6.

50 Alberta Board of Public Utilities Commissioners, *First Annual Report, 1916* (Edmonton: Government Printer, 1917), 4; Gordon Jaremko, *Steward: 75 Years of Alberta Energy Regulation* (Edmonton: Energy Resources Conservation Board, 2013), 29.

51 "Stock salesmen must be licensed to sell securities," *EJ*, March 16, 1916, 6.

52 "Butte grand jury wants oil stock brokers arrested," *CH*, April 28, 1916, 5.

53 Editorial, *CMA*, August 25, 1916, 3.

54 Letter to the Editor, *CH*, August 28, 1916, 6.

55 Alberta Board of Public Utilities Commission, *First Annual Report, 1916* (Edmonton: Government Printer, 1917), 4, 57–58.

56 Alberta Board of Public Utilities Commission, *Second Annual Report, 1917* (Edmonton: Government Printer, 1918), 3–4.

57 "Dunn's report of oil at well was believed by Monarch officials," *CH*, August 22, 1916, 5.

58 Dunn's report of oil at well was believed by Monarch officials," *CH*, August 22, 1916, 5; "Probing of the Monarch Oil Company is commenced," *CNT*, August 22, 1916, 3, 10; "O.S. Chapin admits he never denied oil interviews," *CMA*, August 23, 1916, 5; "Can't remember what he did say about oil strike," *Saskatoon Phoenix*, August 23, 1916, 2.

59 "Dunn's report of oil at well was believed by Monarch officials," *CH*, August 22, 1916, 5; "Probing of the Monarch Oil Company is commenced," *CNT*, August 22, 1916, 3, 10; "O.S. Chapin admits he never denied oil interviews," *CMA*, August 23, 1916, 5; "Can't remember what he did say about oil strike," *Saskatoon Phoenix*, August 23, 1916, 2.

60 "Oil companies are under investigation," *Vancouver Daily World*, August 23, 1916, 13.

61 "Rocky Mountain Oil Co. has nothing in the treasury," *CH*, August 23, 1916, 5.

62 "Probing of the Monarch Oil company is commenced," *CNT*, August 22, 1916, 3.

63 *CMA*, August 24, 1916, 3.

64 *EB*, August 24, 1916, 4.

65 PAA, GR1979.0285, reel 214, file 12695, Calgary District Court, *William Georgeson v. James F.M. Moodie* (1917), Examination for Discovery, James F.M. Moodie, Calgary, October 22, 1917.

66 PAA, GR1979.0285, reel 214, file 12695, Calgary District Court, *William Georgeson v. James F.M. Moodie* (1917), Statement of Claim, Calgary, July 12, 1917.

67 PAA, GR1979.0285, reel 214, file 12695, Calgary District Court, *William Georgeson v. James F.M. Moodie* (1917), Amended Statement of Claim, Calgary, September 25, 1917.

68 "Say Monarch samples showed little oil," *CH*, August 24, 1916, 4.

69 "Startling charge at investigation of oil company," *CNT*, August 24, 1916, 3; "Doubt cast on oil taken from the Monarch well," *CMA*, August 25, 1916, 5; "Claim refined oil was shown as a Monarch product," *EB*, August 25, 1916, 4.

70 PAA, GR1979.0285, reel 214, file 12695, Calgary District Court, *William Georgeson v. James F.M. Moodie* (1917), Examination for Discovery, James F.M. Moodie, Calgary, October 22, 1917.

71 "Inquiry into Monarch Oil Company's affairs resumes," *CNT*, August 29, 1916, 3; "Three companies are under investigation in oil probe," *CMA*, August 30, 1916, 5.

72 "Inquiry into Monarch Oil Company's affairs resumes," *CNT*, August 29, 1916, 3, 10; "Oil inquiry is postponed," *CNT*, August 30, 1916, 3.

73 PAA, GR1986.0166/235c, Attorney General Central Files, Companies Ordinance General File, Letter, G.A. Trainor to A.G. Browning, Calgary, September 6, 1916; Letter, Frank Ford to G.A. Trainor, Edmonton, September 13, 1916.

74 PAA, GR1986.0166/235c, Attorney General Central Files, Companies Ordinance General File, Letter, A.G. Browning to W.H. Short, Edmonton, September 11, 1916; Letter, A.G. MacKay to A.G. Browning, Edmonton, September 15, 1916; Letter, A.G. Browning to M.J. Hewitt (Crown prosecutor), Edmonton, September 16, 1915; Letter, A.G. Browning to Superintendent Horrigan (RNWMP), September 16, 1915.

75 "Oil inquiry comes to an end for lack of witnesses," *CMA*, September 20, 1916, 5; Letter to the Editor, *CH*, September 22, 1916, 6.
76 PAA, GR1979.0285, reel 214, file 12695, Calgary District Court, *William Georgeson v. James F.M. Moodie* (1917), Amended Statement of Claim, Calgary, September 25, 1917; Plaintiff's Factum, Calgary, November 20, 1917.
77 "Alberta will be very large producing field," *CMA*, July 7, 1917, 7.
78 PAA, GR1979.0285, reel 214, file 12695, Calgary District Court, *William Georgeson v. James F.M. Moodie* (1917), Statement of Defence, Calgary, September 1, 1917.
79 In Alberta, a master in chambers is like a judge sitting in chambers. Masters are appointed by the provincial government and derive their power from statutes rather than the Constitution. Their jurisdiction is limited to civil proceedings. "Claims evidence was of privileged nature," *CH*, September 11, 1917, 5.
80 "Slander suit in oil controversy again held over," *CH*, September 28, 1917, 9.
81 PAA, GR1986.0166/235a, Attorney General Central Files, Companies Ordinance General File, Letter, Muir, Jephson, Adams and Brownlee to A.G. Browning, Calgary, September 6, 1917; Memo, E.R. Gording to A.G. Browning, Edmonton, September 6, 1917; Memo, E.R. Gording to A.G. Browning, Edmonton, September 8, 1917; Letter, A.G. Browning to Muir, Jephson, Adams and Brownlee, Edmonton, September 8, 1917.
82 PAA, GR1979.0285, reel 214, file 12695, Calgary District Court, *William Georgeson v. James F.M. Moodie* (1917), Amended Statement of Claim, Calgary, September 25, 1917.
83 PAA, GR1986.0166/235a, Attorney General Central Files, Companies Ordinance General File, Letter, Muir, Jephson, Adams and Brownlee to A.G. Browning, Calgary, September 26, 1917.
84 PAA, GR1986.0166/235a, Attorney General Central Files, Companies Ordinance General File, Orders-in-Council, Edmonton, June 13, 1916.
85 Government of Alberta, *The Alberta Gazette*, vol. 12. no. 13, Edmonton, July 15, 1916, 404.
86 PAA, GR1986.0166/235a, Attorney General Central Files, Companies Ordinance General File, Letter, Muir, Jephson, Adams and Brownlee to A.G. Browning, Calgary, September 26, 1917; Letter, James Muir to A.G. Browning, Calgary, September 27, 1917.
87 PAA, GR1986.0166/235a, Attorney General Central Files, Companies Ordinance General File, Memo, E.R. Gording to A.G. Browning, Edmonton, September 29, 1917; Letter, A.G. Browning to James Muir, Edmonton, October 1, 1917.
88 PAA, GR1987.0246, box 17, file 512, *William Georgeson v. James F.M. Moodie* (1917), Defendant's Factum, November 19, 1917.
89 PAA, GR1987.0246, box 17, file 512, *William Georgeson v. James F.M. Moodie* (1917), Plaintiff's Factum, November 20, 1917.
90 PAA, GR1987.0246, box 17, file 512, *William Georgeson v. James F.M. Moodie* (1917), Judgement of the Honourable Chief Justice Harvey, Edmonton, December 4, 1917.
91 PAA, GR1987.0246, box 17, file 512, *William Georgeson v. James F.M. Moodie* (1917), Judgement of the Honourable Chief Justice Harvey, Edmonton, December 4, 1917; "Georgeson-Moodie suit is dismissed," *CH*, December 5, 1917, 9; "$50,000 damage suit decided," *CNT*, December 5, 1917, 6.

NOTES TO CHAPTER 12

1 "Judge Lees is appointed to probe oil companies," *CNT*, July 24, 1915, 3.
2 PAA, GR1972.0026, box 1, file 1C, Letter, A.G. Browning to James Short, Edmonton, July 18, 1916; Letter, James short to A.G. Browning, Calgary, July 20, 1916.
3 PAA, GR1986.0166/235d, Attorney General Central Files, Companies Ordinance General File, Memo for E. Trowbridge, Edmonton, July 31, 1916.
4 PAA, GR1972.0026, box 1, file 1C, Telegram, A.G. Browning to Paul Wall, Edmonton, July 22, 1916; Telegram, Paul Wall to A.G. Browning, Wichita, July 24, 1916; Letter, A.G. Browning to Paul Wall, Edmonton, July 25, 1916; Letter, Paul Wall to A.G. Browning, Wichita, July 31, 1916; Memo, A.E. Popple, Edmonton, August 18, 1916; Letter, A. G. Browning to James Short, Edmonton, August 18, 1916; Letter, A.G. Browning to Hyndman, Milner, and Matheson, Edmonton, August 18, 1916; Letter, A.G. Browning to James Short, Edmonton, August 22, 1916.

5   PAA, GR1972.0026, box 1, file 1C, Letter, A.G. Browning to Thomas Mulvey, Edmonton, August 22, 1916; Letter, James Short to A.G. Browning, Calgary, August 23, 1916; Letter, Acting Undersecretary of State to A.G. Browning, Ottawa, August 31, 1916; Horan, *On the Side of the Law*, 217.

6   PAA, GR1972.0026, box 1, file 1C, Telegram, James Tweedie to Robert Lansing, Calgary, August 23, 1916; Telegram, Robert Lansing to James Tweedie, Washington, DC, August 24, 1916; Telegram, James Tweedie to Robert Lansing, Calgary, August 25, 1916; Letter, John E. Osborne (Assistant Secretary of State) to James Tweedie, Washington, DC, August 28, 1916.

7   Knafla and Klumpenhouwer, *Lords of the Western Bench*, 191–92; "Bench and bar bid farewell to Judge Winter with fond expressions of affection," *CMA*, April 9, 1926, 3.

8   "September 26 is definitely set as Buck trial date," *CH*, September 8, 1916, 4; "Appeal certain in Buck's case in any event," *CH*, October 28, 1916, 19.

9   PAA, GR1972.0026, box 1, file 1C, Letter, James Short to A.G. Browning, Calgary, August 9, 1916; Letter, James Short to A.G. Browning, Calgary, August 28, 1916; Letter, A.G. Browning to James Short, Edmonton, August 30, 1916; Letter, James Short to A.G. Browning, Calgary October 9, 1916; Letter, James Short to A.G. Browning, Calgary, October 20, 1916; Memo, Popple to A.G. Browning, Edmonton, November 3, 1916.

10 PAA, GR1972.0026, box 1, file 1C, Telegram, J.D. Nicholson to James Short, Great Falls, September 21, 1916; Telegram, James Short to J.D. Nicholson, Calgary, September 21, 1916; J.D. Nicholson, Crime Report, Great Falls, September 22, 1916; Letter, James Short to A.G. Browning, Calgary, September 26, 1916.

11 PAA, GR1972.0026, box 1, file 1C, Telegram, James Short to J.D. Nicholson, Calgary, September 21, 1916; Telegram, J.D. Nicholson to A.G. Browning, Great Falls, October 2, 1916; Letter, A.G. Browning to James Short, Edmonton, October 3, 1916; Telegram, J.D. Nicholson to James Short, Great Falls, October 4, 1916; Telegram, James Short to J.D. Nicholson. Calgary, October 4, 1916; Night letter, J.D. Nicholson to James Short, Great Falls, October 4, 1916; J.D. Nicholson, Crime Report. Edmonton, October 8, 1916; LAC, R927, RG125-A, vol. 398, file 3906, part 1, Affidavit, James Short, Calgary, October 7, 1916.

12 LAC, R927, RG125-A, vol. 398, file 3906, part 1, Supreme Court of Canada, *The King v. George Buck*, Appeal from the Judgment of the Supreme Court of Alberta, Appellate Division, Appeal Book (hereafter cited as "Appeal Book"), 7–9; "The fence not ready, Buck case postponed," *CH*, October 24, 1916, 4; "Counsel for Buck moves to quash the indictments," *CH*, October 26, 1916, 9; "Defence scores a point in trial of Geo. E. Buck," *CMA*, October 27, 1916, 5.

13 Appeal Book, 7–9, 25–32.

14 Appeal Book, 38–39.

15 Appeal Book, 38–47. "Counsel for Buck moves to quash the indictments," *CH*, October 26, 1916, 9.

16 Appeal Book, 59–60.

17 "Defense scores a point in trial of Geo. E. Buck," *CMA*, October 27, 1916, 5; "Three witnesses heard in the Buck case Thursday," *CH*, October 27, 1916, 9.

18 "Defense scores a point in trial of Geo. E. Buck," *CMA*, October 27, 1916, 5.

19 "Defense scores a point in trial of Geo. E. Buck," *CMA*, October 27, 1916, 5.

20 Appeal Book, 85–87, 90, 91–92, 93, 97–99, 125.

21 Appeal Book, 120, 121, 123–24, 126–28; "Case against Buck now on in Calgary," *EB*, October 28, 1916, 1; "Saw sheen of oil on tailing from Black Diamond well," *CMA*, October 28, 1916, 9; "W.W. Cheely testifies in the Buck case," *CH*, October 28, 1916, 4.

22 Appeal Book, 143–48.

23 "Appeal certain in Buck's case in any event," *CH*, October 28, 1916, 19; "Jennie Earl is witness in trial of Geo. E. Buck," *CNT*, October 28, 1916, 20; "More evidence given in Buck case Saturday," *CMA*, October 30, 1916, 5.

24 "Witness swore he poured oil into B.D. well," *CH*, October 30, 1916, 1; "Buck case drawing near a finish in criminal court," *CMA*, October 31, 1916, 5.

25 Appeal Book, 177–80, 218–20, 221–22.

26 PAA, GR1972.0026, box 1, file 1C, Letter, James Short to A.G. Browning, Calgary, November 1, 1916; Appeal Book, 162–66.

27 Appeal Book, 195–209, 229–34; "N. Fletcher's evidence, given at preliminary, read," *CH*, October 31, 1916, 4.

28 Appeal Book, 236–50; "Buck case drawing near a finish in criminal court," *CMA*, October 31, 1916, 5.

29 Appeal Book, 257, 258–60.

30 Appeal Book, 271.

31 Appeal Book, 313, 315–33.
32 Appeal book, 343–48; "Buck will know his fate Monday morning," *CH*, November 1, 1916, 1, 6.
33 Appeal Book, 349–62.
34 PAA, GR1972.0026, box 1, file 1C, Letter, James Short to A.G. Browning, Calgary, November 1, 1916; Letter, A.G. Browning to James Short, Edmonton, November 3, 1916; Memo, Popple to A.G. Browning, Edmonton, November 3, 1916.
35 Appeal Book, 363–67.
36 Appeal Book, 368–72.
37 Appeal Book, 363–76; PAA, GR1972.0026, box 1, file 1C, Warrant of Commitment, *The King v. George Buck*, District Court of Calgary, November 9, 1916.
38 PAA, GR1972.0026, box 1, file 1C, Crime Report, J.D. Nicholson. Edmonton, November 6, 1916; "Buck found guilty and sentenced to four years in jail, *CH*, November 7, 1916, 1, 4; "George E. Buck will appeal his case to higher court," *CMA*, November 8, 1916, 8; "George Buck to turn evangelist when he is free," *CH*, November 11, 1916, 10; Harvey Cameron, *The Law Society of Manitoba, 1877–1977* (Peguis: Winnipeg, 1977), 213–14.
39 Just before Buck's trial began, on October 17, Short's nephew, Lieutenant Eric Harvey, appeared on the casualty list as wounded. No further details emerged about Harvey's condition until November 8, when reports circulated that he still lay in a hospital in France because his wounds were too severe to evacuate him back to England. "Lieut. Eric Harvey has been badly wounded," *CH*, November 8, 1916, 12.
40 PAA, GR1972.0026, box 1, file 1C, Letter, James Short to A.G. Browning, November 7, 1916; Letter, A.G. Browning to James Short, Edmonton, November 6, 1916; Telegram, A.G. Browning to C.W. Cross, Edmonton. November 7, 1916.

NOTES TO CHAPTER 13

1 LAC, R927, RG 125-A, vol. 398, file 3906, part 1, *The King v. George Buck*, J. Anglin, *Buck v. Rex*, 10.
2 PAA, GR1972.0026, box 1, file 1C, Letter, James Short to A.G. Browning, Calgary, November 17, 1916.
3 PAA, GR1972.0026, box 1, file 1C, "Admission of Facts," November 17, 1916.
4 Appeal Book, 398–403.
5 "Geo. E. Buck appeal argued before the Supreme Court," *CMA*, December 13, 1916, 8; "Hearing is started in the Buck appeal," *CH*, December 13, 1916, 11.
6 PAA, GR1972.0026, box 1, file 1C, Letter, James Short to A.G. Browning, Calgary, December 13, 1916; Memo, A.E. Popple to Attorney General Charles Cross, Edmonton, December 13, 1916; "Oil promoter Buck spends Christmas in penitentiary," *EJ*, December 23, 1916, 1.
7 Appeal Book, 407–10.
8 Appeal Book, 411–20.
9 Peter McCormick and Suzanne Maisey, "A Tale of Two Courts II: Appeals from the Manitoba Court of Appeals to the Supreme Court of Canada, 1906–1990," *Manitoba Law Journal* 21, no. 1 (1990): 8.
10 PAA, GR1972.0026, box 1, file 1C, Notice of Appeal to Supreme Court, January 4, 1917; Letter, James Short to A.G. Browning, Calgary, January 4, 1917; Letter, A.G. Browning to Short, Calgary, January 8, 1917; Letter, James Short to A.G. Browning, Calgary, January 9, 1917; Letter, James Short to A.G. Browning, Calgary, January 18, 1917; Letter, A.G. Browning to James Short, Edmonton, January 31, 1917; Letter, A.G. Browning to A.A. McGillivray, Edmonton, February 1, 1917; "Buck's appeal is rejected though the court is divided," *CH*, December 23, 1916, 5.
11 David Ricardo Williams, "Lafleur, Eugene," *Dictionary of Canadian Biography*, vol. 15, University of Toronto/Université Laval, 2003–, accessed April 18, 2023, http://www.biographi.ca/en/bio/lafleur_eugene_15E.html.
12 PAA, GR1972.0026, box 1, file 1C, Letter, A.G. Browning to James Short, Edmonton, February 5, 1917; Letter, A.G. Browning to R.C. Smith, Edmonton, February 5, 1917; Letter, James Short to A.G. Browning, Calgary, February 6, 1917; Letter, James Short to A.G. Browning, Calgary, February 7, 1917; Letter, A.G. Browning to Eugene Lafleur, Edmonton, February 7, 1917; Letter, Eugene Lafleur to A.G. Browning, Montreal, February 12, 1917.
13 Supreme Court of Canada, *The Supreme Court of Canada and Its Justices, 1875–2000* (Toronto: Dundurn, 2000), 5, 48; Jim Phillips, Philip Girard, and R. Blake Brown, *A History of Law in Canada*, vol. 2 (Toronto: University of Toronto Press, 2022), 86.

14   LAC, R927, RG 125-A, vol. 398, file 3906, part 1, *The King v. Buck – Alberta*, A.A. McGillivray, Appellant's Factum, 6–14 (hereafter cited as "Appellant's Factum").
15   Appellant's Factum, 15–21.
16   Appellant's Factum, 22–27.
17   LAC, R927, RG 125-A, vol. 398, file 3906, part 1, *The King v. Buck – Alberta*, James Short, Crown's Factum, 7–8 (hereafter cited as "Crown's Factum").
18   Crown's Factum, 9–14.
19   Crown's Factum, 15–21.
20   James G. Snell and Frederick Vaughan, *The Supreme Court of Canada: History of the Institution* (Toronto: Osgoode Society and University of Toronto Press, 1985), 101–2.
21   LAC, R927, RG 125-A, vol. 398, file 3906, part 1, *The King v. Buck – Alberta*, Chief Justice Opinion, *Buck v. Rex*, 1–3, June 28, 1917.
22   LAC, R927, RG 125-A, vol. 398, file 3906, part 1, *The King v. Buck – Alberta*, J. Idington, *Buck v. Rex*, 1–9.
23   LAC, R927, RG 125-A, vol. 398, file 3906, part 1, *The King v. Buck – Alberta*, J. Anglin, *Buck v. Rex*, 10.
24   PAA, GR1972.0026, box 1, file 1C, Telegram, Smellie and Lewis to A.G. Browning, Ottawa, June 22, 1917; Telegram, A.E. Popple to Smellie and Lewis, Edmonton, June 23, 1917; Telegram, Smellie and Lewis to A.G. Browning, Ottawa, June 25, 1917; Letter, Smellie and Lewis to A.G. Browning, Ottawa, June 29, 1917; "George E. Buck is a free man; appeal allowed," *CMA*, June 23, 1917, 8; "George E. Buck is freed by judgment of Supreme Court," *CH*, June 23, 1917, 23.
25   PAA, GR1972.0026, box 1, file 1C, Telegram, *The News Telegram* to Charles E. Cross, Calgary, June 23, 1917; Telegram, A.E. Popple to *The News Telegram*, Edmonton, June 23, 1917; "Attorney general undecided what to do with Buck," *CMA*, June 25, 1917, 4.
26   PAA, GR1972.0026, box 1, file 1C, Letter, James Short to A.G. Browning, Calgary, March 27, 1917; Letter, McDonell to A.G. Browning, Edmonton.
27   PAA, GR1972.0026, box 1, file 1C, Letter, James Short to A.G. Browning, Calgary, March 27, 1917; Letter, McDonell to A.G. Browning, Edmonton.
28   PAA, GR1972.0026, box 1, file 1C, Letter, James Short to A.G. Browning, Calgary, March 16, 1917; Letter A. G. Browning to James Short, Edmonton, March 17, 1917.
29   PAA, GR1972.0026, box 1, file 1C, Letter, A.G. Browning to McDonell, Edmonton, July 4, 1917; Crime Report, Alberta Provincial Police, Edmonton, July 6, 1917; "Attorney general undecided what to do with Buck," *CMA*, June 25, 1917, 4; "Provincial police place George E. Buck under arrest again," *CH*, July 5, 1917, 1; "George E. Buck is under arrest held in south," *EJ*, July 6, 1917, 7; "George E. Buck still guest of Alberta police," *CH*, July 6, 1917, 9; "Trying to get bail," *CH*, July 7, 1917, 8; "Buck is held till he pays his bail," *CMA*, July 9, 1917, 5.
30   PAA, GR1972.0026, box 1, file 1C, Telegram, James Short to A.E. Popple, Calgary, July 13, 1917; Night Letter, A.E. Popple to James Short, Edmonton, July 13, 1917; Telegram, James Short to A.E. Popple, Calgary, July 14, 1917; Letter, Maynard Mayhood to A.E. Popple, Calgary, July 18, 1917; Letter, A.G. Browning to James Short, Edmonton, July 19, 1917; Draft of Agreement in *The King v. Buck*, n.d.
31   PAA, GR1972.0026, box 1, file 1C, Letter, James Short to A.G. Browning, Calgary, July 24, 1917.
32   PAA, GR1972.0026, box 1, file 1C, "Conundrum: where can a man go who can't go?" *CMA*, August 13, 1917, 4; "Is George E. Buck still in the city," *CH*, August 25, 1917, 21.
33   "Kathleen Buck becomes bride," *Spokane Chronicle*, June 8, 1920, 11.
34   "Chewelan oil evidence grows; history revived," *Spokane Chronicle*, August 2, 1920, 17.
35   "Articles of incorporation," *Washington Standard* (Olympia), August 26, 1921, 6.
36   *Colville Examiner*, February 26, 1921, 4; *Colville Examiner*, September 24, 1921, 4.
37   "Latest on oil search in Spokane," *Spokane Press*, October 22, 1921, 7; "Orders timbers for rig," *Spokesman-Review*, October 25, 1921, 13; "Oppose war finance plan," *Spokesman-Review*, October 29, 1921, 7.
38   "Leases 5000 acres land," *Spokesman-Review*, November 6, 1921, 15.
39   Washington State Division of Mines and Geology. Information Circular No. 29, Vaughn E. Livingston, Jr., "Oil and Gas exploration in Washington, 1900–1957" (Olympia: SPO, 1958); "Oil is magic word in broad Collvile valley," *Spokane Press*, May 13, 1930, 12.
40   In February 1926, two years after the divorce, Ralph Burnett served two years for a grand larceny charge in connection to the disappearance of $2,000 in automobile licence money from the county auditor's office and connected to a love triangle with a married woman from Montana. "Deputy auditor arrested,"

Spokane Chronicle, February 5, 1926, 11; "'I'll be waiting,' says sweetheart of convicted man," *Spokane Chronicle*, February 6, 1926, 1, 2; "Burnett gets two to fifteen years," *Spokane Press*, February 6, 1926, 1.
41 "Judge hates to separate pair," *Spokane Press*, June 10, 1925, 2; "Quarrel ends 30 years' love," *Spokesman-Review*, June 10, 1925, 7; "Court awards three divorces," *Spokane Chronicle*, June 11, 1925, 4.
42 "Conduct rites for Elizabeth Buck, 92," *Valley News*, January 26, 1958, 15.
43 *Spokane Chronicle*, April 1, 1927, 30; *Spokane Chronicle*, April 2, 1927, 6.
44 Alan Brinkley, *Voices of Protest: Huey Long, Father Coughlin and the Great Depression* (New York: Vintage, 1982), 222–26; Kenneth S. Davis, *FDR: The New Deal Years, 1933–1937* (New York: Random House, 1986), 401–2; H.W. Brands, *"A Traitor to His Class:" The Privileged Life and Radical Presidency of Franklin Delano Roosevelt* (New York: Doubleday, 2008), 404; Jean Edward Smith, *FDR* (New York: Random House, 2007), 349; Robert Dallek, *Franklin D. Roosevelt: A Political Life* (New York: Viking, 2017), 188–89.
45 "Buck statement stirs club rank," *Spokane Chronicle*, October 27, 1936, 3; "Landon talker ires Dr. Long," *Spokane Press*. October 27, 1936, 2; "Townsend folk to aid Landon," *Spokesman-Review*, October 28, 1936, 22; "Buck says Landon wins more Townsend votes," *Spokesman-Review*, October 30, 1936, 7; "Townsend votes swing to Landon," *Spokesman-Review*, November 1, 1936, 1.
46 "Fifteen 'live' derricks are busy in Turner Valley field," *Edmonton Bulletin*, May 8, 1926, 15; "Mother earth to be tested by drillers moving out from Turner Valley focal point," *CMA*, May 10, 1929, 30.
47 "Loss of fields in Far East causes hunt for new sources," *EB*, April 9, 1942, 1; "Shell Oil Co., planning great search for oil," *CMA*, April 10, 1942, 8.
48 "Southwest well has big gas flow," *EJ*, July 15, 1948, 23.
49 C.V. Myers, "Anglo-Black Diamond new target for Shell," *CMA*, April 25, 1950, 14; C.V. Myers, "Revival possible in Turner Valley," *EB*, April 25, 1950, 8; C.O. Nickle, "Imperial places four more wells on production," *CH*, April 25, 1950, 25; "Sites selected for wildcats," *CMA*, May 15, 1960, 16; C.V. Myers, "Madison lime 100 feet higher," *EB*, August 14, 1950, 27; "Redwater wells approach 600," *CH*, August 14, 1950, 16; Danforth, "Shady Deals," 74.

NOTES TO CHAPTER 14

1 Fred Kennedy made numerous mentions of Buck over the years. See "The long road to oil, gas," *Calgary Albertan*, May 19, 1977, 6; "From 'salted' well to prosperity," *Calgary Albertan*, April 27, 1978, 6.
2 John Herd Thompson, *The Harvests of War: The Prairie West, 1914–1918* (Toronto: Oxford University Press, 1978), 97.
3 GWRC, M5769, Alberta Stock Exchange Fonds, box 4, file 36, No Author, "History of the Calgary Stock Exchange"; box 4, file 35, Letter, R.C. Carlile to A.E. Graves, June 16, 1955; "Less money in oil," *CMA*, April 13, 1916, 6.
4 Dabbs, *Branded by the Wind*, 36; Breen, *William Stewart Herron*, xxviii.
5 W.S. Herron to H.H. Rowatt, January 24, 1917, In Breen, *William Stewart Herron*, 99.
6 Jim Stott, "... energy resources," *CH*, November 11, 1976, 72.
7 PIOH, William Herron, 1981, 7; Finch, *Hell's Half Acre*, p. 36.
8 "Calgary brokers decide to form oil exchange," *Calgary Albertan*, March 2, 1926, 5; "Stock exchange is decided upon," *CH*, March 2, 1926, 10; "Bond too heavy for oil brokers," *CH*, March 2, 1926, 10.
9 On federal oil and gas policy prior to 1930, see Breen, *Alberta's Petroleum Industry and the Conservation Board*, 25–37.
10 Jaremko, *Steward*, 31.
11 "Says flames are awesome," *CH*, October 25, 1929, 32.
12 Jaremko, *Steward*, 30; Breen, *Alberta's Petroleum Industry*, 101.
13 Latest available figures (2022) from the Canadian Natural Gas Association place Canada's average daily consumption of natural gas at 11.8 billion cubic feet per day. See https://www.ceicdata.com/en/indicator/canada/natural-gas-consumption.
14 Tim McFeely, "The Discovery Defied the Geological Wisdom of 1914," in *Alberta in the 20th Century: A Journalistic History of the Province in Twelve Volumes*, vol. 3: *The Boom and the Bust*, ed. Ted Byfield (Edmonton: United Western Communications, 1994), 374–75.

Index

A

advertisements, 3, 4, 8, 95, 103, 194, 228; as cultural narratives of wealth, risk, and redemption, 7, 8, 10–11, 14, 73, 104, 119–120, 141–142, 168, 170–171, 213, 235, 238–239, 247, 252, 419–422; *Calgary Daily Herald*, 76, 111, 161, 187; *Calgary Morning Albertan*, 119, 131, 133–134, 161, 194, 197–198, 242, 391; *Calgary News Telegram*, 161, 194; progress, 7–8, 11, 12, 97, 102–105, 119–120; salvation narratives, 7–8, 11, 18, 94–95, 97, 102–105, 111–112, 117–121, 163–164, 166, 171–172, 180, 239, 420; *Saskatoon Daily Star*, 210; target the "small investor" and working-class, 63–64, 72, 95–96, 104, 117–121, 163–164, 180, 187, 239

Alberta: anglophilia, 240–241; conservatism, 12, 222; economy, 7, 13, 44, 61; laissez-faire capitalism, 12, 44, 148, 190, 296–297, 421–422, 429; liberalism, 13; limited government, 222, 296, 420

Alberta culture and oil, 12, 73, 96, 183, 218, 420

Alberta attorney general's office, 276, 335, 340; alleged political motives of, 298, 310–312, 313; complaints to, 226–227, 229–230, 234, 255, 259, 270, 271, 274, 353; investigations, 227, 259, 262, 271, 280, 295; Pinkertons, 226–227; pressure on, 254, 327, 367–368; Trainor, Gregory, 271, 277, 298, 299, 301, 303, 304

Alberta exceptionalism: belief in mission, 7–8, 24–25, 72–73, 144; compared to eastern Canada, 73, 149, 168, 169, 170–171, 172; cultural identity, 11, 12, 33, 119, 124, 239, 420–421; "spirit of enterprise" and pioneer legacy, 73, 97, 103–105, 183

Alberta Liberal Party, 12–13, 216, 252, 356, 373

Alberta oil, 40; Admiralty, 10, 97; assumptions, 50–51, 78; automobile demonstration, 47, 48, 233; banks, 44; boosters, 11–12, 35, 47, 51, 56, 57, 65, 77, 83, 86, 89, 97, 102, 109, 121, 141, 150, 170, 217, 232, 252, 258, 271; bootstrap individualism, 12, 97, 172, 420, 422, 424, 426; democratization of wealth, 63–64, 72, 95–96, 104, 117–121, 158–159, 163–164, 180, 186–187, 239; economic saviour, 7–8, 14, 18, 83, 85–86, 94–95, 97, 102–105, 115–116, 111–112, 117–121, 163–164, 166, 171–172, 180, 239, 420; entrepreneurialism, 7, 12, 28, 33, 72, 120, 183, 218, 284, 420; faith in, 12, 15, 50–51, 64, 96, 102, 150–153, 166–167; independent producers, 96; investment, 11, 15, 40, 43–44, 253; laissez-faire capitalism, 44, 55, 82–83, 127; liabilities of, 80–81, 225; markets for, 51; national asset, 81; negative opinions of (*see* critics; knockers); potential, 5, 20; price, 48, 224; private sector development, 222; production costs, 40–41, 71, 223–224, 225; refining, 51; reputation, 13, 15, 176, 216, 252, 255–256, 356, 373; Royal Navy, 49; self-regulation, 44, 96; special qualities, 47, 48; transportation of, 51; US interest and involvement in, 46, 48, 49

Alberta's oil culture: abundance and, 3, 10, 22, 73, 97, 425; advertisements shape/reflect, 95, 97, 101, 239; Alberta Oil Development Association, 82–86; American values, influence on, 46, 239–240; characteristics of, 95–96, 97, 102–103, 218, 239; choice, 55, 93–95, 119, 120, 271; "Christopher Columbus" analogy, 72, 77, 143; crusading impulse, 86, 233; destiny, 51, 72–73, 149, 152; dreams, 13, 53, 64, 65, 97, 102, 189, 191, 194, 238; entrepreneurialism, 7, 11–13, 17, 28, 30, 33, 46, 50, 55, 72, 74, 76, 78–79, 96, 101, 120, 152, 162, 168, 172, 174, 183, 190, 191, 218, 239, 246, 284, 348, 420, 424; faith, 2, 3, 7, 15, 33, 34, 35, 51, 56, 64–65, 68, 69, 72, 74, 79, 81, 97, 102, 119–120, 124, 142, 149, 183, 246, 301, 325, 360, 366, 397, 416; identity and, 85–86, 97;

487

Alberta's oil culture (*continued*); independent producers, 55, 96, 99–102, 104–106, 117, 124, 131–132, 166, 169, 173, 202, 219, 229, 245, 246, 263, 417, 420, 424, 426, 453n4, 454n12; industrialization, 9, 12, 21, 47, 51, 53, 72, 73, 94, 104, 105, 167, 180; insulate against recession, 8, 11, 64, 73, 85, 91, 111, 151, 188, 340; intolerance of criticism, 3, 42, 84, 85–86, 232–234, 235–238; limitless resources, belief in, 50–51, 97, 424–425; local roots, 14, 29, 45–46, 49, 50, 56, 65, 78, 87, 99, 101, 102, 111, 152, 154, 156, 160, 163, 164, 170, 173, 174, 190, 191, 204, 238, 239, 246, 252, 344, 420, 421; modernity, 8, 12, 13, 95, 104, 106, 167; mythmaking, 13–15, 32–33, 50–51, 97; power of nature, 32–33, 74, 78, 97, 103, 118–120; progress, 95, 102–103; prosperity, 3, 8, 11, 12, 35, 61–62, 64, 73, 82, 85, 91, 95, 102–104, 111, 119, 151, 161, 188, 239, 340; religion and, 1–3, 149, 236, 420; rugged individualism, 33, 64, 97, 120, 168, 172, 422, 426, 453n1; strategic significance, 8, 10; strength, 101–103, 105; transformative qualities, 3, 8, 11, 102–105, 166; wealth and, 11, 12, 28, 73, 78, 79, 82, 84, 89, 96, 97, 100, 104, 119, 151, 153, 155, 159, 166, 188, 218, 236, 239, 423

Alberta Oil Development Association (AODA), 82–86, 88–92, 96; *Calgary Daily Herald*, 83–84, 89, 92; *Calgary Morning Albertan*, 84–85; *Calgary News Telegram*, 89

American influence, 46, 239; cross-border legal and regulatory tensions, 45–46, 216, 234–235, 356; migration of US drillers and oil workers to Alberta, 39–40, 49–50, 169–170; influence of US oil culture and technology, 7, 35, 40–41, 119, 341, 343; parallels with Texas, 96, 245, 453n3; role of US investment capital and promoters, 50, 155–156, 158, 171, 213, 235; Standard Oil and Canadian fears, 97–101, 147

Anderson, Hugh, 226

Anderson, "Torchy," 36, 154, 247

Anglo-Persian Oil, 9, 80, 106

anti-Calgary oil campaigns, 213, 216–217; Calgarians response to, 232–234, 235–238; *Chicago Tribune*, 235; *Custer Weekly Chronicle*, 235; *Minneapolis Journal*, 235; *Oregon Daily Journal*, 234–235; reasons for, 13, 60–61, 64–65, 168, 190–191, 216–217, 245, 421; *Regina Leader*, 231, 234; Robson, J.A., 230–231, 262–263; scope of, 238; *Seattle Post-Intelligencer*, 234; *Toronto Daily Star*, 168, 170, 172, 201; *Victoria Colonist*, 231

Athabasca, 97, 165, 197, 203

Athabasca River, 22, 39, 114, 115

B

bank clearings, 160–162, 229

banker, 43, 150, 151, 173, 185, 278, 316

bankruptcy, 4, 6, 136, 138, 260, 342, 352, 363–364

banks, 74, 153, 146, 151, 195, 204, 280, 282, 285; British, 43, 168, 244; Calgary, 173, 197; Canadian, 44; frozen account, 303; private savings, 154, 158, 173, 183, 241; prosperity, 150

Beattie, Harry C., 89, 138, 193–194, 197, 287, 288, 298, 381, 471n60

Beaty, Elizabeth, 2, 138, 194–196

Bennett, Richard B., 29, 133, 288, 341; Alberta Hotel, 342; Calgary Petroleum Products, 32, 34, 96, 448n32; Herron, William S., 424

Berkeley, Mowbray S., 48, 109, 271

Beveridge, Stephen, 76–77, 102; conflict with the *Herald*, 86–87, 88; Rocky Mountain Oil Fields, 110, 258

Black Diamond Oil Fields, 2, 3, 4, 5, 10, 204, 239; ads and promotion, 3–4, 6, 135–136, 198–199; Carpenter Commission, 287, 289–290; claims of strikes and stock manipulation, 7, 123, 141, 195, 196, 206–207, 210, 289; Coalinga Oil Syndicate, 2–3, 128, 133, 183, 192–196, 200, 207, 256, 287, 289, 462n12; Earl, Jennie, 182–183; financial difficulties, 3, 5, 123, 128–129, 136, 191–192, 287–288, 380, 390; International Supply Company, 5, 123, 128–129, 136–137, 192, 209, 211–212, 287–288; investigations of, 14, 227, 271, 289–290, 300, 370, 383, 398; lawsuits, 5–6, 134–135, 208, 287–288; press and public perception, 6, 68, 128–129, 196–197, 199–200, 212; "salting" well, 6–7, 123, 137–139, 209, 212, 390, 398; self-promotion and staged events, 200, 204–205, 242; stock, 4, 5, 146, 191, 193–196

Black, Brian, 9, 32–33, 97, 131

Black Diamond #1, 5, 129, 132, 134, 140, 176, 195–196, 198–199, 205–207, 209–212, 243, 287, 296, 303, 380, 382, 392–393, 416–417

Black Diamond #2, 195, 198, 208, 212, 242, 287–288

Black Diamond Press, 200–201, 235; Knowles, Vernon, 200, 227–228; Rose, Frank, 227–228
Black Diamond v. Carpenter (1916), 354, 365, 366, 367, 369
blue sky laws, 66, 189, 217, 236, 275, 287, 340, 355, 356, 419
boosters, 11–12, 35, 47, 51, 56, 86, 97, 102, 109, 121, 170, 217, 232, 252, 258; advertising campaigns, 7, 8, 10–11, 14, 18, 73, 94–95, 102–105, 111–112, 117–121, 141–142, 163–164, 166, 170–172, 180, 213, 235, 238–239, 247, 252, 419–422; Alberta Oil Development Association, 82–86, 88–92, 96; *Calgary Morning Albertan*, 48, 65, 90, 117, 150–151, 158, 159, 250–251, 271; *Calgary News Telegram*, 73–74, 78–80, 151, 232; Cheely, William, 141; Davidson, William, 57, 65; economic progress, 102; Frost, "Tappy," 83; "Petroleus" op-ed, 78–80; Tucker, J.L., 1, 77, 95
Bow Island, 22, 32, 40
Breen, David, 13–14, 24, 28
Britain, 9, 60, 61, 66, 244, 256, 378 445n1; attempts to attract British capital, 251; Canadian investments by, 43, 61, 155; immigration from, 63, 176–178; oil suppliers, 9, 245; profits, 160; scepticism, 45, 167–168; Webster-Ashburn Treaty 316
brokers, 132, 155, 157–158, 160, 201, 228; aggressiveness, 184; boosterism, 172; Carlile, R.C., 207; Clark, Allan, 235–236; Clarke, Basil, 176–178; commissions, 192–193, 194; incentives, 207; licensing, 184, 186; office spaces, 158–177, 178; price discrepancies, 173–176; profits, 177–178, 207; qualifications, 183–184; self-regulation, 174; spaces, 183; stock sales, 195, 207, 229; women, 178–180
Brown, Joe, 50
Buck, Elizabeth Ada (Beaty), 1, 2, 128, 303, 310, 322, 332, 410, 412, 462n11; divorce, 414–415
Buck, George E.: advertisements, 131, 134, 194, 197–198, 212; appeals and final release, 397–403, 407, 411–413; automobiles, 4, 127–128, 306, 308, 311, 314, 323, 338; Beattie, Harry, 193, 194; Black Diamond #1, 198, 209, 243; Black Diamond #2, 198; Black Diamond Oil Fields, 123, 146; *Black Diamond Press*, 209, 235; *Calgary Daily Herald*, 199, 207, 210–211, 298–299, 314, 323, 331, 332, 336–337, 380, 391, 395; *Calgary Eye Opener*, 140–141, 143, 207, 210, 332, 377, 380, 388, 398, 411, 412, 420; *Calgary Morning Albertan*, 140–141, 143, 207, 210, 332, 377, 380, 388, 398, 411, 412, 420; *Calgary News Telegram,* 139–140, 199–200, 209, 298, 300, 331, 373, 391, 401–402, 406; Carr, Clara, 414–415; Chewelah Basin Oil Company, 413–414; Church of Christ, 127; Clark, Allan, 192–194; Coalinga Oil Syndicate, 128, 192–193; commissions, 192–193, 194; competition, 207; Crandell, E.H., 129–130, 209; criminal trial and appeals of, 376–392, 398–402, 407–409; Cunningham Craig, Edward Hubert, 197; divorce, 414; dreams, 197; Duke and Duchess of Connaught, 242–243; Earl, Jennie, 209, 288, 303, 311; early life, background, and religious convictions, 1–2, 124, 127, 132–133; escalating legal troubles and flight from Calgary, 5–6, 133, 135, 207–208, 287–288, 303, 310–311; evades subpoena, 288–289; evangelical mission of, 1–2, 124, 127, 199, 395; extradition battle in the United States, 306–311, 313–315, 318–321, 324–326, 330; financial instability and the "salting" conspiracy, 3–7, 191–192, 209–210; financial problems, 3, 4, 5, 6, 191–192; Hayes, James, 6, 211, 213; International Supply Company, 123, 129, 192, 209, 211; legacy and impact, 14, 355, 419–420; life after the boom, 413–416; Martin, "Frosty," 192, 198, 209; McGillivray, Alexander A., 271, 289; *Natural Gas and Oil Record*, 128, 134, 185, 242–243; *Oil Finding*, 128, 197; Phillips, "Tiny," 192, 198, 209, 211–212; preacher, 127; promoter, 4, 128, 199, 205, 210–211; promotional tactics and public persona, 4–5, 14, 127–128, 196–197, 416; real estate, 128; *Regina Leader*, 200–201; Rice, Garnet, 210, 211; Ritchie, J.M.D., 205–206; rumours, 196, 199, 206; sales agents, 196; Smith, Fred, 192–194, 197–198; stock manipulation and media control, 191, 193–194, 197, 199–200, 204–205, 207; stock sales, 193–194, 197, 207; Spokane, 299, 413; Texas, 306, 308; transition to oil promotion, 2, 123, 128, 146, 192–193, 197; trial and conviction, 336, 378, 380–383, 385, 390, 393–394; Tucker, J.L., 199–200, 212; United Oils, 131–135, 192; *Vancouver Daily World*, 196–197, 205, 242–243; Wolverton, Grant, 133–134, 207–208; "Wildcat Christianity," 2, 124
bucket shop, 61, 64, 168, 183, 186, 348

C

cable tool rig, 35–38, 51, 80, 246
Calgary, 30; exceptionalism, 78–79, 80; opportunities, 178; real estate boom, 28, 50, 181; reputation, 13, 65, 125, 176, 216, 218–219, 238, 265, 273, 296; unemployed, 61, 63, 150–151, 238, 240, 247; United States, 46
Calgary Board of Trade, 44, 53, 65, 221, 226, 232–233, 237, 244, 256
Calgary Daily Herald, 6, 46, 54, 69, 75, 83, 106, 127, 147, 183, 185, 221–222, 236; advertising, 76, 111, 161, 187; Alberta Oil Development Association, 83–84, 89, 92; banks, 162, 173; Beveridge libel suit, 86–87, 88; Black Diamond Oil Fields, 128–129, 132, 140, 288, 416; Buck, George E., 199, 207, 210–211, 298–299, 314, 323, 331, 332, 336–337, 380, 391, 395; Carpenter Commission, 272, 276, 290; conditions at Turner Valley, 36, 47–48; coverage of Dingman discovery and boom, 140, 150, 155, 158, 161, 173, 180–181, 187, 241–242; critics, 65, 69–70, 71–72, 73, 76–78, 82, 84–85, 103, 109; Cunningham Craig, Edward Hubert, 106, 109, 113, 116; Dingman, Archibald, 34, 41; Dingman #1, 47; ; establishment, 56–57; Flotations series, 68–71, 76–77, 81, 88, 109, 116, 117, 128–129, 169, 285, 452n34; Frost, "Tappy," 233; Herron, William S., 26, 149; letters to the editor, 53, 70, 71, 88, 240, 254, 280, 357, 365; Lees Commission, 354–354, 365; Monarch Oils, 343, 350; role in oil boom and speculation debates, 61, 64–66, 68, 70–71, 76–77, 81–82, 84, 88; Rose, Frank, 229; rumours, 46, 237; Short, James, 472n3; Sifton government and regulation, 254–255, 262–263, 292–293; speculation, 64, 68, 81, 235, 238; stock exchanges, 249, 257, 266; stock quotations, 176; vision of oil, 54–55, 61, 65, 150, 154; women investors, 178–181, 182
Calgary Eye Opener, 59–60; advertising, 143; criticizes the *Herald*, 71; criticizes the oil industry, 236–238, 249, 258–259
Calgary Morning Albertan, 6, 7, 41, 46, 47–48, 50; advertising, 119, 131, 133–134, 161, 194, 197–198, 242, 391; Alberta Oil Development Association, 84–85; Black Diamond Oils, 128–129, 131, 133–134, 140–141, 195, 199, 205–206, 210; Buck, George E., 140–141, 143, 207, 210, 332, 377, 380, 388, 398, 411, 412, 420; Calgary Petroleum Products, 46, 48, 88, 149; Calgary Police Force, 184–185, 186; Carpenter Commission, 271, 275, 276, 283, 286–287; Cheely, William, 141–142, 192, 344–345, 358, 364, 383, 393, 398, 402; counter "flotation" articles, 71–72, 128–129; Cunningham Craig, Edward Hubert, 109–110, 117; Davidson, William M., 55–58, 85, 117, 140–141, 150, 271, 286, 361; Dingman, Archibald, 41, 47; Duke and Duchess of Connaught, 186–187, 242; editorial stance and advocacy, 49, 57, 450n1; establishment and characteristics, 10, 57, 161; Frost, "Tappy," 339, 361, 365; Liberal Party, 87–88; May 9, 1914, article, 143, 192, 344, 377–378, 382–385, 392–394, 398–400, 402, 404, 406–408; Monarch Oils, 341, 343–344, 362; nativism, 84–85; "Oilberta" cartoon, 89, 91; promotional activities and civic boosting, 48, 55–58, 65, 85, 89, 90, 117, 140–141, 150–151, 158, 159, 250–251, 271, 286, 361; regulation, 222, 263; Ritchie, J.M.D., 205–206; role in media debates and feuds, 54, 65, 71–72, 76–77, 82, 84–85, 90, 99–100, 128–129; Rose, Frank, 228; rumors, 46, 199, 203, 207, 210, 295, 349, 352, 359; Sale of Shares Act, 356–357; Short, James, 472n3; Standard Oil, 99–100; stereotypical "oilman," 55; stock exchanges, 173, 186–187, 257, 266; speculation, 55; women investors, 180, 182
Calgary Natural Gas Company, 30, 31–32, 36
Calgary News Telegram, 54, 55, 58, 71, 77, 141; advertising, 161, 194; Alberta Oil Development Association, 89; Alberta's exceptionalism, 73; Black Diamond Oil Fields, 123, 139–40; boosters, 73–74, 78–80, 151, 232; Buck, George E., 139–140, 199, 298, 300, 331, 373, 391, 401–402, 406; Carpenter Commission, 277, 286, 290; challenges critics, 172; criticisms of the *Herald*, 71, 73; Devenish, Oscar, 150; Dingman #1, 100; Dunn, Bird W., 349; independents, 55; Lees Commission, 353, 355, 360; letters to the editor, 71; Monarch Oils, 347; Oil Protective Association, 234; "Petroleus" op-ed, 78–80; regulation, 215, 219, 238; rumours, 209, 228; Standard Oil, 99, 100; Tryon, Charles, 123, 139–140, 387, 404
Calgary Petroleum Products, Ltd., 2, 5, 7, 10, 15, 27, 31, 34–37, 38, 42, 43, 44, 46–47, 88, 117, 120, 123, 146, 148, 156, 179, 191, 202,

203, 207, 343, 423–424; accused of fraud, 232; automobile demonstration, 47; *Calgary Morning Albertan*, 46, 48, 88, 149; Chapin, O.S., 132; Cunningham Craig, Edward Hubert, 49, 115; Dingman, Archibald, 48; drilling costs, 169; Duke and Duchess of Connaught, 244; shareholders, 180–181; stock price, 154, 167, 176, 201, 202; sues Herron, William S., 147

Calgary Petroleum Products #1. *See* Dingman #1

Calgary Police Force, 44, 49, 184–185, 186, 217, 219, 225–226, 465n28; *Calgary Morning Albertan*, 184–185, 186

Calgary real estate boom, 28, 29, 50, 61, 63, 70, 102, 126, 128, 130, 133, 158, 177, 247, 270; difference with oil boom, 64, 70–71, 82, 151, 169, 181–183; Langner, Jullian, 270, 278

Calgary Stock Exchange, 13; incorporation and purpose, 44–45, 54–55, 265; decline and suspension, 207, 253–254, 256–257, 422–423; formation and early operations, 45, 168, 173–174; resumption 424; self-regulation, 44, 168, 174–175, 254, 256–257, 265, 266

Canadian economy: bank clearings, 160–161, 162, 229; British capital, 43, 61, 155, 167–168, 241, 256; domestic capital, 173, 190–191, 231–232, 239, 251, 420–421; foreign investment, 43, 45, 61, 100–101, 155, 167, 171, 173, 239, 251–252, 253–254; investment capital, 13, 15, 39, 43, 74, 191, 221, 222, 257, 264, 423; metropolis-hinterland thesis, 95, 453n3; National Policy, 22; private sector investment, 64, 99, 100, 164, 186, 421; recession, 8, 61, 83, 160–16; role of government, 13–14, 81, 100, 222, 236, 252, 254–255, 421–422; role of natural resources, 21–22, 43, 97, 103–104, 166–167, 236; US capital, 45–46, 50, 61, 155, 171

Canadian Pacific Railway, 22, 24, 26, 35, 57, 60, 64, 77, 98, 125, 126, 146, 148, 154, 159, 182, 181

Canadian Western Natural Gas, 22, 32–33

Carpenter, Alexander A., 270, 271–273, 274–278, 283, 286–287, 290, 292, 294, 340, 353–354

Carpenter Commission: establishment and mandate, 270–272; investigation and findings, 275–277; legacy, 292–293, 295, 340, 354–355, 370, 422; legal challenges, 271, 287, 290–292; press coverage, 271–272, 275–277, 283, 286–287, 290; Western Canadian Oil Company, 270, 277–278, 280–285. *See also Black Diamond v. Carpenter* (1916)

Cheely, William "Bill" Winbourne, 124, 141–143, 149, 171, 349, 359–361, 364, 376–377, 382–384, 386–387, 392–393, 405–406; May 9, 1914, article, 143, 192, 344, 377–378, 382–385, 392–394, 398–400, 402, 404, 406–408; Monarch Oils, 344–346, 349, 358, 478n17

Church of Christ (disciples), 1, 127, 128, 395

Clark, Allan, 235–236; Buck, George E., 192–194

Coalinga Oil Syndicate, 2–3, 128, 133, 182, 183, 200, 287, 289, 462n12; Black Diamond Oil Fields, 2–3, 128, 133, 183, 192–196, 200, 207, 256, 287, 289, 462n12; Buck, George E., 192–194; market manipulation, 192–195, 207

collapse of the boom, 244–247

Coykendall, M. Arthur, 321, 324–327, 328, 329, 330

Companies Ordinance, 217, 218, 219–220, 221, 230, 259, 260, 291, 353–354, 406, 468n33

Coste, Eugene M., 22, 32–34, 35, 50

Crandell, Edward Henry, 129–131, 137, 139, 140, 141, 209, 301, 302, 305, 382, 387, 410, 412, 420

critics: eastern Canada, 149, 168, 169, 170, 172; external, 43–44, 167–169, 245–246; geological, 70, 75–76, 81–82, 110, 113, 165–166, 220, 246, 253, 255; market, 165–166; regulatory, 168, 232, 245, 253, 356; reputational damage, Alberta, 15, 65, 213, 216, 231–232, 245, 253–254, 296; United States, 75–76, 156, 169–170, 216, 235, 245, 356

Cross, A.E., 32

Cross, Charles W., 271, 277, 313, 314, 331, 334, 353, 373, 399, 421

Cuddy, Alfred, 184–186, 220, 221–223, 226, 264, 266, 461n76; and Buck, George E., 298, 299; wildcatters, 220

Cunningham Craig, Edward Hubert, 1, 4, 30, 48–49, 105–111, 449n6; background and expertise, 1, 96–97; cautious assessments and warnings, 109, 113–116; consulting and endorsements, 106–107, 109–111, 113–116, 253; impact and legacy, 96, 99–101, 103–106, 197, 244, 253; *Oil Finding*, 1–2, 106–108, 110, 128, 197; public statements and media coverage, 99–101, 103–106, 109, 244, 253

curb brokers, 13, 64, 168, 174, 176, 177, 180, 184, 186

Index *491*

D

Dabbs, Frank, 24, 25
Dakota sandstone, 17, 18, 22, 27, 113–115, 131, 140–141, 196, 198, 206, 259, 363, 383
Davidson, William M., 420, 472n3; background, 57–58, 71; beliefs and ideology, 56–57, 99–100, 236, 450n1; civic and oil industry boosting, 57, 89–90, 117, 140, 150, 271; rivalry with James Hossack Woods, 54–55, 65, 71–72, 85, 88, 92; *The Morning Albertan* newspaper, 55–58, 85, 117, 140–141, 150, 271, 286, 361
Dawson, George W., 22
Devenish, Oscar, 5, 47, 65, 77, 131, 132–135, 145, 150, 173, 251, 300, 363
deportation, 240, 315, 320–321, 324–330
Dingman #1, 30, 36, 37, 41, 43, 49, 50, 147, 205, 352, 424–425; *Calgary Daily Herald*, 47; "doctored" well allegations, 231–233, 253; Duke and Duchess of Connaught, 244; quality of oil from, 47, 49, 81, 148–149, 153, 156, 170, 224, 253
Dingman, Archibald W., 2, 5, 7, 10, 15, 30–31, 34–35, 41, 44, 46–48; Calgary Petroleum Products, 71; Herron, William S., 32–34, 120, 132, 146–147, 458n1
Dingman, Charles, 36, 149
Dingman, Claude, 36
Dochuk, Darren, 124, 455n2
Dominion of Canada: extradition and international relations, 315–318, 320, 335–336; Geological Survey of Canada, 17, 21–23, 24, 26–27, 31, 81, 109, 113–114, 220; jurisdiction and control of resources, 41, 91–92, 172, 217, 260–261; petroleum regulations, 38–39, 45, 59, 91–92; regulatory role and limitations, 21, 43, 45–46, 92, 98, 220, 236; Royal North West Mounted Police, 86, 217, 225, 298, 376; "specialty principle," 316, 321, 376, 410
Drilling: costs, 37, 40–41, 43; crews, 39, 50; challenges and limitations, 37–41; Geological Survey of Canada, 22, 220; jurisdiction, regulation and oversight, 2, 38, 42–43, 220, 223, 227; safety and technology, 36–40
Duke and Duchess of Connaught, 156, 240, 242–244

E

Earl, Jennie L., 5, 182–183, 193, 195, 205, 209, 288, 303, 313, 445n3; auto accident, 311, 314; investor, 182–183
Edmonton, 40, 57, 128, 189, 220, 221, 241, 271, 327, 330, 424; Appellate court, 290, 360; attorney general's office, 298, 308, 319, 320, 324, 325–326, 331, 335, 337, 409; brokers, 203; Carpenter Commission, 271; crime, 125, 226–227; Dingman, A.W., 30–31; investing, 153–154, 164–165; McDougall, J., 29; McDougall-Segur Exploration company, 30; Nicholson, J.D., 304, 306, 312; oil prospects, 241; penitentiary, 394, 411; Pinkertons, 227; Police force, 126–127; unemployment, 63
Edmonton Bulletin, 56, 242, 262, 361
Edmonton Journal, 10, 46, 57, 154, 190, 274, 419; advertisements, 164–165; boosting, 10; Calgary Petroleum Products, 46–47; Carpenter Commission, 273; Cunningham Craig, Edward Hubert, 116, 164–165; investments in Alberta oil, 253; Monarch Oils, 343; regulation, 262–263, 273, 283
Edwards, Robert Chambers "Bob," 59–60, 71, 93–94, 143, 156–157, 222, 249, 258–259, 292–293, 299, 420
Elder, William, 35, 36, 46, 131
entrepreneurialism and risk, 11–12, 50–51, 67–68, 70, 119–120, 121; bootstrap capitalism, 11–12, 97, 119; independent oil man ideal, 12, 55, 95–101; mythmaking and personal branding, 3–4, 6, 14, 110, 135–138, 143, 194, 196–197, 237, 341, 352; public debates on risk, morality, and market freedom, 54–56, 64–65, 71–72, 167–168, 185, 215–218, 230–231, 234–235, 238; risk-taking and financial desperation, 3–4, 6, 66–67, 136–138, 154, 169, 186, 190–192, 219, 277–278
environmental and economic impact, 10–11, 39, 62–63, 83, 94, 238–239, 247; conservation, 39, 424–425; economic inefficiencies in production, 37–38, 40–41, 102, 169; long-term effects on Alberta's reputation, 13–15, 213, 245, 252–254; Turner Valley flaring and resource waste, 424–426
energy transition, 8, 10–11, 12, 72, 73, 80–81, 103–104, 158, 166
extradition, 286–297, 306, 310, 312–318, 320–321, 324–329, 331, 333, 335–338, 340, 374–376, 378–380, 382, 384, 393, 398–402, 404–410; "specialty principle," 316, 321, 376, 410

F

federal-provincial dynamics, 217, 251–252, 269–271, 317, 320–321; dominion control of natural resources and mineral rights, 38–39; federal petroleum regulations, 38–39, 45, 59, 91–92; jurisdictional gaps and loopholes, 217, 317, 320–321; provincial limitations on oversight, 217–218, 219–220, 222–223, 252, 275, 291–292, 317, 340–341

fraud and deception, 13–14, 124–125, 172, 206, 246, 254–255; fabricated narratives, 194–195, 197, 352, 393–394, 406; insider dealings, 61, 66, 175, 192–193, 266, 270, 275–276, 281–282, 285–286, 344, 384, 393; misleading advertisements and claims, 3–4, 135–136, 197, 207, 222, 237, 259, 279, 360, 385, 393–394; salting and staged discoveries, 11, 123, 137, 138–139, 211–212, 216–217, 300, 340–341, 352, 363, 391, 393–394, 420; techniques and motivations, 6–7, 61, 66, 123, 137–139, 175, 191–192, 195, 197, 218–219, 220, 226, 266, 275–276, 285–286, 302, 325, 341, 344, 358, 380, 394, 398, 399, 405

Frost, Thomas Alfred Presswood "Tappy," 68, 69–70, 83, 89, 102, 243, 244; eastern tour of, 232–233

G

gender and class dynamics, 12, 13, 56, 64, 96, 160, 163–164, 180–182, 220, 234; class-based access to oil wealth, 55, 64, 78 100, 119, 142, 159, 163–164, 204, 220, 232, 234, 239; imagery, 102–103, 105, 163–164, 171, 189–190; social mobility and entrepreneurial aspirations, 159, 160, 163–164, 180–183, 239; women's roles in investment and leadership, 160, 178–181

geology and technology, 1, 21, 24, 26, 30, 106–107, 108, 128, 197, 246, 251, 383; cable tool rig limitations, 36, 37–38, 51, 80, 246; geological surveys and expert opinions, 114–115, 220, 252; Turner Valley's anticline and subsurface complexity, 17, 19, 36, 37, 139, 246, 253

Geological Survey of Canada, 17, 21–23, 24, 26–27, 31, 81, 109, 113–114, 220

Georgeson, William, 124, 132, 204, 349, 420; Americans, views on, 239–240; business interests, 342, 348; Chapin, O.S., 360, 363; Cheely, William, 396; Coste, Eugene, 342; Dunn, B.W., 343, 345, 349–350; faith in Alberta oil, 183, 366; libel lawsuit, 340, 344, 365, 367–370; Lees Commission, 341, 357, 358, 359–361, 365–369; market manipulation, 341; Monarch Oils, 341, 342, 393; Moodie, James, 348, 352, 353, 361, 362, 363; press statements, 346, 351–352, 358–360, 366; Public Inquiries Act, 367–368; reported oil strike, 344, 346, 347, 348, 364; reputation, 342

Gray, Earle, 11, 21, 28

Gray, James, 13, 15, 46, 90, 123, 125, 289

Great War, 15, 241–242, 244–245; alters view of government's role, 252; collapse of investment capital, 61–62, 253–254, 255, 264; decline of exchanges and investor confidence, 255–257, 264–265; failure to attract imperial contracts, 103–104; strategic importance of oil, 103–106

H

hard times, 61, 63, 83, 86, 102, 103, 151, 158, 161, 197, 239; collapse of the Western Land Boom, 8, 61–63, 157–158; decline in economic activity, 8, 61–63, 112, 158, 238

Hayes, James, 5, 6, 7, 206, 211–212, 382, 390, 392

Herron, William Stewart, 15–29, 30, 77, 232, 419, 420; advertisements, 111–112, 119–120, 121, 239; Alberta Oil Development Association, 83, 89; amateur geologist, 26; ambition, 28; booster, 149, 251; Buck, George E., 131; *Calgary Daily Herald*, 26, 149; Calgary Petroleum Products, 34, 35, 120, 132, 147, 424; Carpenter Commission, 277, 286–287; cartage business, 25; cooking demonstration, 32–33, 448n32; Craig, E.H. Cuninigham, 113; Dingman, Archibald W., 32–34, 120, 132, 146–147, 458n1; Herron-Elder Oil Company, 83, 176, 230; mineral rights, 28, 34, 146; Pennsylvania oilfields, 24, 27–28, 447n17; Pinkertons investigation, 230; rental payments, 423

Hovis, Martin, 35, 36, 50

Hume, G.S., 21

I

immigrants, 61, 63, 95–96, 125, 182, 239; Clarke, Basil, 176–178; nativism, 238, 240

infrastructure; pipelines, 14, 26, 32, 33, 141, 98, 113, 165, 342; railroads, 44, 51, 95, 104, 151, 155, 204, 225; railways, 2–3, 128, 133, 183, 192–196, 200, 207, 256, 287, 289, 462n12; refineries, 47, 51, 55, 74, 77, 80, 81, 98, 99, 100, 104, 147, 152, 167, 245, 252, 450n12; roads, 36, 40, 186, 223, 246; storage, 39, 51, 165

Index   *493*

international dimensions: challenges and extradition of Buck, George E., 297, 315–316, 321–322, 327–328; global oil production and strategic importance, 9, 43, 79, 106; international capital and foreign influence, 43, 45–46, 61, 155–156, 171, 239–240; international perceptions and media coverage, 12, 71, 169–171, 213, 216, 235

International Supply Co., 4, 35, 40, 50; Black Diamond Oil Fields, 5, 123, 128–129, 136–137, 192, 209, 211–212, 287–288; Monarch Oil, 342, 343, 360

investors, 15, 197; Calgary Petroleum Products, 180; education of, 68–71, 76–77, 81, 88, 109, 116, 117, 128–129, 169, 285, 452n34; losses incurred by, 194, 226, 247; protection of, 55, 216, 234, 245; small investors, 64, 72, 78, 163–164, 220; warnings to, 64, 66, 216, 217, 220, 231–232, 234; women, 177–183, 187

K

"knockers," 81, 201, 208, 235, 314, 419; definition and characterization, 12, 54; geologists and experts, 110–111, 113–114, 116–117, 169–170, 237; government officials and regulatory bodies, 187, 208, 231; reactions to the "knockers," 1, 71–72, 77, 83, 85, 172, 232; *Calgary Daily Herald*, 78–79, 89; *Chicago Tribune*, 235; *Custer Weekly Chronicle*, 235; *Minneapolis Journal*, 235; *Montreal Gazette*, 110; *Natural Gas and Oil Record*, 6; *Oregon Daily Journal*, 234–235; *Regina Leader*, 231, 234; *Seattle Post-Intelligencer*, 234; *Toronto Daily Star*, 168, 172; *Victoria Colonist*, 231; *Winnipeg*, 232

Knowles, Vernon, 200, 220, 227–228

L

Langner, Julian, 110, 270–271, 278–286, 420, 455n35

Lansing, Robert, 335–336, 374–375, 378, 400, 408

Laramide Orogeny, 20

Lees Commission: challenges and scope, 340, 355, 364–365; formation and mandate, 340, 354, 365, 367, 370; legal challenge and impact, 340–341, 356–357, 365–366, 369–370, 422; Monarch Oil Company hearings, 357–365

legal and regulatory failures, 191; calls for reform and delayed intervention, 4, 13–14, 67, 123–124, 190, 217–220, 225–226, 245, 275–276, 421; jurisdictional ambiguity, 217–218, 220, 225–226, 251, 261–262; lack of oversight, 168, 174–175, 183, 220, 275–276; litigation and discovery, 270–271, 279–283, 283, 285, 291–292, 296, 316, 321, 339–340, 354, 397, 404, 407; self-regulation, 11, 44–45, 56, 83–84, 173, 175, 234, 254

legacies: cultural and social, 7, 11–12, 54, 97, 120, 129, 239–240, 293, 419–420, 425; economic, 13–15, 61, 161–162, 167, 175, 187, 191, 252–253; individual and personal, 13, 123–124, 132–133, 141–142, 207–208, 270, 283, 296, 311, 358, 361; legal and institutional, 14, 123–124, 217, 252, 255, 271, 291, 316, 321, 340, 355, 357, 369, 378–379, 398, 400, 404–405, 407, 420–422; national and imperial, 9–10, 45–46, 91, 100–101, 166–167, 261; political and regulatory, 13–14, 252–255, 291, 294, 421–422, 424–425

local capital and speculation: Calgary, 54–55, 60–61, 64, 71–73, 74, 145, 153, 156–157, 424; Edmonton, 153–154, 165, 203; impact, 103, 150–151, 155, 158, 161–162; land rushes and ticket trading, 49, 66, 168, 185, 285; public participation, 7, 10–11, 154–155, 157–158, 178, 180, 183, 420; Red Deer, 203–204, 349

Lord's Day Act, 185–186

Lougheed, James A., 29, 34, 120, 128, 133, 448n32

Luxton, Eleanor, 29, 186, 241, 255, 447n25

M

Mahan, Alfred Thayer, 9

Martin, Walter Randall "Frosty," 4, 35, 50

McDougall, David, 2, 29–30, 186, 303

McDougall-Segur Exploration Company, 2, 10, 29–30, 42–43, 49, 80, 108, 115, 117, 147–148, 169, 182, 186, 191, 203, 209, 227–229, 236, 358, 449n62

McGillivray, Alexander A., 71, 113, 129–136, 185; appeals Buck's conviction, 384, 397–398, 402, 404–406; background of, 289; Carpenter Commission, 271, 290, 297, 298, 365; legal strategies, 271, 289–290, 378, 379, 383, 384, 386–388, 391

McLaws, William Henry, 34, 390

McWain and Miller Detective Agency, 307, 308–310, 312–313, 317–318, 320–325, 328–330, 331, 337–338

McWain W.A. *See* McWain and Miller Detective Agency

media and messaging: advertising strategies, 97, 100–105, 119, 131, 136, 163, 187, 194; editorial conflicts, 71, 77–78, 82, 84; film and popular culture representations, 8, 10, 91, 94, 95, 101, 103, 105, 118, 152, 153, 163, 164, 170, 190, 201, 224; media ethics, 46–47, 225–226, 228–229, 237, 361, 383; media resistance, 168–169, 172, 216, 231, 234, 236–237, 354; newspapers as promotional tools, 83, 95–96, 140, 142, 161, 198, 200, 232–233, 385
mineral leases, 28, 42, 49, 180–183; acquisition and value of, 1–3, 28, 49; challenges and exploitation of leases, 91, 115, 343; Dominion revenue from, 49; Earl, Jennie, 182–183; Fitzgerald, Jennie 182; legal and regulatory aspects, 38–39, 66, 69–70, 91–92, 152, 168, 200, 220, 261–262, 276, 285; lottery system for, 49, 184–185
Miller, John "Long John." *See* McWain and Miller Detective Agency
Mitchell, John W., 27
Monarch Oil Company, 121, 346, 350, 352, 364; alleged oil strike and promotion, 203, 204, 229, 236, 344–349, 358–359, 362, 478n3, 17; *Calgary Morning Albertan*, 361; *Calgary News Telegram*, 347–348, 349; Carpenter Commission, 272, 341–342; Chapin, O.S., 132, 346, 358, 359, 363; Cheely, William, 344–345, 360; declining fortunes and mounting doubts, 342, 350–352; Dunn, Bird W., 343, 358; founding and initial business strategy, 341–343; Georgeson, William, 204, 239, 340, 342, 348, 358, 360, 366, 369; International Supply Company, 342, 343, 360; investors, 347; leaseholds, 343–344; Lees Commission, 339–340, 353, 357–358, 360; Moodie, James F., 348, 352–353, 361, 363; Morfitt, James 348, 355; motives for a false oil strike, 344, 347, 349, 350, 358; *Natural Gas and Oil Record*, 204, 351; Olds district, 165, 202, 204, 279, 349; Public Inquiries Act (1916), 340; recapitalization, 344, 350, 351; share price, 121, 176, 202, 259, 343, 344, 348, 351, 352; *Vancouver Daily World*, 359
moral hazard, 217–218, 222, 275, 276

N

Natural Gas and Oil Record, 6, 169; advertisements, 105; Black Diamond Oil Fields, 128, 137, 196, 199–200, 212, 229; booster, 77, 94–95, 151–153, 163–164;

brokers, 183; Buck, George E., 128, 134, 185; Coalinga Syndicate, 128; Dominion mineral leases, 93; Duke and Duchess of Connaught, 243–244; exposé of Woods, 77–78; Great War, 25; "Greatest Magnet," 153; Herron, William S., 147; investors, 186, 191; "Scarecrow," 151–152; "Small Investor," 163–164; Stephen Beveridge libel suit, 86, 88; stock exchanges, 175, 176; stock prices, 202; telegram to Southam, 89
National Policy, 22
nativism, 239–240
Nicholson, John D., 304–307, 312–315, 317–340, 373–377, 386–387
Nickle, Carl O., 37, 420

O

oil culture, 7, 8, 11; advertisements, 8, 33, 91; Black, Brian, 131–132; competition, 132; construction of, 12, 33; Intolerance of criticism, 90–92; rule of capture, 132; self-regulation, 13, 45
Oil Finding (book), 1–2, 49, 106–108; Buck, George E., 126
oil industry: California, 9, 28, 48, 50, 79, 101, 109, 116, 117, 119, 131, 135, 147, 149, 152, 165–167, 169, 173, 190, 183–184, 2 24–2 25, 237, 258; exploration and geological context, 9–11, 20–21, 26, 46–47; global scope, 9, 10, 55, 78, 80, 94–95, 111–112, 421; Kansas, 9, 70, 108; Ohio, 50; Oklahoma, 9, 48, 50, 119, 308; Ontario, 21, 43; Pennsylvania, 21, 24, 27, 40–41, 48, 50; salvation, 8, 83; technology, 39; Texas, 9, 37, 50, 51, 96, 119, 45; US, 9, 49–50; wealth generation, 8, 11, 12
Owens, Clarence A., 50, 88–90, 259

P

Pennsylvania, 8, 21, 22, 24, 27, 28, 30, 35, 37, 40–41, 48, 50, 75, 79, 100, 108, 109, 146, 258, 307, 326, 345, 447n17
Phillips, Albert Parker "Tiny," 4, 35, 50
Pinkerton's Detective Agency, 218, 227–228, 230, 262, 421
populism, 12, 13, 22, 98, 100, 105, 163, 265; civic religion and the myth of the independent oil boom, 7, 65, 67, 76, 98–99, 119–120, 124, 158, 171, 238, 251, 349; mistrust of elites and monopolies, 45–46, 63, 76, 98–101, 174, 232, 237–238, 265, 280
prostitution, 64, 125–127, 185

public trust and disillusionment: breakdown of self-regulation, 60–61, 64, 90–91, 234, 291–293, 355, 364; consequences for investors, 175, 191, 226, 235, 247, 249, 254–255; direct losses from fraud, 4, 14, 191–192, 229, 270, 280, 282; false claims, Buck, George, 3–4, 123, 138, 142, 194, 196–197, 199, 211, 206, 390; false claims, other promoters, 66–68, 103, 117–118, 149, 216, 222, 287; growing doubts, 75–76, 109, 112–113, 116, 167–168, 235; investor losses, 194, 226, 247; systemic financial risks, 65, 70, 169, 252–253
Public Utilities Act (1915), 262–263, 271
Public Utilities Commission, 217, 255, 263–264, 355, 357, 422

R

recession. *See* hard times
Red Deer, 164–165, 203–204, 273–274, 289, 343
regulation, 42, 251, 261; federal, 21, 38–39, 43, 45, 59, 91–92, 217, 261; King George Hotel 187–188; provincial, 217–218, 219–220, 222–223, 230, 255, 262, 269–271, 275, 296, 340, 354–357, 421–423. *See also* Companies Ordinance; Public Utilities Commission; Sale of Shares Act (1916); Sale of Shares Act (Manitoba)
regulatory and legal reform, 252, 296; Carpenter and Lees Commissions, 270–272, 275–277, 287, 290–293, 295, 340–341, 354–367, 369–370, 422; government actions, 230–231, 247, 252, 255, 354, 421–422; need for, 12–14, 205, 218, 225, 238, 255; Public Utilities Commission, 255; Sale of Shares Act (1916), 255, 355–357, 422; *Georgeson v. Moodie* and witness privilege, 255, 355–357, 422; Great War and, 252, 421–422
Ritchie, J.M.D., 205–207, 377, 404
Rockefeller, John D., 51, 55, 97, 100, 120, 150, 189, 453n4; as inspiration, 190, 194
Rose, Frank, 227–229
rotary rig, 38, 222, 246, 416
Royal Navy, 9–10, 49, 106, 113, 166, 245, 445n15
Royal North West Mounted Police, 86, 217, 225, 298, 376; Nicholson, John D., 304
rumour, 4, 1, 22, 46, 213, 236–237; motivation for, 200, 210, 229, 237; oversight, 238; Standard Oil, 42; transparency, 237

S

Sale of Shares Act (1916), 255, 355–357, 422
Sale of Shares Act (Manitoba), 231, 263
Sanders, Colonel Gilbert E., 86–88, 185; brokers, 184, 256, 264–265, 266; Buck, George E., 135, 287; Rose, Frank, 228; prostitution, 185
Sayre, A.J., 34, 44, 47
Schmidt, John, 1, 11, 40, 212, 308; Beveridge libel suit, 86; Buck, George E., 127–128; Cheely, William, 478n17
Segur, Ira E., 2, 29, 77, 83, 96, 101, 113, 147, 213, 449n62
self-help, 230–231; advertising ban, 231; anti-Calgary oil campaigns, 232; Calgary Board of Trade, 44, 53, 65, 221, 226, 232–233, 237; Calgary Stock Exchange, 13, 44–45; Oil Protective Association, 234; *Oregon Daily Journal*, 234–235; *Regina Leader*, 231, 234; *Seattle Post-Intelligencer*, 234; "Tappy" Frost's education campaign, 232–233; transparency, 237; *Victoria Colonist*, 231
Shaw, Joseph T., 226–228, 230, 297–298, 301–302, 305
Sheep Creek, 25, 26
Sheep River. *See* Sheep Creek
"shooting" oil well, 345–347, 349–352
Short, James: background and assignment of Buck's prosecution, 297–298, 472n3; initial strategy and difficulties, 305, 321, 334, 373–374; fraud case and conviction, 376, 378–380, 383–387, 388–393, 395; appeals and the Supreme Court of Canada, 397, 398–400, 402–403, 404–407, 410–412
Sifton, Arthur M., 222–223, 224, 297
Sifton government, 14, 217, 231, 254, 255, 262, 263, 267, 270, 271–272, 275, 278, 292, 355, 370–371, 421–422
Skinner, T.J.S., 34
Southam, William, 57, 84–85, 88, 92
speculation, 11, 13, 28, 44, 45, 54, 55, 64, 65, 68, 70, 72, 76, 97, 100, 111, 117, 153, 157, 168, 172, 181–183, 186–187, 213, 219, 223, 231, 235, 238, 239, 245, 252, 263, 283, 350, 450n1; Dingman, A.W., 47, 48, 71, 265; incentives, 187; mineral rights, 109, 261; protection of consumers, 266, 355–356
speculation and investment culture, 10–11, 19, 55, 61–62, 64–66, 93, 100, 169, 190, 216, 245, 450n1; curb brokers and bucket shops, 60–61, 64, 157–158, 176–177, 183–186, 189; small investors and working-class participation, 55, 64, 72, 117–119, 154–155,

159–160, 163–165, 186, 235; stock exchanges and trading practices, 44–45, 168, 137–175, 201, 264–266, 422–424; women in oil investment, 177–183, 187, 424;
Spokane, 85, 158, 201, 202, 207, 415, 416; advertisements, 202, 213; anti-Calgary oil campaign, 234; Black Diamond Oil Fields, 207, 211, 213; broker, 201–202; Buck, George E., 299, 413; Calgary Petroleum Products. Ltd., 201; importance, 171; investment, 156, 171, 213, 347; Ranlett, W.H., 460n66; rumours, 213
Spokane Daily Chronicle, 213, 228; Black Diamond Oil Fields, 211, 213; Buck, George E., 413; Buck, Kathleen, 413; Georgeson, William, 239–240; Langner, Jullian, 279; Monarch Oils, 347; Rose, Frank, 228
Spokane Press, 413
Spokane Spokesman-Review, 171
Standard Oil, 41, 42, 50, 55, 74, 79, 82, 96–101, 160, 147, 148, 165–166, 174, 343, 421, 424
stock certificates, 5, 155, 158, 161, 181, 191, 219, 226, 236, 249, 264, 282, 284, 289, 423; printers and, 155, 158, 161, 249
stock exchange, 44; Calgary Women's Oil Exchange, 178–180; Eureka Women's Oil Exchange, 178; Mason, Blanche, 178–179; unchartered, 168; Woollard's & Company, 178; Wolley-Dod, Annie, 178–179; Women's Oil Brokerage Company, 178
stock market manipulation: artificial scarcity and price inflation, 4, 66, 76–72, 117–119, 137, 194–197, 344, 346; consequences and aftermath, 14, 169, 213, 229, 245, 253–254; exploitation of lax regulations and investor psychology, 64, 66, 175, 190, 210, 213, 217, 229, 280–281, 285–286; painting the tape and staged rallies, 191, 207, 237, 257, 266
stockbrokers: emergence and prevalence, 16, 61, 146, 157–158, 176–178, 254; practices and perceptions, 61, 64, 67, 169, 173, 175, 184, 219–220, 258; provincial interventions, 255–256, 263, 355–357; regulation efforts and challenges, 45, 173–175, 183–184, 254. *See also* Buck, George E.; Georgeson, William; Rose, Frank
Supreme Court of Canada: overview of Chief Justice Sir Charles Fitzpatrick's court, 397, 402–403, 407; George Buck's appeal, 379, 397–398, 402, 404–407; Ruling and implications, 407–411
surface rights, 43, 66, 69, 91, 134–135

T

Texas, 9, 26, 32, 48, 51, 141, 306, 453n4
Thompson, George Marshall, 54, 55, 58–59, 71, 72–75, 80–81, 92, 151, 199–200
Trainor, Gregory, 271, 277, 286, 297–305, 323, 327–328, 352–353, 355, 358–359, 361–364
transparency, 66, 173, 190, 220, 237, 245, 255, 267, 340, 355
Tryon, Charles Elmer, 58, 123, 139–140
Tucker, J.L., 77–78, 199–200, 212, 351; advertising, 95; Black Diamond Oils, 199–200; booster, 1, 77, 95; Buck, George E., 199–200, 212; Devenish, Oscar, 77; Dingman, Archibald, 77; exposé of Woods, 77–78; Herron, William S., 77; Monarch Oils, 351; Segur, Ira 77
Turner, Tom (detective), 228
Turner Valley, 11, 29, 42; cable tool rig, 37–38; conditions, 36; drilling costs, 37, 40–41, 223–224, 246; formation, 19–21, 22; geology, 17–20, 26–27, 32, 36; natural gas, 41; production, 11; production costs, 41, 51, 220, 246; railroads, 51, 104, 151, 151, 204, 225; reserves, 17; roads, 36, 40, 186, 223, 246; rotary rig, 38

U

unemployed, 61, 63, 150–151, 152, 238, 240, 245, 247, 260
United Oils, 117, 131–135, 176, 192, 202, 203, 207
United States: as global power and source of oil industry expertise, 9, 22, 28, 29, 50, 99, 101, 131, 170–171, 239–240; investment and promotional activity in Alberta, 35–36, 40, 45–46, 50, 155–156, 171, 179, 213, 347; US media skepticism and warnings, 232, 234–235; flight of George E. Buck to and extradition from, 301, 303, 305–311, 313–315, 318–321, 324–326, 330, 334–335, 400, 414; 477n96. *See* American influence; anti-Calgary oil campaigns; Canadian economy—US capital; critics—United States

V

Vancouver: investment and capital flow, 30, 166–167, 173, 213, 233–234; newspaper coverage and public perceptions, 158, 171, 196, 232, 236, 242, 279; stock exchanges and brokerages, 174–175

Index *497*

Vancouver Daily World, 116, 149, 158, 196, 203, 205, 242, 256, 359
voluntary organizations, 44, 218. *See also* Alberta Oil Development Association

W

wages, 40, 177–178, 181
Wall, Paul J., 325, 327–333, 378, 398, 399, 404–405, 408
Ware, John, 26
Western Canadian Oil Company: Carpenter Commission, 270, 277–278, 280–285; formation initial operations, 117, 251, 277–278; involvement of Langner, Jullian, 278–283; financial struggles, 279–280;
Western Canadian Sedimentary Basin, 20
Wichita, 297, 306–310, 312–3115, 317–338, 340, 395
wildcat, 13, 213, 219, 220, 229, 232, 234, 236, 237, 356, 421, 424
wildcat Christianity, 124, 424
wildcatters, 14, 84, 117, 131–132, 169, 184, 213, 219, 220–221, 230, 234, 454n12
wildcatting, 71, 77, 173; deceptive practices, 117, 197–198, 212–213, 237; definition and distinctions, 50, 219; financial misconduct and tactics, 137–138, 143, 168, 191–192, 217; impact on investors, 70, 220; lax regulatory environment, 123–124, 168, 190, 218–219, 221, 356; skepticism of, 14, 168, 213, 231–232, 235, 356
Wilson, Woodrow, 326, 334–335, 477n96
Winnipeg: financial and investment connections, 30, 233; newspaper coverage and public perception, 232–233; regulatory actions and opposition to Calgary oil, 187, 227, 230–231, 275, 318
Wolverton, Grant S.: Black Diamond Oil Fields, 5–6, 133–134; Buck, George E., 5–6, 133–134; Devenish, Oscar, 133–134; *Grant S. Wolverton v. Black Diamond Oil Fields et al.* (1914), 207–208, 288–289
Woods, James Hossack, 54–55, 56–57, 60, 64–65, 71–72, 73, 74, 77–78, 84, 86, 88, 89, 92, 103, 238, 450n1
World War I. *See* Great War

www.ingramcontent.com/pod-product-compliance
Lightning Source LLC
Chambersburg PA
CBHW061130031225
36251CB00034BA/604